ATTITUDES

, Function,
and Consequences

Key Readings in Social Psychology

General Editor: ARIE W. KRUGLANSKI, University of Maryland at College Park

The aim of this series is to make available to senior undergraduate and graduate students key articles in each area of social psychology in an attractive, user-friendly format. Many professors want to encourage their students to engage directly with research in their fields, yet this can often be daunting for students coming to detailed study of a topic for the first time. Moreover, declining library budgets mean that articles are not always readily available, and course packs can be expensive and time-consuming to produce. **Key Readings in Social Psychology** aims to address this need by providing comprehensive volumes, each one of which will be edited by a senior and active researcher in the field. Articles will be carefully chosen to illustrate the way the field has developed historically as well as current issues and research directions. Each volume will have a similar structure to include:

- an overview chapter, as well as introduction to sections and articles
- questions for class discussion
- annotated bibliographies
- full author and subject indexes

Published Titles

The Self in Social Psychology	Roy F. Baumeister
Stereotypes and Prejudice	Charles Stangor
Motivational Science	E. Tory Higgins and Arie W. Kruglanski
Emotions in Social Psychology	W. Gerrod Parrott
Social Psychology and Human Sexuality	Roy F. Baumeister
Intergroup Relations	Michael A. Hogg and Dominic Abrams
The Social Psychology of Organizational Behavior	Leigh L. Thompson
Social Psychology: A General Reader	Arie W. Kruglanski and E. Tory Higgins
Social Psychology of Health	Peter Salovey and Alexander J. Rothman
The Interface of Social and Clinical Psychology	Robin M. Kowalski and Mark R. Leary
Political Psychology	John T. Jost and James Sidanius
Close Relationships	Harry T. Reis and Caryl Rusbult
Social Neuroscience	John T. Cacioppo and Gary G. Berntson
Social Cognition	David L. Hamilton
Small Groups	John M. Levine and Richard L. Moreland
Social Comparison Theories	Diederik A. Stapel and Hart Blanton

Titles in Preparation

Attitudes: Persuasion and Change	Richard E. Petty and Russell H. Fazio
Language and Communication	Gün R. Semin
Psychology of Terrorism	Jeff Victoroff and Arie W. Kruglanski

For continually updated information about published and forthcoming titles in the Key Readings in Social Psychology series, please visit: **www.keyreadings.com**

ATTITUDES
Key Readings

Their Structure, Function, and Consequences

Edited by

Russell H. Fazio
Ohio State University, USA

Richard E. Petty
Ohio State University, USA

Psychology Press
Taylor & Francis Group
NEW YORK AND HOVE

Published in 2008
by Psychology Press
270 Madison Avenue
New York, NY 10016
www.psypress.com

Published in Great Britain
by Psychology Press
27 Church Road
Hove, East Sussex BN3 2FA
www.psypress.com

Psychology Press is an imprint of the Taylor & Francis Group, an informa business

Typeset in Times by RefineCatch Limited, Bungay, Suffolk, UK
Printed in the USA by Edwards Brothers, Inc. on acid-free paper
Paperback cover design by Hybert Design
Paperback cover image "Eye of the Beholder" by Valerie Lorimer
(www.valerielorimer.com)

10 9 8 7 6 5 4 3 2 1

Library of Congress Cataloging in Publication Data
A catalog record for this book is available from the Library of Congress.

ISBN13: 978-1-84169-009-4 (hbk)
ISBN13: 978-1-84169-010-0 (pbk)

Dedication

To the mentors who introduced us
to the excitement of theory and research on attitudes

Joel Cooper, Dennis Regan, and Mark Zanna (R.H.F.)

Tim Brock, Bob Cialdini, Tony Greenwald, and Tom Ostrom (R.E.P.)

Contents

About the Editors

Russell H. Fazio received his Ph.D. from Princeton University in 1978. He is currently the Harold E. Burtt Professor of Psychology at Ohio State University. Fazio's program of research focuses upon attitudes, their formation, accessibility from memory, functional value, and the processes by which they influence attention, judgment, and behavior. He served as editor of the *Journal of Experimental Social Psychology* from 1999 to 2003. He has received numerous honors, including the APA Early Career Award (1983) and the Thomas M. Ostrom Award for Outstanding Contributions to Social Cognition (2006).

Richard E. Petty received his B.A. (with high distinction) from the University of Virginia in 1973, and his Ph.D. in social psychology from Ohio State University in 1977. He is currently Distinguished University Professor of Psychology at Ohio State University. Petty's work focuses on attitudes, persuasion, and social cognition. He is former editor of the *Personality and Social Psychology Bulletin* and author of seven books and over 200 journal articles and chapters. He has received various honors including the Distinguished Scientific Contribution Award from the Society for Personality and Social Psychology (2001) and the Society for Consumer Psychology (2000).

Preface

Likes and dislikes constitute a major portion of our daily lives. Through the course of any given day, we make countless choices about what to eat, what to wear, who to see, and what to do. Our conversations often involve discussion of our likes and dislikes, be they movies, political candidates, foods, restaurants, sports teams, or other people. Our behavior as consumers involves a steady stream of purchase decisions that focus heavily on those likes and dislikes. We live in a media-enriched environment in which we are bombarded by attempts to influence what we might like. Advertisers seek to attract us to their products, health care professionals seek to improve our daily routines, politicians seek our endorsements, and charitable organizations seek our donations. It is no wonder, then, that the study of likes and dislikes—what social psychologists refer to as "attitudes"—has been a central focus of the field for decades.

What are attitudes? How can we study and measure them scientifically? How are they formed and changed? Of what functional value, if any, are they? How do they come to influence our attention, perception, judgments, and behavior? These are among the questions that have spurred social psychological research on attitudes, and they are among the issues addressed in this volume.

As any who have taken even an introductory course in social psychology are aware, the literature on attitudes is vast—in part due to the sheer length of time with which the field has been concerned with the concept and in part due to the concept's very centrality having generated so much research. This has made our task as editors very difficult. As we began to contemplate the potential sections of a collection of key readings, it quickly became apparent that we could not accomplish what we envisioned in a single volume. Hence, we decided to divide the literature into two parts and to assemble two volumes, with the thought that they could be used independently or jointly, depending on the focus and scope of any given course. Thus, this collection is devoted to the structure, function, and consequences of attitudes, whereas a companion volume focuses on persuasion and attitude change.

Even after the decision to double the size of the endeavor, the selection of specific readings was not easy. The initial list of articles that we considered for inclusion in this volume was very lengthy. Ultimately, our decisions were influenced heavily by the survey responses provided by 13 leading attitude researchers, whom we wish to thank for their time and effort. These scholars graciously rated over 40 possibilities that we had included in a carefully pruned list. We limited our consideration to those articles that they collectively rated within a range of "essential" to "very desirable" for the volume. By abridging some of the articles (denoted with "[. . .]"), we were able to include all but a few of the highly-rated candidates.

No compilation of readings could ever meet with perfect satisfaction. We have no doubts that every course instructor will be befuddled by the inclusion of one or two of the readings, and will be all the more bewildered by the absence of some others. Nevertheless, we would expect all to agree that the articles reprinted here represent noteworthy developments in the field's understanding of attitudes. Together, the readings provide a representative and broad coverage of the literature, illustrating well what the field has come to learn about the structure, function, and consequences of attitudes. We hope readers enjoy the tour, and come to share the fascination that we long have held for this domain of research.

Russell H. Fazio
Richard E. Petty

Acknowledgments

The editors and publisher are grateful to the following for permission to reproduce the articles in this book:

Reading 1: Zanna, M. P., & Rempel, J. K. (1988). *Attitudes: A new look at an old concept.* In D. Bar-Tal & A. W. Kruglanski (Eds.), *The social psychology of knowledge* (pp. 315–334). New York: Cambridge University Press.

Reading 2: Fazio, R. H., Sanbonmatsu, D. M., Powell, M. C., & Kardes, F. R. (1986). On the automatic activation of attitudes. *Journal of Personality and Social Psychology, 50*, 229–238.

Reading 3: Thurstone, L. L. (1928). Attitudes can be measured. *American Journal of Sociology, 33*, 529–554.

Reading 4: Schwarz, N. (1999). Self-Reports: How the questions shape the answers. *American Psychologist, 54*, 93–105.

Reading 5: Cacioppo, J. T., Petty, R. E., Losch, M. E., & Kim, H. S. (1986). Electromyographic activity over facial muscle regions can differentiate the valence and intensity of affective reactions. *Journal of Personality and Social Psychology, 50*, 260–268.

Reading 6: Fazio, R. H., Jackson, J. R., Dunton, B. C, & Williams, C. J. (1995). Variability in automatic activation as an unobtrusive measure of racial attitudes: A bona fide pipeline? *Journal of Personality and Social Psychology, 69*, 1013–1027.

Reading 7: Greenwald, A. G., McGhee, D. E., & Schwartz, J. L. K. (1998). Measuring individual differences in implicit cognition: The implicit association test. *Journal of Personality and Social Psychology, 74*, 1464–1480.

Reading 8: Fishbein, M. (1963). An investigation of the relationships between beliefs about an object and the attitude toward that object. *Human Relations, 16*, 233–240.

Reading 9: Zajonc, R. B. (1980). Feeling and thinking: Preferences need no inferences. *American Psychologist, 35*, 151–175.

Reading 10: Chaiken, S., & Baldwin, M. W. (1981). Affective–cognitive consistency and the effect of salient behavioral information on the self-perception of attitudes. *Journal of Personality and Social Psychology, 41*, 1–12.

Reading 11: Haddock, G., Zanna, M. P., & Esses, V. M. (1993). Assessing the structure of prejudicial attitudes: The case of attitudes toward homosexuals. *Journal of Personality and Social Psychology, 65*, 1105–1118.

Reading 12: Newby-Clark, I. R., McGregor, I., & Zanna, M. P. (2002). Thinking and caring about cognitive inconsistency: When and for whom does attitudinal ambivalence feel uncomfortable? *Journal of Personality and Social Psychology, 82*, 157–166.

Reading 13: Katz, D. (1960). The functional approach to the study of attitudes. *Public Opinion Quarterly, 24*, 163–204.

Reading 14: Snyder, M., & DeBono, K. G. (1985). Appeals to image and claims about quality: Understanding the psychology of advertising. *Journal of Personality and Social Psychology, 49*, 586–597.

Reading 15: Petty, R. E., & Wegener, D. T. (1998). Matching versus mismatching attitude functions: Implications for scrutiny of persuasive messages. *Personality and Social Psychology Bulletin, 24*, 227–240.

Reading 16: Fein, S., & Spencer, S. J. (1997). Prejudice as self-image maintenance: Affirming the self through derogating others. *Journal of Personality and Social Psychology, 73*, 31–44.

Reading 17: Fazio, R. H., Blascovich, J., & Driscoll, D. M. (1992). On the functional value of attitudes: The influence of accessible attitudes on the ease and quality of decision making. *Personality and Social Psychology Bulletin, 18*, 388–401.

Reading 18: Wilson, T. D., & Schooler, J. W. (1991). Thinking too much: Introspection can reduce the quality of preferences and decisions. *Journal of Personality and Social Psychology, 60*, 181–192.

Reading 19: Hastorf, A. H., & Cantril, H. (1954). They saw a game: A case study. *Journal of Abnormal and Social Psychology, 49*, 129–134.

Reading 20: Lord, C. G., Ross, L., & Lepper, M. R. (1979). Biased assimilation and attitude polarization: The effects of prior theories on subsequently considered evidence. *Journal of Personality and Social Psychology, 37*, 2098–2109.

Reading 21: Ross, M., McFarland, C., & Fletcher, G. J. O. (1981). The effect of attitude on the recall of personal histories. *Journal of Personality and Social Psychology, 40*, 627–634.

Reading 22: Roskos-Ewoldsen, D. R., & Fazio, R. H. (1992). On the orienting value of attitudes: Attitude accessibility as a determinant of an object's attraction of visual attention. *Journal of Personality and Social Psychology, 63*, 198–211.

Reading 23: Sweeney, P. D., & Gruber, K. L. (1984). Selective exposure: Voter information preferences and the Watergate affair. *Journal of Personality and Social Psychology, 46*, 1208–1221.

Reading 24: LaPiere, R. T. (1934). Attitudes vs. actions. *Social Forces, 13*, 230–237.

Reading 25: Lord, C. G., Lepper, M. R., & Mackie, D. (1984). Attitude prototypes as determinants of attitude–behavior consistency. *Journal of Personality and Social Psychology, 46*, 1254–1266.

Reading 26: Ajzen, I., & Fishbein, M. (1973). Attitudinal and normative variables as predictors of specific behaviors. *Journal of Personality and Social Psychology, 27*, 41–57.

Reading 27: Fazio, R. H., & Williams, C. J. (1986). Attitude accessibility as a moderator of the attitude-perception and attitude-behavior relations: An investigation of the 1984 presidential election. *Journal of Personality and Social Psychology, 51*, 505–514.

PART 1

Conceptualizing Attitudes

The term *attitudes* commonly refers to our general evaluations of people, objects, and issues. Although the study of attitudes has been central to the field of social psychology for a long time now, the concept has been viewed in diverse ways over the decades. The term has evolved over time. In order to fully understand and appreciate its current usage, it is useful to know a bit of its history.

Even as long ago as 1935, when Gordon Allport wrote a very influential chapter on attitudes for the *Handbook of Social Psychology*, the term already had a rich history. Allport notes that "attitude" had been used in the field of art to refer to the posture of a figure in a painting or sculpture. There are remnants of this meaning today when we pose the question, "What is your *stance* or *position* on some issue?" This connotation also was evident in what was among the very first usages of the term in experimental psychology—within the study of reaction time. In the late 1800s, numerous studies revealed that participants who were mentally prepared to press a telegraph key upon receiving a signal were able to respond more quickly than those whose attention was directed mainly to the incoming signal and not on the reaction required of them. The importance of this state of preparedness, which sometimes was referred to as a "task-attitude" or "mental set," was demonstrated repeatedly in studies of perception and memory.

In the 1900s, sociologists and psychologists interested in individual differences began to adopt the concept of attitude. In part, this grew from increasing dissatisfaction with the term "instinct" (e.g., an instinct for craftmanship), which fell from favor due to its connotations regarding biological or hereditary influences on behavior. Allport views the desire for a term that placed more emphasis on the role of social and cultural forces as a reason for the emergence of the attitude construct within the social sciences. Indeed, the sociologists Thomas and Znaniecki (1918) are typically credited with this emergence. In a very influential book concerned with the Polish peasant, they used the term to refer to the plans, interests, and sympathies of the average individual. Their enthusiasm for the attitude concept prompted Thomas and Znanieki to define the field of social psychology as the study of attitudes.

Beginning with these early tracings of the attitude concept, Allport (1935) reviewed a large number of definitions that had been offered. His analysis of their common threads and the debates that had appeared regarding the meaning and utility of the construct led him to propose what is certainly the most commonly-cited and widely-known of the early definitions of attitude. "An attitude is a mental and neural state of readiness, organized through experience, exerting a directive or dynamic influence upon the individual's response to all objects and situations with which it is related" (p. 810).

Allport's definition is no longer widely accepted. However, its features provide useful points of departure that help to elucidate the evolution of the concept of attitude into its modern form. Let us consider some key elements of the definition in turn.

"An attitude is a . . . state of readiness . . ." This idea obviously stems from the historical context noted earlier and, in particular, the connotations stemming from use of the term "attitude" in the arts and in early reaction time research. The idea that attitudes "prepare" one to respond in some appropriate manner remains central to the concept of attitude as it is used today, and indeed points to one of the ways in which attitudes prove functional for individuals in daily life—a topic on which we shall focus at a later point in this volume. As we shall see, attitudes serve what is called a knowledge or object appraisal function, enabling the individual to make quick, easy, and efficient decisions about whether to approach or avoid an object.

"An attitude is . . . organized . . ." The idea that an attitude is organized as a mental structure of one sort or another came to be embodied in what is known as the tripartite, three-component, or ABC model of attitudes (Katz & Stotland, 1959; Rosenberg & Hovland, 1960). According to this view, attitudes consist of three classes of information: (a) affective—feelings or emotions that people have in response to the object, (b) behavioral—actions that people have engaged in, or are inclined to engage in, with respect to the attitude object, and (c) cognitive—beliefs that people have about the characteristics of the object. This particular conception is no longer endorsed widely. The reasons for the shift away from the three-component view are detailed in the first reading in this section by Zanna and Rempel (1988). As these authors articulate, the tripartite model implies some degree of consistency among affective, cognitive, and behavioral reactions to an object. Yet, what are we to make of a person who fails to behave consistently with his or her beliefs about some object? Does the person not have an attitude? If the answer were to be "yes," then we are essentially "defining away" what could be interesting questions for empirical research. There is no reason to ask about the

consistency between attitudes and behavior if consistent behavior is a pre-condition for application of the attitude concept. The very definition calls for behavioral consistency. Instead of adopting a definition that prejudges the attitude–behavior relation, Zanna and Rempel endorse a perspective in which attitudes are viewed simply as evaluations—evaluations that themselves can be based on beliefs, feelings, and/or past behavior. As they note, this view encourages the pursuit of questions regarding how attitudes based differentially on affect, cognition, or behavior might differ from one another in terms of the impact they have on behavior and in terms of their persistence over time. The perspective also encourages empirical research regarding the consequences of having affective and cognitive reactions that are consistent with one another versus more contradictory or ambivalent in nature. These questions receive attention in later sections of this volume.

"An attitude . . . [exerts] a directive . . . influence . . ."
The assertion offered here is that attitudes guide subsequent behavior toward the object. So, an individual who thinks highly of a political candidate will vote for the candidate. An individual who regards donating to a charity as a noble gesture will make a monetary contribution. The problem, as we shall see in a later section of the volume, is that such one-to-one correspondence between attitudes and behavior does not necessarily occur. Other variables can intervene. Many qualities of the person, the situation, and the attitude itself can influence the extent to which attitudes guide behavior. Although having a ready guide to behavior is one important reason why people hold attitudes, it does not seem appropriate to assume

attitude–behavior consistency as part of one's very definition of attitude.

"An attitude . . . [exerts] a dynamic . . . influence . . ."
The reference here is to the possibility that attitudes may actually motivate or energize behavior, just as drive states or needs such as hunger and thirst do. This ascription of motivation power to the attitude concept never gained much acceptance. Although the idea that one's evaluations of an object have the potential to direct one's actions regarding the object is unquestionably true, it seems far less plausible that evaluations would, in and of themselves, produce behavior. Sometimes, individuals do actually seek out opportunities to promote their attitudes. Certainly that can be said of some evangelists and political activists. However, such actions seem more a property of the individual's intense personal attachment to the issue than to the favorability per se. Much more than a positive attitude is necessary for individuals to initiate advocacy.

The current perspective. The most commonly accepted modern view of attitudes grew from the concerns that have been noted regarding Allport's definition and the tripartite model. In the interest of avoiding a definition that makes assumptions about the influence that attitudes may or may not exert, most attitude researchers now adopt a fairly simple definition of attitudes. As noted in opening this section, an attitude is a person's evaluation of an object—favorability or unfavorability toward the object. This definition actually can be traced back to the one-component perspective that various early theorists such as Thurstone (1928) espoused. However, as Zanna and Rempel (1988) argued in the first reading, the modern conception explicitly acknowledges that the basis for any given evaluation can vary: the attitude may stem from beliefs, i.e., appraisals of the attributes that characterize the object; it can stem from emotional reactions that the attitude object evokes; it can be based on one's past behaviors and experiences with the object; or it can be based on some combination of these potential sources of evaluative information.

In the second reading, Fazio, Sanbonmatsu, Powell, and Kardes (1986) take this perspective one step further. These authors view the attitude as an association that exists in memory between the attitude object and the summary evaluation of the object. Their model emphasizes that the strength of this association and, as a result, the accessibility of the attitude from memory can vary. In a series of experiments employing a priming paradigm, they demonstrate that attitudes sometimes involve sufficiently strong associations that the evaluation is automatically activated from memory upon mere observation of the attitude object (see Fazio, 2001, for a review of research concerning the priming paradigm). Some people cannot help but experience a negative reaction when they observe a snake. Some have an inescapable positive reaction to the thought of chocolate, or an immediate "yuk" response to the mention of ordering anchovies on a pizza. This view allows for the possibility that attitudes may exert some influence on perceptions, judgments, and behavior without an individual consciously reflecting upon how they evaluate the attitude object. An association in memory can get activated and begin to exert influence simply as a function of its heightened activation. Indeed, attitude accessibility has been found to play an important role with respect to both the power of attitudes and their functional value. These are topics that receive attention in later sections of the volume.

REFERENCES

Allport, G. W. (1935). Attitudes. In C. Murchison (Ed.), *Handbook of social psychology* (pp. 798–844). Worcester, MA: Clark University Press.

Fazio, R. H. (2001). On the automatic activation of associated evaluations: An overview. *Cognition and Emotion*, *15*, 115–141.

Katz, D., & Stotland, E. (1959). A preliminary statement to a theory of attitude structure and change. In S. Koch (Ed.), *Psychology: A study of a science* (Vol. 3, pp. 423–475). New York: McGraw-Hill.

Rosenberg, M. J., & Hovland, C. I. (1960). Cognitive, affective, and behavioral components of attitude. In M. J. Rosenberg *et al.* (Eds.), *Attitude organization and change: An analysis of consistency among attitude components* (pp. 1–14). New Haven, CT: Yale University Press.

Thomas, W. I., & Znaniecki, F. (1918). *The Polish peasant in Europe and America*. Boston, MA: Badger.

Thurstone, L. L. (1928). Attitudes can be measured. *American Journal of Sociology*, *33*, 529–544.

Suggested Readings

Breckler, S. J. (1984). Empirical validation of affect, behavior, and cognition as distinct components of attitude. *Journal of Personality and Social Psychology, 47,* 1191–1205.

Cacioppo, J. T., Gardner, W., & Berntsen, G. (1999). Beyond bipolar conceptualizations and measures: The case of attitudes and evaluative space. *Personality and Social Psychology Review, 1,* 3–25.

Fazio, R. H. (1995). Attitudes as object-evaluation associations: Determinants, consequences, and correlates of attitude accessibility. In R. E. Petty & J. A. Krosnick (Eds.), *Attitude strength: Antecedents and consequences* (pp. 247–282). Hillsdale, NJ: Erlbaum.

Attitudes: A New Look at an Old Concept

Mark P. Zanna and John K. Rempel

The study of attitudes and attitudinal processes has long preoccupied social scientists. Yet despite the concept's venerable and influential history (cf. Fleming 1967), agreement on precisely what an attitude is and how it can be identified has proven to be somewhat elusive (McGuire 1985). There is the general understanding that an attitude has, as its base, an element of evaluation (Ostrom 1969). In his recent work, Fazio (1986) has argued that attitudes primarily fulfill a "knowledge function". Following the functionalist theorists (e.g. Katz 1960), Fazio characterizes attitudes as summary judgments of an object or event which aid individuals in structuring their complex social environments. As such, attitudes can be seen as items of social knowledge, built from the experiences, beliefs, and feelings generated by the attitude objects.

Nevertheless, a number of issues remain unresolved. Briefly, these issues consist of (1) the role played by feelings, beliefs and behaviors in the attitude concept, (2) the dispositional versus episodic nature of attitudes, and (3) the relationship between affect and evaluation. In the following discussion we will present a model of attitudes which will address these various issues. In the process we will consider how an approach to attitudes as knowledge structures can both benefit from and contribute to a more general understanding of social knowledge.

Issues Concerning the Definition of the Attitude Concept

We will begin with a more detailed examination of the issues surrounding attitudinal definition. First we turn to the role of beliefs, feelings, and behavior in the attitude concept. Different theorists tend to advocate definitions which emphasize either a unitary or multicomponent view of attitudes. The most popular definition, at least if one surveys recent social psychology texts, would suggest that attitudes consist of three classes of response (affective, cognitive, and behavioral) to a stimulus, or attitude, object. This view, popularized by Milton Rosenberg and Carl Hovland in the early 1960s (Rosenberg and Hovland 1960), basically suggests that an attitude consists of how we feel, what we think, and what we are inclined to do about an attitude object. Building upon the early work of Ostrom (1969) and Kothandapani (1971), Breckler, in a recent dissertation (Breckler 1983, 1984), has provided impressive evidence supporting this

In addition to the editors and each of the participants of the conference at which this paper was first presented, we wish to thank John Cacioppo, Russell Fazio, Connie Kristiansen, and James Olson for their comments on an earlier draft of the chapter.

so-called three-component or "tripartite" model of attitudes. Using both verbal and nonverbal measures, Breckler's data demonstrate that affect, cognition, and behavior, though related, do have discriminative validity.

Another common definition of attitudes can be traced back to early attitude theorists such as Thurstone (Thurstone and Chave 1929). This view would suggest that attitudes consist of evaluative or affective responses to attitude objects. More recently popularized by Martin Fishbein and Icek Ajzen (1975), this essentially one-component view proposes that affective responses are based upon cognition.

We believe there are conceptual problems with each viewpoint. One concern we have with the three-component view is that it tends to prejudge the attitude–behavior relation, assuming that, almost by definition, such a relation must exist. The early evidence indicating that the attitude–behavior relation was tenuous (Wicker 1969) may have led theorists not only to feel uncomfortable with the tripartite model but to become unduly pessimistic about the notion of attitudes in general.

The one-component view helps resolve the question of attitude–behavior consistency, by making it a theoretical or even empirical question, rather than a definitional necessity. However, the effort to reduce attitudes to a single component may have resulted in an oversimplification. One concern we have with this view, especially as advanced by Fishbein and Ajzen, is that it seems too narrow in its suggestion that evaluative responses are based primarily (if not entirely) on what we would call utilitarian beliefs. To put it another way, there is as yet little or no emphasis on affective experience *per se* or, for that matter, on past behaviors. And, of course, recent models, as well as data, would suggest attitudes can be based upon affect associated with and/or past behaviors relevant to the attitude object.

Robert Zajonc (1980), for example, has recently proposed that one's preferences can be based on affect *per se* and recent empirical work does suggest that affect is an important determinant of evaluation and/or behavior. In a paper which greatly influenced our own thinking, Abelson and

his colleagues (Abelson *et al.* 1982) have demonstrated that affective or emotional states associated with presidential candidates influenced individuals' evaluations of these candidates over and above the conventional beliefs that were held about the candidates. Similar findings, that affect can have a strong and independent effect on attitudes and/or behavior, have now been reported in several other domains, including energy conservation (Seligman *et al.* 1979), health behaviors (Ajzen and Timko 1985), responses to victimization (Tyler and Rasinski 1984), and contraceptive behavior (Fisher 1984).

Daryl Bem, in several influential papers (e.g. Bem 1972), has proposed that attitudes are often inferred from past behaviors, taking into account the conditions under which the behavior was performed. Considerable research has supported this notion (cf. Fazio *et al.* 1977), including a series of elegant studies by Salancik and his colleagues (e.g. Salancik 1974, Salancik and Conway 1975) which demonstrated that subtle manipulations of the salience of past behaviors dramatically influenced individuals' assessments of their attitudes.

Thus the attitude literature is dominated by two conflicting definitions, neither of which seems entirely satisfactory in accounting for the data. By approaching the issue from divergent perspectives, researchers have in effect produced numerous one-component views, each of which emphasizes either cognition, affect, or behavior. By combining the three components into one definition, however, the tenuous relation between attitude and behavior remains problematic.

Some theorists have attempted to deal with the inconsistency among definitions by removing behavior from the attitude equation, and representing attitude as a two-component structure consisting of cognition and affect (Fleming 1967, Zajonc and Markus 1982, Bagozzi and Burnkrant 1979). Others have, in fact, moved toward a loose integration of the one- and three-component views. In this approach, the attitude itself is regarded as a single entity; an evaluative disposition to respond to an object or event in a favorable or unfavorable manner. The three components (beliefs, feelings, and actions) are retained as the three domains in which the attitude is expressed in observable responses (Davis and Ostrom 1984, Ostrom 1969, Ajzen 1984). Greenwald (1968) and subsequently Breckler (1983, 1984) have gone one step further, to argue that the existence of three response categories does not presuppose that they are internally consistent. There is, consequently, no need to assume an *a priori* congruence between attitudes and behavior. Further, these researchers feel that the three components are distinguishable via their developmental roots. Greenwald in particular argues that cognition, affect, and behavioral intentions are coded separately by means of distinct learning processes.

While there is activity among theorists at a conceptual level to move toward integrating the one- and three-component approaches, authors of recent introductory social psychology texts, such as Olson and Zanna (1983) and Myers (1983), have continued to opt for either the one-component or the three-component view. Thus, the distinction continues to provide an important area of conceptual disagreement, at least when presented to an introductory audience.

A second general issue, which is somewhat related to the one-versus-three-component distinction, concerns the extent to which an attitude is dispositional or episodic in nature. Common definitions present attitudes as relatively stable enduring dispositions (cf. Ajzen 1984, Ostrom 1984). In contrast, Bem (1972) has suggested that attitudes may often be the consequence of a relatively superficial inference based on past behavior. From this perspective, attitudinal responses do not reflect an enduring disposition but, rather, indicate a less stable assessment which is more reactive to external cues (see also Salancik 1982). Several researchers have attempted to resolve this controversy by suggesting that superficial attitudinal assessments based on external cues occur when an attitude is either not clearly formed (e.g. Norman 1975, Chaiken and Baldwin 1981) or is inaccessible from internal states (Wood, 1982, Tybout and Scott 1983). Thus these researchers do not assume that an attitudinal response necessarily indicates an enduring disposition toward the attitude object. Further, these views regard issues concerning the

internal consistency of the three attitude components as matters to be resolved by empirical investigation.

A final issue concerns the relationship between affect and evaluation. As was mentioned at the outset, most definitions of attitude rely on some reference to an evaluative element. In some cases the evaluative character of an attitude is regarded as isomorphic with the affective component (Ajzen 1984, Zajonc and Markus 1982, Staats 1968), whereas other researchers see the attitude and its affective component as distinct entities (Mills *et al.* 1976, Abelson *et al.* 1982). We believe that part of the confusion stems from a rather broad and imprecise usage of the term "affect". Affect has been used to refer to any thoughts or actions with overtones of pleasant/unpleasant, good/bad, approach/avoidance, etc. These thoughts or actions may be infused with strong emotion, weak emotion or no feeling at all. We suggest that subsequent usage of the term "affect" be restricted to those cases where emotions or feelings are present in an experiential sense, and that these be distinguished from the cognitive categorization of an object or event along an evaluative dimension. Thus, to use an example from Abelson *et al.*'s (1982) research, individuals are likely to have affects (i.e. emotions or feelings) associated with particular political candidates as well as overall evaluations (i.e. assessments of worth or goodness) of the candidates.

Attitudes: Evaluations based on Beliefs, Feelings, and/or Past Behavior

The definitional issues we have just discussed form the starting-point for our reconceptualization of the attitude construct. Simply stated, we regard an attitude as the categorization of a stimulus object along an evaluative dimension based upon, or generated from, three general classes of information: (1) cognitive information, (2) affective/emotional information, and/or (3) information concerning past behaviors or behavioral intentions.

Let us examine this definition in more detail. First, what do we mean by evaluative dimension?

An evaluative dimension is a dimension on which a comparison can be made between the value or worth of the stimulus object and another object or standard. Thus, in its simplest form the dimension itself consists of a minimum of two discrete categories with the object either judged against an absolute standard (good/bad) or a relative comparison with one or more objects (better than/ worse than). As the number of categories increases the discrete dimension becomes a continuum (e.g. a scale from 1 to 10).

Second, by categorization we refer to a process with at least some minimal cognitive activity. The stimulus object must be perceived and identified at some level before a value judgment can be made. Thus, although, as we will describe shortly, non-cognitive activity may be a basis for an attitude, evaluation itself requires cognitive input.

Describing the attitude concept as cognition is another way of stating that attitudes are, in fact, items of knowledge. Summarizing attitudes at this level of generality, however, masks many of the details which we believe are critical to understanding the implications of the attitude concept. An example may clarify this point. Consider a parent whose child has been killed by a drunk driver. Despite the fact that, when replying to an attitude question toward drivers who drink, the parent is engaging in cognitive activity, the *content* of his or her attitude is, in all likelihood, an intense emotional experience accompanied by a flood of memories containing behaviors and events of the past. The fact that the evaluation is itself a cognitive item of knowledge does not begin to adequately inform the researcher how the attitude is being *experienced*. We argue, therefore, that although it is possible for an attitudinal judgment to be dependent strictly on factual beliefs, attitudes may also be suffused with powerful emotions or may even depend solely on the ways in which the individual has behaved with the attitude object in the past. These sources are not mutually exclusive, of course, and can all be present and acting at the same time. We want to emphasize, however, that beliefs, feelings, and behaviors are more than ways in which individuals can respond to stimulus objects. Rather, they constitute very different ways

in which the attitude is formed and subsequently experienced.

This definition of attitudes has a number of important implications for the issues discussed earlier. First, it leaves open the question of congruence among the attitudinal components. It is possible, within this definition, for an individual to have more than one attitude towards the same object if, over occasions, the evaluative judgment is based on a different source of information. Second, this definition reinforces the position that the dispositional or episodic nature of attitudes must be an empirical rather than a definitional question. We suggest that the answer to the stability of an attitude lies, at least in part, with the source that is playing a dominant role in the attitudinal experience. For example, one source (e.g. behavior) may lead to more stability than some other source (e.g. cognition). And an attitude based on congruent sources may be more stable than an attitude based upon incongruent sources. Finally, this definition clearly takes the position that evaluation and affect or emotion are not the same concept (cf. Simon 1982). As was suggested earlier, emotions may be a component, or even the sole basis, of an evaluation, but the two need not occur together.

Given that we are considering an attitude as knowledge based on three sources, the question necessarily arises, why these particular sources? On the one hand we have suggested why subsuming all sources under the more general category of cognition is undesirable. It is a level of analysis which clouds the important elements that may distinguish the experience of one attitude from another. There is, however, the other side of the coin, and that is, why do we choose to focus at the level of three general categories rather than becoming still more specific? We do so because, first, the tripartite distinction has set a strong historical precedent, not only in attitude theory but in Western philosophy as a whole. Such longevity and pervasive influence, it could be argued, attests the utility and heuristic value of such a distinction. Also, using the tripartite framework allows an easy integration of previous attitude theory and research into the present model.

Finally, recent research (Lingle and Ostrom 1981) suggests that the beliefs upon which an attitude is based may not be accessed when the attitude is subsequently activated. If so, it makes little sense to focus on more specific sources such as different types of belief. More generally, this line of reasoning suggests that attitudes not only act as summary statements (Fazio 1986) but are stored as separate cognitive entities, independent of the specific beliefs and, perhaps, of the feelings and/or behaviors on which they were based.

Why then, however, do we concern ourselves with different sources in the first place, if, as implied, these play no subsequent role in how attitudes are stored? This seeming paradox is resolved by noting that while Lingle and Ostrom did argue that an attitude, once formed, can be accessed without "consulting" the specific beliefs upon which the attitude was originally based, they did not propose that these formative beliefs never come to mind once the attitude is activated. To the extent that there are strong associative networks in memory between the attitude and its constituent beliefs, one would expect the opposite to be the case.

While Lingle and Ostrom focused their research on the cognitive domain, we believe their findings may apply to the domains of feelings and past behavior as well. Regarding feelings or emotions, for example, we would argue that the general evaluative response to an attitude object may be stored and persist even though the more specific emotional reactions which led to the overall evaluative judgment are no longer accessible. Nevertheless, when such an attitude is subsequently activated, it would still generate an emotionally based evaluation and a response with emotional content.

Thus, our interpretation of Lingle and Ostrom suggests that it very well may be useful to focus on sources at the general level of beliefs, feelings, and past behaviors, rather than at more specific levels.

In summary, our reconceptualization can be viewed as an attempt to take existing notions and combine them in a new and heuristically useful way. First, we define attitude as the categorization of a stimulus object along an evaluative dimension (i.e. an evaluation). Second, we propose that such evaluation can be based upon three classes of information: (1) cognitive information, (2) affective information, and (3) information concerning past behaviors. We believe these classes of information can determine evaluations separately or in combination. When, however, evaluations are based primarily on (utilitarian) beliefs about the attitude object, the present model can be reduced to something like the formulation proposed by Fishbein and Ajzen (1975). When evaluations are based primarily on affects produced by or associated with the attitude object, the model can resemble the formulation proposed by Zajonc (1980). Finally, when evaluations are based on inferences from past behavior, the model can be similar to Bem's theory of self-perception (1972). Given past research, we feel that our model of attitudes is an accurate reflection of what attitudes actually are. Further, we believe that such a view can both provide a springboard from which more complex attitude-related phenomena can be explored and at the same time offer a general framework into which research on attitudes can be placed.

Understanding Past Research

If this reconceptualization of the attitude concept is to be useful, it must both help us understand past research and suggest new directions for future research. Let us turn first to past research.

The present model suggests several questions which different researchers, at least implicitly, have addressed in recent years. For example, if attitudes are based on different sources of information, do otherwise equivalent evaluations based on different sources differentially guide (i.e. predict) future behavior? Fazio and Zanna (1981) have been asking just this sort of question. These authors have provided evidence that attitudes based on direct experience with the attitude object predict behavior better than do attitudes based upon indirect experience. In the vocabulary of the current model, Fazio and Zanna have demonstrated that otherwise equivalent evaluations based primarily on past behavior predict future behavior better than evaluations based primarily on cognition. Given the current model's emphasis on three sources of information, an interesting question for future research on direct experience would be whether such experience with an attitude object additionally produces an affective experience, at least under some conditions. That is, does direct experience lead to an attitude based on both past behavioral and affective information?

As mentioned earlier, several researchers have recently demonstrated that one's affects (or feelings) guide behavior, independently from one's cognitions (or beliefs), and perhaps to a greater extent. So, for example, Abelson and his colleagues (Abelson *et al.* 1982) demonstrated that voting preferences were independently (and better) predicted by affects (e.g. whether the candidate made one feel happy or sad) than by cognitions (e.g. whether one thought the candidate was competent or incompetent). In the current model's terms, we would note that evaluations based upon affects seem to guide relevant behavior.

Indeed, a recent series of studies by Wilson and his colleagues (Wilson *et al.* 1984) found that by inducing individuals to analyze the reasons for their affectively based attitudes, the attitude–behavior relation was decreased. According to Wilson, thinking about the reasons why one holds a particular attitude may lead to a reported evaluation based primarily on cognition, rather than upon affect (Wilson *et al.* 1986). If so, and if subsequent behavior continues to be influenced by an evaluation based on one's original feelings, such a "cognitivized" attitude is not likely to guide future behavior.

In future research it would be interesting to determine whether the sort of affect–behavior relation documented by Abelson *et al.* is, in fact, mediated by an overall evaluation (i.e. an attitude). Further, and paralleling the research on direct experience, it would be of interest to ask directly whether the attitude–behavior relation is stronger when attitudes are based primarily on one's feelings rather than on one's beliefs. An intriguing recent study by Millar and Tesser (1985) suggests this question may be put too simply. These authors found strong support for the hypothesis that

evaluations based primarily on beliefs about attitude objects (in this instance analytic puzzles) predicted behavior towards the attitude objects only when the behavior (playing with the puzzles) was undertaken for instrumental reasons (i.e. cognitively driven). When the behavior was performed for consumatory, noninstrumental purposes (i.e. affectively driven), it was much better predicted by attitudes based primarily on feelings. Thus, it appears that the strength of an attitude–behavior relation may depend not only on the source of the attitude, but on the purposes of the behavior as well.

In passing, we might note that the present model also provides a way of conceptualizing symbolic attitudes (cf. Kinder and Sears 1981). The present model would suggest that a symbolic attitude might be thought of as an evaluation based primarily on affects associated with symbolic connections to the attitude object. Certainly, our understanding of symbolic attitudes would be enhanced if researchers were to collect direct measures of affects, cognitions, and past behaviors as well as overall evaluations.

The question of what source of information dominates evaluations is also of interest in the domain of social perception. Here the question becomes: what source of information is the most valid indicator of another person's attitude? Research by Amabile and Kabat (1982) has demonstrated that actions do speak louder than words. However, more recent work by Andersen (Andersen and Ross 1984, Andersen 1984) would suggest that the domination of behavior over cognition may only hold for public deeds and words. Andersen, in fact, has demonstrated that private thoughts/feelings are perceived to be more valid indicators of the real self than are behaviors. We believe it would be of interest for future research in the social perception of attitudes to examine all three sources of information in both private and public domains.

Because the model does not assume consistency among the various sources of information, one might ask if consistency among the sources makes a difference in, say, the prediction of behavior. Several researchers (e.g. Norman 1975, Chaiken and Baldwin 1981, Rosenberg 1968) have, in fact, been asking this sort of question. Norman, working from a traditional three-component view, for example, demonstrated that attitudes high in affective–cognitive consistency better predict behavior than attitudes low in affective–cognitive consistency. Individuals with attitudes low in affective–cognitive consistency are not thought to hold very strong attitudes, or, according to Chaiken and Baldwin (1981), are thought to be aschematic with respect to the attitude object. In the current model's terms, we simply suggest that evaluations based on consistent sources of information, whatever the sources, are more likely to predict behavior. Future research might address two general questions. First, how about other inconsistencies – inconsistencies between affect and past behavior or between cognition and past behavior? Second, should attitudes based upon inconsistent information be considered nonattitudes or, more intriguingly, ambivalent attitudes? If such evaluations are highly unstable or ambivalent, what source of information typically dominates? Or, does the weight given to a particular source of information depend, in part, on situational variables? If so, do evaluations based on chronically inconsistent sources of information predict behavior reasonably well when one or the other source is acutely dominant or salient? These questions, and others, left to the readers' imagination, suggest that studying attitudes based on inconsistent information may be at least as interesting as studying attitudes derived from consistent sources of information – if not more interesting. [. . .]

Conclusion

In the present chapter we have attempted to present the outlines of a model of attitudes that incorporates the main ideas of past conceptualizations in a way that (1) capitalizes on the strengths of several of the most prominent, current models, and (2) provides a framework for future research. We will have fulfilled our purpose if we have piqued the reader's curiosity by the sort of research questions that we believe flow from the model. It is our hope,

however, that these questions will actually capture research attention in the coming years.

By characterizing attitudes as items of knowledge in the form of evaluative summations, we hope to have also added to the understanding of social knowledge in general. Perhaps the most important contribution arises from an examination of the bases or sources of an attitude. In emphasizing multiple sources we suggest that the basis and experience of knowledge in general cannot be simply understood in terms of cognition alone. Rather, social knowledge rests as much on past behaviors and emotions as it does on beliefs. This goes beyond the obvious suggestion that knowledge has multiple sources to argue that the impact a piece of knowledge has on an individual may depend heavily on how it is experienced. In other words, we agree that a study of social knowledge should both give strong consideration to the sources of such knowledge and then go on to consider the impact that such sources have when the knowledge is again called to action.

REFERENCES

Abelson, R. P. (1982). Three modes of attitude–behavior consistency. In M. P. Zanna, E. T. Higgins, and C. P. Herman (eds.), *Consistency in social behavior: the Ontario symposium* (vol. 2). Hillsdale, NJ: Lawrence Erlbaum.

Abelson, R. P., Kinder, D. R., Peters, M. D., and Fiske, S. T. (1982). Affective and semantic components in political person perception. *Journal of Personality and Social Psychology* 42: 619–30.

Ajzen, I. (1984). Attitudes. In R. J. Corsini (ed.), *Wiley encyclopedia of psychology*, vol. 1. New York: Wiley.

Ajzen, I. and Timko, C. (1985). *Correspondence between health attitudes and behavior*. Unpublished manuscript, University of Massachusetts.

Amabile, T. M. and Kabat, L. G. (1982). When self-descriptions contradict behavior: actions do speak louder than words. *Social Cognition* 1: 311–35.

Andersen, S. M. (1984). Self-knowledge and social inference. II: The diagnosticity of cognitive/affective and behavioral data. *Journal of Personality and Social Psychology* 46: 294–307.

Andersen, S. M. and Ross, L. (1984). Self-knowledge and social inference I: The impact of cognitive/affective and behavioral data. *Journal of Personality and Social Psychology* 46: 280–93.

Andersen, S. M. and Williams, M. (1985). *Salience and self-inference: the role of biased recollections in self-inference processes*. Unpublished manuscript, University of California, Santa Barbara.

Bagozzi, R. P. and Burnkrant, R. E. (1979). Attitude organization and the attitude–behavior relationship. *Journal of Personality and Social Psychology* 37: 913–29.

Bem, D. J. (1972). Self-perception theory. In L. Berkowitz (ed.), *Advances in experimental social psychology*, vol. 6. New York: Academic Press.

Breckler, S. J. (1983). *Validation of affect, behavior, and cognition as distinct components of attitude*. Unpublished dissertation, Ohio State University, Columbus.

Breckler, S. J. (1984). Empirical validation of affect, behavior, and cognition as distinct components of attitude. *Journal of Personality and Social Psychology* 47: 1191–205.

Cacioppo, J. T. and Petty, R. E. (1982a). The need for cognition. *Journal of Personality and Social Psychology* 42: 116–31.

Cacioppo, J. T. and Petty, R. E. (1982b). A biosocial model of attitude change. In J. T. Cacioppo and R. E. Petty (eds.), *Perspectives in cardiovascular psychophysiology*. New York: Guilford Press.

Cacioppo, J. T. and Petty, R. E. (1987). Stalking rudimentary processes of social influence: a psychophysiological approach. In M. P. Zanna, J. M. Olson, and C. P. Herman (eds.), *Social influence: the Ontario symposium*, vol. 5. Hillsdale, NJ: Erlbaum.

Chaiken, S. and Baldwin, M. W. (1981). Affective–cognitive consistency and the effect of salient behavioral information on the self-perception of attitudes. *Journal of Personality and Social Psychology* 41: 1–12.

Davis, D. and Ostrom, T. M. (1984). Attitude measurement. In R. J. Corsini (ed.), *Wiley encyclopedia of psychology*, vol. 1. New York: Wiley.

Fazio, R. H. (1986). How do attitudes guide behavior? In R. M. Sorrentino and E. T. Higgins (eds.), *The handbook of motivation and cognition: foundations of social behavior*. New York: Guilford Press.

Fazio, R. H. and Zanna, M. P. (1981). Direct experience and attitude–behavior consistency. In L. Berkowitz (ed.), *Advances in experimental social psychology*, vol. 14. New York: Academic Press.

Fazio, R. H., Zanna, M. P., and Cooper, J. (1977). Dissonance and self-perception: an examination of each theory's proper domain of application. *Journal of Experimental Social Psychology* 13: 464–79.

Fishbein, M. and Ajzen, I. (1975). *Belief, attitude, intention, and behavior: an introduction to theory and research*. Reading, MA: Addison-Wesley.

Fisher, W. A. (1984). Predicting contraceptive behavior among university men: the role of emotions and behavioral intentions. *Journal of Applied Social Psychology* 14: 104–23.

Fleming, D. (1967). Attitude: the history of a concept. In D. Fleming and B. Bailyn (eds.), *Perspectives in American history*, vol. 1. Cambridge, MA: Charles Warren Center in American History, Harvard University.

Greenwald, A. G. (1968). On defining attitude and attitude theory. In A. G. Greenwald, T. C. Brock, and T. M. Ostrom (eds.), *Psychological foundations of attitudes*. New York: Academic Press.

Jung, C. G. (1923). *Psychological types*. London: Constable.

Katz, D. (1960). The functional approach to the study of attitudes. *Public Opinion Quarterly* 24: 163–204.

Kinder, D. R. and Sears, D. O. (1981). Symbolic racism versus racial threats to the good life. *Journal of Personality and Social Psychology* 40: 414–31.

Kothandapani, V. (1971). Validation of feeling, belief, and intention to act as three components of attitude and their contribution to the prediction of contraceptive behaviour. *Journal of Personality and Social Psychology* 19: 321–33.

Lingle, J. H. and Ostrom, T. M. (1981). Principles of memory and cognition in attitude formation. In R. Petty, T. Ostrom, and T. Brock (eds.), *Cognitive responses to persuasion*. Hillsdale, NJ: Lawrence Erlbaum.

Lydon, J., Zanna, M. P., and Ross, M. (in press). Bolstering newly-formed attitudes by autobiographical recall: implications for attitude persistence and selective memory. *Personality and Social Psychology Bulletin*.

McGuire, W. J. (1985). Attitudes and attitude change. In G. Lindzey and E. Aronson (eds.), *Handbook of social psychology*, 3rd ed. Reading, MA: Addison-Wesley.

Millar, M. G. and Tesser, A. (1985). *Effects of affective and cognitive focus on the attitude–behaviour relationship*. Unpublished manuscript, University of Georgia.

Mills, J., Jellison, J. M., and Kennedy, J. (1976). Attribution of attitudes from feelings: effect of positive or negative feelings when the attitude object is benefited or harmed. In J. H. Harvey, W. J. Ickes, and R. F. Kidd (eds.), *New directions in attribution research*, vol. 1. Hillsdale, NJ: Lawrence Erlbaum.

Myers, D. G. (1983). *Social psychology*. New York, NY: McGraw-Hill.

Niedenthal, P. M. and Cantor, N. (1985). *Affect-based categorization and category based affect*. Unpublished manuscript, University of Michigan.

Norman, R. (1975). Affective–cognitive consistency, attitudes, conformity, and behavior. *Journal of Personality and Social Psychology* 32: 83–91.

Olson, J. M. and Zanna, M. P. (1983). Attitude change and behaviour prediction. In D. Perlman and P. C. Cozby (eds.), *Social psychology*. New York: CBS College Publishing.

Ostrom, T. M. (1969). The relationship between the affective, behavioral and cognitive components of attitude. *Journal of Experimental Social Psychology* 5: 12–30.

Ostrom, T. M. (1984). Attitude theory. In R. J. Corsini (ed.), *Wiley encyclopedia of psychology*, vol. 1. New York: Wiley.

Rosenberg, M. J. (1968). Hedonism, inauthenticity, and other goals toward expansion of a consistency theory. In R. P. Abelson *et al.* (eds.), *Theories of cognitive consistency: a sourcebook*. Chicago: Rand McNally.

Rosenberg, M. J. and Hovland, C. I. (1960). Cognitive, affective, and behavioral components of attitude. In M. J.

Rosenberg *et al.* (eds.), *Attitude organization and change: an analysis of consistency among attitude components.* New Haven, CT: Yale University Press.

Ross, M., McFarland, C., Conway, M., and Zanna, M. P. (1983). Reciprocal relation between attitudes and behavioral recall: committing people to newly formed attitudes. *Journal of Personality and Social Psychology* 45: 257–67.

Salancik, G. R. (1974). Inference of one's attitude from behavior recalled under linguistically manipulated cognitive sets. *Journal of Experimental Social Psychology* 10: 415–27.

Salancik, G. R. (1982). Attitude–behavior consistencies as social logics. In M. P. Zanna, E. T. Higgins, and C. P. Herman (eds.), *Consistency in social behavior: the Ontario Symposium*, vol. 2. Hillsdale, NJ: Lawrence Erlbaum.

Salancik, G. R. and Conway, M. (1975). Attitude inferences from salient and relevant cognitive content about behavior. *Journal of Personality and Social Psychology* 32: 829–40.

Seligman, C., Kriss, M., Darley, J. M., Fazio, R. H., Becker, L. J., and Pryor, J. B. (1979). Predicting summer energy consumption from homeowners' attitudes. *Journal of Applied Social Psychology* 9: 70–90.

Simon, H. A. (1982). Comments. In M. S. Clark and S. T. Fiske (eds.), *Affect and cognition*. Hillsdale, NJ: Lawrence Erlbaum.

Staats, A. W. (1968). Social behaviorism and human motivation: principles of the attitude-reinforcer-discriminative system. In A. G. Greenwald, T. C. Brock, and T. M. Ostrom (eds.), *Psychological foundations of attitudes*. New York: Academic Press.

Thurstone, L. L. and Chave, E. J. (1929). *The measurement of attitude*. Chicago: University of Chicago Press.

Tybout, A. M. and Scott, C. A. (1983). Availability of well-defined internal knowledge and the attitude formation process: Information aggregation versus self-perception. *Journal of Personality and Social Psychology* 44: 474–91.

Tyler, T. R. and Rasinski, K. (1984). Comparing psychological images of the social perceiver: role of perceived informativeness, memorability, and affect in mediating the impact of crime victimization. *Journal of Personality and Social Psychology* 46: 308–29.

Wicker, A. W. (1969). Attitudes versus actions: the relationship of verbal and overt behavioral responses to attitude objects. *Journal of Social Issues* 25: 41–78.

Wilson, T. D., Dunn, D. S., Bybee, J. A., Hyman, D. B., and Rotondo, J. A. (1984). Effects of analyzing reasons on attitude–behavior consistency. *Journal of Personality and Social Psychology* 47: 5–16.

Wilson, T. D., Dunn, D. S., Kraft, D., and Lisle, D. J. (1986). *Self-analysis and the cognitivation of attitudes.* Unpublished manuscript, University of Virginia.

Wood, W. (1982). Retrieval of attitude-relevant information from memory: effects on susceptibility to persuasion and on intrinsic motivation. *Journal of Personality and Social Psychology* 42: 798–810.

Zajonc, R. B. (1980). Feeling and thinking: preferences need no inferences. *American Psychologist* 35: 151–75.

Zajonc, R. B. and Markus, H. (1982). Affective and cognitive factors in preferences. *Journal of Consumer Research* 9: 123–31.

Zanna, M. P., Kiesler, C. A., and Pilkonis, P. A. (1970). Positive and negative attitudinal affect established by classical conditioning. *Journal of Personality and Social Psychology* 14: 321–8.

Zanna, M. P., Olson, J. M., and Fazio, R. H. (1981). Self-perception and attitude–behavior consistency. *Personality and Social Psychology Bulletin* 7: 252–6.

On the Automatic Activation of Attitudes

Russell H. Fazio, David M. Sanbonmatsu, Martha C. Powell, and Frank R. Kardes

We hypothesized that attitudes characterized by a strong association between the attitude object and an evaluation of that object are capable of being activated from memory automatically upon mere presentation of the attitude object. We used a priming procedure to examine the extent to which the mere presentation of an attitude object would facilitate the latency with which subjects could indicate whether a subsequently presented target adjective had a positive or a negative connotation. Across three experiments, facilitation was observed on trials involving evaluatively congruent primes (attitude objects) and targets, provided that the attitude object possessed a strong evaluative association. In Experiments 1 and 2, preexperimentally strong and weak associations were identified via a measurement procedure. In Experiment 3, the strength of the object–evaluation association was manipulated. The results indicated that attitudes can be automatically activated and that the strength of the object–evaluation association determines the likelihood of such automatic activation. The implications of these findings for a variety of issues regarding attitudes—including their functional value, stability, effects on later behavior, and measurement—are discussed.

Our focus in this article is on the activation of attitudes from memory. The essential question to be addressed is whether attitudes are capable of being activated automatically upon the individual's encountering the attitude object. Consider such an encounter. One possibility is that the individual's attitude will be activated spontaneously and without any conscious effort on his or her part upon observation of the attitude object. On the other hand, it might be that activation of the attitude

The present research was supported by Grant MH 38832 from the National Institute of Mental Health.

The authors thank Paget Gross, Margaret Intons-Peterson, Steven Sherman, and Richard Shiffrin for their helpful comments on an earlier draft of the article.

Correspondence concerning this article should be addressed to Russell H. Fazio, Department of Psychology, Indiana University, Bloomington, Indiana 47405.

requires that the individual engage in a far more reflective process in which he or she actively considers his or her attitude toward the object. Our concern is with the extent to which the former possibility occurs and the degree to which the likelihood of its occurrence depends upon characteristics of the attitude in question.

The two possibilities regarding attitude activation outlined above correspond to the distinction offered by cognitive psychologists between automatic and controlled processes (e.g., Schneider & Shiffrin, 1977; Shiffrin & Schneider, 1977). Shiffrin and Dumais (1981) characterized as automatic any process that leads to the activation of some concept or response "whenever a given set of external initiating stimuli are presented, regardless of a subject's attempt to ignore or bypass the distraction" (p. 117). The key feature of such automatic activation, then, is its inescapability. The implication for attitudes is that, upon presentation of an attitude object, an individual's attitude would be activated despite the lack of any reflection whatsoever on his or her part. In contrast, a controlled process requires the active attention of the individual. Upon becoming aware of a situational cue implying the importance of considering one's attitude toward an object, the individual might attempt to retrieve a previously stored evaluation of the attitude object or might actively construct such an attitude on the spot. In either case, the process is reflective and active in nature.

The occurrence of an automatic process requires the existence of a previously well-learned set of associations or responses. For example, Shiffrin and Schneider (1977) observed that a target stimulus developed the ability to attract attention automatically only following extensive training. The experimenters first trained subjects to respond to a set of characters (letters). On the critical trials of a subsequent task, these characters served as distractor items. That is, one such character might appear on a display in a location that was irrelevant to the subject's task. Despite this irrelevance, these characters to which the subject had earlier been trained to attend did attract attention, as indicated by relatively poorer performance on the primary task. Shiffrin (in press) reviewed a number of such investigations concerning the development of automatism.

Given that automatic processes require such well-learned responses, it appears doubtful that automatic activation is likely for all of the attitudes that an individual might hold. Only for well-learned ones is the expectation of automatic activation even a possibility. Social psychologists have long recognized that attitudes vary in their "strength". Indeed, a variety of attempts have been made to quantify and assess the centrality or importance of an attitude issue for a given individual. The notion of ego-involvement in the context of social judgment theory serves as an illustration of such an approach (Hovland, Harvey, & Sherif, 1957; M. Sherif & Cantril, 1947). More recently, various indices of the "strength" of an attitude have been identified as moderators of the relation between attitudes and behavior. As examples, the confidence with which an attitude is held (Sample & Warland, 1973; Fazio & Zanna, 1978a, 1978b); how clearly defined the attitude is, as measured by the width of the latitude of rejection (C. Sherif, Kelly, Rodgers, Sarup, & Tittler, 1973; Fazio & Zanna, 1978a); and the consistency between affective and cognitive components of the attitude (Norman, 1975) have each been found to relate to attitude–behavior consistency.

Relevant to this idea of attitudes varying in strength is the so-called *attitude/nonattitude* distinction. A number of years ago, both Hovland (1959) and Converse (1970) attempted to reconcile differences that had been observed between survey and laboratory research on attitude change. In so doing, they each—but Converse in particular—focused on a distinction between attitudes and nonattitudes. The distinction centered on the observation that a person may respond to an item on an attitude survey even though that particular attitude does not really exist in any a priori fashion for the individual. The attitude object may be one that the individual has not even considered prior to administration of the attitude survey. For Converse (1970), the attitude/nonattitude distinction centered on measurement error. An individual's nonattitude was characterized by unreliable measurement (in fact, virtually random responding) across the waves of a panel survey.

The attitude/nonattitude dichotomy might be more fruitfully conceived as a continuum. At one end of the continuum is the nonattitude. No a priori evaluation of the attitude object exists. As we move along the continuum, an evaluation does exist and its accessibility from memory grows increasingly strong. At the other extreme of the continuum, then, is a well-learned attitude that is highly accessible from memory.

A particular conception of attitudes underlies this view of the attitude/nonattitude continuum. In a recent series of experiments concerning attitude accessibility, Fazio and his colleagues (Fazio, Chen, McDonel & Sherman, 1982; Fazio, Powell, & Herr, 1983; Powell & Fazio, 1984) proposed that attitudes be viewed as simple associations between a given object and a given evaluation. The term *object* is used in a broad sense. Individuals may have evaluations of a wide variety of potential attitude objects, including social issues, categories of situations, categories of people, and specific individuals, as well as physical objects. Likewise, the term *evaluation* is used in a broad sense. It may range in nature from a very "hot" affect (the attitude object being associated with a strong emotional response) to a "colder" more cognitively-based judgment of one's affect (feelings of favorability or unfavorability) toward the object (see Abelson, Kinder, Peters, & Fiske, 1982; Zanna & Rempel, 1984).

More relevant to the present purposes is the notion of association between the attitude object and the evaluation, regardless of the precise nature of this evaluation. The definition of an attitude implies that the strength of an attitude, like any other construct based on associative learning, can vary. That is, the strength of the association between the object and the evaluation can vary. This associative strength may determine the accessibility of the attitude from memory and the likelihood that the attitude will be activated automatically upon the individual's encountering the attitude object. Only if it is strongly associated with the attitude object is it likely that the evaluation will be spontaneously activated upon mere presentation of the attitude object. In general, what is being suggested is that the activation of one's affect toward an object (be it a hot or a cold linkage) depends on the strength of the association.

In testing this view of attitudes as object-evaluation associations, Fazio and his associates (Fazio et al., 1982; Powell & Fazio, 1984) employed latency of response to an attitudinal inquiry as a measure of the associative strength. Subjects were asked to indicate as quickly as possible whether they felt positively or negatively toward a given attitude object. Subjects who had been induced to express their attitudes repeatedly—which should have the consequence of strengthening the object–evaluation association—were able to respond relatively quickly to these direct inquiries about their attitudes. For example, Powell and Fazio (1984) manipulated the number of times that an attitude was expressed in a within-subjects design by varying the number of semantic differential scale items that appeared relevant to a given attitude issue. In this way, subjects expressed their attitudes zero, one, three, or six times toward a given object.[1] In a subsequent task, subjects were presented with each attitude object and were instructed to make a good or bad judgment about each object as quickly as possible. Latency of response (from stimulus onset to response) was found to relate to the number of previous attitudinal expressions. The greater the number of expressions, the faster the latency of response to the attitudinal inquiry.

These findings imply that attitudes characterized by strong object–evaluation associations may be more accessible from memory. However, it is important to recognize that these findings are not at all informative with respect to the issue of whether the attitude activation stems from an automatic or a controlled process. Responding quickly to a direct attitudinal inquiry does not necessarily mean that the stored evaluation was activated automatically. Instead, the evaluation simply may have been

---

[1] This manipulation had no effect on the extremity of the final attitudinal expression. Thus, the results appear to be due to the strengthening of the object–evaluation association as a consequence of repeated attitudinal expression.

retrieved efficiently via an effortful, controlled process.

In order to examine the automatic activation of attitudes from memory, the present research employed a priming procedure. The procedure is a variant of a now well-tested method commonly employed to investigate automatic processing. It involves consideration of the extent to which the presentation of a prime automatically activates concepts that facilitate responding to a target word. For example, Neely (1977) found that presentation of a category label as a prime (e.g., bird) facilitated the speed with which subjects could identify a subsequently presented target word as a word, provided that the target was semantically related to the category (e.g., robin). The technique has been used to study activation from memory in a variety of contexts, including text processing (e.g., McKoon & Ratcliff, 1980; Ratcliff & McKoon, 1978) and spatial representations (e.g., McNamara, Ratcliff, & McKoon, 1984), as well as semantic relations (e.g., Neely, 1976, 1977; deGroot, 1983).

In the present context, the subjects' primary task was to indicate as quickly as possible whether a target adjective (e.g., pleasant) had a positive or negative connotation. Latency of response served as the dependent measure. Our concern was with the extent to which such a judgment would be facilitated by the presentation of an attitude object as the prime. We reasoned that presentation of an attitude object would automatically activate any strong association to that object. Such activation is assumed to spread along the paths of the memory network, including any evaluative associations. Consequently, the activation levels of associated evaluations are temporarily increased. If a target word that corresponds in valence to one of these previously activated evaluations is subsequently presented for judgment, then less additional activation is required for the activation level of the target word to reach threshold and, consequently, for a judgment to be made. Responding to a target word that has received some activation as a result of presentation of the prime is thus facilitated. That is, the individual should be able to respond relatively quickly.

As an example, let's assume that the attitude object *vodka* is evaluated positively by an individual. Presentation of vodka as the prime may automatically activate a positive evaluation. If the target adjective that is presented is also positive, then the individual may be able to indicate relatively quickly that the target has a positive connotation. That is, facilitation should occur. In a similar manner, facilitation is expected in the case of a negatively valued object serving as the prime when it is followed by a negative target adjective, as in *cockroach/disgusting*. What is meant by facilitation is simply that the latency is faster in such cases than in a trial involving the same target word preceded by a letter string (e.g., BBB). Such trials provide a no-prime baseline. Thus, the technique relies on the presence of facilitation as an indication that the evaluation associated with the primed attitude object has been activated upon its mere observation.

Of course, we would not expect such facilitation to occur for all attitude objects. Relating the methodology to the previous discussion of the attitude/nonattitude continuum, we would expect facilitation to occur only if the object–evaluation association is quite strong. In Experiments 1 and 2, the strength of the object–evaluation association was assessed with regard to a large number of potential attitude objects and strong versus weak primes were selected on an individual basis for each and every subject. In Experiment 3, the strength of the object–evaluation association was manipulated.

Experiment 1

The first experiment involved selecting attitude objects toward which a given individual possessed a strong versus a weak evaluative association and then testing whether those objects produced facilitation when presented as primes in the major experimental task. In order to assess the strength of object–evaluation associations, we employed the operationalization that had been used successfully in the studies of attitude accessibility mentioned earlier (Fazio et al., 1982; Powell & Fazio, 1984). Recall that the findings from this previous research indicated that latency of response to an attitudinal inquiry appears to index the strength of an object–evaluation association satisfactorily.

In the present experiment, attitude objects toward which a given subject displayed very fast or very slow latencies of response to an attitudinal inquiry were identified. If the latency was fast, we consider the object–evaluation association strong and, hence, facilitation should occur in the procedure described earlier. That is, positive target adjectives should be identified as having a positive connotation relatively more quickly when preceded by a positively valued object. Likewise, negative target adjectives should be identified as having a negative connotation relatively more quickly when preceded by a negatively valued object. Such facilitation is far less likely in the case of a weak object–evaluation association, as indicated by a slow latency of response to the direct inquiry. Thus, the hypothesis leads to a prediction of a three-way interaction (Strength of Association × Valence of Prime × Valence of Target). Greater facilitation is expected on trials involving congruent valences than on trials involving incongruent valences (i.e., a simple interaction of Prime Valence × Target Valence) for primes involving a strong evaluative association but not for primes involving a weak association.

Method

Subjects. Twenty-two Indiana University undergraduates participated in the experiment in partial fulfillment of an introductory psychology course requirement.

Procedure. Subjects were told that the experiment concerned word recognition and meaning and that a number of different tasks relevant to word judgment would be performed during the course of the experiment. They were also told that these

tasks would grow increasingly complex as we progressed through the procedure.

The experimental procedure consisted of two major phases, the first devoted to prime selection and the second involving the actual priming task. A list of 70 attitude objects (including the names of some individuals, animals, foods, social groups, nations, activities, and physical objects) formed the pool of potential primes. Subjects were told that the first and simplest word-judgment task that they would be performing involved the presentation of a single word on the computer screen on any given trial. Their task was to press a key labeled *good* or a key labeled *bad* as quickly as possible to indicate their judgment of the object. Subjects were instructed to maximize both the speed and accuracy of their responses. The presentation was controlled by an Apple II+ computer. The order in which the words were presented was randomized for each subject. A given word remained visible on the screen until the subject responded. A 3-s interval separated each trial. The subject's response was recorded, along with the latency of response (from word onset to response) to the nearest millisecond. Subjects' performance of this task was preceded by a block of practice trials involving different words than those used as the potential primes, so as to familiarize subjects with the procedure.

After performing the task, subjects were excused from the laboratory for a short break. During this time, 16 words were selected on the basis of the subject's data as the primes. Four words were selected in each of four categories: strong good, strong bad, weak good, and weak bad. The 4 words toward which the subject had responded *good* and the 4 toward which the subject had responded *bad* most quickly served as the strong primes. The 4 good and the 4 bad words involving the slowest latencies served as the weak primes.[2]

[2] Which attitude objects from the pool of 70 potential primes were selected for use as primes was quite idiosyncratic across subjects. Nevertheless, the following tabulation is intended to provide the reader with some sense of the nature of the attitude objects that served as priming stimuli. The most frequently selected objects in each of the four prime categories and the number of subjects for whom each object was selected are listed: strong good—gift (7), music (7), party (6), and cake (5); strong bad—death (11), hell (7), guns (6), and crime (5); weak good—crosswords (8), Republicans (7), Democrats (7), and rum (6); and weak bad—mazes (9), radiation (7), Democrats (7), and recession (6). Some of the other objects that also were selected for use as primes relatively frequently, but in varying categories, included vodka (8), snow (8), spider (8), television (7), dentist (6), sports (6), storms (6), Reagan (5), coffee (5), and Iran (4).

These 16 words, along with four different strings of three identical letters (e.g., BBB), which were intended to provide nonprime baselines, were employed as the primes in the next task.

A list of 10 evaluative adjectives that were clearly positive in connotation (e.g., "appealing," "delightful") and a list of 10 adjectives that were clearly negative (e.g., "repulsive," "awful") were prepared. These words served as the target words in the next phase of the experiment. Subjects were told that this task was a more complex one involving their again making a judgment of a word, but that this time they would have to remember another word while making the judgment. They were informed that a memory word would be presented followed by an adjective. They were to press the good or bad key as quickly as possible to indicate whether the adjective had a positive or negative connotation and to then recite the memory word aloud. Subjects were told to recite the memory word, that is the prime, solely to ensure that they attended to the prime. (In the case of a letter string such as BBB, subjects were instructed to recite "Triple B".) A cassette recorder was positioned adjacent to the computer to bolster the presumption that the experimenter was concerned about the subjects' recitation of the memory word.

On any given trial, a prime was presented for 200 ms, followed by a 100-ms interval before onset of the target word. Thus, the interval between prime onset and target onset, commonly referred to as the stimulus onset asynchrony (SOA), was 300 ms. The target word disappeared upon the subject's pressing a key. A 4-s interval passed before presentation of the next prime.

A total of five blocks of trials were presented. Each block consisted of 20 trials, in which each of the 20 primes (including the four letter strings) and each of the 20 target adjectives were presented once. Within each of the five prime categories (strong good, strong bad, weak good, weak bad, and letter string), 2 of the primes were followed by positive adjectives and 2 by negative adjectives. Across blocks, each target adjective was paired once with a prime from each of the five prime categories (strong good, strong bad, weak good, weak bad, and letter string). Thus, a target adjective

appeared equally often in each of the five prime conditions. As with the prime selection task, subjects underwent a series of practice trials before performing the actual task so as to familiarize them with the procedure.

Results and Discussion

Subjects committed very few errors in making judgments of the connotation of the target adjectives. The average error rate across subjects was 1.95%. In these few cases, the latency was excluded from the analysis. For each subject, the mean response latency in each of the 10 cells of the design (Five Prime Categories × Positive vs. Negative Targets) was computed. Facilitation scores were then computed. Each mean in a positive target condition was subtracted from the nonprime baseline provided by trials in which positive targets were preceded by a letter string. The same was done with respect to the negative target conditions.[3] The resulting facilitation scores are depicted in Figure 2.1.

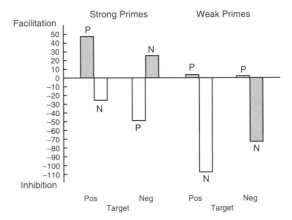

FIGURE 2.1 ■ Mean facilitation scores in Experiment 1 as a function of the strength of the object-evaluation association, the valence of the prime (P = positive; N = negative), and the valence of the target adjective (Pos = positive; Neg = negative). (Conditions involving congruent valences are darkened; incongruent ones are not.)

---

[3] For the benefit of any reader interested in considering raw latencies, the positive target and negative target baselines were 1,065 ms and 1,090 ms, respectively.

A 2 (strength of association) × 2 (prime valence) × 2 (target valence) analysis of variance was performed on the facilitation scores. The analysis revealed that the expected three-way interaction was statistically significant, $F(1, 21) = 6.86$, $p < .02$. In the case of primes involving a strong evaluative association, the predicted interaction between prime valence and target valence was very apparent, $F(1, 21) = 15.30$, $p < .001$. Just as we predicted, facilitation occurred in the cases of congruency between the valence of the primed object and the valence of the target adjective, but not in the cases of incongruency. That is, facilitation is apparent for positively valued attitude objects when followed by a positive target and for negatively valued objects when followed by a negative target. Inhibition is apparent for positively valued attitude objects when followed by a negative target and for negatively valued objects when followed by a positive target.

As indicated by the significant three-way interaction, the data pattern is quite different for those objects involving a weak evaluative association. Most important, there is no interaction between prime valence and target valence, $F < 1$, and no evidence of facilitation in the case of the weak primes. The only effect is a main effect of the valence of the primed object, $F(1, 21) = 14.58$, $p < .001$. Negative objects produced inhibition regardless of the valence of the target adjective. Apparently, the negative objects involving a weak association somehow distracted subjects from the central task. However, this effect should be interpreted cautiously because, unlike the effect observed for strong primes, it does not replicate in the later experiments to be reported.

An important point does need to be made about facilitation versus inhibition in the present procedure. It should be noted that strong primes produced just as much inhibition with regard to targets of incongruent valence as they produced facilitation of targets of congruent valence. The explanation may center on the letter-string trials that were employed as a nonprime baseline. There is considerable discussion in the cognitive literature about the nature of stimuli appropriate for use in baseline trials (see deGroot, Thomassen, &

Hudson, 1982; Jonides & Mack, 1984). Ideally, such stimuli should have no potential for inducing spreading activation, but should be identical to the actual primes in all other respects, including physical appearance, potential to alert subjects, ease of encoding, and memory demands (Jonides & Mack, 1984). Only with the ideal baseline is it appropriate to consider a prime as having produced *facilitation* or *inhibition* in any absolute sense. In recognition of this difficulty, we use these terms in a relative sense throughout this article. Facilitation refers to faster responding to a target word when it is preceded by a prime than when it is preceded by a letter string and inhibition refers to slower responding. Whether the letter-string trials provide an estimate of the true baseline is uncertain. Thus, the zero point of our facilitation–inhibition scale may be a misestimate. What appears to be relative inhibition may actually represent slight facilitation in an absolute sense.

Indeed, we suspect that the letter-string trials may overestimate the true baseline and, consequently, underestimate the amount of absolute facilitation that is occurring. This suspicion is based on the fact that subjects were required to recite the prime aloud at the end of each trial and on the possibility that the letter strings represented less of a memory load than did the attitude object primes. This lesser memory load would allow for responding that is faster than the ideal nonprime, one that is equivalent to the attitude object primes in terms of required memory load.

Regardless of whether a given effect is to be labeled as facilitation or inhibition, the present findings clearly indicate that individuals were able to respond to target adjectives more quickly when the targets were preceded by attitude objects congruent in valence than when they were preceded by attitude objects of incongruent valence. However, as expected, this held true only for attitude objects toward which a strong evaluative association existed.

On the basis of these findings, it appears that at least some attitudes may be activated from memory automatically upon mere presentation of the attitude object. What is critical is that the present evidence for subjects' attitudes having been activated is found in a situation in which the subject was merely exposed to the attitude object. The subjects were never asked during the second phase of the experiment to consider their attitudes. Nor was it to the subjects' advantage to do so, for the subjects' task was simply to respond to the target word and then to recite the memory word. Nevertheless, despite this irrelevance of attitudes to the immediate task concerns, exposure to objects for which subjects presumably possessed strong affective associations appears to have prompted activation of the associated evaluation.

Thus, the very nature of the task leads to the suggestion that the facilitation observed in the case of the strong primes was a result of automatic, rather than controlled, processing. Nevertheless, it might be argued that subjects did for some reason actively consider their evaluations of the prime and, hence, were "prepared" for a target word of congruent valence. To explain the findings, such an interpretation would have to maintain that the SOA that was employed allowed sufficient time for subjects to actively retrieve their evaluation in the case of strong primes, but was insufficient for such active retrieval in the case of weak primes. In order to examine this possibility, a second experiment involving manipulation of the SOA was conducted.

Experiment 2

If the facilitation observed in Experiment 1 were due to a controlled process, then allowing the subjects more time should, if anything, enhance the extent of facilitation. Most important, facilitation might be observed even in the case of weak primes. On the other hand, if the task is such, as we have argued, that the findings in Experiment 1 reflect automatic processing, then no such facilitation is to be expected for weak primes even at a longer SOA.

Assuming that the interpretation in terms of automatism is valid, then whether facilitation in the case of strong primes is observed at a longer SOA will depend on the level of activation of the associated evaluation at the time the target word is presented. If the level of activation has dissipated (possibly due to its irrelevance to the immediate task concerns) then no facilitation is to be expected at the longer SOA. If the level of activation has not yet returned to baseline, then some facilitation might be expected.

Method

Subjects. Twenty-three individuals who had responded to a newspaper advertisement participated in the experiment in return for a payment of $6.

Procedure. The experimental procedure followed that employed in Experiment 1. The only major difference was that, following prime selection, subjects underwent the actual priming task twice. They did so once with an SOA of 300 ms and once with an SOA of 1,000 ms. The order in which they did so was counterbalanced across subjects.

The only other procedural changes made were minor ones aimed at enhancing the power of the experiment. The pool of potential primes employed in the prime selection phase of the experiment was expanded to 92 attitude objects.[4] In addition, a few target adjectives that had produced relatively short or long latencies when preceded by letter strings were replaced by other words.

Results and Discussion

As in Experiment 1, errors were minimal (mean error rate = 1.39%) and when they did occur, the respective latency was omitted from the analysis.

---

[4] The attitude objects most frequently selected for use as primes in each of the four categories (and the number of subjects for whom the object was selected) were as follows: strong good—music (7), friend (7), dancing (5), and cake (5); strong bad—war (8), death (8), cancer (6), and rats (6); weak good—Monday (9), dormitory (5), landlords (5), and Reagan (4); and weak bad—anchovies (8), landlords (6), exams (6), and recession (6). Some of the other objects that also were selected for use as primes relatively frequently, but in varying categories, included priest (8), fraternity (7), dentist (6), liver (6), mosquito (6), worms (6), guns (5), spider (5), taxes (5), and disco (4).

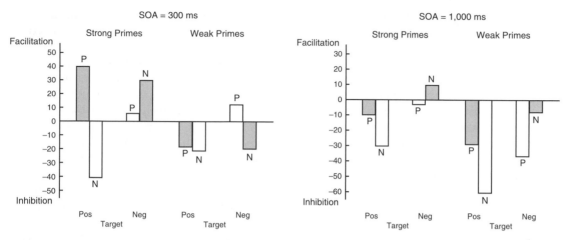

FIGURE 2.2 ■ Mean facilitation scores in Experiment 2 as a function of SOA (stimulus onset asynchrony), the strength of the object–evaluation association, the valence of the prime (P = positive; N = negative), and the valence of the target adjective (Pos = positive; Neg = negative). (Conditions involving congruent valences are darkened; incongruent ones are not.)

Facilitation scores[5] are depicted in Figure 2.2. Because the order of the blocks of trials involving SOAs of 300 versus 1,000 ms did not qualify any of the effects to be reported, the facilitation scores are presented collapsed across the order variable. As is clear from Figure 2.2, left column, the findings with an SOA of 300 ms replicate those observed in Experiment 1 when one considers attitude objects involving a strong evaluative association. Most important, there was a significant interaction of prime and target valence for strong primes at this SOA, $F(1, 22) = 4.87, p < .05$. Facilitation was greater in the case of congruent valences than in the case of incongruent valences. Furthermore, the extent of facilitation in the congruent cases ($M = 37$ ms) differed significantly from zero, $t(22) = 2.17, p < .05$. No significant facilitation was apparent in any of the other cells of the design— strong primes presented at the longer SOA or weak primes at either SOA. This pattern of data led to the observation of a significant SOA × Strength of Association × Prime Valence × Target Valence interaction, $F(1, 22) = 4.35, p < .05$. Only in the case of strong primes and the shorter SOA was

facilitation found on trials involving congruent evaluations.

Thus, even when subjects were provided with additional time, no evidence of facilitation was observed for weak primes. It does not appear that the evaluative association was activated upon presentation of the attitude object when the association was weak in nature. This null finding tends to undermine the plausibility of the controlled processing alternative outlined earlier. If subjects had been actively retrieving their attitudes, then greater facilitation was to be expected at the longer SOA.

Apparently, facilitation in the present task is the result of automatic activation of the evaluation upon presentation of the attitude object. However, such automatic activation requires the existence of a strong association between the attitude object and the evaluation. The findings regarding SOA imply that the level of activation in such cases dissipated quickly (or, conceivably, was actively suppressed). Such quick dissipation may have been a consequence of the irrelevance of the subject's attitudes to the major task that was occupying the subject's attention, that is, identifying the connotation of the target adjective. In effect, presentation of the target adjective 1,000 ms after presentation of the attitude object appears to have been too late for the prime to facilitate responding to adjectives of

[5] The positive and negative target baselines were 830 ms and 880 ms, respectively, at the SOA of 300, and 770 ms and 790 ms, respectively, at the SOA of 1,000.

the same valence. At the 300-ms interval, on the other hand, the level of activation of the associated evaluation was apparently sufficient to facilitate responding to evaluatively congruent adjectives. This finding is reminiscent of one from Neely's (1977) investigation. Subjects had been instructed that the prime *bird* implied that a target word corresponding to a body part would be presented. Despite this instruction, responses to a specific bird exemplar (e.g., robin) as the target were facilitated at a short SOA. However, no such facilitation was observed at a longer SOA. In a fashion parallel to the present case, the level of activation of whatever exemplars had been activated by the presentation of the category prime apparently dissipated quickly.

Experiment 3

In each of the two experiments reported thus far, evidence supportive of the possibility of automatic activation of one's attitude upon mere exposure to the attitude object was found. Such automatic activation was restricted, however, to attitudes involving a strong object–evaluation association. Associative strength was measured via latency of response to an attitudinal inquiry. Attitudes that individuals could report relatively quickly were considered to involve strong object–evaluation associations. Such attitudes were compared to ones that required more time for subjects to report. These two classes of attitudes were found to differ with regard to the likelihood of presentation of the attitude object automatically activating the attitude from memory. We have argued that the strength of the object–evaluation association was the critical difference responsible for this differential likelihood. Nevertheless, as is the case any time a conceptual variable is measured rather than manipulated, other differences might exist between the two classes of attitudes that were identified via our measurement technique.

Experiment 3 was aimed at demonstrating more conclusively the critical importance of the strength of the object–evaluation association by manipulating rather than measuring it. Subjects were induced to express their attitudes toward a number of attitude objects repeatedly, as in the study described earlier by Powell and Fazio (1984). Another set of attitude objects was presented equally often but subjects were asked to make a nonevaluative judgment regarding each of these objects. In this way, the object–evaluation association was strengthened for some attitudes and not for others. These objects then served as primes in the subsequent task. The experimental design was the same as that of Experiment 2. The only difference was that strong versus weak primes were created experimentally rather than being selected on the basis of measured preexperimental strength. A four-way interaction similar to that found in Experiment 2 is to be expected. That is, facilitation should be greater in the cases of congruency between the evaluation of the prime and the evaluation of the target than in the cases of incongruency only for strong primes presented 300 ms before the target words.

Method

Subjects. Eighteen Indiana University undergraduates participated in the experiment in partial fulfillment of an introductory psychology course requirement.

Procedure. As before, subjects were led to believe that the experiment concerned word recognition and that the experimenter was interested in the "speed and accuracy with which people could perform various word recognition tasks." In the initial task, a word and a question appeared simultaneously on the computer screen. In some instances, the question asked "One syllable word?" and the subject was to respond by pressing a yes or no key as quickly as possible. In other instances, the question was "Good or bad?" and subjects responded by pressing the appropriate key as quickly as possible. The words and accompanying question were presented in a random order for each subject. Three seconds separated each trial. Subjects underwent a series of practice trials before performing the actual task so as to ensure their understanding of the task.

A total of 16 attitude objects served as the stimuli that were subject to manipulation. The words were selected from the pool of 92 potential primes employed in Experiment 2 on the basis of the response and response latency data from the prime selection phase of Experiment 2. Two relevant criteria were employed to guide this process. First, objects that were endorsed as positive or negative with near unanimity across the subjects were selected. Second, of these objects that produced nearly uniform responses, the ones with the longest average response latencies across subjects were chosen. In this way, 8 positively valued ("aquarium," "baby, "cake," "chocolate," "eagle," "Friday," "parade," and "silk") and 8 negatively valued ("divorce," "hangover," "litter," "radiation," "recession," "toothache," "virus," and "weeds") attitude objects were selected.[6] These words were then randomly divided into two lists each consisting of 4 positive and 4 negative objects. For any given subject, one list was associated with the attitude expression question and one with the syllable identification question. Which specific list was used for which purpose was counterbalanced across subjects.

The actual task consisted of five blocks of 30 trials each. In any given block, the 16 words of interest appeared once. Thus, across blocks, subjects expressed their attitudes toward 8 of the objects 5 times[7] and answered the syllable question with respect to each of the 8 words from the other list 5 times. In this way, the number of presentations of the critical words was held constant. Filler words were included to bring the number of trials in each block to 30. Sixteen filler words were presented once throughout the series of blocks and another 18 filler words were presented a total of 3 times across all blocks. Half of the filler words were paired with the evaluation question and half with the syllable question.

The 4 positive and the 4 negative objects toward which evaluations had been expressed repeatedly in the above task are referred to as the *repeated expression* primes. The 4 positive and 4 negative objects that had been paired with the syllable question served as the control primes. The actual priming task proceeded as in Experiment 2. Following the priming task, subjects completed a questionnaire that asked them to evaluate each of the 50 attitude objects that had been presented in the first phase of the experiment (i.e., both the experimental and the filler words). These evaluations were made on a 7-point scale with endpoints labeled *very good* and *very bad*.

Results

As in the previous experiments, the number of errors that subjects made in judging the connotation of the target adjectives was minimal (mean error rate = 1.94%). Any latencies associated with a response error were omitted from the analysis.

The facilitation scores[8] are presented in Figure 2.3. An analysis of variance on these data revealed the predicted four-way interaction of SOA × Repeated Expression × Prime Valence × Target Valence, $F(1, 17) = 9.22, p < .01$. Similar to what had been observed for preexperimentally strong primes in Experiment 2, the critical simple interaction of prime and target valence was found for the experimentally created strong primes (repeated expression condition) when the shorter SOA was involved, $F(1, 17) = 8.86, p < .01$. In this case, greater facilitation was observed when positively valued primes were followed by positive targets and when negatively valued primes were followed by negative targets than when the prime-target

---

[6] An additional 6 subjects who participated in the experiment were not included in the analysis because their evaluative judgments of the objects chosen as experimental stimuli were not in accordance with these expectations. Four of these subjects disagreed concerning one of the attitude objects (e.g., judging negatively what had been selected as a positively valued object) and 2 did not concur with respect to two attitude objects.

[7] As is to be expected, subjects were significantly faster at indicating their evaluations the fifth time that they did so ($M = 910$ ms) than the first time ($M = 1,330$ ms), $F(1, 17) = 73.95$, $p < .001$.

[8] The positive and negative target baselines were 780 ms and 840 ms, respectively, at the SOA of 300 ms, 710 ms, and 760 ms, respectively, at the SOA of 1,000.

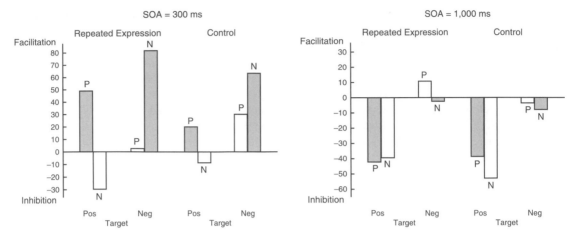

FIGURE 2.3 ■ Mean facilitation scores in Experiment 3 as a function of SOA (stimulus onset asychrony), repeated expression, valence of the prime (P = positive; N = negative), and valence of the target adjective (Pos = positive; Neg = negative). (Conditions involving congruent valences are darkened; incongruent ones are not.)

pairs were incongruent in valence. Furthermore, the extent of facilitation observed on these congruent trials ($M = 73.61$ ms) was once again statistically reliable, $t(17) = 4.37$, $p < .001$. Statistically reliable facilitation ($M = 43.19$ ms) was also apparent on congruent trials with control primes when the trials involved the 300-ms SOA, $t(17) = 3.30$, $p < .005$.[9] However, in a manner that is consistent with the hypothesis, the extent of such facilitation was significantly greater in the repeated expression condition than in the control condition, $t(17) = 2.61$, $p < .02$. No facilitation on congruent trials was apparent with either the repeatedly expressed or the control primes when the trials involved the longer SOA.

Note that the present data regarding the consequences of repeated attitudinal expression are not confounded by attitude extremity. That is, repeated expression did not enhance the extremity of subjects' self-reported attitudes at the end of the experiment. Attitudes toward each of the 16 experimental objects were examined by comparing the attitude scores of those subjects who had repeatedly expressed their attitudes toward the

given object to the attitude scores of those who had not. Only 1 of these 16 comparisons, well within what is to be expected by chance alone, revealed a more extreme attitude among the repeated expression subjects. Such a null effect of repeated expression on attitude extremity is consistent with past research that has employed the repeated attitudinal expression manipulation. Powell and Fazio (1984) did not detect any reliable differences in attitude extremity as a function of repeated expression across 12 attitude issues. Thus, the present findings regarding attitude activation following repeated expression can be attributed to the resulting strength of the object–evaluation association and not to the extremity of the associated evaluation.

General Discussion

Together, the three present experiments suggest that some sorts of attitudes indeed can be activated from memory automatically upon one's mere observation of the attitude object. Such activation appears to be both spontaneous and inescapable. Even though attitude activation was irrelevant to the task that subjects were required to perform, we found evidence that evaluations were activated upon exposure to appropriate attitude objects. However, the likelihood of such automatic acti-

[9] Due to the selection requirement concerning unanimity, the control attitude objects in Experiment 3 involved stronger evaluative associations than did the weak primes in Experiments 1 and 2.

vation of an attitude appears to depend upon the strength of the association between the attitude object and the evaluation. Regardless of whether this associative strength was measured or manipulated experimentally, evidence of automatic activation of the attitude was far stronger when the association could be characterized as strong.

It should be kept in mind that the view of attitude underlying the present research equates it with affect. Thus, the research essentially addresses how affect toward an object might be activated from memory. As mentioned earlier, individuals may have affect toward a wide variety of potential attitude objects, including social issues, categories of people, and specific individuals, as well as physical objects. The present findings, then, are of relevance to any broadly defined "object" toward which an individual possesses some affective linkage. As such, they indicate that affect can be activated automatically from memory in the same way that has been demonstrated previously for semantic knowledge. Just as a knowledge structure concerning some object may consist of bits of information organized in a network of associations to the object, so too may affect be linked to the object (cf. Fiske, 1982; Fiske & Pavelchak, in press). Furthermore, just as activation can spread from one node in the network to another (cf. Anderson & Pirolli, 1984; Ratcliff & McKoon, 1981), the present data indicate a spontaneous spreading of activation from the object to the affective association.

The findings also lend support to the utility of the proposed view of attitudes as evaluative associations with objects. These associations can vary in strength, ranging from *not existing at all* (the case of a nonattitude) to a *weak association* that is unlikely to be capable of automatic activation to a *strong association* that can be activated automatically. This continuum provides an interesting way of conceptualizing the strength of an attitude. The attitudes of two individuals with identical scores from some attitude measurement instrument may still differ markedly with regard to their strength, that is, with regard to their likelihood of activation upon the individual's mere exposure to the object. When they encounter the attitude object in a given

situation, the attitude of one individual may be activated whereas the attitude of the other may not be. As a result, the two individuals may construe any information that is available concerning the object quite differently; that is, selective processing is more likely in the case of the individual whose attitude has been activated. A difference of this sort is apt to have a number of important implications.

First of all, the degree to which the attitude is likely to be evoked automatically is apt to affect the resistance of the attitude to counterinfluence. An attitude involving a strong association is apt to be activated upon the presentation of information concerning the attitude object and, as a result, color one's judgments of the information. Consistent with this notion, Wood (1982) found that attitude change in response to a persuasive communication is moderated by the degree to which individuals can rapidly retrieve from memory beliefs about the attitude object and past behaviours that they had performed relevant to the attitude object. The implication is that the stronger the object–evaluation association, the more resistant the attitude is to change and the greater the stability of the attitude over time.

A second implication concerns attitude–behavior consistency. If an attitude is activated automatically upon the individual's encountering the attitude object, it is far more likely to guide the individual's behavior toward that object than if it is not. Without activation of the attitude, behavior toward the object may proceed without the object having been considered in evaluative terms or on the basis of judgments of whatever features of the object happen to be salient in the immediate situation. In either case, the behavior may not be congruent with the individual's attitude.

Fazio (in press) has proposed a model of the process by which attitudes guide behavior that views activation of the attitude as critical in precisely this manner. The model assumes that behavior in any given situation is largely a function of the individual's definition of the event that is occurring. The critical question concerns the extent to which the attitude will influence one's construction of the event. In some situations, a cue implying the relevance of attitudinal considerations may prompt individuals to access their attitudes from memory. However, in cue-free situations, it is the chronic accessibility of the attitude, that is, the strength of the object–evaluation association, that is important. If the attitude is activated upon one's observation of the attitude object, it is likely to lead to some selective processing of the information available in the immediate situation. Thus, the individual's definition of the event is more likely to be congruent with his or her attitude toward the object in cases involving strong object–evaluation associations than in cases involving weak ones. Consequently, behavior is more likely to follow from a definition of the event that is attitudinally based in the former cases than in the latter.

An additional implication of the present findings for the prediction of behavior from attitude is worth noting. The first two experiments identified attitudes that involved object–evaluation associations sufficiently strong to produce automatic activation. This was accomplished by assessing latency of response to an attitudinal inquiry. The findings imply that such a measure is a fairly good approximation of the likelihood of automatic activation of the evaluation upon mere observation of the attitude object. That is, how long it takes to respond to an attitudinal inquiry is reflective of the likelihood that the attitude will be activated spontaneously upon one's encountering the attitude object.

The very simplicity of the latency measure makes it attractive and potentially feasible for use in surveys in which one is concerned with the prediction of behavior from attitude. Predictive power should be enhanced by taking into account the accessibility of the respondents' attitudes. This notion was tested in a recent field investigation concerning attitudes toward Ronald Reagan (Fazio & Williams, 1985). Approximately 3½ months before the 1984 presidential election, attitudes toward Ronald Reagan and the accessibility of those attitudes (as measured by response latency to the attitudinal inquiry) were assessed. Attitudes were found to be far more predictive of later voting behavior among those respondents who were able to respond relatively quickly to the attitudinal

inquiry than among those who responded relatively slowly.

Thus, there appear to be important implications of automatic attitudinal activation for both persuasion and attitude–behavior consistency. More generally, the present conceptualization and findings are relevant to the very functionality of attitudes. Attitude theorists have long considered one of the major functions served by attitudes to be that of organizing and structuring a rather chaotic universe of objects (Katz, 1960; Smith, Bruner, & White, 1956). An attitude is presumed to provide "a ready aid in 'sizing up' objects and events in the environment" (Smith et al., 1956, p. 41). The degree to which a given attitude actually fulfills this object appraisal function would appear to depend on the likelihood that the attitude is activated automatically when the individual observes the attitude object and, hence, on the strength of the object–evaluation association. Attitudes involving a strong association are highly functional. They free the individual from the processing required for reflective thought about his or her evaluation of the object and, through the process outlined earlier, can guide the individual's behavior in a fairly automatic manner. Thus, the individual is freed from much of the effort of having to engage in deliberate reasoning processes before behaving toward the object in question.

One final implication of the present research concerns attitude measurement. The priming procedure that was used to study the automatic activation of attitudes has the potential of serving as an unobtrusive measure of attitude. Attitude researchers have long searched for a means of assessing attitudes that was not subject to the respondent's self-presentational concerns with social desirability. Despite assurances of anonymity and confidentiality, individuals are not always completely honest when responding to an attitude survey. The most frequently used technique to deal with such assessment concerns has been the bogus pipeline (Jones & Sigall, 1971). This technique relies on an elaborate attempt to convince the respondents that a presumed apparatus has the capacity to discern their true attitudes from various physiological data that are ostensibly being monitored. Because individuals believe that it is not possible to deceive the machine, they respond more truthfully to the survey questions. In contrast, the present approach provides a means of obtaining an estimate of the attitude in a situation in which the individual need not be at all aware that his or her attitude is being assessed. Recall that during the critical priming phase of the experiments the subject was never asked to consider his or her attitude toward the object in question. Yet, it is possible to ascertain from the data the degree to which positive or negative evaluations are activated when the attitude object is encountered. Furthermore, given its automatic nature, such activation is presumably both inescapable and impossible for the individual to control. Whether the present technique is actually useful in measuring attitudes concerning objects or issues for which self-reports might be suspect remains to be tested. However, the present findings suggest that it may be a viable approach.

REFERENCES

Abelson, R. P., Kinder, D. R., Peters, M. D., & Fiske, S. T. (1982). Affective and semantic components in political person perception. *Journal of Personality and Social Psychology, 42,* 619–630.

Anderson, J. R., & Pirolli, P. L. (1984). Spread of activation. *Journal of Experimental Psychology: Learning, Memory, and Cognition, 10,* 791–798.

Converse, P. E. (1970). Attitudes and non-attitudes: Continuation of a dialogue. In E. R. Tufte (Ed.), *The quantitative analysis of social problems* (pp. 168–189). Reading, MA: Addison-Wesley.

deGroot, A. (1983). The range of automatic spreading activation in word priming. *Journal of Verbal Learning and Verbal Behavior, 22,* 417–436.

deGroot, A., Thomassen, A., & Hudson, P. (1982). Associative facilitation of word recognition as measured from a neutral prime. *Memory and Cognition, 10,* 358–370.

Fazio, R. H. (in press). How do attitudes guide behavior? In R. M. Sorrentino & E. T. Higgins (Eds.), *The handbook of motivation and cognition: Foundations of social behavior.* New York: Guilford Press.

Fazio, R. H., Chen, J., McDonel, E. C., & Sherman, S.J. (1982). Attitude accessibility, attitude–behavior consistency, and the strength of the object–evaluation association. *Journal of Experimental Social Psychology, 18,* 339–357.

Fazio, R. H., Powell, M. C., & Herr, P. M. (1983). Toward a process model of the attitude–behavior relation: Accessing one's attitude upon mere observation of the attitude object. *Journal of Personality and Social Psychology, 44,* 723–735.

Fazio, R. H., & Williams, C. (1985). *Attitude accessibility as a moderator of the attitude–perception and attitude–behavior relations: An investigation of the 1984 presidential election.* Unpublished manuscript, Indiana University.

Fazio, R. H., & Zanna, M. P. (1978a). Attitudinal qualities relating to the strength of the attitude–behavior relationship. *Journal of Experimental Social Psychology, 14,* 398–408.

Fazio, R. H., & Zanna, M. P. (1978b). On the predictive validity of attitudes: The roles of direct experience and confidence. *Journal of Personality, 46,* 228–243.

Fiske, S. T. (1982). Schema-triggered affect: Applications to social perception. In M. S. Clark & S. T. Fiske (Eds.), *Affect and cognition: The 17th Annual Carnegie Symposium on Cognition* (pp. 55–78). Hillsdale, NJ: Erlbaum.

Fiske, S. T., & Pavelchak, M. A. (in press). Category-based versus piecemeal-based affective responses: Developments in schema-triggered affect. In R. M. Sorrentino & E. T. Higgins (Eds.), *The handbook of motivation and cognition: Foundations of social behavior.* New York: Guilford Press.

Hovland, C. I. (1959). Reconciling conflicting results derived from experimental and survey studies of attitude change. *American Psychologist, 14,* 8–17.

Hovland, C. I., Harvey, O. J., & Sherif, M. (1957). Assimilation and contrast effects in reactions to communication and attitude change. *Journal of Abnormal and Social Psychology, 55,* 244–252.

Jones, E. E., & Sigall, H. (1971). The bogus pipeline: A new paradigm for measuring affect and attitude. *Psychological Bulletin, 76,* 349–364.

Jonides, J., & Mack, R. (1984). On the cost and benefit of cost and benefit. *Psychological Bulletin, 96,* 29–44.

Katz, D. (1960). The functional approach to the study of attitudes. *Public Opinion Quarterly, 24,* 163–204.

McKoon, G., & Ratcliff, R. (1980). Priming in item recognition: The organization of propositions in memory for text. *Journal of Verbal Learning and Verbal Behavior, 19,* 369–386.

McNamara, T. P., Ratcliff, R., & McKoon, G. (1984). The mental representation of knowledge acquired from maps. *Journal of Experimental Psychology: Learning, Memory, and Cognition, 10,* 723–732.

Neely, J. H. (1976). Semantic priming and retrieval from lexical memory: Evidence for facilitatory and inhibitory processes. *Memory and Cognition, 4,* 648–654.

Neely, J. H. (1977). Semantic priming and retrieval from lexical memory: Roles of inhibitionless spreading activation and limited-capacity attention. *Journal of Experimental Psychology: General, 106,* 225–254.

Norman, R. (1975). Affective-cognitive consistency, attitudes, conformity, and behavior. *Journal of Personality and Social Psychology, 32,* 83–91.

Powell, M. C., & Fazio, R. H. (1984). Attitude accessibility as a function of repeated attitudinal expression. *Personality and Social Psychology Bulletin, 10,* 139–148.

Ratcliff, R., & McKoon, G. (1978). Priming in item recognition: Evidence for the propositional structure of sentences. *Journal of Verbal Learning and Verbal Behavior, 17,* 403–417.

Ratcliff, R., & McKoon, G. (1981). Does activation really spread? *Psychological Review, 88,* 454–462.

Sample, J., & Warland, R. (1973). Attitude and prediction of behavior. *Social Forces, 51,* 292–304.

Schneider, W., & Shiffrin, R. M. (1977). Controlled and automatic human information processing: I. Detection, search, and attention. *Psychological Review, 84,* 1–66.

Sherif, C. W., Kelly, M., Rodgers, H. L., Sarup, G., & Tittler, B. I. (1973). Personal involvement, social judgment, and action. *Journal of Personality and Social Psychology, 27,* 311–328.

Sherif, M., & Cantril, H. (1947). *The psychology of ego involvements.* New York: Wiley.

Shiffrin, R. M. (in press). Attention. In R. C. Atkinson, R. J. Herrnstein, G. Lindzey, & R. D. Luce (Eds.), *Stevens' handbook of experimental psychology* (2nd ed.). New York: Wiley.

Shiffrin, R. M., & Dumais, S. T. (1981). The development of automatism. In J. R. Anderson (Ed.), *Cognitive skills and their acquisition* (pp. 111–140). Hillsdale, NJ: Erlbaum.

Shiffrin, R. M., & Schneider, W. (1977). Controlled and automatic human information processing: II. Perceptual learning, automatic attending, and a general theory. *Psychological Review, 84,* 127–190.

Smith, M. B., Bruner, J. S., & White, R. W. (1956). *Opinions and personality.* New York: Wiley.

Wood, W. (1982). Retrieval of attitude-relevant information from memory: Effects on susceptibility to persuasion and on intrinsic motivation. *Journal of Personality and Social Psychology, 42,* 798–810.

Zanna, M. P., & Rempel, J. K. (1984). *Attitudes: A new look at an old concept.* Paper presented at the Conference on Social Psychology of Knowledge, Tel Aviv.

Received May 9, 1985
Revision received September 8, 1985 ■

PART 2

Measurement of Attitudes

Research concerning attitudes has been able to progress, in no small part, as a result of the advances made in the measurement of attitudes. One of the very first such advances is the classic article by Thurstone (1928) that is reprinted in an abridged manner as the first reading of this section. As shall be apparent, Thurstone proposed a sophisticated and complex scheme for constructing a measure of attitudes toward a given issue. However, the article is just as noteworthy, maybe more so, for the arguments that are provided in support of the bold assertion that constitutes its title: "Attitudes can be measured." Thurstone regards verbal expressions of attitude, which he calls opinions, as symbols of the attitude. Opinion expressions provide a means of measuring attitudes. Thus, his method relies on the individual's agreement or disagreement with each of a set of carefully selected opinion statements ranging from extremely pro to extremely con. The opinion statements that the respondent endorses provide an index of the person's attitude.

Thurstone acknowledges many limitations to this measurement system, the most important of which is that it relies on the respondents' cooperation and truthfulness. Some people may obscure their true feelings about some issues. Thurstone is very explicit in advising that attitude scales be employed only in situations and with respect to issues that involve minimal social pressure to respond in a given way. For example, we certainly would have reason to worry about the validity of a measure of adolescents' attitudes toward beer if that measure were administered orally in the presence of their parents. But, we can take steps to lessen the social pressures; we can ask the parents to leave the testing situation, encourage the adolescents to be truthful, and have them respond on paper anonymously. We can never be completely confident that any given respondent is not misrepresenting his or her attitude. Thurstone effectively argues that distortions of this kind have to be accepted as an "error of measurement" but notes that measurement error also is common when physical qualities are assessed. A thermometer provides a fallible index of the temperature: it may not be working properly, it may require calibration, it may have been positioned in an inappropriate location where it was subjected to some unexpected source of heat. Yet, the obvious presence of measurement error does not stop us from believing that temperature can be measured. Likewise, Thurstone argues, the fact that discrepancies between opinion endorsement and actual attitudes may occur for one reason or another should not lead us to conclude that attitudes cannot be measured.

The specific system that Thurstone proposed for measuring attitudes focused on the acceptance or rejection of opinion statements. It involves a multi-stage scheme for selection of the statements. Statements espousing a wide range of opinions are evaluated by a large number of judges for the extent to which they express a favorable or unfavorable opinion regarding the issue. For example, the judges sometimes are asked to sort the statements into 11 piles, ranging from extreme pro to extreme con, and to try to equalize the intervals between the piles. That is, the difference between the second and third piles should represent as large a difference on the underlying continuum of favorability as the difference between the third and fourth piles. It is for this reason that Thurstone's scaling procedure is often referred to as the method of "equal appearing intervals." Because each interval is assumed to be equal,

consecutive scores (e.g., 1–11) can be assigned to the statements that are sorted into the various piles. Some statements will need to be eliminated because their ambiguity results in insufficient agreement across judges as to where the statements should be placed along the continuum. Such statements can be identified easily by the variability that the judges display and are eliminated from the item pool. Through such elimination, the researcher hopes to arrive at a set of statements whose favorability or unfavorability is very clear. The selected statements are then presented to the sample whose attitudes are being assessed with the instruction that they indicate whether they agree or disagree with each statement. Because each statement has a known scale value of 1–11 associated with it, the average scale value of the statements that the respondent endorses can be computed and this mean serves as the individual's attitude score.

Thurstone's extensive scaling procedure is rarely used today, largely because it is more cumbersome and complicated than is necessary. In 1932, Likert developed a simpler scaling technique that did not rely on judges' assessments of opinion statements. Instead, the opinion statements are presented to the respondents with the instruction that the respondents indicate the extent of their agreement or disagreement with each statement. For example, they might be asked to select one of five options: "Strongly Disagree," "Disagree," "Undecided," "Agree" or "Strongly Agree." These alternatives might be scored as −2 to +2, respectively, if the statement is one that espouses a pro position. If the statement involves a negative stance, it would be reverse-scored as +2 to −2. The scores across the items are summed and serve as the respondent's attitude score, which is why Likert's technique is referred to as the "method of summated ratings." Likert-type scales are very commonly employed in current research.

Yet another popular, and simple, measurement approach is the semantic differential (Osgood, Suci, & Tanenbaum, 1957). This self-report technique asks respondents to directly evaluate an attitude object along a series of, scales (e.g., seven-point), each anchored by bipolar adjectives. Adjectives that seem intuitively relevant to the particular attitude object are typically chosen. However, commonly-employed adjective pairs include: good–bad, favorable–unfavorable, pleasant–unpleasant, wise–foolish, and valuable–worthless. Respondents are asked to check the scale point that best represents their evaluation of the attitude object, i.e., to locate the attitude object along the continuum defined by the two adjectives. The sum or average across the items serves as the respondent's attitude score.

Contemporary attitude research typically involves some form of a Likert or semantic differential scale. These types of scales show reasonable correlations with each other, supporting the notion that they are assessing the same thing. Such attitude measures have the advantage of being fairly easy to construct. In addition, excellent statistical procedures exist for conducting item analyses of the scales and assessing the scale's internal consistency, i.e., the extent to which the items cohere.

Ultimately, however, any ratings that people provide are verbal reports of their attitude. They are responses to a question and, as such, are exercises in communication. The question must be interpreted, its intent understood, and the options by which one might respond must be considered. These inferential processes are addressed in the article by Schwarz (1999) that is reprinted as Reading

4. Schwarz reviews findings regarding how people respond to survey questions in light of various principles of communication. For example, he illustrates how the respondent's construal of the survey question varies as a function of context and how the response alternatives provided are used to disambiguate the meaning of what is being asked. In so doing, Schwarz directs attention to the value of considering questionnaires as conversational devices that enable communication between the researcher and the respondent.

No matter how carefully a questionnaire is constructed, however, there always exists the possibility that the respondent is being less than truthful. The mere awareness that his or her attitude is being assessed may raise concerns for the individual about the types of responses that are socially desirable. For this reason, social psychologists have had a long-standing interest in less direct, unobtrusive measures of attitude—ones that provide an estimate of individuals' attitudes without their awareness that attitudes are being assessed. A very influential book on such nonreactive measures was published by Webb, Campbell, Schwartz, and Sechrest in 1966. The book highlights research that used a variety of clever physical measures, archival records, or behavioral observation techniques to estimate an individual's or a population's attitudes.

The body itself often provides indications of a person's current affective state. Thus, researchers have sometimes turned to physiological measures as a means of assessing attitudes without having to rely on individuals' direct reports. Among the more successful of these approaches is the technique pioneered by Cacioppo, Petty, Losch, and Kim (1986) that is reprinted as Reading 5. These researchers relied on the measurement of electromyographic (EMG) activity over facial muscle regions. Simply put, those facial muscles involved in smiling showed increased activity when pleasant objects or scenes were presented visually, whereas muscles related to frowning responded when negative images were presented. The EMG recordings succeeded in differentiating the positive versus negative stimuli even though the muscular contractions were too slight to produce facial expressions that were observable. Judges observing videotapes of the participants' faces were unable to determine whether participants were looking at positive or negative images.

Unfortunately, recording EMG activity is not an easy endeavor, and tapping into facial expressions seems most likely to reflect attitudes with an emotional rather than a purely cognitive basis. Hence, such measures have not been employed often in attitude research. More recently, social psychologists have turned to measures based on cognitive processes, instead of physiological ones, as a means of obtaining unobtrusive, indirect estimates of individuals' attitudes. In fact, over the last ten years, there has been a remarkable surge of interest in such implicit measures of attitude, as they have come to be known. Like the unobtrusive measures employed decades earlier, these implicit measures seek to obtain an estimate of an individual's attitude without directly asking the individual to consider his or her attitude. In that way, little or no motivation to alter responses in a socially desirable direction should be evoked. However, modern implicit measures go one step further in that they involve responses or processes that are automatic or difficult to control. So, even if participants were motivated to respond in a certain way, the uncontrollability lessens the possibility of their doing so successfully. For this reason, as well as the sheer ease by which they can be implemented with today's

computer technology, implicit measures of attitude have been used with increasing frequency.

The two most commonly-used implicit measures are represented in Readings 6 and 7. The first (Fazio, Jackson, Dunton, & Williams, 1995) is a procedure that grew out of the priming paradigm that had been developed to study the automatic activation of attitudes. This earlier work was presented as Reading 2. Whereas the earlier research aimed to demonstrate that attitudes can be activated automatically from memory upon mere presentation of the attitude object, the adaptation of the procedure as an unobtrusive measure takes advantage of any such automatic activation in order to obtain an estimate of the individual's attitude toward the primed object. A participant's primary task is to indicate the connotation of an evaluative adjective (e.g., "disgusting") as quickly as possible. Doing so will be facilitated if the target adjective is preceded briefly by the presentation of a negatively-valued word or image. For example, the word "cockroach" or a photo of a cockroach will activate negativity automatically for many people and this will enable individuals to more quickly classify the adjective "disgusting" as meaning bad. The extent to which the presentation of a given attitude object as a prime facilitates responding to positive versus negative adjectives can provide an indication of the individual's attitude toward the primed object. Relatively greater facilitation on negative adjectives is indicative of a negative attitude, whereas relatively greater facilitation on positive adjectives suggests a positive attitude.

Fazio *et al.* (1995) used this priming procedure to assess racial attitudes—a topic for which a climate of political correctness creates some mistrust of self-reported attitudes. Their research demonstrated the predictive validity of the unobtrusive measure. The experiments also illustrate the discordance that often is observed between implicit measures and more explicit, self-report measures of racial attitude. Such discordance is shown to stem from motivations to control prejudiced reactions while completing the verbal measure of attitude.

Reading 7 reprints the article in which Greenwald, McGhee, and Schwartz (1998) introduced what is unquestionably the most often used implicit measurement procedure, the Implicit Association Test or IAT. This procedure is also based on response latency. Participants are asked to classify stimuli. However, in the critical portion of the task, four different categories of stimuli must be classified using only two response keys. So, each key has two meanings. In an IAT focused on racial attitudes, the instructions might call for pressing the left key whenever a photo of a Black person is presented and whenever a word with positive connotations (e.g., "peace") is presented. The key might be labeled "Black—Good." The right key, labeled "White—Bad," is to be pressed whenever a photo of a White person is presented or a negative word (e.g., "cancer") appears. Essentially, the procedure provides an indication of how easily participants can remember the dual meanings of a given key, i.e., how easily they can associate, in this case, "Black" with "Good" and "White" with "Bad." What is critically important is how the average speed of responding changes when the response mappings are altered in the next block of trials. Participants respond to the same stimuli, but this time they do so with keys labeled "Black—Bad" and "White—Good." Are they faster or slower with this new arrangement? If they are faster, then they can more easily associate "Blacks" with "Bad" than with "Good."

The IAT has generated a considerable amount of research, excitement, and controversy. Much remains to be learned about the precise mechanisms that underlie the task, the nature of the associations that it measures, and the behaviors that it might predict. It also is the case that the priming measure and the IAT do not always provide corresponding estimates of attitudes, which has raised questions regarding just what each technique is measuring and the conditions under which the two do or do not converge. A recent review of the literature on implicit measures by Fazio and Olson (2003) is a reasonable starting point for any reader who is interested in learning more about these issues (a few additional relevant articles are listed below as "suggested readings"). More extensive information is available in two very recent edited books devoted to the topic of implicit measures (Petty, Fazio, & Briñol, in press; Wittenbrink & Schwarz, 2007). Given all the research activity, relevant findings are accumulating rapidly and progress is being made. Despite the uncertainties, implicit measures represent a very welcome addition to the tools that are available for measuring attitudes.

REFERENCES

Fazio, R. H., & Olson, M. A. (2003). Implicit measures in social cognition: Their meaning and use. *Annual Review of Psychology, 54*, 297–327.

Likert, R. (1932). A technique for the measurement of attitudes. *Archives of Psychology, 140*, 5–53.

Osgood, C. E., Suci, G. J., & Tanenbaum, P. H. (1957). *The measurement of meaning*. Urbana: University of Illinois Press.

Petty, R. E., Fazio, R. H., & Briñol, P. (Eds.) (in press). *Attitudes: Insights from the new implicit measures*. Mahwah, NJ: Erlbaum Associates.

Webb, E. J., Campbell, D. T., Schwartz, R. D., & Sechrest, L. (1966). *Unobtrusive measures: Nonreactive research in the social sciences*. Chicago: Rand McNally.

Wittenbrink, B. & Schwarz, N. (Eds.) (2007). *Implicit measures of attitudes*. New York: Guilford Press.

Suggested Readings

De Houwer, J. (2001). A structural and process analysis of the Implicit Association Test. *Journal of Experimental Social Psychology*, *37*, 443–451.

Himmelfarb, S. (1993). The measurement of attitudes. In A. H. Eagly & S. Chaiken, *The psychology of attitudes* (pp. 23–87). Fort Worth, TX: Harcourt Brace Jovanovich.

McConnell, A. R., & Liebold, J. M. (2001). Relations between the Implicit Association Test, explicit racial attitudes, and discriminatory behavior. *Journal of Experimental Social Psychology*, *37*, 435–442.

Olson, M. A., & Fazio, R. H. (2003). Relations between implicit measures of racial prejudice: What are we measuring? *Psychological Science*, *14*, 636–639.

Olson, M. A., & Fazio, R. H. (2004). Reducing the influence of extra-personal associations on the Implicit Association Test: Personalizing the IAT. *Journal of Personality and Social Psychology*, *86*, 653–667.

Attitudes can be Measured[1]

L. L. Thurstone*

The object of this study is to devise a method whereby the distribution of attitude of a group on a specified issue may be represented in the form of a frequency distribution. The base line represents ideally the whole range of opinions from those at one end who are most strongly in favor of the issue to those at the other end of the scale who are as strongly against it. Somewhere between the two extremes on the base line will be a neutral zone representing indifferent attitudes on the issue in question. The ordinates of the frequency distribution will represent the relative popularity of each attitude. This measurement problem has the limitation which is common to all measurement, namely, that one can measure only such attributes as can be represented on a linear continuum, such attributes as volume, price, length, area, excellence, beauty, and so on. For the present problem we are limited to those aspects of attitudes for which one can compare individuals by the "more and less" type of judgment. For example, we say understandingly that one man is more in favor of prohibition than another, more strongly in favor of the League of Nations than another, more militaristic than some other, more religious than another. The measurement is effected by the indorsement or rejection of statements of opinion. The opinions are allocated to different positions on the base line in accordance with the attitudes which they express. The ordinates of the frequency distribution are determined by the frequency with which each of the scaled opinions is indorsed. The center of the whole problem lies in the definition of a unit of measurement for the base line. The scale is so constructed that two opinions separated by a unit distance on the base line seem to differ as much in the attitude variable involved as any other two opinions on the scale which are also separated by a unit distance. This is the main idea of the present scale construction. The true allocation of an

*University of Chicago.
[1] This is one of a series of papers by the staff of the Behavior Research Fund, Illinois Institute for Juvenile Research, Chicago. Series B No. 110.

The original manuscript for this paper has enjoyed a great deal of friendly criticism, some of which turns on matters of terminology and some on the assumptions which are here stated. In order to keep this paper within reasonable length, the description of the detailed psychophysical methods used and the construction of several attitude scales are reserved for separate publication. This paper concerns then only an outline of one solution to the problem of measuring attitude.

individual to a position on an attitude scale is an abstraction, just as the true length of a chalk line, or the true temperature of a room, or the true spelling ability of a child, is an abstraction. We estimate the true length of a line, the true temperature of a room, or the true spelling ability of a child, by means of various indices, and it is a commonplace in measurement that all indices do not agree exactly. In allocating an individual to a point on the attitude continuum we may use various indices, such as the opinions that he indorses, his overt acts, and his past history, and it is to be expected that discrepancies will appear as the true attitude of the individual is estimated by different indices. The present study is concerned with the allocation of individuals along an attitude continuum based on the opinions that they accept or reject.

The Possibility of Measuring Attitude

The purpose of this paper is to discuss the problem of measuring attitudes and opinions and to offer a solution for it. The very fact that one offers a solution to a problem so complex as that of measuring differences of opinion or attitude on disputed social issues makes it evident from the start that the solution is more or less restricted in nature and that it applies only under certain assumptions that will, however, be described. In devising a method of measuring attitude I have tried to get along with the fewest possible restrictions because sometimes one is tempted to disregard so many factors that the original problem disappears. I trust that I shall not be accused of throwing out the baby with its bath.

In promising to measure attitudes I shall make several common-sense assumptions that will be stated here at the outset so that subsequent discussion may not be fogged by confusion regarding them. If the reader is unwilling to grant these assumptions, then I shall have nothing to offer him. If they are granted, we can proceed with some measuring methods that ought to yield interesting results.

It is necessary to state at the very outset just what we shall here mean by the terms "attitude" and "opinion." This is all the more necessary because the natural first impression about these two concepts is that they are not amenable to measurement in any real sense. It will be conceded at the outset that an attitude is a complex affair which cannot be wholly described by any single numerical index. For the problem of measurement this statement is analogous to the observation that an ordinary table is a complex affair which cannot be wholly described by any single numerical index. So is a man such a complexity which cannot be wholly represented by a single index. Nevertheless we do not hesitate to say that we measure the table. The context usually implies what it is about the table that we propose to measure. We say without hesitation that we measure a man when we take some anthropometric measurements of him. The context may well imply without explicit declaration what aspect of the man we are measuring, his cephalic index, his height or weight or what not. Just in the same sense we shall say here that we are measuring attitudes. We shall state or imply by the context the aspect of people's attitudes that we are measuring. The point is that it is just as legitimate to say that we are measuring attitudes as it is to say that we are measuring tables or men.

The concept 'attitude' will be used here to denote the sum total of a man's inclinations and feelings, prejudice or bias, preconceived notions, ideas, fears, threats, and convictions about any specified topic. Thus a man's attitude about pacifism means here all that he feels and thinks about peace and war. It is admittedly a subjective and personal affair.

The concept 'opinion' will here mean a verbal expression of attitude. If a man says that we made a mistake in entering the war against Germany, that statement will here be spoken of as an opinion. The term "opinion" will be restricted to verbal expression. But it is an expression of what? It expresses an attitude, supposedly. There should be no difficulty in understanding this use of the two terms. The verbal expression is the *opinion*. Our interpretation of the expressed opinion is that the man's *attitude* is pro-German. An opinion symbolizes an attitude.

Our next point concerns what it is that we want to measure. When a man says that we made a mistake in entering the war with Germany, the thing that interests us is not really the string of words as such or even the immediate meaning of the sentence merely as it stands, but rather the attitude of the speaker, the thoughts and feelings of the man about the United States, and the war, and Germany. It is the attitude that really interests us. The opinion has interest only in so far as we interpret it as a symbol of attitude. It is therefore something about attitudes that we want to measure. We shall use opinions as the means for measuring attitudes.[2]

There comes to mind the uncertainty of using an opinion as an index of attitude. The man may be a liar. If he is not intentionally misrepresenting his real attitude on a disputed question, he may nevertheless modify the expression of it for reasons of courtesy, especially in those situations in which frank expression of attitude may not be well received. This has led to the suggestion that a man's action is a safer index of his attitude than what he says. But his actions may also be distortions of his attitude. A politician extends friendship and hospitality in overt action while hiding an attitude that he expresses more truthfully to an intimate friend. Neither his opinions nor his overt acts constitute in any sense an infallible guide to the subjective inclinations and preferences that constitute his attitude. Therefore we must remain content to use opinions, or other forms of action, merely as indices of attitude. It must be recognized that there is a discrepancy, some error of measurement as it were, between the opinion or overt action that we use as an index and the attitude that we infer from such an index.

But this discrepancy between the index and "truth" is universal. When you want to know the temperature of your room, you look at the thermometer and use its reading as an index of temperature just as though there were no error in the index and just as though there were a single temperature reading which is the "correct" one for the room. If it is desired to ascertain the volume of a glass paper weight, the volume is postulated as an attribute of the piece of glass, even though volume is an abstraction. The volume is measured indirectly by noting the dimensions of the glass or by immersing it in water to see how much water it displaces. These two procedures give two indices which might not agree exactly. In almost every situation involving measurement there is postulated an abstract continuum such as volume or temperature, and the allocation of the thing measured to that continuum is accomplished usually by indirect means through one or more indices. Truth is inferred only from the relative consistency of the several indices, since it is never directly known. We are dealing with the same type of situation in attempting to measure attitude. We must postulate an attitude variable which is like practically all other measurable attributes in the nature of an abstract continuum, and we must find one or more indices which will satisfy us to the extent that they are internally consistent.

In the present study we shall measure the subject's attitude as expressed by the acceptance or rejection of opinions. But we shall not thereby imply that he will necessarily *act* in accordance with the opinions that he has indorsed. Let this limitation be clear. The measurement of attitudes expressed by a man's opinions does not necessarily mean the prediction of what he will do. If his expressed opinions and his actions are

---

[2] Professor Faris, who has been kind enough to give considerable constructive criticism to the manuscript for this paper, has suggested that we may be measuring opinion but that we are certainly not measuring attitude. It is in part a terminological question which turns on the concept of attitude. If the concept of attitude as here defined is not acceptable, it may be advisable to change the terminology provided that a distinction is retained between (1) the objective index, which is here called the statement or opinion, and (2) the inferred subjective inclination of the person, which is here called the attitude variable.

inconsistent, that does not concern us now, because we are not setting out to predict overt conduct. We shall assume that it is of interest to know what people *say* that they believe even if their conduct turns out to be inconsistent with their professed opinions. Even if they are intentionally distorting their attitudes, we are measuring at least the attitude which they are trying to make people believe that they have.

We take for granted that people's attitudes are subject to change. When we have measured a man's attitude on any issue such as pacifism, we shall not declare such a measurement to be in any sense an enduring or constitutional constant. His attitude may change, of course, from one day to the next, and it is our task to measure such changes, whether they be due to unknown causes or to the presence of some known persuasive factor such as the reading of a discourse on the issue in question. However, such fluctuations may also be attributed in part to error in the measurements themselves. In order to isolate the errors of the measurement instrument from the actual fluctuation in attitude, we must calculate the standard error of measurement of the scale itself, and this can be accomplished by methods already well known in mental measurement.

We shall assume that an attitude scale is used only in those situations in which one may reasonably expect people to tell the truth about their convictions or opinions. If a denominational school were to submit to its students a scale of attitudes about the church, one should hardly expect intelligent students to tell the truth about their convictions if they deviate from orthodox beliefs. At least, the findings could be challenged if the situation in which attitudes are expressed contains pressure or implied threat bearing directly on the attitude to be measured. Similarly, it would be difficult to discover attitudes on sex liberty by a written questionnaire, because of the well-nigh universal pressure to conceal such attitudes where they deviate from supposed conventions. It is assumed that attitude scales will be used only in those situations that offer a minimum of pressure on the attitude to be measured. Such situations are common enough.

All that we can do with an attitude scale is to measure the attitude actually expressed with the full realization that the subject may be consciously hiding his true attitude or that the social pressure of the situation has made him really believe what he expresses. This is a matter for interpretation. It is something probably worth while to measure an attitude expressed by opinions. It is another problem to interpret in each case the extent to which the subjects have expressed what they really believe. All that we can do is to minimize as far as possible the conditions that prevent our subjects from telling the truth, or else to adjust our interpretations accordingly.

When we discuss opinions, about prohibition for example, we quickly find that these opinions are multidimensional, that they cannot all be represented in a linear continuum. The various opinions cannot be completely described merely as "more" or "less." They scatter in many dimensions, but the very idea of measurement implies a linear continuum of some sort such as length, price, volume, weight, age. When the idea of measurement is applied to scholastic achievement, for example, it is necessary to force the qualitative variations into a scholastic linear scale of some kind. We judge in a similar way such qualities as mechanical skill, the excellence of handwriting, and the amount of a man's education, as though these traits were strung out along a single scale, although they are of course in reality scattered in many dimensions. As a matter of fact, we get along quite well with the concept of a scale in describing traits even so qualitative as education, social and economic status, or beauty. A scale or linear continuum is implied when we say that a man has more education than another, or that a woman is more beautiful than another, even though, if pressed, we admit that perhaps the pair involved in each of the comparisons have little if anything in common. It is clear that the linear continuum which is implied in a "more and less" judgment may be conceptual, that it does not necessarily have the physical existence of a yardstick.

And so it is also with attitudes. We do not hesitate to compare them by the "more and less" type of judgment. We say about a man, for example, that he is more in favor of prohibition than some other, and the judgment conveys its meaning very well with the implication of a linear scale along which people or opinions might be allocated.

The Attitude Variable

The first restriction on the problem of measuring attitudes is to specify an attitude variable and to limit the measurement to that. An example will make this clear. Let us consider the prohibition question and let us take as the attitude variable the degree of restriction that should be imposed on individual liberty in the consumption of alcohol. This degree of restriction can be thought of as a continuum ranging from complete and absolute freedom or license to equally complete and absolute restriction, and it would of course include neutral and indifferent attitudes.

In collecting samples from which to construct a scale we might ask a hundred individuals to write out their opinions about prohibition. Among these we might find one which expresses the belief that prohibition has increased the use of tobacco. Surely this is an opinion concerning prohibition, but it would not be at all serviceable for measuring the attitude variable just mentioned. Hence it would be irrelevant. Another man might express the opinion that prohibition has eliminated an important source of government revenue. This is also an opinion concerning prohibition, but it would not belong to the particular attitude variable that we have set out to measure or scale. It is preferable to use an objective and experimental criterion for the elimination of opinions that do not belong on the specified continuum to be measured, and I believe that such a criterion is available.

This restriction on the problem of measuring attitudes is necessary in the very nature of measurement. It is taken for granted in all ordinary measurement, and it must be clear that it applies also to measurement in a field in which the multi-dimensional characteristics have not yet been so clearly isolated. For example, it would be almost ridiculous to call attention to the fact that a table cannot be measured unless one states or implies what it is about the table that is to be measured; its height, its cost, or beauty or degree of appropriateness or the length of time required to make it. The context usually makes this restriction on measurement. When the notion of measurement is applied to so complex a phenomenon as opinions and attitudes, we must here also restrict ourselves to some specified or implied continuum along which the measurement is to take place.

In specifying the attitude variable, the first requirement is that it should be so stated that one can speak of it in terms of "more" and "less," as, for example, when we compare the attitudes of people by saying that one of them is more pacifistic, more in favor of prohibition, more strongly in favor of capital punishment, or more religious than some other person.

Figure 3.1 represents an attitude variable, militarism-pacifism, with a neutral zone. A person who usually talks in favor of preparedness, for example, would be represented somewhere to the right of the neutral zone. A person who is more interested in disarmament would be represented

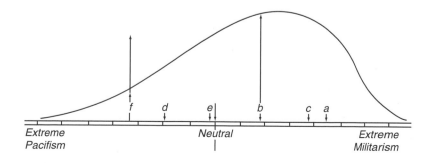

Extreme Pacifism   *Neutral*   *Extreme Militarism*

FIGURE 3.1

somewhere to the left of the neutral zone. It is possible to conceive of a frequency distribution to represent the distribution of attitude in a specified group on the subject of pacifism-militarism.

Consider the ordinate of the frequency distribution at any point on the base line. The point and its immediate vicinity represent for our purpose an attitude, and we want to know relatively how common that degree of feeling for or against pacifism may be in the group that is being studied. It is of secondary interest to know that a particular statement of opinion is indorsed by a certain proportion of that group. It is only to the extent that the opinion is representative of an attitude that it is useful for our purposes. Later we shall consider the possibility that a statement of opinion may be scaled as rather pacifistic and yet be indorsed by a person of very pronounced militaristic sympathies. To the extent that the statement is indorsed or rejected by factors other than the attitude-variable that it represents, to that extent the statement is useless for our purposes. We shall also consider an objective criterion for spotting such statements so that they may be eliminated from the scale. In our entire study we shall be dealing, then, with opinions, not primarily because of their cognitive content but rather because they serve as the carriers or symbols of the attitudes of the people who express or indorse these opinions.

There is some ambiguity in using the term attitude in the plural. An attitude is represented as a point on the attitude continuum. Consequently there is an infinite number of attitudes that might be represented along the attitude scale. In practice, however, we do not differentiate so finely. In fact, an attitude, practically speaking, is a certain narrow range or vicinity on the scale. When a frequency distribution is drawn for any continuous variable, such as stature, we classify the variable for descriptive purposes into steps or class intervals. The attitude variable can also be divided into class intervals and the frequency counted in each class interval. When we speak of "an" attitude, we shall mean a point, or a vicinity, on the attitude continuum. Several attitudes will be considered not as a set of discrete entities, but as a series of class intervals along the attitude scale.

A Frequency Distribution of Attitudes

The main argument so far has been to show that since in ordinary conversation we readily and understandably describe individuals as more and less pacifistic or more and less militaristic in attitude, we may frankly represent this linearity in the form of a unidimensional scale. This has been done in a diagrammatic way in Figure 3.1. We shall first describe our objective and then show how a rational unit of measurement may be adopted for the whole scale.

Let the base line of Figure 3.1 represent a continuous range of attitudes from extreme pacifism on the left to extreme militarism on the right.

If the various steps in such a scale were defined, it is clear that a person's attitude on militarism-pacifism could be represented by a point on that scale. The strength and direction of a particular individual's sympathies might be indicated by the point a, thus showing that he is rather militaristic in his opinions. Another individual might be represented at the point b to show that although he is slightly militaristic in his opinions, he is not so extreme about it as the person who is placed at the point a. A third person might be placed at the point c to show that he is quite militaristic and that the difference between a and c is very slight. A similar interpretation might be extended to any point on the continuous scale from extreme militarism to extreme pacifism, with a neutral or indifference zone between them.

A second characteristic might also be indicated graphically in terms of the scale, namely, the range of opinions that any particular individual is willing to indorse. It is of course not to be expected that every person will find only one single opinion on the whole scale that he is willing to indorse and that he will reject all the others. As a matter of fact we should probably find ourselves willing to indorse a great many opinions on the scale that cover a certain range of it. It is conceivable, then, that a pacifistically inclined person would be willing to indorse all or most of the opinions in the range d to e and that he would reject as too extremely pacifistic most of the opinions to the left of d, and would also reject the whole range of militaristic opinions. His attitude would then be indicated by the average or mean of the range that he indorses, unless he cares to select a particular opinion which most nearly represents his own attitude. The same sort of reasoning may of course be extended to the whole range of the scale, so that we should have at least two, or possibly three, characteristics of each person designated in terms of the scale. These characteristics would be (1) the mean position that he occupies on the scale, (2) the range of opinions that he is willing to accept, and (3) that one opinion which he selects as the one which most nearly represents his own attitude on the issue at stake.

It should also be possible to describe a group of individuals by means of the scale. This type of description has been represented in a diagrammatic way by the frequency outline.

Any ordinate of the curve would represent the number of individuals, or the percentage of the whole group, that indorses the corresponding opinion. For example, the ordinate at b would represent the number of persons in the group who indorse the degree of militarism represented by the point b on the scale. A glance at the frequency curve shows that for the fictitious group of this diagram militaristic opinions are indorsed more frequently than the pacifistic ones. It is clear that the area of this frequency diagram would represent the total number of indorsements given by the group. The diagram can be arranged in several different ways that will be separately discussed. It is sufficient at this moment to realize that, given a valid scale of opinions, it would be possible to compare several different groups in their attitudes on a disputed question.

A second type of group comparison might be made by the range or spread that the frequency surfaces reveal. If one of the groups is represented by a frequency diagram of considerable range or scatter, then that group would be more heterogeneous on the issue at stake than some other group whose frequency diagram of attitudes shows a smaller range or scatter. It goes without saying that the frequent assumption of a normal distribution in educational scale construction has absolutely no application here, because there is no reason whatever to assume that any group of people will be normally distributed in their opinions about anything.

It should be possible, then, to make four types of description by means of a scale of attitudes. These are (1) the average or mean attitude of a particular individual on the issue at stake, (2) the range of opinion that he is willing to accept or tolerate, (3) the relative popularity of each attitude of the scale for a designated group as shown by the frequency distribution for that group, and (4) the degree of homogeneity or heterogeneity in the attitudes of a designated group on the issue as shown by the spread or dispersion of its frequency distribution.

This constitutes our objective. The heart of the problem is in the unit of measurement for the base line, and it is to this aspect of the problem that we may now turn.

A Unit of Measurement for Attitudes

The only way in which we can identify the different attitudes (points on the base line) is to use a set of opinions as landmarks, as it were, for the different parts or steps of the scale. The final scale will then consist of a series of statements of opinion, each of which is allocated to a particular point on the base line. If we start with enough statements, we may be able to select a list of twenty or thirty opinions so chosen that they represent an evenly graduated series of attitudes. The separation between successive statements of opinion would then be uniform, but the scale can be constructed with a series of opinions allocated on the base line even though their base line separations are not uniform. For the purpose of drawing frequency distributions it will be convenient, however, to have the statements so chosen that the steps between them are uniform throughout the whole range of the scale.

Consider the three statements a, c, and d, in Figure 3.1. The statements c and a are placed close together to indicate that they are very similar, while statements c and d are spaced far apart to indicate that they are very different. We should expect two individuals scaled at c and a respectively to agree very well in discussing pacifism and militarism. On the other hand, we should expect to be able to tell the difference quite readily between the opinions of a person at *d* and another person at *c*. The scale separations of the opinions must agree with our impressions of them.

In order to ascertain how far apart the statements should be on the final scale, we submit them to a group of several hundred people who are asked to arrange the statements in order from the most pacifistic to to the most militaristic. We do not ask them for their own opinions. That is another matter entirely. We are now concerned with the construction of a scale with a valid unit of measurement. There may be a hundred statements in the original list, and the several hundred persons are asked merely to arrange the statements in rank order according to the designated attitude variable. It is then possible to ascertain the proportion of the readers who consider statement *a* to be more militaristic than statement *c*. If the two statements represent very similar attitudes we should not expect to find perfect agreement in the rank order of statements *a* and *c*. If they are identical in attitude, there will be about 50 per cent of the readers who say that statement *a* is more militaristic than statement *c*, while the remaining 50 per cent of the readers will say that statement *c* is more militaristic than statement *a*. It is possible to use the proportion of readers or judges who agree about the rank order of any two statements as a basis for actual measurement.

If 90 per cent of the judges or readers say that statement *a* is more militaristic than statement *b* ($p_{a>b} = .90$) and if only 60 per cent of the readers say that statement *a* is more militaristic than statement *c* ($p_{a>c} = .60$) then clearly the scale separation $(a - c)$ is shorter than the scale separation $(a - b)$. [...]

The Construction of an Attitude Scale

The method is as follows. Several groups of people are asked to write out their opinions on the issue in question, and the literature is searched for suitable brief statements that may serve the purposes of the scale. By editing such material a list of from 100 to 150 statements is prepared expressive of attitudes covering as far as possible all gradations from one end of the scale to the other. It is sometimes necessary to give special attention to the neutral statements. If a random collection of statements of opinion should fail to produce neutral statements, there is some danger that the scale will break in two parts. The whole range of attitudes must be fairly well covered, as far as one can tell by preliminary inspection, in order to insure that there will be overlapping in the rank orders of different readers throughout the scale.

In making the initial list of statements several practical criteria are applied in the first editing work. Some of the important criteria are as follows: (1) the statements should be as brief as possible so as not to fatigue the subjects who are asked to read the whole list. (2) The statements should be such that they can be indorsed or rejected in accordance with their agreement or disagreement with the attitude of the reader. Some statements in a random sample will be so phrased that the reader can express no definite indorsement or rejection of them. (3) Every statement should be such that acceptance or rejection of the statement does indicate something regarding the reader's attitude about the issue in question. If, for example, the statement is made that war is an incentive to inventive genius, the acceptance or rejection of it really does not say anything regarding the reader's pacifistic or militaristic tendencies. He may regard the statement as an unquestioned fact and simply indorse it as a fact, in which case his answer has not revealed anything concerning his own attitude on the issue in question. However, only the conspicuous examples of this effect should be eliminated by inspection, because an objective criterion is available for detecting such statements so that their elimination from the scale will be automatic. Personal judgment should be minimized as far as possible in this type of work. (4) Double-barreled statements should be avoided except possibly as examples of neutrality when better neutral statements do not seem to be readily available. Double-barreled statements tend to have a high ambiguity. (5) One must insure that at least a fair majority of the statements really belong on the attitude variable that is to be measured. If a small number of irrelevant statements should be either intentionally or unintentionally left in the series, they will be automatically eliminated by an objective criterion, but the criterion will not be successful unless the majority of the statements are clearly a part of the stipulated variable.

When the original list has been edited with these factors in mind, there will be perhaps 80 to 100 statements to be actually scaled. These statements are then mimeographed on small cards, one statement on each card. Two or three hundred subjects are asked to arrange the statements in eleven piles ranging from opinions most strongly affirmative to those most strongly negative. The detailed instructions will be published with the description of the separate scales. The task is essentially to sort out the small cards into eleven piles so that they *seem* to be fairly evenly spaced or graded. Only the two ends and the middle pile are labelled. The middle pile is indicated for neutral opinions. The reader must decide for each statement which of five subjective degrees of affirmation or five subjective degrees of negation is implied in the statement or whether it is a neutral opinion.

When such sorting has been completed by two or three hundred readers, a diagram like Figure 3.2 is prepared. We shall discuss it with the scale for pacifism-militarism as an example. On the base line of this diagram are represented the eleven apparently equal steps of the attitude variable. The neutral interval is the interval 5 to 6, the most pacifistic interval from 0 to 1, and the most militaristic interval from 10 to 11. This diagram is fictitious and is drawn to show the principle involved. Curve A is drawn to show the manner in which one of the statements might be classified by the three hundred readers. It is not classified by anyone below the value of 3, half of the readers classify it below the value 6, and all of them classify it below the value 9. The scale value of the statement is that scale value below which just one half of the readers place it. In other words, the scale value assigned to the statement is so chosen that one half of the readers consider it more militaristic and one half of them consider it less militaristic than the scale value assigned.

[EDITORS' NOTE: In the next two sections of the paper, Thurstone offers some suggestions for selecting 20–30 statements for actual use as the scale items. For example, some statements should be eliminated because they appear ambiguous. Consider, as Thurstone does, the statements A and B in Figure 3.2. Statement A is characterized by values ranging all the way from 3.5 to 9, suggesting that it is open to a wide range of interpretations. In contrast, statement B has a much smaller range of 2 to 6. It is to be preferred because it is less ambiguous. Using such criteria, the less appropriate statements can be eliminated from the potential pool. Ultimately, the goal is to select a subset of relatively unambiguous statements that represent an evenly graduated series of scale values. For the scale on which Thurstone focused, the chosen items would range from implying extreme pacifism to extreme militarism.]

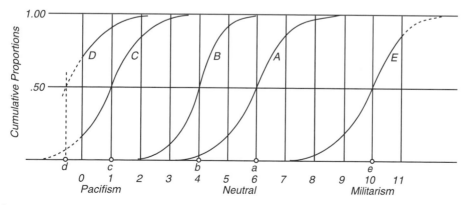

FIGURE 3.2

Measurement with an Attitude Scale

The practical application of the present measurement technique consists in presenting the final list of about twenty-five statements of opinion to the group to be studied with the request that they check with plus signs all the statements with which they agree and with minus signs all the statements with which they disagree. The score for each person is the average scale value of all the statements that he has indorsed. In order that the scale be effective toward the extremes, it is advisable that the statements in the scale be extended in both directions considerably beyond the attitudes which will ever be encountered as mean values for individuals. When the score has been determined for each person by the simple summation just indicated, a frequency distribution can be plotted for the attitudes of any specified group. [. . .]

The essential characteristic of the present measurement method is the scale of evenly graduated opinions so arranged that equal steps or intervals on the scale *seem* to most people to represent equally noticeable shifts in attitude.

Self-Reports: How the Questions Shape the Answers

Norbert Schwarz

Self-reports of behaviors and attitudes are strongly influenced by features of the research instrument, including question wording, format, and context. Recent research has addressed the underlying cognitive and communicative processes, which are systematic and increasingly well-understood. I review what has been learned, focusing on issues of question comprehension, behavioral frequency reports, and the emergence of context effects in attitude measurement. The accumulating knowledge about the processes underlying self-reports promises to improve questionnaire design and data quality.

Self-reports are a primary source of data in psychology and the social sciences. From laboratory experiments to public opinion surveys, researchers rely on the answers that research participants provide to learn about individuals' thoughts, feelings, and behaviors and to monitor societal trends, from the nation's unemployment rate to the development of crime. Unfortunately, self-reports are a fallible source of data, and minor changes in question wording, question format, or question context can result in major changes in the obtained results, as a few examples may illustrate:

- When asked what they consider "the most important thing for children to prepare them for life," 61.5% of a representative sample chose the alternative "To think for themselves" when this alternative was offered on a list. Yet, only 4.6% volunteered an answer that could be assigned to this category when no list was presented (Schuman & Presser, 1981).
- When asked how successful they have been in life, 34% of a representative sample reported high success when the numeric values of the rating scale ranged from −5 to 5, whereas only 13% did so when the numeric values ranged from 0 to

Editor's note. Denise C. Park served as action editor for this article.

Author's note. Correspondence concerning this article should be addressed to Norbert Schwarz, Institute for Social Research, University of Michigan, Ann Arbor, MI 48106–1248. Electronic mail may be sent to nschwarz@umich.edu.

10 (Schwarz, Knäuper, Hippler, Noelle-Neumann, & Clark, 1991).

- When asked how often they experience a variety of physical symptoms, 62% of a sample of psychosomatic patients reported symptom frequencies of more than twice a month when the response scale ranged from "twice a month or less" to "several times a day." Yet, only 39% reported frequencies of more than twice a month when the scale ranged from "never" to "more than twice a month" (Schwarz & Scheuring, 1992).
- Whether we conclude that marital satisfaction is a major or a minor contributor to general life-satisfaction depends on the order in which both questions are asked, with correlations ranging from .18 to .67 as a function of question order and introduction (Schwarz, Strack, & Mai, 1991).

Although findings of this type often come as unpleasant surprises, the underlying cognitive and communicative processes are systematic and increasingly well-understood. Since the early 1980s, psychologists and survey methodologists developed an interdisciplinary field of research that is devoted to understanding the nature of self-reports and to improving the quality of data collection. Research in this field has addressed a wide range of topics: How do respondents make sense of the questions asked of them? What is the role of autobiographical memory in retrospective reports of behaviors and how can we increase the accuracy of these reports? What are the judgmental processes underlying the emergence of context effects in attitude measurement? Do the processes underlying self-reports of behaviors and attitudes change across the adult life span? Which techniques can we use to determine if a question "works" as intended?

Reflecting the need to bring together researchers from diverse disciplines, interdisciplinary conferences played a pivotal role in the development of this area, resulting in a considerable number of edited volumes (Hippler, Schwarz, & Sudman, 1987; Jabine, Straf, Tanur, & Tourangeau, 1984; Jobe & Loftus, 1991; Schwarz, Park, Knäuper, &

Sudman, 1998; Schwarz & Sudman, 1992, 1994, 1996; Sirken et al., 1998; Tanur, 1992). In addition, a recent monograph (Sudman, Bradburn, & Schwarz, 1996) reviewed what has been learned from this research and discussed its implications for questionnaire design.

Although this area of research is typically referred to as "cognitive aspects of survey methodology," the cognitive and communicative processes investigated apply to the question-answering process in all standardized research situations. In this article, I review selected aspects of this work, focusing on basic psychological issues that apply to questionnaire studies as well as laboratory experiments. The first section addresses how respondents make sense of the questions asked of them and highlights the role of conversational inference processes in question comprehension. The second section addresses how respondents answer behavioral questions and relates these questions to issues of autobiographical memory and estimation strategies. Finally, the third section addresses attitude questions and reviews the conditions that give rise to context effects in attitude measurement. Throughout, I focus on how features of the research instrument shape the answers that respondents provide and influence the conclusions that we, as researchers, would draw from the obtained reports.

Making Sense of the Question Asked

Not surprisingly, the first task that respondents face is to understand the question asked of them (Strack & Martin, 1987; Tourangeau, 1984). The key issue is whether the respondent's understanding of the question matches what the researcher had in mind: Is the attitude object, or the behavior, that the respondent identifies as the referent of the question the one that the researcher intended? Does the respondent's understanding tap the same facet of the issue and the same evaluative dimension? From a psychological point of view, question comprehension reflects the operation of two intertwined processes (Clark & Clark, 1977; Clark & Schober, 1992).

The first refers to the semantic understanding of the utterance. Comprehending the *literal meaning* of a sentence involves the identification of words, the recall of lexical information from semantic memory, and the construction of a meaning of the utterance, which is constrained by its context (Anderson, 1980). Not surprisingly, textbooks urge researchers to write simple questions and to avoid unfamiliar or ambiguous terms. However, understanding the words is not sufficient to answer a question. For example, if respondents are asked, "What have you done today?" they are likely to understand the meaning of the words. Yet, they still need to determine what kind of activities the researcher is interested in. Should they report, for example, that they took a shower, or not? Hence, understanding a question in a way that allows an appropriate answer requires not only an understanding of the literal meaning of the question but also involves inferences about the questioner's intention to determine the *pragmatic meaning* of the question.

To infer the pragmatic meaning of a question, respondents rely on the tacit assumptions that govern the conduct of conversation in everyday life. These tacit assumptions were described by Paul Grice (1975), a philosopher of language (see Levinson, 1983, for a detailed introduction). According to Grice's analysis, conversations proceed according to a cooperativeness principle, which can be expressed in the form of four maxims.

First, a *maxim of relation* enjoins speakers to make their contribution relevant to the aims of the ongoing conversation. In research situations, this maxim licenses the use of contextual information in question interpretation and invites respondents to relate the question to the context of the ongoing exchange.

Second, a *maxim of quantity* enjoins speakers to make their contribution as informative as is required, but not more informative than is required. This maxim invites respondents to provide information the questioner seems interested in, rather than other information that may come to mind. Moreover, it discourages the reiteration of information that has already been provided earlier, or that

"goes without saying" (such as "taking a shower" in the above example).

Third, a *maxim of manner* holds that the contribution should be clear rather than obscure, ambiguous, or wordy. In research situations, this maxim entails an "interpretability presumption": research participants can assume that the researcher "chose his wording so they can understand what he meant—and can do so quickly" (Clark & Schober, 1992, p. 27). Hence, the most obvious meaning seems likely to be the correct one, and if there is no obvious meaning, respondents may consult the immediate context to determine one. As numerous studies have shown, the researcher's contributions include formal aspects of questionnaire design, such as the response alternatives provided as part of the question, and respondents draw on these features in interpreting the question.

Finally, a *maxim of quality* enjoins speakers not to say anything they believe to be false or lack adequate evidence for. This maxim is often violated in psychological experiments, for example, when the researcher deliberately presents misleading or uninformative material in a context that suggests otherwise. This topic, however, is beyond the scope of the present article (see Bless, Strack, & Schwarz, 1993; Hilton, 1995; Schwarz, 1994, 1996, for reviews).

In summary, speakers should try to be informative, truthful, relevant, and clear, and listeners interpret the speakers' utterances "on the assumption that they are trying to live up to these ideals" (Clark & Clark, 1977, p. 122). These rules of cooperative conversational conduct are essential for understanding how respondents make sense of the questions asked of them, as the following examples illustrate (see Clark & Schober, 1992; Schober, in press; Schwarz, 1994, 1996; Strack, 1994a, 1994b, for more extended reviews).

Response Alternatives

Open versus closed response formats. Suppose that respondents are asked in an open-response format, "What have you done today?" To give a meaningful answer, respondents have to determine which activities may be of interest to the researcher. In an attempt to be informative, respondents are likely to omit activities that the researcher is obviously aware of (e.g., "I gave a survey interview") or may take for granted anyway (e.g., "I took a shower"), thus observing the maxim of quantity. If respondents were given a list of activities that included giving an interview and taking a shower, most respondents would endorse them. At the same time, however, such a list would reduce the likelihood that respondents would report activities that are not represented on the list (see Schuman & Presser, 1981; Schwarz & Hippler, 1991, for a review of relevant studies). Both of these question-form effects reflect that response alternatives can clarify the intended meaning of a question, in the present example by specifying the activities the researcher is interested in. In addition, response alternatives may remind respondents of material that they may otherwise not consider.

In combination, these processes can result in pronounced and systematic differences between open- and closed-question formats, as a study on parental values illustrated. When asked what they consider "the most important thing for children to prepare them for life," 61.5% of the respondents picked "To think for themselves" when this alternative was offered as part of a list. Yet, only 4.6% provided an answer that could be assigned to this category in an open-response format (Schuman & Presser, 1981, pp. 105–107). Obviously, the researchers would draw very different conclusions about parental values depending on the question format used.

Frequency scales and reference periods. Suppose that respondents are asked how frequently they felt "really irritated" recently. To provide an informative answer, respondents have to determine what the researcher means with "really irritated." Does this term refer to major or to minor annoyances? To identify the intended meaning of the question, they may consult the response alternatives provided by the researcher. If the response alternatives present low-frequency categories, for example, ranging from "less than once a year" to "more than once a

month," respondents may conclude that the researcher has relatively rare events in mind. Hence, the question cannot refer to minor irritations that are likely to occur more often, so the researcher is probably interested in more severe episodes of irritation. In line with this assumption, Schwarz, Strack, Müller, and Chassein (1988; see also Gaskell, O'Muircheartaigh, & Wright, 1994) observed that respondents who had to report the frequency of irritating experiences on a low-frequency scale assumed that the question referred to major annoyances, whereas respondents who had to give their report on a high-frequency scale assumed that the question referred to minor annoyances. Thus, respondents identified different experiences as the target of the question, depending on the frequency range of the response alternatives provided to them.

Similarly, Winkielman, Knäuper, and Schwarz (1998) observed that the length of the reference period can profoundly affect question interpretation. In their studies, respondents were asked how frequently they had been angry either "last week" or "last year." Again, they inferred that the researcher is interested in more frequent and less severe episodes of anger when the question pertained to one week rather than one year, and their examples reflected this differential question interpretation.

These findings have important implications for the comparison of concurrent and retrospective reports of behaviors and emotions. Empirically, individuals report more intense emotions (e.g., Parkinson, Briner, Reynolds, & Totterdell, 1995; Thomas & Diener, 1990), and more severe marital disagreements (e.g., McGonagle, Kessler, & Schilling, 1992), in retrospective than in concurrent reports. Whereas findings of this type are typically attributed to the higher memorability of intense experiences, Winkielman et al.'s (1998) results suggest that discrepancies between concurrent and retrospective reports may in part be due to differential question interpretation: Concurrent reports necessarily pertain to a short reference period, with one day typically being the upper limit, whereas retrospective reports cover more extended periods. Hence, the concurrent and retrospective nature of the report is inherently confounded with the length of the reference period. Accordingly, participants who provide a concurrent report may infer from the short reference period used that the researcher is interested in frequent events, whereas the long reference period used under retrospective conditions may suggest an interest in infrequent events. Hence, respondents may deliberately report on different experiences, rendering their reports incomparable.

Rating scales. Similar considerations apply to psychologists' favorite question format, the rating scale. Suppose respondents are asked, "How successful would you say you have been in life?" accompanied by a rating scale that ranges from "not at all successful" to "extremely successful." To answer this question, respondents have to determine what the researcher means by "not at all successful": Does this term refer to the absence of outstanding achievements or to the presence of explicit failures? To do so, they may draw on what is supposedly a purely formal feature of the rating scale, namely its numeric values. Specifically, Schwarz, Knäuper, et al. (1991) presented the success-in-life question with an 11-point rating scale that ranged either from 0 (*not at all successful*) to 10 (*extremely successful*), or from −5 (*not at all successful*) to 5 (*extremely successful*). The results showed a dramatic impact of the numeric values presented to respondents. Whereas 34% of the respondents endorsed a value between −5 and 0 on the −5 to 5 scale, only 13% endorsed one of the formally equivalent values between 0 and 5 on the 0–10 scale.

Subsequent experiments indicated that this difference reflects differential interpretations of the term "not at all successful." When this label was combined with the numeric value "0," respondents interpreted it to reflect the absence of outstanding achievements. However, when the same label was combined with the numeric value "−5," and the scale offered "0" as the midpoint, they interpreted it to reflect the presence of explicit failures (see also Schwarz, Grayson, & Knäuper, 1998; Schwarz & Hippler, 1995a). In general, a format that ranges from negative to positive numbers conveys that the researcher has a bipolar dimension in mind, where the two poles refer to the presence of opposite attributes. In contrast, a format that uses only positive numbers conveys that the researcher has a unipolar dimension in mind, referring to different degrees of the same attribute.

These and related findings (see Schwarz, 1996, chapter 5, for a review) highlight that respondents draw on apparently formal features of the research instrument to disambiguate the meaning of the questions posed to them. Unless researchers learn to take the informational value of these features into account, we may often be surprised by the answers we obtain.

Question Context

Researcher's epistemic interest. An important but frequently overlooked context variable that may influence respondents' question interpretation is clues provided by the researcher's affiliation. Recall that the norms of conversational conduct (Grice, 1975) require speakers to provide information that the questioner is interested in, which entails inferences about the questioner's likely epistemic interest. A relevant source of information in this regard is the researcher's affiliation. For example, Norenzayan and Schwarz (in press) presented respondents with newspaper accounts of mass murders and asked them to explain why the mass murder occurred. In one condition, the questionnaire was printed on the letterhead of an alleged "Institute for Personality Research," whereas in the other condition it was printed on the letterhead of an "Institute for Social Research." As expected, respondents' explanations showed more attention to personality variables or to social-contextual variables, depending on whether they thought the researcher was a personality psychologist or a social scientist. Apparently, they took the researcher's affiliation into account in determining the kind of information that would be most informative, given the researcher's likely epistemic interest.

Adjacent question. Respondents' interpretation of a question's intended meaning is further influenced by the content of adjacent questions. As an extreme case, consider research in which respondents are asked to report their opinion about a highly obscure, or even completely fictitious, issue, such as the "Agricultural Trade Act of 1978" (e.g., Bishop, Oldendick, & Tuchfarber, 1986; Schuman & Presser, 1981). Public opinion researchers introduced such questions to explore the extent to which respondents are willing to report an opinion in the absence of any knowledge about the topic. In fact, about 30% of any representative sample do offer an opinion on fictitious issues. Yet, their answers may be more meaningful than has typically been assumed.

From a conversational point of view, the sheer fact that a question about some issue is asked presupposes that this issue exists—or else asking a question about it would violate every norm of conversational conduct. But respondents have no reason to assume that the researcher would ask a meaningless question and will hence try to make sense of it. To do so, they are likely to turn to the context of the ambiguous question, much as they would be expected to do in any other conversation. Once they have assigned a particular meaning to the issue, thus transforming the fictitious issue into a subjectively better defined one that makes sense in the context of the questionnaire, they may have no difficulty reporting a subjectively meaningful opinion. Even if they have not given the particular issue much thought, they may identify the broader set of issues to which this particular one apparently belongs, allowing them to derive a meaningful answer.

Supporting this assumption, Strack, Schwarz, and Wänke (1991, Experiment 1) observed that German university students reported different attitudes toward the introduction of a fictitious "educational contribution," depending on the nature of a preceding question. Specifically, some students were asked to estimate the average tuition fees that students have to pay at U.S. universities (in contrast to Germany, where university education is free), whereas others had to estimate the amount of money that the Swedish government pays every student as financial support. As expected, respondents inferred that the fictitious "educational contribution" pertained to students having to pay money when it followed the tuition question, but to students receiving money when it followed the financial support question. Reflecting this differential interpretation, they reported a more favorable attitude toward the introduction of an "educational contribution" in the former than in the latter case—hardly a meaningless response.

Summary

As the preceding examples illustrate, question comprehension is not solely an issue of understanding the literal meaning of an utterance. Rather, question comprehension involves extensive inferences about the speaker's intentions to determine the pragmatic meaning of the question. To make these inferences, respondents draw on the nature of preceding questions as well as the response alternatives. Accordingly, researchers' traditional focus on using the "right words" in questionnaire writing needs to be complemented by a consideration of the conversational processes involved in the question-answering process (see Schwarz, 1996, for a comprehensive review).

To safeguard against unintended question interpretations and related complications, psychologists and survey methodologists have developed a number of procedures that can be used in questionnaire pretesting (see the contributions in Schwarz & Sudman, 1996, for comprehensive reviews). These procedures include the extensive use of probes and think-aloud protocols (summarily referred to as "cognitive interviewing"; e.g., DeMaio & Rothgeb, 1996), detailed codings of interview transcripts (e.g., Bolton & Bronkhorst, 1996; Fowler & Cannell, 1996), and the use of expert systems that alert researchers to likely problems (see Lessler & Forsyth, 1996). In the domain of survey research, these procedures are routinely applied at the questionnaire pretesting stage, and most major survey centers at government agencies, as well as some centers in the academic and private domains, have established "cognitive laboratories" for this purpose. At present, these techniques are less frequently used in psychological research, where questionnaire development is often of a more ad hoc nature.

Once respondents have determined the intended meaning of the question, they face additional tasks (Strack & Martin, 1987; Tourangeau, 1984). These tasks include the recall of relevant information from memory, the computation of a judgment, and the formatting of these judgments in line with the response alternatives provided by the researcher. Moreover, respondents may want to edit their private judgment before they report it to the researcher, due to reasons of social desirability and self-presentation. However, a caveat needs to be added. Although it is conceptually useful to present respondents' tasks as following the above sequence of question comprehension, recall, judgment, and overt report (Strack & Martin, 1987; Tourangeau, 1984), deviations from this sequence are obviously possible. For example, respondents may revise their initial interpretation of a question when their answer does not fit the response alternatives. Next I address these tasks in the context of behavioral questions and attitude questions.

Reporting on One's Behaviors

Many questions require respondents to report on the frequency with which they engaged in a specific behavior during a specified reference period. Ideally, the researcher wants respondents to identify the intended behavior, to search memory for relevant episodes, to date these episodes with regard to the reference period, and to count them up to arrive at a numeric answer. Unfortunately, this is the course of action that respondents are least likely to follow. In fact, unless the behavior is rare and of considerable importance, respondents are unlikely to have detailed episodic representations available in memory. Instead, the individual instances of frequent behaviors blend into generic, knowledge-like representations that lack the time and space markers that allow for episodic recall (see Strube, 1987). Accordingly, a "recall-and-count" model does not capture how people answer questions about frequent behaviors or experiences. Rather, their answers are likely to be based on

some fragmented recall and the application of inference rules to compute a frequency estimate (see Bradburn, Rips, & Shevell, 1987; Sudman et al., 1996, for reviews).

Drawing on basic research into the structure of autobiographical memory, researchers have developed a number of strategies that are designed to facilitate autobiographical recall (for reviews see Schwarz, 1990; Sudman et al., 1996; and the contributions in Schwarz & Sudman, 1994). These strategies are beyond the scope of the present article, which focuses on contextual influences of questionnaire design. Specifically, I address how the frequency alternatives presented as part of a closed-question format influence respondents' frequency estimates and subsequent related judgments.

Frequency Alternatives

Behavioral reports. In many studies, respondents are asked to report their behavior by checking the appropriate alternative from a list of response alternatives of the type shown in Table 4.1. In this example, taken from Schwarz, Hippler, Deutsch, and Strack (1985), German respondents were asked how many hours they watch television on a typical day. To provide their answer, they were presented with a frequency scale that offered either high- or low-frequency response alternatives. Although the selected response alternative is assumed to inform the researcher about the respondent's behavior, it is frequently overlooked that a given set of response alternatives may also constitute a source of information for the respondent, as already seen in the section on question comprehension.

Essentially, respondents assume that the researcher constructs a meaningful scale, based on his or her knowledge of, or expectations about, the distribution of the behavior in the "real world." Accordingly, respondents assume that the values in the middle range of the scale reflect the "average" or "usual" behavioral frequency, whereas the extremes of the scale correspond to the extremes of the distribution. Given this assumption, respondents can use the range of the response alternatives

TABLE 4.1. Reported Daily TV Consumption as a Function of Response Alternatives

Low-frequency alternatives	Daily consumption	High-frequency alternatives	Daily consumption
Up to ½ hour	7.4%	Up to 2½ hours	62.5%
½ hour to 1 hour	17.7%	2½ hours to 3 hours	23.4%
1 hour to 1½ hours	26.5%	3 hours to 3½ hours	7.8%
1½ hours to 2 hours	14.7%	3½ hours to 4 hours	4.7%
2 hours to 2½ hours	17.7%	4 hours to 4½ hours	1.6%
More than 2½ hours	16.2%	More than 4½ hours	0.0%

Note: N = 132. From "Response Categories: Effects on Behavioral Reports and Comparative Judgments," by N. Schwarz, H. J. Hippler, B. Deutsch, & F. Strack, 1985, *Public Opinion Quarterly, 49*, p. 391. Copyright 1985 by The University of Chicago Press. Adapted with permission.

as a frame of reference in estimating their own behavioral frequency.

This strategy results in higher estimates along scales that present high- rather than low-frequency response alternatives, as shown in Table 4.1. In this study (Schwarz et al., 1985), only 16.2% of a sample of German respondents reported watching TV for more than two and a half hours a day when the scale presented low-frequency response alternatives, whereas 37.5% reported doing so when the scale presented high-frequency response alternatives. Similar results have been obtained for a wide range of different behaviors, including sexual behaviors (e.g., Schwarz & Scheuring, 1988; Tourangeau & Smith, 1996), consumer behaviors (e.g., Menon, Raghubir, & Schwarz, 1995), and reports of physical symptoms (e.g., Schwarz & Scheuring, 1992; see Schwarz, 1990, 1996, for reviews).

For example, Schwarz and Scheuring (1992) asked 60 patients of a German psychosomatic clinic to report the frequency of 17 symptoms along a low-frequency scale that ranged from "never" to "more than twice a month," or along a high-frequency scale that ranged from "twice a month or less" to "several times a day." Across 17 symptoms, 62% of the respondents reported average frequencies of more than twice a month when presented with the high-frequency scale, whereas only 39% did so when presented with the low-frequency scale, resulting in a mean difference of 22 percentage points. This impact of response alternatives was most pronounced for the ill-defined symptom of "responsiveness to changes in the weather," to which 75% of the patients reported

a frequency of more than twice a month along the high-frequency scale, whereas only 21% did so along the low-frequency scale. Conversely, the influence of response alternatives was least pronounced for the better defined symptom "excessive perspiration," with 50% versus 42% of the respondents reporting a frequency of more than twice a month in the high- and low-frequency scale conditions, respectively.

As expected on theoretical grounds, the impact of response alternatives is more pronounced the more poorly the behavior is represented in memory, thus forcing respondents to rely on an estimation strategy. When the behavior is rare and important, and hence well-represented in memory, or when the respondent engages in the behavior with high regularity (e.g., "every Sunday"), the impact of response alternatives is small because no estimation is required (see Menon, 1994; Menon et al., 1995, for a discussion). Moreover, the influence of response alternatives is particularly pronounced when the behavior is ill-defined (as seen above), in which case the response alternatives influence respondents' interpretation of the question (Schwarz et al., 1988) as well as the estimation strategy used. I return to the methodological implications of these findings below.

Subsequent judgments. In addition to affecting respondents' behavioral reports, response alternatives may also affect subsequent judgments. For example, a frequency of "2½ hours a day" constitutes a high response on the low-frequency scale, but a low response on the high-frequency scale shown in Table 4.1. A respondent who checks this alternative may therefore infer that her own TV consumption is above average in the former case, but below average in the latter. As a result, Schwarz et al. (1985) observed that respondents were less satisfied with the variety of things they do in their leisure time when the low-frequency scale suggested that they watch more TV than most other people (see Schwarz, 1990, for a review). Similarly, the psychosomatic patients in Schwarz and Scheuring's (1992) study reported higher health satisfaction when the high-frequency scale suggested that their own symptom frequency is below average than when the low-frequency scale suggested that it is above average. Note that this higher report of health satisfaction was obtained despite the fact that the former patients reported a higher symptom frequency in the first place, as seen above. Findings of this type reflect that respondents extract comparison information from their own placement on the scale and use this information in making subsequent comparative judgments.

However, not all judgments are comparative in nature. When asked how satisfied we are with our health, we may compare our own symptom frequency with that of others. Yet, when asked how much our symptoms bother us, we may not engage in a social comparison but may instead draw on the absolute frequency of our symptoms. In this case, we may infer that our symptoms bother us more when a high-frequency scale leads us to estimate a high symptom frequency. Accordingly, other patients who reported their symptom frequency on one of the above scales reported that their symptoms bother them more when they received a high- rather than a low-frequency scale (Schwarz, in press). Thus, the same high frequency scale elicited subsequent reports of higher health satisfaction (a comparative judgment) or of higher subjective suffering (a noncomparative judgment), depending on which judgment followed the symptom report.

Users of respondents' reports. Finally, the use of frequency scales as a frame of reference in making comparative judgments is not limited to patients, but has also been observed for their physicians.

Schwarz, Bless, Bohner, Harlacher, and Kellenbenz (1991, Experiment 2) asked practicing physicians with an average professional experience of eight and a half years to participate in a study allegedly designed to "test if a standard health survey could be shortened without a decrease in usefulness and reliability." As part of this study, practitioners were presented with vignettes that described a patient who had allegedly reported his or her symptoms along one of the scales shown in Figure 4.1.

For example, in one vignette, "Mr. Z., 25 years old" checked that he suffered twice a week from "aching loins or back," and in another vignette, "Mrs. K., 41 years old" checked that she suffered from a "lack of energy," also twice a week. Note that "twice a week" constitutes a high response on the low-frequency scale, but a low response on the high-frequency scale. On the basis of these materials, the physicians rated the severity of the symptoms and the extent to which they saw a need for medical consultation. As expected, suffering from a given symptom "twice a week" was rated as more severe, and as more likely to require consultation, when "twice a week" represented a high- rather than a low-frequency response on the respective scale.

Methodological implications. The reviewed findings have important methodological implications of the assessment of frequency reports (see Schwarz, 1990, for more detailed discussions).

First, the numeric response alternatives presented as part of a frequency question may influence respondents' interpretation of what the question refers to, as seen in the section on question comprehension. Hence, the same question stem in combination with different frequency alternatives may result in the assessment of somewhat different behaviors. This is more likely the less well-defined the behavior is.

Second, respondents' use of the frequency scale as a frame of reference influences the obtained behavioral reports. Aside from calling the interpretation of the absolute values into question, this also implies that reports of the same behavior along different scales are not comparable, often

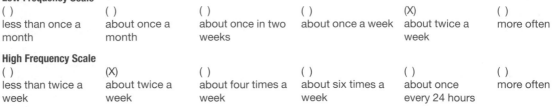

Low Frequency Scale

( )	( )	( )	( )	(X)	( )
less than once a month	about once a month	about once in two weeks	about once a week	about twice a week	more often

High Frequency Scale

( )	(X)	( )	( )	( )	( )
less than twice a week	about twice a week	about four times a week	about six times a week	about once every 24 hours	more often

FIGURE 4.1 ■ Response alternatives used in medical judgment study. "Response Scales as Frames of Reference: The Impact of Frequency Range on Diagnostic Judgment," by N. Schwarz, H. Bless, G. Bohner, U. Harlacher, and M. Kellenbenz, 1991, *Applied Cognitive Psychology, 5*, p. 43. Copyright 1991 by John Wiley & Sons. Reprinted with permission.

rendering comparisons among different studies difficult.

Third, the impact of response alternatives is more pronounced the less respondents can recall relevant episodes from memory. This implies that reports of behaviors that are poorly represented in memory are more affected than reports of behaviors that are well-represented. When behaviors of differential memorability are assessed, this may either exaggerate or reduce any actual differences in the relative frequency of the behaviors, depending on the specific frequency range of the scale.

Fourth, for the same reason, respondents with poorer memory for the behavior under study are more likely to be influenced by response alternatives than respondents with better memory. Such a differential impact of response alternatives on the reports provided by different groups of respondents can result in misleading conclusions about actual group differences.

Finally, the range of response alternatives may further influence subsequent comparative and non-comparative judgments. Hence, respondents may arrive at evaluative judgments that are highly context-dependent and may not reflect the assessments they would be likely to make in daily life.

To avoid these systematic influences of response alternatives, it is advisable to ask frequency questions in an open-response format, such as, "How many hours a day do you watch TV?—hours per day." Note that such an open format needs to specify the relevant units of measurement, for example, "hours per day," to avoid answers like "a few."

As another alternative, researchers are often tempted to use vague quantifiers, such as "sometimes," "frequently," and so on. This, however, is the worst possible choice (see Moxey & Sanford, 1992; Pepper, 1981, for reviews). Most important, the same expression denotes different frequencies in different content domains. Thus, "frequently" suffering from headaches reflects higher absolute frequencies than "frequently" suffering from heart attacks. Moreover, different respondents use the same term to denote different objective frequencies of the same behavior. For example, suffering from headaches "occasionally" denotes a higher frequency for respondents with a medical history of migraines than for respondents without that history. Accordingly, the use of vague quantifiers reflects the objective frequency relative to respondents' subjective standard, rendering vague quantifiers inadequate for the assessment of objective frequencies, despite the popularity of their use.

Reporting the Answer

After having determined a frequency estimate, respondents have to report their estimate to the researcher (Strack & Martin, 1987; Tourangeau, 1984). The estimate they communicate may deviate from their private estimate due to considerations of social desirability and self-presentation (see DeMaio, 1984, for a review). Survey researchers have developed a number of techniques to reduce this "editing" of the communicated response. Most of these techniques emphasize the respondent's anonymity and the confidentiality of the collected data (see Sudman & Bradburn, 1983, for a review and good practical advice).

In the context of the preceding discussion of frequency scales, one may wonder to what extent these scales contribute to response editing: Do respondents hesitate to endorse a frequency that seems "deviant" in the context of the scale? This possibility has been suggested by Bradburn and Danis (1984) in a discussion of higher reports of alcohol consumption in an open- as opposed to a closed-response format, but has received little empirical support. Specifically, this self-presentation hypothesis suggests that the impact of response alternatives should be more pronounced when respondents report about their own behavior than when they report about the behavior of distant others, reflecting that self-presentation considerations are of less concern in the latter case. In contrast, the estimation hypothesis advanced above predicts that the impact of response alternatives increases with decreasing memory for the behavior. If so, the impact of response alternatives should be more pronounced for reports about others than for reports about self, reflecting that one usually knows more about one's own behavior. The available data support the latter prediction (Schwarz & Bienias, 1990). Nevertheless, it is conceivable that self-presentation concerns elicited by highly threatening questions may be compounded if the respondent discovers that his or her report requires the endorsement of a response alternative that seems extreme in the context of the scale. If so, response alternatives may also affect behavioral reports at the editing stage of the response sequence, although compelling empirical evidence for this possibility has yet to be provided.

Summary

In summary, research into behavioral reports consistently demonstrated that mundane and frequent behaviors are poorly represented in memory, for-

cing respondents to rely on estimation strategies (Bradburn et al., 1987; Schwarz & Sudman, 1994; Strube, 1987; Sudman et al., 1996). One of these strategies entails the use of frequency response alternatives as a frame of reference, resulting in systematic biases in behavioral reports and subsequent related judgments. Other strategies, which are beyond the scope of this article, include the decomposition of the behavior into easier to estimate parts (e.g., Blair & Burton, 1987) and the use of subjective theories of stability and change over time as a framework for reconstructing one's personal history (Ross, 1989). In combination, the bulk of the work in this area highlights that retrospective behavioral reports are highly fallible and strongly affected by the specifics of the research instrument used.

Reporting on One's Attitudes

Public opinion researchers have long been aware that attitude measurement is highly context-dependent. Numerous studies have demonstrated that preceding questions may influence the responses given to subsequent ones (see Schuman & Presser, 1981; Schwarz & Strack, 1991; Sudman et al., 1996; Tourangeau & Rasinski, 1988; and the contributions in Schwarz & Sudman, 1992, for research examples and reviews). Moreover, when a self-administered questionnaire is used, subsequent questions may also influence preceding ones (e.g., Schwarz & Hippler, 1995b) because self-administered questionnaires allow respondents to go back and forth between questions. In recent years, considerable conceptual and empirical progress has been made in this domain, and several related theoretical models have been offered (Feldman, 1992; Feldman & Lynch, 1988; Schwarz & Bless, 1992a; Schwarz & Strack, 1991; Strack & Martin, 1987; Tourangeau, 1987, 1992; Tourangeau & Rasinski, 1988). Below I draw on Schwarz and Bless's (1992a) inclusion–exclusion model, which specifies the conditions under which question-order effects emerge and predicts their direction, their size, and their generalization across related issues.

The Construal of Targets and Standards

In a nutshell, the model assumes that individuals who are asked to form a judgment about some target stimulus first need to form some mental representation of it. As numerous studies in social cognition have shown (see Bodenhausen & Wyer, 1987; Higgins, 1996; Schwarz, 1995, for reviews), individuals do not retrieve all knowledge that may potentially bear on the target. Instead, they truncate the search process as soon as enough information has come to mind to form a judgment with sufficient subjective certainty. Accordingly, the judgment is based on the subset of potentially relevant information that is most accessible at the time of judgment. Some of this information may always come to mind when the individual thinks about this topic and is hence called *chronically accessible*. Other information may only come to mind due to contextual influences, for example, because it was addressed in a preceding question. Such information is called *temporarily accessible* (see Higgins, 1996). An example may illustrate the difference. Suppose a respondent who suffers from a severe illness is asked to report on her life-satisfaction. Although she may draw on numerous different aspects of her life, her health problems are likely to be chronically accessible, and she will probably consider them independent of whether a preceding question brought health-related issues to mind or not. On the other hand, she may only draw on the quality of her housing arrangements when this aspect was brought to mind by a preceding question, and healthy respondents may not consider their health unless their attention is drawn to it. The influence of preceding questions on the temporary accessibility of information in memory is a primary source of context effects in self-reports, whereas chronically accessible information is a source of context-independent stability in reports.

To form an evaluative judgment, however, it is not sufficient to have a mental representation of the target. In addition, respondents need a mental representation of a standard against which the target is evaluated. Much as the mental representation of the target, the mental representation of a relevant standard is formed on the spot and is based on

chronically or temporarily accessible information that happens to come to mind (see Kahneman & Miller, 1986; Schwarz & Bless, 1992a).

How a given piece of accessible information influences the judgment depends on how it is *used* in forming these different representations. For example, Strack, Schwarz, and Gschneidinger (1985) asked respondents to report either three positive or three negative life-events that recently happened to them. Not surprisingly, respondents who had to recall positive events subsequently reported *higher* happiness and life-satisfaction than respondents who had to recall negative events, as shown in the first row of Table 4.2. This reflects that they included the recent events in the mental representation of their current lives. Other respondents, however, were asked to report three positive or negative events that happened to them at least five years ago. These respondents reported *lower* current happiness and life-satisfaction after recalling past positive events than after recalling past negative events, as shown in the second row of Table 4.2. This contrast effect reflects that the distant events did not directly pertain to respondents' current lives and were hence not included in the representation formed of the target "my-life-now." Instead, the accessible past events were used in forming a mental representation of the standard against which respondents evaluated their current lives—and compared with the fun (or trouble) they had five years ago, life now seemed pretty bland (or rather good, respectively).

In general, information that is included in the representation formed of the target of judgment results in *assimilation effects*, that is, more positive

TABLE 4.2. Subjective Well-Being: The Impact of Valence of Event and Time Perspective

Time perspective	Valence of event	
	Positive	Negative
Recent events	8.9	7.1
Past events	7.5	8.5

Note: Shown are mean scores of happiness and life-satisfaction, ranging from 1 to 11, with higher values indicating reports of higher well-being. Adapted from Experiment 1 of Strack, Schwarz, and Gschneidinger (1985).

judgments when positive rather than negative information comes to mind. On the other hand, information that is used in constructing a standard of comparison results in *contrast effects*. In this case, positive (negative) information results in a more positive (or negative, respectively) standard of comparison, against which the target is evaluated more negatively (or positively, respectively). Hence, the same information may influence the judgment in opposite directions, depending on whether it is used in forming a mental representation of the target or of the standard against which the target is evaluated (see Schwarz & Bless, 1992a, for more detail).

To further illustrate the basic logic of these mental construal processes, I review a recent experiment that explored the impact of thinking about Colin Powell on evaluations of the Republican party and of Bob Dole (Stapel & Schwarz, 1998).

The Republican Who Did Not Want to Become President: Context Effects in Political Judgment

In November 1995, retired General Colin L. Powell declined to compete in the 1996 Presidential race as a Republican candidate, admitting that his candidacy would require "a passion and commitment that, despite my every effort, I do not have for political life" (New York Times, 1995). Simultaneously, however, he also announced that he had just joined the Republican party. How would this dual decision affect judgments of the Republican party and of Bob Dole?

When asked to evaluate the Republican party, respondents presumably draw on information that bears on this party. When the highly popular Colin Powell comes to mind and is included in the representation formed of this party, the party should be evaluated more positively. To test this prediction, Stapel and Schwarz (1998) asked some respondents, "General Colin L. Powell, the hero of the Gulf War, recently decided to become a member of a political party. Do you happen to know which party that is?" As expected, these respondents subsequently evaluated the Republican party more

positively than respondents who were not asked a question about Powell.

Other respondents were also asked a question about Colin Powell, yet this question was designed to set Powell aside from the Republican party. It read, "General Colin L. Powell, the hero of the Gulf War, has recently been wooed by a political party to run as its candidate in the 1996 Presidential elections. He decided not to run. Do you happen to know which party it was that made Powell an offer he rejected?" As expected, these respondents subsequently evaluated the party more negatively than respondents who were not asked a question about Powell.

Thus, bringing Colin Powell to mind through a preceding question always influenced respondents' judgments of the Republican party. The direction of the influence, however, depended on whether Colin Powell was included in the representation formed of this party or excluded from it. In the former case, the judgment became more positive (an assimilation effect), whereas in the latter case Powell served as a very positive standard of comparison, relative to which the party looked less good (a contrast effect). Hence, we need to consider the accessibility as well as the use of contextual information to understand the emergence and direction of context effects, as already seen in the life-satisfaction example discussed above (Strack et al., 1985).

Next, consider how the above questions about Colin Powell may influence judgments of Bob Dole, who ran as the Republican candidate in the 1996 elections. When asked about Bob Dole, respondents presumably draw on information pertaining to this person. When Colin Powell comes to mind, he is unlikely to be included in the representation formed of Bob Dole: The target category "Bob Dole" has only one member, in contrast to the more inclusive target category "Republican party." Hence, Colin Powell should serve as a standard of comparison whenever he comes to mind, independent of which of the two context questions is asked. Confirming this prediction, respondents evaluated Bob Dole more negatively when either of the context questions brought Colin Powell to mind, compared with a condition in which no question about Powell was presented.

This differential impact of Colin Powell on judgments of Bob Dole and the Republican party reflects the categorical relationship between the contextual information and the target of judgment: When the judgment pertains to a target category that is superordinate (Republican party) to the context information (Colin Powell), the contextual information can be included in, as well as excluded from, the representation formed of the target. Unless the context question elicits exclusion (as in the above experiment), inclusion is more likely. Hence, assimilation effects are more likely to be obtained than contrast effects when the judgment pertains to a superordinate target. Conversely, target categories that are lateral (Bob Dole) to the context information (Colin Powell) do not allow for the inclusion of the context information. Hence, the context information is used in constructing a standard of comparison, resulting in contrast effects (see Schwarz & Bless, 1992a, for a more detailed discussion).

Scandals and the Trustworthiness of Politicians

The diverging impact of the same context information on evaluations of superordinate and lateral target categories often leads to surprising results. Suppose respondents are asked to evaluate the trustworthiness of American politicians and Richard Nixon and his role in the Watergate scandal come to mind due to a preceding question. Nixon is likely to be included in the representation of the superordinate target "American politicians," resulting in judgments of low trustworthiness. Yet, suppose that the question does not pertain to American politicians as a group but to specific exemplars, such as Newt Gingrich. In this case, Nixon cannot be included in the representation of the lateral target "Newt Gingrich" and will serve as a standard of comparison, relative to which Newt Gingrich will look more trustworthy than would otherwise be the case. A study with German respondents, and the German equivalent of Watergate, confirmed these predictions: Thinking about a politician who was involved in this scandal decreased the trustworthiness of politicians in general, but increased the trustworthiness of all individual politicians assessed (Schwarz & Bless, 1992b; see also Bless & Schwarz, 1998).

Such diverging evaluations of groups and exemplars are often observed in public opinion research. For example, Americans distrust Congress, but trust their own representative (e.g., Erikson, Luttberg, & Tedin, 1988). Similarly, they are likely to favor capital punishment in general, but much less likely to favor its application in any specific case (e.g., Ellsworth & Gross, 1994). Moreover, women and minorities report considerable discrimination against their group as a whole, yet evaluate their own personal experiences as more benign (e.g., Taylor, Wright, & Porter, 1994). These patterns are to be expected because media coverage renders extreme cases of untrustworthiness, hideous crime, and severe discrimination highly accessible in memory. And these extreme examples can be included in the representation formed of the issue in general, yet they serve as a standard of comparison in evaluating individual instances. As a result, the general and specific judgments diverge in the manner observed above.

Conversational Norms and Information Use: Does Marital Satisfaction Contribute to Life-Satisfaction?

In the preceding examples, the use of temporarily accessible information was determined by the categorical relationship between the context information and the target of judgment. In addition, a host of other variables may influence the use of contextual information (see Schwarz & Bless, 1992a, for a comprehensive review). One of these variables is the norms of conversational conduct discussed in the section on question comprehension. Recall that the maxim of quantity (Grice, 1975) enjoins speakers to provide information that is new to the recipient and to avoid redundancy. Consequently, respondents deliberately exclude information from further consideration when it seems redundant in the context of the ongoing conversation.

A study on marital satisfaction and life-satisfaction illustrates this process (Schwarz, Strack, & Mai, 1991; see also Strack, Martin, & Schwarz, 1988; Tourangeau, Rasinski, & Bradburn, 1991). In one condition, respondents were first asked how satisfied they are with their life as a whole and subsequently how satisfied they are with their marriage. In this case, the two judgments correlated $r = .32$. When the question order was reversed, however, this correlation increased to $r = .67$. This reflects that the marital satisfaction question brought marriage-related information to mind, which could be included in the representation formed of one's life as a whole, resulting in an assimilation effect. In a third condition, the two questions were introduced by a joint lead-in, designed to evoke the norm of nonredundancy. This lead-in informed respondents that they would be asked two questions related to their well-being, namely one about their marriage and one about their life as a whole. In this case, the previously observed correlation of $r = .67$ under the same order condition dropped to a nonsignificant $r = .18$. Apparently, respondents interpreted the general life-satisfaction question as if it were worded, "Aside from your marriage, which you already told us about, how satisfied are you with other aspects of your life?" Confirming this interpretation, a control condition in which the general life-satisfaction question was reworded in this way resulted in a highly similar correlation of $r = .12$.

This impact of question order and conversational norms was also reflected in respondents' mean life-satisfaction judgments, as the reports of unhappily married respondents may illustrate (i.e., the reports of the third of the sample with the lowest marital satisfaction). Compared with the condition where the general life-satisfaction question was asked first ($M = 6.8$ on an 11-point scale, with $11 = very$ $satisfied$), these respondents reported lower general life-satisfaction ($M = 5.8$) when the preceding question brought their unhappy marriage to mind. Yet, when the joint lead-in induced them to disregard their marriage, the rest of life didn't seem so bad by comparison ($M = 8.0$). The reports of the happily married respondents provided a mirror image of these results.

Quite obviously, with correlations ranging from .18 to .67, we would draw very different conclusions about the contribution of marital satisfaction to overall life-satisfaction depending on the order in which these questions were presented and whether they were introduced by a joint lead-in. Moreover, these contextual influences would profoundly affect the outcome of structural equation models based on these data.

Summary

As the reviewed examples illustrate, attitude measurement is subject to pronounced context effects. In fact, some readers may wonder if the reviewed results suggest that we mostly collect artifacts when we ask attitude questions. I do *not* think so (see Sudman et al., 1996, chapter 5, for a more detailed discussion). Human judgment is always context-dependent, in research situations as in real life, and attitude judgments are no exception to this rule. We construct these judgments on the spot, when needed (Schwarz & Bless, 1992a; Strack, 1994a, 1994b; Wilson & Hodges, 1992), by drawing on the information that is most accessible at that point in time (Higgins, 1996). Some of this information is chronically accessible, whereas other information may only come to mind because it has been addressed in an earlier question or the recent news. Whereas the chronically accessible information provides for some stability in judgments, the temporarily accessible information is the basis of context effects. The direction of context effects depends on how the accessible information is *used*—and the same information may result in assimilation as well as contrast effects, reflecting the mental construal processes discussed above. These processes are systematic and apply in "real life" as well as in research situations—and many readers will agree that they see their life differently, depending, for example, on whether they take their marriage into account or not. The "problem" is not the context dependency of human judgment but researchers' hope that this context dependency may—miraculously—not apply to their own study. Unfortunately, this hope is unwarranted, and any given result may lead us astray when we do not take its contextual nature into account. To be alerted to contextual influences, researchers are well-advised to include context manipulations in the design of their studies, a piece of advice that is more often offered than heeded.

Concluding Remarks

Psychologists and social scientists have long been aware that collecting data by asking questions is an exercise that may yield many surprises (e.g., Cantril, 1944; Payne, 1951)—some obvious ones (as when the researcher is left wondering, "When this is the answer, what was the question?"), and some so nonobvious that they can only be detected when we compare responses to different question wording, format, or order conditions. Whereas the obvious surprises are merely annoying, the nonobvious ones may lead us to erroneous conclusions about the substantive issue under study if we do not become aware of them. Over the last decade, psychologists and survey methodologists have made considerable progress in understanding the cognitive and communicative processes underlying the question-answering process, rendering some of these "surprises" less surprising than they have been in the past. In fact, we can produce findings like the ones reviewed in this article in a reliable and replicable way when we deliberately write questions to satisfy theoretical criteria. Yet, this does not imply that we can always predict how a *given* question will "behave" when colleagues ask us for advice: In many cases, the given question is too mushy an operationalization of theoretical variables to allow for predictions (although we typically feel we know what would happen if the question were tinkered with, in one way or another, to bring it in line with theoretical models). Nevertheless, the accumulating insights (reviewed in Sudman et al., 1996) are helpful in guiding researchers to avoid many of the more common pitfalls associated with collecting self-reports. Most important, they alert us to likely problems and help us in identifying questions and question sequences that need systematic experimental testing before they are used in a large-scale study.

The most important lesson that has emerged from this research is rather general in nature (Schwarz, 1996). As researchers, we tend to view our questionnaires as "measurement devices" that elicit information from respondents. What we frequently overlook is that our questionnaires are also a source of information that respondents draw on in order to determine their task and to arrive at a useful and informative answer. Far from reflecting "artifacts" or "shallow responding," findings of the type reviewed in this article indicate that respondents do their best to be cooperative communicators. Consistent with the assumptions that underlie the conduct of conversation in daily life, they assume that all contributions of the researcher are relevant to the goals of the ongoing exchange, and they take these contributions into account in arriving at an answer. Unfortunately, as researchers we are often not fully aware of the information that our questionnaires—or our experimental procedures (see Hilton, 1995; Schwarz, 1994, 1996)—provide, and hence miss the extent to which the questions we ask determine the answers we receive.

REFERENCES

Anderson, J. R. (1980). *Cognitive psychology and its implications*. San Francisco: Freeman.

Bishop, G. F., Oldendick, R. W., & Tuchfarber, A. J. (1986). Opinions on fictitious issues: The pressure to answer survey questions. *Public Opinion Quarterly, 50*, 240–250.

Blair, E., & Burton, S. (1987). Cognitive processes used by survey respondents to answer behavioral frequency questions. *Journal of Consumer Research, 14*, 280–288.

Bless, H., & Schwarz, N. (1998). Context effects in political judgment: Assimilation and contrast as a function of categorization processes. *European Journal of Social Psychology, 28*, 159–172.

Bless, H., Strack, F., & Schwarz, N. (1993). The informative functions of research procedures: Bias and the logic of conversation. *European Journal of Social Psychology, 23*, 149–165.

Bodenhausen, G. V., & Wyer, R. S. (1987). Social cognition and social reality: Information acquisition and use in the laboratory and the real world. In H. J. Hippler, N. Schwarz, & S. Sudman (Eds.), *Social information processing and survey methodology* (pp. 6–41). New York: Springer Verlag.

Bolton, R. N., & Bronkhorst, T. M. (1996). Questionnaire pretesting: Computer assisted coding of concurrent protocols. In N. Schwarz & S. Sudman (Eds.), *Answering questions: Methodology for determining cognitive and communicative processes in survey research* (pp. 37–64). San Francisco: Jossey-Bass.

Bradburn, N., & Danis, C. (1984). Potential contributions of cognitive research to survey questionnaire design. In T. B. Jabine, M. L. Straf, J. M. Tanur, & R. Tourangeau (Eds.), *Cognitive aspects of survey methodology: Building a bridge between disciplines* (pp. 101–129). Washington, DC: National Academy Press.

Bradburn, N. M., Rips, L. J., & Shevell, S. K. (1987). Answering autobiographical questions: The impact of memory and inference on surveys. *Science, 236,* 157–161.

Cantril, H. (1944). *Gauging public opinion.* Princeton, NJ: Princeton University Press.

Clark, H. H., & Clark, E. V. (1977). *Psychology and language.* New York: Harcourt, Brace, Jovanovich.

Clark, H. H., & Schober, M. F. (1992). Asking questions and influencing answers. In J. M. Tanur (Ed.), *Questions about questions* (pp. 15–48). New York: Russell Sage Foundation.

DeMaio, T. J. (1984). Social desirability and survey measurement: A review. In C. F. Turner & E. Martin (Eds.), *Surveying subjective phenomena* (Vol. 2, pp. 257–281). New York: Russell Sage Foundation.

DeMaio, T. J., & Rothgeb, J. M. (1996). Cognitive interviewing techniques: In the lab and in the field. In N. Schwarz & S. Sudman (Eds.), *Answering questions: Methodology for determining cognitive and communicative processes in survey research* (pp. 177–196). San Francisco: Jossey-Bass.

Ellsworth, P. C., & Gross, S. R. (1994). Hardening of the attitudes: Americans' views on the death penalty. *Journal of Social Issues, 50,* 19–52.

Erikson, R. S., Luttberg, N. R., & Tedin, K. T. (1988). *American public opinion* (3rd ed.). New York: Macmillan.

Feldman, J. M. (1992). Constructive processes in survey research: Explorations in self-generated validity. In N. Schwarz & S. Sudman (Eds.), *Context effects in social and psychological research* (pp. 49–61). New York: Springer Verlag.

Feldman, J. M., & Lynch, J. G. (1988). Self-generated validity and other effects of measurement on belief, attitude, intention, and behavior. *Journal of Applied Psychology, 73,* 421–435.

Fowler, F. J., & Cannell, C. F. (1996). Using behavioral coding to identify cognitive problems with survey questions. In N. Schwarz & S. Sudman (Eds.), *Answering questions: Methodology for determining cognitive and communicative processes in survey research* (pp. 15–36). San Francisco: Jossey-Bass.

Gaskell, G. D., O'Muircheartaigh, C. A., & Wright, D. B. (1994). Survey questions about the frequency of vaguely defined events: The effects of response alternatives. *Public Opinion Quarterly, 58,* 241–254.

Grice, H. P. (1975). Logic and conversation. In P. Cole & J. L. Morgan (Eds.), *Syntax and semantics: Vol. 3, Speech acts* (pp. 41–58). New York: Academic Press.

Higgins, E. T. (1996). Knowledge activation: Accessibility, applicability, and salience, In E. T. Higgins & A. Kruglanski (Eds.), *Social psychology: Handbook of basic principles* (pp. 133–168). New York: Guilford Press.

Hilton, D. J. (1995). The social context of reasoning: Conversational inference and rational judgment. *Psychological Bulletin, 118,* 248–271.

Hippler, H. J., Schwarz, N., & Sudman, S. (Eds.). (1987). *Social information processing and survey methodology.* New York: Springer Verlag.

Jabine, T. B., Starf, M. L., Tanur, J. M., & Tourangeau, R. (Eds.). (1984). *Cognitive aspects of survey methodology: Building a bridge between disciplines.* Washington, DC: National Academy Press.

Jobe, J., & Loftus, E. (Eds.) (1991). Cognitive aspects of survey methodology [Special issue]. *Applied Cognitive Psychology, 5.*

Kahneman, D., & Miller, D. (1986). Norm theory: Comparing reality to its alternatives. *Psychological Review, 93,* 136–153.

Lessler, J. T., & Forsyth, B. H. (1996). A coding system for appraising questionnaires. In N. Schwarz & S. Sudman (Eds.), *Answering questions: Methodology for determining cognitive and communicative processes in survey research* (pp. 259–292). San Francisco: Jossey-Bass.

Levinson, S. C. (1983). *Pragmatics.* Cambridge, England: Cambridge University Press.

McGonagle, K. A., Kessler, R. C., & Schilling, E. A. (1992). The frequency and determinants of marital disagreements in a community sample. *Journal of Social & Personal Relationships, 9,* 507–524.

Menon, G. (1994). Judgments of behavioral frequencies: Memory search and retrieval strategies. In N. Schwarz & S. Sudman (Eds.), *Autobiographical memory and the validity of retrospective reports* (pp. 161–172). New York: Springer Verlag.

Menon, G., Raghubir, P., & Schwarz, N. (1995). Behavioral frequency judgments: An accessibility-diagnosticity framework. *Journal of Consumer Research, 22,* 212–228.

Moxey, L. M., & Sanford, A. J. (1992). Context effects and the communicative functions of quantifiers: Implications for their use in attitude research. In N. Schwarz & S. Sudman (Eds.), *Context effects in social and psychological research* (pp. 279–296). New York: Springer Verlag.

New York Times. (1995, November 9). *Excerpts from General Powell's news conference,* p. A11.

Norenzayan, A., & Schwarz, N. (in press). Telling what they want to know: Participants tailor causal attributions to researchers' interests. *European Journal of Social Psychology.*

Parkinson, B., Briner, R. B., Reynolds, S., & Totterdell, P. (1995). Time frames for mood: Relations between momentary and generalized ratings of affect. *Personality and Social Psychology Bulletin, 21,* 331–339.

Payne, S. L. (1951). *The art of asking questions.* Princeton, NJ: Princeton University Press.

Pepper, S. C. (1981). Problems in the quantification of frequency expressions. In D. W. Fiske (Ed.), *Problems with language imprecision: New directions for methodology of social and behavior science* (Vol. 9, pp. 25–41). San Francisco: Jossey-Bass.

Ross, M. (1989). The relation of implicit theories to the construction of personal histories. *Psychological Review, 96,* 341–357.

Schober, M. F. (in press). Making sense of questions: An interactional approach. In M. Sirken, D. Hermann, S. Schechter, N. Schwarz, J. Tanur, & R. Tourangeau (Eds.), *Cognition and survey research.* New York: Wiley.

Schuman, H., & Presser, S. (1981). *Questions and answers in attitude surveys.* New York: Academic Press.

Schwarz, N. (1990). Assessing frequency reports of mundane behaviors: Contributions of cognitive psychology to questionnaire construction. In C. Hendrick & M. S. Clark (Eds.), *Research methods in personality and social psychology: Review of personality and social psychology* (Vol. 11, pp. 98–119). Beverly Hills, CA: Sage.

Schwarz, N. (1994). Judgment in a social context: Biases, shortcomings, and the logic of conversation. In M. Zanna (Ed.), *Advances in experimental social psychology* (Vol. 26, pp. 123–162). San Diego, CA: Academic Press.

Schwarz, N. (1995). Social cognition: Information accessibility and use in social judgment. In E. E. Smith & D. N. Osherson (Eds.), *Thinking: An invitation to cognitive science* (2nd ed., Vol. 3, pp. 345–376). Cambridge, MA: MIT Press.

Schwarz, N. (1996). *Cognition and communication: Judgmental biases, research methods, and the logic of conversation.* Hillsdale, NJ: Erlbaum.

Schwarz, N. (in press). Frequency reports of physical symptoms and health behaviors: How the questionnaire determines the results. In D. C. Park, R. W. Morrell, & K. Shifren (Eds.), *Processing medical information in aging patients: Cognitive and human factors perspectives.* Mahwah, NJ: Erlbaum.

Schwarz, N., & Bienias, J. (1990). What mediates the impact of response alternatives on frequency reports of mundane behaviors? *Applied Cognitive Psychology, 4,* 61–72.

Schwarz, N., & Bless, H. (1992a). Constructing reality and its alternatives: Assimilation and contrast effects in social judgment. In L. L. Martin & A. Tesser (Eds.), *The construction of social judgments* (pp. 217–245). Hillsdale, NJ: Erlbaum.

Schwarz, N., & Bless, H. (1992b). Scandals and the public's trust in politicians: Assimilation and contrast effects. *Personality and Social Psychology Bulletin, 18,* 574–579.

Schwarz, N., Bless, H., Bohner, G., Harlacher, U., & Kellenbenz, M. (1991). Response scales as frames of reference: The impact of frequency range on diagnostic judgment. *Applied Cognitive Psychology, 5,* 37–50.

Schwarz, N., Grayson, C. E., & Knäuper, B. (1998). Formal features of rating scales and the interpretation of question meaning. *International Journal of Public Opinion Research, 10,* 177–183.

Schwarz, N., & Hippler, H. J. (1991). Response alternatives: The impact of their choice and ordering. In P. Biemer, R. Groves, N. Mathiowetz, & S. Sudman (Eds.), *Measurement error in surveys* (pp. 41–56). Chichester, England: Wiley.

Schwarz, N., & Hippler, H. J. (1995a). The numeric values of rating scales: A comparison of their impact in mail surveys and telephone interviews. *International Journal of Public Opinion Research, 7,* 72–74.

Schwarz, N., & Hippler, H. J. (1995b). Subsequent questions may influence answers to preceding questions in mail surveys. *Public Opinion Quarterly, 59,* 93–97.

Schwarz, N., Hippler, H. J., Deutsch, B., & Strack, F. (1985). Response categories: Effects on behavioral reports and comparative judgments. *Public Opinion Quarterly, 49,* 388–395.

Schwarz, N., Knäuper, B., Hippler, H. J., Noelle-Neumann, E., & Clark, F. (1991). Rating scales: Numeric values may change the meaning of scale labels. *Public Opinion Quarterly, 55,* 570–582.

Schwarz, N., Park, D., Knäuper, B., & Sudman, S. (Eds.). (1998). *Aging, cognition, and self-reports.* Washington, DC: Psychology Press.

Schwarz, N., & Scheuring, B. (1988). Judgments of relationship satisfaction: Inter- and intraindividual comparison strategies as a function of questionnaire structure. *European Journal of Social Psychology, 18,* 485–496.

Schwarz, N., & Scheuring, B. (1992). Selbstberichtete verhaltens- und symptomhäufigkeiten: Was befragte aus anwortvorgaben des fragebogens lernen [Frequency reports of psychosomatic symptoms: What respondents learn from response alternatives]. *Zeitschrift für Klinische Psychologie, 22,* 197–208.

Schwarz, N., & Strack, F. (1991). Context effects in attitude surveys: Applying cognitive theory to social research. *European Review of Social Psychology, 2,* 31–50.

Schwarz, N., Strack, F., & Mai, H. P. (1991). Assimilation and contrast effects in part-whole question sequences: A conversational logic analysis. *Public Opinion Quarterly, 55,* 3–23.

Schwarz, N., Strack, F., Müller, G., & Chassein, B. (1988). The range of response alternatives may determine the meaning of the question: Further evidence on informative functions of response alternatives. *Social Cognition, 6,* 107–117.

Schwarz, N., & Sudman, S. (Eds.). (1992). *Context effects in social and psychological research.* New York: Springer Verlag.

Schwarz, N., & Sudman, S. (1994). *Autobiographical memory and the validity of retrospective reports.* New York: Springer Verlag.

Schwarz, N., & Sudman, S. (1996). *Answering questions: Methodology for determining cognitive and communicative processes in survey research.* San Francisco: Jossey-Bass.

Sirken, M., Hermann, D., Schechter, S., Schwarz, N., Tanur, J., & Tourangeau, R. (Eds.). (in press). *Cognition and survey research.* New York: Wiley.

Stapel, D. A., & Schwarz, N. (1998). The Republican who did

not want to become President: An inclusion/exclusion analysis of Colin Powell's impact on evaluations of the Republican Party and Bob Dole. *Personality and Social Psychology Bulletin, 24,* 690–698.

Strack, F. (1994a). *Zur psychologie der standardisierten befragung* [The psychology of standardized interviews]. Heidelberg, Germany: Springer Verlag.

Strack, F. (1994b). Response processes in social judgment. In R. S. Wyer & T. K. Srull (Eds.), *Handbook of social cognition* (2nd ed., Vol. 1, pp. 287–322). Hillsdale, NJ: Erlbaum.

Strack, F., & Martin, L. (1987). Thinking, judging, and communicating: A process account of context effects in attitude surveys. In H. J. Hippler, N. Schwarz, & S. Sudman (Eds.), *Social information processing and survey methodology* (pp. 123–148). New York: Springer Verlag.

Strack, F., Martin, L. L., & Schwarz, N. (1988). Priming and communication: The social determinants of information use in judgments of life-satisfaction. *European Journal of Social Psychology, 18,* 429–442.

Strack, F., Schwarz, N., & Gschneidinger, E. (1985). Happiness and reminiscing: The role of time perspective, mood, and mode of thinking. *Journal of Personality and Social Psychology, 49,* 1460–1469.

Strack, F., Schwarz, N., & Wänke, M. (1991). Semantic and pragmatic aspects of context effects in social and psychological research. *Social Cognition, 9,* 111–125.

Strube, G. (1987). Answering survey questions: The role of memory. In H. J. Hippler, N. Schwarz, & S. Sudman (Eds.), *Social information processing and survey methodology* (pp. 86–101). New York: Springer Verlag.

Sudman, S., & Bradburn, N. M. (1983). *Asking questions.* San Francisco: Jossey-Bass.

Sudman, S., Bradburn, N. M., & Schwarz, N. (1996). *Thinking about answers: The application of cognitive processes to survey methodology.* San Francisco, CA: Jossey-Bass.

Tanur, J. M. (Ed.). (1992). *Questions about questions.* New York: Russell Sage Foundation.

Taylor, D. M., Wright, S. C., & Porter, L. E. (1994). Dimensions of perceived discrimination: The personal/group discrimination discrepancy. In M. P. Zanna & J. M. Olson (Eds.), *The psychology of prejudice: The Ontario symposium* (Vol. 7, pp. 233–255). Hillsdale, NJ: Erlbaum.

Thomas, D. L., & Diener, E. (1990). Memory accuracy in the recall of emotions. *Journal of Personality and Social Psychology, 59,* 291–297.

Tourangeau, R. (1984). Cognitive science and survey methods: A cognitive perspective. In T. Jabine, M. Straf, J. Tanur, & R. Tourangeau (Eds.), *Cognitive aspects of survey methodology: Building a bridge between disciplines* (pp. 73–100). Washington, DC: National Academy Press.

Tourangeau, R. (1987). Attitude measurement: A cognitive perspective. In H. J. Hippler, N. Schwarz, & S. Sudman (Eds.), *Social information processing and survey methodology* (pp. 149–162). New York: Springer Verlag.

Tourangeau, R. (1992). Attitudes as memory structures: Belief sampling and context effects. In N. Schwarz & S. Sudman (Eds.), *Context effects in social and psychological research* (pp. 35–47). New York: Springer Verlag.

Tourangeau, R., & Rasinski, K. A. (1988). Cognitive processes underlying context effects in attitude measurement. *Psychological Bulletin, 103,* 299–314.

Tourangeau, R., Rasinski, K. A., & Bradburn, N. (1991). Measuring happiness in surveys: A test of the subtraction hypothesis. *Public Opinion Quarterly, 55,* 255–266.

Tourangeau, R., & Smith, T. W. (1996). Asking sensitive questions: The impact of data collection, mode, question format, and question context. *Public Opinion Quarterly, 60,* 275–304.

Wilson, T. D., & Hodges, S. D. (1992). Attitudes as temporary constructions. In L. L. Martin & A. Tesser (Eds.), *The construction of social judgments* (pp. 37–65). Hillsdale, NJ: Erlbaum.

Winkielman, P., Knäuper, B., & Schwarz, N. (1998). Looking back at anger: Reference periods change the interpretation of (emotion) frequency questions. *Journal of Personality and Social Psychology, 75,* 719–728.

READING 5

Electromyographic Activity over Facial Muscle Regions can Differentiate the Valence and Intensity of Affective Reactions

John T. Cacioppo, Richard E. Petty, Mary E. Losch, and Hai Sook Kim

Physiological measures have traditionally been viewed in social psychology as useful only in assessing general arousal and therefore as incapable of distinguishing between positive and negative affective states. This view is challenged in the present report. Sixteen subjects in a pilot study were exposed briefly to slides and tones that were mildly to moderately evocative of positive and negative affect. Facial electromyographic (EMG) activity differentiated both the valence and intensity of the affective reaction. Moreover, independent judges were unable to determine from viewing videotapes of the subjects' facial displays whether a positive or negative stimulus had been presented or whether a mildly or moderately intense stimulus had been presented. In the full experiment, 28 subjects briefly viewed slides of scenes that were mildly to moderately evocative of positive and negative affect. Again, EMG activity over the brow (corrugator supercilia), eye (orbicularis oculi), and cheek (zygomatic major) muscle regions differentiated the pleasantness and intensity of individuals' affective reactions to the visual stimuli even though visual inspection of the videotapes again indicated that expressions of emotion were not apparent. These results suggest that gradients of EMG activity over the muscles of facial expression can provide objective and continuous probes of affective processes that are too subtle or fleeting to evoke expressions observable under normal conditions of social interaction.

This research was supported by National Science Foundation Grants BNS 8217096 and BNS 8444909.

The data reported in this paper are based in part on masters theses conducted by the third and fourth authors. The advice of committee members Hariett Shaklee, Carolyn Cutrona, Robert Baron, and Donal Carlston and the helpful comments of Louis G. Tassinary, Barbara L. Andersen, and several anonymous reviewers are acknowledged with thanks.

Portions of this paper were presented at the annual meeting of the Society for Psychophysiological Research, October 1984, in Milwaukee, Wisconsin.

Correspondence concerning this article should be addressed to John T. Cacioppo, Department of Psychology, University of Iowa, Iowa City, Iowa 52242 or to Richard E. Petty, Department of Psychology, University of Missouri, Columbia, Missouri 65211.

In focusing on the powerful situational factors governing behavior, social psychologists have sometimes ignored or dismissed physiological factors and measures as being irrelevant, at least at present, to the study of social processes and behavior. When physiological principles or measures have been used, the analyses have oftentimes been untestable (Wilson, 1975) or crude and accompanied by the disclaimer that they reflected the "state of the art in social psychology" (cf. Kiesler & Pallak, 1976, p. 1015). The primary physiological construct to have had a major impact on social psychological research and theory during the past half century is the notion of general, diffuse, and misattributable arousal (cf. Lindzey & Aronson, 1985). Yet the notion of arousal has its limits. In reviewing past literature on physiological arousal, Fowles (1980) noted that

> The effect of attempting to assimilate all of these traditions to a single arousal theory was to create a model in which the reticular activating system was assumed to serve as a generalized arousal mechanism which responded to sensory input of all kinds, energized behavior, and produced both EEG and sympathetic nervous system activation . . . As is well-known, this model failed the empirical test rather badly. (p. 88)

For years the notion of general arousal, which has been based largely on single physiological measures (e.g., Breckler, 1984), analyses of tonic changes in somatovisceral activity (e.g., Elkin & Leippe, 1985), performance on "drive sensitive tasks" (Pallak & Pittman, 1972), or simple self-reports or misattributions of bodily sensations (e.g., Higgins, Rhodewalt, & Zanna, 1979), has overshadowed the theoretically compatible notion that subtle changes in efference, particularly within the facial muscles, are exquisitely sensitive to variations in intrapersonal (e.g., transient affective reactions) and interpersonal (e.g., veridical and deceptive communications among individuals)

processes. For instance, physiological measures have traditionally been viewed in social psychology as useful only in assessing general arousal and therefore as incapable of distinguishing between positive and negative affective states (e.g., Fishbein & Ajzen, 1975, p. 94; Schachter, 1964)—despite long-standing suggestions to the contrary:

> The low visibility of the affects and the difficulties to be encountered in attempting to identify the primary affects have already been described. Yet our task is not as difficult as it might otherwise have been, for the primary affects, before the transformations due to learning, seem to be innately related in a one-to-one fashion with an organ system which is extraordinarily visible. (Tomkins, 1962, p. 204)

Tomkins was of course referring to the facial efference system—an organ system we know from common experience is capable of more complex and variable actions than are captured by the notion of general arousal.[1] Why this might be so is apparent when the purpose of efference is considered. The somatic nervous system is the final pathway through which people interact with and modify their physical and social environments. That the pattern of efference is not always as intended (e.g., as when one performs clumsily), not always a veridical reflection of goals (e.g., as when one deceives), and not always obvious (e.g., as when one hides feelings) is important to recognize (e.g., see Ekman & Friesen, 1975). But without efference, individuals do not communicate, do not affiliate, do not proliferate, do not interact—in short, are not social. It is conceivable, therefore, that analyses of the patterns of efference may be of interest to social psychologists. Even efferent discharges that are too subtle or fleeting to be observable under normal conditions of social interaction may be of interest because these are less likely to undergo the same distortions as overt actions and expressions.

Moreover, the muscles of facial expression may be especially noteworthy to social psychologists in that these somatic effectors are linked to connective tissue and fasciae rather than to skeletal structures; their influence on the social environment, therefore, is often mediated by the construction of

---

[1] We use the term *efference* rather than *response*, following Zajonc's (1985) argument that the former has fewer a priori implications regarding the role of efference in the production of affect.

facial configurations rather than by direct action through the movement of the skeletal structure (Ekman & Friesen, 1975; Izard, 1971; Rinn, 1984). There is now a growing literature on these facial configurations (a) supporting Darwin's (1872/1965) notions regarding their evolutionary history and adaptive utility (e.g., Ekman, 1972, 1982a; Ekman, Friesen, & Ellsworth, 1982), (b) highlighting their capacity as social stimuli (e.g., Englis, Vaughan, & Lanzetta, 1982; Lanzetta & Orr, 1980, 1981; Sorce, Emde, Campos, & Klinnert, 1981), and (c) documenting the associated movements accompanying intrapersonal processes such as silent language processing and emotion (see recent reviews by Ekman & Oster, 1979; Fridlund, Ekman, & Oster, in press; McGuigan, 1978; Zuckerman, DePaulo, & Rosenthal, 1981). We are concerned in the present article with the latter focus.

Not all intrapersonal processes are accompanied by visually or socially perceptible expressive facial actions and, although there are several notable exceptions (cf. Ekman, 1972; Ekman, Friesen, & Ancoli, 1980; Haggard & Isaacs, 1966), this fact has limited the utility of research linking facial actions to psychological processes of interest in social psychology. Rajecki (1983, pp. 204–207), for instance, compared subjects' aggressive behavior using a standard social psychological measure—the Buss (1961) aggression machine test—with their simultaneous facial expressions. Rajecki reported that although "angry" subjects delivered significantly greater electric shock to their partner than did "not angry" subjects, there was no consistent relationship between aggression measured in the standard fashion and motivation or emotion as revealed in subjects' visually observable facial expressions. Similarly, Graham (1980) attempted to assess viewers' emotional responses to television advertisements using Ekman and Friesen's (1978) exhaustive Facial Action Coding System (FACS). Although Graham noted that his results are still preliminary, analyses of the data from 20 subjects indicated "too few content-related facial expressions were displayed to make FACS scoring worthwhile" (p. 342). However, the neural activation of the striated muscles results in muscle action potentials (MAPs) that can be detected using electromyography (EMG) even when there are no perceptible muscle contractions. This raises the interesting possibility that social processes too fleeting or subtle to evoke an overt expression can nevertheless be tracked.

Existing data provide support for this idea. For instance, Love (1972) videotaped people's facial expressions while they were exposed to a proattitudinal or counterattitudinal appeal and reported detecting no differences in overt expression. Cacioppo and Petty (1979) subsequently replicated this (null) finding while also demonstrating that the mean amplitude of EMG activity recorded over selected muscle regions of facial expression (e.g., corrugator supercilia, zygomatic major, depressor anguli oris) differentiated subjects exposed to a proattitudinal appeal from those exposed to a counterattitudinal appeal. Expanding on the research by Ekman et al. (1980), McHugo (1983) examined the facial EMG responses of individuals as they viewed excerpts of videotapes. McHugo found that the EMG activity over the zygomatic major (cheek) and corrugator supercilium (brow) muscle regions varied as a function of subjects' emotional reactions to the excerpts. The procedures employed in this research make it unlikely that socially observable expressions of emotion were evinced by subjects, although assessments regarding the overt nature of the facial actions observed using EMG were not reported.

Studies of emotional and attitudinal imagery have provided further evidence that, even in the absence of overt facial movements, positive and negative affective states can lead to localized changes in facial EMG activity. Fridlund, Schwartz, and Fowler (1984), for instance, demonstrated the utility of facial EMG activity in discriminating among subtle facial expressions observed during distinctive emotional imagery states, and Cacioppo, Petty, and Marshall-Goodell (1984) found that localized changes in EMG activity differentiated trials on which subjects imagined reading agreeable and disagreeable editorials. The most consistent finding in this area of research is that EMG activity over the corrugator supercilium muscle (whose action draws the brows together) region is higher and that EMG activity over the zygomatic major muscle (whose action draws the end of the mouth up and back) region is lower during negative than positive emotional episodes (cf. Cacioppo & Petty, 1981; Fridlund & Izard, 1983; Schwartz, 1975). It should be noted, however, that whether or not these facial EMG responses mark the intensity as well as the valence of positive and negative affective reactions has yet to be determined.

Pilot Study

To provide preliminary data regarding the idea that EMG activity over the muscles of facial expression generally, and over the brow and cheek regions in particular, varies as a function of the valence and intensity of people's affective reactions to mildly evocative stimuli, 16 undergraduates were exposed to mildly and moderately positive and negative visual and auditory stimuli. A paradigm similar to that used by Zanna, Kiesler, and Pilkonis (1970) was employed in this study. Positive scenes were accompanied by a mildly pleasant tone, and negative scenes were accompanied by a mildly unpleasant tone. The scenes and tones were presented simultaneously for 4.5 s, and each compound experimental stimulus was preceded and followed by a 0.5-s presentation of a neutral polygon. Subjects were told that the polygons were presented as focal points to ensure that subjects could avoid moving and focus on the screen throughout the presentation of the pictorial scene. Each subject was exposed to 20 pleasant and 20 unpleasant stimuli during the session. Surface EMG activity was measured over the corrugator supercilia (brow), zygomatic major (cheek), orbicularis oculi (lower eyelid), medial frontalis (forehead), orbicularis oris (lip), and superficial forearm flexor muscle regions during trials, and after each trial subjects responded to several questions about the depicted scene, including how much they liked it. Skin conductance was also monitored to examine the effects of the mildly evocative stimuli on sympa-

thetic activity. Finally, subjects' faces were videotaped unobtrusively throughout the session, and periods during which subjects were exposed to the positive and negative stimuli were identified.

As expected, subjects reported liking the pleasant stimuli more than the unpleasant stimuli, $F(1, 14) = 480.69$, $p < .01$. Each subject's set of ratings was used to distinguish between the scenes that were mildly versus moderately liked and between the scenes that were mildly versus moderately disliked, and 2 (valence: positive or negative) × 2 (intensity: mild or moderate) analyses of variance (ANOVAS) were performed to examine the separable effects of affective valence and affective intensity on physiological responding. The ANOVAS of the mean amplitude of the EMG activity over the corrugator supercilia and zygomatic major muscle regions produced the expected main effects for valence: $F(1, 14) = 21.47$, $p < .01$, and $F(1, 14) = 5.02$, $p < .05$, respectively. There was also a Valence × Intensity interaction on the measure of EMG activity over the corrugator supercilia region, $F(1, 14) = 9.03$, $p < .01$. Briefly, the facial efference to the brow region decreased as the subjects' affective reaction to the compound stimulus became more positive, whereas the efference to the cheek region was simply higher during positive than negative stimulus presentations. Analyses also revealed several unexpected effects. Positive stimulus presentations evoked higher EMG activity over the orbicularis oculi region, $F(1, 14) = 6.46$, $p < .05$, and lower EMG activity over the medial frontalis muscle region, $F(1, 14) = 9.40$, $p < .05$, than did negative stimulus presentations. In addition, a Valence × Intensity interaction on the measure of EMG activity over the medial frontalis region, $F(1, 14) = 5.15$, $p < .05$, reflected equivalent levels of activity in response to mildly positive and negative stimuli but higher levels of EMG activity in response to moderately negative than to moderately positive stimuli. Also, a Valence × Intensity interaction on the forearm flexor muscle region, $F(1, 14) = 6.54$, $p < .05$, reflected the fact that EMG activity was highest during mildly negative stimulus presentations and lowest during mildly positive stimulus presentations.[2]

Despite the general nature of the somatic activity associated with the experimental stimuli, these pilot data are consistent with the notion that facial EMG activity varies as a function of both the intensity and valence of people's affective reactions. Indeed, analyses of skin conductance responding (frequency and amplitude) revealed no significant effects or interactions, which suggests that the experimental stimuli were sufficiently mild to prevent the evoking of sympathetic activation.

These data, of course, do not address whether the facial actions evoked by the experimental stimuli were sufficiently incipient to be indistinguishable visually in social contexts. To examine this question, eight independent judges attempted to determine the emotional valence and the intensity of the experimental stimulus shown to subjects. Each judge was seated approximately .75 m directly in front of a 48.26-cm (19-in.) color monitor and viewed a random sample of 160 videotape excerpts of subjects' faces during 80 positive and 80 negative experimental trials. After the presentation of each excerpt, judges indicated whether their impression from viewing the subject's face led them to believe the excerpt was from a positive or negative trial and whether the stimulus had been classified as mildly or moderately intense by the subject. Analyses revealed that each of the eight judges performed at chance level. In addition, judges indicated that they perceived so few

changes in subjects' facial appearances that they too viewed the majority of their ratings as mere guesses. Hence, the EMG responses to the experimental stimuli reflected affective processes that were not apparent in overt facial expressions—at least under normal viewing conditions.

We conducted a conceptual replication of the pilot study using simpler affective stimuli and procedures to check the reliability of the finding that EMG activity over selected muscles of expression varied as a function of the valence and intensity of affective stimuli. EMG activity was recorded from the brow, cheek, eye, forehead, lip, and forearm muscle regions while subjects viewed mildly to moderately affectively evocative slides. Subjects' faces were also unobtrusively videotaped during stimulus presentations.

Method

Subjects and Design

Twenty-eight healthy women between 18 and 24 years of age served as subjects in a 2 (replication) × 2 (affective valence: positive or negative) × 2 (affective intensity: mild or moderate) × 8 (trials) mixed-model factorial, with the first factor varied between subjects.[3] The experimental stimuli were ordered randomly across trials, and a separate random order was used for each of the two replications. Although the first and second within-subjects factors could be ordered in terms of their pleasantness and treated as a single factor with four levels (moderately unpleasant, mildly unpleasant, mildly pleasant, moderately pleasant), we partitioned these conditions into a 2 × 2 design to examine the separate effects attributable to affective valence and affective intensity. If a measure varies simply as a function of the pleasantness of a stimulus, however, a main effect for valence and a Valence × Intensity interaction result.

[2] Although not directly pertinent to the present discussion, it should be noted that for any given subject a pair of neutral polygons was associated with the onset of pleasant stimuli and the offset of unpleasant stimuli, and a second pair of neutral polygons was associated with the onset of unpleasant stimuli and the offset of pleasant stimuli (cf. Zanna, Kiesler, & Pilkonis, 1970). A funnel interview at the conclusion of the study indicated that subjects knew nothing about the unique relationship between particular polygons and affective stimuli. Analyses revealed that neither the measures of EMG activity obtained during the presentation of the polygons nor the measures of subjects' attitudes obtained at the end of the study provided any evidence of attitude conditioning. The absence of attitude conditioning might be due to the mild nature of the affectively evocative stimuli with which the polygons were paired.

[3] Women alone served as subjects to minimize the error variance attributable to sex differences (e.g., regarding what visual stimuli are slightly pleasant versus slightly unpleasant) and to maintain same-sex conditions between subjects and experimenters.

Stimulus Materials

The affectively evocative slides to which subjects were exposed were selected in preliminary research using volunteers from the same subject population. Twenty-four photographs were selected because they were judged consistently to be mildly to moderately pleasant, and 24 were chosen because they were consistently judged to be mildly to moderately unpleasant. An attempt was made to select a wide variety of scenes, some of which were mildly exciting or upsetting to view (e.g., a mountain cliff or a bruised torso) and others of which were mildly relaxing or boring to view (e.g., an ocean beach or a polluted roadway). Pilot testing also revealed that although there was consistency across individuals in their ratings of the affective valence of a given photograph, there was little consistency across individuals in terms of the rated intensity of the affect evoked by a given photograph. Hence, we decided following pilot testing (a) to use the a priori classifications for the affective valence factor but (b) to perform a median split of the liking ratings provided by each subject to determine which positive stimuli were liked mildly versus moderately and (c) to perform a second median split to determine which negative stimuli were disliked mildly versus moderately. Thus, each subject's median likeability rating within each affective valence condition was used to define affective intensity.[4] Although using each subject's own rating of emotional arousal after each 5-s trial to define the intensity factor means that one cannot determine whether the affective experience resulted in efferent discharges or the facial efference influenced the affective experience, or both, the present investigation is not compromised because the issue is whether an association exists between facial efference and people's transient and idiosyncratic affective reactions.

---

[4] Larry Gant and Kathy Morris were very helpful in the selection and pilot testing of these stimuli. Their assistance is gratefully acknowledged.

Procedure

To reduce apprehension about participating in the study, subjects attended an introductory lecture on psychophysiological recording, were led to believe that the study concerned the effects of affective stimuli on involuntary neural processes, completed several questionnaires (e.g., a health status questionnaire), and toured the laboratory several weeks prior to their participation. Subjects were unaware that physiological responses over which they had control were being monitored (cf. Cacioppo, Petty, & Marshall-Goodell, 1985).

Surface EMG activity was recorded using miniature Ag/AgCl electrodes placed in pairs over the corrugator supercilia, zygomatic major, orbicular oris, orbicularis oculi, and medial frontalis regions on the left side of the face to gauge the MAPs from the regions of the muscles of facial expression, and over the nonpreferred superficial forearm flexors to assess somatic activity in a peripheral region. To reduce subject awareness of the experimental hypotheses, subjects were told that the study concerned the natural, involuntary physiological reactions evoked by complex visual stimuli such as photographs, and additional dummy electrodes were placed on the head and torso to divert attention from the face as the particular site of interest. EMG signals obtained from surface, in contrast to needle, electrodes are less precise in isolating the specific source of MAPs because they generally reflect the MAPs from a cluster of heterogeneous motor units rather than from a single unit. However, although the details of individual MAPs are lost in surface EMG recordings, the discrete microvolt discharges from individual MAPs summate spatially and temporally during motor-unit recruitment to yield an aggregate indicating the action (or inaction) of motoneuron pools. Moreover, this aggregate response develops in an orderly manner from the individual MAPs such that progressively larger motoneurons are added to, or progressively smaller units are subtracted from, the total input from a motoneuron pool. Thus, changes in the amplitude of the integrated EMG provide a reliable and valid index of changes in MAP activity (e.g., Henneman, 1980; Lippold, 1967; cf.

Cacioppo, Marshall-Goodell, & Dorfman, 1983; Fridlund & Izard, 1983).

Prior to the onset of the experimental trials, subjects underwent a 10-min period of progressive relaxation to minimize general somatic activity. Subjects were then instructed to examine each slide projected onto a screen, which was situated 1.5 m in front of them, and to answer the questions posed after the presentation of each scene. Questions were posed on a 22.86-cm (9-in.) videoscreen suspended in front of the subject, and responses were made using a numeric keypad.

Subjects were exposed to an initial 16 buffer slides to ensure habituation to the procedure and to another 32 slides during which data were collected. Subjects were unaware of the total number of trials or of the transition between the buffer and experimental trials. Each slide was presented for 5 s. After each presentation, subjects used 9-point scales to rate how much they liked the depicted scene (1 = *disliked*, 9 = *liked*), how aroused it made them feel (1 = *relaxed*, 9 = *aroused*), and how familiar the scene appeared (1 = *novel*, 9 = *familiar*). A closed-loop baseline was employed such that the next slide was presented only after subjects had returned to and maintained basal levels of somatic activity for 5 s (cf. McHugo & Lanzetta, 1983).[5]

Data Reduction

The EMG signals were relayed through shielded cable to Grass wide-band ac-preamplifiers, where they were rectified and smoothed using contour-following integrators with time constants of 0.02 s. The preamplifiers were calibrated to yield a full-scale deflection of an 80-μV signal, and the integrator thresholds were adjusted to place the zero signal at 2% of full-scale deflection. Each channel of EMG was transmitted online to a laboratory computer, digitized at a rate of 100 samples per second, and stored on a hard disk. In addition, dur-

ing the study the rectified and smoothed EMG recordings were displayed on a polygraph, raw EMG recordings were intermittently checked using an oscilloscope, and subjects were monitored and videotaped using a videocamera housed unobtrusively in a speaker. Subsequently, data were deleted for trials on which artifacts were detected or for which the response exceeded full-scale deflection (i.e., 80 μV). Finally, EMG activity recorded over each region was denoised in quadrature, mean amplitude of EMG activity over each region was determined, and the mean amplitudes were averaged across trials but within subjects to obtain more reliable and normally distributed estimates of treatment effects.[6]

Results

Self-Report Measures

Discriminable episodes of mildly and moderately positive and negative affect were identified in the present study. The large F ratio for affective valence, $F(1, 25) = 199.58$, $p < .01$, indicated, as suggested earlier, that subjects in this study responded to the pleasant and unpleasant stimuli in the same manner as did subjects in the pilot testing. The Valence × Intensity interaction was of course also

---

[5]There was no difference across conditions in the time required by subjects to reach the criterion before proceeding to the next experimental trial. For an excellent discussion of the closed-loop baseline, see McHugo and Lanzetta (1983).

---

[6]The videotapes of subjects were visually inspected to determine whether noticeable facial expressions were exhibited during the 5-s stimulus period. The data obtained during trials in which a change in facial expression could be detected were deleted prior to analyses, and in all but one case such instances were rare (i.e., < 3%) and equally distributed across conditions. One subject, however, consistently displayed detectable facial actions during this period. Because data from most of the trials for this individual exceeded 80 μV, her data were deleted prior to analyses.

We also wish to thank A. J. Fridlund for his advice concerning denoising in quadrature, which is a procedure designed to maximize the signal-to-noise ratio in complex waveforms such as the EMG. The transformation used is

$$[Y_i^2 - Y_{(min)}^2]^{1/2},$$

where $Y_{(min)}$ represents the minimum signal observed in a given channel during a given session (expressed in microvolts) and Y_i represents the ith element in the digital array corresponding to the EMG activity during a given trial.

significant, because the intensity factor was operationalized using subjects' responses on this scale, $F(1, 25) = 344.82$, $p < .01$. Cell means and pairwise comparisons are summarized in Table 5.1.

Analysis of the extent to which the scenes were reported to be arousing revealed main effects for affective valence, $F(1, 25) = 24.02$, $p < .01$, and affective intensity, $F(1, 25) = 27.21$, $p < .01$, and a Valence × Intensity interaction, $F(1, 25) = 9.39$, $p < .01$. Inspection of Table 5.1 reveals that unlike the preceding pattern of data, photographs of moderately negative scenes were rated as being more arousing than were the remaining photographs. The analysis of the familiarity ratings also revealed main effects for affective valence, $F(1, 25) = 54.37$, $p < .01$, and affective intensity, $F(1, 25) = 13.83$, $p < .01$, and a Valence × Intensity interaction, $F(1, 25) = 28.71$, $p < .01$. Briefly, the positive scenes were rated as being equally and relatively familiar, whereas the moderately unpleasant scenes were rated as being relatively novel (see Table 5.1).

Electromyographic Measures

A multivariate analysis of variance in which the mean amplitude of EMG activity over each of the six muscle regions served as a dependent measure revealed that the affectively evocative scenes had significant effects on EMG activity. The multivariate main effect for affective valence was signifi-cant, Wilk's criterion $F(6, 20) = 6.08$, $p < .01$, and as expected it was qualified by a significant multivariate Valence × Intensity interaction, Wilk's criterion $F(6, 20) = 7.80$, $p < .01$.

Follow-up univariate analyses of variance revealed significant main effects for affective valence on the measures of EMG activity over the region of the corrugator supercilia, $F(1, 25) = 22.54$, $p < .01$, zygomatic major, $F(1, 25) = 9.19$, $p < .01$, and orbicularis oculi, $F(1, 25) = 4.95$, $p < .05$. As summarized in Table 5.1, EMG activity over the corrugator supercilia muscle region was greater when unpleasant than when pleasant scenes were presented, whereas EMG activity over the zygomatic major and orbicularis oculi regions was greater when pleasant than when unpleasant scenes were presented.

Analyses also revealed Affective Valence × Affective Intensity interactions for EMG activity over the facial regions of the corrugator supercilia, $F(1, 25) = 21.43$, $p < .01$, and the orbicularis oculi, $F(1, 25) = 5.57$, $p < .05$. As can be seen in Table 5.1, these significant interactions were attributable to the fact that EMG activity over the muscle region responsible for lowering and drawing the eyebrows together (corrugator supercilia) tended to be higher for moderately than for mildly intense unpleasant affective reactions, whereas it was lower for moderately than for mildly intense pleasant reactions. EMG activity over the muscle region controlling

TABLE 5.1. Mean Verbal Descriptions and Electromyographic Responses as a Function of Affective Valence and Intensity

Measure	Negative		Positive	
	Moderately	Mildly	Mildly	Moderately
Verbal descriptions				
Liking	2.09$_a$	5.23$_b$	5.78$_c$	8.42$_d$
Arousal	6.64$_a$	5.27$_b$	4.94$_b$	5.08$_b$
Familiarity	3.16$_a$	4.82$_b$	5.50$_c$	5.74$_c$
Electromyographic responses[a]				
Corrugator supercilia	47.37$_a$	46.21$_b$	45.27$_b$	42.22$_c$
Zygomatic major	23.12$_a$	23.50$_{ab}$	24.04$_b$	24.16$_b$
Orbicularis oculi	28.39$_a$	28.56$_a$	28.83$_a$	30.32$_b$
Orbicularis oris	33.02$_a$	33.73$_a$	32.82$_a$	33.58$_a$
Medial frontalis	29.07$_{ab}$	29.35$_b$	28.65$_a$	28.82$_{ab}$
Superficial forearm flexor	23.50$_a$	23.56$_a$	23.25$_a$	23.57$_a$

Note: Means in a row with a similar subscript do not differ significantly by the Duncan multiple-range test ($p < .05$).
[a] Entries represent the mean amplitude of transformed scores for EMG activity.

the actions of squinting (orbicularis oculi) showed the opposite pattern. No other tests were significant.[7]

Discussion

The present results challenge the conventional wisdom in social psychology that physiological measures are sensitive only to changes in general arousal and therefore cannot be used to distinguish between positive and negative affect. The obtained pattern of EMG data indicates a selective activation and inhibition of MAP activity across specific facial muscle regions. This result, together with the electrodermal data from the pilot study and verbal reports regarding felt arousal from the main study, makes it unlikely that the detected EMG responses are due simply to a general increase in arousal or to an increased tensing of the muscles during the presentation of a positive or negative stimulus. Recall, too, that a given positive or negative scene served as a mild affective stimulus for some subjects whereas it served as a moderate affective stimulus for others. Hence the gradations of facial EMG activity found in the present study are more likely to be attributable to the subjects' psychological reaction to the stimuli than to some irrelevant physical feature (e.g., luminosity). Moreover, the pleasantness of emotional reactions has been shown previously to influence the facial actions over the brow (corrugator supercilia) and/or cheek (zygomatic major) regions (e.g., Ekman et al., 1980; Ekman & Friesen, 1978; McHugo, 1983; Schwartz, 1975). The EMG responses obtained in the present study

fit well with this previous research and suggest that facial expressions of emotion—like perioral activity during silent language processing and bodily activity during imagery—can occur so subtly as to go unnoticed in normal social settings (cf. Cacioppo & Petty, 1981).

The one unexpected outcome in the present study concerned the EMG activity obtained over the orbicularis oculi (periocular) muscle region. EMG recordings from this region have been shown to be heightened by expressions of pain, squinting, and so forth (e.g., Englis et al., 1982). Activity over this region in the present study, therefore, may simply reflect eye movements and fixations rather than incipient facial actions associated with affect. On the other hand, EMG activity over this muscle region was greater when positive than when negative stimuli were presented even when a focal point was used (see Pilot Study).

Yet another interesting account for these data is based on Ekman and Friesen's (1982) important work on "felt" smiles. Ekman and Friesen (1982) suggest that people display a smile—whether happy or not—when they wish to present a happy image but that people display both a smile and crow's feet at the outer edges of their eyes when they *feel* happy. Ekman and Friesen (1982) hypothesize that the common elements in the facial expression of the person who actually experiences a positive emotion are the action of two muscles: "the zygomatic major pulling the lip corners upwards towards the cheekbone; and the orbicularis oculi which raises the cheek and gathers skin inwards from around the eye socket" (p. 242). Because there was no reason in the present setting for subjects to feign positive affective reactions to

---

[7] We initially considered and rejected the notion of performing linear trend analyses on these means because (a) there is a long history of attempts to detect distinct physiological reactions that mark both the valence and the intensity of momentarily reportable affective states (e.g., see Cook & Selltiz, 1964) and (b) trend analyses are inappropriate because the valence and intensity conditions represent qualitative rather than quantitative categories (cf. Winer, 1971, pp. 388–390). A reviewer requested that we nevertheless calculate linear contrasts to test more directly our hypothesis that facial EMG activity over localized areas varies as a function of the

pleasantness/unpleasantness of the affective reaction. We did so and, as expected, the results revealed significant linear trends for mean amplitude over the corrugator supercilia, $F(1, 25) = 65.05$, $p < .01$, orbicularis oculi, $F(1, 25) = 14.82$, $p < .01$, and zygomatic major, $F(1, 25) = 8.48$, $p < .01$, muscle regions.

Finally, Spearman correlation coefficients were calculated to examine the relation between the mean level of EMG activity recorded over each site and the reported familiarity and arousing effects of the stimuli. None of these correlations approached significance ($-.10 < rs < .10$).

the experimental stimuli, it is possible that the heightened EMG activity over the orbicularis oculi region, which we found to differentiate the affective nature of the experimental stimuli, may have been related to the variations in the subjects' *feelings* of positive regard for the depicted scenes.

Indeed, a general congruence between results based on facial EMG recordings and those obtained through fine-grain analyses of overt expressions is to be expected because

> facial expressions are principally the result of stereotyped movements of facial skin and fascia (connective tissue) due to contraction of the facial muscles in certain combinations. Such contractions create folds, lines, and wrinkles in the skin and cause movements of facial landmarks such as mouth corners and eyebrows. (Rinn, 1984, p. 52)

Yet the redundancy between these procedures is only partial. For instance, EMG recordings can reveal MAP activity too small to evoke detectable movements and/or whose corresponding muscle contraction is counteracted by contraction of an antagonist.[8] In an interesting illustration of this principle, Ekman, Schwartz, and Friesen (reported in Ekman, 1982b) simultaneously secured video-recordings and surface EMG recordings of individuals as they deliberately intensified the contraction of specific facial muscles (corrugator supercilia and medial frontalis). Results revealed that measurements from FACS and from surface EMG over these muscle regions were highly correlated ($r = .85$). Nevertheless, reliable EMG signals emerged at levels of MAP activity that were lower than could reliably be detected visually. An implication of the former result is that the wealth of information that exists regarding overt facial displays during communication, deception, and emotion should provide a rich theoretical resource for research on subtler, more fleeting discharges of facial efference. An implication of Ekman,

Friesen, and Schwartz's latter finding is that the absence of visually detectable facial actions does not rule out the possibility of tracking at least limited features of moment-by-moment affective processes.

The social context in which facial efference is measured is also important (cf. Ekman & Friesen, 1975). Facial actions can serve communicative and emotionally expressive functions, but they can also serve to deceive; they are controllable, yet they are not always controlled:

> Whereas sounds and the body movements that illustrate speech are intermittent, the face even in repose may provide information about some emotion or mood state. Many nonverbal behaviors simply do not occur when a person is alone, or at least do so very rarely. For example, it would be unusual for someone to shrug or gesture hello when totally alone. Yet facial expressions of emotion may be quite intense even when a person is alone. They are not occasioned only by the presence of others. In fact, social situations can dampen facial expression of emotion. (Ekman, 1982b, p. 45)

The display rules and contingencies that govern overt facial expressions in social contexts may well be less powerful and less likely to influence patterns of facial efference when the efference is so subtle or fleeting as to be undetectable by observers. If this is in fact the case, then discrepancies between the MAP activity underlying covert versus overt facial expressions may be of interest in much the same manner as are discrepancies between private and public actions. For instance, consider an individual who, upon seeing a familiar person approaching at a distance, shows an elevation in EMG activity over the corrugator supercilia muscle region, a diminution in EMG activity over the zygomatic major and orbicularis oculi regions, and yet maintains what appears to be an expressionless face. As the two approach more closely, the pattern of efference changes dramatically as the individual smiles broadly. The striking discrepancy between the facial efference associated with incipient versus public facial displays would at least raise the otherwise unnoticed possibility that the former

---

[8] FACS, on the other hand, remains the only available comprehensive coding system for quantifying observable facial actions. For further discussion of the unique advantages of visual scoring procedures, see Ekman (1982b).

individual was repulsed by the other. To summarize thus far, then, measures of facial EMG and of observable facial actions each have unique advantages and disadvantages, with neither necessarily being "better" or capable of capturing completely the information provided by the other.

Because the present research indicates that facial EMG activity varies as a function of the direction and the intensity of affective reactions, and because the absence of a physiological measure that varied as a function of the direction and intensity of affective reactions has long been held to be a major obstacle in the development of a physiological measure of attitudes (cf. McGuire, 1985), the utility of facial EMG as a physiological measure of attitudes warrants comment. Electrodermal activity (e.g., Rankin & Campbell, 1955), pupil size (e.g., Hess, 1965), and heart rate (e.g., Katz, Cadoret, Hughes, & Abbey, 1965) have all been used to study attitudes, but these physiological measures have at best proven sensitive to variations in the extent of strong emotion underlying an attitude (cf. Cacioppo & Sandman, 1981; Petty & Cacioppo, 1983; Zanna, Detweiler, & Olson, 1984). Although measures of facial efference may overcome this particular problem, we do not envision facial EMG as an effective physiological measure of attitudes in many contexts. At the simplest level, people are capable of suppressing, falsifying, and distorting their facial expressions, which makes it difficult to determine their true feelings toward a stimulus using measures of facial actions, at least in some settings (Zuckerman, Larrance, Spiegel, & Klorman, 1981; cf. Cacioppo & Petty, in press-a).

Second, attitudes are generally conceived of as global and enduring evaluations of a stimulus (e.g., Petty & Cacioppo, 1981; Zanna & Rempel, 1984). People's positive attitudes toward their children endure despite moments of displeasure and occasional thoughts of abandonment. Facial efference, on the other hand, can be extremely transient and specific, marking perhaps a positive thought and feeling one moment and the realization of an undesirable consequence the next. This is not to say that attitudes and facial EMG will never covary; when people are left to simply think about an unequivocally counterattitudinal versus proattitudinal topic, for instance, the predominant thought and feeling can be expected to vary so dramatically and consistently that facial EMG should differentiate the individuals in these conditions (Cacioppo & Petty, 1979). But the same general factors mitigating attitude–behavior correspondence when comparing a general measure of attitude with a specific measure of behavior can also be expected to vitiate the correspondence between a person's general and enduring attitude toward a stimulus and the facial efference associated with transient, specific, and possibly issue-irrelevant (e.g., a speaker's facial expression; cf. McHugo, Lanzetta, Sullivan, Masters, & Englis, 1985) affective reactions.

Third, conditions can be anticipated in which even *general* expressions of attitudes and of affect diverge. Avid smokers, for instance, may generally hold that the consumption of cigarettes is foolish, harmful, and negative but nevertheless have consistent and general positive affective reactions to the act of smoking cigarettes (Fishbein, 1980; see also Englis et al., 1982).

Finally, the accessing of one's attitude toward a stimulus can but need not be accompanied by an unequivocal affective reaction. For instance, mild affective reactions habituate with repeated presentations of a stimulus, yet people's evaluations of the stimulus need not become neutral (e.g., Hare, 1973). Similarly, individuals appear able to categorize a familiar stimulus as being good or bad with minimal, if any, affective involvement (e.g., Cacioppo & Petty, 1980; Cacioppo, Petty, & Morris, 1985; Gordon & Holyoak, 1983). This is not to suggest that affect cannot precede inferences, but simply to suggest that individuals, like well-programmed computers, can access a previously formulated attitude and can perhaps even apply a set of criteria to categorize a stimulus as being "good" or "bad," "wise" or "foolish", or "harmful" or "beneficial" without invoking emotion. To the extent that this analysis is accurate, at least in relative if not in absolute terms, then interesting questions arise regarding the differences in the consequences of social judgments (e.g., attitudes, attributions, and inferences) grounded primarily in cognition and those based primarily in affect.

Although the present research was not designed to address questions about the role of facial efference in affective experience, the observed correspondence between subtle patterns of facial efference and subjects' transient and idiosyncratic affective reactions is certainly consistent with the view that facial efference is a significant determinant of emotion. It is also consistent with the view emphasized earlier that facial efference can serve as emotional readout. It is possible, for instance, that subjects in the present study rated their affective reactions as more intense *because* greater discriminably patterned feedback had been evoked. Research on the temporal specificity of striated muscular activity (e.g., Henneman, 1980; Willis & Grossman, 1977), facial actions (e.g., Ekman & Friesen, 1978), and facial EMG activity (e.g., Cacioppo et al., 1984) is clearly consistent with recent arguments that the temporal parameters of the efference resulting from spontaneous versus deliberate facial actions are distinguishable, just as are the spatial parameters that differentiate the feedback resulting from expressions of, say, happiness and sadness (cf. Tomkins, 1981).

As is well known, evidence has also been reported questioning the contributions of facial efference to affective experience (cf. Tourangeau & Ellsworth, 1979). However, several mechanisms of action linking spontaneous facial efference to affective experience can be suggested that do not cast the relation between facial efference and affective experience as an invariant. In addition to innate afferent mechanisms (e.g., Izard, 1977; Tomkins, 1962, 1963), one might point to the processes of classical conditioning (wherein facial feedback from spontaneous expressions of emotion has been paired so frequently with particular emotional experiences that this feedback has come to serve as a conditioned stimulus), self-perception (e.g., why would one smile spontaneously at another unless liking was involved), and behavioral confirmation (e.g., facial expressions, like overt actions toward another, should influence the social feedback individuals receive). Although deliberate facial expressions of emotion may invoke some of these mechanisms in a weakened form (e.g., even the effects attributable to social feedback should be weakened by leakage from other channels—cf. Zuckerman, Larrance, et al., 1981), the construction and maintenance of a deliberate expression of emotion and the monitoring of the communicative effectiveness of the expression can also subsume processing capacity. When an individual's processing resources are sufficiently limited in an emotionally evocative context that the capacity allocated to the construction, maintenance, and monitoring of an expressive display diminishes what can be allocated to the evocative stimulus, then one might expect deliberate expressions of emotion to actually attenuate the affective experience or to experience or to introduce feelings of negative affect such as anxiety or distress. For instance, expressing and maintaining an unfelt smile in the face of danger may prove to be an effective means of attenuating fear because of the disruption of the normal (i.e., spontaneous) pattern of efference and feedback found in this situation *and* because of the reduction in the processing capacity that can be allocated to the fear-evoking situation.[9]

In sum, previous research has demonstrated that overt facial expressions vary as a function of people's emotional reactions and that the electromyogram is an effective technology for examining neuromuscular actions in the absence of overt muscle contractions. The results of the present research point to a procedure for tracking affective processes. Specifically, results indicated that facial EMG can mark the valence and intensity of transient and specific affective reactions even in the absence of emotional expressions that are noticeable, at least under normal viewing conditions. Although the pattern of facial efference is unlikely to yield a satisfactory physiological marker of attitudes per se, the present results do suggest that

---

[9] Of course, deliberately constructed facial expressions should not have this effect on affective experience when the expression is automatic, the emotionally evocative stimulus requires little processing capacity, or the emotionally evocative stimulus persists sufficiently long that any diminution of processing resources that can be allocated to the stimulus becomes trivial.

facial EMG may provide a useful technology for tracking the rudimentary positive or negative feelings a person has toward a stimulus and the more elementary processes underlying a variety of social judgments and behaviors such as attitude development and change. For instance, whether episodes of "instrumental" and "hostile" aggression studied in social psychological laboratories differ in terms of their emotional underpinnings (cf. Rajecki, 1983) and whether cognitive dissonance is characterized phenomenologically by the perception of arousal or by an unpleasant affective reaction (see recent reviews by Fazio & Cooper, 1983; Cacioppo & Petty, in press-b) are questions that should be amenable to psychophysiological probes.

REFERENCES

Breckler, S. J. (1984). Empirical validation of affect, behavior, and cognition as distinct components of attitude. *Journal of Personality and Social Psychology, 47*, 1191–1205.

Buss, A. H. (1961). *The psychology of aggression*. New York: Wiley.

Cacioppo, J. T., Marshall-Goodell, B., & Dorfman, D. D. (1983). Skeletomuscular patterning: Topographical analysis of the integrated electromyogram. *Psychophysiology, 20*, 269–283.

Cacioppo, J. T., & Petty, R. E. (1979). Attitudes and cognitive response: An electrophysiological approach. *Journal of Personality and Social Psychology, 37*, 2181–2199.

Cacioppo, J. T., & Petty, R. E. (1980). The effects of orienting task on differential hemispheric EEG activation. *Neuropsychologia, 18*, 675–683.

Cacioppo, J. T., & Petty, R. E. (1981). Electromyograms as measures of extent and affectivity of information processing. *American Psychologist, 36*, 441–456.

Cacioppo, J. T., & Petty, R. E. (in press-a). Physiological responses and advertising effects: Is the cup half full or half empty? *Psychology and Marketing*.

Cacioppo, J. T., & Petty, R. E. (in press-b). Social processes. In M. G. H. Coles, E. Donchin, & S. Porges (Eds.), *Psychophysiology: Systems, processes, and applications*. New York: Guilford Press.

Cacioppo, J. T., Petty, R. E., & Marshall-Goodell, E. (1984). Electromyographic specificity during simple physical and attitudinal tasks: Location and topographical features of integrated EMG responses. *Biological Psychology, 18*, 85–121.

Cacioppo, J. T., Petty, R. E., & Marshall-Goodell, E. (1985). Physical, social, and inferential elements of psychophysiological measurement. In P. Karoly (Ed.), *Measure-ment strategies in health psychology* (Vol. 1, pp. 263–300). New York: Wiley.

Cacioppo, J. T., Petty, R. E., & Morris, K. J. (1985). Semantic, evaluative, and self-referent processing: Memory, cognitive effort, and somatovisceral activity. *Psychophysiology, 22*, 371–384.

Cacioppo, J. T., & Sandman, C. A. (1981). Psychophysiological functioning, cognitive responding, and attitudes. In R. E. Petty, R. M. Ostrom, & T. C. Brock (Eds.), *Cognitive responses in persuasion*. Hillsdale, NJ: Erlbaum.

Cook, S. W., & Selltiz, C. (1964). A multiple-indicator approach to attitude measurement. *Psychological Bulletin, 62*, 36–55.

Darwin, C. (1965). *The expression of the emotions in man and animals*. Chicago: University of Chicago Press. (Originally published 1872).

Ekman, P. (1972). Universal and cultural differences in facial expressions of emotion. In J. Cole (Ed.), *Nebraska Symposium on Motivation* (Vol. 19). Lincoln: University of Nebraska Press.

Ekman, P. (1982a). *Emotion in the human face* (2nd ed.). Cambridge, England: Cambridge University Press.

Ekman, P. (1982b). Methods for measuring facial action. In K. R. Scherer & P. Ekman (Eds.), *Handbook of methods in nonverbal behavior research* (pp. 45–90). Cambridge, England: Cambridge University Press.

Ekman, P., & Friesen, W. V. (1975). *Unmasking the face*. Englewood Cliffs, NJ: Prentice-Hall.

Ekman, P., & Friesen, W. V. (1978). *Facial coding action system (FACS): A technique for the measurement of facial actions*. Palo Alto, CA: Consulting Psychologists Press.

Ekman, P., & Friesen, W. V. (1982). Felt, false, and miserable smiles. *Journal of Personality and Social Psychology, 39*, 1125–2234.

Ekman, P., Friesen, W. V., & Ancoli, S. (1980). Facial signs of emotional experience. *Journal of Personality and Social Psychology, 39*, 1125–1134.

Ekman, P., Friesen, W. V., & Ellsworth, P. (1982). Research foundations. In P. Ekman (Ed.), *Emotion in the human face* (2nd ed., pp. 1–143). New York: Cambridge University Press.

Ekman, P., & Oster, H. (1979). Facial expressions of emotion. *Annual Review of Psychology, 30*, 527–554.

Elkin, R. A., & Leippe, M. R. (1985). *Physiological arousal, dissonance, and attitude change: Evidence for a dissonance-arousal link and a "don't remind me" effect*. Manuscript submitted for publication.

Englis, B. G., Vaughn, K. B., & Lanzetta, J. T. (1982). Conditioning of counter-emphatic emotional responses. *Journal of Experimental Social Psychology, 18*, 375–391.

Fazio, R. H., & Cooper, J. (1983). Arousal in the dissonance process. In J. T. Cacioppo & R. E. Petty (Eds.), *Social psychophysiology: A source-book* (pp. 122–152). New York: Guilford Press.

Fishbein, M. (1980). A theory of reasoned action: Some applications and implications. In H. Howe & M. Page (Eds.),

Nebraska Symposium on Motivation (Vol. 27). Lincoln: University of Nebraska Press.

Fishbein, M., & Ajzen, I. (1975). *Belief, attitude, intention, and behavior: An introduction to theory and research.* Reading, MA.: Addison-Wesley.

Fowles, D. C. (1980). The three arousal model: Implications of Gray's two-factor learning theory for heart rate, electrodermal activity, and psychopathy. *Psychophysiology, 17,* 87–104.

Fridlund, A. J., Ekman, P., & Oster, H. (in press). Facial expressions of emotion: Review of literature, 1970–1983. In A. Siegman (Ed.), *Nonverbal communication.* Hillsdale, NJ: Erlbaum.

Fridlund, A. J., & Izard, C. E. (1983). Electromyographic studies of facial expressions of emotions and patterns of emotion. In J. T. Cacioppo & R. E. Petty (Eds.), *Social psychophysiology: A sourcebook* (pp. 243–286). New York: Guilford Press.

Fridlund, A. J., Schwartz, G. E., & Fowler, S. C. (1984). Pattern recognition of self-reported emotional state from multiple-site facial EMG activity during affective imagery. *Psychophysiology, 21,* 622–637.

Gordon, P. C., & Holyoak, K. J. (1983). Implicit learning and generalization of the "mere exposure" effect. *Journal of Personality and Social Psychology, 45,* 492–500.

Graham, J. L. (1980). A new system for measuring nonverbal responses to marketing appeals. *1980 AMA Educator's Conference Proceedings, 46,* 340–343.

Haggard, E. A., & Isaacs, F. S. (1966). Micromentary facial expressions as indicators of ego mechanisms in psychotherapy. In C. A. Gottschalk & A. Averback (Eds.), *Methods of research in psychotherapy.* New York: Appleton-Century-Crofts.

Hare, R. D. (1973). Orienting and defensive responses to visual stimuli. *Psychophysiology, 10,* 453–464.

Henneman, E. (1980). Organization of the motoneuron pool: The size principle. In V. E. Mountcastle (Ed.), *Medical physiology* (14th ed., Vol. 1). St. Louis, MO: Mosby.

Hess, E. H. (1965). Attitude and pupil size. *Scientific American, 212,* 46–54.

Higgins, E. T., Rhodewalt, F., & Zanna, M. P. (1979). Dissonance motivation: Its nature, persistence, and reinstatement. *Journal of Experimental Social Psychology, 15,* 16–34.

Izard, C. E. (1971). *The face of emotion.* New York: Appleton-Century-Crofts.

Izard, C. E. (1977). *Human emotions.* New York: Plenum Press.

Katz, H., Cadoret, R., Hughes, K., & Abbey, D. (1965). Physiological correlates of acceptable and unacceptable statements. *Psychological Reports, 17,* 78.

Kiesler, C. A., & Pallak, M. S. (1976). Arousal properties of dissonance manipulations. *Psychological Bulletin, 83,* 1014–1025.

Lanzetta, J. T., & Orr, S. P. (1980). Influence of facial expressions in the classical conditioning of fear. *Journal of Personality and Social Psychology, 39,* 1081–1087.

Lanzetta, J. T., & Orr, S. P. (1981). Stimulus properties of facial expressions and their influence on the classical conditioning of fear. *Motivation & Emotion, 5,* 225–234.

Lindzey, G., & Aronson, E. (1985). *Handbook of social psychology* (3rd ed.). New York: Random House.

Lippold, O. C. J. (1967). Electromyography. In P. H. Venables & I. Martin (Eds.), *Manual of psychophysiological methods* (pp. 245–298). New York: Wiley.

Love, R. E. (1972). *Unobtrusive measurement of cognitive reactions to persuasive communications.* Unpublished doctoral dissertation, Ohio State University.

McGuigan, F. J. (1978). *Cognitive psychophysiology: Principles of covert behavior.* Englewood Cliffs, NJ: Prentice-Hall.

McGuire, W. J. (1985). Attitudes and attitude change. In G. Lindzey & E. Aronson (Eds.), *Handbook of social psychology* (3rd ed., Vol. 2, pp. 233–346). New York: Random House.

McHugo, G. (1983, September). *Facial EMG and self-reported emotion.* Paper presented at the meeting of the Society for Psychophysiological Research, Asilomar, CA.

McHugo, G., & Lanzetta, J. T. (1983). Methodological decisions in social psychophysiology. In J. T. Cacioppo & R. E. Petty (Eds.), *Social psychophysiology: A sourcebook* (pp. 630–665). New York: Guilford Press.

McHugo, G., Lanzetta, J. T., Sullivan, D. G., Masters, R. D., & Englis, B. G. (1985). Emotional reactions to a political leader's expressive displays. *Journal of Personality and Social Psychology, 49,* 1513–1529.

Pallak, M. S., & Pittman, E. S. (1972). General motivation effects of dissonance arousal. *Journal of Personality and Social Psychology, 21,* 349–358.

Petty, R. E., & Cacioppo, J. T. (1981). *Attitudes and persuasion: Classic and contemporary approaches.* Dubuque, IA: William C. Brown.

Petty, R. E., & Cacioppo, J. T. (1983). The role of bodily responses in attitude measurement and change. In J. T. Cacioppo & R. E. Petty (Eds.), *Social psychophysiology: A sourcebook* (pp. 51–101). New York: Guilford Press.

Rajecki, D. W. (1983). Animal aggression: Implications for human aggression. In R. G. Geen & E. J. Donnerstein (Eds.), *Aggression: Theoretical and empirical reviews* (Vol. 1, pp. 189–211). New York: Academic Press.

Rankin, R. E., & Campbell, D. T. (1955). Galvanic skin response to Negro and white experimenters. *Journal of Abnormal and Social Psychology, 51,* 30–33.

Rinn, W. E. (1984). The neuropsychology of facial expression: A review of the neurological and psychological mechanisms for producing facial expression. *Psychological Bulletin, 95,* 52–77.

Schachter, S. (1964). The interaction of cognitive and physiological determinants of emotion. In P. H. Leiderman & D. Shapiro (Eds.), *Psychobiological approaches to social behavior.* Stanford, CA: Stanford University Press.

Schwartz, G. E. (1975). Biofeedback, self-regulation, and the patterning of physiological processes. *American Scientist, 63*, 314–324.

Sorce, J., Emde, R., Campos, J., & Klinnert, M. (1981, April). *Maternal emotional signaling; its effects on the visual cliff of one-year-olds.* Paper presented at the meeting of the Society for Research in Child Development, Boston.

Tomkins, S. S. (1962). *Affect, imagery, consciousness: The positive affects* (Vol. 1). New York: Springer.

Tomkins, S. S. (1963). *Affect, imagery, consciousness: The negative affects* (Vol. 2). New York: Springer.

Tomkins, S. S. (1981). The role of facial response in the experience of emotion: A reply to Tourangeau and Ellsworth. *Journal of Personality Social Psychology, 40*, 355–357.

Tourangeau, R., & Ellsworth, P. C. (1979). The role of facial response in the experience of emotion. *Journal of Personality and Social Psychology, 37*, 1519–1531.

Willis, W. D., & Grossman, R. G. (1977). *Medical neurobiology* (2nd ed.). St. Louis, MO: Mosby.

Wilson, E. O. (1975). *Sociobiology.* Cambridge, MA: Harvard University Press.

Winer, B. J. (1971). *Statistical principles in experimental design* (2nd ed.). New York: McGraw Hill.

Zajonc, R. B. (1985). Emotion and facial efference: A theory reclaimed. *Science, 228*, 15–21.

Zanna, M. P., Detweiler, R. A., & Olson, J. M. (1984). Physiological mediation of attitude maintenance, formation, and change. In W. Waid (Ed.), *Sociophysiology* (pp. 133–196). New York: Springer-Verlag.

Zanna, M. P., Kiesler, C. A., & Pilkonis, P. A. (1970). Positive and negative attitudinal affect established by classical conditioning. *Journal of Personality and Social Psychology, 14*, 321–328.

Zanna, M. P., & Rempel, J. R. (1984). *Attitudes: A new look at an old concept.* Paper presented at the Conference on Social Psychology of Knowledge, Tel Aviv, Israel.

Zuckerman, M., DePaulo, B. M., & Rosenthal, R. (1981). Verbal and nonverbal communication of deception. *Advances in Experimental Social Research, 14*, 1–59.

Zuckerman, M., Larrance, D. T., Spiegel, N. H., & Klorman, R. (1981). Controlling nonverbal displays: Facial expressions and tone of voice. *Journal of Experimental Social Psychology, 17*, 506–524.

Received February 1, 1985
Revision received July 30, 1985 ■

Variability in Automatic Activation as an Unobtrusive Measure of Racial Attitudes: A Bona Fide Pipeline?

Russell H. Fazio, Joni R. Jackson, Bridget C. Dunton, and
Carol J. Williams

The research examines an unobtrusive measure of racial attitudes based on the evaluations that are automatically activated from memory on the presentation of Black versus White faces. Study 1, which concerned the technique's validity, obtained different attitude estimates for Black and White participants and also revealed that the variability among White participants was predictive of other race-related judgments and behavior. Study 2 concerned the lack of correspondence between the unobtrusive estimates and Modern Racism Scale (MRS) scores. The reactivity of the MRS was demonstrated in Study 3. Study 4 observed an interaction between the unobtrusive estimates and an individual difference in motivation to control prejudiced reactions when predicting MRS scores. The theoretical implications of the findings for consideration of automatic and controlled components of racial prejudice are discussed, as is the status of the MRS.

Russell H. Fazio, Joni R. Jackson, Bridget C. Dunton, and Carol J. Williams, Department of Psychology, Indiana University Bloomington.

This research was supported by Research Scientist Development Award MH00452 and Grant MH38832 from the National Institute of Mental Health and by an American Psychological Association Minority Fellowship. Portions of the data from Studies 1 and 3 were presented at the 1994 and 1995 Midwestern Psychological Association conventions (Jackson & Fazio, 1994, 1995).

We thank Michael Bailey, who developed and tested the software used to present the high-resolution color images as primes and to collect the response latency data. We also thank Teresa Robeson and Jennifer Bradley for so capably serving as experimenters in Studies 1 and 2 and Study 3, respectively, and Edward Hirt for his helpful comments on an earlier version of the article.

Correspondence concerning this article should be addressed to Russell H. Fazio, Department of Psychology, Indiana University, Bloomington, Indiana 47405–1301.

The present research concerns the validity of a technique for measuring racial attitudes unobtrusively. The technique stems from a now widely used procedure, introduced by Fazio, Sanbonmatsu, Powell, and Kardes (1986), for examining the automatic activation of attitudes from memory. The procedure involves priming and permits assessment of the extent to which the presentation of an attitude object automatically activates an associated evaluation from memory. On each trial, the prime that is presented is the name of an attitude object. Its presentation is followed by the display of a positive or negative evaluative adjective. The participant's task is to indicate the connotation of the target word as quickly as possible. Does it mean "good" or "bad"? The latency with which this judgment is made constitutes the dependent measure.

For example, assume that the attitude object *snake* is evaluated negatively by an individual. Presentation of *snake* as the prime may automatically activate the negative evaluation. If the target adjective that is subsequently presented is also negative (e.g., *disgusting*), then the individual is able to indicate the connotation of the target adjective relatively quickly; that is, responding is facilitated. Thus, the technique relies on the presence of facilitation as an indication that the evaluation associated with the primed attitude object has been activated on presentation of the object. Precisely such attitude-congruent facilitation effects have been observed in many experiments using this basic procedure (e.g., Bargh, Chaiken, Govender, & Pratto, 1992; Fazio, 1993; Fazio et al., 1986; Hermans, De Houwer, & Eelen, 1994; Sanbonmatsu & Fazio, 1986; Sanbonmatsu, Osborne, & Fazio, 1986).

In our first report regarding automatic attitude activation (Fazio et al., 1986), we raised the possibility that the procedure might have utility as an unobtrusive measure of attitude. Essentially, the pattern of facilitation that is exhibited on positive versus negative adjectives can provide an indication of the individual's attitude toward the primed object. Relatively more facilitation on positive adjectives would be indicative of a more positive attitude, and relatively more facilitation on negative adjectives would be indicative of a negative attitude. Furthermore, these estimates are obtained in a situation in which the individual is not aware that his or her attitude is being assessed. During the critical priming task, the participant is not asked to consider his or her attitude toward the object in question. Yet, it is possible to ascertain from the facilitation data the degree to which positive or negative evaluations are activated when the attitude object is presented.

Relatively recent technological advances provide all the more reason to believe that the basic technique might represent a useful and valid unobtrusive measure of attitude. It now is possible to present not words (i.e., not names of attitude objects), but high-resolution color images as primes. Thus, a digitized photo of an attitude object—a color photo of a snake, for example— can now be presented as the prime. Using this new technology, our laboratory has typically observed stronger facilitation effects than in our earlier work using words as primes. The present research used such a methodology to investigate racial attitudes.

Racial attitudes provide an excellent context for consideration of the difficulties that can arise when attempting to assess individuals' attitudes. Either because they are unaware of their true sentiments (Banaji & Greenwald, 1994; Greenwald & Banaji, 1995; Nisbett & Wilson, 1977) or because they are reluctant to reveal negativity toward Blacks (e.g., Crosby, Bromley, & Saxe, 1980; Gaertner & Dovidio, 1986; Sigall & Page, 1971), individuals' self-reported attitudes may be suspect. For example, an individual may be reluctant to provide a response that would indicate a negative attitude toward Blacks and, hence, might lead to him or her being labeled as prejudiced. Precisely such concerns about the validity of direct self-reports have motivated pleas for the use of more indirect, unobtrusive measures of racial attitudes (e.g., Crosby et al., 1980; Dovidio & Fazio, 1992).

Various techniques have been promoted over the years as means of circumventing the reactivity of direct measures. The most well known of these is Jones and Sigall's (1971) bogus pipeline technique. By convincing participants that an apparatus, ostensibly recording their physiological responses, is capable of revealing their true attitudes, this technique seeks to induce participants to provide truthful self-reports. Indeed, this technique has been successful in revealing disparities between participants' self-reports on traditional measures and their self-reports when attached to the bogus pipeline (Jones & Sigall, 1971; Sigall & Page, 1971). However, the technique requires an elaborate deception to convince participants of the capacity of the apparatus to discern their true attitudes.

Another type of measure that has been used to examine racial attitudes is the Modern Racism Scale (McConahay, 1986). The Modern Racism Scale was purportedly designed as a nonreactive measure of anti-Black feelings. The scale asks respondents to agree or disagree with a set of beliefs that Whites may or may not hold about Blacks (e.g., "It is easy to understand the anger of Black people in America"). According to McConahay (1986), this instrument allows participants to express negative affect toward a minority without apprehension that this expression might be labeled as prejudiced or racist: "The wording of the items in the Modern Racism Scale permit the expression of negative affect because giving the prejudiced response in each instance can be explained by racially neutral ideology or nonprejudiced race-relevant attributions" (p. 100).

Ultimately, both the bogus pipeline technique and the Modern Racism Scale rely on the individual's self-report. In contrast, the technique we are proposing provides an estimate of participants' attitudes without ever asking them to consider their attitudes. That is, we try to "get inside the head" of the participant. In this respect, the technique represents a potentially bona fide, not a bogus, pipeline.

Various priming paradigms have been used in past research on stereotypes as a means of documenting their automatic activation from memory. Included among these are investigations of racial stereotypes (e.g., Devine, 1989b; Dovidio, Evans, & Tyler, 1986; Dovidio & Gaertner, 1991; Gaertner & McLaughlin, 1983; Gilbert & Hixon, 1991), ageism (e.g., Perdue & Gurtman, 1990), and in-groups versus out-groups (Perdue, Dovidio, Gurtman, & Tyler, 1990). Such research has succeeded

in demonstrating the operation of stereotypes at an automatic processing level; stereotype-related constructs were activated by the various primes. In a similar fashion, implicit memory paradigms have recently been used to examine gender stereotyping, demonstrating the occurrence of sexism at an unconscious level (Banaji & Greenwald, 1995). The present research extended beyond such work, however, in that our goal was not merely to demonstrate the activation of differential evaluations as a function of priming but to explore the utility of using each participant's pattern of facilitation as an individual-differences measure. Our initial study aimed to examine the validity of the priming technique as an indirect, unobtrusive measure of attitude.

However, a second, related aim was more theoretical in nature. Devine (1989a, 1989b) has proposed a very influential model of prejudice. Much like our Motivation and Opportunity as Determinants (MODE) model of attitude–behavior processes (Fazio, 1986, 1990), her model focuses on automatic and controlled components of prejudice. The model assumes that high- and low-prejudiced individuals are equally knowledgeable of cultural stereotypes and that these socially shared, cultural stereotypes are likely to be accessible and automatically activated in the presence of a minority group member. What distinguishes prejudiced and unprejudiced individuals is not this automatic component but the controlled component. Nonprejudiced people are presumed to hold personal beliefs that motivate them to inhibit the influences of the automatically activated cultural stereotype. Thus, the model suggests that personal beliefs must be consciously attended to via controlled processes to exert any influence. In contrast, our approach emphasizes the automatic component far more and suggests that there will be meaningful variability in the nature of the evaluations that are activated from memory automatically. We argue that what is automatically activated from memory is not necessarily some socially shared, cultural stereotype but personal evaluations.

In one study testing her model, Devine (1989b) examined the effects of subliminally priming stereotypes commonly held about Blacks in

Western culture. The primes included words that were social category labels (e.g., *Blacks* and *Negroes*) and stereotypic descriptors (e.g., *poor* and *athletic*). Participants' perceptions of the ambiguous behavior of a target person whose race was unspecified served as the dependent variable. Devine found that priming of the stereotype associated with Blacks affected participants' perceptions of the target person's behavior. Those participants primed with the cultural stereotype of Blacks rated the ambiguous behavior of the target person as more hostile. This effect occurred equally for both high- and low-prejudiced participants, as identified by the Modern Racism Scale.

These findings raise two questions. First, which concept, the cultural stereotype or one's personal evaluation, is automatically activated in the presence of a minority group member? Devine (1989b) suggested that this commonly held stereotype, rather than one's personal evaluation, is activated automatically. Yet, her study primed the cultural stereotype of Blacks directly. The primes included words such as *lazy, ghetto*, and *welfare* that tend to evoke negative images. In contrast, priming with the faces of Black individuals would provide an opportunity to examine whether personal evaluations, as opposed to shared cultural stereotypes, are activated on observation of a minority person.

The second issue raised by Devine's (1989b) study concerns the validity of the Modern Racism Scale. Devine found no difference between high- and low-prejudiced participants. Although this lack of a difference may reflect the activation of a similar, culturally shared stereotype (as Devine suggested), it also is possible that the null finding stems from a failure on the part of the Modern Racism Scale to provide a valid measure of an individual's level of racism.

The present study was designed to examine both of these issues, as well as the validity of the indirect technique as a measure of racial attitudes. The automatic activation of attitudes was tested among groups of participants scoring high and low on the Modern Racism Scale. Participants were presented with photographs of faces of White and Black male and female undergraduates and asked to make judgments about the connotation of target adjectives that followed the presentation of each face. If the face (prime) automatically activated evaluations from memory, responding in the adjective connotation task should be affected differently for positive versus negative adjectives. Inferences regarding the participant's attitude toward the individuals represented in the photographs can be drawn from the pattern of facilitation. Relatively greater facilitation on negative than positive adjectives when those adjectives are preceded by Black faces than when they are preceded by White faces would be indicative of a more negative attitude toward Blacks.

More specifically, the goals of the present research were threefold. First, the study explored Devine's assumption about cultural stereotypes versus personal evaluations. In the present study, group membership (i.e., White or Black), rather than the cultural stereotype, was primed. If, as Devine suggested, the shared cultural stereotype is activated in the presence of a minority group, one would expect little meaningful variation in the pattern of facilitation across participants. On the other hand, if it is one's personal evaluation that is activated in the presence of a minority group member, the variation across participants would be more substantial and predictive of race-relevant behaviors.

Such predictive validity constituted the second aim of the present study. The ability of both the Modern Racism Scale and the attitude estimate based on facilitation scores to predict judgment and behavior was examined. To do so, we obtained two additional measures of participants' behaviors and judgments: (a) ratings of an interaction between each participant and a Black experimenter and (b) participants' responses to a number of questions regarding the Rodney King verdict and the ensuing 1992 Los Angeles riots. The data from these two measures were correlated with Modern Racism Scale scores and the unobtrusive attitude estimates to examine the link between the participants' attitudes, as measured by both techniques, and their judgments and behaviors.

Finally, the serendipitous inclusion of a sample of Black students in the study permitted the comparison of patterns of facilitation in the priming task for Black versus White individuals. Thus, estimates of racial attitudes based on facilitation scores could be examined for the degree to which they distinguished Black and White participants. Such discriminability would provide further evidence regarding the validity of the unobtrusive technique.

Study 1

Method

Participants. Fifty-three individuals (45 Whites and 8 Blacks) participated for payment or as partial fulfillment of an introductory psychology course requirement. These individuals were among 479 students who had participated in an earlier mass survey that included the Modern Racism Scale. Scores on the Modern Racism Scale can range from −14 (low prejudice) to 14 (high prejudice). Twenty-five students had scores that placed them among the top 10% of respondents (scores of 2 to 12); 28 had scores that placed them among the bottom 10% (scores of −14). Seven of the 8 Black students were from this latter group.

Stimulus materials. Forty-eight color photographs of White, Black, and other ("other" being Asian and Hispanic) male and female undergraduates served as primes. All photographs were head shots taken against a common background. Volunteers, who were paid $5, signed consent agreement forms permitting the use of their photographs for research purposes. The photographs were digitized as 256 color, 640 × 480 resolution image files. Thirty-two black-and-white yearbook photographs were selected from the 1991 Indiana University yearbook for use in the second and third phases of the experiment described subsequently.

Procedure. On arrival, students were greeted by an Asian female experimenter unaware of their Modern Racism Scale scores. Students were told that the experiment involved word meaning as an automatic skill and that a variety of different tasks would be performed during the experiment. The

experimental procedure consisted of six phases, the fourth phase involving the actual priming task.

The first word-meaning task, whose purpose was to obtain baseline data, involved the presentation of a single word on the computer screen. The student's task was to press a key labeled *good* or a key labeled *bad* as quickly as possible to indicate his or her judgment of the word. The list of words consisted of 12 adjectives that were positive in connotation (e.g., attractive, likable, and wonderful) and 12 adjectives that were negative in connotation (e.g., annoying, disgusting, and offensive). Students were instructed to maximize the speed and accuracy of their responses. The order in which the adjectives were presented was randomized for each student. A row of asterisks preceded the presentation of each adjective, serving as a warning signal that the target adjective was about to appear. A given adjective remained on the screen until the student responded or for a maximum of 1.75 s. A 2.5-s interval separated each trial. The student's response was recorded, along with the latency of response (from adjective onset to response) to the nearest millisecond. Students' performance of this task was preceded by a block of practice trials involving different adjectives to familiarize students with the procedure. Students performed two blocks of trials, each block consisting of 24 adjectives. The average latency for the two trials involving any given adjective served as the student's baseline latency for that adjective.

The next two phases of the experiment were intended to prepare students for the priming task that would involve presentation of faces as primes and adjectives as targets. The second and third phases were presented to students as face learning and detection tasks.

The second phase ostensibly involved the ability to learn faces for a later recognition task. The students' task was simply to attend to the faces (targets) presented on the computer screen. They were told that they would be asked to recall the targets in the next task. The stimuli consisted of 16 black-and-white yearbook photographs of White, Black, and Asian male and female faces. Each photograph was presented twice, once in each of two blocks.

The third phase involved a recognition test of the faces presented in the previous task. The photographs from the previous task were presented on the computer screen. Students were told that their task was to press the key labeled *yes* if the face had appeared in the previous task or to press the key labeled *no* if the face had not appeared in the previous task. Each face remained on the screen for a maximum of 5 s. A 2.5-s interval separated each trial. Students made such judgments about 32 faces, 16 "target" faces that had appeared in the previous task and 16 "filler" faces not previously presented.

The fourth phase involved the actual priming task. Students were told that the previous tasks would now be combined. They were told that our interest was in determining the degree to which the judgment of word meaning was an automatic skill. The experimenter said that if such a judgment was truly an automatic skill, individuals should be able to perform just as well as in the very first phase of the experiment even if they had to do something else at the same time. Thus, students were led to believe that this phase of the experiment involved both the learning of the faces and the judgment of the connotation of the adjectives.

The instructions and procedures were identical to the first task, with one exception. Students were told it was important that they attend to the faces presented because they would be asked to recall the faces in the next task. The row of asterisks was replaced by 48 color photographs of White, Black, and "other" male and female faces. These photographs served as primes. On any given trial, a prime was presented for 315 ms, followed by a 135-ms interval before onset of the target adjective. Thus, the interval between prime onset and target onset, stimulus onset asynchrony, was 450 ms.[1] A 2.5-s interval separated each trial. After an initial practice block involving different faces and adjectives, four blocks of trials were presented. Each

block consisted of 48 trials in which each of the primes appeared once, followed by one of the 24 adjectives. Over the course of the four blocks, each prime was paired with 2 positive and 2 negative adjectives. Each Black face and each "other" face were randomly paired with a same-sex White face. The paired faces were followed by an identical set of 4 adjectives. Trials involving the 12 matched pairs of Black and White faces constituted the actual trials of the experiment. The trials involving the 12 "other" faces and their 12 matched White faces served as fillers. These trials were included to reduce the overall proportion of Black faces to which the student was exposed and, thus, minimize the likelihood that students would become aware of the interest in the race shown in the photograph.

The fifth phase of the experiment was the detection task that students had been led to expect during the instructions for the fourth phase. This detection task involved the presentation of the 48 color photographs used during the priming task, along with 48 filler photographs not previously presented. Students were instructed to press the key labeled *yes* if the face was presented in the priming task or the key labeled *no* if the face had not been presented in the priming task. The instructions for this task were identical to those given in the third phase of the experiment. Each photograph appeared on the screen for 5 s or until the student pressed a key. A 2.5-s interval separated each trial. Each photograph was presented once.

The sixth and final phase involved ratings of attractiveness of the color photographs (primes). This phase was intended to bolster the cover story and to provide the basis for the "debriefing" that students were to receive later (see later discussion). Students were told that we were interested in assessing the extent to which the attractiveness of a face determined the degree to which it had distracted them from their task of judging word meaning during the fourth phase. Hence, we were asking

---

[1] This stimulus onset asynchrony of 450 ms was selected on the basis of earlier pilot testing and experimentation involving photos of objects as primes. Just as in Experiments 2 and 3 of Fazio et al. (1986), the Valence of the Attitude Object × Valence of the Adjective interaction was not observed at a longer stimulus onset asynchrony, but was apparent at the stimulus onset asynchrony of 450 ms. With even shorter prime durations, participants had difficulty identifying and naming the pictures that were presented.

them to rate the attractiveness of each photo. Students were instructed to press one of nine keys (1 = *not at all attractive*, 9 = *very attractive*) to indicate their rating of the attractiveness of the photograph. Each photograph appeared on the screen for 15 s or until the student pressed a key.

Additional measures. Two additional measures were collected to examine the possibility that the direct measure (Modern Racism Scale) or an indirect measure (one based on facilitation scores) of students' racial attitudes (or both measures) would be predictive of their behavior. The first measure involved the students interacting with a second experimenter, a Black woman, who was unaware of students' Modern Racism Scale scores. After completing the computer tasks, the students were introduced to the second experimenter with the explanation that this person would take a few minutes to explain the experiment and pay them. During the debriefing session, this experimenter provided an explanation of the experiment, focusing on the possibility of attractiveness as a distraction in the performance of the word-meaning task. The experimenter answered any questions the students may have had at this time. Each debriefing session lasted approximately 10 min. On the basis of this interaction, the experimenter rated each student in terms of friendliness and interest in psychology on scales ranging from *not at all* (−3) to *very* (3). In making these judgments, the experimenter was especially attentive to such factors as smiling, eye contact, spatial distance, and body language. The purpose of these measures was to obtain some indication of the nature of the student's behavior during an interaction with a Black target person and to assess whether a student's Modern Racism Score, indirect attitude score, or both scores would predict such behavior.

As students were leaving the laboratory after the debriefing, the first experimenter stopped each one to ask him or her to complete a survey ostensibly unrelated to this study. This constituted the second measure. Students were asked to complete a questionnaire for a colleague at another university. This "college student national opinion survey" contained a number of items related to the 1992

Rodney King trial and the ensuing Los Angeles riots.[2] The survey asked respondents to indicate the extent to which they agreed or disagreed with statements regarding the trial verdict ("Was it just?") and the anger of the Black community after the verdict ("Was the community justified?"). In addition, respondents were asked to indicate the degree to which they would attribute responsibility for the riots to the following groups: Whites, Blacks, Koreans, the media, and the Los Angeles Police Department. After they had completed the questionnaire, students placed it in an envelope, sealed the envelope, and then placed the sealed envelope in a large manila envelope posted on a bulletin board. This envelope was clearly addressed to a scientist at another university. The students were under the impression that the packet would be mailed to the individual.

Results

Detection data. During the priming phase, students had been instructed to attend to the photographs for recall in a later task. In compliance with the cover story, students later participated in a detection task in which they had to indicate whether a given photograph had or had not been presented during the priming phase of the experiment. These data were examined to check whether the students had followed the instruction to attend to the faces. Detection scores were calculated for each student by subtracting the proportion of false alarms (filler not previously presented that the student incorrectly identified as having been presented) from the proportion of correctly identified hits (previously presented faces correctly identified as such). Performance at chance levels would be indicated by a score of zero on this detection index. Students performed at better than chance levels; their mean score was .65, which was statistically reliable, $t(53) = 26.18$, $p < .001$.

Facilitation scores. For each student, baseline

---

[2] In 1992, four White police officers were acquitted in the brutal beating of a Black motorist, Rodney King. The verdict resulted in looting and rioting in Los Angeles.

latency for each adjective was computed from the average of the two presentations of the adjective during the initial asterisk task. The latency for any given target adjective when preceded by a given face was subtracted from the baseline for that adjective to arrive at a facilitation score. Average facilitation scores on positive target adjectives and negative target adjectives were computed for each face. For each student, mean positive and mean negative facilitation scores were computed within each cell of the 2 (race of face) × 2 (sex of face) design. The latencies for any trials on which the student made an error, which averaged 3.52%, were not included in these computations.

Effects of race of student.   Of the 53 students, 8 were Black. Thus, an initial analysis examined the effects of the student's race. The data were analyzed in a mixed analysis of variance (ANOVA) involving one between-subjects variable (race of student) and three within-subject variables (race and sex of the photograph and valence of the adjective). This overall analysis revealed main effects for race of the photo, $F(1, 51) = 5.67, p = .021$, and valence of the adjective, $F(1, 51) = 5.29, p = .026$. However, both main effects were qualified by a significant three-way Race of Student × Race of Photo × Valence of Adjective interaction, $F(1, 51) = 25.88, p < .001$. No significant effects concerning sex of the face were observed; therefore, subsequent analyses have collapsed across this variable.

As a means of exploring the nature of the interaction, separate ANOVAs were conducted among the White and among the Black students. The analysis among White students revealed a significant interaction between the race of the prime and the valence of the target adjective, $F(1, 43) = 32.49, p < .001$. The means for this interaction are displayed in the left panel of Figure 6.1. Greater facilitation[3] occurred when positive adjectives had been preceded by White than by Black primes and when negative adjectives had been preceded by Black than by White primes. This pattern of facilitation suggests that White students, on average, held negative attitudes toward Blacks.

Among Black students, the analysis again revealed a significant interaction between the race of the prime and the valence of the target adjective, $F(1, 7) = 9.36, p = .018$. However, in this case, the pattern of facilitation was in the opposite direction (see the right panel of Figure 6.1). Greater facilitation occurred when positive adjectives had been preceded by Black than by White primes and when negative adjectives had been preceded by White than by Black primes.

As noted earlier, the differential patterns of facilitation for Black and White students produced a highly significant Race of Student × Race of Photo × Valence of Adjective interaction. This outcome provides the first indication that the unobtrusive technique has some validity. Black and White students displayed very different patterns of facilitation.

Effects of level of modern racism.   Subsequent analyses focused on only the White students to allow examination of the effects of level of racism, as measured by the Modern Racism Scale. A mixed ANOVA involving three within-subject variables (race of face, sex of face, and valence of adjective) and one between-subjects variable (level of racism, as defined by the Modern Racism Scale) was conducted. This analysis revealed that level of racism did not interact with any other variable. The critical Race of Face × Valence of Adjective interaction that had been observed earlier was not qualified by level of racism, $F < 1$. For both

---

[3] Throughout this article, the term *facilitation* is used in a relative sense. To speak of absolute facilitation requires the assessment of a true no-prime baseline that is identical to the primes in such respects as ease of encoding and memory demands (for further discussion of this issue, see Fazio et al., 1986; Jonides & Mack, 1984). In the present case, the task instructions clearly demanded that the students attend to and familiarize themselves with the faces that appeared as primes. Hence, it is not surprising that responding to the adjectives generally took longer during the priming phase of the experiment than during the baseline assessment phase, when the students' sole task was to indicate the connotation of the adjective.

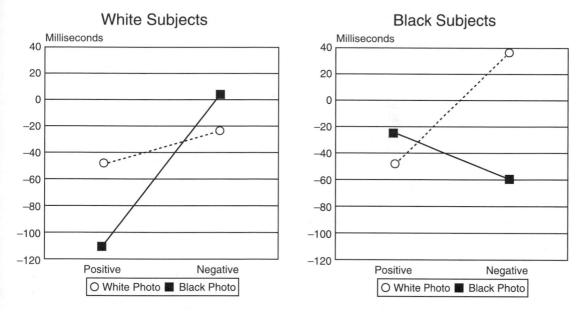

FIGURE 6.1 ■ Mean facilitation scores in Study 1 for positive and negative adjectives preceded by photos of White and Black faces.

low- and high-prejudiced White students, greater facilitation occurred when positive adjectives had been preceded by White primes and when negative adjectives had been preceded by Black primes. Thus, the pattern of facilitation held constant regardless of the level of racism, as measured by the Modern Racism Scale. This null effect parallels Devine's (1989b) finding. As noted earlier, the priming effects observed in her study were not moderated by scores on the Modern Racism Scale.

Attitude estimates based on facilitation scores. The facilitation data can be represented in another form, one that proves useful for other purposes. We wished to reduce the facilitation data for any given student to a single index that would serve as an estimate of the student's attitude toward Blacks. Given that multiple observations were available for each student (i.e. facilitation data for 12 White faces and 12 Black faces), it was possible to examine the Race of Photo × Valence of Adjective interaction for each and every student. We computed the effect size of this interaction for each student as our estimate of the student's attitude. In more precise terms, the steps (see Rosenthal, 1991)

involved (a) computation of the difference between the average facilitation score for positive adjectives and that for negative adjectives for each and every face, (b) computation of a pairwise t test comparing the difference scores for the White faces and their matched Black counterparts, (c) transformation of the t value to a correlation coefficient, and (d) further transformation of this coefficient via Fisher's r-to-z transformation. For the resulting index, more negative scores reflected a pattern of facilitation indicating greater negativity toward Blacks.

A frequency distribution of these attitude estimates is displayed in Figure 6.2. Note, first of all, the relative position of the Black versus White students in this distribution. Reiterating what was observed in the ANOVAs, the White students were characterized, on average, by negative attitude scores; their mean score was $-.26$, which was significantly different from zero, $t(44) = 6.33$, $p < .001$. The Black students were characterized by positive attitude scores; their mean score was $.33$, $t(7) = 2.51$, $p < .05$. The two means differed significantly from one another, $t(51) = 5.32$, $p < .001$. However, it is also worth noting that there existed

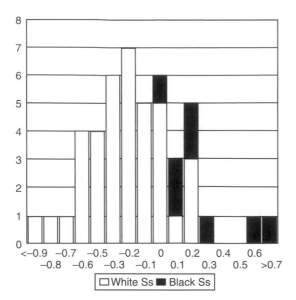

FIGURE 6.2 ■ Frequency distribution of attitude estimates among White and Black subjects. More negative scores reflect more negativity toward Blacks.

considerable variability among the White students. Some of them were characterized by relatively extreme negative attitude estimates. However, some of them were not, and, in fact, some displayed data similar to those displayed by some of the Black students.

Predicting judgment and behavior. One of our goals was to examine how well the attitude estimates, as well as the Modern Racism Scale, served as predictors of judgment and behavior. The value of having reduced the facilitation data to a single attitude estimate for each student is that we could

easily examine how the unobtrusive estimates correlated with some of the other measures that were collected. The correlations presented were calculated only among the White students. The question of interest is the extent to which the variability that was observed among the White students is meaningful in the sense that it is predictive of other judgments and behavior.

The Black experimenter had rated the friendliness and interest that each student had exhibited during the debriefing. These two ratings, which correlated significantly ($r = .37$, $p < .02$), were standardized, and their average was computed as an indication of the overall tone of the interaction. As shown in Table 6.1 the indirect attitude estimates correlated significantly with this measure, whereas the level of modern racism (high vs. low, as indicated by whether the student had been selected on the basis of his or her falling in the top or bottom 10% of the distribution of Modern Racism Scale scores in the mass survey) did not.

In addition to the behavioral measure obtained during the debriefing, students' assessments of the Rodney King trial verdict and the subsequent riots were collected in the opinion survey. Students rated how just the verdict was and how justified the anger of the Black community was. The average of these two ratings, which correlated significantly ($r = .42$, $p = .005$), was computed. This assessment of the verdict correlated well with the level of modern racism but did not correlate with the unobtrusive estimates of attitude based on facilitation scores (see Table 6.1).

However, the unobtrusive attitude estimates did correlate with students' assignment of

TABLE 6.1. Correlation Matrix of Variables in Study 1

Variable	1	2	3	4	5	6
1. Unobtrusive estimate	–					
2. Modern racism level	.15	–				
3. Interaction rating	.31**	−.09	–			
4. Rodney King verdict	−.06	−.53***	.02	–		
5. Responsibility	.32*	−.41***	.26*	.52***	–	
6. Attractiveness	.18	−.35**	.07	.39***	.20	–

Note: Higher scores on the unobtrusive estimate, the interaction rating, the verdict, and the responsibility and attractiveness measures reflect a more favorable response to Blacks. Higher scores on the modern racism level variable reflect a more negative response.
* $p < .10$. ** $p < .05$. *** $p < .01$.

responsibility for the escalation of tension and violence that ensued after the verdict. The responsibility measure was simply the difference between the responsibility assigned to Whites and that assigned to Blacks. This measure correlated well with both our unobtrusive estimates and the level of modern racism.

Although attractiveness ratings were collected in the final phase of the experiment largely for the purpose of setting the stage for the Black experimenter's debriefing of the student, the relation of these data to the other variables also was examined. For each student, a point-biserial correlation was computed between a dichotomous variable representing Black versus White photos and the attractiveness ratings. These within-subject correlations were transformed via Fisher's r-to-z transformation. For the resulting index, more negative scores reflected having rated the Blacks as less attractive than the Whites. This measure correlated significantly with scores on the Modern Racism Scale (more prejudiced students were more likely to rate the Black faces as relatively less attractive) but not with our unobtrusive measure (see Table 6.1).

A factor analysis of these six variables was conducted in the hope of gaining further insight into the nature of their interrelations. Two factors emerged with eigenvalues greater than one; together, these factors accounted for 61.4% of the variance. The factor loadings, following a varimax rotation, are displayed in Table 6.2. The level of modern racism and the unobtrusive estimates clearly loaded on different factors, thus reiterating the independence of modern racism and automatically activated evaluations noted earlier. Consistent with our observations from the correlation

TABLE 6.2. Factor Loadings

Variable	Factor 1	Factor 2
Unobtrusive estimate	−.10	.84
Modern racism level	−.83	.08
Interaction rating	.10	.68
Rodney King verdict	.84	.10
Responsibility	.59	.55
Attractiveness	.66	.05

matrix, the two factors clearly reflect variables that are related to level of modern racism versus those related to the unobtrusive estimates. The interaction rating loaded much more highly on the unobtrusive estimate factor, whereas the Rodney King verdict variable and the attractiveness variable loaded more highly on the modern racism factor. The responsibility variable loaded about equally on both factors. (These two factors receive further discussion later in the context of the findings of the subsequent studies.)

Discussion

The present data are certainly encouraging for what they imply about our unobtrusive measure of attitude. Two findings, in particular, suggest that the measure has some validity. First, the attitude estimates for Black and White students differed markedly. Black and White students displayed very different patterns of facilitation in response to primes that consisted of Black versus White faces. Whereas White students exhibited more negativity in response to Black faces than in response to White faces, Black students displayed the opposite pattern of relatively more negativity toward Whites.

Second, the variability that existed among White students appears meaningful in the sense that it was predictive of at least some race-related judgments and behaviors. Although the attitude estimates for White students were, on average, indicative of negativity toward Blacks, some students displayed more negativity than others. These attitude estimates related significantly to the Black experimenter's ratings of the quality of the interaction that she had with the student. Those students with more negative attitudes toward Blacks, according to the unobtrusive measure, behaved in a less friendly and less interested manner. The measure also proved predictive of the extent to which students assigned responsibility to Blacks versus Whites for the riots in Los Angeles after the Rodney King verdict. In summary, there are a number of indications that the indirect estimates obtained from the pattern of facilitation evident on trials involving positive versus negative adjectives form a valid, unobtrusive measure of attitudes toward Blacks.

These findings are of theoretical, as well as methodological, import. The data illustrate the importance of evaluations that are activated automatically from memory. The meaningful variability that we observed among the White students suggests that a personal evaluation, rather than a socially shared cultural stereotype, is automatically activated on encountering a Black person. Thus, at a theoretical level, the data point to the importance of considering the variability that exists in the automatic component of prejudice.

In addition, the research provides corroboration for the MODE model's (Fazio, 1990) depiction of a spontaneous attitude-to-behavior process and, in particular, for the emphasis that it places on evaluations that are activated from memory automatically. To our knowledge, our consideration of the relation between our unobtrusive measure and behavior toward the Black experimenter represents the very first effort to directly examine the correspondence between automatically activated evaluations and behavior. Although numerous investigations have examined how attitude–behavior consistency varies as a function of attitude accessibility (i.e., the likelihood that the attitude will be activated from memory automatically on encountering the attitude object; see Fazio, 1995, for a review), the present investigation is the first to directly assess the nature of the evaluations that are automatically activated from memory and to use the resulting individual-differences measure as a predictor of behavior.

This is not to say that motivations to control the influences of any negativity that is automatically activated, in the manner that Devine (1989b) has proposed, are irrelevant. It is certainly reasonable to believe that some individuals may experience such automatically activated negativity toward Blacks but work to counter the influence of such negativity so as not to appear prejudiced to themselves or others, or both. As Devine has noted,

change from the status of racially prejudiced to unprejudiced may involve precisely such a stage of attempting to consciously monitor and control one's judgments and behaviors (Devine, 1989a; Devine, Monteith, Zuwerink, & Elliot, 1991; Monteith, Devine, & Zuwerink, 1993). Some such judgments and behavior may be more difficult to control fully than others. It is for such relatively uncontrollable classes of behavior that the effects of any automatically activated personal evaluations are likely to be most apparent.

The single perplexing aspect of the findings from the present investigation was the lack of any apparent relation between our unobtrusive measure and what is probably the most commonly used self-report measure of racial prejudice, namely, the Modern Racism Scale. At the very outset of the investigation, we had been concerned about the relatively unprejudiced nature of a college student population. Indeed, the distribution of scores on the Modern Racism Scale was heavily skewed in our mass survey of nearly 500 students. Relatively few scores fell at the prejudiced end of the scale. It was for this reason that the students who participated in the study were selected from the top and bottom 10% of the distribution. The low-prejudiced students all scored at the endpoint of the scale (-14). The high-prejudiced students scored at 2 or higher.[4] Despite having sampled two groups whose scores differed so markedly, we found no signs of an effect of modern racism level on our facilitation data. The basic Race of Photo × Valence of Adjective interaction was not moderated by modern racism level. Moreover, our unobtrusive measure and modern racism loaded on two distinct factors.

In summary, the present findings suggest that the priming methodology may yield a valid, unobtrusive measure of racial attitudes. However, the discordance between our unobtrusive estimates and scores on the Modern Racism Scale is puzzling. If the unobtrusive measure is as valid as the preliminary findings lead us to believe and if the

---

[4] It was this selection criterion that led to the serendipitous sampling of so many Blacks in our sample. Eight of our 53 students were Blacks, which is much higher than the percentage of Black students on the Bloomington campus. Seven of these 8 Blacks had scores of -14.

Modern Racism Scale is characterized by the validity with which it has been portrayed, then it is reasonable to expect the two measures to correlate with one another. This is the puzzle to which we turned our attention in the next three studies.

The first issue that required attention was whether the null relation observed in Study 1 would replicate. Study 2 attempted such a replication. Moreover, the participants in Study 2 were recruited with different criteria in mind. Study 1 had involved students from the top or bottom 10% of the distribution of Modern Racism Scale scores. In the case of the nonprejudiced group, the students all had the most extreme score possible on the scale (i.e., −14). Thus, they had a response of −2 to each of the seven items on the scale. Although it does not seem very likely, one might argue that there is something unusual about people who consistently use the endpoint of the scale. In addition, the lack of variability within the nonprejudiced group made it impossible to meaningfully examine the relation between our unobtrusive estimates and each of the items of the Modern Racism Scale individually. For these reasons, Study 2 involved a sample of participants recruited so as to form roughly a normal distribution of scores on the Modern Racism Scale.

Study 2

Method

Participants. Forty-nine students, all of whom were White, participated in the study. They were selected from a large sample of students who had completed the Modern Racism Scale as part of a mass survey early in the semester. The students were recruited with the goal of obtaining a roughly normal distribution of scores on the Modern Racism Scale centered around the scale value of 0. This effort was successful and resulted in a sample with a mean score of 0.33 and a standard deviation of 5.11.

Procedure. The stimulus materials and procedure for Study 2 were identical to those used in Study 1.

Results

Facilitation scores, as well as attitude estimates based on the facilitation data, were calculated in the same manner as for Study 1. These attitude estimates, for which lower scores reflect greater negativity toward Blacks, averaged −.14, which was significantly different from zero, $t(48) = 3.27$, $p < .002$. Just as in Study 1, then, students displayed relatively greater facilitation when positive adjectives had been preceded by White than by Black primes and when negative adjectives had been preceded by Black than by White primes.

The attitude estimates were correlated with scores on the Modern Racism Scale, for which higher scores are presumed to reflect greater prejudice. The correlation was .28 ($p < .06$). Although the coefficient did not reach a conventional level of statistical significance, this correlation was in the direction opposite to what was expected. People with less prejudiced scores on the Modern Racism Scale exhibited more negativity toward Blacks on our measure of automatically activated evaluations. That is, more negative scores on the unobtrusive measure tended to be associated with lower, less prejudiced scores on the Modern Racism Scale. When the correlations between the unobtrusive measure and each of the seven scale items were examined individually, none were found to yield a significant correlation in the expected direction; six, three of which were statistically reliable, produced a correlation in the unexpected direction. Thus, just like in Study 1, the data from Study 2 failed to reveal the expected relation between attitude estimates based on the priming technique and Modern Racism Scale scores.

Discussion

Essentially, then, the second study substantiates what was observed in the first. Even when a normally distributed sample was selected, the expected relation between Modern Racism Scale scores and our unobtrusive estimates based on automatically activated evaluations was not observed. What, then, is the Modern Racism Scale measuring?

We have focused our attention on two potential

difficulties with the Modern Racism Scale as the basis for the discordance between the scale and our unobtrusive measure. One issue concerns a confounding variable, and the other concerns the potential reactivity of the scale. First, the scale appears to confound prejudice and political conservatism. Recall that the wording of the items was intended to permit an individual's giving the prejudiced response to be "explained by racially neutral ideology" (McConahay, 1986, p. 100). The racially neutral ideology here is conservatism. Given the nature of the items (e.g., "Over the past few years, the government and news media have shown more respect to Blacks than they deserve" and "Over the past few years, Blacks have gotten more economically than they deserve"), it would appear quite difficult for a political conservative—one who does not value government intervention—to score at the low-prejudiced end of the scale. This confounding has been emphasized by critics of the modern racism perspective, especially Sniderman and Tetlock (1986a, 1986b). In fact, empirical work has documented the existence of a correlation between individuals' self-identification as politically conservative and scores on the Modern Racism Scale (Weigel & Howes, 1985). Yet, experimental results have demonstrated that political conservatives, although less supportive than liberals of governmental assistance of any form, are, if anything, more supportive of such assistance for Black claimants than for White claimants (Sniderman & Piazza, 1993; Sniderman, Piazza, Tetlock, & Kendrick, 1991).

Thus, there appears to be no reason to believe that politically conservative individuals are necessarily racially prejudiced. Nevertheless, such a confounding is implied by Weigel and Howes's (1985) finding and also is readily apparent within our own studies. In our work, the Modern Racism Scale items had been embedded in an opinion survey. Many of these filler items concerned political

issues and were such that a liberal versus conservative side to the issue could be identified. Thirteen of these filler items served as our measure of conservatism. They covered a wide range of topics (e.g., abortion rights, capital punishment, gay rights, censorship, tax increases, defense spending, and sex education) but yielded a scale with quite satisfactory internal consistency (Cronbach's α = .72). This measure of political conservatism was correlated with Modern Racism Scale scores. When our two samples of White students were combined, the correlation was highly significant ($r = .47$, $p < .001$), with more conservative individuals having Modern Racism Scale scores presumably indicative of greater prejudice. Thus, it seems very possible for someone to obtain a high score on the Modern Racism Scale not because he or she is prejudiced but simply because he or she is conservative.[5]

The second difficulty with the Modern Racism Scale concerns its potential reactivity. Despite the claims to the contrary, the scale items appear very obvious and even blatant. The evidence that has been marshalled in support of the scale's nonreactivity comes from research by McConahay, Hardee, and Batts (1981). These researchers had participants complete the modern racism items, as well as the so-called old-fashioned racism items. The latter included such even more blatant and inflammatory statements as "Black people are generally not as smart as Whites" and "It was wrong for the U.S. Supreme Court to outlaw segregation in its 1954 decision." The questionnaire was administered by either a Black or a White experimenter. In each of two experiments, scores on the old-fashioned items, but not the modern items, were influenced by the race of the experimenter. In a third experiment, participants rated the extent to which agreement (or disagreement) with a given item was indicative of a negative attitude toward Blacks. The old-fashioned items were perceived as more indicative of negativity than were the modern racism items, although even the latter were viewed as having significant racial implications relative to filler items that bore no relation to issues of race. On the basis of these findings, McConahay et al. (1981) concluded that

---

[5] In this vein, it is interesting to note that the single Black student from Experiment I whose Modern Racism Scale score led to inclusion in the high-prejudice group had the second highest conservatism score in the entire sample.

these experiments demonstrate that the modern racism scale is a nonreactive measure in this period of history. When there were incentives to fake being less prejudiced, items measuring old-fashioned racism were the ones that subjects could spot and figure out how to fake in a consistently less prejudiced direction. Though the modern racism items might have been recognized as having racial implications, they were not altered very much or very consistently. (p. 577)

It is our belief that the participants' recognition of the racial implications of the modern racism items points to a serious problem in and of itself. The participants in McConahay et al.'s (1981) Experiment 3 perceived agreement with the modern racism items to be indicative of a negative attitude. The failure of participants in the other two experiments to shift toward a less prejudiced direction when the questionnaire was administered by a Black experimenter may bear little relation to the potential reactivity of the scale. They may not have shifted because they may have believed that the attitudes they were expressing were such that they would not offend the Black experimenter. Indeed, the participants were not very prejudiced, according to their Modern Racism Scale scores. At the time, the scale included only six items, ranging from *strongly disagree* (−2) to *strongly agree* (2); possible total scores ranged from −12 (least prejudiced) to 12 (most prejudiced). The mean in the White experimenter condition was −4.2, on the nonprejudiced side of the neutral point. Thus, these participants may have believed that they held the "correct" attitudes on the modern racism items and, hence, felt little pressure to alter their responses in the presence of a Black experimenter. In contrast, they may not have perceived their slight disagreement with the even more blatant, old-fashioned items as sufficiently extreme to satisfy the Black experimenter.

Whether it be for this reason or simply because times have changed since the McConahay et al. (1981) study was conducted, we thought that it would be useful to conduct an experimental test of the reactivity of the Modern Racism Scale. All of our students had participated in a mass survey that included the Modern Racism Scale early in the

semester. As a means of ensuring our sample might have reason to modify their responses, all of the students who participated in the study had scores of at least −1 on the current (−14 to 14) version of the Modern Racism Scale. Thus, our least prejudiced score was considerably more prejudiced than the average score in the McConahay et al. study. The students were administered an opinion survey that included the modern racism items by either a Black or a White experimenter.

Study 3

Method

Participants.   Fifty-eight students participated for payment or partial fulfillment of an introductory psychology course requirement. These individuals were among 552 students who had participated in an earlier mass survey that included the Modern Racism Scale. Students were selected on the basis of their scores on the Modern Racism Scale; those with the highest scores (i.e., high prejudiced) were selected (scores ranged from −1 to 7). Pairs of students were created by matching students with identical scores on the Modern Racism Scale. One member of each pair was then randomly assigned to the Black or the White experimenter condition.

Procedure.   Students were recruited for participation in the experiment 2 to 3 months after the mass survey. On their arrival, students were greeted by a Black or a White female experimenter unaware of their scores on the Modern Racism Scale.

Students were told that they would be completing three short questionnaires. The first questionnaire included the Modern Racism Scale; the other two measures were not related to the present concerns. Each experimenter stressed that because the questionnaires were not computer administered, she would personally input the student's responses into the computer at a later time. This statement was intended to underscore that the experimenter would be aware of the student's responses to questionnaire items.

The format of the Modern Racism Scale was

modified from the format used during the earlier mass survey to minimize the possibility that students would recognize the scale, but the wording and order of the modern racism items were not changed. As before, the items were embedded in a larger opinion survey. However, new filler items were used, the questionnaire was printed on paper of a different color, and the format of the 5-point scale was altered.

Results

The mean Modern Racism Scale scores in the two conditions are presented in Figure 6.3. Naturally, given our creation of matched pairs, the scores in the two conditions were identical when considering the scale completed in the mass survey. However, at Time 2, the scores shifted toward the less prejudiced end of the scale. This was true of both the White experimenter condition, $t(28) = 2.21, p < .04$, and the Black experimenter condition, $t(28) = 6.34, p < .001$. However, as is apparent in Figure 6.3, the movement toward the less prejudiced end of the

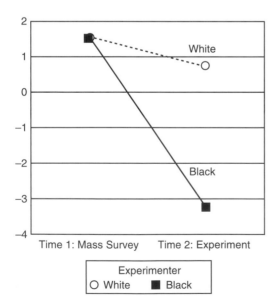

FIGURE 6.3 ■ Mean scores on the Modern Racism Scale at Time 1 and Time 2 in the White and in the Black experimenter conditions. Higher numbers indicate more prejudice.

scale was especially pronounced when the scale was administered by the Black experimenter. An ANOVA revealed the Time × Race of Experimenter interaction to be highly significant, $F(1,56) = 18.19, p < .001$.

Additional analyses revealed that the movement induced by the Black experimenter did not simply shift the entire distribution in a less prejudiced direction. Instead, the relative rank ordering of the students was affected. The correlation between Modern Racism Scale scores obtained in the initial mass survey and the scores obtained at Time 2 was .68 ($p < .001$) when the Time 2 experimenter was White and .29 ($p = .12$) when she was Black. A test of the difference between the two correlations revealed a marginally significant difference ($z = 1.93, p < .054$).

Discussion

On the basis of the present findings, it certainly appears that the Modern Racism Scale is a reactive measure. Students did indeed respond in a less prejudiced manner when interacting with the Black experimenter. Apparently, students were not only aware of the racial implications of the scale items but also motivated to respond in a less prejudiced manner as a result. Thus, the experiment provides evidence that the Modern Racism Scale, like traditional self-report measures, is subject to social desirability concerns.

How might one account for the difference between our results and those of McConahay et al. (1981)? Students in the present sample had average Modern Racism Scale scores that placed them on the prejudiced side of the scale. In contrast, McConahay et al.'s participants had scores that placed them on the nonprejudiced side of the scale. Thus, participants in the present study may have been more motivated to shift toward the nonprejudiced end of the scale than those in McConahay et al.'s study. Participants in McConahay et al.'s (1981) study may not have felt this same pressure because their responses were sufficiently nonprejudiced to raise little concern about social desirability.

Alternatively, or in addition, the difference

between the outcomes of the two studies may simply reflect the possibility that the scale items have become outdated, a possibility that McConahay et al. (1981) seem to have forecast when they concluded that their findings indicated the Modern Racism Scale to be a "nonreactive measure in this period of history" (p. 577). Although McConahay et al.'s (1981) participants were aware of the racial implications of the scale items, they may not have labeled these items as blatantly racist. However, statements that were perceived as subtle and nonracist more than a decade ago may now be perceived as blatantly racist. Indeed, recent research by Swim, Aikin, Hall, and Hunter (1995) suggests that old-fashioned and modern racism scale items are no longer as empirically distinct as they once were. Whether it was because we selected a sample with relatively prejudiced Modern Racism Scale scores or simply because times have changed, the present data clearly contradict the conclusion that the Modern Racism Scale is nonreactive.

It should be emphasized that the Black–White experimenter manipulation merely provides a convenient and effective means of examining the scale's inherent reactivity. It by no means suggests that scores on the Modern Racism Scale are valid with a White experimenter. In our view, social desirability concerns are accentuated when it is evident that a Black experimenter will see the participant's questionnaire. However, the extent to which such factors concern a given individual and the extent to which the concerned individual adjusts his or her responses varies considerably, as is suggested by the differential correlations of Modern Racism Scores across time in the two conditions. Moreover, these concerns are likely to arise for some individuals even when the scale is distributed by a White experimenter (as it was during the initial mass survey), simply as a consequence of the blatantly obvious wording of the scale items. Were it not for the language of the Modern Racism Scale items, the race of the experimenter would matter little. As a result, some truly prejudiced individuals obtain scores presumably indicative of low prejudice, no matter how the scale is administered.

In this context, it is interesting to speculate about the relation that was observed in Study 2 between Modern Racism Scale scores and our unobtrusive estimates of attitude. Recall that the correlation was in the unexpected direction; students for whom more negativity was automatically activated in response to Black faces had lower, less prejudiced scores on the scale. The inherent reactivity of the Modern Racism Scale may have prompted students for whom negative attitudes were automatically activated to present themselves as relatively unprejudiced on the scale items. When faced with such social desirability concerns, these students may have, in effect, overcompensated (i.e., presented themselves as even less prejudiced than individuals for whom little or no negativity toward Blacks is automatically activated).

As noted earlier, another force that contributes to the manner in which respondents complete the Modern Racism Scale is their political conservatism. The Modern Racism Scale appears to be confounded with conservatism. Thus, some truly nonprejudiced individuals obtain scale scores presumably indicative of prejudice simply because they are conservative. It is our contention that these two forces—the scale's reactivity and its confounding with conservatism—yield a distribution of Modern Racism Scale scores that bears little resemblance to the extent to which negative evaluations are automatically activated on encountering a Black individual. These arguments suggest that the Modern Racism Scale may amount to a measure of "willingness to express" negativity toward Blacks that is confounded with political conservatism. This reasoning was tested in Study 4.

Study 4

According to the MODE model (Fazio, 1990), attitudes can influence judgments and behavior via either a spontaneous or a deliberative process. However, the model explicitly postulates the possibility of attitude–behavior processes that are neither purely spontaneous nor purely deliberative but instead are "mixed" processes involving a combination of automatic and controlled components. The MODE model also proposes that a deliberative process, or any controlled component within a mixed sequence, requires that the individual both be motivated to engage in the necessary cognitive effort and have the opportunity to do so.

It is this theoretical perspective that underlies our reasoning regarding individuals' responses to the Modern Racism Scale. Any automatically activated negativity toward Blacks is potentially tempered by a controlled process among individuals who are so motivated. The reactivity that was observed in Study 3 suggests that at least some individuals experience such motivation when responding to the items of the Modern Racism Scale. In Study 4, we directly assessed this motivation to control seemingly prejudiced reactions. Scores on the Modern Racism Scale were predicted to be a function of political conservatism and the joint influence of automatically activated evaluations and the motivation to control prejudice. Thus, when conservatism is controlled, Modern Racism Scale scores should be more predictable from our unobtrusive estimates of automatically activated attitudes as the motivation to control seemingly prejudiced reactions decreases.

Method

Participants. During each of two consecutive semesters, students were selected from a large sample of those who had completed the Modern Racism Scale as part of a mass survey early in the semester. One hundred seventeen students were recruited with the goal of obtaining a wide range of scores on the Modern Racism Scale. The sample's mean score on the scale was −2.33, with a standard deviation of 7.39.

Procedure. The same experimenter conducted the priming procedure in each of the two semesters. Students participated in the same first five procedural tasks used in Study 1, with the exception that 16 Black faces and 16 White faces were paired for the target trials. The remaining 16 photos (Whites, Hispanics, and Asians) were used on the filler trials. Given time constraints and the lack of any need to set the stage for a debriefing by a

Black experimenter, attractiveness ratings were not collected in Study 4.

Motivation to control racial prejudice. Students completed a 17-item scale assessing their motivation to control seemingly prejudiced reactions. The survey included such statements as "In today's society it's important that one not be perceived as prejudiced in any manner"; "If I have a prejudiced thought or feeling, I keep it to myself"; and "It's never acceptable to express one's prejudices." Students responded to each item on a scale ranging from *strongly disagree* (−3) to *strongly agree* (3). The scale's internal consistency within the present sample was more than adequate (Cronbach's α = .81). All of the scale items, as well as additional psychometric details, have been reported by Dunton and Fazio (1995).

Students in one semester completed the scale as their final task in an ostensibly unrelated second session conducted by a different experimenter 1 week after the priming procedure. In the other semester, the scale was included as part of the mass survey.

Political conservatism. As in Studies 1 and 2, political conservatism was estimated by students' responses to relevant filler items in the opinion survey in which the Modern Racism Scale items had been embedded. As before, the internal consistency of this scale was satisfactory (Cronbach's α = .68).

Results

Estimates of automatically activated attitudes were calculated from facilitation scores in the same manner as in Studies 1 and 2. Although not as extremely as in the earlier studies, the average attitude estimate tended to be negative (M = −.046), $t(116)$ = 1.74, p = .084. Moreover, there was considerable variability around this mean (SD = .287).

Complete data (i.e., unobtrusive estimates, motivation to control prejudice scores, and conservatism scores) were available for 111 of the 117 students. The major hypothesis was tested by a multiple regression equation predicting scores on the Modern Racism Scale from conservatism, attitude estimates, motivation scores, and the interaction between the last two variables. When entered simultaneously, the three main effects accounted for a significant proportion of the variance, $R = .57$, $F(3, 107) = 17.57$, $p < .001$. Conservatism was a highly significant predictor, $t(107) = 6.90$, $p < .001$, such that more politically conservative individuals had higher, more prejudiced Modern Racism Scale scores. This finding replicates what was observed earlier in Studies 1 and 2. Higher motivation to control prejudice was significantly associated with lower, less prejudiced scores on the Modern Racism Scale, $t(107) = 2.68$, $p = .01$. No main effect of the attitude estimate was apparent, $t < 1$.

The interaction between attitude estimates and motivation to control prejudice was entered as the next step in the equation and yielded a significant increase of .03 in the squared multiple correlation, $F(1,106) = 5.38$, $p < .025$. Other interaction terms were tested but were not found to add to the prediction of Modern Racism Scale scores. Nor did the semester in which the students participated yield a main effect or any interactions.

The nature of the Attitude × Motivation interaction can be readily discerned from Figure 6.4, which displays the regression lines predicting Modern Racism Scale scores from attitude estimates for motivation to control prejudice scores of 1.07 and −0.59 (one standard deviation above and below the mean of 0.24). As motivation to control prejudice decreases, the relation between the unobtrusive attitude estimates and Modern Racism Scale scores grows stronger, such that more negative automatically activated attitudes are associated with more prejudiced Modern Racism Scale scores. In other words, motivation to control prejudice matters little among those for whom little or no negativity is automatically activated in response to Black faces. However, motivation to control seemingly prejudiced reactions exerts a strong influence among those individuals for whom negativity is automatically activated. Those with little such motivation feel free to respond to the Modern Racism Scale items in a manner that is indicative

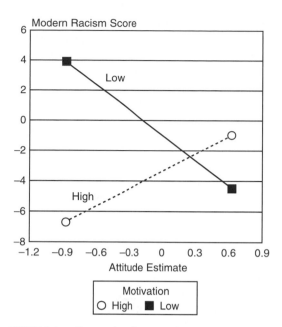

FIGURE 6.4 ■ Regression lines predicting scores on the Modern Racism Scale as a function of the unobtrusive attitude estimates and motivation to control prejudice. Higher scores indicate more prejudice.

of prejudice, whereas more motivated individuals present themselves as far less prejudiced.

Discussion

The results of Study 4 confirm the predictions advanced by the MODE model and our reasoning regarding the Modern Racism Scale, as well as attesting further to the predictive validity of our unobtrusive estimates of racial attitude. As suggested earlier, the Modern Racism Scale assesses willingness to express prejudice and conservatism. Unprejudiced individuals can score high on the scale if they endorse a conservative political philosophy. Truly prejudiced individuals will score high on the scale, provided that they are not motivated to control prejudiced reactions. Relatively low scores on the Modern Racism Scale, on the other hand, can emanate either from individuals' being truly unprejudiced or from their being motivated to control their prejudiced reactions.

Obviously, individuals can control their responses to the Modern Racism Scale items if they are motivated to do so. The interaction that was observed between automatically activated attitudes and motivation indicates that individuals who lack such motivation respond in a manner that is consistent with their automatically activated attitudes. In contrast, individuals who are motivated to control prejudiced reactions do not respond in accord with their automatically activated attitudes. Indeed, the positive slope that was observed among those with high motivation suggests that individuals who are highly motivated to control their automatically activated negativity may actually overcompensate. They presented themselves as even less prejudiced than similarly motivated individuals for whom negativity is not automatically activated. This observation is consistent with our earlier conjecture regarding the positive correlation between Modern Racism Scale scores and our unobtrusive estimates in Study 2, a correlation that was in the direction opposite to what was expected. Apparently, a preponderance of the students in Study 2 were relatively motivated to control prejudiced reactions.

The findings certainly suggest that researchers need to be extremely cautious in using the Modern Racism Scale. Given the myriad of factors that influence individuals' responses to the scale items, it will be difficult to draw any clear inferences from findings based on the scale scores. This is not to say that the Modern Racism Scale is not without predictive validity. Indeed, it was found to be predictive of some race-related judgments in Study 1. Given that the Modern Racism Scale measures willingness to express negativity toward Blacks, along with conservatism, it should be predictive of any judgments that themselves involve either or both of these dimensions. Thus, for example, it should correlate reasonably well with any judgment that is itself influenced by conservatism.[6] Likewise, it should correlate reasonably well with any judgment that provokes the same concerns with social sensitivity. In this case, individuals who are willing to express negativity on the Modern Racism Scale are equally likely to be willing to express negativity on some other clearly race-related judgment.

General Discussion

The major aim of the present research concerned the value of using the priming paradigm that has been used to study automatic attitude activation as an unobtrusive measure of racial attitudes. The priming procedure appears to provide a bona fide pipeline for attitude measurement. It permits assessment of the extent to which judgments of positive versus negative adjectives are facilitated by primes consisting of Black faces relative to primes consisting of White faces. As noted earlier, the findings of Study 1 suggest that attitude estimates derived from the resulting patterns of facilitation have some validity. Similarly, the results of Study 4 indicate that the unobtrusive attitude estimates are predictive of responses to the Modern Racism Scale for individuals who are relatively unmotivated to control any prejudiced reactions that they may experience.

The results of the research clearly attest to the importance of the variability that exists among people with respect to the evaluations that are likely to be activated from memory automatically on encountering a minority individual. The theoretical assumption offered by Devine (1989a, 1989b) concerning the automatic activation of a socially shared, cultural stereotype involving negativity toward Blacks does not appear tenable in light of the present results. Nevertheless, the findings, especially those from Study 4, imply that it may be useful to identify, broadly speaking, three types of individuals, one of whom is very appropriately characterized by Devine's model. The three types vary with respect to the evaluation that is automatically activated and with respect to the extent to which the evaluation is countered by a subsequent controlled process. First, some indi-

---

[6] In fact, conservatism scores did correlate significantly with judgments of the Rodney King verdict ($r = .35$, $p < .025$). More conservative individuals viewed the verdict as more appropriate, which may have contributed to the relation observed between modern racism level and verdict judgments.

viduals do not experience the automatic activation of any negative evaluation from memory on encountering a Black person (or may experience activation of a positive evaluation relative to what occurs when they encounter a White target). We would label these individuals as truly nonprejudiced. Second, negativity is automatically activated for other individuals. Some such people may have no qualms about their experiencing such negativity or about expressing it. It seems appropriate to label these individuals as truly prejudiced. Third, as Devine (1989a, 1989b) has postulated, some individuals for whom negativity is automatically activated may be motivated to counter the effects of that negativity.[7] This motivation may vary from a sincere distaste for the negative reaction that was automatically evoked on encountering a Black individual to a more strategic self-presentation dictated by perceptions of the social norms for the particular situation in which the individual was encountered. In either case, the expression of judgments and the performance of overt behavior may be carefully and deliberately monitored so as to avoid the appearance of a prejudiced response. The more the efforts to inhibit and control one's automatically activated negativity stem from a sincere displeasure with one's having experienced such negativity, the more one would appear to be moving toward a truly nonprejudiced stand. The importance of such self-dissatisfaction has been documented by recent research concerned with the process of prejudice reduction (Devine et al., 1991; Monteith, 1993; Monteith et al., 1993).

We believe that the MODE model (Fazio, 1990) provides a useful theoretical framework for considering the influence of automatic and controlled processes in race-related judgments and behavior (see Dovidio & Fazio, 1992). As noted earlier, the model asserts that motivation is necessary to engage in the cognitive effort required to counter any automatically activated negativity. In this particular domain, the relevant motivation concerns a desire to control and avoid seemingly prejudiced responses. Whether this motivation is engaged in any given situation will depend on individuals' construal of the situation and the judgmental or behavioral response that is being requested of them. Construing the situation and requested response as related to their racial attitudes will evoke such motivation among any individuals who share these concerns.

The interactive influence of automatically activated attitudes and motivation to control prejudice that characterized responses to the Modern Racism Scale in Study 4 presumably stemmed from such construals. In fact, the reactivity that was demonstrated in Study 3 illustrates that the scale items are perceived as related to racial attitudes. We would suggest that any requested judgment or behavior that is construed as related to racial attitudes will evoke motivational concerns. Study 1's assessments of the Rodney King verdict and of the attractiveness of the Black and White faces, both of which were found to load highly on the same factor as the Modern Racism Scale, are likely to have been of this sort. To some extent, the same may have been true of Study 1's assessment of Black versus White responsibility for the riots that followed announcement of the verdict, a measure that loaded highly on both the modern racism and the unobtrusive estimate factors.

According to the MODE model, the opportunity factor will be the key determinant of whether any motivation that is activated can successfully counter the influence of automatically activated negativity. As mentioned earlier, efforts to control any automatically activated negativity may vary in their likelihood of success. Some behaviors may be more easily monitored and controlled than others.

---

[7] A fourth class of individuals, one that can be viewed as a subcategory of the second class, may be identifiable. As noted earlier, some individuals may have negative evaluations of Blacks but not be aware of their sentiments or experience any automatically activated negativity phenomenologically (see Greenwald & Banaji, 1995). Nevertheless, such individuals' behavior would presumably be influenced by their automatically activated attitudes. Yet, they may not realize that there is any need for them to monitor and control their behavior. In this sense, such individuals are similar to individuals who are aware of their negativity but have no reservations about expressing it. For both such types, the automatically activated negativity is not tempered by a controlled process.

Likewise, some situations (e.g., those that do not place the individual under any time pressure to respond) may offer a greater opportunity for the motivated individual to engage in the desired controlling effort than other situations (Jamieson & Zanna, 1989; Kruglanski & Freund, 1983; Sanbonmatsu & Fazio, 1990). Judgments and behaviors that provide the opportunity for controlling one's response should be predictable from the joint, interactive influence of automatically activated attitudes and motivation to control prejudice, just as we observed for the Modern Racism Scale. Such controllable responses also are likely to be well predicted from other measures, like the Modern Racism Scale, that are similarly influenced by the extent to which the individual is willing to express a response that is identifiable as prejudiced. However, as opportunity decreases, either because the behavior is not easily controllable or because the situation itself limits the opportunity, the behavior should be less influenced by motivational concerns and more directly influenced by any automatically activated evaluations. Thus, as the opportunity to satisfy one's motivation to control prejudice decreases, the behavior should be more and more predictable from attitude estimates based on automatically activated evaluations.

Nonverbal behavior, in particular, may be subject to "leakage" of the negativity that an individual is experiencing, despite the individual's effort to behave in a nonprejudiced manner (see Ambady & Rosenthal, 1992; Rosenthal & DePaulo, 1979). Indeed, one of the most interesting of our findings may be the ability of our unobtrusive measure to predict the Black experimenter's judgment of the quality of the interaction she had with the student. Apparently, those students for whom negative evaluations were automatically activated on the presentation of a Black face behaved more distantly during their interaction with her. Given what is known about nonverbal behavior and leakage, this automatically activated negativity would be difficult for such an individual to conceal during an interaction with a Black. Such leakage may have played a role in the correspondence that was observed between the unobtrusive attitude estimates and the experimenter's ratings of the quality

of the interaction. Obviously, this finding requires replication before any conclusions can be reached with confidence. Yet, the finding does suggest that our unobtrusive measure can directly predict behavior, especially when the behavior measure is one that is likely to be difficult to control strategically and, hence, is influenced largely by automatically activated attitudes unmoderated by any motivation to control prejudice. We look forward to future research pursuing these possibilities in a systematic and detailed fashion.

REFERENCES

Ambady, N., & Rosenthal, R. (1992). Thin slices of expressive behaviors as predictors of interpersonal consequences: A meta-analysis. *Psychological Bulletin, 111,* 256–274.

Banaji, M. R., & Greenwald, A. G. (1994). Implicit stereotyping and prejudice. In M. Zanna & J. Olson (Eds.), *The psychology of prejudice: The Ontario symposium* (Vol. 7, pp. 55–76). Hillsdale, NJ: Erlbaum.

Banaji, M. R., & Greenwald, A. G. (1995). Implicit gender stereotyping in judgments of fame. *Journal of Personality and Social Psychology, 68,* 181–198.

Bargh, J. A., Chaiken, S., Govender, R., & Pratto, F. (1992). The generality of the automatic activation effect. *Journal of Personality and Social Psychology, 62,* 893–912.

Crosby, F., Bromley, S., & Saxe, L. (1980). Recent unobtrusive studies of Black and White discrimination and prejudice: A literature review. *Psychological Bulletin, 87,* 546–563.

Devine, P. G. (1989a). Automatic and controlled processes in prejudice: The role of stereotypes and personal beliefs. In A. R. Pratkanis, S. J. Breckler, & A. G. Greenwald (Eds.), *Attitude structure and function* (pp. 181–212). Hillsdale, NJ: Erlbaum.

Devine, P. G. (1989b). Stereotypes and prejudice: Their automatic and controlled components. *Journal of Personality and Social Psychology, 56,* 5–18.

Devine, P. G., Monteith, M. J., Zuwerink, J. R., & Elliot, A. J. (1991). Prejudice with and without compunction. *Journal of Personality and Social Psychology, 60,* 817–830.

Dovidio, J. F., Evans, N., & Tyler, R. B. (1986). Racial stereotypes: The contents of their cognitive representations. *Journal of Experimental Social Psychology, 22,* 22–37.

Dovidio, J. F., & Fazio, R. H. (1992). New technologies for the direct and indirect assessment of attitudes. In J. Tanur (Ed.), *Questions about questions: Inquiries into the cognitive bases of surveys* (pp. 204–237). New York: Russell Sage Foundation.

Dovidio, J. F., & Gaertner, S. L. (1991). Changes in the nature and expression of racial prejudice. In H. Knopke, J. Norrell, & R. Rogers (Eds.), *Opening doors: An appraisal of race* relations in contemporary America (pp. 201–241). Tuscaloosa: University of Alabama Press.

Dunton, B. C., & Fazio, R. H. (1995). *An individual difference measure of motivation to control prejudiced reactions.* Unpublished manuscript, Indiana University, Bloomington.

Fazio, R. H. (1986). How do attitudes guide behavior? In R. M. Sorrentino & E. T. Higgins (Eds.), *The handbook of motivation and cognition* (pp. 204–243). New York: Guilford Press.

Fazio, R. H. (1990). Multiple processes by which attitudes guide behavior: The MODE model as an integrative framework. In M. P. Zanna (Ed.), *Advances in experimental social psychology.* (Vol. 23, pp. 75–109). New York: Academic Press.

Fazio, R. H. (1993). Variability in the likelihood of automatic attitude activation: Data re-analysis and commentary on Bargh, Chaiken, Govender, and Pratto (1992). *Journal of Personality and Social Psychology, 64,* 753–758, 764–765.

Fazio, R. H. (1995). Attitudes as object-evaluation associations: Determinants, consequences, and correlates of attitude accessibility. In R. E. Petty & J. A. Krosnick (Eds.), *Attitude strength: Antecedents and consequences* (pp. 247–282). Hillsdale, NJ: Erlbaum.

Fazio, R. H., Sanbonmatsu, D. M., Powell, M. C., & Kardes, F. R. (1986). On the automatic activation of attitudes. *Journal of Personality and Social Psychology, 50,* 229–238.

Gaertner, S. L., & Dovidio, J. F. (1986). The aversive form of racism. In J. F. Dovidio & S. L. Gaertner (Eds.), *Prejudice, discrimination, and racism* (pp. 61–89). Orlando, FL: Academic Press.

Gaertner, S. L., & McLaughlin, J. P. (1983). Racial stereotypes: Associations and ascriptions of positive and negative characteristics. *Social Psychology Quarterly, 46,* 23–30.

Gilbert, D. T., & Hixon, J. G. (1991). The trouble of thinking: Activation and application of stereotypic beliefs. *Journal of Personality and Social Psychology, 60,* 509–517.

Greenwald, A. G., & Banaji, M. R. (1995). Implicit social cognition: Attitudes, self-esteem, and stereotypes. *Psychological Review, 102,* 4–27.

Hermans, D., De Houwer, J., & Eelen, P. (1994). The affective priming effect: Automatic activation of evaluative information in memory. *Cognition and Emotion, 8,* 515–533.

Jackson, J. R., & Fazio, R. H. (1994, May). *Assessment of racial attitudes.* Paper presented at the annual meeting of the Midwestern Psychological Association, Chicago.

Jackson, J. R., & Fazio, R. H. (1995, May). *The effect of race of experimenter on responses to the Modern Racism Scale: A test of reactivity.* Paper presented at the annual meeting of the Midwestern Psychological Association, Chicago.

Jamieson, D. W., & Zanna, M. P. (1989). Need for structure in attitude formation and expression. In A. R. Pratkanis, S. J. Breckler, & A. G. Greenwald (Eds.), *Attitude structure and function* (pp. 383–406). Hillsdale, NJ: Erlbaum.

Jones, E. E., & Sigall, H. (1971). The bogus pipeline: A new paradigm for measuring affect and attitude. *Psychological Bulletin, 76,* 349–364.

Jonides, J., & Mack, R. (1984). On the cost and benefit of cost and benefit. *Psychological Bulletin, 96,* 29–44.

Kruglanski, A. W., & Freund, T. (1983). The freezing and unfreezing of lay-inferences: Effects on impressional primacy, ethnic stereotyping, and numerical anchoring. *Journal of Experimental Social Psychology, 19,* 448–468.

McConahay, J. B. (1986). Modern racism, ambivalence, and the modern racism scale. In J. F. Dovidio & S. L. Gaertner (Eds.), *Prejudice, discrimination, and racism* (pp. 91–125). Orlando, FL: Academic Press.

McConahay, J. B., Hardee, B. B., & Batts, V. (1981). Has racism declined in America? It depends on who is asking and what is asked. *Journal of Conflict Resolution, 25,* 563–579.

Monteith, M. J. (1993). Self-regulation of prejudiced responses: Implications for progress in prejudice-reduction efforts. *Journal of Personality and Social Psychology, 65,* 469–485.

Monteith, M. J., Devine, P. G., & Zuwerink, J. R. (1993). Self-directed versus other-directed affect as a consequence of prejudice-related discrepancies. *Journal of Personality and Social Psychology, 64,* 198–210.

Nisbett, R. E., & Wilson, T. D. (1977). Telling more than we know: Verbal reports on mental processes. *Psychological Review, 84,* 231–259.

Perdue, C. W., Dovidio, J. F., Gurtman, M. B., & Tyler, R. B. (1990). "Us" and "them": Social categorization and the process of intergroup bias. *Journal of Personality and Social Psychology, 59,* 475–486.

Perdue, C. W., & Gurtman, M. B. (1990). Evidence for the automaticity of ageism. *Journal of Experimental Social Psychology, 26,* 199–216.

Rosenthal, R. (1991). *Meta-analytic procedures for social research.* Newbury Park, CA: Sage.

Rosenthal, R., & DePaulo, B. M. (1979). Sex differences in accommodation in nonverbal communication. In R. Rosenthal (Ed.), *Skill in nonverbal communication: Individual differences* (pp. 68–103). Cambridge, MA: Oelgeschlager, Gunn, & Hain.

Sanbonmatsu, D. M., & Fazio, R. H. (1986, October). *The automatic activation of attitudes toward products.* Paper presented at the meeting of the Association for Consumer Research, Toronto, Ontario, Canada.

Sanbonmatsu, D. M., & Fazio, R. H. (1990). The role of attitudes in memory-based decision making. *Journal of Personality and Social Psychology, 59,* 614–622.

Sanbonmatsu, D. M., Osborne, R. E., & Fazio, R. H. (1986, May). *The measurement of automatic attitude activation.* Paper presented at the annual meeting of the Midwestern Psychological Association, Chicago, IL.

Sigall, H., & Page, R. (1971). Current stereotypes: A little fading, a little faking. *Journal of Personality and Social Psychology, 19,* 247–255.

Sniderman, P. M., & Piazza, T. (1993). *The scar of race.* Cambridge, MA: Harvard University Press.

Sniderman, P. M., Piazza, T., Tetlock, P. E., & Kendrick, A.

(1991). The new racism. *American Journal of Political Science, 35,* 423–447.

Sniderman, P. M., & Tetlock, P. E. (1986a). Reflections on American racism. *Journal of Social Issues, 42,* 173–187.

Sniderman, P. M., & Tetlock, P. E. (1986b). Symbolic racism: Problems of motive attribution in political analysis. *Journal of Social Issues, 42,* 129–150.

Swim, J. K., Aikin, K. J., Hall, W. S., & Hunter, B. A. (1995). Sexism and racism: Old-fashioned and modern prejudices. *Journal of Personality and Social Psychology, 68,* 199–214.

Weigel, R. H., & Howes, P. W. (1985). Conceptions of racial prejudice: Symbolic racism reconsidered. *Journal of Social Issues, 41,* 117–138.

Received January 19, 1995
Revision received July 5, 1995
Accepted July 10, 1995 ■

Measuring Individual Differences in Implicit Cognition: The Implicit Association Test

Anthony G. Greenwald, Debbie E. McGhee, and Jordan L. K. Schwartz

An implicit association test (IAT) measures differential association of 2 target concepts with an attribute. The 2 concepts appear in a 2-choice task (e.g., flower vs. insect names), and the attribute in a 2nd task (e.g., pleasant vs. unpleasant words for an evaluation attribute). When instructions oblige highly associated categories (e.g., flower + pleasant) to share a response key, performance is faster than when less associated categories (e.g., insect + pleasant) share a key. This performance difference implicitly measures differential association of the 2 concepts with the attribute. In 3 experiments, the IAT was sensitive to (a) near-universal evaluative differences (e.g., flower vs. insect), (b) expected individual differences in evaluative associations (Japanese + pleasant vs. Korean + pleasant for Japanese vs. Korean subjects), and (c) consciously disavowed evaluative differences (Black + pleasant vs. White + pleasant for self-described unprejudiced White subjects).

Consider a thought experiment. You are shown a series of male and female faces, to which you are to respond as rapidly as possible by saying "hello" if the face is male and "goodbye" if it is female. For a second task, you are shown a series of male and female names, to which you are to respond rapidly with "hello" for male names and "goodbye" for female names. These discriminations are both designed to be easy—the faces and names are unambiguously male or female. For a final task you are asked to perform both of these discriminations alternately. That is, you are shown

Anthony G. Greenwald, Debbie E. McGhee, and Jordan L. K. Schwartz, Department of Psychology, University of Washington.

This research was partially supported by Grant SBR-9422242 from the National Science Foundation and Grant MH 41328 from the National Institute of Mental Health. For comments on a draft of this article, the authors thank Mahzarin Banaji, Shelly Farnham, Laurie Rudman, and Yuichi Shoda.

Correspondence concerning this article should be addressed to Anthony G. Greenwald, Department of Psychology, Box 351525, University of Washington, Seattle, Washington 98195-1525. Electronic mail may be sent to agg@u.washington.edu.

a series of alternating faces and names, and you are to say "hello" if the face or name is male and "goodbye" if the face or name is female. If you guess that this combined task will be easy, you are correct.

Now imagine a small variation of the thought experiment. The first discrimination is the same ("hello" to male faces, "goodbye" to female faces), but the second is reversed ("goodbye" to male names, "hello" to female names). As with the first experiment, each of these tasks, by itself, is easy. However, when you contemplate mixing the two tasks ("hello" to male face or female name and "goodbye" to female face or male name), you may suspect that this new combined task will be difficult. Unless you wish to make many errors, you will have to respond considerably more slowly than in the previous experiment.

The expected difficulty of the experiment with the reversed second discrimination follows from the existence of strong associations of male names to male faces and female names to female faces. The attempt to map the same two responses ("hello" and "goodbye") in opposite ways onto the two gender contrasts is resisted by well-established associations that link the face and name domains. The (assumed) performance difference between the two versions of the combined task indeed measures the strength of gender-based associations between the face and name domains. This pair of thought experiments provides the model for a method, the implicit association test (IAT), that is potentially useful for diagnosing a wide range of socially significant associative structures. The present research sought specifically to appraise the IAT method's usefulness for measuring evaluative associations that underlie implicit attitudes (Greenwald & Banaji, 1995).

Measuring Implicit Attitudes

Implicit attitudes are manifest as actions or judgments that are under the control of automatically activated evaluation, without the performer's awareness of that causation (Greenwald & Banaji, 1995, pp. 6–8).[1] The IAT procedure seeks to measure implicit attitudes by measuring their underlying automatic evaluation. The IAT is therefore similar in intent to cognitive priming procedures for measuring automatic affect or attitude (e.g., Bargh, Chaiken, Govender, & Pratto, 1992; Fazio, Sanbonmatsu, Powell, & Kardes, 1986; Fazio, 1993; Greenwald, Klinger, & Liu, 1989; Perdue, Dovidio, Gurtman, & Tyler, 1990; Perdue & Gurtman, 1990).[2]

One might appreciate the IAT's potential value as a measure of socially significant automatic associations by changing the thought experiment to one in which the to-be-distinguished faces of the first task are Black or White (e.g., "hello" to African American faces and "goodbye" to European American faces) and the second task is to classify words as pleasant or unpleasant in meaning ("hello" to pleasant words, "goodbye" to unpleasant words). The two possible combinations of these tasks can be abbreviated as Black + pleasant and White + pleasant.[3] Black + pleasant should be easier than White + pleasant if there is a stronger association between Black Americans and pleasant meaning than between White Americans and pleasant meaning. If the preexisting associations are opposite in direction—which might be expected for White subjects raised in a culture imbued with pervasive residues of a history of anti-Black discrimination—the subject should find White + pleasant to be easier.

A possible property of the IAT—and one that is

----

[1] Greenwald and Banaji (1995) defined implicit attitudes as "introspectively unidentified (or inaccurately identified) traces of past experience that mediate favorable or unfavorable feeling, thought, or action toward social objects" (p. 8).

[2] A few recent studies have indicated that priming measures may be sensitive enough to serve as measures of individual differences in the strength of automatic attitudinal evaluation (Dovidio & Gaertner, 1995; Fazio, Jackson, Dunton, & Williams, 1995). At the same time, other studies have indicated that priming is relatively unaffected by variations in attitude strength (Bargh et al., 1992; Chaiken & Bargh, 1993), implying that it may be limited in sensitivity to intra- or interindividual differences.

[3] *Black + pleasant* means that African American faces and pleasant words share the same response; it could equally have been described as *White + unpleasant*.

similar to a major virtue of cognitive priming methods—is that it may resist masking by self-presentation strategies. That is, the implicit association method may reveal attitudes and other automatic associations even for subjects who prefer not to express those attitudes.

Design of the IAT

Figure 7.1 describes the sequence of tasks that constitute the IAT measures in this research and illustrates this sequence with materials from the present Experiment 3. The IAT assesses the association between a *target-concept discrimination* and an *attribute dimension*. The procedure starts with introduction of the target-concept discrimination. In Figure 7.1, this initial discrimination is to distinguish first names that are (in the United States) recognizable as Black or African American from

ones recognizable as White or European American. This and subsequent discriminations are performed by assigning one category to a response by the left hand and the other to a response by the right hand. The second step is introduction of the attribute dimension, also in the form of a two-category discrimination. For all of the present experiments, the attribute discrimination was evaluation, represented by the task of categorizing words as pleasant versus unpleasant in meaning. After this introduction to the target discrimination and to the attribute dimension, the two are superimposed in the third step, in which stimuli for target and attribute discriminations appear on alternate trials. In the fourth step, the respondent learns a reversal of response assignments for the target discrimination, and the fifth (final) step combines the attribute discrimination (not changed in response assignments) with this reversed target discrimination. If the target categories are

Sequence	1	2	3	4	5
Task description	*Initial target-concept discrimination*	*Associated attribute discrimination*	*Initial combined task*	*Reversed target-concept discrimination*	*Reversed combined task*
Task instructions	● BLACK WHITE ●	● pleasant unpleasant ●	● BLACK ● pleasant WHITE ● unpleasant ●	BLACK ● ● WHITE	BLACK ● ● pleasant ● WHITE unpleasant ●
Sample stimuli	MEREDITH ○ ○ LATONYA ○ SHAVONN HEATHER ○ ○ TASHIKA KATIE ○ BETSY ○ ○ EBONY	○ lucky ○ honor poison ○ grief ○ gift disaster ○ ○ happy hatred ○	○ JASMINE ○ pleasure PEGGY ○ evil ○ COLLEEN ○ ○ miracle ○ TEMEKA bomb ○	○ COURTNEY ○ STEPHANIE SHEREEN ○ ○ SUE-ELLEN TIA ○ SHARISE ○ ○ MEGAN MICHELLE ○	peace LATISHA ○ filth ○ ○ LAUREN ○ rainbow SHANISE ○ accident ○ NANCY

FIGURE 7.1 ■ Schematic description and illustration of the implicit association test (IAT). The IAT procedure of the present experiments involved a series of five discrimination tasks (numbered columns). A pair of target concepts and an attribute dimension are introduced in the first two steps. Categories for each of these discriminations are assigned to a left or right response, indicated by the black circles in the third row. These are combined in the third step and then recombined in the fifth step, after reversing response assignments (in the fourth step) for the target-concept discrimination. The illustration uses stimuli for the specific tasks for one of the task-order conditions of Experiment 3, with correct responses indicated as open circles.

differentially associated with the attribute dimension, the subject should find one of the combined tasks (of the third or fifth step) to be considerably easier than the other, as in the male–female thought experiments. The measure of this difficulty difference provides the measure of implicit attitudinal difference between the target categories.

Overview of Research

Because the present three experiments sought to assess the IAT's ability to measure implicit attitudes, in each experiment the associated attribute dimension was evaluation (pleasant vs. unpleasant).[4] Each experiment investigated attitudes that were expected to be strong enough to be automatically activated.

Experiment 1 used target concepts for which the evaluative associations were expected to be highly similar across persons. Two of these concepts were attitudinally positive (flowers and musical instruments) and two were negative (insects and weapons). Experiment 2 used two groups of subjects (Korean American and Japanese American) to assess ethnic attitudes that were assumed to be mutually opposed, stemming from the history of military subjugation of Korea by Japan in the first half of the 20th century. The IAT method was expected to reveal these opposed evaluations even for subjects who would deny, on self-report measures, any antipathy toward the out-group. Experiment 3 used the IAT to assess implicit attitudes of White subjects toward White and Black racial categories. For these subjects we expected that the IAT might reveal more attitudinal discrimination between White and Black categories than would be revealed by explicit (self-report) measures of the same racial attitudes.

Experiment 1

Experiment 1 used the IAT to assess implicit attitudes toward two pairs of target attitude concepts for which subjects were expected to have relatively uniform evaluative associations. A second purpose was to examine effects on IAT measures of several procedural variables that are intrinsic to the IAT method. Subjects in Experiment 1 responded to two target-concept discriminations: (a) flower names (e.g., *rose, tulip, marigold*) versus insect names (e.g., *bee, wasp, horsefly*) and (b) musical instrument names (e.g., *violin, flute, piano*) versus weapon names (e.g., *gun, knife, hatchet*). Each target-concept discrimination was used in combination with discrimination of pleasant-meaning words (e.g., *family, happy, peace*) from unpleasant-meaning words (e.g., *crash, rotten, ugly*). The IAT procedure was expected to reveal superior performance for combinations that were evaluatively compatible (flower + pleasant or instrument + pleasant) than for noncompatible combinations (insect + pleasant or weapon + pleasant).

Method

After being seated at a table with a desktop computer in a small room, subjects received all instructions from a computer display and provided all of their responses via the computer keyboard.

Subjects

Thirty-two (13 male and 19 female) students from introductory psychology courses at the University of Washington participated in exchange for an optional course credit.[5] Data for 8 additional subjects were not included in the analysis because of their relatively high error rates, which were associated with responding more rapidly than appropriate

---

[4] The IAT can be used also to measure implicit stereotypes and implicit self-concept (see Greenwald & Banaji, 1995) by appropriate selection of target concept and attribute discriminations.

[5] Another group of 32 subjects participated in a prior replication of Experiment 1 that, however, lacked the paper-and-pencil explicit measures that were included in the reported replication. With one minor exception (mentioned in Footnote 11), there were no discrepancies in findings between the two replications.

for the task.[6] Data were unusable for one additional subject who, for unknown reasons, neglected to complete the computer-administered portion of the experiment.

Materials

The experiment's three classification tasks used 150 stimulus words: 25 insect names, 25 flower names, 25 musical instrument names, 25 weapon names, 25 pleasant-meaning words, and 25 unpleasant-meaning words. The pleasant and unpleasant words were selected from norms reported by Bellezza, Greenwald, and Banaji (1986). Many of the items for the other four categories were taken from category lists provided by Battig and Montague (1969), with additional category members generated by the authors. The selected flower, insect, instrument, and weapon exemplars were ones that the authors judged to be both familiar to and unambiguously classifiable by members of the subject population. The 150 words used as stimuli in Experiment 1 are listed in Appendix A.

Apparatus

Experiment 1 was administered on IBM-compatible (80486 processor) desktop computers.[7] Subjects viewed this display from a distance of about 65 cm and gave left responses with left forefinger (using the A key) and right responses with right forefinger (using the 5 key on the right-side numeric keypad).

Overview

Each subject completed tasks for two IAT measures in succession, one using flowers versus insects

as the target-concept discrimination, and the other using musical instruments versus weapons. The first IAT used the complete sequence of five steps of Figure 7.1: (a) initial target-concept discrimination, (b) evaluative attribute discrimination, (c) first combined task, (d) reversed target-concept discrimination, and (e) reversed combined task. The second IAT did not need to repeat practice of the evaluative discrimination, and so included only four steps: (f) initial target-concept discrimination, (g) first combined task, (h) reversed target-concept discrimination, and (i) reversed combined task. One IAT measure of attitude was obtained by comparing performance in steps (c) and (e), and the second by comparing performance in steps (g) and (i).

Design

The two IAT measures obtained for each subject were analyzed in a design that contained five procedural variables, listed here and described more fully in the *Procedure* section: (a) order of the two target-concept discriminations (flowers vs. insects first or instruments vs. weapons first), (b) order of compatibility conditions within each IAT (evaluatively compatible combination of discriminations before or after noncompatible combination), (c) response key assigned to pleasant items (left or right), (d) category set sizes for discriminations (5 items or 25 items per category), and (e) interval between response and next item presentation for the combined task (100, 400, or 700 ms). The first four of these were two-level between-subjects variables that were administered factorially, such that 2 subjects received each of the 16 possible combinations; the last was a three-level within-subjects variation.

Procedure

Trial blocks.   All tasks were administered in trial blocks of 50 trials. Each trial block started with instructions that described the category discrimination(s) for the block and the assignments of response keys (left or right) to categories. Reminder labels, in the form of category names

---

[6] Use of data from these 8 subjects (instead of those who replaced them in the design) would have reduced power of statistical tests. As it turns out, this would not have altered any conclusions. The higher power obtained by replacing them was desirable because of the importance of identifying possible procedural influences on the IAT method.

[7] The programs used for all of the present experiments were Windows 95-based and written primarily by Sean C. Draine.

appropriately positioned to the left or right, remained on screen during each block. Each new category discrimination—in Steps (a), (b), and (f) described in the *Overview* section—consisted of a practice block of 50 trials followed by a block for which data were analyzed. Combined tasks consisted of a practice block followed by three blocks of data collection, each with a different intertrial interval (see next paragraph).

Timing details. The first trial started 1.5 s after the reminder display appeared. Stimuli were presented in black letters against the light gray screen background, vertically and horizontally centered in the display and remaining on screen until the subject's response. The subject's keypress response initiated a delay (intertrial interval) before the next trial's stimulus. For all simple categorization and combined-task practice trials, the intertrial interval was 400 ms. For the three blocks of combined-task data collection, the interval was either 100, 400, or 700 ms. Half of the subjects received these intervals in ascending order of blocks (100, 400, 700), and the remainder in the opposite order. Throughout the experiment, after any incorrect response, the word *error* immediately replaced the stimulus for 300 ms, lengthening the intertrial interval by 300 ms. At the end of each 50-trial block, subjects received a feedback summary that gave their mean response latency in milliseconds and percentage correct for the just-concluded block.

Stimuli. Words were selected randomly and without replacement (independently for each subject) until the available stimuli for a task were exhausted, at which point the stimulus pool was replaced if more trials were needed. For example, in single-discrimination tasks (a) in the 25-items-per-category condition, each 50-trial block used each of the 50 stimuli for the two categories once, and (b) in the 5-items-per-category condition, each of the 10 stimuli was used five times each. Selection of subsets of five items for the 5-items-per-category conditions was counterbalanced so that all stimuli were used equally in the experiment. For the combined tasks, stimuli were selected such that (a) for subjects assigned to 25-item categories,

each of the 100 possible stimuli—50 target-concept items and 50 evaluative items—appeared twice in a total of 200 combined-task trials, or (b) for those assigned to 5-item categories, each of the 20 possible stimuli appeared 10 times. In all combined tasks, items for the target-concept discrimination and the attribute discrimination appeared on alternating trials.

Explicit attitude measures. After the computer tasks, subjects completed paper-and-pencil questionnaire measures of their attitudes toward the four target concepts. On the feeling thermometer, subjects were asked to describe their general level of warmth or coolness toward flowers, insects, musical instruments, and weapons (in that order) by making a mark at the appropriate position on an illustration of a thermometer. The thermometer was numerically labeled at 10-degree intervals from 0 to 99 and anchored at the 0, 50, and 99 points with the words *cold or unfavorable, neutral,* and *warm or favorable,* respectively. Next, subjects completed a set of five semantic differential items for each of the four object categories. These 7-point scales were anchored at either end by polar-opposite adjective pairs: *beautiful–ugly, good–bad, pleasant–unpleasant, honest–dishonest,* and *nice–awful.* Subjects were instructed to mark the middle of the range if they considered both anchoring adjectives to be irrelevant to the category. The semantic differential was scored by averaging the five items for each concept, scored on a scale ranging from –3 (*negative*) to 3 (*positive*).

Results

Data reduction

The data for each trial block included response latencies (in milliseconds) and error rates. Prior to conducting other analyses, distributions of these measures were examined, revealing the usual impurities (for speeded tasks) in the form of small proportions of extremely fast and extremely slow responses. These outlying values typically indicate, respectively, responses initiated prior to perceiving the stimulus (anticipations) and momentary inattention. The values in these tails of the latency distribution are problematic not only because they lack theoretical interest but also because they distort means and inflate variances. The solution used for these was to recode values below 300 ms to 300 ms and those above 3,000 ms to 3,000 ms.[8] We then log-transformed latencies in order to use a statistic that had satisfactory stability of variance for analyses.[9] Also, the first two trials of each block were dropped because of their typically lengthened latencies. Analyses of error rates are not described in detail. However, they (a) revealed relatively low error rates, averaging just under 5% in Experiment 1, and (b) were consistent with latency analyses (higher error rates were obtained for conditions that produced longer latencies), but (c) also revealed considerably weaker effects of task-compatibility combinations than were obtained in analyses of latencies.

A summary measure of IAT effect

Figure 7.2 displays mean latencies for the nine successive tasks of Experiment 1 (see *Overview* section), presented separately for the two levels of the only procedural variable that substantially influenced the data, whether subjects performed evaluatively compatible combinations before noncompatible ones, or vice versa. Evaluatively compatible combinations (either flower + pleasant or instrument + pleasant) are shown as white bars in Figure 7.2, and noncompatible combinations (insect + pleasant or weapon + pleasant) as black

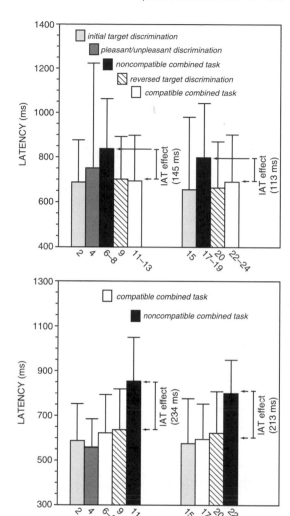

FIGURE 7.2 ■ Mean (untransformed) latency results of Experiment 1 (*N* = 32), separately for subjects who performed at evaluatively noncompatible combinations before evaluatively compatible ones (upper panel) and those who performed compatible combinations first (lower panel). Data were combined for subjects for whom the first implicit attitude test (IAT) measure used a target discrimination of flowers versus insects and those for whom the first target discrimination was weapons versus instruments. Because results were indistinguishable for the two target-concept discriminations (flower vs. insect and instrument vs. weapon) data for both were collapsed over this design factor in the figure. The first block that introduced each new discrimination or combined task was treated as practice and not included in the figure. Error bars are standard deviations for the 16 subjects contributing to each mean.

---

[8] This recoding solution to the problem of outlying data is an alternative to simply dropping trials outside the 300- and 3,000-ms (or other such) boundaries. It has the advantage of being relatively insensitive to (a) differences among conditions in the proportions of trials in the upper versus lower tails, and (b) the choice of specific lower and upper boundaries. Selection of alternative nearby boundaries would yield unchanged conclusions.

[9] Additional analyses were also conducted on speeds (1,000 ÷ latency in milliseconds, a reciprocal conversion that is interpretable as items per second), which is an alternative method of stabilizing latency variance. All conclusions based on analyses of log-transformed latencies were equally evident on the speed measure.

bars. An *IAT effect* is defined as the difference in mean latency between these two conditions (noncompatible minus compatible). For the data presented in Figure 7.2, IAT effects averaged 129 ms when noncompatible combinations preceded compatible (upper panel) and 223 ms when compatible combinations came first. For this effect of compatibility order, $F(1, 16) = 10.12$, $p = .006$.

In Experiment 1, IAT effects indicating more positive attitudes toward flowers than insects or toward musical instruments than weapons were expected and were also quite clearly obtained. That is, subjects performed faster for flower + pleasant or instrument + pleasant combinations than for insect + pleasant or weapon + pleasant. Using the pooled standard deviation (for compatible and noncompatible conditions) as the effect size unit and collapsing across all design factors other than order of compatibility conditions, effect sizes for the IAT effect (i.e., differences from zero) were $d = 0.78$ and $d = 2.30$, respectively, for the noncompatible first and compatible first conditions. (By convention, $d = 0.8$ is considered to be a large effect size.) Statistical significance tests for difference of these IAT effects from zero were, respectively, $F(1, 8) = 25.62$, $p = .001$, and $F(1, 8) = 134.53$, $p = 10^{-6}$.[10]

Effects of procedural variables

The design had five procedural factors, one varied within-subject (intertrial interval) and four varied between-subjects: Combination compatibility order (compatible combination first or second), category set size (5 or 25 items), key assignment for pleasant category (left or right key), and target-

concept order (flowers vs. insects or instruments vs. weapons as the first target-concept discrimination). The main effect of combination compatibility order has already been noted and described in Figure 7.2. Aside from an uninterpretable four-way interaction effect, there were no other significant effects of these procedural variables.[11]

IAT compared with explicit attitude measures

The IAT effect index is proposed as a measure of subjects' relative implicit attitudes toward the categories under study. That is, better performance in the flower + pleasant condition than in the insect + pleasant condition is taken to indicate a stronger association between flowers and pleasant meaning than between insects and pleasant meaning and, thus, a more positive attitude toward flowers than insects.

Table 7.1 presents data for the IAT latency measure along with corresponding attitude measures derived from the feeling thermometer and semantic differential measures. All measures are difference scores, with positive scores indicating more favorable attitudes toward flowers than insects, or toward musical instruments than weapons. For all of these measures, attitude differences were observed.

Correlations among the explicit and implicit attitude measures are shown in Table 7.2. The table presents correlations between measures for the flower–insect contrast above the diagonal and those for the musical instrument–weapon contrast below the diagonal. All of the correlations in Table 7.2 are in the expected positive direction. Notably,

---

[10] These statistical tests were based on the log-transformed latencies. Here and elsewhere in this report, p values are reported as approximately exact values, rather than as inequalities relative to a Type I error criterion (e.g., $p < .05$). This follows the suggestion by Greenwald, Gonzalez, Guthrie, and Harris (1996) not to obscure information provided by p values. Values smaller than .0001 are rounded to the nearest exponent of 10. This treatment of p values notwithstanding, the primary reporting of data is in terms of descriptively more useful raw and standardized effect sizes. For comparison, analysis of untransformed latencies yielded $F(1, 8)$ ratios of 18.97 and

72.45, ps = .002 and 10^{-5}, respectively. Analyses of reciprocally transformed latencies (speeds) yielded $F(1, 8)$ ratios of 26.72 and 198.15, ps = .0009 and 10^{-6}, respectively.

[11] Fortunately, the uninterpretable four-way interaction did not appear in the prior replication (see Footnote 5) and so appears not to call for effort at interpretation. In other respects, however, the prior replication produced IAT effects that were very similar in magnitude to those shown in Figure 7.2, and it also revealed the same effect of combination compatibility order that was obtained in Experiment 1.

TABLE 7.1. Summary Statistics for Difference-Score Attitude Indexes

Attitude measure	M	SD	d[a]	t(31)	p
Flowers vs. insects					
Feeling thermometer	51.1	31.8	1.61	9.09	10^{-10}
Semantic differential	2.58	1.50	1.72	9.75	10^{-10}
IAT (log latency)	.234	.173	1.35	7.66	10^{-8}
IAT (latency)	166.8	140.2	1.19	6.73	10^{-7}
Instruments vs. weapons					
Feeling thermometer	46.4	42.2	1.10	6.22	10^{-6}
Semantic differential	2.94	1.28	2.30	13.01	10^{-14}
IAT (log latency)	.246	.148	1.66	9.42	10^{-10}
IAT (latency)	185.5	134.9	1.37	7.78	10^{-8}

Note: Positive scores indicate preference for flowers relative to insects, and musical instruments relative to weapons. The thermometer range was –99 to 99, and the semantic differential range was –6 to 6. IAT = implicit association test.
[a] The effect size measure **d** = M ÷ SD. Conventional small, medium, and large values of **d** are .2, .5, and .8, respectively.

TABLE 7.2. Correlations Among Implicit and Explicit Attitude Measures

Measure	Explicit attitude		Implicit attitude	
	1	2	3	4
1. Thermometer	*.53*	.70	**.13**	**.16**
2. Semantic differential	.79	*.27*	**.12**	**.20**
3. IAT effect (log latency)	**.29**	**.19**	*.59*	.95
4. IAT effect (latency)	**.27**	**.19**	.93	*.57*

Note: Correlations above the diagonal involve the flower–insect contrast, below the diagonal are those for the instrument–weapon contrast, and on the main diagonal, in italics, are correlations between corresponding measures for the two contrasts. Correlations between explicit and implicit attitude measures are printed in bold. All measures were scored so that higher scores indicate more positive attitude toward flowers or musical instruments. N = 32 for all correlations; two-tailed p values of .10, .05, .01, .005, and .001 are associated, respectively, with r values of .30, .35, .45, .49, and .56. IAT = implicit association test.

however, scores on the explicit measures for both the flower–insect and instrument–weapon contrasts were only weakly correlated with implicit attitude scores derived from the IAT.

Discussion

Experiment 1 tested the principal assumption underlying the implicit association test: that associations can be revealed by mapping two discrimination tasks alternately onto a single pair of responses. Confirming expectation, consistently superior performance was observed when associatively compatible (compared with associatively noncompatible) categories were mapped onto the same response. In Experiment 1, both flower–insect and instrument–weapon discriminations were performed more rapidly when their evaluatively positive categories (flowers or musical instruments) shared a response with pleasant-meaning words than when those categories shared a response with unpleasant-meaning words. Of importance, the data (Figure 7.2) indicated that compatible task combinations were performed about as rapidly as the uncombined target concept or attribute discriminations, whereas noncompatible combinations were performed considerably more slowly. These findings were clearly encouraging regarding the possibility that the IAT method can effectively measure implicit attitudes. In summary, Experiment 1's IAT measures were highly sensitive to evaluative discriminations that are well established in the connotative meaning structure of the English language.

Experiment 1 was remarkable for the near absence of moderating effects of procedural variables on the measures of evaluative associations that were revealed by the IAT procedure. The effect of task–combination compatibility was not noticeably affected (a) by intertrial intervals (100, 400, or 700 ms), (b) by the set size of categories used in discrimination tasks (5 or 25 items), (c) by the assignment of response key (left or right) to the pleasant category, or (d) by position of the IAT measure within the experiment (first or second internal replication). The variation of order in which compatible and noncompatible task combinations were performed produced a moderate effect, such that the IAT measure of differential evaluation was larger when the compatible combination was performed first. This effect is examined also in Experiments 2 and 3.

Last, Experiment 1 provides the first of a series of findings of low correlations between explicit and implicit measures (see Table 7.2). The correlations between explicit measures of different contrasts (flower–insect with instrument–weapon, average $r = .41$) and between implicit measures of different contrasts (average $r = .58$) were strikingly greater than those between explicit and implicit measures of the same contrast (average $r = .19$).[12] This pattern indicates the likely presence of systematic method variance for both types of measures, along with a divergence in the constructs measured by the two types of measures. This conceptual divergence between the implicit and explicit measures is of course expected from theorization about implicit social cognition (Greenwald & Banaji, 1995), as well as from previous research findings such as those already mentioned by Dovidio and Gaertner (1995) and Fazio, Jackson, Dunton, and Williams (1995). It is also plausible, however, that these correlations are low because of relative lack of population variability in the attitudes being assessed (e.g., uniformity in liking for flowers or disliking for insects).

Experiment 2

Experiment 1 demonstrated the IAT's ability to detect presumed near-universal evaluative associations involving the semantic contrasts of flowers versus insects and instruments versus weapons. Perhaps because the evaluative aspects of these contrasts are so nearly uniform in the population, they are not typically considered to be attitudinal. Experiment 2 sought to extend the IAT method to a domain that is more typically attitudinal, by using it to discriminate differences between Japanese Americans and Korean Americans in their evaluative associations toward Japanese and Korean ethnic groups. The history of Japanese–Korean antagonism provided the basis for a known-groups study in which it could be expected that each ethnic group would have not only a typical in-group-directed positive attitude but also a likely negative attitude toward the out-group.[13] To supplement the IAT results, we also obtained explicit measures of these ethnic attitudes along with measures intended to gauge participants' level of immersion in the cultures of their respective ethnicities.

Method

Subjects

The subjects were 17 self-described Korean American (8 female and 9 male) and 15 Japanese American (10 female and 5 male) students who participated in return for optional course credit for their introductory psychology courses at the University of Washington. Data for one of the Korean Americans were not included in analyses because of an IAT error rate of about 50%, indicative of random responding. These subjects were recruited in response to a request for volunteers belonging to the two ethnic groups. As part of the consent procedure prior to participation, subjects were informed that the experiment could reveal attitudes that they would prefer not to express and were reminded that they were free to withdraw at any time.

Materials and apparatus

In addition to the 25 pleasant-meaning and 25 unpleasant-meaning words used in Experiment 1, 25 Korean and 25 Japanese surnames were used.

---

[12] All averaged correlations were computed by averaging the Fisher's Z conversions of r values, then reconverting the average of these Fisher Zs to r.

[13] From 1905 to 1945, the Japanese occupied Korea, exploiting Koreans economically and repressing them politically. At present, Koreans are a discriminated against minority in Japan.

These Korean and Japanese surnames were selected with the help of two Korean and two Japanese judges, who were asked to rate the typicality and ease of categorizing each of a larger set of surnames that had been selected on the basis of their frequency in the Seattle telephone directory. Because Japanese names are typically longer than Korean names, a set of 25 truncated Japanese names was generated from the 25 selected Japanese surnames, such that for each Korean name, there was a truncated Japanese name of the same length. For example, the Japanese name *Kawabashi* was truncated to *Kawa* to match the length of the Korean name *Youn* while retaining the Japanese character of the name. The truncated Japanese names were used only after subjects had received several exposures to the full-length versions. Evaluative words were presented in lowercase, whereas Korean and Japanese names were presented in uppercase. The apparatus was the same as used for Experiment 1.

Procedure

IAT measures. As in Experiment 1, subjects completed two IAT measures. For the first IAT measure, the target-concept discrimination was Korean names versus full-length Japanese names. For the second, the discrimination was Korean names versus truncated Japanese names. Other than the replacement of Experiment 1's target-concept discriminations with the Japanese versus Korean name discrimination, Experiment 2 had only two substantial differences of procedure from Experiment 1. First, the intertrial interval independent variable was dropped, and all blocks of trials were conducted with a 250 ms interval between response to one stimulus and presentation of the next. Second, combined tasks consisted of one practice block followed by two data-collection blocks (contrasted with Experiment 1's use of three data-collection blocks, each with a different intertrial interval). For half of the subjects, Japanese names were initially assigned to the left key, Korean to the right; the reverse assignment was used for the remaining subjects. Throughout the experiment, all subjects responded to unpleas-

ant words with the left key and pleasant words with the right key. (The omission of counterbalancing for key assignment was a consequence of Experiment 1's finding that key assignment for the pleasant–unpleasant discrimination did not affect findings.)

The second IAT differed from the first in (a) omitting practice of the pleasant–unpleasant discrimination (as in Experiment 1), (b) using the truncated Japanese names in place of the full-length ones, and (c) using opposite key assignments for the initial target-concept discrimination. The last of these three changes was instituted because of Experiment 1's demonstration that order of performance for the target discrimination and its reversal influenced magnitude of observed IAT effect. The consequence of the change was that subjects who performed the first IAT with the Japanese + pleasant combination first performed the second IAT with the Korean + pleasant combination first.

Ethnic identity and attitude questionnaires. After the computer administered IAT tasks, subjects completed several paper-and-pencil questionnaire measures. The first three measures, which were prepared specifically for this experiment, assessed the extent to which subjects were involved in sociocultural networks that were ethnically Japanese or Korean.

The first measure asked subjects to provide initials of "up to twenty people, *not family members*, that you know." Subjects were instructed that listing close friends was preferable but that they could also list acquaintances. The instructions did not alert subjects to the researchers' interest in ethnicity of these acquaintances (information that was to be requested later), although subjects could well have been sensitized to ethnicity from both the inclusion of ethnic name discriminations in the IAT procedure and their knowledge of having been recruited by virtue of their ethnicity. After completing the next two measures, subjects were instructed to turn back to the list of initials and to mark each to indicate which of the following labels provided the best description: Korean, Korean American,

Japanese, Japanese American, none of the above, or don't know. This acquaintances measure was scored to indicate the percentage of those listed who were ethnically Korean or Korean American and the percentage who were ethnically Japanese or Japanese American.

For the second measure, subjects were asked to indicate the number of members of their family who would be described by each of the following labels: Korean, Korean American, Japanese, Japanese American, and American. This yielded percentage scores of those mentioned who were ethnically Korean and ethnically Japanese, treating each Korean American as 50% Korean and 50% American, and similarly for Japanese Americans.

The third measure asked subjects to respond to eight yes–no items, four each concerned with Korean and Japanese language. These items asked, respectively, whether subjects could understand, speak, read, and write each language, each answered on a 3-point scale with $0 = no$, $1 = somewhat$, and $2 = yes$. This yielded 9-point language scales (summing responses, range 0–8) for both the Korean and the Japanese language.

Next followed feeling thermometer and semantic differential measures of attitude toward Japanese and Koreans, which were identical to the corresponding measures of Experiment 1 except for the change of concepts for which responses were requested. All of the first five measures were scored by conversion to a difference score (Korean minus Japanese), for which positive values indicated numerically greater scores for the Korean submeasure.

A sixth and final questionnaire measure was the 23-item Suinn–Lew Asian Self-Identity Acculturation Scale (Suinn, Rickard-Figueroa, Lew, & Vigil, 1987). Unlike the preceding five measures, all of which yielded a comparison of involvement in or attitude toward Korean and Japanese cultures, the Suinn–Lew acculturation measure indicated involvement in Asian (relative to American) culture.

Results and Discussion

IAT effects

Figure 7.3 presents Experiment 2's results separately for the counterbalanced variable of order of performing the Korean + pleasant versus Japanese + pleasant combinations, and also separately for the Korean American and Japanese American subject subsamples. The expectation for Experiment 2's data was that ethnically Korean subjects would find it more difficult to perform the Japanese + pleasant than the Korean + pleasant combination (appearing as higher white than black bars in Figure 7.3) and that the reverse should be true for ethnically Japanese subjects (higher black than white bars). Figure 7.3 reveals these expected patterns (higher white than black bars in the left panels; higher black than white bars in the right panels). Using the log-latency IAT-effect measure as a dependent variable, analyses for the effect of subject ethnicity yielded $F(1, 28)$ ratios of 28.53 and 31.93 for the subexperiments with full-length and truncated Japanese names, respectively (both $ps = 10^{-5}$). There were no other significant effects in the design that included also Japanese name length (first vs. second subexperiment) and order of administration of the task combinations. The IAT effect was very similar in magnitude for the first subexperiment with full length Japanese names (mean IAT effect = 105.3 ms) and the second one with truncated Japanese names ($M = 92.8$ ms), $F(1, 27) = 0.58$, $p = .45$. Also, there was a weak order effect of the same type found in Experiment 1: IAT effects were slightly larger when own-ethnicity + pleasant was performed first ($M = 117.0$ ms) than when other-ethnicity + pleasant was performed first ($M = 84.3$ ms). This difference, however, was nonsignificant, $F(1, 27) = 0.37$, $p = .55$.

IAT compared with explicit measures

Table 7.3 presents Korean and Japanese subject means for the log-latency IAT measure, along with those for the five paper-and-pencil measures that yielded Korean–Japanese difference scores, with all measures scored so that higher numbers were expected for Korean subjects. For example, the

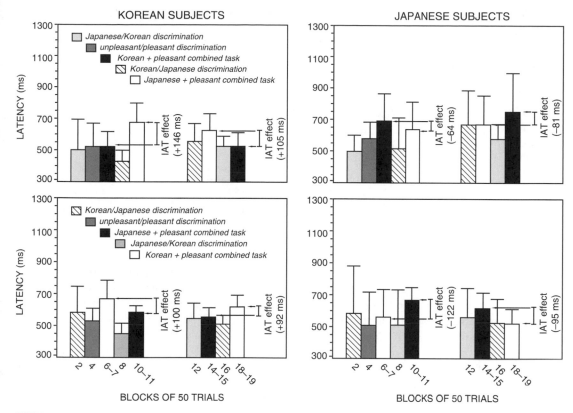

FIGURE 7.3 ■ Mean (untransformed) latency results of Experiment 2, separately for 16 Korean American and 15 Japanese American subjects and for subjects who received the two orders of presentation for own-ethnicity + pleasant combination and other-ethnicity + pleasant combinations. Error bars are within-cell standard deviations for the 7 to 9 observations (subjects) contributing to each mean. IAT = implicit association test.

TABLE 7.3. Summary Statistics for Difference Scores in Comparison of Ethnicity Discrimination by Seven Measures

Attitude measure[a]	Korean M	Japanese M	SD	d[c]	t[d]	p
Feeling thermometer	18.88	−2.43	12.81	1.65	4.51	.0001
Semantic differential	0.43	−0.31	0.83	0.89	2.33	.02
IAT (full names)	.159	−.144	.161	1.88	5.26	10^{-5}
IAT (truncated names)	.139	−.119	.126	2.04	5.70	10^{-5}
Acquaintances	36.0	−6.4	22.4	1.89	4.88	10^{-5}
Family	64.5	−38.0	38.62	2.65	7.02	10^{-7}
Language	5.50	−2.50	3.37	2.37	6.58	10^{-7}

Note: All difference measures were scored so that positive differences are expected for ethnically Korean subjects and negative differences for ethnically Japanese subjects. Implicit association test (IAT) measures were based on natural logarithm transformations. Effect sizes were slightly smaller for untransformed latency measures.

[a] For Korean/Japanese groups, respectively, $N = 16/14$ for feeling thermometer and semantic differential; $N = 16/15$ for IAT names (full and truncated); $N = 16/13$ for acquaintances; $N = 14/14$ for family; and $N = 16/14$ for language.
[b] Standard deviation is the pooled within-cell values for the two-group (Japanese vs. Korean) design.
[c] The effect size measure **d** is computed by dividing the Korean minus Japanese mean difference by the pooled standard deviation. Conventional small, medium, and large values for **d** are .2, .5, and .8, respectively.
[d] For *t* tests, degrees of freedom varied from 26 to 30 depending on sample size (see Note a).

TABLE 7.4. Correlations Among Explicit and Implicit Measures of Ethnic Attitudes and Measures of Acculturation

Measure	Explicit attitude		Implicit attitude		Ethnic identity		
	1	2	3	4	5	6	7
1. Feeling thermometer	—						
2. Semantic differential	.43	—					
3. IAT (full names)	**.64**	**.12**	—				
4. IAT (truncated names)	**.53**	**−.04**	.85	—			
5. Acquaintances	.70	.48	*.60*	*.52*	—		
6. Family	.77	.39	*.67*	*.65*	.65	—	
7. Language	.69	.34	*.74*	*.70*	.69	.86	—

Note: Measures are the same as those in Table 7.3, scored so that higher scores are expected for ethnically Korean than for ethnically Japanese subjects. $N = 31$ (16 Korean, 15 Japanese), reduced to 28, 29, or 30 for correlations involving Measures 5–7. For $N = 28$, two-tailed *p* values of .10, .05, .01, .005, and .001 are associated, respectively, with *r* values of .32, .37, .46, .52, and .58. Correlations between explicit attitude measures (Nos. 1 and 2) and implicit measures (Nos. 3 and 4) are in bold, and correlations between implicit measures and ethnic identity measures (Nos. 5, 6, and 7) are in italics. IAT = implicit association test.

language score was computed by subtracting the 9-point measure of the subject's knowledge of Japanese language from the corresponding measure for the Korean language. Perhaps the most noteworthy result in the table is that the IAT's measure of ethnic attitudes discriminated Korean from Japanese subjects more effectively than did three of the five questionnaire measures. Only the language and family measures discriminated Japanese American from Korean American subjects with greater effect sizes (**d**s = 2.65 and 2.37) than did the two IAT measures (**d**s = 2.04 and 1.88).

Correlations of the two IAT log-latency measures with the other five measures of Table 7.3 are shown in Table 7.4. All but one correlation was in the expected positive direction. Surprisingly, the semantic differential was uncorrelated with the two IAT measures. This observation strongly suggests that the semantic differential and the IAT measured different constructs.

The strength of correlations of the implicit measures with the acquaintances, family, and language measures suggested the possibility of an analysis using individual differences within the Korean American and Japanese American subsamples. For this analysis, the acquaintances, family, and language measures were converted to absolute values and rescaled so that all were on a 0–100 scale. The acculturation measure was also converted to a 0–100 range. The resulting four measures were averaged to construct an index that was

interpretable as measuring immersion in Asian culture. It was expected that the IAT effect measure should show greater Korean–Japanese differentiation for subjects who were immersed in their particular Asian culture (i.e., had high proportions of family members and acquaintances in that culture and were familiar with the language). The analysis to test this expectation is shown in Figure 7.4, where it can be seen that, indeed, IAT differentiation between the Korean and Japanese subsamples was greater with higher immersion in Asian culture. The test of significance for difference in slopes for the subsample regression functions in Figure 7.4 yielded an $F(1, 26)$ of 9.83, $p = .004$. Remarkably, the intersection of the two regression functions near the left side of Figure 7.4 indicates that an IAT effect of approximately zero would be expected for subjects who had zero immersion in their Asian culture.[14]

Unexpectedly, the feeling thermometer explicit measure was correlated more highly with the IAT measure (average $r − .59$) than it was with another explicit attitude measure, the semantic differential

---

[14] By contrast, neither explicit measure showed the same property. Interaction $F(1, 26)$ ratios were 2.69, $p = .11$, and 0.04, $p = .85$, for feeling thermometer and semantic differential measures, respectively. The nonsignificant interaction effect on the thermometer was, however, directionally the same as that for the IAT.

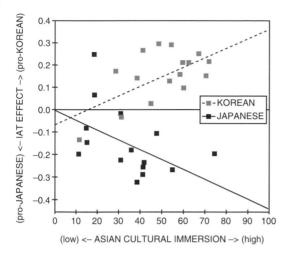

FIGURE 7.4 ■ Implicit association test (IAT) effect data of Experiment 2 (N = 30) as a function of an index of immersion in Asian culture that combined four measures. The trend lines are the individual regression slopes for the Korean American and Japanese American subsamples. The IAT measure is the average of the two measures obtained for each subject (one using full-length and one using truncated Japanese names).

($r = .43$). The semantic differential measure itself was uncorrelated with the IAT (average $r = .04$) but was modestly correlated with the three ethnic identity measures (average $r = .41$). Although this pattern is somewhat puzzling, it does not undermine the impressive evidence for validity of the IAT provided by the data in Figure 7.4. There, it can be seen that the IAT was most effective in diagnosing ethnicity for subjects who were highly involved with their Asian American culture. These findings indicate that the IAT is sensitive to the expected covariation of positivity of ethnic-name-to-evaluation associations with level of exposure to the culture of one's ethnic group.

Experiment 3

Experiment 3 was motivated by several previous demonstrations of automatic expressions of race-related stereotypes and attitudes that are consciously disavowed by the subjects who display them (Crosby, Bromley, & Saxe, 1980; Devine, 1989; Fazio et al., 1995; Gaertner & McLaughlin,

1983; Greenwald & Banaji, 1995; Wittenbrink, Judd, & Park, 1997). This experiment used the IAT procedure to measure an implicit attitude that might not readily be detected through explicit self-report measures. Experiment 3's IAT method combined the tasks of classifying Black versus White names and discriminating pleasant versus unpleasant word meanings.

Method

Subjects

The subjects were 14 female and 12 male White American students from introductory psychology courses at the University of Washington. The students received optional course credit in return for participation. As in Experiment 2, the pre-experiment consent procedure advised subjects that the experiment could reveal attitudes that they might find objectionable and reminded them that they could withdraw at any time.

Materials and procedure

With the exception of two unpleasant words that were changed, the 25 pleasant-meaning and 25 unpleasant-meaning words used in Experiment 3 were the same as those used in Experiments 1 and 2. Two 50-item sets of first names were also used, one consisting of 25 male names that had been judged by introductory psychology students to be more likely to belong to White Americans than to Black Americans (e.g., Brandon, Ian, and Jed) and 25 male names that had been judged to be more likely to belong to Blacks than to Whites (e.g., Darnell, Lamar, and Malik). The other set consisted of 50 female first names, similarly selected (e.g., White: Betsy, Katie, and Nancy; Black: Ebony, Latisha, and Tawanda). Evaluative words were presented in lowercase and names were presented in uppercase.

Except for the replacement of Japanese and Korean names with Black and White names, Experiment 3 was virtually identical to Experiment 2. Like Experiment 2, Experiment 3 also contained two subexperiments, the first using male names and the second using female names.

After completing the computer-administered IAT tasks, subjects responded to five questionnaire measures of race-related attitudes and beliefs. To allow subjects to know that they would be responding in privacy, they completed these questionnaires in their experimental booths and were informed that they would be placing their completed questionnaires in an unmarked envelope before returning them to the experimenter. The measures included feeling thermometer and semantic differential measures similar to those of the previous two experiments (but targeted at the racial concepts of Black and White), the Modern Racism Scale (MRS; McConahay, Hardee, & Batts, 1981), and two measures developed by Wittenbrink, Judd, and Park (1997), their Diversity and Discrimination scales. The Diversity Scale assesses attitudes about the value of multiculturalism, and the Discrimination Scale assesses beliefs about the causes and pervasiveness of discrimination in American society.

Results and Discussion

IAT effects

The data of Experiment 3 (see Figure 7.5) clearly revealed patterns consistent with the expectation that White subjects would display an implicit attitude difference between the Black and White racial categories. More specifically, the data indicated an implicit attitudinal preference for White over Black, manifest as faster responding for the White + pleasant combination (white bars in Figure 7.5) than for the Black + pleasant combination (black bars). The magnitude of this IAT effect averaged 179 ms over the four White + pleasant versus Black + pleasant contrasts shown in Figure 7.5. For the separate tests with male names and female names, respectively, Fs$(1, 21) = 41.94$ and 28.83, ps $= 10^{-6}$ and 10^{-5}. This finding indicates that, for the White college-student subjects of Experiment 3, there was a considerably stronger association of White (than of Black) with positive evaluation. For comparison, these effects, measured in milliseconds, were larger than those observed for the Korean–Japanese contrast in Experiment 2, and even slightly larger than those for the flower–insect

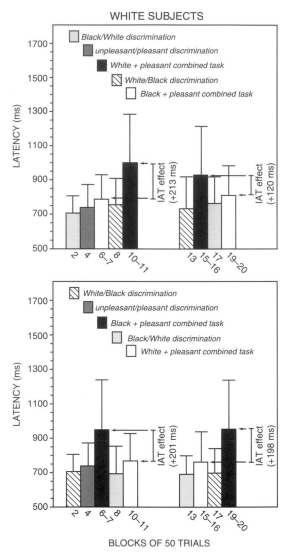

FIGURE 7.5 ■ Mean untransformed latency data of Experiment 3 ($N = 26$). Results are shown separately for subjects who performed the White + pleasant combination first ($n = 13$) and those who performed the Black + pleasant combination first ($n = 13$). Error bars are standard deviations for the 13 observations included in each mean. IAT = implicit association test.

and instrument–weapon contrasts in Experiment 1. However, measured in log-latency units or effect sizes, Experiments 3's IAT effects were smaller than those of Experiment 1.

There were no significant effects of order of administering task combinations in Experiment 3,

$Fs(1, 21) = 0.03$ and 2.01, $ps = .86$ and .17, respectively, for the tests with male and female names. The direction of this weak and nonsignificant effect indicated, once again, that IAT effects are slightly larger when an evaluatively compatible task combination precedes an evaluatively noncompatible one. (This assumes that for the White subjects of Experiment 3, it is appropriate to call the White + pleasant combination evaluatively compatible, relative to the Black + pleasant combination.)

IAT compared with explicit measures

Table 7.5 presents the IAT measures from the two subexperiments (for male and female names) along with the feeling thermometer and semantic differential measures, each in the form of a difference score for which the value 0.0 indicates equivalent attitudes toward Black and White. The four measures in Table 7.5 were computed so that positive

numbers would indicate preference for Black relative to White.

As can be seen in Table 7.5, the IAT measures indicated considerably stronger relative preference for White than did either the feeling thermometer or semantic differential measure. Remarkably, the semantic differential index indicated a virtual absence of racial preference, reminiscent of the weak sensitivity of Experiment 2's semantic differential measure to Korean versus Japanese ethnicity (see Table 7.3). The thermometer index, along with the two IAT measures, indicated statistically significant relative preference for White. The magnitude (effect size) of the pro-White preference was approximately twice as great for the IAT measures as for the thermometer measure.

Table 7.6 presents the correlations involving the four measures of Table 7.5, along with the three additional explicit (self-report questionnaire) measures that were obtained (the MRS and the Diversity and Discrimination scale measures).

TABLE 7.5. Summary Statistics for Difference Score Attitude Indexes

Measure	M	SD	d[a]	t(25)	p
Feeling thermometer	−8.73	15.06	−0.58	−2.96	.01
Semantic differential	0.008	0.559	0.01	0.07	.95
IAT (male names)	−.181	.139	−1.30	−6.61	10^{-7}
IAT (female names)	−.145	.141	−1.03	−5.26	10^{-5}

Note: Positive scores indicate preference for Black relative to White. The feeling thermometer range was −99 to 99, and the semantic differential range was −6 to 6. Latency measures were transformed to natural logarithms for this analysis. IAT = implicit association test.
[a] The effect size measure $d = M \div SD$. Conventional small, medium, and large values of **d** are .2, .5, and .8, respectively.

TABLE 7.6. Correlations Among Implicit and Explicit Measures of Racial Attitudes and Explicit Measures of Racist Beliefs

Measure	Explicit attitude 1	2	Implicit attitude 3	4	Racist beliefs 5	6	7
1. Feeling thermometer	—						
2. Semantic differential	.36	—					
3. IAT (male names)	**.19**	**.30**	—				
4. IAT (female names)	**.07**	**.11**	.46	—			
5. Modern Racism Scale	.29	.48	.11	.03	—		
6. Diversity Index	.24	.18	.19	.28	.69	—	
7. Discrimination Index	.54	.52	.12	.01	.79	.67	—

Note: Scores on Measures 5–7 were reversed (relative to their usual scoring) so that high scores on all measures would indicate pro-Black attitudes or beliefs. $N = 26$ for all correlations; two-tailed p values of .10, .05, .01, .005, and .001 are associated, respectively, with r values of .33, .39, .50, .54, and .61. Correlations between explicit and implicit attitude measures are printed in bold, and correlations of implicit measures with racist belief measures are in italics. IAT = implicit association test.

Scores on the three additional explicit measures were reversed relative to their usual scoring, so that high scores on all seven measures would indicate pro-Black attitudes or beliefs. All correlations were therefore expected to be positive. The five explicit measures (feeling thermometer, semantic differential, the MRS, and the Diversity and Discrimination scales) formed a cluster that accounted for all of the correlations that were greater than .50 (average r = .50). By contrast, the average correlation of explicit measures with implicit measures was r = .14. Consistent with the results of Experiment 1, this again indicates a divergence between the constructs assessed by the implicit and explicit measures.

An important purpose of Experiment 3 was to determine whether the IAT would reveal an implicit White preference among subjects who explicitly disavowed any Black–White evaluative difference. Figure 7.6 provides a scatter plot that relates the semantic differential measure of racial evaluative preference to the average of Experiment 3's two IAT measures. Two striking features of Figure 7.6 indicate that the IAT may indeed

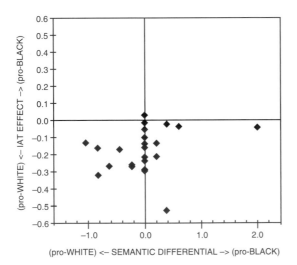

FIGURE 7.6 ■ Relationship of semantic differential and implicit association test (IAT) measures of Black–White evaluative preference. Data are from Experiment 3 (N = 26 White American subjects). Both measures have meaningful zero points that indicate absence of preference. The major feature of the data is the indication of substantial White preference on the IAT measure.

implicitly reveal explicitly disavowed prejudice. First, Figure 7.6 indicates that a majority of Experiment 3's White subjects (19 of 26) explicitly endorsed a position of either Black–White indifference (zero on the semantic differential) or Black preference (a positive semantic differential score). Second, it can be seen in Figure 7.6 that all but one of these subjects had negative IAT scores, indicating White preference. Indeed, only one of the 26 White subjects had a positive IAT score. At the same time that these findings are encouraging in regard to usefulness of the IAT to measure implicit attitudes, they are discouraging in indicating the pervasiveness of unconscious forms of prejudice.

In Experiment 3, the implicit measures were no more than weakly correlated with explicit measures of either attitude (feeling thermometer and semantic differential, average r = .17) or racist belief measures (MRS and Diversity and Discrimination scales; average r = .12). Although these correlations provide no evidence for convergent validity of the IAT, nevertheless—because of the expectation that implicit and explicit measures of attitude are not necessarily correlated—neither do they damage the case for construct validity of the IAT.

Of course, construct validity of the IAT measure cannot be assumed just from the suspicion that virtually all White Americans may have automatic negative associations to African American names. There is a plausible alternative interpretation: that Experiment 3's White college student subjects were much less familiar with the African American stimulus names than they were with the White-American stimulus names. This differential familiarity, coupled with the expectation of greater liking for more familiar stimuli (Zajonc, 1968), could explain the IAT results. This possible alternative to the implicit racism interpretation is considered further in the General Discussion.

General Discussion

Each of the present three experiments produced findings consistent with the supposition that the IAT procedure is sensitive to automatic evaluative associations. These findings are encouraging in regard to usefulness of the IAT to measure implicit attitudes but do not establish that usefulness beyond doubt. Key issues still to be considered are (a) the IAT's immunity to self-presentation forces and (b) possible alternative interpretations of IAT results in terms of variables that may be confounded with evaluative differences among the categories examined in the three experiments.

Immunity to Self-Presentational Forces

All three experiments used two explicit self-report measures of attitude that could be compared with the IAT measures. These two measures were a feeling thermometer measure that used a 100-point scale single-item rating for each category used in the experiment and a semantic differential measure that averaged ratings for each category on five 7-point bipolar evaluative items. Comparison of results obtained for the IAT measures and these self-report measures provides important indications that the IAT may be more resistant to self-presentational factors than are the explicit measures.

Experiment 1's attitude objects were familiar semantic categories for which evaluations are widely shared and presumably not socially sensitive. Subjects should have had little concern about being perceived as liking flowers more than insects or as liking musical instruments more than weapons. For the feeling thermometer and semantic differential explicit measures, indeed, subjects apparently had no reluctance to express these expected attitudes. Effect sizes for Experiment 1's explicit measures (mean d = 1.68) were greater than the average effect sizes for the IAT log-latency measures (mean d = 1.50; see Table 7.1).

Experiment 2 sought to assess socially more sensitive attitudes involving mutual ethnic regard of Japanese Americans and Korean Americans. By contrast with Experiment 1, the average effect sizes were substantially smaller for the two explicit measures (mean d = 0.49) than for IAT measures (mean d = 0.99; see Table 7.3).[15] Experiment 3 assessed a presumably even more socially sensitive attitude domain, involving the Black–White racial

evaluative contrast for White American subjects. In Experiment 3, effect sizes for the two explicit measures were even smaller (mean d = 0.30) than those in Experiment 2 and were considerably smaller than Experiment 3's IAT-measured effect sizes (mean d = 1.13).

The much greater variation across experiments in effect sizes of explicit measures, relative to those of the IAT measures, suggests that the explicit measures might have been more responsive to self-presentational forces that can mask subjects' attitudes. Because of the anonymity and privacy conditions under which both the IAT and explicit-measure data were collected in all three experiments, the self-presentation forces operating in them may belong more in the category of private self-presentation (self-presentation to self: Breckler & Greenwald, 1986; Greenwald & Breckler, 1985) than in the category of impression management (self-presentation to others).

Convergent Validity of IAT Attitude Measures

A measure's convergent validity is established by demonstrating that it displays theoretically expected correlations with other measures. In Experiment 1, an expected correlation was demonstrated in that the IAT effect measures were in agreement with common views regarding evaluative differentiations among semantic categories (such as weapons vs. musical instruments). In Experiment 2, the expected correlation was in the relationship of an IAT measure of attitude difference between Korean and Japanese ethnicities and subjects' self-described ethnic identities. Further, this correlation was moderated in theoretically expected fashion by subjects' level of immersion in the cultures of their ethnic groups (Figure 7.4). Unlike the known-groups design of Experiment 2,

---

[15] The effect sizes in Table 7.3 are for differences between two subject samples, Korean American and Japanese American. The mean ds of 0.49 and 0.99 were obtained by dividing Table 7.3's effect sizes in half, making them more directly comparable to the one-sample effect sizes available for Experiments 1 and 3.

Experiment 3 had a single subject group, White Americans. For this group, the IAT indicated an implicit in-group preference (for Whites, relative to Blacks) that was expected on the basis of others' investigations of implicit attitudes (Crosby et al., 1980; Devine, 1989; Fazio et al., 1995; Gaertner & McLaughlin, 1983; Greenwald & Banaji, 1995; Wittenbrink, Judd, & Park, 1997), even though it was not expressed on the explicit (self-report) attitude measures of Experiment 3.

Discriminant Validity of IAT Attitude Measures

Two issues relating to discriminant validity merit consideration. The first is evidence bearing on the supposition that the IAT and the self-report measures assessed different constructs that might be identified, respectively, as implicit and explicit attitudes. Second is evidence bearing on the possibility that the IAT procedure is sensitive (in an undesired fashion) to differential familiarity with the stimulus items used to represent target concepts.

Explicit versus implicit

In addition to the convergent validity evidence obtained in the form of the expected patterns of results just described, each experiment also examined correlations of IAT measures of implicit attitudes with semantic differential and feeling thermometer measures of explicit attitudes. On average, these two explicit measures were better correlated with each other (average $r = .60$) than they were with the IAT measures of the same attitudes (average $r = .25$). It is clear that these implicit–explicit correlations should be taken not as evidence for convergence among different methods of measuring attitudes but as evidence for divergence of the constructs represented by implicit versus explicit attitude measures.

Differential familiarity with IAT stimuli

In all three experiments, target-concept stimuli for IAT measures were words or names that were associated with naturally occurring categories. This allowed possible confounding of implicit attitude differences with any other differences that existed naturally among the stimulus words or names used for the various categories. The most obvious possible confounding was that of positive evaluation with amount of prior exposure to the target concept stimuli. This possible confounding raises a concern about discriminant validity: Does the IAT measure implicit attitude, or is it an artifact of amount of exposure to the stimuli used to represent target concepts?

In both Experiments 2 and 3, it was virtually certain that subjects were more familiar with names associated with their own ethnic group than with names associated with the contrasting group. For example, the Japanese American and Korean American subjects in Experiment 2 were undoubtedly more familiar with names of their own ethnicity than the other, and the White subjects in Experiment 3 were similarly more familiar with the White first names used in that experiment than with the contrasting Black names.

Although it is plausible that IAT measures possibly tapped prior exposure differences in Experiments 2 and 3, this alternative explanation cannot apply to Experiment 1. In Experiment 1, the evaluatively negative categories (insects and weapons) consisted of words that have substantially higher frequency in the language than did the words used for the evaluatively positive categories (flowers and musical instruments). Thus, even if relative familiarity of stimulus items plays some role in the IAT effect, it cannot explain the full set of findings for all three studies. This aspect of Experiment 1's design notwithstanding, it is desirable to pursue alternative strategies to resolve the discriminant validity question concerning differential item familiarity.[16]

---

[16] Preliminary findings of experiments using multiple strategies to examine the effect of item familiarity have, so far, produced findings indicating that the implicit in-group preferences observed in Experiments 2 and 3 are not artifacts of greater familiarity with in-group-related stimuli (Dasgupta, McGhee, Greenwald, & Banaji, 1998).

Comparison of IAT With Other Automatic Evaluation Measures

The chief method previously investigated for the assessment of automatic evaluative associations is evaluative semantic priming (e.g., Bargh et al., 1992; Fazio et al., 1986; Greenwald et al., 1989). In the evaluative priming method, subjects classify each of a series of target words based on the target word's evaluative meaning, with each target word immediately preceded by a to-be-ignored prime word. Prime-target evaluative congruence facilitates responding to the target, producing variations in response latencies that can be used to measure automatic evaluation of the prime category. The more a category of words speeds judgments of positive evaluated targets or hinders judgments of negatively evaluated targets, the more evaluative positivity is indicated for that category. Studies of evaluative priming have used prime stimulus categories much like the target-concept categories of the present experiments. Perdue and Gurtman (1990) examined automatic evaluation associated with the prime categories of old and young. Perdue et al. (1990) contrasted automatic evaluation evoked by words representing concepts of in-group (such as we or us) and out-group (they or them). Fazio et al. (1995) used an evaluative priming method to assess relative automatic evaluations toward Black and White race categories.

In comparing usefulness of the IAT method with that of the priming method, it is appropriate to compare effect sizes obtained by the two procedures with similar materials. The priming studies of Fazio et al. (1986), Perdue and Gurtman (1990), Perdue et al. (1990), and Fazio et al. (1995) were considered suitable for comparison with the present research, although only one of three experiments in the last of these provided latency data that could be used for comparison. Treating each of the seven comparison priming experiments as an independent estimate, and combining them in unweighted fashion, yielded an average priming effect (latency difference for evaluative-category contrasts) of 64.0 ms, with an average effect size of **d** = .62. For comparison, the IAT effects in the present three experiments averaged 153.5 ms, with effect sizes averaging **d** = 1.21. (These figures are unweighted averages of data from the present three experiments as given in Tables 7.1, 7.3, and 7.5, halving the figures in Table 7.3 in order to treat the data from the Korean and Japanese subsamples as individual subexperiments.) This comparison suggests that the IAT method has about twice the priming method's sensitivity to evaluative differences. The implications of a doubling of effect size are substantial, perhaps chiefly because doing so permits experiments at fixed levels of statistical power to be conducted with a quarter of the sample size. Of course, it would be much superior to compare the IAT and priming methods' effect sizes in a single experiment, using the same stimulus categories with each method.

IAT measures share some important properties with semantic priming measures: (a) Both procedures measure attitude as the evaluative difference between two categories (target concepts in the IAT and priming item categories in semantic priming), and (b) the procedure juxtaposes items from categories for which an attribute is to be measured (target concepts in the IAT, or priming categories in priming) with items that have well-established attribute values (attribute categories in the IAT and target items in priming).

Effect of Procedural Variables on IAT

Order of task-compatibility combinations

Experiment 1 tested the impact of five procedural factors on the IAT's sensitivity to evaluative associations. Only one procedural variable was demonstrated to moderate the IAT: the order of performing compatible and noncompatible concept–attribute combinations. When a compatible combination (for example, pleasant + flowers) precedes a noncompatible one (pleasant + insects), the IAT's measure of evaluative difference between the positive (flowers) and negative (insects) concepts is increased. Although this compatibility–order effect was statistically significant only in Experiment 1, it was also found directionally in Experiments 2 and 3. This procedural effect does not appear to undermine the IAT's sensitivity to individual differences in implicit attitudes, but it does compromise the location of a zero point. For example, a person truly characterized by no implicit attitude difference between the Black and White racial categories would appear to be mildly pro-White if given an IAT in which White + pleasant preceded Black + pleasant but would appear mildly pro-Black if this ordering were reversed. Fortunately, the effect of this procedural variable appears to be removable by reducing the number of trials used in each component of the IAT. As already mentioned, the effect was statistically non-significant in Experiments 2 and 3, both of which used reduced numbers of trials in the critical combined task portions of the IAT. Subsequent (as yet unreported) data collections indicate that the compatibility–order effect can be eliminated completely by further reducing the numbers of combined-task trials.

Category set sizes

Of the several procedural factors tested in Experiment 1 and found not to influence IAT measures, perhaps the most practically significant was the variation of 5 versus 25 items used to represent each category in Experiment 1. If the IAT can be administered equally effectively with 5-item and 25-item categories, it should be relatively easy to extend its method to new domains in which there may be relatively few items available to represent either target concepts or associated attributes. It remains possible, also, that the IAT may be successfully usable with even fewer than five items per category.

Extension of the IAT Method to Stereotypes and Self-Concept

A reason for strong interest in the IAT method is its potential for easy extension both to additional attitude–object categories and to attribute dimensions other than evaluation. For example, by using male versus female names as the target concept pair and replacing the pleasant–unpleasant attribute contrast of the present experiments with a strong–weak contrast, the IAT method can be used to assess a stereotypic differentiation between males and females on the strong–weak attribute dimen-

sion (Rudman, Greenwald, & McGhee, 1996). By using me versus not me (i.e., self vs. other) as the target–concept contrast together with the pleasant–unpleasant contrast, one can obtain a measure of evaluative associations that underlie self-esteem (Farnham & Greenwald, 1998; Farnham, Greenwald, & Banaji, in press). By combining the self–other target concepts with any of various attribute dimensions, one should also be able to determine whether each attribute dimension is associated with a person's self-concept. This last possibility offers a new method for measuring the self-schema construct that was introduced by Markus (1977).

Conclusion

Findings of three experiments consistently confirmed the usefulness of the IAT (implicit association test) for assessing differences in evaluative associations between pairs of semantic or social categories. The findings also suggested that the IAT may resist self-presentational forces that can mask personally or socially undesirable evaluative associations, such as the ethnic and racial attitudes investigated in Experiments 2 and 3. The IAT method offers the further advantage of being adaptable to assess a wide variety of associations, including those that comprise stereotypes and self-concept.

REFERENCES

Bargh, J. A., Chaiken, S., Govender, R., & Pratto, F. (1992). The generality of the automatic attitude activation effect. *Journal of Personality and Social Psychology, 62*, 893–912.

Battig, W. F., & Montague, W. E. (1969). Category norms for verbal items in 56 categories: A replication and extension of the Connecticut category norms. *Journal of Experimental Psychology Monographs, 80*(3, Pt. 2), 1–46.

Bellezza, F. S., Greenwald, A. G., & Banaji, M. R. (1986). Words high and low in pleasantness as rated by male and female college students. *Behavior Research Methods, Instruments, & Computers, 18*, 299–303.

Breckler, S. J., & Greenwald, A. G. (1986). Motivational facets of the self. In E. T. Higgins & R. Sorrentino (Eds.), *Handbook of motivation and cognition* (pp. 145–164). New York: Guilford Press.

Chaiken, S., & Bargh, J. A. (1993). Occurrence versus moderation of the automatic attitude activation effect: Reply to Fazio. *Journal of Personality and Social Psychology, 64*, 759–765.

Crosby, F., Bromley, S., & Saxe, L. (1980). Recent unobtrusive studies of Black and White discrimination and prejudice: A literature review. *Psychological Bulletin, 87,* 546–563.

Dasgupta, N., McGhee, D. E., Greenwald, A. G., & Banaji, M. R. (1998). *Measuring implicit racism using the Implicit Association Test.* Unpublished manuscript, University of Washington.

Devine, P. G. (1989). Stereotypes and prejudice: Their automatic and controlled components. *Journal of Personality and Social Psychology, 56,* 5–18.

Dovidio, J. F., & Gaertner, S. L. (1995, October). *Stereotyping, prejudice, and discrimination: Spontaneous and deliberative processes.* Paper presented at the meeting of the Society of Experimental Social Psychology, Washington, DC.

Farnham, S. D., & Greenwald, A. G. (1998, May). *Implicit balance of personal and social identity: I am good + I am female = female is good.* Paper presented at the meetings of the Midwestern Psychological Association, Chicago.

Farnham, S. D., Greenwald, A. G., & Banaji, M. R. (in press). Implicit self-esteem. In D. Abrams & M. A. Hogg (Eds.), *Social cognition and social identity.* London: Blackwell.

Fazio, R. H. (1993). Variability in the likelihood of automatic attitude activation: Data reanalysis and commentary on Bargh, Chaiken, Govender, and Pratto (1992). *Journal of Personality and Social Psychology, 64,* 753–758.

Fazio, R. H., Jackson, J. R., Dunton, B. C., & Williams, C. J. (1995). Variability in automatic activation as an unobtrusive measure of racial attitudes: A bona fide pipeline? *Journal of Personality and Social Psychology, 69,* 1013–1027.

Fazio, R. H., Sanbonmatsu, D. M., Powell, M. C., & Kardes, F. R. (1986). On the automatic activation of attitudes. *Journal of Personality and Social Psychology, 50,* 229–238.

Gaertner, S. L., & McLaughlin, J. P. (1983). Racial stereotypes: Associations and ascriptions of positive and negative characteristics. *Social Psychology Quarterly, 46,* 23–30.

Greenwald, A. G., & Banaji, M. R. (1995). Implicit social cognition: Attitudes, self-esteem, and stereotypes. *Journal of Personality and Social Psychology, 102,* 4–27.

Greenwald, A. G., & Breckler, S. J. (1985). To whom is the self presented? In B. R. Schlenker (Ed.), *The self and social life* (pp. 126–145). New York: McGraw-Hill.

Greenwald, A. G., Gonzalez, R., Guthrie, D. G., & Harris, R. J. (1996). Effect sizes and p-values: What should be reported and what should be replicated? *Psychophysiology, 33,* 175–183.

Greenwald, A. G., Klinger, M. R., & Liu, T. J. (1989). Unconscious processing of dichoptically masked words. *Memory and Cognition, 17,* 35–47.

Markus, H. (1977). Self-schemata and processing information about the self. *Journal of Personality and Social Psychology, 35,* 63–78.

McConahay, J. B., Hardee, B. B., & Batts, V. (1981). Has racism declined in America? It depends on who is asking and what is asked. *Journal of Conflict Resolution, 25,* 563–579.

Perdue, C. W., Dovidio, J. F., Gurtman, M. B., & Tyler, R. B. (1990). Us and them: Social categorization and the process of intergroup bias. *Journal of Personality and Social Psychology, 59,* 475–486.

Perdue, C. W., & Gurtman, M. B. (1990). Evidence for the automaticity of ageism. *Journal of Experimental Social Psychology, 26,* 199–216.

Rudman, L., Greenwald, A. G., & McGhee, D. E. (1996, October). *Powerful women, warm men? Implicit associations among gender, potency, and nurturance.* Paper presented at the meeting of the Society of Experimental Social Psychology, Sturbridge, MA.

Suinn, R., Rickard-Figueroa, K., Lew, S., & Vigil, P. (1987). The Suinn–Lew Asian Self-Identity Acculturation Scale: An initial report. *Educational and Psychological Measurement, 47,* 401–407.

Wittenbrink, B., Judd, C. M., & Park, B. (1997). Evidence for racial prejudice at the implicit level and its relationship with questionnaire measures. *Journal of Personality and Social Psychology, 72,* 262–274.

Zajonc, R. B. (1968). Attitudinal effects of mere exposure. *Journal of Personality and Social Psychology, 9*(Supp. 2, Pt. 2).

[Appendices deleted . . .]

PART 3

Affective, Cognitive, and Behavioral Bases of Attitudes

Like people, attitudes come in varying shapes and sizes. They can be based on very different classes of information. Although, as noted in the introduction to the first set of readings, the field has drifted away from the three-component view of attitudes, theorists continue to recognize attitudes as stemming from affective, cognitive, and/or behavioral information. Sometimes, attitudes toward an object, person, place, or event stem directly from the emotions that it evokes. For some, a rollercoaster evokes feelings of excitement; for others, fear and dread. Those differential emotions obviously produce different attitudes regarding the prospect of riding a rollercoaster. Sometimes, our attitudes stem from a reasoned analysis of the consequences that are likely to accrue from selecting a particular option among those available to us. For example, in this age of online travel booking, we might scrutinize the information that a website makes available to us regarding a particular hotel option. We can consider the location, its proximity to attractions and restaurants, the number of stars the hotel has earned as its rating, the room rate, etc. and arrive at an overall evaluation of the option. At other times, our attitudes stem not from a consideration of the characteristics of the object, but directly from our experiences and from observation of our own relevant behavior. For example, finding oneself tightly grasping the armrests of an airplane seat at the first sign of turbulence is a very informative behavioral cue regarding one's attitude toward flying. The articles reprinted in this section are intended to illustrate these various potential bases of attitudes.

Beliefs. Attitudes can be formed on the basis of our consideration of our beliefs about the attitude object. A belief about an object simply refers to a characteristic or attribute that it possesses. So, just as an attitude can be thought of as an object–evaluation association, a belief can be viewed as an object–attribute association. Historically, one of the most significant approaches to the study of attitudes—the expectancy-value framework—has focused on the value associated with such attributes. According to this perspective, people sometimes form attitudes quite rationally on the basis of syllogistic reasoning regarding the value that they associate with the attributes that characterize an object. Essentially, there are two premises involved in the syllogism: (1) the expectancy, or belief, refers to the probability that the object is characterized by a given attribute, and (2) the value refers to how favorably or unfavorably we view the attribute. This information leads to a logical conclusion about our attitude toward the object. So, if it seems very probable that a new brand of a multi-vitamin pill provides the recommended daily amounts of all essential vitamins (the belief) and if meeting the recommended guidelines is viewed favorably (the value), then the brand of vitamins is logically viewed positively (the attitude).

Reading 8 reprints a classic article by Fishbein (1963) illustrating the expectancy-value framework. Although much of the content and language would not be regarded as politically correct today in terms of current cultural norms, the research provides an excellent illustration of how even a topic as complex as racial attitudes can be approached by a consideration of relevant beliefs.

Affect. Some attitudes have a strong emotional basis: something frightens or disgusts us, leading to the development of a negative attitude; or it thrills us, leading to a positive attitude. A politician's stance on some vital national issue might actually anger us (Abelson, Kinder, Peters, & Fiske, 1982), prompting a decision to vote against him. A photo of a starving, malnourished child may evoke strong feelings of empathy and pity, encouraging us to donate to the charitable foundation that promises to offer assistance to such children.

Obviously, the affect that an object evokes can be a powerful determinant of our attitudes. Reading 9 is an influential article by Zajonc (1980) in which he espouses a very strong position regarding the importance of affect. Zajonc argues that affective reactions often are "primary" in that they can occur prior to any thoughtful consideration, or even conscious recognition, of the attitude object. The argument is fascinating and, just as would be expected, has generated considerable debate (e.g., Lazarus, 1982, 1984; Zajonc, 1984). Regardless of the ultimate conclusion one might reach regarding the primacy of affect, the arguments that Zajonc offers, and the research that he reviews, make it very evident that individuals can experience affective reactions to an object, despite the involvement of minimal cognition and thought.

Behavior. Sometimes, we infer our attitudes from our behavior. That proposition forms the core of Bem's (1972) self-perception theory, which certainly ranks among the most important theories concerning attitudes. Bem argued that: "Individuals come to 'know' their own attitudes, emotions, and other internal states partially by inferring them from observation of their own behavior and/or the circumstances in which this behavior occurs" (p. 2). As long as the behavior is not attributable to some external force, one's attitude can be inferred directly from the behavior. Essentially, individuals ask themselves "what must my attitude be if I am willing to behave in this fashion in this situation?"

A considerable amount of evidence has accumulated in support of this basic proposition. Reading 10 is one such article. In this classic experiment, Chaiken and Baldwin (1981) employed an intriguing linguistic manipulation to make salient to individuals either pro-ecology or anti-ecology behaviors that they had performed. Due to how the adverbs "occasionally" and "frequently" were paired with various ecology-related behaviors, participants found themselves indicating that they had performed many pro and few anti behaviors, or vice versa. Consistent with the tenets of self-perception theory, this linguistically-biased review of their past behaviors led participants to differential views of their favorability toward environmentalism.

What makes the Chaiken and Baldwin article all the more interesting is that it also tested another aspect of self-perception theory. Bem's core proposition included an important proviso, suggesting that individuals would engage in such a behavioral inference process only "to the extent that internal cues are weak, ambiguous, or uninterpretable" (Bem, 1972, p. 2). Thus, acknowledging that individuals' attitudes can vary in their strength, the theory suggests that individuals would not need to engage in a consideration of their behavior if they already know their attitudes well. Chaiken and Baldwin operationalized attitude strength via the consistency of participants' responses across varying measures of attitude. Essentially, they presumed that anyone who had a clear, well-defined attitude toward environmentalism would respond equivalently to two different ways of assessing attitudes. Indeed, the

attitudes of such people were not affected by the behavioral salience manipulation. Only those who responded relatively inconsistently, suggesting that they lacked clear knowledge of their attitudes, were influenced by the linguistically-biased recall of past behaviors. Thus, this study points to yet another sense in which attitudes come in varying shapes and sizes. Some attitudes are stronger and more resistant to the influence of momentarily salient information than are other attitudes. The topic of what makes some attitudes stronger than others has become a well-researched one (see Petty & Krosnick, 1995).

Why attitude bases matter. The final two readings illustrate both the complexity involved in considering the varying bases of attitudes and the importance of doing so. Reading 11 is an article by Haddock, Zanna, & Esses (1993) in which they report research assessing the structure of attitudes toward homosexuals. The studies consider how those attitudes vary as a function of individuals' beliefs about typical homosexuals, beliefs about the extent to which homosexuals block or facilitate various values, the emotions they experience when they encounter a homosexual, and their past experiences with homosexuals. The findings reveal that these various predictors vary in their importance, with some carrying more weight than others for different kinds of people.

Reading 12 focuses on a possibility of which we are all aware. Sometimes, we have both positive and negative reactions to an object. For example, our hearts and our minds may not be in agreement. An appointment with the dentist can evoke feelings of fear and apprehension, and yet one remains aware that the time in the dentist's chair is both necessary and valuable. The article by Newby-Clark, McGregor, and

Zanna (2002) concerns the experience of such attitudinal ambivalence. Their research focuses on the conditions under which conflicting evaluations of an object produce feelings of discomfort and the kind of person for whom such subjective ambivalence is most pronounced.

REFERENCES

Abelson, R. P., Kinder, D. R., Peters, M. D., & Fiske, S. T. (1982). Affective and semantic components in political person perception. *Journal of Personality and Social Psychology*, *42*, 619–630.

Bem, D. J. (1972). Self-perception theory. In L. Berkowitz (Ed.), *Advances in experimental social psychology* (Vol. 6, pp. 1–62). New York: Academic Press.

Lazarus, R. S. (1982). Thoughts on the relations between emotion and cognition. *American Psychologist*, *37*, 1019–1024.

Lazarus, R. S. (1984). On the primacy of cognition. *American Psychologist*, *39*, 124–129.

Petty, R. E., & Krosnick, J. A. (Eds.) (1995). *Attitude strength: Antecedents and consequences*. Mahwah, NJ: Erlbaum.

Zajonc, R. B. (1984). On the primacy of affect. *American Psychologist*, *39*, 117–123.

Suggested Readings

Chaiken, S., Pomerantz, E. M., & Giner-Sorolla, R. (1995). Structural consistency and attitude strength. In R. E. Petty & J. A. Krosnick (Eds.), *Attitude strength: Antecedents and consequences* (pp. 387–412). Mahwah, NJ: Erlbaum.

Crites, S., Fabrigar, L., & Petty, R. E. (1994). Measuring the affective and cognitive properties of attitudes: Conceptual and methodological issues. *Personality and Social Psychology Bulletin*, *20*, 619–634.

De Houwer, J., Thomas, S., & Baeyens, F. (2001). Associative learning of likes and dislikes: A review of 25 years of research on human evaluative conditioning. *Psychological Bulletin*, *127*, 853–869.

Fazio, R. H. (1987). Self-perception theory: A current perspective. In M. P. Zanna, J. M. Olson, & C. P. Herman (Eds.), *Social influence: The Ontario symposium* (Vol. 5, pp. 129–150). Hillsdale, NJ: Erlbaum.

Fazio, R. H., & Zanna, M. P. (1981). Direct experience and attitude-behavior consistency. In L. Berkowitz (Ed.), *Advances in experimental social psychology* (Vol. 14, pp. 161–202). New York: Academic Press.

Priester, J. R., & Petty, R. E. (1996). The gradual threshold model of ambivalence: Relating the positive and negative bases of attitudes to subjective ambivalence. *Journal of Personality and Social Psychology*, *71*, 431–449.

Reber, R., Winkielman, P., & Schwarz, N. (1998). Effects of perceptual fluency on affective judgments. *Psychological Science*, *9*, 45–48.

Strack, F., Martin, L. L., & Stepper, S. (1988). Inhibiting and facilitating conditions of the human smile: A nonobtrusive test of the facial feedback hypothesis. *Journal of Personality and Social Psychology*, *54*, 768–777.

Wells, G. L., & Petty, E. (1980). The effects of overt head movements on persuasion: Compatibility and incompatibility of responses. *Basic and Applied Social Psychology*, *1*, 219–230.

An Investigation of the Relationships between Beliefs about an Object and the Attitude toward that Object[1]

Martin Fishbein[2]

In a recent paper, Fishbein (1961) proposed a theory of the relationships between beliefs about an object and the attitude toward that object. Consistent with the theoretical formulations of Osgood, Suci & Tannenbaum (1957) and of Fishbein & Raven (1962), attitudes are defined as 'the evaluative dimension of a concept'—e.g. is the concept 'good' or 'bad'?—and they are described as mediating evaluative responses. Similarly, beliefs are defined as 'the probability dimension of a concept'—e.g. is the concept 'probable' or 'improbable'? Further, Fishbein & Raven (1962) distinguished between *beliefs in* the existence of an object and *beliefs about* an object, describing the latter as 'the probability of a relationship between the object of belief and any other object, concept, or goal'. Thus, a belief about an object may be defined as the probability dimension of a 'concept' where the 'concept' is a relational statement (e.g. 'Negroes have a dark skin').

Fishbein's (1961) theory may essentially be stated as follows: (1) an individual holds many beliefs about any given object, i.e. many different characteristics, attributes, values, goals, and objects are positively or negatively associated with a given object; (2) associated with each of these 'related objects' is a mediating evaluative response, i.e. an attitude; (3) these evaluative responses summate; (4) through the mediation process, the summated evaluative response is associated with the attitude object, and thus (5) on future occasions the attitude object will elicit this summated evaluative response, i.e. this attitude.

According to the theory, then, an individual's attitude toward any object is a function of his beliefs about the object (i.e. the probability that the object is associated with other objects, concepts, values, or goals) and the evaluative aspect of those beliefs (i.e. the attitude toward the 'related objects'). Algebraically, it may be predicted that an individual's attitude toward any object =

[1] This paper is adapted from a dissertation submitted in partial fulfillment of the requirements for the degree of doctor of philosophy at the University of California, Los Angeles. The project was supported by the Group Psychology Branch of the Office of Naval Research, Contract Nonr-233 (54).

[2] The author wishes to acknowledge his indebtedness to Dr Bertram H. Raven for his direction, aid, and encouragement during the entire project; and to Dr Irving Maltzman, Dr Alexander C. Rosen, Dr Harry C. Triandis and many of his other colleagues for their critical reading of an earlier draft of this paper.

$$\sum_{i=1}^{N} B_i a_i,$$ where B_i = belief 'i' about the object, a_i = the evaluative aspect of B_i, and N = the number of beliefs. Although this hypothesis is similar to hypotheses proposed by other investigators (e.g. Rosenberg, 1956, 1960; Zajonc, 1954; Peak, 1955), several theoretical and methodological differences have been noted elsewhere (e.g. Fishbein, 1961).

Before turning to the test of the hypothesis, one point should be made. A review of the literature on attitude organization and change clearly indicates that there is some question about the types of beliefs that are related to, and/or function as determinants of, attitudes. For example, many investigators (e.g. Krech & Crutchfield, 1948; Katz & Stotland, 1959; Abelson & Rosenberg, 1958; Rosenberg & Abelson, 1960, etc.) attempt to distinguish between beliefs that are 'attitudinal' in nature (i.e. beliefs that are related to an S's attitude) and beliefs that are 'purely descriptive or reportorial'. Indeed, with very few exceptions (e.g. Zajonc, 1954; Campbell, 1950), most investigators have tended to ignore descriptive or reportorial beliefs in their investigations of attitudes.

From the point of view of Fishbein's theory (1961), all beliefs about an object (e.g. descriptive beliefs, instrumental beliefs, beliefs about the object's relations with other objects, beliefs about what should be done with respect to the object, etc.) are related to an individual's attitude since all beliefs about an object contain an evaluative aspect. Since most investigators of attitude have tended to ignore 'descriptive beliefs', it was felt that this type of belief would provide the severest test of the hypothesis. Further, it seems reasonable to assume that the strongest beliefs about an object that an individual holds are those beliefs that serve to define and describe the object for him, i.e. descriptive beliefs. Since the strongest beliefs an individual holds should have the greatest influence on his attitude, descriptive beliefs should play a major role in theories of attitude organization and change.

As a result of these considerations, the following hypothesis was formulated:

An individual's attitude toward 'Negroes' is a function of (1) his beliefs about the characteristics and components of Negroes (B_i) and (2) the evaluative aspect of those beliefs (a_i).

Operationally, there should be a high positive correlation between the predicted attitude toward Negroes (i.e. $\sum_{i=1}^{N} B_i a_i$) and some obtained measure of that attitude (A_0).

Method

In order to test the above hypothesis, it is necessary to obtain (1) an individual's beliefs about the attitude object, (2) a measure of each belief *and* its evaluative aspect, and (3) a measure of his attitude toward the object. The experiment was run in two sessions. The first session was concerned with obtaining Ss' beliefs, and the second session obtained all the other necessary measurements.

Obtaining the Beliefs

One hundred and twenty-five undergraduate Ss volunteered to take part in an experiment entitled 'The Perception of Persons'. Following the procedure of Maltzman, Bogartz & Breger (1958), each S gave different associations to the same stimulus words in a free association situation. Ss were told that the purpose of the experiment was to find out 'what you believe the characteristics of different groups of people are'. A list of ten stimulus words, including the word 'Negro', representing ethnic and national groups (e.g. American, Jew) was read to the Ss. Ss were told to respond to each word with what they 'believed to be a characteristic of the group'. The list was read four more times, and on each presentation S was told to give a different response for each word. Thus, each S responded with five different characteristics of Negroes.

Originally, it was planned to select the ten most frequent responses to Negro, and use these to construct ten belief statements. However, since many different responses referred to the same characteristic, response categories were established. For example, three of the most common responses to Negro were 'dark skin', 'dark', and 'black'. Rather than being viewed as indicating different beliefs about Negroes, these responses, and others such as 'colored', 'color', 'brown skin', etc., were all taken as indications of the same characteristic. Since the most frequent response among these was 'dark skin', this response was used as the designation of the response category. The ten response categories representing the most frequent characteristics of Negroes were then used to construct ten belief statements. The ten characteristics and the ten belief statements may be seen in Table 8.1.

The Measurement of Beliefs and their Evaluative Aspects

Two weeks after obtaining the beliefs that were most common to all Ss, 50 of the Ss who took part in the first session of the experiment returned for a second session. All Ss were presented with 22-page booklets with the standard instructions for using the Semantic Differential as the first page (Osgood et al., 1957, pp. 82–4).

The measurement of the evaluative aspect of belief. The next ten pages of the booklet contained a form of Fishbein and Raven's (1962) A Scale. This scale is a modified form of the Semantic Differential containing five, empirically

determined evaluative scales (e.g. 'good—bad', 'clean—dirty', etc.) and five filler scales. Previous research has demonstrated the reliability and validity of the Semantic Differential as a measure of attitudes (e.g. Osgood et al., 1957; Fishbein & Raven, 1962). Above each A Scale, Ss found one of the ten characteristics of Negroes. The Ss evaluated the characteristics first because it was felt that if the characteristics were rated after the belief statements, the evaluation of the characteristics would be some function of the evaluation of Negroes. Since all of these characteristics were also elicited with respect to *at least* one of the other stimulus words in Part I of the experiment, it could be assumed that, to some extent, the evaluation of each of the characteristics was being made independent of any one of the stimulus groups. The order in which the characteristics were rated may be seen in Table 8.1.

The measurement of belief. The next ten pages of the booklet contained Fishbein & Raven's (1962) B Scale, another modified form of the Semantic Differential designed to measure belief. The B Scale consists of five, empirically determined probabilistic scales (e.g. 'probable—improbable', 'likely—unlikely', etc.) and five filler scales. Evidence for the reliability and validity of the B Scale as a measure of belief has been presented by Fishbein & Raven (1962). An additional test of validity will be discussed below. Each S rated each of the ten belief statements on the B Scales. The

TABLE 8.1. The Ten Most Common Characteristics of Negroes and the Belief Statements Derived from Them

Order[a]	Characteristic	Frequency[b]	Order[a]	Belief statement	Mean B score[c]
5	Dark skin	72	5	Negroes have dark skin	13.30
9	Curly (Kinky) hair	31	10	Negroes have curly (Kinky) hair	12.18
2	Musical	31	9	Negroes are musical	9.62
3	Athletic	27	7	Negroes are athletic	11.24
7	Friendly	19	4	Negroes are friendly	6.02
6	Tall	14	1	Negroes are tall	5.12
1	Uneducated	11	6	Negroes are uneducated	4.83
10	Unintelligent	10	3	Negroes are unintelligent	1.47
4	Hard workers	9	8	Negroes are hard workers	2.84
8	Lazy	8	2	Negroes are lazy	2.50

[a] Order refers to order of presentation in Part II of the experiment.
[b] Based on an N = 125.
[c] B scores can range from –15 (complete disbelief) to +15 (complete belief) for each statement.

order in which the statements were rated may be seen in Table 8.1.

The Measurement of Attitude toward the Negro

The final page of the booklet contained the A Scale described above. Each S rated the concept Negro on this scale. It should be noted that one of the reasons for selecting the concept Negro as the attitude object was that previous research by Osgood *et al.* (1957) specifically tested the validity of the Semantic Differential as a measure of attitude toward the Negro. For an N of 50, these investigators obtained a correlation of ·82 between attitude toward the Negro as measured on the evaluative scales of the Semantic Differential and attitude toward the Negro as measured by a Thurstone Scale.

To summarize briefly, responses to the word 'Negro' were obtained from 125 Ss. The ten most frequent characteristics of Negro (e.g. dark skin) were then used to construct ten belief statements (e.g. Negroes have dark skin). Two weeks later, 50 Ss returned for a second session. Each S rated each of the characteristics on Fishbein & Raven's (1962) A Scale (a measure of 'a_i') and then rated each of the belief statements on Fishbein & Raven's (1962) B Scale (a measure of B_i). Finally, each S rated the concept Negro on the A Scale (a measure of A_0).

Results and Discussion

I. A Validity Test of the B Scale

Before testing the major hypothesis, it was first necessary to establish the validity of the B Scale as a measure of beliefs about an object. Although Fishbein & Raven (1962) provided evidence for the validity of the B Scale as a measure of belief, these investigators were concerned with *beliefs in* the existence of an object rather than with *beliefs about* an object. In order to test the validity of the B Scale, an independent criterion of belief strength had to be established. Placement of the concept of

belief within the framework of behavior theory suggests such a criterion. According to Fishbein (1961), a belief system may be described as a habit-family-hierarchy of responses. The assumption underlying the conception of a habit-family-hierarchy is that the higher the response is in the hierarchy, the stronger is the association between the stimulus (i.e. the attitude object) and the response (i.e. the object or concept associated with the attitude object). That is, the higher the response in the hierarchy, the stronger the belief. Thus, if the B Scale is valid, the B score obtained when an S rates a belief statement (i.e. the stimulus + the association + the response) should correlate highly with the position of the response in the habit-family-hierarchy. In Part I of the experiment, a habit-family-hierarchy of responses to Negro was obtained. Thus, the most frequent response to Negro should represent the strongest belief that the population holds about Negroes. Table 8.1 presents the frequency of the ten most common responses to Negro and the obtained mean B scores. The rank-order correlation between the obtained scores and the frequency of responses = ·942 ($N = 10$, $p < $ ·001). The data strongly support the validity of the B scale as a measure of beliefs about an object.

II. The Test of the Hypothesis

Having found that the measure of B_i, like the measures of a_i and A_0, is valid, we may now turn to a test of the major hypothesis. Using the algebraic formula presented above, an estimated attitude score was computed for each of the 50 Ss. Since each B_i and each a_i could range from −15 to +15 (i.e. both the A and the B Scales are comprised of five, seven-place bipolar adjective scales), the possible range of estimated attitude scores was between −2,250 and +2,250. The actual range of estimated scores was between −471 and +856. Similarly, the possible range of obtained scores (A_0) was between −15 and +15 (i.e. A_0 was measured on a single A scale) and the actual range of obtained scores was between −11 and +14. In support of the hypothesis, the Spearman rank-order correlation between estimated and obtained attitude scores = ·801 ($p < $ ·001, $N = 50$). In addition to correlating the estimated and obtained attitude scores, $\sum_{i=1}^{N} B_i$ and $\sum_{i=1}^{N} a_i$ were also correlated with the obtained attitudes. The correlations were $\cdot 017$ (n.s.) and $\cdot 468$ ($p < \cdot 01$, $N = 50$). Both of these are significantly lower than the correlation with the estimated attitude ($p < \cdot 01$). However, if $\sum_{i=1}^{N} B_i$ is computed in a manner that takes into account the evaluative aspect of B_i, i.e. if S is given a positive score for indicating disbelief in a statement with a negative evaluative aspect, then the correlation between $\sum_{i=1}^{N} B_i$ and the obtained attitude = $\cdot 653$ ($p < \cdot 01$, $N = 50$).[3] Thus, although a better than chance prediction of an individual's attitude can be made *either* on the basis of the evaluative aspect of his beliefs *or* on the basis of a variable derived from his beliefs about the object, a significantly better estimate of attitude is obtained by taking both the belief and its evaluative aspect into account.

It should be noted, however, that although a correlational procedure provides a test of the relation between the estimated and the obtained attitude scores, it does not take the direction of the attitude, i.e. the 'positiveness' or 'negativeness', into account directly. That is, theoretically it is possible to get a perfect positive correlation between two sets of scores when one set is all positive and the other is all negative. As an additional test of the hypothesis, the sign of the estimated attitude was compared with the sign of the obtained attitude. A two-tailed sign test for $N > 25$ was used to test the equivalence of the signs of estimated and obtained scores. In support of the hypothesis, the results indicate that the direction of the estimated attitude

is equal to the direction of the obtained attitude significantly more often than would be expected by chance ($z = 3.54$, $p < .001$).

In conclusion, then, the results strongly support the hypothesis that an individual's attitude toward Negroes is a function of his beliefs about the characteristics of Negroes and the evaluative aspect of those beliefs. This finding, along with the previous findings of Zajonc (1954), Rosenberg (1956, 1960), and others, provides strong support for the general hypothesis that an individual's attitude toward any object is a function of his beliefs about the object and the evaluative aspect of those beliefs. In addition, the present study has attempted to demonstrate that descriptive or reportorial beliefs about an object are important determinants of an individual's attitude toward that object. Since these beliefs are among the strongest beliefs about an object that an individual holds, it is suggested that more emphasis be placed upon them in future studies of attitude organization and change.

Summary

This paper tests the hypothesis that an individual's attitude toward any object is a function of (1) his beliefs about that object (i.e. the probability that the object is related to other objects, concepts, values, or goals) and (2) the evaluative aspect of those beliefs (i.e. the attitude toward the related objects). On the basis of ten descriptive beliefs about Negroes (e.g. 'Negroes have dark skin'), 50 Ss' attitudes toward Negroes were predicted. In support of the hypothesis, the correlation between predicted and obtained attitude scores =.801 ($p < .001$).

---

[3] The technique of reversing the scoring for beliefs statements with negative evaluative aspects is similar to the technique used in scoring Likert scales: i.e. when the statement is taken as an indication of a favorable attitude, agreement is given a score of 5 and disagreement a score of 1; when the statement is taken as an indication of an unfavorable attitude, disagreement is given a score of 5 and agreement a score of 1.

REFERENCES

Abelson, R. P. & Rosenberg, M. J. (1958). Symbolic psychologic: a model of attitudinal cognition. *Behavioral Science* **3**, 1–13.

Campbell, D. T. (1950). The indirect assessment of social attitudes. *Psychol. Bull.* **47**, 15–38.

Fishbein, M. (1961). An investigation of the relationships between beliefs about an object and the attitude toward that object. University of California, Los Angeles. Tech. Rep. No. 6, Contract Nonr-233 (54).

Fishbein, M. & Raven, B. H. (1962). The AB scales: an operational definition of belief and attitude. *Hum. Relat.* **15,** 35–44.

Katz, D. & Stotland, E. (1959). A preliminary statement to a theory of attitude structure and change. In S. Koch (Ed.), *Psychology: a study of a science*. Vol. 3, *Formulations of the person and the social context*. New York: McGraw-Hill.

Krech, D. & Crutchfield, R. S. (1948). *Theory and problems of social psychology*. New York: McGraw-Hill.

Maltzman, I., Bogartz, W. & Breger, L. (1958). A procedure for increasing word association originality and its transfer effects. *J. exp. Psychol.* **56,** 392–8.

Osgood, C. E., Suci, G. J. & Tannenbaum, P. H. (1957). *The measurement of meaning*. Urbana: Univ. of Illinois Press.

Peak, H. (1955). Attitude and motivation. In M. Jones (Ed.), *Nebraska symposium on motivation, 1955*. Lincoln: Univ. of Nebraska Press.

Rosenberg, M. J. (1956). Cognitive structure and attitudinal affect. *J. abnorm. soc. Psychol.* **53,** 367–72.

Rosenberg, M. J. (1960). An analysis of affective-cognitive consistency. In Rosenberg *et al.*, *Attitude organization and change*. New Haven: Yale Univ. Press.

Rosenberg, M. J. & Abelson, R. P. (1960). An analysis of cognitive balancing. In Rosenberg *et al.*, *Attitude organization and change*. New Haven: Yale Univ. Press.

Zajonc, R. B. (1954). Structure of the cognitive field. Unpublished doctor's dissertation, University of Michigan.

READING 9

Feeling and Thinking: Preferences Need No Inferences

R. B. Zajonc

Affect is considered by most contemporary theories to be postcognitive, that is, to occur only after considerable cognitive operations have been accomplished. Yet a number of experimental results on preferences, attitudes, impression formation, and decision making, as well as some clinical phenomena, suggest that affective judgments may be fairly independent of, and precede in time, the sorts of perceptual and cognitive operations commonly assumed to be the basis of these affective judgments. Affective reactions to stimuli are often the very first reactions of the organism, and for lower organisms they are the dominant reactions. Affective reactions can occur without extensive perceptual and cognitive encoding, are made with greater confidence than cognitive judgments, and can be made sooner. Experimental evidence is presented demonstrating that reliable affective discriminations (like–dislike ratings) can be made in the total absence of recognition memory (old–new judgments). Various differences between judgments based on affect and those based on perceptual and cognitive processes are examined. It is concluded that affect and cognition are under the control of separate and partially independent systems that can influence each other in a variety of ways, and that both constitute independent sources of effects in information processing.

This article was the Distinguished Scientific Contribution Award address given at the meeting of the American Psychological Association, New York, New York, September 2, 1979. It was prepared with the support of a John Simon Guggenheim Fellowship.

I benefited greatly by discussing these ideas with several people, and I am very indebted to them. I am especially grateful to Hazel Markus, Phoebe Ellsworth, Allan Paivio, and Robyn Dawes, who all made extensive and helpful comments on an earlier draft.

Requests for reprints should be sent to R. B. Zajonc, Research Center for Group Dynamics, University of Michigan, Ann Arbor, Michigan 48106.

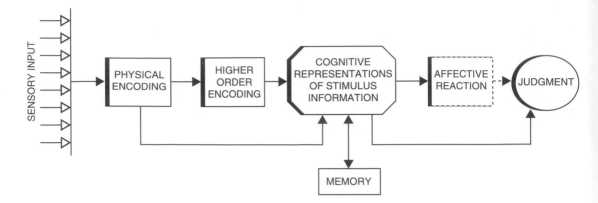

FIGURE 9.1 ■ Typical information-processing model of affect.

The intellectual contact between psychology and poetry is scarce and, when it takes place, often tends to be exploitative. If we happen to come across a poem that appears to support one of our favorite generalizations, we are tempted to cite it (not as evidence, of course, but more in the form of a testimonial). Or we might confer upon it the status of an epigraph in one of our forthcoming chapters (commonly, to the detriment of both the poem and the chapter). But when poetry disagrees with us we are apt to ignore the conflict altogether. Nevertheless, this paper begins with a poem by E. E. Cummings (1973), the first stanza of which affirms a premise tacitly rejected by psychology many decades ago:

> since feeling is first
> who pays any attention
> to the syntax of things
> will never wholly kiss you (p. 160)

In it, Cummings takes for granted that feelings are primary and, by implication, that they are fundamental. They are precedent to the intellective qualities and elements of experience, and they are nearer to its essence: They are nearer to an inner "truth."

In contrast, contemporary psychology regards feelings as last. Affect is postcognitive. It is elicited only after considerable processing of information has been accomplished (see Figure 9.1). An affective reaction, such as liking, disliking, preference, evaluation, or the experience of pleasure or displeasure, is based on a prior cognitive process in which a variety of content discriminations are made and features are identified, examined for their value, and weighted for their contributions. Once this analytic task has been completed, a computation of the components can generate an overall affective judgment. Before I can like something I must have some knowledge about it, and in the very least, I must have identified some of its discriminant features. Objects must be cognized before they can be evaluated.

Most of us will not be deeply distressed by discovering that our current theories are in conflict with a controversial poet of the 1920s. But contemporary psychology not only contradicts Cummings, it also contradicts one of its very own founding fathers. Thirty years before Cummings published his poem on feelings, Wundt (1907) wrote in a similar vein:

> When any physical process rises above the threshold of consciousness, it is the affective elements which as soon as they are strong enough, first become noticeable. They begin to force themselves energetically into the fixation point of consciousness *before anything is perceived of the ideational elements*[1] ... They are sometimes states of pleasurable or unpleasurable character,

---

[1] The italics are mine. The original is even more to the point. "Affective elements" were "Gefühlselemente," and the italicized part of the citation was "ehe noch von den Vorstellungselementen irgend etwas wahrgenommen wird" (Wundt, 1905, p. 262).

sometimes they are predominantly states of strained expectation. . . . Often there is vividly present . . . the special affective tone of the forgotten idea, although the idea itself still remains in the background of consciousness. . . . In a similar manner . . . the clear apperception of ideas in acts of cognition and recognition is always preceded by feelings. (pp. 243–244)

Whatever happened to Wundt's affective primacy idea? Is there compelling evidence to reject it?[2] Or to accept it, for that matter? Strictly speaking, we have no better evidence today than Wundt had in 1896. Perhaps a bit better.

In part, my concern in this paper is with Wundt's assertion. More specifically, building on the scanty evidence we now have, I have tried to develop some notions about the possible ways in which affect is processed as part of experience and have attempted to distinguish affect from processing of information that does not have affective qualities.

This article is confined to those aspects of affect and feeling that are generally involved in preferences. These aspects are reflected in the answers to such questions as "Do you like this person?" "How do you feel about capital punishment?" "Which do you prefer, Brie or Camembert?" "Are you pleased with the review your recent book received?" In short, I deal with some hot cognitions (as Abelson [1963] christened them) and try to distinguish them from the cold ones. The class of feelings considered here is that involved in the general quality of behavior that underlies the approach–avoidance distinction. Thus, for the present purposes, other emotions such as surprise, anger, guilt, or shame, which have been identified in the literature and extensively analyzed by Tomkins (1962, 1963), Izard (1977), and others, are ignored.

Unlike experimental psychologists,[3] social psychologists are deeply concerned with affect and

---

[2] It is a fact that only 12 years after the first edition of Wundt's *Grundriss* was published, Nakashima (1909a; 1909b) tested Wundt's assertion by collecting reaction times of psychophysical (pitch, hue, temperature, etc.) and affective (preference) judgments made on the same sets of stimuli. He did not find shorter reaction times for judgments of preference than for judgments of pitch, hue, temperature, etc., and thus disagreed with Wundt with regard to the primacy of feelings. But his study alone could not have buried Wundt's idea. Actually, Nakashima's data were rather inconclusive, since he failed to control for levels of discriminability associated with the two types of judgments. Thus, for example, subjects can detect very small differences in hue yet feel quite indifferent in their preference for stimuli that differ so little. Since reaction times for comparisons vary with the size of the difference, these times can be compared meaningfully only if the stimuli are preselected so that difference thresholds for the two types of judgments are the same.

[3] Contemporary cognitive psychology simply ignores affect. The words *affect, attitude, emotion, feeling,* and *sentiment* do not appear in the indexes of any of the major works on cognition (Anderson, 1976; Anderson & Bower, 1973; Bobrow & Collins, 1975; Crowder, 1976; Kintsch, 1974; Lachman, Lachman, & Butterfield, 1979; Norman & Rumelhart, 1975; Schank & Abelson, 1977; Tulving & Donaldson, 1972). Nor do these concepts appear in Neisser's (1967) original work that gave rise to the cognitive revolution in experimental psychology. And in the six volumes and the 2,133 pages of the *Handbook of Learning and Cognitive Processes* (Estes, 1975–1978), there is only one entry for *affect* and only one for

attitude. It is worth noting that both of these entries are in Volume 3 in a contribution written by a social psychologist. In the last three volumes—those principally devoted to cognition—there are no references to affect whatsoever.

The notable exceptions are Mandler's (1975) work on thought and emotion, Neisser's 1976 essay, and Miller and Johnson-Laird's (1976) recent volume on language and perception from which the following revealing quotation is taken:

The information-processing system that emerges from these remarks is fearfully cognitive and dispassionate. It can collect information, remember it, and work toward objectives, but it would have no emotional reaction to what is collected, remembered, or achieved. Since in this respect it is a poor model of a person, we should add at least one more predicate to this list of those that take "person" as their first argument. We will use *Feel* (person, *x*) to indicate that people have feelings as well as perceptions, memories, and intentions. It might be possible to subsume *Feel* under *Perceive* on the grounds that our feelings are a special class of perception of inner states. Or we might discuss feelings under *Remember*; the recognition that some word or object is familiar, is after all, a matter of feeling a certain way about it. Or, since we have already recognized that there is a strong affective component to our intentions, we might link *Feel* to *Intend.* . . . All these considerations testify to the systematic importance of this psychological predicate. Nevertheless, we will have little to say about *Feel* in the following pages. (pp. 111–112)

Thus, Miller and Johnson-Laird explicitly acknowledge the

with hot cognitions. The extensive work on attitudes, research on cognitive dissonance and cognitive balance, the Schachter and Singer (1962) studies on emotion, and Heider's (1958) attempts to describe the cognitive representation of affect that characterizes interpersonal relationships are all clear manifestations of this concern.[4] There are practically no social phenomena that do not implicate affect in some important way. Affect dominates social interaction, and it is the major currency in which social intercourse is transacted. The vast majority of our daily conversations entail the exchange of information about our opinions, preferences, and evaluations. And affect in these conversations is transmitted not only by the verbal channel but by nonverbal cues as well—cues that may, in fact, carry the principal components of information about affect. It is much less important for us to know whether someone has just said "You are a friend" or "You are a fiend" than to know whether it was spoken in contempt or with affection. Argyle and his colleagues (Argyle, Salter, Nicholson, Williams, & Burgess, 1970) found that 22 times more variance is accounted for by the tone of one's voice than by the content of the utterance when people are asked to interpret utterances. In fact, even when the content of recorded utterances is nearly completely obliterated by means of electronic masking, filtering, or random splicing of the tape, subjects still can encode the emotions expressed in these utterances quite reliably (Dawes & Kramer, 1966; Scherer, Koivumaki, & Rosenthal, 1972). And we have no difficulty in identifying emotions expressed by members of unknown cultures speaking unknown languages. In a recent volume on person perception, Schneider, Hastorf, and Ellsworth (1979) noted that "inferences based on nonverbal cues are primarily inferences about relationships and feelings, and thus are among the most important inferences we make" (p. 142). One cannot be introduced to a person without experiencing some immediate feeling of attraction or repulsion and without gauging such feelings on the part of the other. We evaluate each other constantly, we evaluate each others' behavior, and we evaluate the motives and the consequences of their behavior. And you have already made up your mind about this paper!

Nor is the presence of affect confined to *social* perception. There are probably very few perceptions and cognitions in everyday life that do not have a significant affective component, that aren't hot, or in the very least tepid. And perhaps all perceptions contain some affect. We do not just see "a house": we see "a *handsome* house," "an *ugly* house," or "a *pretentious* house." We do not just read an article on attitude change, on cognitive dissonance, or on herbicides. We read an "exciting" article on attitude change, an "important" article on cognitive dissonance, or a "trivial" article on herbicides. And the same goes for a sunset, a lightning flash, a flower, a dimple, a hangnail, a cockroach, the taste of quinine, Saumur, the color of earth in Umbria, the sound of traffic on 42nd Street, and equally for the sound of a 1000-Hz tone and the sight of the letter Q.[5]

---

significance of feelings as part of experience, yet they decide to devote minimal attention to them. Their decision is noteworthy in the light of their belief that "*Feel* is an indispensable predicate for any complete psychology and that it probably lies much closer than *Perceive, Remember*, and *Intend* to the basic sources of energy that keep the whole system running" (p. 112).

Beyond these volumes there are some isolated theoretical attempts directed toward the understanding of the role of motivational and emotional factors in perception and cognition (Broadbent, 1977; Erdelyi, 1974; Posner & Snyder, 1975a).

[4] While such studies as those of Byrne (1961), Berscheid and Walster (1978), or Rubin (1973), which deal with interpersonal attraction, also have a concern with affect, they do not contain specific analyses of how affect is represented as part of experience. And in studies that compare the effects of

conditions that differ on the affective dimension (such as self- vs. nonself-relevance, ego-involvement), it is generally not the affective quality per se in these conditions that is examined as the major source of variation.

[5] This conjecture probably does not apply to incidental perceptions where the attentive processes are at minimum, although it is not inconceivable that the traces of these incidental perceptions still might recruit affect upon retrieval and thus become hot. In fact, Izard (1979) assumes that some emotion is *always* present in consciousness. Normally, it is the emotion of "interest" that dominates behavior. This emotion, which directs and sustains attention and exploration, is absent only when other emotions such as distress or anger "achieve consciousness" (p. 165).

Feeling and Thinking

According to the prevalent models for affect (e.g., Figure 9.1), preferences are formed and expressed only after and only as a result of considerable prior cognitive activity. How fully and completely must objects be cognized before they can be evaluated? I argue, along with Wundt and Cummings, that to arouse affect, objects need to be cognized very little—in fact, minimally.

In order to consider this possibility more specifically it is important to distinguish between thoughts and feelings. At the genotypic level, this distinction is not an easy one to make, for it hovers dangerously near the mind-body duality. Some conceptual elements of this distinction, however, may be identified for purposes of clarity. While feelings and thoughts both involve energy and information, the first class of experiences is heavier on energy, whereas the second is heavier on information (e.g., Inhelder & Piaget, 1958; pp. 347–348). In the pure case, the analysis of feelings attends primarily to energy transformations, for example, the transformation of chemical or physical energy at the sensory level into autonomic or motor output. In contrast, the analysis of thoughts focuses principally on information transformations. In nearly all cases, however, feeling is not free of thought, nor is thought free of feelings. Considerable cognitive activity most often accompanies affect, and Schachter and Singer (1962) consider it a necessary factor of the emotional experience. Thoughts enter feelings at various stages of the affective sequence, and the converse is true for cognitions. Feelings may be aroused at any point of the cognitive process: registration, encoding, retrieval, inference, etc. But this converse relation is not totally symmetrical. I will later argue for Wundt's conjecture that affect is *always* present as a companion to thought, whereas the converse is not true for cognition. In fact, it is entirely possible that the very first stage of the organism's reaction to stimuli and the very first elements in retrieval are affective. It is further possible that we can like something or be afraid of it before we know precisely what it is and perhaps even *without* knowing what it is. And when we try

to recall, recognize, or retrieve an episode, a person, a piece of music, a story, a name, in fact, anything at all, the affective quality of the original input is the first element to emerge. To be sure, the early affective reaction is gross and vague. Nevertheless, it is capable of influencing the ensuing cognitive process to a significant degree. Needless to say, after some cognitive activity has been executed, there may be new feeling to the stimulus. But the fact that cognitions *can* produce feelings—as in listening to a joke, for example, where affect comes at the end with a punch line or as a result of post-decision dissonance—need not imply that cognitions are necessary components of affect. What I want to argue is that the form of experience that we came to call feeling accompanies *all* cognitions, that it arises early in the process of registration and retrieval, albeit weakly and vaguely, and that it derives from a parallel, separate, and partly independent system in the organism.

At the phenotypic level, we can support Wundt's conjecture by spelling out in somewhat greater detail some of the ways in which affective judgments and reactions, or hot cognitions, differ from their cold cognitive counterparts, keeping in mind that the first category is represented by the prototype "I like Joe," and the second by "Joe is a boy."

Affective Reactions are Primary

Wundt and Cummings are joined by Bartlett and Osgood in the view that feelings come first. Bartlett (1932) observes in his book on remembering,

> Attitude names a complex psychological state or process which it is very hard to describe in more elementary psychological terms. It is, however, as I have often indicated, very largely a matter of feeling, or affect. . . . [When] a subject is being asked to remember, very often the first thing that emerges is something of the nature of attitude. The recall is then a construction, made largely on the basis of this attitude, and its general effect is that of a justification of the attitude. (pp. 206–207)

In his analysis of environments as perceptual targets, Ittelson (1973) asserts that "the first level of response to the environment is affective. The direct emotional impact of the situation, perhaps largely a global response to the ambiance, very generally governs the directions taken by subsequent relations with the environment. It sets the motivational tone and delimits the kinds of experiences one expects and seeks" (p. 16). Preferences influence language comprehension and language production as well (Premack, 1976). Osgood (1962) was impressed with the primacy of affect in a different way:

> First, I must confess that, when we began this research over ten years ago, I had the expectation that the major factors of the semantic space would represent the ways in which our sensory apparatus divides up the world—e.g., would parallel Boring's "dimensions of consciousness." ... The accumulating data have proved my expectation wrong ... the dominant factors of *evaluation, potency* and *activity* that keep appearing certainly have a response-like character, reflecting the ways we can react to meaningful events rather than the ways we can receive them.
>
> But these major factors also seem to have an *affective* as well as a response-like character. As a matter of fact, the similarity of our factors to Wundt's (1896) tridimensional theory of *feeling*—pleasantness-unpleasantness, strain-relaxation, and excitement-quiescence—has been pointed out to me." (pp. 19–20)

It is significant also that at least three social-psychological conceptions labeled "cognitive" consistency theories focus not on consistency of content but on the consistency of affect (Abelson & Rosenberg, 1958; Heider, 1958; Osgood & Tannenbaum, 1955).

Decisions are another area where thought and affect stand in tension to each other. It is generally believed that *all* decisions require some conscious or unconscious processing of pros and cons. Somehow we have come to believe, tautologically, to be sure, that if a decision has been made, then a cognitive process must have preceded it. Yet there is no evidence that this is indeed so. In fact, for most decisions, it is extremely difficult to demonstrate that there has actually been *any* prior cognitive process whatsoever. One might argue that these are cases in which one alternative so

overwhelmingly dominates all the others that only a minimum of cognitive participation is required and that that is why the cognitive involvement preceding such decisions is so hard to detect. But this argument must confront the observation that if all decisions involve the evaluation of alternatives, then when choices appear quite lopsided to the decision maker, it is even more important to scrutinize the alternatives that appear inferior, for it is entirely possible that one of them possesses some hidden but overriding virtue. It is therefore not without merit to suppose that in many decisions affect plays a more important role than we are willing to admit. We sometimes delude ourselves that we proceed in a rational manner and weigh all the pros and cons of the various alternatives. But this is probably seldom the actual case. Quite often "I decided in favor of X" is no more than "I liked X." Most of the time, information collected about alternatives serves us less for making a decision than for justifying it afterward. Dissonance is prevalent just because complete and thorough computation is not performed before the decision (Festinger, 1964). We buy the cars we "like," choose the jobs and houses that we find "attractive," and then justify those choices by various reasons that might appear convincing to others who never fail to ask us, "Why this car?" or "Why this house?" We need not convince ourselves.[6] *We know what we like.*

In a study of consumer behavior, Quandt (1956) found that buyers often do not attend to the features of the article that they consider criterial for their decisions and often base their choices on features that they previously dismissed as irrelevant. And Kahneman and Tversky (1979) have demonstrated that numerous axioms of decision theory that give decisions their rational flavor are blatantly contradicted by experimental results.

---

[6] Phoebe Ellsworth (Note 1) illustrates the role of affect in her own recent decision experience. In trying to decide whether to accept a position at another university, she says, "I get half way through my Irv Janis balance sheet and say, 'Oh hell, it's not coming out right! Have to find a way to get some pluses over on the other side!' "

Affect is Basic

In one of her last books, which bears the provocative title of *Mind: An Essay on Human Feeling*, Susan K. Langer (1967) tried to show "that the entire psychological field—including human conception, responsible action, rationality, knowledge—is a vast and branching development of feeling" (p. 23). Affect is the first link in the evolution of complex adaptive functions that eventually differentiated animals from plants. And unlike language or cognition, affective responsiveness is universal among the animal species. A rabbit confronted by a snake has no time to consider all the perceivable attributes of the snake in the hope that he might be able to infer from them the likelihood of the snake's attack, the timing of the attack, or its direction. The rabbit cannot stop to contemplate the length of the snake's fangs or the geometry of its markings. If the rabbit is to escape, the action must be undertaken long before the completion of even a simple cognitive process—before, in fact, the rabbit has fully established and verified that a nearby movement might reveal a snake in all its coiled glory. The decision to run must be made on the basis of minimal cognitive engagement.

It is thus significant that in categorizing facial expressions, about 50% of the variance is explained by the pleasant–unpleasant dimension (Abelson & Sermat, 1962; Hastorf, Osgood, & Ono, 1966), and the same value is obtained for the multidimensional scaling of similarities among photographs of faces (Milord, 1978). Similarly, it is a typical result in semantic differential studies that among the three factors Evaluation, Potency, and Activity, all of which Osgood considers to be affective components of meaning, it is the first that accounts for about 50% of the variance.[7] And it is no accident, according to Osgood (1969), that

these three factors of the semantic space are found repeatedly among diverse sets of concepts:

> In my opinion, it is the innateness of the emotional reaction system of the human animal that underlies the universality of the affective E-P-A components of meaning. In other words, the "innateness" of E-P-A ... is really the pan-humanes of emotional reactions, and these obviously have evolutionary significance for the survival of any species. Organisms without other specialized adaptive mechanisms (e.g., armor, coloration, poisons, etc.) which were unable to represent for themselves the good versus bad implications of things (antelope versus saber-toothed tiger), the strong versus weak of things (saber-toothed tiger versus mosquito), and the quick versus slow of things (saber-toothed tiger versus quicksand) would have little chance of survival. In the human species these "gut" reactions to things appear as the affective meaning system (the E-P-A components of total meaning), and it is these components which provide us with what might most appropriately be called the "feeling tones" of concepts as a part of their total meaning. (p. 195)

Affective Reactions are Inescapable

Unlike judgments of objective stimulus properties, affective reactions that often accompany these judgments cannot always be voluntarily controlled. Most often, these experiences occur whether one wants them to or not. One might be able to control the expression of emotion but not the experience of it itself. It is for this very reason that law, science, sports, education, and other institutions of society keep devising ever new means of making judgments "objective." We wish some decisions to be more independent of these virtually inescapable reactions.

We may completely fail to notice a person's hair color or may hardly remember what it was shortly after meeting the person. But we can seldom escape the reaction that the person impressed us as pleasant or unpleasant, agreeable or disagreeable, as someone to whom we were drawn or someone by whom we were repelled. And these affective reactions—and, more important, the retrieval of affect—occur without effort. In contrast, some

---

[7] It is therefore something of a paradox that so little attention is paid to affect in information-processing studies. Most of the tasks in experiments on information processing are verbal. Most of them involve some forms of *semantic* memory. If the semantic space is primarily an *affective* space, as Osgood argues, then the affective components and qualities of information need to be given as much attention as their phonemic, graphemic, lexical, semantic, conceptual, or pictorial counterparts.

cognitive judgments require substantial effort. Chess contestants typically lose several pounds of their weight in the course of a tournament.

Because affective judgments are inescapable, they cannot be focused as easily as perceptual and cognitive processes. They are much more influenced by the context of the surround, and they are generally holistic. Affective reactions are thus less subject to control by attentive processes.[8]

Affective Judgments Tend to be Irrevocable

Once a cognitive judgment has been made—for example, that at the forthcoming social hour there will be more scotches drunk than bourbons—one can still be persuaded that it may turn out otherwise. It can be pointed out, say, that the distribution of ages of the guests is different than that we *really* like scotch better than bourbon, is greater than the supply of scotch. We can readily accept the fact that we can be wrong. But we are never wrong about what we like or dislike. Hot cognitions are seldom subjectively false. It would be much harder to persuade us that we *really* like scotch better than bourbon, given that we feel otherwise. Once formed, an evaluation is not readily revoked. Experiments on the perseverance effect, the strong primacy effects in impression formation, and the fact that attitudes are virtually impervious to persuasion by communication all attest to the robust strength and permanence of affect. Affect often persists after a complete invalidation of its original cognitive basis, as in the case of the perseverance phenomenon when a subject is told that an initial experience of success or failure has been totally fabricated by the experimenter (Ross, Lepper, & Hubbard, 1975).

The reason why affective judgments seem so irrevocable is that they "feel" valid. We are not easily moved to reverse our impression of a person or of a piece of music. We trust our reactions, we believe that they are "true" and that they accurately represent an internal state or condition. Perhaps the subjective validity of affective judgments and reactions and our confidence in these judgments derive from the Cartesian tradition[9] that allows us to doubt everything except our own feelings, especially the feelings of doubt. Perhaps it reflects a basic reality.[10]

Affective Judgments Implicate the Self

When we evaluate an object or an event, we are describing not so much what is in the object or in the event, but something that is in ourselves. Cognitive judgments deal with qualities that reside in the stimulus: "This cat is black," "Camembert and Brie are soft-ripened cheeses." These judgments are made on I-scales that are orders of stimuli (Coombs, 1964). Affective judgments, however, are made on J-scales, that is, scales on which are located jointly the various stimuli as well as the ideal preference point of the person. "I dislike this black cat" or "I prefer Camembert to Brie" are judgments on J-scales. Thus, affective judgments are *always* about the self. They identify the state of the judge in relation to the object of judgment.

Affective Reactions are Difficult to Verbalize

The remarkable aspect of first impressions of persons is their immediacy. When we meet a stranger, we know within a fraction of a second whether we like the person or not. The reaction is instantaneous

---

[8] The existentialists (e.g., Sartre, 1947) ascribe a substantial voluntary component to emotion. "The existentialist does not believe in the power of passion. He will never agree that a sweeping passion is a ravaging torrent, which fatally leads a man to certain acts and is therefore an excuse. He thinks that man is responsible for his passion" (pp. 27–28). Because of the participation of sensory, cognitive, and motor processes, the argument that emotions have some voluntary component is not without basis.

[9] Hume (1898), too, held that emotions (passions) cannot be false. "A passion must be accompanied with some false judgment, in order to its being unreasonable; and even then 'tis not the passion properly speaking, which is unreasonable, but the judgment" (p. 196).

[10] Because nonverbal cues exchanged in social interaction are dominated by affect, they are perceived as having such properties as trustworthiness and freedom from voluntary control (Schneider, Hastorf, & Ellsworth, 1979, pp. 123–127).

and automatic. Perhaps the feeling is not always precise, perhaps we are not always aware of it, but the feeling is always there. If our later experience with the stranger conflicts with the first impression, we are terribly surprised. We consider it an exception. Paradoxically, this subjective validity of affective reaction, this certainty that we "know what we like," is often accompanied by our inability to verbalize the reasons for our attraction or repulsion to the person.[11] When asked why we like someone, we say that we like the person because he or she is "nice," "pleasant," or "interesting." But these adjectives describe our reactions to the person, not the person. There simply aren't very effective verbal means to communicate why we like people and objects or what it is that we like about them.

The communication of affect, therefore, relies much more on the nonverbal channels (Ekman & Friesen, 1969; Schneider, Hastorf, & Ellsworth, 1979). Yet it is remarkably efficient. And it is in the realm of nonverbal expression of feelings that their basic nature is again revealed. The universality of emotional expression strongly suggests our evolutionary continuity with other species and the fundamental nature of affect. The facial expressions of humans upon biting into a sour apple and their expressions of surprise, anger, delight, or serenity are remarkably similar across all cultures and are not far removed from the expressions of the great apes. Perhaps we have not developed an extensive and precise verbal representation of feeling just because in the prelinguistic human this realm of experience had an adequate representation in the nonverbal channel.

The role of affective communication is particularly significant in the social interaction among animals. The effectiveness of communication of affect and the accuracy of recognition of affective expression are illustrated by the results of Pratt and Sackett (1967). They raised rhesus monkeys in conditions that allowed complete contact with peers, in conditions that allowed only visual and auditory access, and in complete isolation. The monkeys were then examined for the kinds of animals they preferred to approach. Those raised under the same conditions preferred each other twice as much as those raised under different conditions, even when the stimulus animals were total strangers to the test monkeys. While it could not be determined what sorts of cues allowed the animals to make these fine discriminations, it is very likely that the three groups developed during the course of their previous experience distinct patterns of emotional responding to new stimuli and to strange individuals, and that the animals raised under the same conditions found each other more attractive because of the familiarity of these emotional patterns.

The reliance of affect on nonverbal means of communication has, I believe, implications for the way it is processed. For if affect is not always transformed into semantic content but is instead often encoded in, for example, visceral or muscular symbols, we would expect information contained in feelings to be acquired, organized, categorized, represented, and retrieved somewhat differently than information having direct verbal referents. Recent electromyographic research provides strong evidence for the participation of muscular activity in the imagination, recall, and production of emotional states (Lang, 1979; Schwartz, Fair, Salt, Mandel, & Klerman, 1976). In light of these intuitions, it is not unreasonable to speculate that the processing of affect is closer to the acquisition and retention of motor skills than of word lists.

Affective Reactions Need Not Depend on Cognition

At the turn of the century, Nakashima (1909a, 1909b) tried to find support for Wundt's affective-primacy conjecture by comparing reaction times for psychophysical judgments and for preferences. He failed. But he did find evidence that judgments

---

[11] Mandler (1975), Neisser (1967), and Nisbett and Wilson (1977) pointed out that individuals have no access to the cognitions that occasion, mediate, or cause their actions, that are parts of their attitudes, or that determine their preferences. On the basis of an extensive review of the social psychological literature, Nisbett and Wilson (1977) concluded that introspective reports about influences on the subjects' evaluations, decisions, and actions were so unreliable as not to be trusted.

of pleasantness were independent of sensory qualities and that these judgments could not have been mediated by these qualities. Similar independence, based on multidimensional scaling, has been reported more recently, for example, in studying the perceptions of and preferences for soft drinks. Cooper (1973) found that similarity scaling yielded a space dominated by a "cola-ness" dimension, whereas preference scaling generated a space dominated by popularity of the drinks. Generally, it appears that similarity judgments predict preferences only when the similarity judgments are themselves highly evaluative, as in the case of admissions officers judging college candidates (Klahr, 1969) or art-trained students judging paintings (Berlyne, 1975; O'Hare, 1976). Osgood (1962) took it as a given that the affective reaction system "is independent of any particular sensory modality" (p. 21).

If there is indeed a separation between affect and cognition, then it is not surprising that research on preferences, attitudes, attractions, impressions, aesthetic judgments, and similar affective responses—research that commonly has invoked cognitive mediators—has not been terribly successful. If overall preferences were simply a matter of calculating the combination of weighted component preferences, and if component preferences were nothing more than cognitive representations of object features marked with affect, then the problems of predicting attitudes, decisions, aesthetic judgments, or first impressions would have been solved long ago. After all, these problems have been around for nearly a century. Yet except for trivial cases or cases in which the responses are highly cognitive (e.g., Yntema & Torgerson's [1961] study of judgments of ellipses), the cognition-based solutions to these problems have rarely predicted more than 20% of the total variance.

The dismal failure in achieving substantial attitude change through various forms of communication or persuasion is another indication that affect is fairly independent and often impervious to cognition. If attitudes consist of information units that have affect or utilities attached to them, then to change an individual's attitude, what could be

simpler than providing the individual with alternative information units that have the same sort of affect as that attached to the desired attitude? If a person believes that Candidate A is honest, we can simply give the person information proving that A is not honest. Or, we could change the centrality or the weight of honesty. Yet this approach has been the least successful in attitude change. Even the most convincing arguments on the merits of spinach won't reduce a child's aversion to this vegetable. Direct persuasion effects have been so weak that researchers have instead turned to more pernicious avenues of attitude change, such as insufficient justification, persuasion through distraction, the foot-in-the-door technique, or the bogus pipeline.

It is unlikely that calculations based on discriminable component features and their affective values will reliably predict our overall affective reactions to objects and events. These reactions do not seem to be composites of such elements. An affective reaction to a person we meet emerges long before any of these features can be identified, let alone evaluated. The assumption that component affect, utilities, or values attach themselves *to the very same* features that the subject attends to in a typical detection, recognition, discrimination, or categorization task is likely to be wrong.[12] The analysis of preferences is not simply an analysis of cold cognitive representations that have become hot, that is, cognitive representations that have some affect attached to them.[13] The stimulus features that serve us so well in discriminating, recognizing, and categorizing objects and events may not be useful at all in evaluating these objects. If

---

[12] I did not have the slightest doubt of this assumption, however, when I wrote my dissertation (Zajonc, 1955), which employed it without question.

[13] The term *hot cognition* has been used fairly indiscriminately, although it generally refers to cases when affect *accompanies* or *qualifies* information. 'I have a malignant tumor' is a hot cognition. However, the emotional experience of listening to one's favorite piece of music performed by one's favorite artist is less likely to receive the label of *hot cognition*. It is even less meaningful to speak of *hot cognitions* when affect becomes separated from the original cognitions.

this is indeed the case, then there must exist a class of features that can combine more readily with affect and thereby allow us to make these evaluations, to experience attraction, repulsion, pleasure, conflict, and other forms of affect, and to allow us to have these affective reactions quite early after the onset of the sensory input. These features might be quite gross, vague, and global. Thus, they might be insufficient as a basis for most cognitive judgments—judgments even as primitive as recognition, for example. In order to distinguish this class of features from simple discriminanda, I call them *preferenda* (Zajonc, Note 2).

I cannot be very specific about preferenda. If they exist they must be constituted of interactions between some gross object features and internal states of the individual—states that can be altered while the object remains unchanged, as, for example, when liking for a stimulus increases with repeated experience. Color preferences are a case in point. Similarity scaling of color yields three dimensions—brightness, hue, and saturation—that explain almost all of the variance in similarity judgments. But on the basis of Nakashima's (1909a) research and according to unpublished work of Premack and Kintsch (Note 3), the scaling of color for preference would not reveal these three factors. If we did not know from other sources that brightness, hue, and saturation exhaust the entire range of differences among colors, then we would not discover them by means of preference scaling. Abstract preferences for color and color preferences for classes of objects, such as hair, cars, or houses, are still more problematic if we insist on using brightness, hue, and saturation in quantifying them. And the same applies to face recognition: Physical features do not serve as discriminanda for faces (Milord, 1978; Patterson & Baddeley, 1977). It is therefore an interesting problem to discover what it is in color that "holds" affect if it isn't brightness, hue, and saturation and what it is in a face that "holds" affect if it isn't physical features. The answer to this problem is probably that *some* physical aspects, perhaps vague, gross, or configural, are involved, but not alone. Preferenda must consist of an interaction of these global features

with some internal state or condition of the individual.

Affective Reactions May Become Separated from Content

It sometimes happens that we are reminded of a movie or of a book whose contents we are unable to recall. Yet the affect present when leaving the movie or our general impression of the book are readily accessible. Or we are reminded of an interpersonal conflict of long ago. The cause of the conflict, the positions taken, the matter at issue, who said what, may have all been forgotten, and yet the affect that was present during the incident may be readily retrieved. Such experiences, together with such clinical phenomena as free-floating anxiety, hysteria, or posthypnotically induced moods, all point to the possibility that some aspects of affective processes might well be separate and partly independent of cold cognitions. Occasions when they are not include those when an affective experience has been communicated to someone else or when it has been thought of a great deal. On such occasions an elaborate cognitive representation of affect occurs that may be processed very much like any other type of information. It is important to observe, however, that not all affective experiences are accompanied by verbal or other cognitive representations and that when they are, such representations are imprecise and ambiguous.

Preferences Need No Inferences: Empirical Evidence

The prevalent approach to the study of preferences and related affective phenomena holds that affective reactions follow a prior cognitive process: Before I can like something I must first know what it is. According to this prevalent view, therefore, such cold cognitive processes as recognition or categorization are primary in aesthetic judgments, in attitudes, in impression formation, and in decision making: They come first. If we say, for example, that we like John *because* he is intelligent, rich, and compassionate, it follows that we must have gained some impression of John's intelligence, wealth, and compassion, and combined them, before we formed an attraction to him. This must be especially so in the case of judgments of novel stimuli before the component units become fused into an integrated structure. Thus, if the complexity of polygons is an important basis of their attractiveness, then polygons that are judged pleasing (or displeasing) must have previously been somehow examined for their complexity. Otherwise, the calculus of preferences makes little sense.[14]

The first indication that affect may not require extensive participation of cold cognitive processes appeared in studies of the exposure effect, that is, the phenomenon of increasing preference for objects that can be induced by virtue of mere repeated exposure (Harrison, 1977; Zajonc, 1968). While the empirical results that established the phenomenon were quite consistent, their explanation continued to be very elusive. Theories that attempted to account for the mere exposure effect, such as Harrison's (1968) response competition hypothesis or Berlyne's (1970) optimal arousal theory, treated affect as resulting from a prior cognitive process. Both theories contained the remnants of Titchener's (1910) thesis on familiarity. In explaining the preference for familiar objects, Titchener attributed a critical role to recognition, which he thought gave the individual a "glow of warmth, a sense of ownership, a feeling of intimacy" (p. 411). The majority of subsequent findings bearing on the explanation of the exposure effect, however, have revealed that recognition must play a relatively minor role, as must the subjective feeling of recognition.

Matlin (1971) was the first to discover that the role of recognition in the exposure effect may have been overstated. During an initial experimental session, she presented Turkish-like words either three times or six times. Subsequently, these words, together with others that were not shown at all, were rated for liking and also for familiarity. That is, for each word the subjects had to decide whether they saw it previously in the exposure series and to report how much they liked it. Table 9.1 shows Matlin's results. Liking is averaged as a function of objective familiarity and as a function of subjective familiarity. Note that there is an effect due to subjective familiarity, that is, when the subjects thought a stimulus was old they rated it more positively than when they thought it was new. However, the *objective* history of the individual's experience with the stimulus is just as effective in influencing liking. Stimuli that the subjects had actually seen were liked better than stimuli not seen, independently of whether the subjects thought of them as "old" or "new."

Similar results were obtained recently by Moreland and Zajonc (1977, 1979), using Japanese ideographs. Subjects were given 0, 1, 3, 9, and 27 prior exposures, counterbalanced, of course, with the stimuli. Following these exposures, the subjects made a variety of recognition and liking judgments. A number of findings are of interest. Many stimuli shown in the first series, some of them 27 times, were not recognized as familiar when shown later. Taking only those stimuli that were so judged, and relating the rated attractiveness of these stimuli to their actual number of exposures, we obtained correlations of .43 in one experiment and of .50 in another. An objective history of

---

[14] Affective reactions to objects that have been encountered and evaluated many times may become automated, thus gaining some independence from the component processes (Shiffrin & Schneider, 1977). As such, they may have different properties than *first* reactions. It is those first affective reactions (that is, those elicited when individuals are asked to evaluate objects totally novel to them) that I wish to consider at this point.

TABLE 9.1. Average Stimulus Affect Ratings as a Function of Objective Familiarity (Old–New) and Subjective Familiarity ("Old"–"New")

Objective familiarity	Subjective familiarity		
	"Old"	"New"	*M*
Old	4.90	4.20	4.47
New	4.20	3.90	4.01
M	4.55	4.05	

Note: Data are from Matlin (1971).

exposure influenced liking of stimuli for which the subjects could not have felt a "glow of warmth" or a "sense of ownership."

We also performed another type of analysis. Because we had a sufficient number of measures, we were able to use linear structural equation analyses to evaluate various causal models of our data. We used the LISREL III program (see Jöreskog & Sörbom, 1977) to calculate maximum likelihood estimates for causal models that assign different roles to the recognition factor. The program distinguishes between latent variables (constructs) and their observed indicators (measures). By estimating the unknown coefficients in a system of simultaneous equations for any particular model, the program describes the pattern of relations among the latent variables, distinguishing causal effects from unexplained variation in each case.

The results of this analysis are shown in Figure 9.2. Latent variables are shown in ellipses, while measures of those variables are shown in rect-

angles. The coefficients linking the ellipses with the boxes represent the validities with which particular latent variables were assessed by their measures. Path coefficients linking the latent variables to each other represent causal relations. Unexplained variation in the latent variables (V_1 and V_2) and error in the various measures (E_1 through E_5) are also shown. Some parameters (shown in parentheses) had to be set equal to some a priori value in the maximum likelihood solution so that variance in all of the latent variables could be identified.

The first model tested was one postulating that stimulus exposure has two mutually independent effects, one cognitive and one affective, or one cold and one hot. We supposed that under the impact of repeated exposure, people gain an increasing ability to recognize the stimulus—They achieve a feeling of subjective familiarity and an awareness of recognition, which authors since Titchener have thought to be the necessary conditions for an increased positive affect toward the stimulus. This

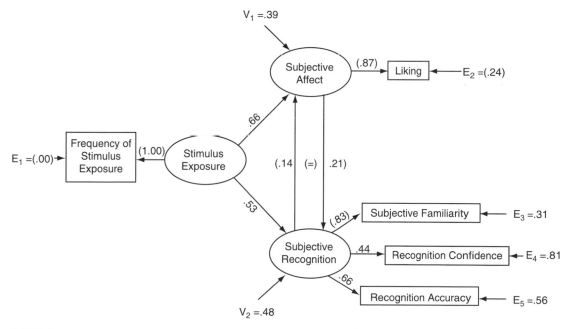

FIGURE 9.2 ■ Causal model for independent affect; goodness of fit is χ^2 (5) = 39.0. V = variable; E = error. (From "Exposure Effects May Not Depend on Stimulus Recognition" by R. L. Moreland and R. B. Zajonc, *Journal of Personality and Social Psychology*, 1979, 37, 1085–1089. Copyright 1979 by the American Psychological Association. Reprinted by permission.)

is the purely cold effect that is capable of generating the eventual "glow of warmth." However, we wanted to know as well whether, quite independently of this cold cognitive effect, there is also an affective change, or hot effect—that is, whether subjects acquire a more positive attitude toward the object as exposure increases, independently of recognition. They do. While the path coefficient from stimulus exposure to subjective recognition is substantial (.53), indicating that recognition improves with exposure, there also is a hot effect: There is a strong path from stimulus exposure to subjective affect that is *independent of recognition* (.66).

We can compare this model with one that is entirely cold, that is, with one that requires the entire process to be mediated by cognitive factors, by the discriminanda. This model, shown in Figure 9.3, says essentially that whatever affective changes take place as a result of exposure are entirely mediated by stimulus recognition. The result of requiring affect to be mediated by recognition is a substantial reduction in the efficiency of prediction. The χ^2 in the previous model was 39.0 ($df = 5$) and in this model is 83.6 ($df = 6$), generating a significant ($p < .01$) difference between the two models of χ^2 (1) = 44.6.

The experiments just described all involved presentation of stimuli under optimal conditions; that is, there was nothing to prevent the subjects from registering what was shown and from memorizing the information presented to them. Subjective recognition and the likelihood of recognition were controlled by statistical techniques. And the results

showing that stimulus recognition was not a necessary condition for the exposure effect were correlational.

Much firmer evidence, however, that hot cognition is quite short on cognition was collected by W. R. Wilson (1975), who controlled for recognition experimentally by means of an ingenious technique. He employed the method of dichotic listening in order to reduce recognition to a chance level. Random sequences of tones, such as those constructed by Vitz (1964), were presented to one ear, and a story was simultaneously presented to the other. Subjects were asked to track the story on a written page to verify whether what they heard corresponded to the printed text. The melodies were played five times each. The subjects were subsequently given a recognition memory test in which the earlier melodies and other melodies that they had never heard were played. But now there was no interference from the other channel, and no other task was required of the subject. The subjects also rated all the melodies for liking, some subjects giving their recognition memory judgments before, others after, the ratings for liking. The procedure succeeded in reducing recognition memory nearly to the chance level. The accuracy of recognition was 59% in one experiment and only 53% in another.

Table 9.2 shows the results of these experiments. Again, as in the case of previous results, liking varies with subjective recognition. But apart from this effect, liking also varies with the objective history of stimulus exposure. With recognition

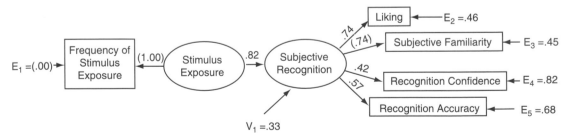

FIGURE 9.3 ■ Causal model for mediated affect; goodness of fit is χ^2 (6) = 83.6. V = variable; E = error. (From "Exposure Effects May Not Depend on Stimulus Recognition" by R. L. Moreland and R. B. Zajonc, *Journal of Personality and Social Psychology*, 1979, *37*, 1085–1089. Copyright 1979 by the American Psychological Association. Reprinted by permission.)

TABLE 9.2. Average Stimulus Affect Ratings as a Function of Objective Familiarity (Old–New) and Subjective Familiarity ("Old" –"New")

Objective familiarity	Subjective familiarity		
	"Old"	"New"	M
Old			
Experiment I	4.20	4.03	4.12
Experiment II	3.51	3.85	3.66
New			
Experiment I	3.75	3.07	3.30
Experiment II	3.03	3.02	3.03
M			
Experiment I	4.02	3.52	
Experiment II	3.29	3.40	

Note: Data are from Wilson (1975).

reduced nearly to the chance level, differential affective reaction to the stimuli is obtained as a consequence of mere repeated exposure. Random melodies presented five times were liked better than melodies never heard, even though the subjects could not discriminate the former from the latter for familiarity.

In a follow-up of these studies, Kunst-Wilson (who is the same person as W. R. Wilson) and I tried to reproduce the effect in a visual mode (Kunst-Wilson & Zajonc, 1980). Random polygons were constructed and presented for an extremely brief time interval—in fact, only 1 millisecond. Subsequently, the subjects rated the polygons for liking and were tested for their recognition memory. Judgments were made in paired comparisons to avoid possible response bias. Again, recognition was at a chance level: 48%. However, of the stimuli that were liked, 60% were old and 40% were new. Sixteen of 24 subjects liked objectively old stimuli better than new stimuli, but only 5 of 24 recognized them as such at better than chance level. And of the 24 subjects, 17 showed better discrimination between objectively old and objectively new stimuli in their affective judgments than in their recognition responses, while only 4 showed such superiority of recognition over affective judgments. Thus, the subjects were able to distinguish between the old and new stimuli if they used liking as their response, but they were not

able to distinguish between them if they had to identify them as "old" or "new." This result may be taken as evidence that a class of features (preferenda) exists that allows individuals to experience affect toward objects but does not allow them to accomplish cognitive tasks as simple as those in recognition memory tests.

These experiments establish, I believe, that affective reactions to a stimulus may be acquired by virtue of experience with that stimulus even if not accompanied by such an elementary cold cognitive process as conscious recognition. Thus, a theory that assumes that subjective experiences of novelty and familiarity mediate the affective response acquired during the course of exposures must contend with the results showing that with the subjective experience of novelty held constant, systematic variations in affect can be obtained just by means of an objective manipulation of exposure.

However, one should not assume that no form of recognition occurred. Obviously, some discrimination, however primitive or minimal, must have taken place, even though it must have been at a level not accessible to the subject's awareness. It is somewhat surprising that any effect at all was obtained with exposures as short as 1 millisecond, but it should be noted that the stimuli were high contrast (black on white) and that no mask was used. Detectable effects with 1-millisecond exposures were also obtained by Shevrin and Fritzler (1968) and by Shevrin, Smith, and Fritzler (1971). These authors reported differential evoked potentials and word associations to critical and control stimuli presented for 1 millisecond—stimuli that the subject could neither recognize nor identify. Even more pertinent is the work of Marcel (Note 4). He presented over a large number of trials either a single word or a blank always followed by a mask. The exposure duration of the word was varied. The subjects were then asked whether anything had been presented before the mask. If they answered yes, two words were then presented to them under optimal conditions. The subjects were then asked which of these two words was more *visually* similar to the one shown before the mask. Finally, they were asked which of these same two words was more *semantically* similar to the stimulus shown before the mask. With decreasing stimulus exposure, all three types of judgments tended to become less accurate, and eventually all three reached the chance level. But the first to become totally unreliable were judgments regarding the actual presence of the stimulus words. The second type of judgment to be reduced to a chance level by the decreasing exposures was that concerned with physical similarity. And when the subjects were totally unable to rise above chance in comparing physical similarities of the words, they were still judging their semantic similarities quite reliably.

Marcel's results are reminiscent of those reported by Broadbent and Gregory (1967), who found that unpleasant words (such as "blood") were more often misperceived as other unpleasant words (such as "death") than as equally probable neutral words. Marcel's results, moreover, are of particular interest if we consider the consistent findings from the semantic differential literature showing that meaning is very highly saturated with affect. If it is indeed affect that allows subjects to make a semantic match in the absence of conscious recognition, then deciding which of two given words is *emotionally* more similar to a stimulus word should be at least as easy as deciding which is semantically more similar. This experiment, in fact, is now being carried out by Moreland and myself.

Another consequence derives from the prevalent approach to affect and cognition. Prevalent theories, especially the one developed by the late Daniel Berlyne (1967), generally assume that the affective reaction occurs in response to the level of arousal,

which in turn is mediated by collative variables such as complexity, novelty, or congruity. If complexity, congruity, and novelty mediate liking, in that objects and events are liked just because they are optimally complex or simple, novel or familiar, then the judgments of objects along these dimensions should, in general, be more stable, more consistent, and made sooner than affective judgments. At the very least, these judgments should not be slower, more inconsistent, unstable, or inefficient than affective ratings. In particular, we would expect that recognition judgments, for example, which reflect the operation of the collative variable of novelty, should be made with greater confidence than liking judgments. Figure 9.4 shows the results from our previous study with Kunst-Wilson using 1-millisecond exposures. The results show that compared to liking judgments, recognition judgments are made with much less confidence. The differences are, in fact, huge – more than 6 times their standard errors. Even if we take only the recognition judgments on which the subject was correct, this effect remains true.[15]

One more bit of data. According to the prevalent view, attending to discriminanda alone should be easier and quicker than attending to discriminanda tagged with values. Since the latter involve more information, more detail must be attended to, and the subject would consequently require more processing time. If familiarity mediates the affective reaction generated as the result of repeated exposures, then judgments of familiarity should be made quicker than judgments of liking. If anything, however, our results showed the opposite. Although of only borderline significance, affective

[15] We suspected that these results may be due to the fact that the subjects knew they could be wrong on the old–new judgments, and awareness of this fact might have induced caution in them. But they could not be "wrong" on their liking judgments. These latter judgments express opinions, and people generally feel free to hold any opinions whatsoever. We tried, therefore, to "objectify" affective judgments and to "subjectify" recognition judgments in order to determine whether the confidence ratings would be reversed. To obtain "objectified" affective ratings, subsequent to stimulus exposures, we asked subjects in another experiment to rate the polygons for their "aesthetic value." We told them also in this connection that our polygons had all been rated for aesthetic value by art critics. To obtain "subjectified" recognition judgments, we told the subjects that one of the two polygons in each slide might appear more "familiar" than the other and asked the subjects to indicate which one did in fact appear more familiar. Thus, the subjects could now be "wrong" in their affective judgments, whereas recognition became much more a matter of subjective impression. The results did not change a great deal. Confidence was a little greater for subjective familiarity judgments than for the old–new judgments and a little weaker for aesthetic judgments than for judgments of outright liking. But these differences were quite small. The means were 2.01 and 2.41 for familiarity and aesthetic judgments, whereas they were 1.60 and 2.29 for recognition and liking.

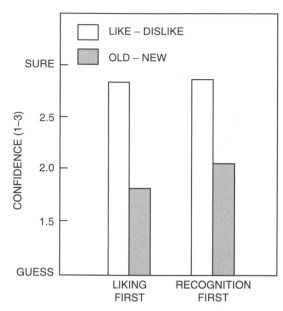

FIGURE 9.4 ■ Confidence in liking and recognition judgments. (Drawn from data reported by Kunst-Wilson & Zajonc, 1980).

judgments of polygons were made faster than recognition judgments.

Feeling and Thought: Two Systems?

About 10 years ago, Hyde and Jenkins (1969) carried out an experiment in which subjects were tested for recall of word lists to which they were exposed under different conditions. Some subjects were simply exposed to the words with the instruction to pay close attention. Of three other groups, one was instructed to count the number of letters in each word, another to report the presence of the letter E, and a third to rate each word for pleasantness. In some groups the subjects were warned that they would be tested for recall; in others they were not warned. Hyde and Jenkins's results were quite strong. Among both the subjects who were warned about a future recall test and those who were not warned, those asked to rate pleasantness showed the best recall. Hyde and Jenkins took their data to mean that items are "arranged" differently in storage depending on the context prevailing during acquisition. The superior performance of subjects

who rated the words for pleasantness was due to the fact that these subjects acquired the words as "units of meaning" and could therefore recruit for them supportive components of associative structures. When words are examined for number of letters or the presence of the letter E, such "structures are not activated and the recall is unorganized" (Hyde & Jenkins, 1969, p. 480).

Since, as we have seen earlier, the semantic content of verbal material is saturated with affect, the facilitation that occurred as a result of prior pleasantness ratings in the Hyde and Jenkins experiment could have strong affective components. Two conditions of a recent experiment by Rogers, Kuiper, and Kirker (1977) are of particular interest in this respect. In all conditions, their subjects were tested for recall of previously shown adjectives. In one condition, the subjects had to check the adjectives to see if they were printed in the same or different type as a sample print (structural), and in another whether they rhymed with comparison words (phonemic). But in two conditions the subjects were required to engage in extensive semantic processing of the adjectives: In one they checked the adjectives to see if they meant the same as comparison words (semantic) and in another to see whether they described the subject (self-reference). Note that while these last two conditions both activate semantic structures within which the adjectives are imbedded, the self-reference condition brings the subject into a cognitive domain greatly charged with affect. Rogers, Kuiper, and Kirker's findings are especially significant in view of the virtual discontinuity of the self-reference effects. Of the 10 self-reference adjectives, 2.84 were correctly recalled. In contrast, only .34, .68, and 1.33 adjectives were correctly recalled in the structural, phonemic, and semantic treatments, respectively.

Another group of similar studies that used recognition memory rather than recall also suggests strong participation of affect in information processing. Formulating their experimental problem in depth-of-processing terms (Craik & Lockhart, 1972), Bower and Karlin (1974) showed photographs of faces to subjects with instructions to judge the photographs for gender, honesty, or likeability. Following exposures, subjects were tested for recognition memory in two experiments. The hit rate was higher when the subjects rated photographs for honesty or likeability than when they reported gender. Strnad and Mueller (1977) replicated Bower and Karlin's results in a between-subjects design, and Warrington and Ackroyd (1975) found parallel effects when comparing these effects for faces and words, also in a between-subjects design. According to Bower and Karlin (1974), deeper processing facilitates recognition because it forces the subject to attend to a greater variety of detail. "Judgment of honesty of face would appear to require comparison to an idiosyncratic set of vague prototype criteria regarding the patterning of features such as distance between the eyes, size of pupils, curvature of the mouth, thickness of lips, and so on" (p. 756). They went on to say that "if you want to remember a person's face, try to make a number of difficult personal judgments about his face when you are first meeting him" (pp. 756–757). Patterson and Baddeley (1977) asked subjects to do just that: In one condition their subjects rated photographs of faces for the length of nose, distance between the eyes, roundness of face, or fullness of lips. In another condition the ratings were vague and less detailed but much more likely to recruit affect: nice–nasty, reliable–unreliable, intelligent–dull, and lively–stolid. Recognition memory, as reflected by d' and by hit- and false-alarm rates, was clearly superior for what Patterson and Baddeley called "personality" ratings. Patterson and Baddeley (1977) thus disagreed with Bower and Karlin and concluded that their own "results clearly did not implicate analysis of facial features as a critical or optimal basis for face recognition" (p. 411). Instead, they believed that should they "ever find an optimum strategy for encoding of faces, analysis of individual features is unlikely to be its focus" (p. 417).

There seems to be general agreement that when judgments of pleasantness are made of faces or of adjectives, individuals engage in forms of deeper information processing. What is not agreed upon is the type of content that is accessed at these deeper levels. Patterson and Baddeley (1977) doubt that face recognition is based on the sorts of discriminanda that we would intuitively suspect of serving recognition. But if these discriminanda are not the basis of face recognition, what is? Is face recognition, then, based on preferenda? Recall in this respect that the scaling of faces for similarity yields pleasantness as the major factor, explaining about 50% of the variance, whereas physical features play a relatively minor role. Clearly, the contribution of affect to face recognition has been underestimated. Early face discrimination is based primarily on affective reactions. Infants smile at an approaching face as early as 10 weeks of age, and at 12 weeks they smile differently at familiar and unfamiliar faces (Izard, 1978).

Curiously enough, none of the above studies mention the possible role of affect in processing face information. And none of the studies on recognition memory of faces collected reaction time data to verify whether the assumed deeper processing was accompanied by longer response latencies. However, in one recent study, Keenan and Bailett (1979) used methods similar to those of Rogers, Kuiper, and Kirker (1977) but instead administered recognition memory tests. They report results that have an important bearing on the form of information processing that may emerge when affect is involved. As in the previous studies, a number of adjectives were presented, and the subjects were required to check them against a number of criteria. For example, subjects were asked whether the given adjective described themselves, a best friend, a parent, another friend, a teacher or boss, a favorite TV character, or Jimmy Carter. Also asked for some adjectives was a semantic encoding question: "Means the same as ——?" Following the initial series, subjects were given a recognition memory task in which the original adjectives were interspersed among an equal number of similar distractor items. Keenan and Bailett's results are very clear. Self-reference generated by far the highest recognition performance (over 90%), whereas reference to Jimmy Carter produced a recognition rate of less than 65%. The other recognition rates were arranged according to the social significance that the target had for the subject: best friend, parent, friend, and teacher.

If the superior recognition memory for the

self-reference items was due to deeper processing, one would expect that response times for these items would be longer than response times for items processed at shallow levels. However, the results were quite the opposite and very strikingly so. Encoding times for self-reference items were by far the shortest. The longest reaction time was found for items referred to Jimmy Carter (note that the experiment was run in 1977 when Carter was not quite as well known as he is now). Moreover, the other targets had response times that varied directly with the proportion of correct recognitions.

Keenan and Bailett (1979) attempt a variety of cognitive interpretations, but at the conclusion of what is truly a valiant effort, they offer the possibility that in the course of processing self-referent information, "the crucial dimension underlying memory is not what the subject knows or the amount of knowledge that is used in encoding the item, but rather what the subject feels about what he knows" (p. 25). It is no longer clear that deeper processing necessarily requires more time. Structures that are highly integrated and that have been frequently "tuned in" may process information quite rapidly. The relation between reaction time and depth of processing cannot be predicted, therefore, for all tasks (Baddeley, 1978). Keenan and Bailett's study may be taken as evidence against the levels-of-processing approach. But it may also be taken as evidence that the participation of affect in processing information of some types may increase efficiency to a remarkable degree. The beneficial role of affect in memory is dramatically illustrated in a paired-associates study in which Sadalla and Loftness (1972) asked subjects to form pleasant, unpleasant, and nonemotional images for each pair and found considerably poorer performance for the neutral pairs than for either the pleasant or the unpleasant pairs.

It is this type of result that suggests the possibility of some separation between affect and cognition. Consider the task in those experiments where the subject is asked to verify if a given adjective, say "honest," describes him or her. It is most unlikely that the process of this verification involves checking the item for its presence in a list, as some information-processing models would

have it. For one thing, no evidence suggests even vaguely that the self is represented as a list of trait adjectives (Markus, 1977). For another, the question is probably not interpreted by the subject to mean "Is the trait 'honest' true of you?" but more likely to mean "Is the trait 'honest' consistent with your perception of yourself?" If this is indeed the interpretation that the subject imposes upon the task, then we must inquire what may be meant by "consistent with your perception of yourself?" To some extent this consistency may involve absence of content that is mutually contradictory; for example, the person could not be both tall and short. But more important, some form of affective consistency is probably involved. That is, the self as used in this task is probably some global and general impression suffused with affective quality. What is matched is primarily the affective quality of the item with the affective quality of the impression. Of course, the shorter processing times for self-referent items may be due to the fact that we have more integrated and better structured impressions of ourselves and of people who are important to us. But it is equally true that the self is a target charged with strong, widespread, and clear affect, and an emotional match would therefore be quite easy for the subject to verify. There is a need in these studies to separate the elaboration and integration of the cognitive structure from the affect that pervades it, but such a control procedure is difficult, for the two properties are highly correlated.

That the affective qualities in impression formation are processed differently and perhaps separately from the cognitive content that "carries" that impression is shown both by Anderson and Hubert (1963) and by Posner and Snyder (1975b). In a typical impression formation task, the first authors found strong primacy effects for impressions (i.e., the overall affective rating of the person was influenced more by early trait adjectives in the list) and an equally strong recency effect for the recall of the adjectives. Anderson and Hubert (1963) suggested that "the impression response is based on a different memory system than that which underlies the verbal recall" (p. 388). They did not go on to specify how these two systems might differ except to say that "as each adjective is received, its meaning is extracted and combined with the current impression, thus yielding a changed impression. Once this is done, memory for the adjective *per se* is no longer necessary for the impression process" (pp. 390–391).

Dreben, Fiske, and Hastie (1979) found similar order effects for impressions, and Hamilton, Katz, and Leirer (in press) obtained better recall when subjects organized items into an impression of a person than when subjects regarded these items as discrete units. More important for the dual-process hypothesis, however, is the finding of Dreben, Fiske, and Hastie that the weights calculated for the adjectives did not predict their recall. That is, the adjectives assumed to be contributing the most to impression are not necessarily also the ones that are best recalled. Following his cognitive response theory, Greenwald (1980) suggested that cues effective in helping the individual retrieve content may not be the same ones that are effective in helping retrieve the evaluative aspects of the content. It is not unreasonable to suppose that the major difference between these two types of cues may be the difference between discriminanda and preferenda. And it is perhaps the difference between these cues that is also involved in the perseverance effect (Ross, Lepper, & Hubbard, 1975), in that details of initial information about success (or failure) are used only to construct an overall impression of one's own task competence and are soon discarded. Thus, in debriefing, when the experimenter tells the subjects that their success (or failure) was rigged, this new information may no longer be capable of making contact with the original input (which by then has been recoded and discarded) and may therefore have little effect on its original affective consequences.

Posner and Snyder (1975b) also argue for a dual memory. In their experiments, subjects are shown a sentence such as "James is honest, loyal, and mature," and in a subsequent display a probe word such as "foolish" is flashed. Two tasks are studied. In one the subject is asked to verify if the word itself was among those in the preceding sentence. In another, the required match is between the emotional tone of the word and that of the preceding sentence. The interesting result these authors obtain is that, as the length of the list increases, reaction times increase for word matching and decrease for emotional tone matching. Posner and Snyder (1975b) agree with Anderson and Hubert about the two memory systems for the component adjectives and for the overall impression, but they doubt that the "emotional information concerning impression is handled in any different way than other semantic dimensions in the memory system" (p. 80). Their doubts should be weakened by a recent impression-formation experiment in which the pattern of recall of individual adjectives was effectively manipulated in the hope of thereby affecting the primacy of impressions. Riskey (1979) was able to change the recall of adjectives, but the primacy of impressions nevertheless remained unchanged.

While these authors propose separate systems, it is always separate *cognitive* systems that they propose. In contrast, the separation being considered here is between an affective and a cognitive system—a separation that distinguishes between discriminanda and preferenda and that takes us back to Wundt and Bartlett, who speculated that the overall impression or attitude has an existence of its own, independent of the components that contributed to its emergence. The question that cannot be answered with the data thus far collected is whether the affect–content separation is simply a matter of separate storage (as Anderson and Hubert, on the one hand, and Posner and Snyder, on the other, have proposed) or whether there isn't some separation already at the point of registration and encoding. The rapid processing times of affect suggest a more complete separation of the two processes at several junctures.

One is necessarily reminded in this context of the dual coding hypothesis proposed by Paivio (1975) for the processing of pictures and words. Paivio (1978a) suggested a number of differences between the processing of these types of content, for example, that representations of pictures emerge as perceptual isomorphs or analogs (imagens), whereas parallel units in the verbal system are linguistic components (logogens). He also proposed that pictorial information is organized in a synchronous and spatially parallel manner, whereas verbal information is discrete and sequential. Finally, he suggested that the processing of pictures is more likely to be the business of the right-brain hemisphere, whereas the processing of words is the business of the left. Paivio's proposal for a dual coding theory kindled a controversy of some vigor. While Anderson (1978) has recently argued that the controversy cannot be resolved with what we now know about these processes, it has nevertheless stimulated some exciting empirical and theoretical work (e.g., Banks & Flora, 1977; Kerst & Howard, 1977; Kosslyn & Pomerantz, 1977; Paivio, 1978b; Pylyshyn, 1973; Shepard, 1978).

Most relevant for my discussion, however, is Paivio's (1978c) finding that reaction times for pleasant-unpleasant ratings are faster for pictures than for words. Paivio takes this result to indicate that "the analog information involved in pleasantness and value judgments is more closely associated with the image system than with the verbal system" (p. 207). This

> analog pleasantness information is "carried by" affective and motor processes that are closely associated with visual memory representations of things. Such processes presumably originate as reactions to things and persist as affective or motor memories that can be activated by pictures of the referent objects, or, more indirectly, by their names when accompanied by the appropriate contextual cues. More specifically, pleasantness and value judgments might be based on continuously variable interoceptive reactions and approach or avoidance tendencies that are activated jointly by the comparison stimuli and the task instructions. (p. 207)

However, the specific responses of the autonomic nervous system are not readily discriminable, since there are not many receptors to register the fine changes in autonomic processes (Averill, 1969; Mandler, Mandler, Kremen, & Sholiton, 1961). Moreover, interoceptive process and motor memories are slower than the affective responses they are presumed to activate.

It is a fact, of course, that *all* sorts of judgments are faster and more efficient for pictures than for words, and this may be so just because pictures are able to evoke an affective reaction more directly and faster than words. An affective reaction aroused early in the encoding process—earlier than it is possible for the interoceptive and motor memories to become effective—might facilitate a complex cognitive encoding sequence by an initial categorization along affective lines, which, as we have seen, requires minimal stimulus information. Such facilitation through early affective sorting that relies not only on discriminanda but on preferenda as well may also induce a constructive process that can more readily recruit stored content by searching for congruent affective tags.[16]

This review suggests that a separation between affect and cognition may well have a psychological and a biological basis.[17] Recall that in contrast with

---

[16] Another area of research in which affect may be implicated (although it had not been so suspected) is the frequency-judgment paradigm. Typically, in these experiments subjects are shown stimuli in different frequencies, and two types of judgments are collected afterwards. In one condition, the subjects are shown the old stimuli interspersed among new ones and are asked to report for each item whether it is new or old. In the other condition, the subjects must say how often each stimulus occurred. It turns out that the frequency judgment generates greater accuracy than the binary recognition memory judgment (e.g., Proctor, 1977; Proctor & Ambler, 1975). Two findings are of interest in the present context. First, subjects have remarkable confidence in their frequency judgments (Howell, 1971). Second, warning the subjects that they will be estimating frequencies of events (vs. simply recalling them) and varying the length of the list both influence free recall but have little if any effect on frequency estimation

(Howell, 1973). It thus appears that frequency judgments behave like affective judgments. It is possible, therefore, that frequency estimation is more likely to invoke an underlying affective reaction (which accrues from repeated stimulus exposures) than the binary recognition memory task. It may be hotter. Since frequency judgment makes exposure effects salient and since it requires finer discrimination than recognition memory, it may recruit affect as an auxiliary source of information. In fact, it has been suggested that recognition memory responses and frequency estimation are not made from the same sources of information (Wells, 1974), although what these sources are and how they differ from each other is not altogether clear (Hintzman, 1976).

[17] Multiple processing systems and multiple channel conceptions are today more the rule than the exception in the study of sensory processes (Graham & Nachmias, 1971; Trevarthen, 1968).

cold cognitions, affective responses are effortless, inescapable, irrevocable, holistic, more difficult to verbalize, yet easy to communicate and to understand. [. . .]

Affective reactions are primary in ontogeny. The infant knows to cry and to smile long before it acquires any semblance of verbal skills (Izard, 1978, 1979). Meltzoff and Moore (1977) report that human infants can imitate emotional expressions at 12 days of age, long before they acquire language. And good–bad is one of the very first discriminations that children learn.

More important, however, affect is clearly primary in philogeny. Affect was there before we evolved language and our present form of thinking. The limbic system that controls emotional reactions was there before we evolved language and our present form of thinking. It was there before the neocortex, and it occupies a large proportion of the brain mass in lower animals. Before we evolved language and our cognitive capacities, which are so deeply dependent on language, it was the affective system alone upon which the organism relied for its adaptation. The organism's responses to the stimuli in its environment were selected according to their affective antecedents and according to their affective consequences. Thus, if the most recent version of homo sapiens specifies that affective reactions are mediated by prior cognitive processes—as contemporary cognitive views would have it—then at some point in the course of evolution, affect must have lost its autonomy and acquired an intermediary in the form of cold cognition. This scenario seems most unlikely. When nature has a direct and autonomous mechanism that functions efficiently—and there is no reason to suppose that the affective system was anything else—it does not make it indirect and entirely dependent on a newly evolved function. It is rather more likely that the affective system retained its autonomy, relinquishing its exclusive control over behavior slowly and grudgingly. At most, the formerly sovereign affective system may have accepted an alliance with the newly evolved system to carry out some adaptive functions jointly. These conjectures make a two-system view more plausible than one that relegates affect to a secondary role mediated and dominated by cognition.

Because it is so heavily rooted in verbal skills, the cognitive system in humans has properties that are quite distinct from those of affect. Above all, the cognitive system is infinitely more diverse and flexible than the affective system. Anything at all can be said and thought with various degrees of precision, and these things can be said and thought in an infinite variety of ways. But there are only a handful of emotions and feelings that can be felt, and they can be felt only in some few, very constrained ways. And for reasons that must be rooted in the partial separation of the two systems, affect can be communicated much more efficiently and accurately than thought in spite of the fact that its vocabulary is quite limited. It was a wise designer who provided separately for each of these processes instead of presenting us with a multiple-purpose appliance that, like the rotisserie-broiler-oven-toaster, performs none of its functions well.

Conclusion

[. . .] I began this paper with a quotation from Wundt, and it must be apparent that another spirit has emerged as I have developed my arguments—that of Freud. The separation of affect and cognition, the dominance and primacy of affective reactions, and their ability to influence responses when ordinary perceptual recognition is at chance level are all very much in the spirit of Freud, the champion of the unconscious. In terms of my formulation, there seem to be at least two different forms of unconscious processes. One emerges where behavior, such as that occurring in discrimination among stimuli, is entirely under the influence of affective factors without the participation of cognitive processes. Included here are such phenomena as perceptual defense and vigilance, subliminal perception and discrimination, state dependent recall, and mood and context effects. Another form of unconscious process is implicated in highly overlearned, and thus automated, sequences of information processing; this form includes cognitive acts but has collapsed them into larger molar chunks that may conceal their original component links (cf. Shiffrin & Schneider, 1977). And there may be other forms of process in which the separation between affect and cognition prevents the individual from apprehending the potential connection between them.

Because the language of my paper has been stronger than can be justified by the logic of the argument or the weight of the evidence, I hasten to affirm that one of my purposes was to convince you that affect should not be treated as unalterably last and invariably postcognitive. The evolutionary origins of affective reactions that point to their survival value, their distinctive freedom from attentive control, their speed, the importance of affective discriminations for the individual, the extreme forms of action that affect can recruit—all of these suggest something special about affect. People do not get married or divorced, commit murder or suicide, or lay down their lives for freedom upon a detailed cognitive analysis of the pros and cons of their actions. If we stop to consider just how much variance in the course of our lives is controlled by cognitive processes and how much by affect, and how much the one and the other influence the important outcomes in our lives, we cannot but agree that affective phenomena deserve far more attention than they have received from cognitive psychologists and a closer cognitive scrutiny from social psychologists.

REFERENCE NOTES

1. Ellsworth, P. Personal communication, May 13, 1979.
2. Zajonc, R. B. *Preferenda and discriminanda: Processing of affect.* Paper presented at the First Ontario Symposium on Personality and Social Psychology, London, Ontario, Canada, August 1978.
3. Premack, D., & Kintsch, W. Personal communication, July 1979.
4. Marcel, J. *Unconscious reading: Experiments on people who do not know that they are reading.* Paper presented to the British Association for Advancement of Science, Lancaster, England, 1976.
5. Katz, R. J. Personal communication, February 1979.

REFERENCES

Abelson, R. P. Computer simulation of "hot cognitions." In S. Tomkins & S. Mesick (Eds.), *Computer simulation of personality.* New York: Wiley, 1963.

Abelson, R. P., & Rosenberg, M. J. Symbolic psychologic: A model of attitudinal cognition. *Behavioral Science,* 1958, *3,* 1–13.

Abelson, R. P., & Sermat, V. Multidimensional scaling of facial expressions. *Journal of Experimental Psychology,* 1962, *63,* 546–554.

Anderson, J. R. *Language, memory, and thought.* Hillsdale, N.J.: Erlbaum, 1976.

Anderson, J. R. Arguments concerning representations for mental imagery. *Psychological Review,* 1978, *85,* 249–277.

Anderson, J. R., & Bower, G. H. *Human associative memory.* Washington, D.C.: Winston, 1973.

Anderson, N. H., & Hubert, S. Effects of concomitant verbal recall on order effects in personality impression formation. *Journal of Verbal Learning and Verbal Behavior,* 1963, *2,* 379–391.

Argyle, M., Salter, V., Nicholson, H., Williams, M., & Burgess, P. The communication of inferior and superior attitudes by verbal and non-verbal signals. *British Journal of Social and Clinical Psychology,* 1970, *9,* 222–231.

Averill, J. R. Autonomic response patterns during sadness and mirth. *Psychophysiology,* 1969, *5,* 399–414.

Baddeley, A. D. The trouble with levels: A re-examination of Craik and Lockhart's framework for memory research. *Psychological Review,* 1978, *85,* 139–152.

Banks, W. P., & Flora, J. Semantic and perceptual processes in symbolic comparisons. *Journal of Experimental Psychology: Human Perception and Performance,* 1977, *3,* 278–290.

Barlett, F. C. *Remembering: A study in experimental and social psychology.* Cambridge, England: Cambridge University Press, 1932.

Berlyne, D. E. Arousal and reinforcement. In D. Levine (Ed.), *Nebraska Symposium on Motivation* (Vol. 15). Lincoln: University of Nebraska Press, 1967.

Berlyne, D. E. Novelty, complexity, and hedonic value. *Perception and Psychophysics,* 1970, *8,* 279–286.

Berlyne, D. E. Dimensions of perception of exotic and pre-renaissance paintings. *Canadian Journal of Psychology,* 1975, *29,* 151–173.

Berscheid, E., & Walster, E. *Interpersonal attraction.* Reading, Mass.: Addison-Wesley, 1978.

Blum, G. S., & Barbour, J. S. Selective inattention to anxiety-linked stimuli. *Journal of Experimental Psychology: General,* 1979, *108,* 182–224.

Bobrow, D. G., & Collins, A. *Representation and understanding.* New York: Academic Press, 1975.

Bower, G. H., & Karlin, M. B. Depth of processing pictures of faces and recognition memory. *Journal of Experimental Psychology,* 1974, *103,* 751–757.

Broadbent, D. E. The hidden preattentive processes. *American Psychologist,* 1977, *32,* 109–118.

Broadbent, D. E., & Gregory, M. H. P. The perception of emotionally toned words. *Nature,* 1967, *215,* 581–584.

Byrne, D. Interpersonal attraction and attitude similarity.

Journal of Abnormal and Social Psychology, 1961, *62*, 713–715.

Carmon, A., & Nachson, I. Ear asymmetry in perception of emotional non-verbal stimuli. *Acta Psychologica*, 1973, *37*, 351–357.

Coombs, C. H. *A theory of data*. New York: Wiley, 1964.

Cooper, L. G. A multivariate investigation of preferences. *Multivariate Behavioral Research*, 1973, *8*, 253–272.

Craik, F. I. M., & Lockhart, R. S. Levels of processing: A framework for memory research. *Journal of Verbal Learning and Verbal Behavior*, 1972, *11*, 671–684.

Crowder, R. G. *Principles of learning and memory*. Hillsdale, N.J.: Erlbaum, 1976.

Cummings, E. E. *Complete poems* (Vol. I). Bristol, England: McGibbon & Kee, 1973.

Dawes, R. M., & Kramer, E. A proximity analysis of vocally expressed emotion. *Perceptual and Motor Skills*, 1966, *22*, 571–574.

De Renzi, E., & Spinnler H. Facial recognition in brain-damaged patients. *Neurology*, 1966, *16*, 145–152.

Diamond, S. J., Farrington, L., & Johnson, P. Differing emotional response from right and left hemisphere. *Nature*, 1976, *261*, 690–692.

Dreben, E. K., Fiske, S. T., & Hastie, R. The independence of evaluative and item information: Impression and recall order effects in behavior-based impression formation. *Journal of Personality and Social Psychology*, 1979, *37*, 1758–1768.

Ekman, P., & Friesen, W. V. The repertoire of nonverbal behavior: Categories, origins, usage, and coding. *Semiotica*, 1969, *1*, 49–98.

Erdelyi, M. H. A new look at the New Look: Perceptual defense and vigilance. *Psychological Review*, 1974, *81*, 1–25.

Estes, W. K. (Ed.). *Handbook of learning and cognitive processes* (Vols. 1–6). Hillsdale, N.J.: Erlbaum, 1975–1978.

Festinger, L. *Conflict, decision, and dissonance*. Stanford, Calif.: Stanford University Press, 1964.

Gainotti, G. Emotional behavior and hemispheric side of the lesion. *Cortex*, 1972, *8*, 41–55.

Graham, N., & Nachmias, J. Detection of grating patterns containing two spatial frequencies: A comparison of single-channel and multiple-channels models. *Vision Research*, 1971, *11*, 251–259.

Greenwald, A. G. Cognitive response analysis: An appraisal. In R. E. Petty, T. M. Ostrom, & T. C. Brock (Eds.), *Cognitive responses in persuasive communication*. Hillsdale, N.J.: Erlbaum, 1980.

Hamilton, D. L., Katz, L. B., & Leirer, V. O. Organizational processes in impression formation. In R. Hastie, T. Ostrom, E. Ebbesen, R. Wyer, D. Hamilton, & D. Carlston (Eds.), *Person memory*. Hillsdale, N.J.: Erlbaum, in press.

Harrison, A. A. Response competition, frequency, exploratory behavior, and liking. *Journal of Personality and Social Psychology*, 1968, *9*, 363–368.

Harrison, A. A. *Mere exposure*. In L. Berkowitz (Ed.),

Advances in experimental social psychology (Vol. 10). New York: Academic Press, 1977.

Hastorf, A. H., Osgood, C. E., & Ono, H. The semantics of facial expressions and the prediction of the meanings of stereoscopically fused facial expressions. *Scandinavian Journal of Psychology*, 1966, *7*, 179–188.

Heider, F. *The psychology of interpersonal relations*. New York: Wiley, 1958.

Hintzman, D. L. Repetition and memory. In G. H. Bower (Ed.), *The psychology of learning and motivation* (Vol. 10). New York: Academic Press, 1976.

Howell, W. C. Uncertainty from internal and external sources: A clear case of overconfidence. *Journal of Experimental Psychology*, 1971, *89*, 240–243.

Howell, W. C. Representation of frequency in memory. *Psychological Bulletin*, 1973, *80*, 44–53.

Hume, D. *A treatise on human nature* (Vol. 2). London: Longmans, Green, 1898.

Hyde, T. W., & Jenkins J. J. The differential effects of incidental tasks on the organization of recall of a list of highly associated words. *Journal of Experimental Psychology*, 1969, *82*, 472–481.

Inhelder, B., & Piaget, J. *The growth of logical thinking from childhood to adolescence*. New York: Basic Books, 1958.

Ittelson, W. H. Environment perception and contemporary perceptual theory. In W. H. Ittelson (Ed.), *Environment and cognition*. New York: Seminar Press, 1973.

Izard, C. E. *Human emotions*. New York: Plenum Press, 1977.

Izard, C. E. On the development of emotions and emotion-cognition relationship in infancy. In M. Lewis & L. Rosenblum (Eds.), *The development of affect*. New York: Plenum Press, 1978.

Izard, C. E. Emotions as motivations: An evolutionary-developmental perpective. In R. Dienstbier (Ed.), *Nebraska Symposium on Motivation* (Vol. 27). Lincoln: University of Nebraska Press, 1979.

Johnston, J. C., & McClelland, J. L. Perception of letters: Seek not and ye shall find. *Science*, 1974, *184*, 1192–1194.

Jöreskog, K. G., & Sörbom, D. Statistical models and methods for analysis of longitudinal data. In D. J. Aigner & A. S. Goldberger (Eds.), *Latent variables in socio-economic models*. Amsterdam: North-Holland, 1977.

Kahneman, D., & Tversky, A. Prospect theory: An analysis of decision under risk. *Econometrica*, 1979, *47*, 263–291.

Keenan, J. M., & Bailett, S. D. Memory for personally and socially significant events. In R. S. Nickerson (Ed.), *Attention and performance VIII*. Hillsdale, N.J.: Erlbaum, 1979.

Kerst, S. M., & Howard, J. H., Jr. Mental comparisons for ordered information on abstract and concrete dimensions. *Memory and Cognition*, 1977, *5*, 227–234.

Kintsch, W. *The representation of meaning in memory*. Hillsdale, N.J.: Erlbaum, 1974.

Klahr, D. Decision making in a complex environment: The use of similarity judgments to predict preferences. *Management Science*, 1969, *15*, 595–618.

Kosslyn, S. M., & Pomerantz, J. R. Imagery, propositions, and the form of internal representations. *Cognitive Psychology*, 1977, *9*, 52–76.

Kunst-Wilson, W. R., & Zajonc, R. B. Affective discrimination of stimuli that cannot be recognized. *Science*, 1980, *207*, 557–558.

Lachman, R., Lachman, J. L., & Butterfield, E. C. *Cognitive psychology and information processing*. Hillsdale, N.J.: Erlbaum, 1979.

Lang, P. J. A bio-informational theory of emotional imagery. *Psychophysiology*, 1979, *16*, 495–512.

Langer, S. K. *Mind: An essay on human feeling* (Vol. 1). Baltimore, Md.: Johns Hopkins University Press, 1967.

Ley, R. G., & Bryden, M. P. Hemispheric differences in processing emotions and faces. *Brain and Language*, 1979, *7*, 127–138.

Mandler, G. *Mind and emotion*. New York: Wiley, 1975.

Mandler, G., Mandler, J. M., Kremen, I., & Sholiton, R. D. The response to threat: Relations among verbal and physiological indices. *Psychological Monographs*, 1961, *75*(9, Whole No. 513).

Markus, H. Self-schemata and processing of information about the self. *Journal of Personality and Social Psychology*, 1977, *35*, 63–78.

Marshall, J. C., & Newcombe, F. Syntactic and semantic errors in paralexia. *Neuropsychologia*, 1966, *4*, 169–176.

Matlin, M. W. Response competition, recognition, and affect. *Journal of Personality and Social Psychology*, 1971, *19*, 295–300.

Meltzoff, A. N., & Moore, M. K. Imitation of facial and manual gestures by human neonates. *Science*, 1977, *198*, 75–78.

Miller, G. A., & Johnson-Laird, P. N. *Language and perception*. Cambridge, Mass.: The Belknap Press of Harvard University Press, 1976.

Milner, B. Visual recognition and recall after right temporal-lobe excision in man. *Neuropsychologia*, 1968, *6*, 191–209.

Milord, J. T. Aesthetic aspects of faces: A (somewhat) phenomenological analysis using multidimensional scaling methods. *Journal of Personality and Social Psychology*, 1978, *36*, 205–216.

Moore, E. F., & Shannon, C. E. Reliable circuits using less reliable relays. Part I. *Journal of the Franklin Institute*, 1956, *262*, 191–208.

Moreland, R. L., & Zajonc, R. B. Is stimulus recognition a necessary condition for the occurrence of exposure effects? *Journal of Personality and Social Psychology*, 1977, *35*, 191–199.

Moreland, R. L., & Zajonc, R. B. Exposure effects may not depend on stimulus recognition. *Journal of Personality and Social Psychology*, 1979, *37*, 1085–1089.

Moscovitch, M., Scullion, D., & Christie, D. Early versus late stage of processing and their relation to functional hemispheric asymmetries in face recognition. *Journal of Experimental Psychology: Human Perception and Performance*, 1976, *2*, 401–416.

Nakashima, T. Contribution to the study of the affective processes. *American Journal of Psychology*, 1909, *20*, 157–193. (a)

Nakashima, T. Time-relations of the affective process. *Psychological Review*, 1909, *16*, 303–339. (b)

Neisser, U. *Cognitive psychology*. Englewood Cliffs, N.J.: Prentice-Hall, 1967.

Neisser, U. *Cognition and reality*. San Francisco: Freeman, 1976.

Nisbett, R. E., & Wilson, T. D. Telling more than we can know: Verbal reports on mental processes. *Psychological Review*, 1977, *84*, 231–259.

Norman, D. A., & Rumelhart, D. E. *Explorations in cognition*. San Francisco: Freeman, 1975.

O'Hare, D. Individual differences in perceived similarity and preference for visual art: A multidimensional scaling analysis. *Perception & Psychophysics*, 1976, *20*, 445–452.

Osgood, C. E. Studies on the generality of affective meaning systems. *American Psychologist*, 1962, *17*, 10–28.

Osgood, C. E. On the whys and wherefores of E, P, and A. *Journal of Personality and Social Psychology*, 1969, *12*, 194–199.

Osgood, C. E., & Tannenbaum, P. H. The principle of congruity in the prediction of attitude change. *Psychological Review*, 1955, *62*, 42–55.

Paivio, A. Perceptual comparisons through the mind's eye. *Memory and Cognition*, 1975, *3*, 635–647.

Paivio, A. Dual coding: Theoretical issues and empirical evidence. In J. M. Scandura & C. J. Brainerd (Eds.), *Structural/process models of complex human behavior*. Leiden, The Netherlands: Nordhoff, 1978. (a)

Paivio, A. Images, propositions, and knowledge. In J. M. Nicholas (Ed.), *Images, perception, and knowledge. The Western Ontario Series in Philosophy of Science* (No. 8). Dordrecht, The Netherlands: Reidel, 1978. (b)

Paivio, A. Mental comparisons involving abstract attributes. *Memory and Cognition*, 1978, *3*, 199–208. (c)

Patterson, K. E., & Baddeley, A. D. When face recognition fails. *Journal of Experimental Psychology: Human Learning and Memory*, 1977, *3*, 406–417.

Posner, M. I., & Snyder, C. R. R. Attention and cognitive control. In R. L. Solso (Ed.), *Information processing and cognition: The Loyola Symposium*. Hillsdale, N.J.: Erlbaum, 1975. (a)

Posner, M. I., & Snyder, C. R. R. Facilitation and inhibition in the processing of signals. In P. M. A. Rabbitt & S. Dornic (Eds.), *Attention and performance V*. New York: Academic Press, 1975. (b)

Pratt, C. L., & Sackett, G. P. Selection of partners as a function of peer contact during rearing. *Science*, 1967, *155*, 1133–1135.

Premack, D. *Intelligence in ape and man*. Hillsdale, N.J.: Erlbaum, 1976.

Proctor, R. W. The relationship of frequency judgments to recognition: Facilitation of recognition and comparison to recognition-confidence judgments. *Journal of Experimental Psychology: Human Learning and Memory*, 1977, *3*, 679–689.

Proctor, R. W., & Ambler, B. A. Effects of rehearsal strategy on memory for spacing and frequency. *Journal of Experimental Psychology: Human Learning and Memory*, 1975, *1,* 640–647.

Pylyshyn, Z. W. What the mind's eye tells the mind's brain: A critique of mental imagery. *Psychological Bulletin*, 1973, *80,* 1–24.

Quandt, R. E. A probabilistic theory of consumer behavior. *Quarterly Journal of Economics*, 1956, *70,* 507–536.

Riskey, D. R. Verbal memory process in impression formation. *Journal of Experimental Psychology: Human Learning and Memory*, 1979, *5,* 271–281.

Rogers, T. B., Kuiper, N. A., & Kirker, W. S. Self-reference and the encoding of personal information. *Journal of Personality and Social Psychology*, 1977, *35,* 677–688.

Ross, L., Lepper, M. R., & Hubbard, M. Perseverance in self-perception and social perception: Biased attributional processes in the debriefing paradigm. *Journal of Personality and Social Psychology*, 1975, *32,* 880–892.

Rubin, Z. *Liking and loving*. New York: Holt, Rinehart & Winston, 1973.

Sadalla, E. K., & Loftness, S. Emotional images as mediators in one-trial paired-associates learning. *Journal of Experimental Psychology*, 1972, *95,* 295–298.

Safer, N. A., & Leventhal, H. Ear differences in evaluating emotional tones of voice and verbal content. *Journal of Experimental Psychology: Human Perception and Performance*, 1977, *3,* 75–82.

Sartre, J. P. *Existentialism*. New York; Philosophical Library, 1947.

Schachter, S., & Singer, J. Cognitive, social, and physiological determinants of emotional state. *Psychological Review*, 1962, *65,* 379–399.

Schank, R. C., & Abelson, R. P. *Scripts, plans, goals, and understanding*. Hillsdale, N.J.: Erlbaum, 1977.

Scherer, K. R., Koivumaki, J., & Rosenthal, R. Minimal cues in the vocal communication of affect: Judging emotions from content-masked speech. *Journal of Psycholinguistic Research*, 1972, *1,* 269–285.

Schneider, D. J., Hastorf, A. H., & Ellsworth, P. C. *Person perception*. Reading, Mass.: Addison-Wesley, 1979.

Schwartz, G. E., Davidson, R. J., & Maer, F. Right hemisphere lateralization for emotion in the human brain: Interactions with cognition. *Science*, 1975, *190,* 286–288.

Schwartz, G. E., Fair, P. L., Salt, P., Mandel, M. R., & Klerman, G. L. Facial muscle patterning to affective imagery in depressed and nondepressed subjects. *Science*, 1976, *192,* 489–491.

Shepard, R. N. The mental image. *American Psychologist*, 1978, *33,* 125–137.

Shevrin, H., & Fritzler, D. E. Visual evoked response correlates of unconscious mental process. *Science*, 1968, *161,* 295–298.

Shevrin, H., Smith, W. H., & Fritzler, D. E. Average evoked response and verbal correlates of unconscious mental processes. *Psychophysiology*, 1971, *8,* 149–162.

Shiffrin, R. M., & Schneider, W. Controlled and automatic human information processing: II. Perceptual learning, automatic attending, and a general theory. *Psychological Review*, 1977, *84,* 127–190.

Smoke, W. H., & Zajonc, R. B. On the reliability of group judgments and decisions. In J. Criswell, H. Solomon, & P. Suppes (Eds.), *Mathematic methods in small group process*. Stanford, Calif.: Stanford University Press, 1962.

Strnad, B. N., & Mueller, J. H. Levels of processing in facial recognition memory. *Bulletin of the Psychonomic Society*, 1977, *9,* 17–18.

Suberi, M., & McKeever, W. F. Differential right hemispheric memory storage of emotional and non-emotional faces. *Neuropsychologia*, 1977, *15,* 757–768.

Titchener, E. B. *A textbook of psychology*. New York: Macmillan, 1910.

Tomkins, S. S. *Affect, imagery, consciousness: Vol. 1. The positive affects*. New York: Springer, 1962.

Tomkins, S. S. *Affect, imagery, consciousness: Vol. 2. The negative affects*. New York: Springer, 1963.

Trevarthen, C. B. Two mechanisms of vision in primates. *Psychologische Forschung*, 1968, *31,* 299–337.

Tulving, E., & Donaldson, W. *Organization of memory*. New York: Academic Press, 1972.

Vitz, P. C. Preferences for rates of information presented by sequences of tones. *Journal of Experimental Psychology*, 1964, *68,* 176–183.

Warrington, E. K., & Ackroyd, C. The effect of orienting tasks on recognition memory. *Memory and Cognition*, 1975, *3,* 140–142.

Wells, J. E. Strength theory and judgments of recency and frequency. *Journal of Verbal Learning and Verbal Behavior*, 1974, *13,* 378–392.

Wilson, W. R. *Unobtrusive induction of positive attitudes*. Unpublished doctoral dissertation, University of Michigan, 1975.

Wilson, W. R. Feeling more than we can know: Exposure effects without learning. *Journal of Personality and Social Psychology*, 1979, *37,* 811–821.

Wundt, W. *Grundriss der Psychologie*. Leipzig: Wilhelm Engelmann, 1905.

Wundt, W. *Outlines of psychology*. Leipzig: Wilhelm Engelmann, 1907.

Yntema, D. B., & Torgerson, W. S. Man–computer cooperation in decision requiring common sense. *IRE Transactions of the Professional Group on Human Factors in Electronics 1961,* Vol. HRE-2, No. 1, 20–26.

Zajonc, R. B. *Cognitive structure and cognitive tuning*. Unpublished doctoral dissertation, University of Michigan, 1955.

Zajonc, R. B. Attitudinal effects of mere exposure. *Journal of Personality and Social Psychology Monograph*, 1968, *9*(2, Part 2, 1–28).

Zajonc, R. B., & Smoke, W. H. Redundancy in task assignment and group performance. *Psychometrika*, 1959, *24,* 361–369.

Affective-Cognitive Consistency and the Effect of Salient Behavioral Information on the Self-Perception of Attitudes

Shelly Chaiken* and Mark W. Baldwin**

Subjects with well-defined or poorly defined prior attitudes toward being an environmentalist/conservationist were identified by assessing the structural consistency between the affective and cognitive components of their attitudes. After subjects completed one of two versions of a questionnaire designed to make salient either past pro-ecology or past anti-ecology behaviors, their final attitudes were assessed. The hypothesis that the self-perception account of attitude expression holds primarily for individuals with poorly defined prior attitudes was supported: Low-consistency subjects, with presumably poorly defined attitudes, but not high-consistency subjects, with well-defined attitudes, expressed postmanipulation environmentalist attitudes that were congruent with the pro- or anti-ecology behaviors made salient by the questionnaire manipulation. The additional finding that high-consistency (vs. low-consistency) subjects' beliefs on five ecology-related issues were more highly intercorrelated supported the assumption that the consistency construct appropriately indexes the degree to which individuals possess well-defined attitudes. A comparison of theory and research on self-schemata with research on the affective–cognitive consistency variable suggested that the latter may be a useful measure of attitude schematicity.

* University of Toronto, Ontario, Canada.
** University of Waterloo, Ontario, Canada.
The present research was supported by a grant to the first author from the Humanities and Social Sciences Committee of the Research Board of the University of Toronto. The authors thank John Bassili, Alice Eagly, Jonathan Freedman, Michael Ross, Diane Ruble, Wendy Wood, Mark Zanna, and two anonymous reviewers for their comments on an earlier draft of this manuscript.

Self-perception theory (Bem, 1972) asserts that people often infer their attitudes (and other internal states) from observations of their overt behaviors and the contexts in which these behaviors occur. Empirical support for this theory is fairly widespread. For example, researchers studying counterattitudinal advocacy (e.g., Bem, 1967, 1972; Bem & McConnell, 1970), pro attitudinal advocacy (e.g., Fazio, Zanna, & Cooper, 1977; Kiesler, Nisbett, & Zanna, 1969), and intrinsic motivation (e.g., Calder & Staw, 1975; Deci, 1971; Lepper, Greene, & Nisbett, 1973; Ross, 1976) have demonstrated that the less people perceive their behaviors to be under the control of contextual stimuli such as reward or justification, the greater is their tendency to express attitudes that correspond to, or are consistent with, these behaviors.

Most self-perception research has examined the relationship between expressed attitudes and behaviors that subjects are induced to perform immediately prior to the time their attitudes are assessed. More recently, Salancik (1974; Salancik & Conway, 1975) demonstrated that attitude inferences can also be influenced by manipulating perceivers' recall of past attitudinally relevant behaviors. For example, before assessing subjects' religious attitudes, Salancik and Conway used a linguistic device to vary the saliency of subjects' past proreligious and antireligious behaviors. Subjects for whom past proreligious behaviors had been made salient perceived themselves as more religious and expressed more positive attitudes toward being religious than did subjects for whom antireligious behaviors had been made salient.

Notwithstanding Salancik and Conway's (1975) demonstration that information about past as well as recent behaviors affects attitude judgments, their findings are consistent with other self-perception research in suggesting that persons' attitude expressions represent "top of the head" (cf., Taylor & Fiske, 1978) evaluative judgments, constructed largely on the basis of contemporaneous and salient contextual and behavioral information. This research tradition, then, has tended to regard attitudes as epiphenomena and has focused on the external nature of the information underlying attitude judgments. In contrast, most other attitudinal research (e.g., persuasion, attitude–behavior relations) has been guided by the traditional theoretical view (e.g., Allport, 1935; McGuire, 1969) that attitudes represent relatively enduring learned predispositions of persons. Consistent with this conceptualization, information-processing models of attitude such as those proposed by Fishbein and Ajzen (1975) and others (e.g., Anderson, 1968; Wyer, 1974) have assumed that the locus of much information underlying attitude judgments is internal in the sense that it consists of people's private knowledge of or memory for prior beliefs about and past affective reactions to the attitude object (for an elaborated discussion of self-perception vs. traditional attitude theory perspectives, see Greenwald, 1968, and Wood, 1980).

Both conceptualizations of attitude and assumptions regarding the primary locus of information underlying attitude judgments have received empirical support, and most researchers would probably concur that the two view points can be subsumed under a more general cognitive theory explicitly acknowledging the influence of both internal and external cue information on attitude judgments (cf., Eagly & Himmelfarb, 1978; Wood, 1980). Yet, despite this probable consensus and despite Bem's (1972) original proviso that the self-perception process he described held only to the extent that "internal cues are weak, ambiguous, or uninterpretable" (p. 2), self-perception research has been strikingly successful in demonstrating that subjects' attitude inferences can be so strongly influenced by contemporaneous external cues and that prior attitudes are often not salient for subjects (Bem & McConnell, 1970). Such empirical success leads one to wonder when, if ever, internal cue information (i.e., prior attitudes) might approach the salience of contemporaneous external cues and thus diminish or override the impact of the latter information on people's attitude judgments.

It might be that this concern that people often underutilize internal cue information when queried about their attitudes is unwarranted. As others have noted (e.g., Kelley, quoted in Harvey, Ickes, & Kidd, 1978; Salancik & Conway, 1975; Wood, 1980), self-perception studies often employ experimental tasks or attitude topics that are novel or unfamiliar to subjects. Given the likelihood that subjects have not yet formulated attitudes toward such stimuli, it is understandable that their attitude inferences would be strongly affected by contemporaneous external cues. However, at least some self-perception research has used more familiar experimental tasks (e.g., drawing: Lepper et al., 1973) or attitude objects (e.g., "being religious": Salancik & Conway, 1975) toward which most subjects might reasonably be expected to have prior attitudes. Yet this research, too, has revealed the strong impact of contemporaneous informational cues on attitude judgments.

The present study was explicitly designed to test Bem's (1972) proviso concerning the moderating impact of internal cues, or prior attitudes, on the influence of contemporaneous external cues on attitude inferences. Guiding the present research was the assumption that, independent of the extremity of people's scores on some standard premeasure of attitude, they will differ in the strength or degree of definition of those attitudes. In the experiment, we assessed the extent to which our subjects possessed well-defined prior attitudes. We assumed that internal cue information would rival or override the salience of external cues for subjects with well-defined prior attitudes but not for subjects with poorly defined attitudes. Thus, we hypothesized that only the attitude inferences of the latter subject group would be strongly influenced by salient behavioral information.

In the study, we investigated subjects' attitudes toward "being an environmentalist conservationist." At the first of two experimental sessions, subjects with well-defined (vs. poorly defined) attitudes on this topic were identified by assessing the structural consistency between the affective and cognitive components of their attitudes (Rosenberg, 1960, 1968; Rosenberg & Hovland, 1960). According to Rosenberg (1960, 1968), people whose attitudes are characterized by high affective–cognitive consistency (i.e., similar scores on affective and cognitive indices of attitude) are likely to have "well-articulated," "well-thought-out" attitudes reflecting a stable underlying disposition, whereas people whose attitudes are low in

such consistency are likely to have "poorly articulated" attitudes that do not reflect a stable disposition toward the attitude object. Consistent with this hypothesis, Rosenberg (1968) showed that greater affective–cognitive consistency was associated with greater attitudinal stability and resistance to persuasion. In addition, Norman (1975), although not Fazio and Zanna (1978), found that higher affective–cognitive consistency was predictive of higher attitude–behavior consistency. At our first experimental session, we attempted to adduce further evidence for Rosenberg's hypothesis by assessing subjects' beliefs on a number of ecology-related issues (e.g., nuclear power, solar energy). We expected that the relationship between subjects' environmentalist attitudes and their ecology-related beliefs, as well as the relationship among these beliefs, would be stronger for subjects exhibiting high (vs. low) affective–cognitive consistency.

At the second experimental session, we employed the linguistic device developed by Salancik and Conway (1975) to make either past pro-ecology or anti-ecology behaviors salient for subjects. Immediately afterward, we reassessed subjects' environmentalist self-perceptions and attitudes. Self-perception theory predicts that subjects for whom pro-ecology (vs. anti-ecology) behaviors are made salient will express more positive attitudes toward being environmentalists/conservationists and, to a greater extent, perceive themselves as being environmentalists. We anticipated, however, that this prediction would be borne out only among subjects previously identified as low in affective–cognitive consistency.

Method

Subjects

Subjects were male and female University of Toronto undergraduates who participated during regular lecture meetings of the first author's introductory psychology course. At the first experimental session, all 99 students in attendance completed questionnaires. Ninety-four students attended class the evening of the second session, and all responded to the experimental materials. Data from 14 of these subjects, who did not attend the first session, were discarded. Both sessions occurred early in the semester and were conducted by the senior author. The experiment and its findings were subsequently discussed during a lecture on attitudes.

Procedure and Measuring Instruments

First experimental session. After describing the study as a "survey of people's attitudes," the course instructor distributed a nine-page questionnaire to subjects. On page 1, subjects indicated their name, sex, and age, and responded to five items pertaining to the attitude object, "being an environmentalist/conservationist." Subjects first indicated their favorability (vs. unfavorability) toward the attitude object (11-point scale) and then rated the attitude object on five 7-point bipolar adjective scales (good vs. bad, wise vs. foolish, pleasant vs. unpleasant, healthy vs. sick, beneficial vs. harmful). Subjects' responses to the five scales were summed to form one semantic differential index of attitude. Both the favorability rating and the semantic differential index assessed subjects' *affect* toward the attitude object and, in addition to serving as attitude premeasures, were used in determining affective–cognitive consistency (see-below). The next item (self-perception premeasure) requested subjects to rate the extent to which they considered themselves an environmentalist/conservationist (11-point scale). Finally, subjects indicated the extent to which they had *thought* about the attitude object in the past and how *personally important* they considered the attitude object (9-point scales).

The next four questionnaire pages consisted of 22 items designed to assess the *cognitive* component of subjects' attitudes. Following Rosenberg (1960, 1968), each item pertained to 1 of 22 values (e.g., happiness, a world of beauty, a sense of accomplishment, world harmony, pleasure, human welfare, good health) and consisted of two 9-point rating scales.[1] On the first scale, subjects rated the extent to which attainment of a particular value

(e.g., happiness) would be helped (vs. hindered) by "being an environmentalist/conservationist." On the second scale, subjects rated how positive (vs. negative) they considered the value. The weighted cognitive index of subjects' attitudes was calculated by multiplying their two ratings for each item and then summing the resulting 22 products (Rosenberg, 1960). Along with the affective indices described earlier, this index was used in determining affective–cognitive consistency (see below). Prior to the experiment, 89 pilot subjects completed the 22-item instrument. Analysis of their data indicated that the instrument possessed satisfactory reliability (average item total $r = .58$, coefficient $a = .88$).

The next three questionnaire pages consisted of 5 opinion statements on ecology-related issues and 14 filler statements on other topics. Subjects indicated their agreement with these opinion statements on 15-point scales. The ecology-related statements were: "More nuclear power stations should be built," "Nonreturnable soft drink bottles should be outlawed," "Aerosol spray cans are damaging to the environment and should be banned," "The government should make the development of solar energy technology its highest energy priority," and "nonbiodegradable consumer goods such as colored tissue and toilet paper should be outlawed."

Finally, the last questionnaire page consisted of the 33-item Crowne-Marlowe social desirability scale (Crowne & Marlowe, 1964). This scale was included in order to explore, and hopefully to rule out, the possibility that social desirability concerns underlie persons' tendencies to exhibit affective–cognitive consistency.

After subjects had completed and handed in their questionnaires (a task requiring approximately 30 minutes), the instructor began the evening's lecture. While noting that the questionnaires

---

[1] These 22 values were selected on the basis of pretesting with a group of subjects ($n = 26$) who indicated, for each of a large set of values, whether the value was relevant to the attitude object. These subjects also indicated whether there were redundancies among values.

would be discussed later in the term, the instructor made no mention of a second experimental session.

Second experimental session. At the beginning of class 2 weeks later, subjects were asked to complete two one-page questionnaires. On the first questionnaire, subjects indicated, for each of 26 ecology-related behavioral statements, whether or not the particular behavior was self-descriptive: Subjects were instructed to place a check mark next to behaviors they considered "true" for them and to leave blank behaviors they considered "not true." Two versions of this questionnaire, representing the two levels of the pro-ecology (vs. anti-ecology) behavior saliency manipulation (see below), were randomly distributed to subjects. On the second questionnaire, subjects indicated their name and responded to the experiment's major dependent measures. Except for minor differences in scale length, these postmanipulation measures were identical to the self-perception and two attitude premeasures: Subjects indicated the extent to which they considered themselves environmentalists/conservationists, their favorability (vs. unfavorability) toward being an environmentalist/conservationist (both 15-point scales), and rated "being an environmentalist/conservationist" on the five 7-point adjective scales described earlier.

Independent Variables

Affective–cognitive consistency. As suggested by Rosenberg (1968) and Norman (1975), affective–cognitive consistency was determined in the following way: Subjects ($N = 99$) were rank ordered on the basis of an affective index (average of each subject's Z scores on the two attitude premeasures) and also on the basis of the overall favorability implied by the weighted cognitive index. The absolute value of the discrepancy between each subject's standing in the two rankings was defined as his or her level of affective–cognitive consistency. Lower (higher) discrepancy scores reflected higher (lower) consistency. Subjects ($n = 50$) whose discrepancy scores were below the median (18.4, range = 1–98) were considered high in consistency,

whereas subjects ($n = 49$) whose scores fell above the median were designated low in consistency.

Saliency manipulation. The first questionnaire distributed at the second session consisted of 13 pro-ecology and 13 anti-ecology behavioral statements of the general form "I do (or refuse to do) X," where X is pro- or anti-ecology behavior. Using the linguistic device developed by Salancik and Conway (1975), we prepared two versions of this questionnaire, one designed to make pro-ecology behaviors salient and the other designed to make anti-ecology behaviors salient. The linguistic device is based on the tested assumption (Salancik & Conway, 1975) that the probability of endorsing a statement "I do X *on occasion*" is higher than the probability of endorsing a statement "I do X *frequently*." Implementation of this device involved systematically varying the wording of the 26 behavioral statements such that, in the pro-ecology version, pro-ecology behaviors were paired with "on occasion" (or "occasionally") whereas anti-ecology behaviors were paired with "frequently" (e.g., "I occasionally pick up other persons' garbage and take it to the trash can," "I occasionally carpool rather than drive separately," "I frequently litter," "I frequently leave on lights in rooms I'm not using"). Opposite pairings were used to create the anti-ecology version of the questionnaire (e.g., "I frequently pick up other persons' garbage . . .," "I frequently carpool . . .," "I occasionally litter," "I occasionally leave on lights . . .").

Results

The design included two levels each of the saliency manipulation, affective–cognitive consistency, and subject sex. Since preliminary analyses yielded no significant effects involving sex, all reported analyses ignored this variable.

Check on Experimental Conditions

Saliency manipulation. To assess the success of the saliency manipulation, an analysis of variance was performed on a "salient behavior" index. This index was derived from subjects' responses to the 26-item questionnaire designed to manipulate their pro-ecology (vs. anti-ecology) behavioral endorsements and represented the number of pro-ecology statements minus the number of anti-ecology statements that subjects actually endorsed. As expected, the main effect for the saliency manipulation proved highly significant on this index, $F(1, 76) = 29.40$, $p < .0001$: Subjects who completed the pro-ecology version of the questionnaire endorsed significantly more proecology (vs. anti-ecology) behaviors as self-descriptive than did subjects who completed the anti-ecology version (M's = 5.69 vs. .58). Separate analyses on each component of the index revealed that both were affected by the manipulation: pro-ecology behaviors, $F(1, 76) = 8.32$, $p < .005$, and anti-ecology behaviors, $F(1, 76) = 36.11$, $p < .0001$. Although a marginally significant Consistency × Saliency Manipulation interaction on the salient behavior index, $F(1, 76) = 3.11$, $p = .09$, suggested that the manipulation had a slightly greater impact on the pro- and anti-ecology behavior endorsements of low-consistency (vs. high-consistency) subjects, the main effect for the saliency manipulation proved significant within both subject groups ($ps < .025$ and .001 for high- and low-consistency subjects, respectively). Further, when the influence of subjects' initial attitudes and self-perceptions on their behavioral endorsements was partialed out in an analysis of covariance on the salient behavior index, the saliency manipulation main effect remained highly significant, $F(1, 73) = 26.21$, $p < .0001$, whereas the Consistency × Saliency Manipulation interaction disappeared, $F(1, 73) = 1.42$, $p = .24$. It should also be noted that the two-way interaction proved nonsignificant in the analysis of variance on the pro- and anti-ecology components of the salient behavior index ($ps = .17$ and .12, respectively). Finally, the analyses of the salient behavior index and its two components revealed no overall differences between high- and low-consistency subject samples in terms of their means ($Fs < 1.0$) or variances ($Fs < 1.33$).

Affective–cognitive consistency. As expected, the correlation between the affective and cognitive indices used to determine affective–cognitive consistency was significant for high-consistency subjects ($r = .83$, $p < .001$) but nonsignificant for low-consistency subjects ($r = -.20$). It is important to note that the two consistency groups did not differ significantly in terms of their means or variances on the affective and cognitive indices of their attitudes (all $Fs < 1.0$). Thus, prior to the saliency manipulation, high- and low-consistency subjects evidenced no difference in the extremity or variability of their attitudes toward being an environmentalist conservationist.

Analyses on the remaining measures assessed at the first experimental session also revealed little difference between the two consistency samples. High- and low-consistency subjects did not differ in the extent to which they reported thinking about their environmental attitudes in the past or in the extent to which they considered the attitude object personally important ($Fs < 1.0$). Whereas low-consistency (vs. high-consistency) subjects indicated greater agreement with the statement "More nuclear power stations should be built" ($p < .01$), the opinions of the two subject groups did not differ on the remaining four ecology-related issues ($Fs = 1.23$ or smaller). Finally, the fact that the two consistency groups did not differ in their Crowne-Marlowe scores ($F < 1.0$) suggests that social desirability concerns do not underlie persons' tendencies to manifest high or low affective–cognitive consistency.

Self-Perceptions and Attitudes

Analysis of variance revealed no significant differences among experimental conditions on either the self-perception premeasure or the two attitude premeasures (favorability ratings, semantic differential index). Thus, the three corresponding postmanipulation measures were treated by analyses of variance.[2]

Cell means for the postmanipulation measures appear in Table 10.1. The saliency manipulation

---

[2] Each postmanipulation measure was also submitted to an analysis of covariance, using its corresponding premeasure as the covariate. The results of these analyses were virtually identical to those reported in the text.

TABLE 10.1. Mean Postmanipulation Self-Perception and Attitude Scores as a Function of Affective–Cognitive Consistency and Salience of Pro- Versus Anti-Ecology Behaviors

Dependent variable	High consistency		Low consistency	
	P-E	A-E	P-E	A-E
Self-perceptions	9.00	9.68	11.33	8.25
Semantic differential index	29.13	28.72	31.25	26.38
Favorability ratings	11.73	11.00	12.17	10.62

Note: P-E = pro-ecology behaviors salient; A-E = anti-ecology behaviors salient. Higher numbers indicate a greater tendency to describe oneself as an environmentalist/conservationist and more positive attitudes toward being an environmentalist/conservationist. Cell *n*s ranged from 15 to 25.

main effect was significant on all three post measures: favorability ratings $F(1, 76) = 8.48$, $p < .005$; semantic differential index, $F(1, 76) = 10.05$, $p < .005$; and self-perceptions, $F(1,76) = 4.08$, $p < .05$. Overall, subjects for whom pro-ecology (vs. anti-ecology) behaviors were made salient in the context of the second experimental session reported more positive attitudes toward "being an environmentalist/conservationist" and, to a greater extent, perceived themselves as being environmentalists. These findings replicate those reported by Salancik and Conway (1975), who studied self-perceptions and attitudes about religiosity, and thus lend further support to the self-perception account of attitude expression.

More important, however, the Consistency × Saliency manipulation interaction proved significant on subjects' semantic differential scores, $F(1, 76) = 7.01$, $p < .01$, and their self-perception scores, $F(1, 76) = 9.64$, $p < .005$. The patterning of the interaction on these variables, as well as a similar but nonsignificant patterning on subjects' favorability ratings, $F(1, 76) = 1.06$, supports our hypothesis that the saliency manipulation would more strongly influence the self-reported attitudes and self-perceptions of low-consistency (vs. high-consistency) subjects (see Table 10.1). Indeed, planned comparisons revealed that for low-consistency subjects, the contrast between pro- and anti-ecology conditions was significant on all three postmanipulation measures (Fs 7.91, $ps < .01$ or smaller). For high-consistency subject, however, the pro- versus anti-ecology contrast proved nonsignificant on all three postmeasures ($Fs \leq 1.71$, $ps > .15$ or larger).

Correlational analyses provided additional evidence regarding the differential informational determinants of high- and low-consistency subjects' postmanipulation responses. As expected, correlations computed between subjects' salient behavior scores (i.e., number of pro- minus anti-ecology behavioral endorsements on the manipulation questionnaire) and their postmanipulation self-perceptions and attitudes were generally higher for low-consistency (vs. high-consistency) subjects: self-perceptions, $rs = .59$ versus .38, $p < .10$; favorability ratings, $rs = .57$ versus .34, $p < .10$; and semantic differential scores, $rs = .25$ versus .25, *ns*. In contrast, correlations between subjects' premanipulation and postmanipulation self-perceptions/attitudes tended to be greater for high-consistency (vs. low-consistency) subjects: self-perceptions, $rs = .61$ versus .50, $p = .23$; favorability ratings, $rs = .58$ versus .15, $p < .025$; and semantic differential scores, $rs = .33$ versus .18, $p = .23$.[3] To explore more directly the relative influence

[3] In evaluating these findings, it is important to note that the high- and low-consistency samples differed little in terms of their within-group standard deviations on the seven variables included in the correlational analyses. The F tests yielded only two significant group differences (all other comparisons were nonsignificant, $Fs[39, 39] = 1.40$ or smaller, $ps > .10$ or larger): High-consistency (vs. low-consistency) subjects manifested less variability in their premanipulation semantic differential scores ($SDs = 3.49$ vs. 5.19, $p < .01$) but greater variability in their postmanipulation favorability ratings ($SD = 2.05$ vs. 1.48, $p < .05$). To the extent that a restricted range on a variable reduces the magnitude of the correlation that may be observed between that variable and others, we may have overestimated (in favor of our hypothesis) the difference in correlations between consistency groups in one case (*r* between

TABLE 10.2. *F* Values and β Weights for Predictor Variables and Partial Correlations Between Predictor and Criterion Variables in Multiple Regression Equations

Criterion variable and predictor variables	High-consistency subjects (n = 40)			Low-consistency subjects (n = 40)		
	F value	β weight	Partial r	F value	β weight	Partial r
Postmanipulation self-perceptions						
Initial self-perceptions	17.78****	.55	.57****	5.01**	.31	.34**
Salient behavior index	3.30	.24	.28**	11.56***	.47	.49****
Postmanipulation favorability ratings						
Initial favorability ratings	15.08****	.52	.54****	.62	.10	.13
Salient behavior index	2.38	.21	.24	17.86****	.56	.57****
Postmanipulation semantic differential scores						
Initial semantic differential scores	4.08*	.31	.32**	.39	.10	.10
Salient behavior index	2.00	.22	.23	1.54	.21	.20

Note: For tabled *F* values, *dfs* = 1, 37; for tabled partial *rs* (one-tailed tests), *dfs* = 37.
* $p ≈ .06$. ** $p < .05$. *** $p < .01$. **** $p < .001$.

of initial attitudes/self-perceptions versus contemporaneous behavioral information on subjects' final attitudes/self-perceptions, we performed three multiple regression analyses for each consistency group. Each analysis regressed one postmanipulation measure (i.e., self-perception, favorability, or semantic differential scores) on (a) its corresponding premanipulation measure and (b) the salient behavior index. The results of these analyses are shown in Table 10.2. Examination of the *F* (and associated *p*) values, partial *rs*, and beta weights for the two predictors (where comparison of $β^2$ for the two predictors reflects their relative importance in explaining variation in the criterion variable; cf. McNemar, 1969, p. 195) reveals that the postmanipulation self-perceptions and attitudes of high-consistency subjects were better predicted by their initial self-perceptions and attitudes than by the environmental behaviors they were induced to endorse. In contrast, low-consistency subjects' postmanipulation responses were better predicted by the environmental behaviors they endorsed than by their initial self-perceptions and attitudes.

premanipulation and postmanipulation favorability ratings) and underestimated (in opposition to our hypothesis) group differences in two cases (*r* between premanipulation and postmanipulation semantic differential scores and *r* between salient behavior index and postmanipulation favorability ratings).

Affective–Cognitive Consistency and Ecology-Related Beliefs

Correlational analyses explored the relationship between subjects' (premanipulation) attitudes toward being an environmentalist/conservationist and their beliefs on five ecology-related issues as well as the interrelatedness of these beliefs. These analyses included data from all 99 subjects who attended the first experimental session.

Attitude–belief relationship. Subjects' agreement with the five ecology-related opinion statements were summed to form one index, with higher scores implying greater favorability toward the environment. As expected, the correlations between this opinion index and the two attitude indices (i.e., affective and weighted cognitive index) were larger for high-consistency (vs. low-consistency) subjects: affective index, $rs = .55$ versus 12, $p < .01$; and cognitive index, $rs = .43$ versus .18, $p < .08$ (both one-tailed *z*s). Further, when the two attitude measures were correlated with subjects' opinions on each of the five issues, the correlation coefficient was larger for high-consistency subjects in 9 out of 10 possible group comparisons. The average correlations between subjects' ecology-related beliefs and the affective (cognitive) index were .398 (.313) and .068 (.114) for high- and low-consistency subjects, respectively.

TABLE 10.3. Correlations Among Ecology-Related Beliefs for Combined Samples of High- and Low-Consistency Subjects

	1	2	3	4	5
1. Nuclear power	3.71 (3.58)	−.05	−.16	.06	.19*
2. Solar energy	.19*	3.02 (3.28)	.26**	.19*	.15
3. Nonreturnable bottles	.32***	.40***	3.45 (3.11)	.55***	.42***
4. Aerosol sprays	.21*	.13	.39***	3.20 (3.05)	.45***
5. Biodegradable products	.34***	.31***	.58***	.57***	3.40 (3.81)

Note: Intercorrelations for high-consistency subjects (*n* = 94) appear below the diagonal and those for low-consistency subjects (*n* = 94) appear above the diagonal. Within-group standard deviations (shown without [with] parentheses for high-consistency [low-consistency] subjects) for the belief measures appear along the diagonal. No significant group variance differences were obtained (*F*s = 1.26 or smaller). Higher scores on the belief measures indicated less agreement that more nuclear plants should be built and greater agreement that solar energy technology should be supported, nonreturnable bottles outlawed, aerosol spray cans banned, and nonbiodegradable products outlawed (see Method section for exact wording of belief statements).
* *p* < .05. ** *p* < .01. *** *p* < .005.

Relationship among beliefs. As we anticipated, the ecology-related beliefs of high-consistency (vs. low-consistency) subjects tended to be more highly interrelated. The average intercorrelation among beliefs was .347 for high-consistency subjects and .238 for low-consistency subjects, and in 7 of 10 possible group comparisons, the pair-wise correlation coefficient was higher for high-consistency subjects. Because pilot subjects (*n* = 89) had also completed the opinion questionnaire and the procedure used to classify subjects into high and low consistency groups was identical for the experimental and pilot samples (i.e., the same median consistency score obtained in both samples), the two samples were combined. For this larger sample, the average relationship among beliefs was .354 and .216 for high- and low-consistency subjects, respectively. Further, as Table 10.3 indicates, 8 of the 10 group comparisons yielded a larger pair-wise correlation for high-consistency subjects (*p* < .10, one-tailed, by Mann-Whitney *U* test).[4]

Among the filler items appearing on the opinion questionnaire completed by experimental subjects

were five statements dealing with the United States' cultural domination over Canada (e.g., "The number of U.S. programs shown on Canadian television should be reduced"). If, as Rosenberg (1960) claimed, the consistency construct is domain specific rather than a reflection of a general individual difference, high- and low-consistency subjects (whose consistency was assessed with respect to their environmental attitudes) should show no difference in the degree to which their beliefs about cultural domination are interrelated. In line with this reasoning, the average intercorrelation among these beliefs proved quite similar for high- and low-consistency subjects (mean *r*s = .343 and .391, respectively). Further, of 10 possible group comparisons, 4 yielded a larger pair-wise correlation for high-consistency subjects, whereas 5 yielded a larger correlation for low-consistency subjects (one comparison yielded a tie).

Discussion

Our hypothesis that the self-perception account of attitude expression holds primarily for individuals who do not possess well-defined prior attitudes toward the target attitude object was supported. At the second experimental session, the attitude judgments and self-perceptions of subjects with poorly defined prior attitudes were strongly affected by the contemporaneous behavioral cues made available to them. Low-consistency subjects for whom past pro-ecology (vs. anti-ecology)

---

[4] A separate analysis of the beliefs expressed by high-consistency (vs. low-consistency) pilot subjects revealed that the average belief intercorrelation was .358 (vs. .215) and that 8 of the 10 possible group comparisons yielded a larger pair-wise correlation for high-consistency subjects. It should also be noted that the pair-wise correlations accounting for the 2 reversals to the overall pattern (larger *r*s for high-consistency subjects) in the pilot sample and the pair-wise correlations accounting for the 3 reversals in the experimental sample showed no overlap.

behaviors were made salient expressed significantly more favorable attitudes toward being environmentalists and significantly heightened perceptions of being environmentalists. Further, the regression analyses revealed that the postmanipulation responses of low-consistency subjects were better predicted by the pro- or anti-ecology nature of the behaviors they were induced to endorse than by their prior self-perceptions and environmentalist attitudes.

In contrast to these findings, subjects who were high in affective–cognitive consistency were not significantly affected by the pro-ecology (vs. anti-ecology) behavior manipulation. Although the manipulation was successful in inducing these subjects, like low-consistency subjects, to endorse pro-ecology (vs. anti-ecology) behaviors as self-descriptive, their postmanipulation attitude judgments, and self-perceptions reflected no appreciable reliance on these contemporaneous behavioral cues. Presumably, high-consistency subjects possessed strong internal cues regarding their feelings and self-perceptions about being environmentalists and thus did not need to "infer" their attitudes from currently available behavioral information. Consistent with this interpretation, the regression findings indicated that the postmanipulation responses of high-consistency subjects were better predicted by their prior attitudes and self-perceptions than by the contemporaneous pro- and anti-ecology behavioral cues available to them.

Although these findings strongly support our major hypothesis, it is important that their implications for self-perception theory not be overstated. We think it would be inappropriate to conclude that the self-perception account of attitude expression holds *only* for individuals with poorly defined prior attitudes or, more specifically, that persons with well-defined attitudes *never* express attitudes that reflect, at least in part, the impact of salient and contemporaneous external cues. (Indeed, had our saliency manipulation been more potent, the final attitudes expressed by high-consistency subjects might have begun to reflect—albeit to a lesser extent than the final attitudes of low-consistency subjects—the impact of currently available behavioral cues.) Although our results indicate that both internal cue information (i.e., prior attitudes) and external cue information can influence attitudinal judgments, we suspect that the latter kind of information often predominates. As Taylor and Fiske (1978) recently suggested, individuals may frequently respond with little thought to the most salient stimuli in their environment and thus may typically express "top of the head" opinions (and other judgments) that reflect little or no information beyond that available to them in the immediate situation.

Affective–Cognitive Consistency

The fact that high- and low-consistency subjects responded in the predicted manner to our saliency manipulation, as well as the fact that their postmanipulation attitudes and self-perceptions were best predicted by internal and external cue information, respectively, is consistent with Rosenberg's (1968) hypothesis that the affective–cognitive consistency construct appropriately indexes the extent to which people possess well-defined attitudes with respect to a particular object. Our correlational analyses provided further evidence regarding the validity of the consistency construct. The relationships between subjects' environmentalist attitudes and their ecology-related beliefs, as well as the relationships among these beliefs, were stronger for high-consistency (vs. low-consistency) subjects. These findings indicate that persons who score high on the affective–cognitive consistency dimension can be distinguished from those who score low on this dimension on the basis of the presence (vs. absence) of an organized set of supporting cognitions in relation to the attitude object. In this regard, it is important to note that our two consistency groups manifested little difference in the degree to which their beliefs on a nonecology topic (cultural domination of Canada by the United States) were interrelated. This result is compatible with other research that has obtained nonsignificant correlations between subjects' consistency scores in different attitudinal domains (Norman, 1975; Chaiken & Garisto, Note 1) and provides additional evidence for the assumption that the affective–cognitive consistency construct is truly domain specific rather than simply reflective of a more general individual difference.

Although the above findings support the utility and validity of the consistency construct as an index of attitude definition, it should be noted that we found no differences between high- and low-consistency subjects on several ancillary measures where differences had been anticipated. Thus, we found no greater tendency for high-consistency (vs. low-consistency) subjects to consider the attitude object personally important or to report thinking about their attitudes in the past. Correlations between subjects' consistency scores and these measures were also low and nonsignificant (rs = .12 and .09 for thought and importance ratings, respectively).[5] In addition, Fazio and Zanna (1978) found no relationship between affective–cognitive consistency and several other potential indicants of attitude strength: self-reported certainty of attitude and number of past direct experiences with the attitude object.

The lack of a relationship between quantity of direct experiences with the attitude object and structural consistency does not necessarily undermine the validity of this construct. Certainly, people seem capable of forming strong, well-defined attitudes toward objects with which they have had no personal direct experiences (e.g., capital punishment, abortion). The possibility that structural consistency is unrelated to individuals' self-reports of the personal importance of the attitude object, the amount of time they have spent thinking about their attitudes in the past, and their attitudinal certainty is somewhat more disconcerting, since it seems reasonable that people would be more likely to form well-defined attitudes toward objects of greater personal importance and that

people possessing well-defined attitudes would have thought more about and would express greater confidence in their attitudes. Clearly, more research examining the relationship between affective–cognitive consistency and these and other possible indicants of attitudinal strength or definition, as well as research exploring possible antecedents of structural consistency, is necessary before the validity of this construct can be fully accepted. Given the apparent lack of relationship between affective–cognitive consistency and various self-report indicants of attitudinal strength, such research might also entertain the interesting possibility that people whose attitudes are characterized by high (vs. low) structural consistency and whose behavior, in our own and previous research (Norman, 1975; Rosenberg, 1968), indicates that they possess strong, well-defined attitudes are, for whatever reason, not especially aware of this fact.

Before we conclude, two additional points about the affective–cognitive consistency construct deserve mention. First, it is important to note that this construct assumes the validity of a multicomponent view of attitudes (cf., Bagozzi, 1978; Katz & Stotland, 1959; Kothandapani, 1971; Ostrom, 1969; Rosenberg, 1968). Although popular at one time, this conceptualization has been largely superseded in recent years by a unidimensional view that regards the cognitive and affective (and conative) components of attitude as alternative measures of the same underlying affective dimension rather than as distinguishable constructs (cf. Fishbein & Ajzen, 1974, 1975). The present findings, as well as previous research on affective–cognitive consistency (Norman, 1975; Rosenberg, 1968), support the idea that affect and cognition represent differentiable components of attitude. Further, using confirmatory factor analysis, Bagozzi and Burnkrant (1979) recently substantiated the validity of a two-component (affective/cognitive), but not a single-component (affective), model of attitude. The view that attitude is a multidimensional construct clearly deserves renewed empirical attention by attitude researchers. To illustrate only one possible direction that such research might take, we are currently pursuing Greenwald's (1968) suggestion that the affective and cognitive

---

[5] Norman (1975), who studied attitudes toward volunteering for psychological research, also found no relationship between subjects' consistency scores and the extent to which they considered the attitude object important or reported thinking about the attitude object in the past. Also in line with our findings, Norman found no differences between his high- and low-consistency subjects in the extremity of their attitudes. Thus, there is little reason to believe that individuals whose attitudes are characterized by high (vs. low) consistency will necessarily possess highly polarized attitudes.

components of attitude may have separate antecedents (Chaiken & Garisto, Note 1).

Finally, it is interesting to compare the affective–cognitive consistency construct and existing research on this variable with recent theorizing and research in personality psychology regarding self-schemata (Kuiper & Rogers, 1979; Markus, 1977; Rogers, Kuiper, & Kirker, 1977). According to self theorists (e.g., Markus, 1977), individuals who are schematic (vs. aschematic) along a particular trait dimension (e.g., independence–dependence) are people who possess well-articulated cognitive generalizations about the self in that trait domain. Because an attitude can be regarded as a judgment concerning the self's orientation toward some object, an individual whose attitude toward some object is characterized by high (vs. low) affective–cognitive consistency might plausibly be labeled *attitude schematic* (vs. *aschematic*).

Existing research indicates that self-schemata facilitate the processing of information about the self and that schematics (vs. aschematics) can supply more behavioral evidence supporting their self-perceptions, are more resistant to counterschematic information, and exhibit greater confidence in predicting their behaviors on schema-related dimensions (Kuiper & Rogers, 1979; Markus, 1977; Rogers et al., 1977). Schematics are also postulated to manifest greater cross-situational consistency in their trait-related behaviors (Markus, 1977). The idea that affective–cognitive consistency may be a schemalike concept is given credence by Norman's (1975) demonstration that people who exhibit high (vs. low) structural consistency manifest greater attitude–behavior correspondence. Also compatible with this notion are Rosenberg's (1968) demonstration that higher affective–cognitive consistency confers greater resistance to persuasion and the present study's results, since both experiments could be interpreted as indicating that attitude-schematic individuals are more resistant to counterschematic information.

We believe that it would be premature to assert that the assessment of affective–cognitive consistency provides an acceptable method for identifying persons whose stated attitudes do or do not reflect a well-articulated schema in a particular attitudinal domain. Nevertheless, we are intrigued by the theoretical and empirical parallels that seem to exist between the affective–cognitive consistency literature and the literature on self-schemata, and feel that further research exploring the utility of the consistency construct as a measure of attitude schematicity is warranted. As suggested by the literature on self-schemata, such research might investigate whether greater structural consistency facilitates the processing of attitude-relevant information, whether high- and low-consistency persons differ in their predictions regarding the likelihood of performing attitude-consistent behaviors, and whether they differ in their ability to provide behavioral or cognitive evidence supporting their stated attitudes.

REFERENCE NOTE

1. Chaiken, S., & Garisto, B. *Experiential antecedents of affective–cognitive consistency.* Research in progress, University of Toronto, 1981.

REFERENCES

Allport, G. W. Attitudes. In C. Murchison (Ed.), *Handbook of social psychology.* Worcester, Mass.: Clark University Press, 1935.

Anderson, N. H. A simple model for information integration. In R. P. Abelson et al. (Eds.), *Theories of cognitive consistency: A sourcebook.* Chicago: Rand McNally, 1968.

Bagozzi, R. P. The construct validity of the affective, behavioral and cognitive components of attitude by analysis of covariance structures. *Multivariate Behavioral Research,* 1978, *13,* 9–31.

Bagozzi, R. P., & Burnkrant, R. E. Attitude organization and the attitude–behavior relationship. *Journal of Personality and Social Psychology,* 1979, *37,* 913–929.

Bem, D. J. Self-perception: An alternative interpretation of cognitive dissonance phenomena. *Psychological Review,* 1967, *74,* 183–200.

Bem, D. J. Self-perception theory. In L. Berkowitz (Ed.), *Advances in experimental social psychology* (Vol. 6). New York: Academic Press, 1972.

Bem, D. J., & McConnell, H. K. Testing the self-perception explanation of dissonance phenomena: On the salience of premanipulation attitudes. *Journal of Personality and Social Psychology,* 1970, *14,* 23–31.

Calder, B. J., & Staw, B. M. Self-perception of intrinsic and extrinsic motivation. *Journal of Personality and Social Psychology,* 1975, *31,* 599–605.

Crowne, D., & Marlowe, D. *The approval motive.* New York: Wiley, 1964.

Deci, E. L. Effects of externally mediated rewards on intrinsic motivation. *Journal of Personality and Social Psychology,* 1971, *18,* 105–115.

Eagly, A. H., & Himmelfarb, S. Attitudes and opinions. *Annual Review of Psychology,* 1978, *29,* 517–554.

Fazio, R. H., & Zanna, M. P. Attitudinal qualities relating to the strength of the attitude–behavior relationship. *Journal of Experimental Social Psychology,* 1978, *14,* 398–408.

Fazio, R. H., Zanna, M. P., & Cooper, J. Dissonance versus self-perception: An integrative review of each theory's proper domain of application. *Journal of Experimental Social Psychology,* 1977, *13,* 464–479.

Fishbein, M., & Ajzen, I. Attitudes toward objects as predictors of single and multiple behavioral criteria. *Psychological Review,* 1974, *81,* 59–74.

Fishbein, M., & Ajzen, I. *Belief, attitude, intention, and behavior: An introduction to theory and research.* Reading, Mass.: Addison-Wesley, 1975.

Greenwald, A. G. On defining attitude and attitude theory. In A. G. Greenwald, T. C. Brock, & T. M. Ostrom (Eds.), *Psychological foundations of attitudes.* New York: Academic Press, 1968.

Harvey, J. H., Ickes, W., & Kidd, R. F. A conversation with Edward E. Jones and Harold H. Kelley. In J. H. Harvey, W. Ickes, & R. F. Kidd (Eds.), *New directions in attribution research* (Vol. 2). Hillsdale, N.J.: Erlbaum, 1978.

Katz, D., & Stotland, E. A preliminary statement to a theory of attitude structure and change. In S. Koch (Ed.), *Psychology: A study of a science* (Vol. 3). New York: McGraw-Hill, 1959.

Kiesler, C. A., Nisbett, R. E., & Zanna, M. P. On inferring one's beliefs from one's behavior. *Journal of Personality and Social Psychology,* 1969, *11,* 321–327.

Kothandapani, V. Validation of feeling, belief, and intention to act as three components of attitude and their contribution to prediction of contraceptive behavior. *Journal of Personality and Social Psychology,* 1971, *19,* 321–333.

Kuiper, N. A., & Rogers, T. B. Encoding of personal information: Self–other differences. *Journal of Personality and Social Psychology,* 1979, *37,* 499–514.

Lepper, M. R., Greene, D., & Nisbett, R. E. Undermining children's intrinsic interest with extrinsic reward: A test of the overjustification hypothesis. *Journal of Personality and Social Psychology,* 1973, *28,* 129–137.

Markus, H. Self-schemata and processing information about the self. *Journal of Personality and Social Psychology,* 1977, *35,* 63–78.

McGuire, W. J. The nature of attitudes and attitude change. In G. Lindsey & E. Aronson (Eds.), *The handbook of social psychology* (Vol. 3, 2nd ed.). Reading, Mass.: Addison-Wesley, 1969.

McNemar, Q. *Psychological statistics* (4th ed.). New York: Wiley, 1969.

Norman, R. Affective–cognitive consistency, attitudes, conformity, and behavior. *Journal of Personality and Social Psychology,* 1975, *32,* 83–91.

Ostrom, T. M. The relationship between the affective, behavioral, and cognitive components of attitude. *Journal of Experimental Social Psychology,* 1969, *5,* 12–30.

Rogers, T. B., Kuiper, N. A., & Kirker, W. S. Self-reference and the encoding of personal information. *Journal of Personality and Social Psychology,* 1977, *35,* 677–688.

Rosenberg, M. J. A structural theory of attitude dynamics. *Public Opinion Quarterly,* 1960, *24,* 319–341.

Rosenberg, M. J. Hedonism, inauthenticity, and other goals toward expansion of a consistency theory. In R. P. Abelson, et al. (Eds.), *Theories of cognitive consistency: A sourcebook.* Chicago: Rand McNally, 1968.

Rosenberg, M. J., & Hovland, C. I. Cognitive, affective, and behavioral components of attitudes. In M. J. Rosenberg, et al. (Eds.), *Attitude organization and change.* New Haven, Conn.: Yale University Press, 1960.

Ross, M. The self-perception of intrinsic motivation. In J. H. Harvey, W. J. Ickes, & R. F. Kidd (Eds.), *New directions in attribution research* (Vol. 1). Hillsdale, N.J.: Erlbaum, 1976.

Salancik, G. R. Inference of one's attitude from behavior recalled under linguistically manipulated cognitive sets. *Journal of Experimental Social Psychology,* 1974, *10,* 415–427.

Salancik, G. R., & Conway, M. Attitude inferences from salient and relevant cognitive content about behavior. *Journal of Personality and Social Psychology,* 1975, *32,* 829–840.

Taylor, S. E., & Fiske, S. T. Salience, attention, and attribution: Top of the head phenomena. In L. Berkowitz (Ed.), *Advances in experimental social psychology* (Vol. 11). New York: Academic Press, 1978.

Wood, W. *The retrieval of attitudinally-relevant information from memory: Effects on susceptibility to persuasion and on intrinsic motivation.* Unpublished doctoral dissertation, University of Massachusetts, 1980.

Wyer, R. S., Jr. *Cognitive organization and change: An information processing approach.* Potomac, Md.: Erlbaum, 1974.

Received June 4, 1980
Revision received December 16, 1980 ■

Assessing the Structure of Prejudicial Attitudes: The Case of Attitudes toward Homosexuals

Geoffrey Haddock, Mark P. Zanna, and Victoria M. Esses

Two studies assessed the structure of attitudes toward homosexuals. In Study 1, Ss completed measures of stereotypes, symbolic beliefs, and affective associates as well as attitudes toward homosexuals. They also completed the right-wing authoritarianism (RWA) scale. The results revealed that (a) stereotypes did not provide a complete representation of attitudes, (b) RWA was negatively correlated with attitudes toward homosexuals, (c) the relative importance of the predictor variables differed for high and low RWAs, and (d) the three predictors accounted for more variance in the attitudes of low RWAs than of high RWAs. Study 2 also included measures of past experiences and perceived value dissimilarity. Results revealed that past experiences significantly added to the prediction of attitudes only for high RWAs and that much of the RWA–attitude relation was accounted for by the consideration of symbolic beliefs and perceived value dissimilarity.

Until recently, the psychological literature on homosexuality has been dominated by research on diagnosis, cause, and cure. In a review of the literature from 1967 to 1974, Morin (1977) found that less than 10% of the research on homosexuality dealt with attitudes toward lesbians and gay

Geoffrey Haddock and Mark P. Zanna, Department of Psychology, University of Waterloo, Waterloo, Ontario, Canada; Victoria M. Esses, Department of Psychology, University of Western Ontario, London, Ontario, Canada.

Preparation of this article was facilitated by a Social Sciences and Humanities Research Council of Canada Doctoral Fellowship to Geoffrey Haddock. The research on which this article is based was supported by a research grant from the Social Sciences and Humanities Research Council of Canada to Victoria M. Esses and Mark P. Zanna.

We would like to thank Wendy Wood and three anonymous reviewers for their comments on earlier drafts of this article. In addition, we would like to thank the University of Waterloo Psych Society for their assistance in Study 2.

Correspondence concerning this article should be addressed to Geoffrey Haddock, Department of Psychology, University of Waterloo, Waterloo, Ontario, Canada N2L 3G1.

men. However, in the past decade, research assessing attitudes toward homosexuals has become increasingly common (see, for example, reviews by Herek, 1991, and Kite, 1984).[1] Numerous studies have now concluded that attitudes toward lesbians and gay men are negative (Herek, 1991). Many of these studies, in addition to assessing attitudes, have also sought to discover individual difference variables that correlate with such attitudes. Although this process has been useful in determining the type of individual most likely to express prejudice toward homosexuals, few researchers have studied the *underlying structure* of these attitudes. The primary goal of this series of studies is to assess the relative importance of cognitive and affective information in predicting attitudes toward homosexuals. A second goal is to assess the extent to which the individual difference variable of right-wing authoritarianism (RWA; Altemeyer, 1981, 1988) moderates the relative importance of cognition and affect in predicting such attitudes.

Previous Research Assessing the Correlates of Attitudes toward Homosexuals

Although there is now a large volume of research assessing attitudes toward lesbians and gay men, only a small proportion of this research has examined the correlates of these attitudes. Generally, the variables studied as potential correlates have taken on two forms: (a) individual difference variables, and (b) social and demographic variables (Herek, 1991).

A variety of individual difference variables have been associated with attitudes toward homosexuals (see, e.g., Kite & Deaux, 1986). One variable relevant to our research is that of authoritarianism (Adorno, Frenkel-Brunswik, Levinson, & Sanford,

1950; Altemeyer, 1981, 1988). Through the years, a number of researchers have been interested in assessing the relation between authoritarianism and anti-gay attitudes. Perhaps not surprising is that high authoritarians have been consistently documented as maintaining particularly negative attitudes toward homosexuals (Altemeyer, 1988; Herek, 1988; Larsen, Reed, & Hoffman, 1980).

What social and demographic variables have been associated with attitudes toward lesbians and gay men? A review by Herek (1984) revealed that a variety of factors, such as personal contact, self-reports of homosexual experiences, perceptions of peers' attitudes, and education level are all related to attitudes toward lesbians and gay men (see Herek, 1984, for a more complete description of these variables).

Finally, several studies have assessed the content of individuals' stereotypes of lesbians and gay men. For example, Kite and Deaux (1987) explored the content of stereotypes toward male and female homosexuals in reference to the inversion theory of sexuality (i.e., the assumption that homosexuals are perceived as similar to opposite-sex heterosexuals). Consistent with their predictions, male homosexuals were perceived as being "positive toward males," "feminine," and possessing a "high-pitched voice," Female homosexuals were perceived as being "positive toward females," "masculine," and having "short hair" (see also Jackson & Sullivan, 1990; Page & Yee, 1985).

Despite the research on the content of stereotypes, the extent to which these beliefs are related to attitudes remains unclear. Although Herek (1991, p. 66) has pointed out that "strongly correlated with negative attitudes toward lesbians and gay men is acceptance of negative stereotypes," the magnitude of this association is unknown.

As this review suggests, the study of anti-gay attitudes has tended to lack a theoretical framework. As Larsen et al. (1980, p. 246) pointed out, there is "a need to develop a theoretical framework to understand the ... factors predicting heterosexual attitudes toward homosexuality." To date, the most complete model for predicting attitudes toward lesbians and gay men is that described by Herek (1988). On the basis of a review of earlier

[1] The American Psychological Association's Committee on Lesbian and Gay Concerns (1991) has recently suggested that the terms *lesbians* and *gay males* be used rather than the term *homosexuals*. However, this latter term is often used in this article because our subjects were asked to provide their perceptions of the group "homosexuals."

research, he sought to determine the relative importance of religiosity, adherence to traditional ideologies of family and gender, perceptions of friends' agreement with one's own attitudes, and past interactions with lesbians and gay men in predicting attitudes. Although none of these variables individually emerged as most predictive of attitudes, Herek (1988) found in a series of studies that these variables together explained between 45% and 62% of the variance in attitudes toward lesbians and gay men.

A New Theoretical Perspective for Understanding The Structure of Attitudes toward Homosexuals

The framework from which the current research is derived comes from contemporary theorizing in the general area of attitudes. In the attitude literature, it has recently been suggested that evaluations, cognitions, and affective responses are separable yet related aspects of attitudes (e.g., Eagly & Chaiken, 1993; Zanna & Rempel, 1988). This consideration leads us to our definition of attitude. Drawing on recent theoretical perspectives on the attitude concept presented by Zanna and Rempel (1988) and Eagly and Chaiken (1993), we define an attitude as an overall categorization of an attitude object along an evaluative dimension (e.g., favorable–unfavorable, positive–negative). Both Zanna and Rempel (1988) and Eagly and Chaiken (1993) perceived such evaluations as having multiple antecedents. According to this perspective, the attitude concept is viewed as being based on three general sources of information: (a) cognitive information (e.g., beliefs about the attitude object), (b) affective information (e.g., feelings or emotions associated with the attitude object), and (c) information concerning past behaviors or behavioral intentions toward the attitude object.

How does this multicomponent formulation of the attitude concept lend itself to the study of intergroup attitudes? Recently, we have suggested that an intergroup attitude be defined as a favorable or unfavorable overall evaluation of a social group that is based on cognitive and affective sources of information (Esses, Haddock, & Zanna, 1993). In terms of the role of cognition in intergroup attitudes, we have postulated that two separate types of beliefs are relevant to the cognitive component of prejudice. One type of cognitive information is stereotypic beliefs, that is, the characteristics attributed to typical members of a target group (e.g., the belief that typical members of a group are friendly, unintelligent, or both). This is the most popular conception of the cognitive component of prejudice (Ashmore & Del Boca, 1981), with a long history in social psychology (e.g., Katz & Braly, 1933). Traditionally, the *evaluative implications* of stereotypes have been taken as the cognitive component of intergroup attitudes (Fishbein, 1963; Harding, Proshansky, Kutner, & Chein, 1969), with the suggestion that such implications entirely account for individual differences in intergroup attitudes. Cognitions about social groups, however, may not be derived entirely from stereotypic beliefs. For instance, Rokeach (1968) discovered that perceived similarity in *values* serves as an important determinant of interpersonal attraction. In addition, recent research on the importance of values in the expression of symbolic racism (e.g., McConahay, 1986; Sears, 1988) has led us to believe that other general, more abstract beliefs are also relevant to the cognitive component of intergroup attitudes. We refer to these beliefs as symbolic beliefs. Symbolic beliefs are beliefs that social groups violate or promote the attainment of cherished values, customs, and traditions (e.g., the perception that typical members of a group promote freedom of expression, violate the attainment of world peace, or both) These beliefs, however, are different from the concept of symbolic racism in that the latter concept focuses on affect and values, whereas symbolic beliefs focus solely on the importance of values in relation to intergroup attitudes.

In contrast, the affective component of intergroup attitudes focuses on the evaluative implications of the emotions that are elicited by members of different social groups (e.g., typical group members may evoke feelings of fear, admiration, or both). Although not entirely independent of the cognitive component of prejudice, assessing the affective component of intergroup attitudes provides information that is not captured by simply assessing individuals' beliefs. For example, research by Dijker (1987) and Stangor, Sullivan, and Ford (1991) has found that emotional responses toward social groups make a significant contribution to the prediction of intergroup attitudes.

The conceptualization of attitude as an overall evaluation based on multiple sources of information is an important development in that it extends previous models (e.g., the theory of reasoned action; Ajzen & Fishbein, 1980; Fishbein & Ajzen, 1975) that conceptualize attitude as being based entirely on the evaluative implications of beliefs associated with the attitude object. For instance, as originally formulated, the theory of reasoned action would suggest that stereotypic beliefs should play a dominant role in predicting intergroup attitudes. Indeed, Fishbein (1963), using a theoretical perspective consistent with the theory of reasoned action, that is, Attitude = Σ(Belief $\times$ Evaluation), assessed the extent to which the evaluative implications of stereotypes toward African-Americans were associated with the favorability of subjects' attitudes toward the group. It is not surprising that Fishbein found a strong association between attitudes and the evaluative implications of individuals' beliefs (see also Ajzen, 1989). The multicomponent conceptualization of intergroup attitudes extends stereotype-based perspectives by suggesting that the evaluative implications of symbolic beliefs and affective responses should also serve to predict intergroup attitudes, above and beyond the prediction obtained by the sole consideration of the evaluative implications of stereotypic beliefs.

How effectively do stereotypes, symbolic beliefs, and affective associates serve as predictors of intergroup attitudes? First, it should be made clear that these sources of information are not entirely redundant. In addition, research using these variables as predictors of attitudes toward a range of target groups has revealed that the relative importance of cognition and affect is dependent on a variety of factors, such as the specific target group under evaluation, situational determinants, and characteristics of the individual making the evaluative judgment (Esses et al., 1993). Nonetheless, consistent with the multicomponent conceptualization of attitude, our past research has revealed that (a) the evaluative implications of stereotypes, on their own, are associated with the favorability of attitudes, and (b) the consideration of symbolic beliefs and affect significantly increases one's ability to predict prejudice (e.g., Esses et al., 1993; Haddock, Zanna, & Esses, 1993; Haddock & Zanna, in press). These findings are important because they suggest that prejudice is more than simply a reflection of the stereotypes maintained toward a group. Thus, to fully comprehend the nature of intergroup attitudes, researchers need to examine the evaluative implications of other sources of information (e.g., symbolic beliefs and affective responses).

How does the multicomponent perspective of intergroup attitudes that we have proposed compare with that of Herek (1988)? These perspectives share some similarities but are in many ways different. In terms of similarities, Herek's variables of religiosity and adherence to traditional ideologies of family and gender appear to be relevant to the concept of symbolic beliefs. For example, homosexuals might be perceived by some individuals as violating "God's laws" and "proper family values," which might lead these individuals to express extremely negative attitudes. On this basis, one might expect symbolic beliefs to be highly predictive of the attitudes of these traditionally minded individuals. One major difference between our approach and that of Herek's lies in their generality. Although our perspective can be applied to predict attitudes toward a wide range of target groups (see Esses et al., 1993; Haddock & Zanna, in press; Haddock et al., 1993), some of the variables in Herek's framework seem relevant only for attitudes toward lesbians and gay men. In addition, the variables that we have presented may be more direct determinants of attitudes. For instance, the association between religiosity and negative attitudes toward homosexuals documented by Herek might be mediated by what we refer to as symbolic beliefs.

Study 1

The primary purpose of Study 1 was to determine the relative importance of stereotypes, symbolic beliefs, and affective associates in predicting attitudes toward homosexuals. Consistent with our theoretical conceptualization of intergroup attitudes and with past research, we predicted that the evaluative implications of stereotypes, on their own, would be related to attitudes but that the consideration of the evaluative implications of both symbolic beliefs and affective information would significantly increase our ability to predict prejudice. In particular, symbolic beliefs may play the most prominent role in uniquely predicting negative attitudes, especially if homosexuals are perceived as violating cherished values and norms.

A second goal of Study 1 was to assess the extent to which the individual difference variable of RWA (Altemeyer, 1981, 1988) might (a) be related to the favorability of attitudes toward homosexuals and (b) moderate the relative importance of stereotypes, symbolic beliefs, and affective associates in predicting attitudes toward homosexuals. RWA refers to a combination of three attitudinal clusters: conventionalism, authoritarian submission, and authoritarian aggression. As described by Altemeyer (1988), high authoritarians are extremely self-righteous individuals who maintain a strong acceptance of traditional (i.e., Judeo-Christian) values and norms, possess a general willingness to submit to legitimate authority, and display a general tendency to aggress against others (especially those who threaten their conventional values and norms). High authoritarians are characterized as being most committed to maintaining the traditional family structure as well as being threatened by "liberalization" and individuals who threaten their conventional and traditional values.

Recent research has discovered that, in addition to simply maintaining traditional values, high authoritarians give values themselves an extremely important role in their lives. For instance, using a value importance rating procedure developed by Schwartz (1992), Haddock and Zanna (1993b) have found that authoritarianism is positively cor-

related with value importance ratings in both college ($r = .40$) and adult ($r = .35$) samples (both $ps < .01$). Thus, not only do high authoritarians maintain traditional values, they also rate their values as more important in guiding their everyday lives than do low authoritarians.

How might authoritarianism be related to the favorability and structure of attitudes toward homosexuals? First, consistent with past research (e.g., Altemeyer, 1988), we expect high RWAs to maintain particularly negative attitudes toward lesbians and gay men. As for a possible moderating effect of authoritarianism on the relative importance of stereotypes, symbolic beliefs, and affective responses in predicting attitudes, high RWAs, as described earlier, are strongly committed to traditional social norms and values and are threatened by groups that violate or challenge their conventional value system. As a result of their more traditional outlook and the more important role of values in guiding their lives, high RWAs might be especially likely to perceive homosexuals as maintaining and promoting values that violate their highly conventional value system, perhaps leading to these beliefs serving as a primary determinant of their (negative) attitude. Thus, the evaluative implications of symbolic beliefs might function as an especially important source of information in predicting the attitudes of these individuals. Indeed, past research has revealed that attitudes toward groups that are evaluated particularly negatively by high authoritarians are usually based primarily on symbolic beliefs (Esses et al., 1993). In contrast, low authoritarians might be more willing to perceive value differences as acceptable, thus letting symbolic beliefs play a less important role in predicting the attitudes of these individuals. Consequently, stereotypes, affective responses, or both might be particularly important in predicting the attitudes of low authoritarians.

Method

Subjects

One hundred sixty-four students enrolled in introductory psychology classes at the University of

Waterloo participated in return for partial course credit. The data from 19 subjects were discarded because they did not follow the instructions, yielding a total of 145 subjects (73 women and 72 men) for analysis.[2]

Materials

Assessment of attitudes. To measure attitudes, subjects were asked to complete a 101-point *evaluation thermometer*. This measure was adapted from the "feeling thermometer" used in past research (e.g., Campbell, 1971) but modified to remove its affective nature and make it more purely evaluative. Subjects were asked to "provide a number between 0° and 100° to indicate (their) overall evaluation of typical members of the target group." The extreme ends of the scale, 0° and 100°, were labeled *extremely unfavorable* and *extremely favorable*, with the adjectives *very, quite, fairly,* and *slightly unfavorable* or *favorable* marked at 10° increments. The midpoint of the scale, 50°, was labeled *neither favorable nor unfavorable*. The thermometer measure has been successfully used in past research in the domain of intergroup attitudes (e.g., Esses et al., 1993; Sears, 1988; Stangor et al., 1991).

The evaluation thermometer was selected over other possible attitude measures for two main reasons. First, this measure is purely evaluative, in the sense that it contains no specific dimensions on which the group is to be rated.[3] Second, although there are a number of existing scales assessing attitudes toward homosexuals and homosexuality (e.g., Black & Stevenson, 1984; Herek, 1988; Kite & Deaux, 1986; Larsen et al., 1980), we felt that these measures did not sufficiently conform with our definition of attitude.

Assessment of stereotypic beliefs. Using a procedure independently developed by Esses and Zanna (1989) and Eagly and Mladinic (1989), stereotypes were assessed by asking subjects to list the characteristics they would use to describe typical members of the group. Having completed this task, they were asked to rate each characteristic on a 5-point scale ranging from −2 (*very negative*) to +2 (*very positive*). Finally, subjects were asked to indicate the percentage of group members who possess each characteristic.

A stereotype score was calculated in the following manner. First, the valence of each characteristic was multiplied by the proportion (percentage/100) of group members believed to possess that characteristic. Second, these scores were summed and then divided by the number of characteristics listed.[4]

Assessment of symbolic beliefs. To assess symbolic beliefs, subjects were asked to list the values, customs, and traditions that they believed are blocked or facilitated by typical group members. On the completion of this task, they were asked to rate the extent to which each value, custom, or tradition is blocked or facilitated by typical group members, on a 5-point scale ranging from −2 (*almost always blocked*) to +2 (*almost always facilitated*). As well, subjects were asked to indi-

---

[2] The consideration of gender differences in attitudes was not a primary purpose of this study. In both studies, men expressed less favorable attitudes than did women.

[3] It was suggested to us that a single-item attitude measure might be less reliable than multi-item measures. However, research by Jaccard, Weber, and Lundmark (1975) has revealed that single-item attitude measures that are purely evaluative are as reliable as multi-item measures and yield the same results as multiple-item assessment devices. In addition, in Study 2 (to be reported later), the attitudes of the last 63 subjects were reassessed after 2 weeks, using the evaluation thermometer and a five-item semantic differential measure (Cronbach α = .92) that has been used in recent research on

intergroup attitudes by Eagly and her colleagues (e.g., Eagly & Mladinic, 1989). The test–retest reliability of the evaluation thermometer was .77. Furthermore, the evaluation thermometer correlated .70 with the semantic differential measure. The magnitude of this latter correlation is similar to that obtained by Stangor, Sullivan, and Ford (1991), who found a correlation of −.73 between scores on an evaluation thermometer for the target group Jews and scores on a 10-item Anti-Semitism scale.

[4] Evans (1991) has warned against using correlational analyses for assessing the relation between a multiplicative composite and other variables. However, high correlations (all > .90) between the composite measure and a Σ valence/*n* measure suggest that this is not a problem in analyzing these data.

cate the percentage of group members whom they believed block or facilitate each value. A symbolic belief score was calculated in the same manner as for the measure of stereotypes.

Assessment of affect. To assess affect, subjects were asked to list the feelings or emotions they experience when they see, meet, or think about typical members of the group. As with the stereotype measure, they were asked to indicate the valence of each emotion on a 5-point scale ranging from −2 (*very negative*) to +2 (*very positive*). Finally, they were asked to indicate the percentage of group members who evoke each emotion. An affect score was calculated in the same manner as for the measure of stereotypes.

Assessment of RWA. RWA was assessed through the use of a short form of the RWA scale (Altemeyer, 1988). The RWA scale is a 30-item, 9-point scale with higher scores representing higher levels of authoritarianism. Respondents were asked to indicate the extent of their agreement or disagreement with statements such as, "In these troubled times laws have to be enforced without mercy, especially when dealing with the agitators and revolutionaries who are stirring things up" and "People should pay less attention to the Bible and the other traditional forms of religious guidance and instead develop their own personal standards of what is moral and immoral" (this item reverse scored). In our study, an abbreviated 10-item version of the scale was used (Cronbach α = .75). In a separate sample, the abbreviated measure correlated .89 with the complete thirty-item scale.

Procedure

Subjects, most often in groups of 3 or 4, arrived at the laboratory knowing that the study was intended to measure group evaluations. They were then given general instructions as to the procedure of the study, including instructions designed to reduce the demands of listing only positive information. Subjects were told that "almost everyone has positive and negative things to say about most groups," and the anonymous nature of their responses was

made salient. Subjects were then provided a consent form to sign. No subject declined participation at this point. After signing the consent form, subjects completed the measures, which took approximately 45 min. Homosexuals were one of five target groups that subjects evaluated during the session (the others being English Canadians, French Canadians, Native Indians, and Pakistanis). Whereas all subjects completed the attitude measure first, the order of the predictor variables and of the target groups was counterbalanced across subjects. Finally, subjects completed the abbreviated RWA scale, provided demographic information, and were fully debriefed as to the goals of the study.

Results

Evaluation thermometer and predictor variables

How favorable or unfavorable were subjects in their perceptions of homosexuals? The mean attitude and predictor variable scores are presented in the first column of Table 11.1. Overall, subjects' attitudes toward homosexuals were negative ($M = 40.84$, $SD = 25.48$) and were significantly more unfavorable than their attitudes toward any of the other target groups studied. In comparison, the mean attitude scores for the other target groups ranged from 81.08 (for the target group English Canadians) to 58.01 (for the target group Pakistanis).

The means for the predictor variables are also

TABLE 11.1. Mean Perceptions of Homosexuals: Studies 1 and 2

Variable	Study 1		Study 2	
	M	SD	M	SD
Attitude	40.84	25.48	40.87	21.71
Stereotypes	−.17	.85	.08	.71
Symbolic beliefs	−.27	1.04	−.06	.78
Affect	−.57	.82	−.32	.65
Past experiences	–	–	.01	.44

Note: For the attitude variable, possible range = 0 to 100; for the remaining variables, possible range = −2 to +2.

presented in Table 11.1. In each case, the mean predictor score is negative. In addition, each of the predictors contained large amounts of variability, indicating that different subjects were willing to provide disparate beliefs and feelings.

Intercorrelations among the predictor variables

To ensure that the predictor variables were not redundant, Pearson product–moment correlations were computed among these variables. These correlations are presented in the upper section of Table 11.2. It is not surprising that the correlations are all positive, meaning that positive stereotypes were typically associated with positive symbolic beliefs and positive affective associates. However, the

correlations were not high enough to suggest that the variables were eliciting completely overlapping information.

The different types of information elicited by the different measures are also revealed through a content analysis of subjects' open-ended responses. The three most frequently mentioned statements for each predictor variable are provided in the upper section of Table 11.3. With respect to stereotypes, subjects most frequently reported that homosexuals are effeminate, friendly, and normal. Kite and Deaux (1987) discovered that male homosexuals were often perceived as being feminine, implying that our subjects probably construed the term *homosexuals* to refer to gay men. For the symbolic beliefs measure, homosexuals were perceived as promoting freedom, blocking

TABLE 11.2. Correlations Among Predictor Variables: Studies 1 and 2

| Variable | Study 1 (*N* = 145) | | | | |
	1	2	3		
1. Stereotypes	–	.44**	.61**		
2. Symbolic beliefs		–	.36**		
3. Affect			–		

| Variable | Study 2 (*N* = 151) | | | | |
	1	2	3	4	5
1. Stereotypes	–	.36**	.29**	.28**	−.35**
2. Symbolic beliefs		–	.30**	.14	−.42**
3. Affect			–	.23*	−.24*
4. Past experiences				–	−.20*
5. Perceived value dissimilarity					–

$* p < .01.$ $** p < .001.$ All two-tailed tests.

TABLE 11.3. Most Frequently Elicited Responses: Studies 1 and 2

Stereotype	Symbolic belief	Affect	Past experiences
	Study 1		
Effeminate	Promote freedom	Disgust	–
Friendly	Block family	Discomfort	–
Normal	Promote peace	Confusion	–
	Study 2		
Effeminate	Promote freedom	Disgust	School experiences
Normal	Block family	Discomfort	Partners in public
Friendly	Block religion	Curiosity	Conversations

the attainment of the traditional family, and promoting peace. The emotions most frequently elicited by homosexuals were feelings of disgust, discomfort, and confusion.

Prediction of attitudes

To what extent were stereotypes, symbolic beliefs, and affective associates related to attitudes toward homosexuals? The correlation between each of these variables and the attitude measure is shown in the first column of the top panel of Table 11.4. All three predictor variables were positively and significantly correlated with subjects' attitudes.

To determine the relative importance of stereotypes, symbolic beliefs, and affective associates in predicting attitudes toward homosexuals, a hierarchical regression analysis was performed in which the stereotype score was entered in a first block, followed by a second block in which the symbolic belief and affect scores were entered simultaneously. This hierarchical method of analysis allowed us to (a) assess the extent to which stereotypes, on their own, predict attitudes toward homosexuals; (b) discover the increase in explanatory power afforded by including symbolic beliefs and affective associates as predictor variables; (c) determine the total proportion of variance in

attitudes accounted for by the three predictor variables; and (d) assess the unique contribution of stereotypes, symbolic beliefs, and affect to the prediction of attitudes toward homosexuals. As described earlier in this article, we hypothesized that, overall, stereotypes, on their own, would be associated with attitudes but that the consideration of the evaluative implications of symbolic beliefs and affective associates would significantly add to the prediction of attitudes.

The results of this analysis are presented in the top panel of Table 11.4. The analysis revealed that stereotypes, on their own, accounted for 20.7% of the variance in attitudes, $F(1, 143) = 37.40$, $p < .001$. The entry of symbolic beliefs and affective associates in a second block accounted for an additional 19.4% of the variance in attitudes, $F_{change} = 22.86$, $p < .001$. Thus, the evaluative implications of stereotypic beliefs do not entirely account for variability in intergroup attitudes. Together, the three predictor variables accounted for 40.1% of the variance in attitudes toward homosexuals. The standardized regression coefficients for each predictor variable are also presented in Table 11.4. These coefficients reveal that both symbolic beliefs ($\beta = .379$, $p < .001$) and affective associates ($\beta = .303$, $p < .001$) uniquely contributed to the prediction of attitudes. Stereotypes, on the other hand, were not uniquely predictive of attitudes ($\beta = .102$, ns).

TABLE 11.4. Hierarchical Regression Analyses: Study 1

Variable	Correlation[a]	R^2 change (%)	Final beta coefficient
All subjects ($N = 145$)			
Stereotypes	.455***	20.7***	.102
Symbolic beliefs	.534***		.379***
Affect	.503***	19.4***	.303***
High RWAs ($N = 48$)			
Stereotypes	.091	0.8	−.214
Symbolic beliefs	.315*		.343*
Affect	.223	15.2*	.318
Low RWAs ($N = 48$)			
Stereotypes	.698***	48.7***	.434***
Symbolic beliefs	.464***		.157
Affect	.650***	11.5**	.348**

Note: RWAs = right-wing authoritarians.
[a] Correlation between variable and attitude measure.
* $p < .05$. ** $p < .01$. *** $p < .001$. All two-tailed tests.

RWA and the prediction of attitudes

Consistent with past research (e.g., Altemeyer, 1988), there was a significant negative correlation between authoritarianism and attitudes toward homosexuals ($r = −.42$, $p < .001$). High authoritarians expressed less favorable attitudes than did low authoritarians. For the purposes of our regression analyses, subjects were assigned to high and low RWA groups on the basis of a tertile split of our sample. High RWAs were those individuals who scored greater than 54 on the RWA scale, whereas low RWAs were operationalized as those scoring less than 42. Mean attitudes toward homosexuals for high and low RWAs were 27.06 and 51.67, respectively. In addition to holding more negative attitudes, high authoritarians were also more likely to express negative stereotypes, symbolic beliefs, and affective associates toward homosexuals than were low authoritarians (all $ps < .05$).

To assess the relative importance of stereotypes, symbolic beliefs, and affective associates in predicting attitudes toward homosexuals for high and low authoritarians, a separate regression analysis was performed for each of these groups. The stereotype measure was entered in a first block, followed by a second block in which the symbolic belief and affect measures were entered simultaneously. Conducting separate analyses for high and low RWAs not only allowed us to assess differences in the unique contribution of each predictor variable, it also provided us the opportunity to determine whether the three predictor variables accounted for equivalent proportions of variance in attitudes toward homosexuals for high and low RWAs. The results of these analyses are also presented in Table 11.4. For high RWAs, stereotypes, on their own, were unrelated to attitudes, accounting for less than 1% of the variance in attitudes, $F(1, 46) = .39$, ns. The entry of symbolic beliefs and affective associates accounted for an additional 15.2% of the variance in attitudes, $F_{change} = 3.96$, $p < .05$. Together, the three predictor variables accounted for 16.0% of the variance in attitudes held by high authoritarians. The standardized regression coefficients are also presented in Table 11.4. The unique contribution of symbolic beliefs was significant ($\beta = .343$, $p < .05$), whereas the unique contribution of affect approached significance ($\beta = .318$, $p < .085$). Stereotypes did not uniquely contribute to the prediction of attitudes for high RWAs ($\beta = -.214$, ns).

For low RWAs, stereotypes, on their own, accounted for 48.7% of the variance in attitudes, $F(1, 46) = 43.70$, $p < .001$. The entry of symbolic beliefs and affective associates accounted for an additional 11.5% of the variance, $F_{change} = 6.35$, $p < .01$. Thus, the three predictor variables together accounted for 60.2% of the variance in attitudes held by low RWAs. The standardized regression coefficients reveal that the unique contribution of both stereotypes ($\beta = .434$, $p < .001$) and affective associates ($\beta = .348$, $p < .01$) were significant. In contrast, symbolic beliefs were not uniquely predictive of attitudes ($\beta = .157$, ns) for low RWAs.

Discussion

The results of Study 1 demonstrate that attitudes toward homosexuals are negative and that the most unfavorable attitudes are expressed by high authoritarian subjects. In addition, the stereotypes, symbolic beliefs, and affective information associated with homosexuals are also negative (and especially negative for high authoritarians).

Overall, how effective were stereotypes, symbolic beliefs, and affective information in predicting attitudes toward homosexuals? Based on our past research, we expected that the evaluative implications of stereotypic beliefs, on their own, would be related to attitudes toward homosexuals but that the consideration of the evaluative implications of both symbolic beliefs and affective associates would significantly increase our ability to predict prejudice. Overall, this finding was confirmed. Stereotypes were correlated with subjects' attitudes but provided little unique contribution to the prediction of attitudes upon the consideration of symbolic beliefs and affective associates. Thus, to more effectively predict attitudes toward homosexuals, one must measure more than simply the evaluative implications of stereotypic beliefs.

It was suggested that the relative importance of stereotypes, symbolic beliefs, and affective associates might differ as a function of individual differences in RWA. Among high authoritarians, stereotypes, on their own, were unrelated to attitudes toward homosexuals. The attitudes of these individuals were best predicted by symbolic beliefs. Conversely, stereotypic beliefs and affective associates were very useful in predicting the attitudes of low authoritarians. For these individuals, symbolic beliefs were not uniquely predictive of attitudes toward homosexuals.

As described earlier, homosexuals was not the only target group included in our study. For our conceptualization of intergroup attitudes to be considered useful, the results obtained with regard to homosexuals should, at least to some extent, generalize to the other groups that were assessed during the experimental session. Indeed, the results obtained with the other target groups were similar to those for homosexuals in that, overall, (a) stereotypes, on their own, were correlated with attitudes; (b) the consideration of symbolic beliefs and affect added to the prediction of attitudes; and (c) stereotypes were not uniquely predictive of attitudes toward any of the target groups. In addition, for the target group where authoritarianism was associated with more negative attitudes (i.e., Pakistanis), symbolic beliefs served as the best unique predictor of attitudes for high authoritarians (see also Esses et al., 1993). This pattern of findings has also been replicated in a recent study assessing the structure of attitudes toward feminists (Haddock & Zanna, in press).[5]

What is it about symbolic beliefs that led them to play an important role in predicting the attitudes toward homosexuals expressed by high authoritarians? As described earlier, high RWAs maintain traditional values and have been found to rate values as extremely important in life (relative to low RWAs). Perhaps high authoritarians perceive homosexuals as maintaining a value system markedly different from their own and these perceived differences in values serve as the primary determinant of their (negative) attitudes. Some evidence for the relation between perceptions of basic differences and negative attitudes toward homosexuals comes from research by Krulewitz and Nash (1980), who examined the impact of attitude similarity on men's rejection of male homosexuals. They discovered that men holding traditional sex role attitudes were less accepting of homosexuals than were men endorsing relatively liberal sex role attitudes. Their results also suggested that "homosexuals are disliked because they are perceived as (maintaining) different (attitudes)" (Krulewitz & Nash, 1980, p. 72). On the basis of this hypothesis, we thought it would be useful to investigate in our next study the extent to which perceived differences in values are related to symbolic beliefs and attitudes, particularly for high authoritarians.

An unexpected finding in this study was the

difference in the proportion of variance accounted for by the three predictor variables as a function of authoritarianism. Although stereotypes, symbolic beliefs, and affective associates accounted for only 16% of the variance in attitudes toward homosexuals for high RWAs, these same predictor variables accounted for more than 60% of the variance in the attitudes of low RWAs. This result was not attributable to differences between high and low RWAs in the amount of variance in the variables. In fact, there was slightly more variation for high RWAs on all three predictor variables and the criterion variable. This led us to consider other sources of information that might be especially relevant for high authoritarians. Recall that the Zanna and Rempel (1988) formulation of the attitude concept posited that information concerning past behaviors or behavioral intentions serve as a source of available information during the evaluative process. We thought it might be useful to assess this source of information in our next study, to determine if the evaluative implications of behavioral information are differentially important in predicting the attitudes of high and low authoritarians. [. . .]

[EDITORS' NOTE: In addition to the measures administered in the first study, the second included an assessment of past experiences with homosexuals. Participants were asked to list the most recent experiences they shared with members of the target group. They then rated the valence of each listed experience and indicated the percentage of group members with whom they had shared the experience. These data were employed to compute a past experiences score in the same manner as had been done for the other measures. Study 2 successfully replicated the findings of the first study. It also revealed that participants' reports regarding the quality of their behavioral experiences with members of the target group related to their attitude scores. However, as seen in Table 11.5, this was more true for the high RWA participants than the low. Thus, symbolic beliefs and past experiences proved to be important predictors of the attitudes of the high RWAs, whereas stereotypes and affect were the more important predictors of attitude scores among the low RWAs.]

---

[5] Comparative data for other target groups are available from the authors on request.

TABLE 11.5. Hierarchical Regression Analyses: Study 2

Variable	Correlation[a]	R^2 change (%)	Final beta coefficient
All subjects ($N = 151$)			
Stereotypes	.393***	15.4***	.130
Symbolic beliefs	.494***		.346***
Affect	.418***	20.3***	.216**
Past experiences	.411***	7.0***	.278***
High RWAs ($N = 58$)			
Stereotypes	.206	4.2	.063
Symbolic beliefs	.409**		.262*
Affect	.356**	18.5**	.222
Past experiences	.448***	14.6***	.387***
Low RWAs ($N = 46$)			
Stereotypes	.444**	19.7**	.392*
Symbolic beliefs	.244		−.055
Affect	.402**	8.4	.306*
Past experiences	.275	0.1	−.009

Note: RWAs = right-wing authoritarians.
[a] Correlation between variable and attitude measure.
* $p < .05$. ** $p < .01$. *** $p < .001$. All two-tailed tests.

General Discussion

Previous research has revealed that attitudes toward homosexuals are negative and are correlated with RWA. However, research examining the underlying structure of these attitudes has been virtually nonexistent. This series of studies was intended to determine the relative importance of stereotypes, symbolic beliefs, affective associates, and, in Study 2, past experiences, in the prediction of individuals' attitudes toward homosexuals.

Study 1 confirmed that attitudes toward homosexuals are negative and that the most negative attitudes are expressed by high authoritarians. Furthermore, symbolic beliefs were especially useful in predicting the attitudes of high authoritarians, whereas the attitudes of low authoritarians were best predicted by stereotypic beliefs and affective associates. It is interesting that the variability in attitudes accounted for by the cognitive and affective variables was substantially higher for low authoritarians than for high authoritarians.

Study 2 was performed in an attempt to replicate and extend the findings of Study 1. First, in an attempt to increase the variance in attitudes

accounted for, especially for high authoritarians, a measure assessing individuals' past experiences with the target group was devised and administered along with the cognitive and affective measures. Second, in an attempt to gain further understanding of subjects' symbolic beliefs, subjects were asked to complete a measure of perceived value dissimilarity by rating a series of values in terms of their perceived importance to themselves and to typical homosexuals. As in Study 1, the relative importance of symbolic beliefs, stereotypes, and affective associates in predicting attitudes differed as a function of authoritarianism. Symbolic beliefs were especially predictive of the attitudes of high authoritarians, whereas stereotypes and affective associates were especially predictive of the attitudes of low authoritarians. Past experiences accounted for a significant proportion of variance in attitudes toward homosexuals, but only among high authoritarians. As for perceived value dissimilarity, it was associated with our measure of symbolic beliefs, but only among high authoritarians. Controlling for the symbolic belief and perceived value dissimilarity measures greatly decreased the magnitude of the RWA–attitude relation.

Our initial work assessing the impact of perceived value dissimilarity suggests that it is an integral part of prejudice toward lesbians and gay men. Additional research assessing perceived value dissimilarity is necessary to determine its effects on attitudes toward other outgroups (see, e.g., Struch & Schwartz, 1989). In addition, a more complete understanding of the content of these differences is required. For instance, perceived value dissimilarity can be conceptualized as containing two components: (a) actual differences in values and (b) inaccuracy in the perception of others' values. Thus, one can examine the extent to which perceived dissimilarity is determined by actual differences in values as compared with inaccurate perceptions and also determine whether the authoritarianism–perceived value dissimilarity relation is primarily mediated by larger actual differences in values, or greater perceptual inaccuracy on the part of high authoritarians, or both.

Prejudice toward homosexuals is not simply the expression of a negative attitude; it is often accompanied by discriminatory behavior. To begin to explore the role of authoritarianism and attitudes in predicting one form of anti-gay discrimination, we had the last 63 participants from Study 2 return for a second session 2 weeks after completing the main set of measures. In this second session, subjects first completed the evaluation thermometer and a semantic differential measure of attitudes toward homosexuals (which were assessed to collect information concerning the reliability and validity of the evaluation thermometer; see footnote 3). After completing these measures, they were asked to complete a short survey ostensibly given on behalf of the University of Waterloo Psych Society (i.e., undergraduate psychology association). Subjects were (mis)informed that researchers within the psychology department had been approached by the Psych Society and asked to distribute to introductory psychology students a short survey concerning the funding of student organizations. In a letter introducing the survey, subjects were told that the student government was being forced to cut funding to student organizations by 20% and that the Psych Society was interested in soliciting psychology students' impressions of this issue. They were further informed that the results of the survey would be presented to the student government. Subjects were then given a subset of 10 campus organizations and the funding that they ostensibly received for the 1992–1993 academic year. They were then asked to indicate the amount of funding they believed each group should be allocated for 1993–1994, with the restriction that, overall, the funds for the 10 groups should be reduced by 20%. Embedded among the various academic, social, and recreational clubs used in the survey was the university's organization for lesbians and gay men, the Gay and Lesbian Liberation of Waterloo (GLLOW).[6]

To what extent did proposed funding allocations for GLLOW differ as a function of authoritarianism and the favorability of individuals' attitudes? To explore this question, we conducted a 2 × 2

(Unfavorable/Favorable Attitude × High/Low Authoritarianism) analysis of variance (ANOVA). A median split of authoritarianism was used because of our small sample size. Of course, we expected those individuals with negative attitudes to propose the most substantial funding reductions. Moreover, among those individuals with unfavorable attitudes, we expected the high authoritarians to be especially harsh in their proposed funding allocations, as a result of their negative attitudes being based on symbolic beliefs.

This analysis revealed a significant main effect of authoritarianism, $F(1, 53) = 6.05, p < .05$. High authoritarians (derived on the basis of a RWA median split score of 45) proposed an average reduction of 37%, whereas low RWAs advocated a mean reduction of 25%. There was also a marginal main effect of attitude favorability, $F(1, 53) = 3.13$, $p = .08$. Individuals expressing unfavorable attitudes (i.e., below 50 on the evaluation thermometer) proposed an average reduction of 35%, whereas individuals expressing favorable attitudes advocated a smaller decrease (25%). However, both main effects were qualified by their two-way interaction, $F(1, 53) = 4.08, p < .05$. Of those individuals expressing unfavorable attitudes, high authoritarians proposed a significantly greater funding reduction (mean reduction = 45%) than low RWAs (25%), $t = 2.56, p < .05$. This difference in behavior existed even though these individuals maintained equally unfavorable attitudes (M_{high} = 28.61; $M_{low} = 32.14, t < 1$). In contrast, among high and low authoritarians maintaining favorable attitudes ($M_{high} = 65.00; M_{low} = 60.33, t < 1$), there was no difference in proposed funding to GLLOW ($M_{high} = 27\%; M_{low} = 26\%, t < 1$).[7]

---

[6] Only three subjects expressed any suspicion concerning this procedure. Consequently, their data were discarded. One additional subject elected not to complete the survey.

[7] To more directly test the notion that attitudes based on symbolic beliefs would lead to more negative behavior, we also conducted an analysis in which we derived an index that allowed us to quantify the source of information most consistent with the individual's attitude. If negative attitudes based on symbolic beliefs lead to particularly negative funding proposals, it would provide evidence that these beliefs have important consequences concerning discriminatory actions directed against homosexuals. Before conducting the appropriate analysis, we first needed to compute an index that would allow us to quantify the consistency between individuals' attitudes, symbolic beliefs, and stereotypes. Following

Thus, these GLLOW funding results suggest that individual differences in authoritarianism and the favorability of individuals' attitudes toward homosexuals have important implications for one form of discriminatory behavior directed against homosexuals. Although promising, these results need to be generalized to other forms of behavior. One interesting avenue for future research would be to investigate the extent to which differences in authoritarianism and the favorability of attitudes lead to differences in other types of discriminatory behavior that are more hostile in nature.

The results of our studies also have implications for attempts to eliminate prejudice against lesbians and gay men. Herek (1991) has described two techniques thought to be successful in reducing the prevalence of negative attitudes toward homosexuals. First, heterosexuals' attitudes toward homosexuals have been documented as becoming more favorable following an educational program about homosexuality (see Herek, 1991, for a review). Two explanations for the success of this approach have been that (a) it refutes stereotypes about lesbians and gay men and (b) it provides an opportunity to develop positive feelings toward lesbians and gay men (Herek, 1991). On the basis of the results of our study, one might expect this

technique to be most successful in changing the attitudes of low authoritarians. To change the attitudes of high authoritarians, approaches intended to increase contact and reduce perceived value differences would probably be necessary. Accordingly, the second technique described by Herek (1991) may be somewhat effective in reducing the negative attitudes of high authoritarians. This technique focuses on positive personal contact. As Herek (1991, pp. 76–77) has pointed out, "Knowing an openly gay person is predictive of supportive attitudes even in demographic groups where hostility is the norm." Unfortunately, few high authoritarians have homosexual acquaintances. For example, Altemeyer (1988) discovered that less than 25% of a large sample of high RWAs had a homosexual acquaintance. Optimistically, however, it should also be noted that the high RWAs in Altemeyer's sample who reported having a homosexual acquaintance had more favorable attitudes toward homosexuals than did those without such an acquaintance, although the direction of causality is, of course, unknown (see also Pryor, Reeder, & McManus, 1991, for a discussion of educational programs aimed at changing attitudes toward persons with acquired immunodeficiency syndrome).

Despite the coherence of the results of our studies, their correlational nature prevents definitive causal inferences. For example, we have suggested

---

the work of Chaiken and her colleagues (Chaiken, Pomerantz, & Giner-Sorolla, in press), we computed scores that represented the extent to which individuals' symbolic belief and stereotype scores were consistent with their attitudes (see also Haddock & Zanna, 1993a). This index was computed by first standardizing subjects' scores on the three measures. Second, we calculated the absolute difference between the attitude and symbolic belief scores (ATT/SYM scores) and the attitude and stereotype scores (ATT/STR scores). The ATT/SYM score was then subtracted from the ATT/STR score to create an index that represented the degree to which attitudes are based on symbolic beliefs vs. stereotypic beliefs. A more positive score on this consistency index would represent a smaller discrepancy (and, therefore, greater consistency) between individuals' attitudes and symbolic beliefs. Using a tertile split on attitude favorability and a median split on the consistency index, we conducted a 3 × 2 (Relatively Favorable/Neutral/Unfavorable Attitude × Attitude Most Consistent With Either Symbolic Beliefs or Stereotypes) ANOVA using subjects' funding allocation for GLLOW as the dependent variable. This analysis revealed a main effect of attitude favorability; subjects with relatively unfavorable attitudes proposed greater

cuts to GLLOW's funding (mean percentage funding reduction = 42%) than did subjects with relatively neutral (25%) or favorable attitudes (27%). More important, the analysis revealed a marginally significant interaction between favorability and basis of attitudes ($p < .10$). Subjects whose negative attitudes were based on (i.e., more consistent with) symbolic beliefs proposed the largest funding cut for GLLOW (reducing funds by an average of 52%) and proposed significantly greater cuts than those subjects with relatively neutral (22%) or favorable (25%) attitudes based on symbolic beliefs. In contrast, subjects whose negative attitudes were based on (i.e., more consistent with) stereotypic beliefs proposed cuts (36%) that were not different from those of subjects with relatively neutral (28%) or favorable (29%) attitudes based on stereotypes. Finally, among those subjects with relatively negative attitudes, those based primarily on symbolic beliefs tended to propose greater cuts than those based primarily on stereotypes ($p < .10$, one-tailed). Thus, these results provide preliminary evidence that symbolic beliefs have important behavioral consequences in that negative attitudes based on these beliefs are translated into negative behavior toward homosexuals.

that for low authoritarians, negative stereotypes contribute to unfavorable attitudes. It is also conceivable that unfavorable attitudes might lead low authoritarians to create or recall stereotypes that are congruent with their evaluations. This suggests that future research might examine the effect of changing stereotypes versus symbolic beliefs on attitudes. In addition, a developmental study examining naturally occurring changes in attitudes and their components appears warranted.

In sum, the results of this series of studies suggest that cognitive, affective, and behavioral information are all relevant to the understanding of attitudes toward homosexuals. Furthermore, different sources of information were uniquely predictive of attitudes as a function of authoritarianism. We have suggested (and obtained preliminary evidence) that attitudes based on different sources of information have different effects and that attempts to change attitudes might be more or less effective, depending on the primary correlate or correlates of the attitude. Our hope is that future research in this area will consider this model as an appropriate theoretical framework for studying attitudes toward lesbians and gay men, and that the model will lead to advances in our understanding of anti-gay prejudice.

REFERENCES

Adorno, T. W., Frenkel-Brunswik, E., Levinson, D. J., & Sanford, R. N. (1950). *The authoritarian personality*. New York: Harper & Row.

Ajzen, I. (1989). Attitude structure and behavior. In A. R. Pratkanis, S. J. Breckler, & A. G. Greenwald (Eds.), *Attitude structure and function* (pp. 241–274). Hillsdale, NJ: Erlbaum.

Ajzen, I., & Fishbein, M. (1980). *Understanding attitudes and predicting social behavior*. Englewood Cliffs, NJ: Prentice Hall.

Altemeyer, B. (1981). *Right-wing authoritarianism*. Winnipeg: University of Manitoba Press.

Altemeyer, B. (1988). *Enemies of freedom: Understanding right-wing authoritarianism*. San Francisco: Jossey-Bass.

American Psychological Association, Committee on Lesbian and Gay Concerns (1991). Avoiding heterosexual bias in language. *American Psychologist, 46,* 973–974.

Ashmore, R. D., & Del Boca, F. K. (1981). Conceptual approaches to stereotypes and stereotyping. In D. L. Hamilton (Ed.), *Cognitive processes in stereotyping and intergroup behavior* (pp. 1–36). Hillsdale, NJ: Erlbaum.

Black, K. N., & Stevenson, M. R. (1984). The relationship of self-reported sex-role characteristics and attitudes toward homosexuality. *Journal of Homosexuality, 10,* 83–93.

Campbell, D. T. (1971). *White attitudes toward Black people*. Ann Arbor, MI: Institute for Social Research.

Chaiken, S., Pomerantz, E. M., & Giner-Sorolla, R. (in press). Structural consistency and attitude strength. In R. E. Petty & J. A. Krosnick (Eds.), *Attitude strength: Antecedents and consequences*. Hillsdale, NJ: Erlbaum.

Cohen, J., & Cohen, P. (1983). *Applied multiple regression/correlation analysis for the behavioral sciences*. Hillsdale, NJ: Erlbaum.

Dijker, A. J. M. (1987). Emotional reactions to ethnic minorities. *European Journal of Social Psychology, 17,* 305–325.

Eagly, A. H., & Chaiken, S. (1993). *The psychology of attitudes*. Fort Worth, TX: Harcourt Brace Jovanovich.

Eagly, A. H., & Mladinic, A. (1989). Gender stereotypes & attitudes toward women and men. *Personality and Social Psychology Bulletin, 15,* 543–558.

Esses, V. M., Haddock, G., & Zanna, M. P. (1993). Values, stereotypes, and emotions as determinants of intergroup attitudes. In D. M. Mackie & D. L. Hamilton (Eds.), *Affect, cognition and stereotyping: Interactive processes in group perception* (pp. 137–166). New York: Academic Press.

Esses, V. M., & Zanna, M. P. (1989, August). *Mood and the expression of ethnic stereotypes*. Paper presented at the 97th Annual Convention of the American Psychological Association, New Orleans, LA.

Evans, M. (1991). The problem of analyzing multiplicative composites: Interactions revisited. *American Psychologist, 46,* 6–15.

Fishbein, M. (1963). An investigation of the relationships between beliefs about an object and the attitude toward the object. *Human Relations, 16,* 233–259.

Fishbein, M., & Azjen, I. (1975). *Belief, attitude, intention, and behavior: An introduction to theory and research*. Reading, MA: Addison-Wesley.

Gardner, R. C., Lalonde, R. N., Nero, A. M., & Young, M. Y. (1988). Ethnic stereotypes: Implications of measurement strategy. *Social Cognition, 6,* 40–60.

Haddock, G., & Zanna, M. P. (1993a). Predicting prejudicial attitudes: The importance of affect, cognition, and the feeling–belief dimension. In L. McAlister & M. L. Rothschild (Eds.), *Advances in consumer research* (Vol. 20, pp. 315–318). Provo, UT: Association for Consumer Research.

Haddock, G., & Zanna, M. P. (1993b). *Right-wing authoritarianism and the importance of human values*. [Unpublished raw data]

Haddock, G., & Zanna, M. P. (in press). Preferring "Housewives" to "Feminists": Categorization and the favorability of attitudes toward women. *Psychology of Women Quarterly*.

Haddock, G., Zanna, M. P., & Esses, V. M. (1993). *The (limited) role of trait-based stereotypes in predicting attitudes toward Native Peoples*. Manuscript submitted for publication.

Harding, J., Proshansky, H., Kutner, B., & Chein, I. (1969). Prejudice and ethnic relations. In G. Lindzey (Ed.), *Handbook of social psychology* (Vol. 5, pp. 1–76). Reading, MA: Addison-Wesley.

Herek, G. M. (1984). Beyond "homophobia": A social psychological perspective on attitudes toward lesbians and gay men. *Journal of Homosexuality, 10,* 1–21.

Herek, G. M. (1988). Heterosexuals' attitudes toward lesbians and gay men: Correlates and gender differences. *The Journal of Sex Research, 25,* 451–477.

Herek, G. M. (1991). Stigma, prejudice, and violence against lesbians and gay men. In J. C. Gonsiorek & J. D. Weinrich (Eds.), *Homosexuality: Research implications for public policy* (pp. 60–80). Newbury Park, CA: Sage.

Jaccard, J., Weber, J., & Lundmark, J. (1975). A multitrait–multimethod analysis of four attitude assessment procedures. *Journal of Experimental Social Psychology, 11,* 149–154.

Jackson, L. A., & Sullivan, L. A. (1990). Cognition and affect in evaluations of stereotyped group members. *Journal of Social Psychology, 129,* 659–672.

Katz, D., & Braly, K. (1933). Racial stereotypes in 100 college students. *Journal of Abnormal and Social Psychology, 28,* 280–290.

Kite, M. S. (1984). Sex differences in attitudes toward homosexuals: A meta-analytic review. *Journal of Homosexuality, 10,* 69–81.

Kite, M. S., & Deaux, K. (1986). Attitudes toward homosexuality: Assessment and behavioral consequences. *Basic and Applied Social Psychology, 7,* 137–162.

Kite, M. S., & Deaux, K. (1987). Gender belief systems: Homosexuality and the implicit inversion theory. *Psychology of Women Quarterly, 11,* 83–96.

Krulewitz, J. E., & Nash, J. E. (1980). Effects of sex role attitudes and similarity on men's rejection of male homosexuals. *Journal of Personality and Social Psychology, 38,* 67–74.

Larsen, K. S., Reed, M., & Hoffman, S. (1980). Attitudes of heterosexuals toward homosexuality: A Likert-type scale and construct validity. *The Journal of Sex Research, 16,* 245–257.

McConahay, J. B. (1986). Modern racism, ambivalence, and the modern racism scale. In J. F. Dovidio & S. L. Gaertner (Eds.), *Prejudice, discrimination, and racism* (pp. 84–105). New York: Academic Press.

Morin, S. F. (1977). Heterosexual bias in psychological research. *American Psychologist, 32,* 629–637.

Page, S., & Yee, M. (1985). Conception of male and female homosexual stereotypes among university undergraduates. *Journal of Homosexuality, 12,* 109–117.

Pryor, J. B., Reeder, G. D., & McManus, J. A. (1991). Fear and loathing in the workplace: Reactions to AIDS-infected co-workers. *Personality and Social Psychology Bulletin, 17,* 133–139.

Rokeach, M. (1968). *Beliefs, attitudes, and values: A theory of organization and change.* San Francisco: Jossey-Bass.

Schwartz, S. H. (1992). Universals in the content and structure of values: Theoretical advances and empirical tests in 20 countries. In M. P. Zanna (Ed.), *Advances in experimental social psychology* (Vol. 25, pp. 1–65). San Diego, CA: Academic Press.

Schwartz, S. H., & Struch, N. (1989). Values, stereotypes, and intergroup antagonism. In D. Bar-Tal, C. F. Graumann, A. W. Kruglanski, & W. Stroebe (Eds.), *Stereotyping and prejudice: Changing conceptions* (pp. 151–168). New York: Springer-Verlag.

Sears, D. O. (1988). Symbolic racism. In P. A. Katz & D. A. Taylor (Eds.), *Eliminating racism* (pp. 53–84). New York: Plenum Press.

Stangor, C., Sullivan, L. A., & Ford, T. E. (1991). Affective and cognitive determinants of prejudice. *Social Cognition, 9,* 359–391.

Struch, N., & Schwartz, S. H. (1989). Intergroup aggression: Its predictors and distinctness from in-group bias. *Journal of Personality and Social Psychology: 56,* 364–373.

Zanna, M. P., & Rempel, J. K. (1988). Attitudes: A new look at an old concept. In D. Bar-Tal & A. W. Kruglanski (Eds.), *The social psychology of knowledge* (pp. 315–334). Cambridge, England: Cambridge University Press.

Received June 5, 1992
Revision received July 9, 1993
Accepted July 9, 1993 ■

Thinking and Caring about Cognitive Inconsistency: When and for Whom does Attitudinal Ambivalence Feel Uncomfortable?

Ian R. Newby-Clark, Ian McGregor, and Mark P. Zanna

The relation between conflicting evaluations of attitude objects (potential ambivalence) and associated unpleasant feelings (felt ambivalence) was investigated. Participants indicated their potential and felt ambivalence about capital punishment (Studies 1 and 2) and abortion (Studies 1–3). The simultaneous accessibility (J. N. Bassili, 1996) of participants' potential ambivalence (i.e., how quickly and equally quickly conflicting evaluations came to mind) was measured using response latency (Studies 1–3) and manipulated by repeated expression (Study 3). The relation between potential ambivalence and felt ambivalence was strongest when potential ambivalence was high in simultaneous accessibility (Studies 1–3). This pattern was most pronounced for participants who were high in preference for consistency (Study 3; R. B. Cialdini, M. R. Trost, & T. J. Newsom, 1995). Similarities of ambivalence and cognitive dissonance constructs are discussed.

Ian R. Newby-Clark, Department of Psychology, University of Windsor, Windsor, Ontario, Canada; Ian McGregor, Department of Psychology, York University, Toronto, Ontario, Canada; Mark P. Zanna, Department of Psychology, University of Waterloo, Waterloo, Ontario, Canada.

This research was supported by an Ontario graduate scholarship granted to Ian R. Newby-Clark, a Social Sciences and Humanities Research Council of Canada (SSHRCC) doctoral fellowship granted to Ian McGregor, and an SSHRCC research grant to Mark P. Zanna. The results of Studies 1 and 2 were reported at the 105th Annual Convention of the American Psychological Association, Chicago, August 1997. The results of Study 3 were reported at the first annual meeting of the Society for Personality and Social Psychology, Nashville, Tennessee, February 2000. We thank Steve Bauer, Jeff Bennett, Clay Boutilier, Jill Dickinson, Bill Eickmeier, Sharon Schroeder, and the Registrar's Office at the University of Waterloo for their assistance during various phases of this project. We thank Ziva Kunda and Steven Spencer for their feedback on drafts of this article.

Correspondence concerning this article should be addressed to Ian R. Newby-Clark, Department of Psychology, University of Windsor, Windsor, Ontario N9B 3P4, Canada. E-mail: newby@uwindsor.ca

Our lives can be rife with cognitive inconsistency, both prosaic and profound. We might conduct an internal debate over which television show to watch or, while viewing a program about capital punishment, realize that our desire for vengeance conflicts with our love of all life, no matter how vile. Our inconsistent thoughts might cause uncomfortable mixed emotions and feelings of being torn about the value of state-sanctioned execution. When the program ends and our thoughts turn to what is in the refrigerator, though, we may no longer feel torn. Also, some of us may not be particularly bothered when we are aware of our inconsistent thoughts about capital punishment. The conditions under which people experience negative emotions about their cognitive inconsistency, if they do at all, are explored in the current investigation.

A person who feels mixed emotions and is torn about an attitude object feels ambivalent about it (Jamieson, 1993). The experience of such negative affect is partly determined by attitudinal ambivalence—that is, positive and negative evaluations of an attitude object. If a person has both a highly positive and a highly negative evaluation of capital punishment, then he or she is attitudinally ambivalent and could experience mixed emotions about the issue. If that same person has only a highly negative evaluation of capital punishment, then he or she is not attitudinally ambivalent and probably will not feel torn about the issue (Priester & Petty, 1996; Thompson, Zanna, & Griffin, 1995).

Researchers usually measure attitudinal ambivalence by separately asking people about their positive and negative unipolar evaluations of an attitude object. Researchers obtain unipolar evaluations by instructing respondents to ignore their positive evaluations of an attitude object when giving their negative evaluations, and vice versa (Kaplan, 1972). The unipolar responses are then put into an ambivalence formula that produces an attitudinal ambivalence score (e.g., Priester & Petty, 1996; Scott, 1968; Thompson et al., 1995). As positive and negative evaluations become increasingly and equally extreme, attitudinal ambivalence increases (Kaplan, 1972; Priester & Petty, 1996; Scott, 1968; Thompson et al., 1995).

Feelings of ambivalence, in contrast, are measured with self-report scales that assess how torn or conflicted an individual feels about a certain attitude object (e.g., Jamieson, 1993; Priester & Petty, 1996). As might be expected, attitudinal ambivalence is correlated with feelings of ambivalence, though the correlation is not particularly high. Thompson et al. (1995) found that attitudinal ambivalence correlated only $r = .40$ with feelings of ambivalence (for a similar finding, see Priester & Petty, 1996). This somewhat low correlation suggests that the potential to feel ambivalent (i.e., *potential ambivalence*), as measured by unipolar attitudinal ambivalence questions, does not necessarily entail feelings of ambivalence (i.e., *felt ambivalence*).[1] In the studies reported here, we focus on two moderators of the potential ambivalence–felt ambivalence relation: *simultaneous accessibility* (Bassili, 1996) and *preference for consistency* (PFC; Cialdini, Trost, & Newsom, 1995).

Simultaneous Accessibility

Festinger (1957) held that cognitive inconsistency (i.e., dissonance) causes a negative affective experience. This aversive experience is eliminated by resolution of the inconsistency that caused it. Zanna, Lepper, and Abelson (1973) demonstrated the role of awareness of cognitive inconsistency in that dissonance process. They used a forbidden toy paradigm (e.g., Aronson & Carlsmith, 1963) and manipulated awareness of inconsistency. Children in the awareness condition were reminded during a temptation period that they were not playing with a favorite toy even though the punishment for doing so was relatively mild. Those children derogated the once-favored toy more than did children who were not reminded of their inconsistency. Presumably, toy derogation increased cognitive harmony because self-contradiction (e.g., "I am not playing

---

[1] In Priester and Petty's (2001) terms, potential ambivalence is intrapersonal ambivalence and felt ambivalence is subjective ambivalence.

with a toy that I like even though the punishment for doing so is mild") became self-consistency (e.g., "I am not playing with a toy that I do not like"). In accord with Festinger (1957), Zanna et al. reasoned that the more pronounced reduction of cognitive inconsistency in the awareness condition occurred because children in that condition experienced more negative affect when their inconsistent cognitions were made salient.

The Zanna et al. (1973) findings suggest that an experience of inconsistency-related discomfort is more likely to occur when a person is simultaneously aware of his or her contradictory cognitions. However, because Zanna et al. inferred the existence of such discomfort from attitude change, any conclusion about the effect of simultaneous awareness on the experience of negative affect must remain tentative. Indeed, because cognitive dissonance studies typically infer the existence of discomfort, there has been substantial debate about the existence of negative affect caused by dissonance (Bem, 1967; cf. Fazio, Zanna, & Cooper, 1977). There is controversy at the other end of the dissonance paradigm as well. The forced compliance methods typically used to induce dissonance have led some to conclude that participants may indeed feel uncomfortable but that discomfort arises from self-threat and not cognitive inconsistency (Abelson et al., 1968; Steele, 1988).

We chose to explore the dynamics and effects of cognitive inconsistency within the ambivalence paradigm because doing so allowed us to sidestep the methodological controversies surrounding the dissonance paradigm. The ambivalence paradigm provides unambiguous methods for assessing cognitive inconsistency (i.e., potential ambivalence) and experienced discomfort (i.e., felt ambivalence). There is also a promising precedent in the ambivalence literature for assessing the simultaneous awareness of cognitive inconsistency (Bassili, 1996). To determine the simultaneous accessibility of people's potential ambivalence, researchers measure their latencies in responding to unipolar evaluation questions. Those response latencies are then submitted to an ambivalence-like formula to obtain a simultaneous accessibility score. Thus, simultaneous accessibility scores have

the same properties as do potential ambivalence scores. As unipolar evaluations come to mind more quickly and equally quickly, simultaneous accessibility increases.

Bassili (1998) demonstrated the utility of the simultaneous accessibility construct in his study of intrapsychic conflict about affirmative action. It is not surprising that participants were slower to express their opinion (i.e., were more conflicted) about affirmative action when they were high in potential ambivalence (i.e., when they held contradictory values that related to the issue). Most interesting from the present perspective, the relation between response latency and potential ambivalence was more pronounced for those whose contradictory values were relatively high in simultaneous accessibility.

We propose that the simultaneous accessibility of potential ambivalence determines the strength of the relation between potential and felt ambivalence. The relation between potential and felt ambivalence increases in strength as the simultaneous accessibility of the potential ambivalence increases. Thus, inconsistent evaluations are necessary but may not be sufficient for the experience of ambivalence. All three studies presented here test our simultaneous accessibility hypothesis.

PFC

We also suspect that even when inconsistent cognitions are fully in awareness, not all people experience discomfort to the same degree. Indeed, the proposition that inconsistent cognitions are aversive for everyone (e.g., Abelson et al., 1968) has been redressed in the cognitive dissonance literature. Cialdini et al. (1995) demonstrated individual differences in the extent to which people are apparently averse to cognitive inconsistency. Cialdini et al. developed a measure of individuals' PFC and found that dissonance reduction (i.e., attitude change) was more pronounced for those who were high in PFC. As in the Zanna et al. (1973) study, though, Cialdini et al. did not directly measure negative affect associated with inconsistent cognitions. Therefore, in this study we directly investigate the role of PFC in the experience of feeling mixed emotions and feeling torn.

We hypothesize that the moderating effect of simultaneous accessibility on the relation between potential and felt ambivalence is, in turn, moderated by PFC. We expect that high-PFC people who are aware of their conflicted evaluations of an attitude object will feel the most discomfort. In contrast, awareness of conflicting evaluations will not translate into uncomfortable feelings for low-PFC people, because cognitive inconsistency concerns them less.

The Current Studies

In three studies, we examined the relation between potential and felt ambivalence as a function of simultaneous accessibility (Studies 1–3) and PFC (Study 3). Our measure of potential ambivalence consisted of Kaplan's (1972) unipolar evaluation questions. Our measure of felt ambivalence consisted of two questions from the Jamieson (1993) scale that ask about feelings of ambivalence (i.e., mixed emotions and feeling torn).[2] In the first two studies we obtained correlational evidence for our claim that the relation between potential ambivalence and feelings of ambivalence is moderated by the simultaneous accessibility of the potential ambivalence. We used a phone survey in the first study and computer-driven trials in the second study. Both studies focus on ambivalence about capital punishment and abortion. In the third study, we extended our empirical and theoretical analysis in two ways. First, we manipulated simultaneous accessibility instead of only measuring it. We thus aimed to demonstrate that increased simultaneous accessibility of potential ambivalence causes a corresponding experience of that ambivalence. Second, we attempted to demonstrate that PFC

moderates the hypothesized effect of simultaneous accessibility.

Study 1

We conducted a phone survey study using a computer-assisted telephone interviewing (CATI) methodology developed by Bassili and Fletcher (1991; see also Bassili, 1996). An interviewer used a computer to administer a questionnaire about capital punishment and abortion and record participants' response latencies.

Method

Participants

Participants were 198 undergraduate students (76 men and 122 women) enrolled in full-time studies at the University of Waterloo.

Questions asked

Participants were asked potential and felt ambivalence questions about capital punishment and abortion. Following Kaplan (1972), for potential ambivalence we asked participants three pairs of questions about each issue. There was a positive evaluation question and a negative evaluation question within each pair. An example of a positive evaluation question is as follows:

> Your options for responding are *not at all favorable, slightly favorable, quite favorable*, and *extremely favorable*. [For all questions, the four response options were scored 0–3, respectively]. Think about your evaluation of capital punishment. Considering only the favorable aspects of capital punishment and ignoring the unfavorable aspects, how favorable is your evaluation of capital punishment?

An example of a negative evaluation question is as follows:

> Your options for responding are *not at all unfavorable, slightly unfavorable, quite unfavorable* and *extremely unfavorable*. Think about your evaluation of capital punishment. Considering

---

[2] The other four items on the Jamieson (1993) scale are less relevant to the current investigation because they concern participants' thoughts or a combination of their thoughts and feelings. To be exhaustive, though, we included the full scale in all three studies. Results are parallel but somewhat weaker in Study 3 when the full scale is used.

only the unfavorable aspects of capital punishment and ignoring the favorable aspects, how unfavorable is your evaluation of capital punishment?

The other two pairs of questions involved the dimensions *positive–negative* and *beneficial–harmful*. To ensure that participants were familiar with the response format, we began the potential ambivalence questions with two practice questions (one about coffee and one about police radar).

Participants rated six felt ambivalence statements on an 11-point scale ranging from −5 (*strongly disagree*) to 5 (*strongly agree*). The two items that formed the felt ambivalence index in this study and in Studies 2 and 3 were, "I have strong mixed emotions both for and against capital punishment [abortion], all at the same time" and "I do not find myself feeling torn between the two sides of the issue of capital punishment [abortion]; my feelings go in one direction only" (reverse scored).

Procedure

The interviewer used an IBM-compatible computer that ran a survey program written in C code. A phone list of undergraduates was provided by the registrar's office. The interview began once the interviewer outlined the nature and duration of the study (a survey on social issues that would take 10 min) and consent was obtained.

Participants were asked two blocks of questions. The order of the two blocks was randomly counterbalanced across participants. One block consisted of the potential ambivalence questions about capital punishment and abortion. The other block consisted of the felt ambivalence questions about the two issues. Within both blocks, the abortion questions were asked as a subblock, as were the capital punishment questions. The order of the subblocks was randomly counterbalanced across participants and was the same within the two blocks.

The computer program guided the administration of the interview. The interviewer read the questions displayed on the computer screen aloud. Response latencies were recorded in the following manner: After uttering the last syllable of a question, the interviewer pressed the space bar. Doing so caused a timer in the computer to start. When a participant began to give his or her response, the interviewer pressed the space bar, which stopped the timer. The interviewer then judged the validity of the response latency. If the timer was started or stopped too early or too late or if a participant's response to a query did not meet the question format (e.g., the participant asked a clarification question), the response latency was coded as invalid and not included in subsequent analyses.

At the end of the survey, participants were debriefed, told that their response latencies had been recorded, and given the option of having their response latencies deleted from the database. No participant chose to have his or her response latencies deleted.

Results and Discussion

Initial data screening, calculations, and analyses

Felt ambivalence. Responses to the two felt ambivalence questions of interest were highly correlated for capital punishment, $r(192) = .75$, $p < .001$, and for abortion, $r(185) = .69$, $p < .001$. Thus, we created an index of felt ambivalence for each issue using those two items. Four participants did not provide any valid responses to the questions concerning abortion. They were therefore excluded from analyses involving abortion.

Potential ambivalence. For the three pairs of potential ambivalence questions for each issue, a potential ambivalence score was derived using the D. W. Jamieson (personal communication, June 23, 1991; from Scott, 1968) calculation, in which the less extreme evaluation is squared and divided by the stronger evaluation (i.e., weak^2 / strong).[3]

---

[3] We chose the Jamieson (1993) formula because it is parallel to Bassili's (1996) calculation of simultaneous accessibility. Another technique for calculating potential ambivalence, proposed by Thompson et al. (1995), was highly correlated with the Jamieson formula (all $rs > .90$). Thus, the pattern of results was virtually identical for both measures.

For each attitude object, the three measures of potential ambivalence were interrelated ($rs > .30$, $ps < .001$). Thus, we averaged the three measures for each issue to create potential ambivalence indices.

Response latencies and simultaneous accessibility. Valid response latencies were first reciprocally transformed because of skewness in the distributions. The response latency scores therefore became speed scores, with higher numbers indicating quicker responses. As with the calculation of potential ambivalence, simultaneous accessibility was calculated for the three pairs of potential ambivalence questions associated with each issue. As suggested by Bassili (1996), we used a formula similar to that of Jamieson (1993): For a given pair of questions, the slower speed score was squared and divided by the faster. This method of calculation entailed that simultaneous accessibility scores mirrored the properties of potential ambivalence scores. That is, just as potential ambivalence scores represent the extent to which inconsistent cognitions are extreme and equally extreme, simultaneous accessibility scores represent the extent to which inconsistent cognitions come to mind quickly and equally quickly. For each of the two issues, the three measures of simultaneous accessibility were interrelated ($rs > .30$, $ps < .01$). Thus, we averaged the three measures to create simultaneous accessibility indices for each issue.

Response latencies associated with the potential ambivalence questions were coded as invalid an average of 15.3% of the time (15.7% for abortion and 14.9% for capital punishment). The data of 194 participants were included in the capital punishment analyses, and the data of 187 participants were included in the abortion analyses. There were no sex of participant or counterbalancing effects in this or subsequent studies.

Main analyses

Our hypothesis was confirmed for both attitude objects. Participants who reported highly conflicted evaluations of capital punishment and abortion indicated that they experienced more ambivalence when their evaluations came to mind quickly and equally quickly.

Capital punishment. As expected from previous findings (e.g., Thompson et al., 1995), potential and felt ambivalence about capital punishment were correlated, $r(192) = .18$, $p < .025$. We next conducted a regression analysis in which felt ambivalence about capital punishment was the criterion and potential ambivalence, simultaneous accessibility, and the interaction of the two were entered simultaneously as predictors. As suggested by Aiken and West (1991), we first centered the potential ambivalence and simultaneous accessibility indices before calculating the product of the two (representing the interaction). We obtained an effect for potential ambivalence, $\beta = .18$, $t(190) = 2.57$, $p < .025$,[4] and a marginal effect for simultaneous accessibility, $\beta = -.13$, $t(190) = 1.84$, $p < .07$, indicating that higher simultaneous accessibility was related to less felt ambivalence. Because the simultaneous accessibility effect itself is not relevant to our hypothesis and did not occur reliably across studies, it is not discussed further.

The hypothesized Potential Ambivalence × Simultaneous Accessibility interaction was significant, $\beta = .14$, $t(190) = 2.18$, $p < .05$ (see Table 12.1 for the complete regression equation). Also as suggested by Aiken and West (1991), we subsequently explored the nature of this interaction by recalculating the full regression equation for simultaneous accessibility values one standard deviation above and below the simultaneous accessibility mean ($SD = 0.14$). At high simultaneous accessibility, the relation between felt and potential ambivalence was positive and significant, $\beta = .32$, $t(190) = 3.30$, $p < .01$. At low simultaneous accessibility, the relation was not significant, $\beta = .04$, $t(190) = 0.41$, *ns.*

Abortion. The correlation between potential and felt ambivalence about abortion was $r(185) = .39$,

---

[4] Because this effect is essentially redundant with the potential–felt ambivalence correlations we report in all studies, it is not discussed here or reported in subsequent analyses.

TABLE 12.1. Regression Statistics for Capital Punishment and Abortion: Felt Ambivalence as a Function of Potential Ambivalence, Simultaneous Accessibility, and Potential Ambivalence × Simultaneous Accessibility (Study 1)

Variable	B	β	t	p <
Capital punishment				
Constant	−0.58		2.55	.025
Potential ambivalence	1.08	.18	2.57	.025
Simultaneous accessibility	−3.02	−.13	1.84	.07
Potential Ambivalence × Simultaneous Accessibility	6.04	.14	2.18	.05
Abortion				
Constant	−0.43		1.94	.06
Potential ambivalence	2.52	.37	5.58	.001
Simultaneous accessibility	−3.17	−.12	1.79	.08
Potential Ambivalence × Simultaneous Accessibility	9.57	.18	2.74	.01

Note: Potential ambivalence and simultaneous accessibility scores were centered before the product term was calculated. Betas were calculated in separate regression analyses in which all variables were standardized, the product term calculated, and the unstandardized solution used (Aiken & West, 1991). *n* = 194 for capital punishment, and *n* = 187 for abortion. For capital punishment, *t*(190); for abortion, *t*(183).

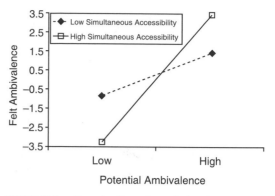

FIGURE 12.1 ■ For abortion, the relation between felt ambivalence and potential ambivalence as a function of simultaneous accessibility (Study 1).

$p < .001$. Regression analysis revealed the hypothesized Potential Ambivalence × Simultaneous Accessibility interaction, $\beta = .18$, $t(183) = 2.74$, $p < .01$. There was a strong relation between potential and felt ambivalence at high simultaneous accessibility (one standard deviation above the mean; $SD = 0.13$), $\beta = .55$, $t(183) = 5.82$, $p < .001$, and a weaker but still reliable relation at low simultaneous accessibility, $\beta = .19$, $t(183) = 2.01$, $p < .05$ (one standard deviation below the mean). See Table 12.1 for the complete regression equation and Figure 12.1 for an illustration.[5]

Study 2

Though the CATI paradigm used in Study 1 allowed us to contact many people, our ability to

accurately record all response latencies was somewhat hampered. Indeed, many response latencies were coded as invalid. Consequently, some participants were excluded from analyses. In addition, three aspects of Study 1 detracted from our measurement of response latencies. First, it was possible for participants to begin thinking about an answer before the interviewer stopped asking the question. Second, requiring the interviewer to start and stop the timer was somewhat imprecise. Third, telephone interviews do not afford control over the interview environment, and there was likely large variability in external distractions (e.g., a television or other people in the background) that might have influenced response latencies. In Study 2, we moved to a technique that enabled us to more consistently record response latencies, exert greater experimental control, and at the same time establish the reliability of our hypothesized effect.

Participants were brought into the lab and interacted with a computer program that prompted them for their positive and negative evaluations of capital punishment and abortion. The program presented participants with the relevant response set prior to their knowing what the attitude object was. Thus, as opposed to Study 1, it was not possible for participants to think of the answer to an inquiry before the start of the timer.

[5] Comparable figures of the capital punishment analyses for Study 1 and both attitude objects for Study 2 are available on request from Ian R. Newby-Clark.

Method

Participants

Ninety-five undergraduate students (34 men and 61 women) at the University of Waterloo participated for course credit. Prior to data entry and analysis, the experimenter (a research assistant) categorized participants as to whether they understood and followed all directions. Primarily because of their difficulties with the English language, many participants (i.e., 26) did not understand the computer procedure (which was rather complex). They were excluded from all analyses reported here. Sixty-nine participants (25 men and 44 women) remained.

Procedure

The experimenter outlined the procedure for participants and demonstrated how their fingers should be placed on the computer keyboard for responding. From left to right, four adjacent keys in the center of the keyboard were labeled with the numbers 1–4. Participants were instructed to place the index and middle fingers of each hand on the four keys. They were asked not to move their fingers off of the keys while the study was in progress. They then followed instructions presented to them on the computer screen.

A trial, similar in many respects to a potential ambivalence question from Study 1, proceeded as follows. An evaluation instruction (e.g., "Ignoring the unfavorable aspects and focusing on the favorable aspects") appeared in the upper left of the computer screen along with four options for responding (e.g., *not at all favorable, slightly favorable, quite favorable, extremely favorable*). As in Study 1, regardless of the dimension of evaluation, the order and numbering of the response options always ranged from *not at all* (1) to *extremely* (4). If the dimension of evaluation was "unfavorable," the response set was *not at all unfavorable* (1) through *extremely unfavorable* (4). Also as in Study 1, there were six potential ambivalence questions for each attitude object (i.e., "favorable," "unfavorable," "positive," "negative," "beneficial," "harmful") that were scored *not at all*

(0) through *extremely* (3). The sequence of trials was randomized.

Once participants familiarized themselves with a question and the associated responses, they pressed the space bar with their thumb while keeping their fingers positioned over the labeled keys. After a randomly determined delay of 250, 500, or 750 ms, a word representing an attitude object (e.g., *abortion*) appeared in the center of the screen. The participant then evaluated the attitude object by pressing the numbered key associated with his or her response. Participants were instructed to answer the questions as quickly as possible while maintaining accuracy. Response latencies were measured by the computer as the time between the appearance of the word and a participant's key press. After the computer trials, participants indicated their felt ambivalence about capital punishment and abortion by filling out a paper-and-pencil version of Jamieson's (1993) scale. Response options ranged from *strongly disagree* (1) to *strongly agree* (6). Participants were subsequently debriefed and excused.

Results and Discussion

Initial data screening, calculations, and analyses

As in Study 1, the two felt ambivalence questions of interest were highly correlated for both issues ($rs > .70$). For each issue, the three potential ambivalence scores were interrelated ($rs > .37, ps < .001$), as were the three simultaneous accessibility scores ($rs > .29, ps < .025$). We therefore created felt ambivalence, potential ambivalence, and simultaneous accessibility indices for both attitude objects (as in Study 1).

Main analyses

Our hypothesis was again confirmed for both attitude objects.

Capital punishment. The correlation between potential and felt ambivalence about capital punishment was $r(67) = .29, p < .025$. Regression analysis, with felt ambivalence about capital punishment as the criterion, revealed the hypothesized Potential Ambivalence × Simultaneous Accessibility interaction, $\beta = .27$, $t(65) = 2.19$, $p < .05$. See Table 12.2 for the full equation. There was a significant relation between potential and felt ambivalence at high simultaneous accessibility, $\beta = .60$, $t(65) = 3.16$, $p < .01$ (one standard deviation above the mean; $SD = 0.15$), and a nonsignificant relation at low simultaneous accessibility, $\beta = .06$, $t(65) = 0.38$, ns (one standard deviation below).

Abortion. The results were much the same for abortion. The correlation between potential and felt ambivalence was $r(67) = .35$, $p < .01$. Regression analysis revealed a significant Potential Ambivalence × Simultaneous Accessibility interaction, $\beta = .15$, $t(65) = 2.06$, $p < .05$ (see Table 12.2). For high simultaneous accessibility (one standard deviation above the mean, $SD = 0.17$), there was a significant relation between potential and felt ambivalence, $\beta = .46$, $t(65) = 3.80$, $p <$

TABLE 12.2. Regression Statistics for Capital Punishment and Abortion: Felt Ambivalence as a Function of Potential Ambivalence, Simultaneous Accessibility, and Potential Ambivalence × Simultaneous Accessibility (Study 2)

Variable	B	β	t(65)	p <
Capital punishment				
Constant	3.43		20.10	.001
Potential ambivalence	0.80	.33	2.76	.01
Simultaneous accessibility	−0.46	−.04	0.38	.75
Potential Ambivalence × Simultaneous Accessibility	4.53	.27	2.19	.05
Abortion				
Constant	2.91		18.40	.001
Potential ambivalence	0.82	.30	2.72	.01
Simultaneous accessibility	−2.54	−.30	2.62	.025
Potential Ambivalence × Simultaneous Accessibility	2.43	.15	2.06	.05

Note: Potential ambivalence and simultaneous accessibility scores were centered before the product term was calculated. Betas were calculated in separate regression analyses in which all variables were standardized, the product term calculated, and the unstandardized solution used (Aiken & West, 1991). $N = 69$.

.001, and a nonsignificant relation for low simultaneous accessibility (one standard deviation below the mean), $\beta = .15$, $t(65) = 1.02$, ns.

Study 3

In the first two studies, we obtained correlational evidence that simultaneous accessibility moderates the relation between potential and felt ambivalence. We next attempted to demonstrate that increased simultaneous accessibility of potential ambivalence causes the relation between potential ambivalence and felt ambivalence to be more pronounced. We adapted a repeated expression paradigm to manipulate the simultaneous accessibility of people's potential ambivalence. Fazio, Chen, McDonel, and Sherman (1982) demonstrated that repeatedly expressing an evaluation of an attitude object increases the accessibility of that evaluation. Repeated expression of positive and negative evaluations of an attitude object, therefore, should increase the simultaneous accessibility of potential ambivalence.

We also established the role of PFC (Cialdini et al., 1995) in this last study. We expected the moderating effect of simultaneous accessibility on the relation between potential and felt ambivalence to be more pronounced for those who were high in PFC. Thus, we hypothesized a Potential Ambivalence × Repeated Expression × PFC interaction.

We focus on the issue of abortion in this last study. To conduct a sensitive test of our hypotheses, we first identified a sample that considered the abortion issue to be important. We suspected that women would rate abortion (i.e., an issue involving pregnancy) as more important than would men. As part of a mass pretesting session some weeks prior to the study, we asked 342 women and 119 men to rate the importance of abortion on a 7-point scale with the options labeled from *extremely unimportant* (1) to *extremely important* (7). Women indeed rated abortion as more important ($M = 5.23$) than did men ($M = 4.46$), $t(459) = 5.52$, $p < .001$. We thus elected to recruit female participants only. We measured potential ambivalence about abortion in the same mass pretesting session. Thus, in using the repeated expression manipulation, we aimed to render preexisting potential ambivalence simultaneously accessible.

Study Overview

Participants either did or did not repeatedly express their unipolar evaluations of abortion and then answered felt ambivalence questions about abortion. The simultaneous accessibility of participants' potential ambivalence about abortion and their PFC were subsequently assessed.

Method

Participants

We gave 154 female University of Waterloo students either course credit or $7 for their participation.

Procedure

Premeasure of potential ambivalence. In the mass pretesting session, introductory psychology stuents completed a booklet of questionnaires in exchange for course credit. Included in that booklet was a questionnaire concerning participants' unipolar positive and negative evaluations of abortion. Potential ambivalence scores for participants in the current study were calculated using those unipolar evaluations[6]

Experimental session. On arrival, participants were informed that the study concerned people's views of various social issues. They were randomly assigned to one of two conditions. In the repeated expression condition, participants filled out a potential ambivalence questionnaire, in which they indicated their unipolar evaluations of abortion. Next, the experimenter informed participants that

other researchers wished to have access to their responses. Each participant was required to copy her responses onto two additional questionnaires, which (they were told) would be passed along to the other researchers. The two new questionnaires contained the same questions as the original, but the order of the questions differed from the original and from each other. Participants were thus instructed to copy their responses carefully and deliberately. Participants in the control condition did not fill out the three potential ambivalence questionnaires. Next, participants in both conditions filled out Jamieson's (1993) felt ambivalence questionnaire about abortion. The scale ranged from *strongly disagree* (−3) to *strongly agree* (3). To service our cover story that the study concerned an investigation of attitudes toward several social issues, all participants then filled out two other felt ambivalence questionnaires: one concerning capital punishment, and one concerning euthanasia.

We then assessed the simultaneous accessibility of participants' potential ambivalence about abortion using the computer procedure from Study 2. Participants first engaged in practice trials (i.e., questions about coffee and sports cars) before answering questions about abortion. Also in service of the cover story and to ensure that participants did not know which attitude object would be presented on a particular trial, the computer prompted participants for their unipolar evaluations of capital punishment and euthanasia in addition to abortion.

After participants completed the computer trials, they filled out the short form of Cialdini et al.'s (1995) PFC measure. Participants rated their agreement with nine items on a 9-point scale, with the endpoints labeled *strongly disagree* (1) and *strongly agree* (9). Examples of items are "The appearance of consistency is an important part of the image I present to the world" and "It doesn't bother me much if my actions are inconsistent" (reverse scored). Participants were subsequently probed for suspicion, debriefed, and remunerated. No participant expressed suspicion about the procedure.

---

[6] In a further effort to exclude those who were indifferent to abortion, we selected female participants who indicated at least some ambivalence about the issue.

Results and Discussion

Initial data screening, calculations, and analyses

As in the previous two studies, the two felt ambivalence questions were highly correlated, $r(152) = .68$, $p < .001$. The response latencies were logarithmically transformed prior to reciprocal transformation.[7] The three simultaneous accessibility measures (corresponding to the three pairs of potential ambivalence questions) were reasonably interrelated ($rs > .39$, $ps < .001$) and, thus, combined into an index. The PFC scale was acceptably reliable ($\alpha = .86$). The items were combined into a PFC index, which, although measured after the accessibility manipulation, was not affected by it, $t < 1$ ($M = 5.03$ overall). Also, participants' potential ambivalence scores from the mass pretesting session did not differ significantly between conditions, $t < 1$.

Manipulation check

An analysis of covariance with mean speed score of the practice questions as the covariate revealed that participants in the repeated expression condition had higher simultaneous accessibility scores than did those in the control condition, $F(1, 150) = 3.91$, $p < .05$.[8] A subsequent regression analysis established that PFC did not account for significant variance in simultaneous accessibility scores (main effect and interaction $ts < 1.10$, $ps > .25$). Also, using participants' responses to the unipolar questions from the computer task, we confirmed that repeated expression did not significantly affect potential ambivalence, $t < 1$.

Main analysis

The correlation between potential ambivalence (measured at mass pretesting) and felt ambivalence

about abortion was $r(152) = .36$, $p < .001$. Potential ambivalence and PFC were centered and experimental condition was contrast coded (-1 for the control condition and 1 for the repeated expression condition). The three 2-way and one 3-way interaction terms were then computed (Aiken & West, 1991). We conducted a regression analysis in which felt ambivalence about abortion was the criterion and all main effects and interactions were entered on the same step. We obtained a significant Potential Ambivalence × Repeated Expression interaction, $\beta = .18$, $t(146) = 2.37$, $p < .025$. That interaction was qualified by the hypothesized Potential Ambivalence × Repeated Expression × PFC interaction, $\beta = .18$, $t(146) = 2.37$, $p < .025$.

We interpreted the three-way interaction by solving the regression equation for individuals whose PFC scores were one standard deviation above or below the mean on PFC ($SD = 1.29$). See Figures 12.2A and 12.2B for the results for high- and low-PFC participants, respectively. As expected, for high-PFC participants the Potential Ambivalence × Repeated Expression interaction was significant, $\beta = .36$, $t(146) = 3.18$, $p < .01$. There was a significant relation between potential and felt ambivalence for high-PFC participants in the repeated expression condition, $\beta = .77$, $t(146) = 4.81$, $p < .001$, and no significant relation for high-PFC participants in the control condition, $\beta = .05$, $t < 1$. For low-PFC participants, the Potential Ambivalence × Repeated Expression interaction was not significant, $\beta = .01$, $t < 1$.[9]

General Discussion

Our simultaneous accessibility hypothesis was confirmed and twice replicated. In all three studies, people's conflicted evaluations of attitude objects manifested more strongly as mixed emotions and

---

[7] This initial logarithmic transformation was necessary because the reciprocal transformation alone did not completely eliminate skewness in the response latency distributions.

[8] One participant did not provide any valid responses during the computer task and was therefore excluded from the simultaneous accessibility analysis.

[9] As suggested by the slope difference between low- and high-PFC participants in the repeated expression condition, there was a significant PFC × Potential Ambivalence interaction for those participants in the repeated expression condition, $\beta = .20$, $t(146) = 2.14$, $p < .05$.

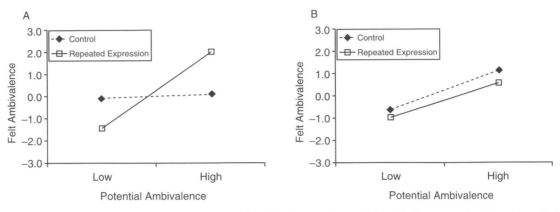

FIGURE 12.2 ■ For abortion, the relation between felt ambivalence and potential ambivalence as a function of repeated expression for (A) participants with a high preference for consistency and (B) participants with a low preference for consistency (Study 3).

feelings of being torn when those evaluations were simultaneously accessible. In the third study, heightened simultaneous accessibility of potential ambivalence caused the experience of ambivalence about abortion.

If, as our results suggest, simultaneous accessibility moderates the relation between inconsistent cognitions and the experience of negative affect, why are so many cognitive dissonance studies successful despite the lack of a simultaneous accessibility manipulation? Put simply, we suggest that those studies were implicitly, if not explicitly, designed to render participants' inconsistent cognitions simultaneously accessible. Consider, for example, the study of hypocrisy (e.g., Stone, Aronson, Crain, Winslow, & Fried, 1994). In those experiments, participants were reminded of a past act (e.g., not using condoms) that directly contradicted a just-performed behavior (e.g., preparing and giving a speech on safer sex). Thus, simultaneous accessibility was presumably high (Stone et al., 1994; see also McGregor, Newby-Clark, & Zanna, 1999).

We do not mean to suggest, however, that mere simultaneous accessibility of conflicting cognitions can account for dissonance effects. It is now established that dissonance effects are multiply determined. They are moderated by variables such as self-presentation (Baumeister & Tice, 1984), perceived choice (Linder, Cooper, & Jones, 1967),

importance (Simon, Greenberg, & Brehm, 1995), self-affirmation (Steele, Spencer, & Lynch, 1993), attributions (Zanna & Cooper, 1974), aversive consequences (Cooper & Fazio, 1984), culture (Heine & Lehman, 1997), and individual differences in PFC (Cialdini et al., 1995) and repression sensitization (Zanna & Aziza, 1976). The current studies suggest, though, that whatever produces cognitive inconsistency, an experience of discomfort will result only when that inconsistency is simultaneously accessible.

If cognitive dissonance researchers go to some lengths to create experimental situations that increase awareness of cognitive inconsistency, perhaps inconsistent cognitions are typically low in simultaneous accessibility. Indeed, because cognitive inconsistency is psychologically aversive (Elliot & Devine, 1994; Festinger, 1957), people may exert some effort to maintain chronically low simultaneous accessibility. People might distract themselves, for example. In a study of dissonance and distraction (Brock, 1962), half of the participants' attention was directed away from the content of their counterattitudinal essay and toward its grammar. Those participants shifted their attitudes toward the position of the essay less than did the half of the participants who were not distracted (see also Zanna & Aziza, 1976). Perhaps the simultaneous accessibility of distracted participants' inconsistent cognitions was lower than that of undistracted participants, thereby leading to reduced negative affect and, thus, little compensatory attitude shift.

According to dissonance theory, people are motivated to get their minds off their cognitive inconsistency only if they experience negative affect associated with that inconsistency (Festinger, 1957). From the results of Study 3, it appears that high-PFC people are more motivated than are low-PFC people to self-distract or otherwise lower the simultaneous accessibility of their inconsistent cognitions. High-PFC participants experienced negative affect when their highly inconsistent cognitions were rendered simultaneously accessible. In contrast, low-PFC participants' experience of ambivalent feelings was not affected when the simultaneous accessibility of their potential ambivalence increased. PFC differences in self-distraction and other means by which simultaneous accessibility of cognitive inconsistency could be lowered should be investigated in future studies.

At the same time, the circumstances under which cognitive inconsistency becomes simultaneously accessible should be investigated. With respect to ambivalence, Priester and Petty (2001) tested and confirmed the balance theory notion that perceived disagreement with parents or friends about an attitude object is associated with greater felt ambivalence when that attitude object is important. Perhaps when an attitude object is important, perceived disagreement (i.e., the discrepancy between one's own and another's attitude) is high in simultaneous accessibility (Roese & Olson, 1994). It might be interesting to determine whether the simultaneous accessibility of one's own and another's attitude moderates the perceived attitude disagreement–felt ambivalence relation.

Throughout this article, we have entwined theory and findings in ambivalence and cognitive dissonance. Indeed, we derived our ambivalence hypotheses in part from cognitive dissonance research (e.g., Cialdini et al., 1995; Zanna et al., 1973). There are important differences between our ambivalence studies and cognitive dissonance paradigms that must be noted, however. Participants

in dissonance studies typically write counterattitudinal essays (e.g., Collins & Hoyt, 1972; Elliot & Devine, 1994; Harmon-Jones, 2000a; Scher & Cooper, 1989), choose between equally attractive alternatives (e.g., Brehm, 1956; Gerard & White, 1983; Younger, Walker, & Arrowood, 1977), or are made aware of their hypocrisy (Aronson, Fried, & Stone, 1991; Stone et al., 1994). In such studies, researchers assume, probably reasonably, that cognitive dissonance exists for most participants and that it causes an experience of negative affect (McGregor et al., 1999). Investigating cognitive inconsistency within the ambivalence paradigm, in contrast, allows us to measure the extent of each participant's cognitive inconsistency (i.e., potential ambivalence). Also, in accord with Elliot and Devine (1994) and Harmon-Jones (2000a), we elicited self-reports of negative affect associated with attitudinal ambivalence (i.e., felt ambivalence).

Although the methods typically used by dissonance and ambivalence researchers are different and the literatures remain largely unintegrated, we believe the two literatures can complement and inform one another. In both, there is an assumption that cognitive inconsistency is aversive. Furthermore, the ambivalence and dissonance constructs involve cognitive inconsistency about an attitude object. Researchers usually assess ambivalence by measuring an individual's positive and negative evaluations of an attitude object. They often create cognitive dissonance by inducing participants to perform a behavior that is inconsistent with a prior attitude. Presumably, the "freely chosen" counterattitudinal behavior implies an attitude that contradicts the prior one.

Thus, the two literatures may simply represent different ranges of focus. Dissonance researchers, on the one hand, tend to neglect assessment and quantification of inconsistency and subsequent affective response in favor of manipulating inconsistency and assessing social–cognitive consequences of the assumed affective response. Ambivalence researchers, on the other hand, focus on mapping the inner workings of how cognitive inconsistency translates into experienced discomfort. Together, the two literatures provide a more complete picture than either alone can offer.

We contend that, despite the differing methodologies and foci of the paradigms, the ambivalence and dissonance constructs are remarkably similar and may share functional roots. Personal uncertainty arising from inconsistent evaluations of attitude objects may impede decision making about what to approach and what to avoid and disrupt one's ability to act efficiently. This may be why, from an evolutionary perspective, it makes sense for cognitive inconsistency to feel bad and why people are apparently motivated to defend against it (Beckmann & Irle, 1984; Harmon-Jones, 2000b; McGregor, Zanna, Holmes, & Spencer, 2001).

REFERENCES

Abelson, R. P., Aronson, E., McGuire, W. J., Newcomb, T. M., Rosenberg, M. J., & Tannenbaum, P. H. (1968). *Theories of cognitive consistency: A sourcebook*. Chicago: Rand McNally.

Aiken, L. S., & West, S. G. (1991). *Multiple regression: Testing and interpreting interactions*. Newbury Park, CA: Sage.

Aronson, E., & Carlsmith, J. M. (1963). Effect of the severity of threat on the valuation of forbidden behavior. *Journal of Abnormal and Social Psychology, 66,* 584–588.

Aronson, E., Fried, C., & Stone, J. (1991). Overcoming denial and increasing the intention to use condoms through the induction of hypocrisy. *American Journal of Public Health, 81,* 1636–1638.

Bassili, J. N. (1996). The "how" and "why" of response latency measurement in telephone surveys. In N. Schwarz & S. Sudman (Eds.), *Answering questions: Methodology for determining cognitive and communicative processes in survey research* (pp. 319–346). San Francisco: Jossey-Bass.

Bassili, J. N. (1998, July). Simultaneous accessibility: A prerequisite to heated intrapsychic conflict. In J. N. Bassili (Chair), *Response time measurement in survey research*. Symposium conducted at the meeting of the International Society of Political Psychology, Montreal, Canada.

Bassili, J. N., & Fletcher, J. F. (1991). Response time measurement in survey research: A method for CATI and a new look at nonattitudes. *Public Opinion Quarterly, 55,* 331–346.

Baumeister, R. R., & Tice, D. M. (1984). Role of self-presentation and choice in cognitive dissonance under forced compliance: Necessary or sufficient causes? *Journal of Personality and Social Psychology, 46,* 5–13.

Beckmann, J., & Irle, M. (1984). Dissonance and action control. In J. Kuhl & J. Beckmann (Eds.), *Action control: From cognition to behavior* (pp. 129–146). Berlin, Germany: Springer-Verlag.

Bem, D. J. (1967). Self-perception: An alternative interpretation of cognitive dissonance phenomena. *Psychological Review, 74,* 183–200.

Brehm, J. W. (1956). Postdecision changes in the desirability of alternatives. *Journal of Abnormal and Social Psychology, 52,* 384–389.

Brock, T. C. (1962). Cognitive restructuring and attitude change. *Journal of Abnormal and Social Psychology, 64,* 264–271.

Cialdini, R. B., Trost, M. R., & Newsom, T. J. (1995). Preference for consistency: The development of a valid measure and the discovery of surprising behavioral implications. *Journal of Personality and Social Psychology, 69,* 318–328.

Collins, B. E., & Hoyt, M. F. (1972). Personal responsibility-for-consequences: An integration and extension of the "forced compliance" literature. *Journal of Experimental Social Psychology, 8,* 558–593.

Cooper, J., & Fazio, R. H. (1984). A new look at dissonance theory. In L. Berkowitz (Ed.), *Advances in experimental social psychology* (pp. 229–266). Orlando, FL: Academic Press.

Elliot, A. J., & Devine, P. (1994). On the motivational nature of cognitive dissonance: Dissonance as psychological discomfort. *Journal of Personality and Social Psychology, 67,* 382–394.

Fazio, R. H., Chen, J., McDonel, E. C., & Sherman, S. J. (1982). Attitude accessibility, attitude–behavior consistency, and the strength of the object-evaluation association. *Journal of Experimental Social Psychology, 18,* 339–357.

Fazio, R. H., Zanna, M. P., & Cooper, J. (1977). Dissonance and self-perception: An integrative view of each theory's proper domain of application. *Journal of Experimental Social Psychology, 13,* 464–479.

Festinger, L. (1957). *A theory of cognitive dissonance*. Evanston, IL: Row, Peterson.

Gerard, H. B., & White, G. L. (1983). Post-decisional reevaluation of choice alternatives. *Personality and Social Psychology Bulletin, 9,* 365–369.

Harmon-Jones, E. (2000a). Cognitive dissonance and experienced negative affect: Evidence that dissonance increases experienced negative affect even in the absence of aversive consequences. *Personality and Social Psychology Bulletin, 26,* 1490–1501.

Harmon-Jones, E. (2000b). A cognitive dissonance theory perspective on the role of emotion in the maintenance and change of beliefs and attitudes. In N. H. Frijda, A. R. S. Manstead, & S. Bem (Eds.), *Emotions and beliefs* (pp. 185–211). Cambridge, England: Cambridge University Press.

Heine, S. J., & Lehman, D. R. (1997). Culture, dissonance, and self-affirmation. *Personality and Social Psychology Bulletin, 23,* 389–400.

Jamieson, D. W. (1993, August). *The attitude ambivalence construct: Validity, utility, and measurement*. Paper presented at the annual meeting of the American Psychological Association, Toronto.

Kaplan, K. J. (1972). On the ambivalence–indifference problem in attitude theory and measurement: A suggested modification of the semantic differential technique. *Psychological Bulletin, 77*, 361–372.

Linder, D. E., Cooper, J., & Jones, E. E. (1967). Decision freedom as a determinant of the role of incentive magnitude in attitude change. *Journal of Personality and Social Psychology, 6*, 245–254.

McGregor, I., Newby-Clark, I. R., & Zanna, M. P. (1999). "Remembering" dissonance: Simultaneous accessibility of inconsistent cognitive elements moderates epistemic discomfort. In E. Harmon-Jones & J. Mills (Eds.), *Cognitive dissonance: Progress on a pivotal theory in social psychology* (pp. 325–353). Washington, DC: American Psychological Association.

McGregor, I., Zanna, M. P., Holmes, J. G., & Spencer, S. J. (2001). Compensatory conviction in the face of personal uncertainty: Going to extremes and being oneself. *Journal of Personality and Social Psychology, 80*, 472–488.

Priester, J. R., & Petty, R. E. (1996). The gradual threshold model of ambivalence: Relating the positive and negative bases of attitudes to subjective ambivalence. *Journal of Personality and Social Psychology, 71*, 431–449.

Priester, J. R., & Petty, R. E. (2001). Extending the bases of subjective attitudinal ambivalence: Interpersonal and intrapersonal antecedents of evaluative tension. *Journal of Personality and Social Psychology, 80*, 19–34.

Roese, N. J., & Olson, J. M. (1994). Attitude importance as a function of repeated attitude expression. *Journal of Experimental Social Psychology, 30*, 39–51.

Scher, S. J., & Cooper, J. (1989). Motivational basis of dissonance: The singular role behavioral consequences. *Journal of Personality and Social Psychology, 56*, 899–906.

Scott, W. A. (1968). Measures of cognitive structure. *Multivariate Behavior Research, 1*, 391–395.

Simon, L., Greenberg, J., & Brehm, J. (1995). Trivialization:

The forgotten mode of dissonance reduction. *Journal of Personality and Social Psychology, 68*, 247–260.

Steele, C. M. (1988). The psychology of self-affirmation: Sustaining the integrity of the self. In L. Berkowitz (Ed.), *Advances in experimental social psychology* (pp. 261–302). San Diego, CA: Academic Press.

Steele, C. M., Spencer, S. J., & Lynch, M. (1993). Self-image resilience and dissonance: The role of affirmational resources. *Journal of Personality and Social Psychology, 64*, 885–896.

Stone, J., Aronson, E., Crain, A. L., Winslow, M. P., & Fried, C. B. (1994). Inducing hypocrisy as a means of encouraging young adults to use condoms. *Personality and Social Psychology Bulletin, 20*, 116–128.

Thompson, M. M., Zanna, M. P., & Griffin, D. W. (1995). Let's not be indifferent about (attitudinal) ambivalence. In R. E. Petty & J. A. Krosnick (Eds.), *Attitude strength: Antecedents and consequences* (pp. 361–386). Hillsdale, NJ: Erlbaum.

Younger, J. C., Walker, L., & Arrowood, A. J. (1977). Postdecision dissonance at the fair. *Personality and Social Psychology Bulletin, 3*, 284–287.

Zanna, M. P., & Aziza, C. (1976). On the interaction of repression-sensitization and attention in resolving cognitive dissonance. *Journal of Personality, 44*, 577–593.

Zanna, M. P., & Cooper, J. (1974). Dissonance and the pill: An attribution approach to studying the arousal properties of dissonance. *Journal of Personality and Social Psychology, 29*, 703–709.

Zanna, M. P., Lepper, M. R., & Abelson, R. P. (1973). Attentional mechanisms in children's devaluation of a forbidden activity in a forced-compliance situation. *Journal of Personality and Social Psychology, 28*, 355–359.

Received January 27, 2001
Revision received June 20, 2001
Accepted June 21, 2001 ■

PART 4

Functions of Attitudes

One of the many interesting sets of questions to have been asked about attitudes concerns their functional value. What functions do attitudes serve for people? What do they accomplish?

This functional perspective was first highlighted decades ago in two classic contributions: a book by Smith, Bruner, and White (1956) and an article by Katz (1960). Both attempted to delineate the functional value of attitudes (and, in fact, articulated roughly parallel functions), and both continue to influence attitude theory and research.

Katz's article is reprinted, in abridged fashion, as Reading 13. Katz discussed four primary functions served by attitudes. The first he labeled the *instrumental, adjustive, or utilitarian* function, which stems from the undeniable premise that individuals develop favorable attitudes toward objects that satisfy needs and unfavorable attitudes toward ones that thwart needs. Thus, the focus here is on the utilitarian value of the attitude object, i.e., the extent to which it is instrumental to the attainment of pleasure and/or avoidance of pain. Objects associated with reward or success come to be valued, whereas those associated with punishment or failure are devalued.

In many ways, this is more a theoretical assertion about a basis for developing positive or negative attitudes than it is a function served by the attitudes per se. However, Katz's observation about the utilitarian value of an object assumes more importance when this function is contrasted to one of the other functions he elaborates. Katz notes that attitudes also serve a *value-expressive* function. They reflect our cherished values and self-image and, hence, are one means by which individuals project who they are and the social groups with which they identify. (This is even clearer in Smith *et al.*'s (1956) label for this function; they used the term *social adjustment* function.) Thus, attitudes can situate us in our social world, allowing us to express our self-image and, in that way, establish our connections to the social groups and principles that we value. This social focus is strikingly different from the sheer utilitarian value of the object itself.

The distinction between these two functions is nicely illustrated in Reading 14, which reprints an important article by Snyder and DeBono (1985). These researchers consider the potential effectiveness of two very different advertising strategies—appeals to the image that a product portrays versus claims about the quality of the product. The latter maps on to the utilitarian function, emphasizing the inherent merit of a product for accomplishing some desired objective. The former relates to the social adjustment function. What does my use of this product convey to others about who I am? The experiments conducted by Snyder and DeBono establish that appeals to image versus quality can be differentially effective for different kinds of people. Some people are more responsive to the utilitarian function, whereas others are relatively more sensitive to the social adjustment function. More specifically, these researchers related the effectiveness of different advertisements for the very same product to the individual difference measure of self-monitoring. Snyder's (1974) self-monitoring scale identifies and contrasts people who are very adept at monitoring situations and tailoring their behavior to fit the demands of the situation (high self-monitors) from those who typically do not attempt to mold their behavior to any given situation (low self-monitors). The research findings revealed that high self-monitors were more persuaded by image appeals, whereas low self-monitors were more influenced by advertisements that focused on the quality of the product.

In Reading 15, Petty and Wegener (1998) expand upon the relation between self-monitoring and image-versus quality-oriented advertisements. Like Snyder and DeBono, they tested one of the major hypotheses advanced by the classic functional theories—the matching hypothesis. This proposition maintains that persuasive messages that match the functional basis of a given individual's attitude will be more effective at producing attitude change than messages that are unrelated to that function. Snyder and DeBono's findings provide empirical support for this matching hypothesis. Petty and Wegener essentially ask why matching is effective. They provide a careful and broad consideration of the implications of matching, relating the functional bases of attitudes to a well-established model of the processes underlying persuasion, the Elaboration Likelihood Model (Petty & Cacioppo, 1986). The experimental findings lead to a clear conclusion about one of the underlying mechanisms by which matching proves effective. When individuals are exposed to messages that match the functional basis for their attitudes, they are more engaged by the message. They experience more motivation to process the arguments carefully than if the message content does not relate to the function associated with their attitudes. Provided that those arguments are strong and convincing, individuals are more persuaded by the functionally matched message.

Yet another function that Katz elaborates as attitudes potentially serving is what he termed the *ego-defensive* function. Attitudes can serve to bolster or maintain one's self-esteem. Evaluations of our own skills, abilities, traits, and performance may be inflated in a self-serving manner. The attitudes we develop toward others also may have the consequence of affirming one's self-image. Those with whom we share some characteristic may be viewed more positively than those who are different from us. Such ingroup favoritism is a well-documented phenomenon (see Brewer, 1999). Finally, those who are different may also be derogated, in the interest of feeling better about ourselves by comparison.

Such outgroup derogation is illustrated in the article by Fein and Spencer (1997), which is reprinted as Reading 16. Their research demonstrates the complex dynamics by which prejudicial attitudes are linked to self-esteem concerns. Especially when threatened by negative feedback, individuals are likely to derogate an outgroup member and, by comparison, view themselves more positively. Thus, threats to self-esteem can promote derogation, and the resulting prejudicial attitudes can play a role in the maintenance of self-esteem.

The final function that Katz discusses, the *knowledge* function, refers to the fact that attitudes serve to organize and structure the environment. Smith *et al.* (1956) used the term *object appraisal* to refer to this same function. In many ways, this can be considered the primary value of attitudes in terms of their functional utility. Its essence is perfectly captured by Smith *et al.* (1956) when they assert that: ". . . an attitude provides a ready aid in 'sizing up' objects and events in the environment . . . Presented with an object or event, [the individual] may categorize it in some class of objects and events for which a predisposition to action and experience exists. Once thus categorized, it becomes the focus of an already-established repertory of

reactions and feelings, and the person is saved the energy-consuming and sometimes painful process of figuring out *de novo* how he shall relate himself to it" (p. 41).

Thus, the knowledge or object appraisal function is broader or more general than any of the other functions that have been delineated. Some attitudes are based on the utilitarian value of the object, some allow us to communicate our values and self-image, and some facilitate the maintenance of self-esteem. But all attitudes, regardless of their basis, serve this knowledge function. There is value simply in knowing whether we like or dislike some object—whether we view it positively or negatively. Such summary assessment can guide our tendencies to approach or avoid the object, and it can do so without our having to engage in effortful deliberation each and every time we encounter the object.

This functional value of attitudes is highlighted in the final two readings in this section. The article by Fazio, Blascovich, and Driscoll (1992; Reading 17) reports a series of experiments demonstrating the benefits of having pre-existing and accessible attitudes stored in memory. When faced with the task of deciding which of two alternatives they preferred under rushed conditions, people who had not earlier developed and rehearsed attitudes toward the alternatives displayed elevated blood pressure. Thus, they actually had to muster more physiological resources to cope with the demands of the decision task. In yet another experiment, individuals lacking attitudes required more time to make their preference decisions. Thus, these experiments illustrate how attitudes can save individuals from the "energy-consuming" reflective process of which Smith *et al.* (1956) spoke.

An additional finding to emerge from this research concerned the quality of the decisions that were made. Even though they were rushed, individuals who had developed accessible attitudes in the earlier phase of the experiment made preference decisions that more closely matched the judgments that they made later under unlimited time. In other words, those lacking attitudes were more likely to make preference decisions when rushed that did not concur with the judgments they expressed when they had unlimited time to consider the alternatives. In that sense, these individuals seem to have regretted their decisions and to wish to change their minds.

Such decision quality forms the very focus of Reading 18, an article by Wilson and Schooler (1991). These researchers considered how well individuals' preferences corresponded to expert opinion. They offer the provocative hypothesis that introspection—at least of a certain form—can have the surprising consequence of reducing the quality of decisions. In this research, the experimenters compared a control condition, in which participants were simply exposed to the attitude objects, to one in which participants were asked to list their reasons for liking or disliking each object. The need to verbalize reasons apparently led participants to focus on some attributes of the object that they otherwise would not have considered or weighted heavily. Their final evaluations of the alternatives differed from those who had not been asked to analyze reasons, with the latter more closely aligning with the judgments of experts. One reason why analyzing reasons can reduce the quality of

decision is that it puts emphasis on the cognitive bases of attitudes and tends to underestimate the emotional bases.

Similar evidence was obtained in subsequent research that focused on post-choice satisfaction. Wilson *et al.* (1993) demonstrated that introspecting about reasons for preferring one poster over others resulted in a poorer choice about which poster to accept as a bonus for having participated in the experiment. Weeks later, these participants showed signs of being less satisfied with the poster they had selected than participants who had not analyzed reasons before making their choice. Apparently, then, there is value to following one's attitudes ("going with one's gut") and not attempting to analyze and verbalize why one's attitudes are what they are, at least when the attitude object is one for which liking is based primarily on affect (e.g., a poster, candy, one's significant other). In such cases, introspection can lead one astray.

REFERENCES

Brewer, M. B. (1999). The psychology of prejudice: Ingroup love or outgroup hate? *Journal of Social Issues, 55,* 429–444.

Petty, R. E., & Cacioppo, J. T. (1986). The elaboration likelihood model of persuasion. In L. Berkowitz (Ed.), *Advances in experimental social psychology* (Vol. 19, pp. 123–205). San Diego, CA: Academic Press.

Smith, M. B., Bruner, J. S., & White, R. W. (1956). *Opinions and Personality.* New York: Wiley.

Snyder, M. (1974). Self monitoring of expressive behavior. *Journal of Personality and Social Psychology, 30,* 526–537.

Wilson, T. D., Lisle, D. J., Schooler, J. W., Hodges, S. D., Klaaren, K. J., & LaFleur, S. J. (1993). Introspecting about reasons can reduce post-choice satisfaction. *Personality and Social Psychology Bulletin, 19,* 331–339.

Suggested Readings

Fazio, R. H. (2000). Accessible attitudes as tools for object appraisal: Their costs and benefits. In G. R. Maio & J. M. Olson (Eds.), *Why we evaluate: Functions of attitudes* (pp. 1–36). Mahwah, NJ: Erlbaum.

Jamieson, D. W., & Zanna, M. P. (1989). Need for structure in attitude formation and expression. In A. R. Pratkanis, S. J. Breckler, & A. G. Greenwald (Eds.), *Attitude structure and function* (pp. 383–406). Hillsdale, NJ: Erlbaum.

Maio, G. R. & Olson, J. M. (Eds.) (2000). *Why we evaluate: Functions of attitudes.* Mahwah, NJ: Erlbaum.

Shavitt, S. (1990). The role of attitude objects in attitude functions. *Journal of Experimental Social Psychology, 26,* 124–148.

Snyder, M., & DeBono, K. G. (1989). Understanding the functions of attitudes: Lessons from personality and social behavior. In A. R. Pratkanis, S. J. Breckler, & A. G. Greenwald (Eds.), *Attitude structure and function* (pp. 361–381). Hillsdale, NJ: Erlbaum.

The Functional Approach to the Study of Attitudes

Daniel Katz

At the psychological level the reasons for holding or for changing attitudes are found in the functions they perform for the individual, specifically the functions of adjustment, ego defense, value expression, and knowledge. The conditions necessary to arouse or modify an attitude vary according to the motivational basis of the attitude. Ego-defensive attitudes, for example, can be aroused by threats, appeals to hatred and repressed impulses, and authoritarian suggestion, and can be changed by removal of threat, catharsis, and self-insight. Expressive attitudes are aroused by cues associated with the individual's values and by the need to reassert his self-image and can be changed by showing the appropriateness of the new or modified beliefs to the self-concept. Brain washing is primarily directed at the value-expressive function and operates by controlling all environmental supports of old values. Changing attitudes may involve generalization of change to related areas of belief and feeling. Minimal generalization seems to be the rule among adults; for example, in politics voting for an opposition candidate does not have much effect upon party identification.

The study of opinion formation and attitude change is basic to an understanding of the public opinion process even though it should not be equated with this process. The public opinion process is one phase of the influencing of collective decisions, and its investigation involves knowledge of channels of communication, of the power structures of a society, of the character of mass media, of the relation between elites, factions and masses, of the role of formal and informal leaders, of the institutionalized access to officials. But the raw material out of which public opinion develops is to be found in the attitudes of individuals, whether they be followers or leaders and whether

The author is Professor of Psychology at the University of Michigan, former president of the Society for the Psychological Study of Social Issues, and co-editor of *Research Methods in the Behavioral Sciences* and *Public Opinion and Propaganda*.

these attitudes be at the general level of tendencies to conform to legitimate authority or majority opinion or at the specific level of favoring or opposing the particular aspects of the issue under consideration. The nature of the organization of attitudes within the personality and the processes which account for attitude change are thus critical areas for the understanding of the collective product known as public opinion.

Early Approaches to the Study of Attitude and Opinion

There have been two main streams of thinking with respect to the determination of man's attitudes. The one tradition assumes an irrational model of man: specifically it holds that men have very limited powers of reason and reflection, weak capacity to discriminate, only the most primitive self-insight, and very short memories. Whatever mental capacities people do possess are easily overwhelmed by emotional forces and appeals to self-interest and vanity. The early books on the psychology of advertising, with their emphasis on the doctrine of suggestion, exemplify this approach. One expression of this philosophy is in the propagandist's concern with tricks and traps to manipulate the public. A modern form of it appears in *The Hidden Persuaders*, or the use of subliminal and marginal suggestion, or the devices supposedly employed by "the Madison Avenue boys." Experiments to support this line of thinking started with laboratory demonstrations of the power of hypnotic suggestion and were soon extended to show that people would change their attitudes in an uncritical manner under the influence of the prestige of authority and numbers. For example, individuals would accept or reject the same idea depending upon whether it came from a positive or a negative prestige source.[1]

The second approach is that of the ideologist who invokes a rational model of man. It assumes that the human being has a cerebral cortex, that he seeks understanding, that he consistently attempts to make sense of the world about him, that he possesses discriminating and reasoning powers which will assert themselves over time, and that he is capable of self-criticism and self-insight. It relies heavily upon getting adequate information to people. Our educational system is based upon this rational model. The present emphasis upon the improvement of communication, upon developing more adequate channels of two-way communication, of conferences and institutes, upon bringing people together to interchange ideas, are all indications of the belief in the importance of intelligence and comprehension in the formation and change of men's opinions.

Now either school of thought can point to evidence which supports its assumptions, and can make fairly damaging criticisms of its opponent. Solomon Asch and his colleagues, in attacking the irrational model, have called attention to the biased character of the old experiments on prestige suggestion which gave the subject little opportunity to demonstrate critical thinking.[2] And further exploration of subjects in these stupid situations does indicate that they try to make sense of a nonsensical matter as far as possible. Though the same statement is presented by the experimenter to two groups, the first time as coming from a positive source and the second time as coming from a negative source, it is given a different meaning dependent upon the context in which it appears.[3] Thus the experimental subject does his best to give some rational meaning to the problem. On the other hand, a large body of experimental work indicates that there are many limitations in the rational approach in that people see their world in terms of

[1] Muzafer Sherif, *The Psychology of Social Norms*, New York, Harper, 1936.

[2] Solomon E. Asch, *Social Psychology*, New York, Prentice-Hall, 1952.

[3] *Ibid.*, pp. 426–427. The following statement was attributed to its rightful author, John Adams, for some subjects and to Karl Marx for others: "those who hold and those who are without property have ever formed distinct interests in society." When the statement was attributed to Marx, this type of comment appeared: "Marx is stressing the need for a redistribution of wealth." When it was attributed to Adams, this comment appeared: "This social division is innate in mankind."

their own needs, remember what they want to remember, and interpret information on the basis of wishful thinking. H. H. Hyman and P. Sheatsley have demonstrated that these experimental results have direct relevance to information campaigns directed at influencing public opinion.[4] These authors assembled facts about such campaigns and showed conclusively that increasing the flow of information to people does not necessarily increase the knowledge absorbed or produce the attitude changes desired.

The major difficulty with these conflicting approaches is their lack of specification of the conditions under which men do act as the theory would predict. For the facts are that people do act at times as if they had been decorticated and at times with intelligence and comprehension. And people themselves do recognize that on occasion they have behaved blindly, impulsively, and thoughtlessly. A second major difficulty is that the rationality-irrationality dimension is not clearly defined. At the extremes it is easy to point to examples, as in the case of the acceptance of stupid suggestions under emotional stress on the one hand, or brilliant problem solving on the other; but this does not provide adequate guidance for the many cases in the middle of the scale where one attempts to discriminate between rationalization and reason.

Reconciliation of the Conflict in a Functional Approach

The conflict between the rationality and irrationality models was saved from becoming a worthless debate because of the experimentation and research suggested by these models. The findings of this research pointed toward the elements of truth in each approach and gave some indication of the conditions under which each model could make fairly accurate predictions. In general the irrational approach was at its best where the situation

imposed heavy restrictions upon search behavior and response alternatives. Where individuals must give quick responses without adequate opportunities to explore the nature of the problem, where there are very few response alternatives available to them, where their own deep emotional needs are aroused, they will in general react much as does the unthinking subject under hypnosis. On the other hand, where the individual can have more adequate commerce with the relevant environmental setting, where he has time to obtain more feedback from his reality testing, and where he has a number of realistic choices, his behavior will reflect the use of his rational faculties.

[. . .] There is a growing interest in a more comprehensive framework for dealing with the complex variables and for bringing order within the field. [. . . A] point of departure is represented by two groups of workers who have organized their theories around the functions which attitudes perform for the personality. Sarnoff, Katz, and McClintock, in taking this functional approach, have given primary attention to the motivational bases of attitudes and the processes of attitude change.[5] The basic assumption of this group is that both attitude formation and attitude change must be understood in terms of the needs they serve and that, as these motivational processes differ, so too will the conditions and techniques for attitude change. Smith, Bruner, and White have also analyzed the different functions which attitudes perform for the personality.[6] Both groups present essentially the same functions, but Smith, Bruner, and White give more attention to perceptual and cognitive processes and Sarnoff, Katz, and McClintock to the specific conditions of attitude change.

The importance of the functional approach is threefold.

(1) Many previous studies of attitude change have dealt with factors which are not genuine

[4] Herbert H. Hyman and Paul B. Sheatsley, "Some Reasons Why Information Campaigns Fail," *Public Opinion Quarterly*, Vol. 11, 1947, pp. 413–423.

[5] Irving Sarnoff and Daniel Katz, "The Motivational Bases of Attitude Change," *Journal of Abnormal and Social Psychology*, Vol. 49, 1954, pp. 115–124.
[6] M. Brewster Smith, Jerome S. Bruner, and Robert W. White, *Opinions and Personality*, New York, Wiley, 1956.

psychological variables, for example, the effect on group prejudice of contact between two groups, or the exposure of a group of subjects to a communication in the mass media. Now contact serves different psychological functions for the individual and merely knowing that people have seen a movie or watched a television program tells us nothing about the personal values engaged or not engaged by such a presentation. If, however, we can gear our research to the functions attitudes perform, we can develop some generalizations about human behavior. Dealing with nonfunctional variables makes such generalization difficult, if not impossible.

(2) By concerning ourselves with the different functions attitudes can perform we can avoid the great error of oversimplification—the error of attributing a single cause to given types of attitude. It was once popular to ascribe radicalism in economic and political matters to the psychopathology of the insecure and to attribute conservatism to the rigidity of the mentally aged. At the present time it is common practice to see in attitudes of group prejudice the repressed hostilities stemming from childhood frustrations, though Hyman and Sheatsley have pointed out that prejudiced attitudes can serve a normative function of gaining acceptance in one's own group as readily as releasing unconscious hatred.[7] In short, not only are there a number of motivational forces to take into account in considering attitudes and behavior, but the same attitude can have a different motivational basis in different people.

(3) Finally, recognition of the complex motivational sources of behavior can help to remedy the neglect in general theories which lack specification of conditions under which given types of attitude will change. Gestalt theory tells us, for example, that attitudes will change to give better cognitive

organization to the psychological field. This theoretical generalization is suggestive, but to carry out significant research we need some middle-level concepts to bridge the gap between a high level of abstraction and particularistic or phenotypical events. We need concepts that will point toward the types of motive and methods of motive satisfaction which are operative in bringing about cognitive reorganization. [. . .]

Four Functions which Attitudes Perform for the Individual

The major functions which attitudes perform for the personality can be grouped according to their motivational basis as follows:

1. *The instrumental, adjustive, or utilitarian function* upon which Jeremy Bentham and the utilitarians constructed their model of man. A modern expression of this approach can be found in behavioristic learning theory.
2. *The ego-defensive function* in which the person protects himself from acknowledging the basic truths about himself or the harsh realities in his external world. Freudian psychology and neo-Freudian thinking have been preoccupied with this type of motivation and its outcomes.
3. *The value-expressive function* in which the individual derives satisfactions from expressing attitudes appropriate to his personal values and to his concept of himself. This function is central to doctrines of ego psychology which stress the importance of self-expression, self-development, and self-realization.
4. *The knowledge function* based upon the individual's need to give adequate structure to his universe. The search for meaning, the need to understand, the trend toward better organization of perceptions and beliefs to provide clarity and consistency for the individual, are other descriptions of this function. The development of principles about perceptual and cognitive structure have been the contribution of Gestalt psychology.

---

[7] Herbert H. Hyman and Paul B. Sheatsley, "The Authoritarian Personality: A Methodological Critique," in Richard Christie and Marie Jahoda, editors, *Studies in the Scope and Method of the Authoritarian Personality*, Glencoe, Ill., Free Press, 1954, pp. 50–122.

Stated simply, the functional approach is the attempt to understand the reasons people hold the attitudes they do. The reasons, however, are at the level of psychological motivations and not of the accidents of external events and circumstances. Unless we know the psychological need which is met by the holding of an attitude we are in a poor position to predict when and how it will change. Moreover, the same attitude expressed toward a political candidate may not perform the same function for all the people who express it. And while many attitudes are predominantly in the service of a single type of motivational process, as described above, other attitudes may serve more than one purpose for the individual. A fuller discussion of how attitudes serve the above four functions is in order.

1. *The adjustment function.* Essentially this function is a recognition of the fact that people strive to maximize the rewards in their external environment and to minimize the penalties. The child develops favorable attitudes toward the objects in his world which are associated with the satisfactions of his needs and unfavorable attitudes toward objects which thwart him or punish him. Attitudes acquired in the service of the adjustment function are either the means for reaching the desired goal or avoiding the undesirable one, or are affective associations based upon experiences in attaining motive satisfactions.[8] The attitudes of the worker favoring a political party which will advance his economic lot are an example of the first type of utilitarian attitude. The pleasant image one has of one's favorite food is an example of the second type of utilitarian attitude.

In general, then, the dynamics of attitude formation with respect to the adjustment function are dependent upon present or past perceptions of the utility of the attitudinal object for the individual. The clarity, consistency, and nearness of rewards and punishments, as they relate to the individual's activities and goals, are important factors in the acquisition of such attitudes. Both attitudes and habits are formed toward specific objects, people, and symbols as they satisfy specific needs. The closer these objects are to actual need satisfaction and the more they are clearly perceived as relevant to need satisfaction, the greater are the probabilities of positive attitude formation. These principles of attitude formation are often observed in the breach rather than the compliance. In industry, management frequently expects to create favorable attitudes toward job performance through programs for making the company more attractive to the worker, such as providing recreational facilities and fringe benefits. Such programs, however, are much more likely to produce favorable attitudes toward the company as a desirable place to work than toward performance on the job. The company benefits and advantages are applied across the board to all employees and are not specifically relevant to increased effort in task performance by the individual worker.

Consistency of reward and punishment also contributes to the clarity of the instrumental object for goal attainment. If a political party bestows recognition and favors on party workers in an unpredictable and inconsistent fashion, it will destroy the favorable evaluation of the importance of working hard for the party among those whose motivation is of the utilitarian sort. But, curiously, while consistency of reward needs to be observed, 100 per cent consistency is not as effective as a pattern which is usually consistent but in which there are some lapses. When animal or human subjects are invariably rewarded for a correct performance, they do not retain their learned responses as well as when the reward is sometimes skipped.[9]

2. *The ego-defensive function.* People not only seek to make the most of their external world and what it offers, but they also expend a great deal of their energy on living with themselves. The mechanisms by which the individual protects his ego from his own unacceptable impulses and from the knowledge of threatening forces from without, and

[8] Katz and Stotland, *op.cit.*, pp. 434–443.

[9] William O. Jenkins and Julian C. Stanley, "Partial Reinforcement: A Review and Critique," *Psychological Bulletin*, Vol. 47, 1950, pp. 193–234.

the methods by which he reduces his anxieties created by such problems, are known as mechanisms of ego defense. A more complete account of their origin and nature will be found in Sarnoff's article in this issue.[10] They include the devices by which the individual avoids facing either the inner reality of the kind of person he is, or the outer reality of the dangers the world holds for him. They stem basically from internal conflict with its resulting insecurities. In one sense the mechanisms of defense are adaptive in temporarily removing the sharp edges of conflict and in saving the individual from complete disaster. In another sense they are not adaptive in that they handicap the individual in his social adjustments and in obtaining the maximum satisfactions available to him from the world in which he lives. The worker who persistently quarrels with his boss and with his fellow workers, because he is acting out some of his own internal conflicts, may in this manner relieve himself of some of the emotional tensions which beset him. He is not, however, solving his problem of adjusting to his work situation and thus may deprive himself of advancement or even of steady employment.

Defense mechanisms, Miller and Swanson point out, may be classified into two families on the basis of the more or less primitive nature of the devices employed.[11] The first family, more primitive in nature, are more socially handicapping and consist of denial and complete avoidance. The individual in such cases obliterates through withdrawal and denial the realities which confront him. The exaggerated case of such primitive mechanisms is the fantasy world of the paranoiac. The second type of defense is less handicapping and makes for distortion rather than denial. It includes rationalization, projection, and displacement.

Many of our attitudes have the function of defending our self-image. When we cannot admit to ourselves that we have deep feelings of inferiority we may project those feelings onto some convenient minority group and bolster our egos by attitudes of superiority toward this underprivileged group. The formation of such defensive attitudes differs in essential ways from the formation of attitudes which serve the adjustment function. They proceed from within the person, and the objects and situation to which they are attached are merely convenient outlets for their expression. Not all targets are equally satisfactory for a given defense mechanism, but the point is that the attitude is not created by the target but by the individual's emotional conflicts. And when no convenient target exists the individual will create one. Utilitarian attitudes, on the other hand, are formed with specific reference to the nature of the attitudinal object. They are thus appropriate to the nature of the social world to which they are geared. The high school student who values high grades because he wants to be admitted to a good college has a utilitarian attitude appropriate to the situation to which it is related.

All people employ defense mechanisms, but they differ with respect to the extent that they use them and some of their attitudes may be more defensive in function than others. It follows that the techniques and conditions for attitude change will not be the same for ego-defensive as for utilitarian attitudes.

Moreover, though people are ordinarily unaware of their defense mechanisms, especially at the time of employing them, they differ with respect to the amount of insight they may show at some later time about their use of defenses. In some cases they recognize that they have been protecting their egos without knowing the reason why. In other cases they may not even be aware of the devices they have been using to delude themselves.

3. *The value-expressive function.* While many attitudes have the function of preventing the individual from revealing to himself and others his true nature, other attitudes have the function of giving positive expression to his central values and to the type of person he conceives himself to be. A man may consider himself to be an enlightened conservative or an internationalist or a liberal, and will hold attitudes which are the appropriate indication

[10] See pp. 251–279 [of *Public Opinion Quarterly*, *24*, 1960].
[11] Daniel R. Miller and Guy E. Swanson, *Inner Conflict and Defense*, New York, Holt, 1960, pp. 194–288.

of his central values. Thus we need to take account of the fact that not all behavior has the negative function of reducing the tensions of biological drives or of internal conflicts. Satisfactions also accrue to the person from the expression of attitudes which reflect his cherished beliefs and his self-image. The reward to the person in these instances is not so much a matter of gaining social recognition or monetary rewards as of establishing his self-identity and confirming his notion of the sort of person he sees himself to be. The gratifications obtained from value expression may go beyond the confirmation of self-identity. Just as we find satisfaction in the exercise of our talents and abilities, so we find reward in the expression of any attributes associated with our egos.

Value-expressive attitudes not only give clarity to the self-image but also mold that self-image closer to the heart's desire. The teenager who by dress and speech establishes his identity as similar to his own peer group may appear to the outsider a weakling and a craven conformer. To himself he is asserting his independence of the adult world to which he has rendered childlike subservience and conformity all his life. Very early in the development of the personality the need for clarity of self-image is important—the need to know "who I am." Later it may be even more important to know that in some measure I am the type of person I want to be. Even as adults, however, the clarity and stability of the self-image is of primary significance. Just as the kind, considerate person will cover over his acts of selfishness, so too will the ruthless individualist become confused and embarrassed by his acts of sympathetic compassion. One reason it is difficult to change the character of the adult is that he is not comfortable with the new "me." Group support for such personality change is almost a necessity, as in Alcoholics Anonymous, so that the individual is aware of approval of his new self by people who are like him.

The socialization process during the formative years sets the basic outlines for the individual's self-concept. Parents constantly hold up before the child the model of the good character they want him to be. A good boy eats his spinach, does not hit girls, etc. The candy and the stick are less in evidence in training the child than the constant appeal to his notion of his own character. It is small wonder, then, that children reflect the acceptance of this model by inquiring about the characters of the actors in every drama, whether it be a television play, a political contest, or a war, wanting to know who are the "good guys" and who are the "bad guys." Even as adults we persist in labeling others in the terms of such character images. Joe McCarthy and his cause collapsed in fantastic fashion when the telecast of the Army hearings showed him in the role of the villain attacking the gentle, good man represented by Joseph Welch.

A related but somewhat different process from childhood socialization takes place when individuals enter a new group or organization. The individual will often take over and internalize the values of the group. What accounts, however, for the fact that sometimes this occurs and sometimes it does not? Four factors are probably operative, and some combination of them may be necessary for internalization. (1) The values of the new group may be highly consistent with existing values central to the personality. The girl who enters the nursing profession finds it congenial to consider herself a good nurse because of previous values of the importance of contributing to the welfare of others. (2) The new group may in its ideology have a clear model of what the good group member should be like and may persistently indoctrinate group members in these terms. One of the reasons for the code of conduct for members of the armed forces, devised after the revelations about the conduct of American prisoners in the Korean War, was to attempt to establish a model for what a good soldier does and does not do. (3) The activities of the group in moving toward its goal permit the individual genuine opportunity for participation. To become ego-involved so that he can internalize group values, the new member must find one of two conditions. The group activity open to him must tap his talents and abilities so that his chance to show what he is worth can be tied into the group effort. Or else the activities of the group must give him an active voice in group decisions. His particular talents and abilities may not be tapped but he does have the opportunity to enter into group decisions, and thus his need for self-determination is satisfied. He then identifies with the group in which such opportunities for ego-involvement are available. It is not necessary that opportunities for self-expression and self-determination be of great magnitude in an objective sense, so long as they are important for the psychological economy of the individuals themselves. (4) Finally, the individual may come to see himself as a group member if he can share in the rewards of group activity which includes his own efforts. The worker may not play much of a part in building a ship or make any decisions in the process of building it. Nevertheless, if he and his fellow workers are given a share in every boat they build and a return on the proceeds from the earnings of the ship, they may soon come to identify with the ship-building company and see themselves as builders of ships.

4. *The knowledge function.* Individuals not only acquire beliefs in the interest of satisfying various specific needs, they also seek knowledge to give meaning to what would otherwise be an unorganized chaotic universe. People need standards or frames of reference for understanding their world, and attitudes help to supply such standards. The problem of understanding, as John Dewey made clear years ago, is one "of introducing (1) *definiteness* and *distinction* and (2) *consistency* and *stability* of meaning into what is otherwise vague and wavering."[12] The definiteness and stability are provided in good measure by the norms of our culture, which give the otherwise perplexed individual ready-made attitudes for comprehending his universe. Walter Lippmann's classical contribution to the study of opinions and attitudes was his description of stereotypes and the way they provided order and clarity for a bewildering set of complexities.[13] The most interesting finding in Herzog's familiar

study of the gratifications obtained by housewives in listening to daytime serials was the unsuspected role of information and advice.[14] The stories were liked "because they explained things to the inarticulate listener."

The need to know does not of course imply that people are driven by a thirst for universal knowledge. The American public's appalling lack of political information has been documented many times. In 1956, for example, only 13 per cent of the people in Detroit could correctly name the two United States Senators from the state of Michigan and only 18 per cent knew the name of their own Congressman.[15] People are not avid seekers after knowledge as judged by what the educator or social reformer would desire. But they do want to understand the events which impinge directly on their own life. Moreover, many of the attitudes they have already acquired give them sufficient basis for interpreting much of what they perceive to be important for them. Our already existing stereotypes, in Lippmann's language, "are an ordered, more or less consistent picture of the world, to which our habits, our tastes, our capacities, our comforts and our hopes have adjusted themselves. They may not be a complete picture of the world, but they are a picture of a possible world to which we are adapted."[16] It follows that new information will not modify old attitudes unless there is some inadequacy or incompleteness or inconsistency in the existing attitudinal structure as it relates to the perceptions of new situations. [. . .]

In the foregoing analysis we have attempted to clarify the functions which attitudes perform and to give some psychological specifications of the conditions under which they are formed, elicited, and changed. This material is summarized in Table 13.1. [. . .]

---

[12] John Dewey, *How We Think*, New York, Macmillan, 1910.
[13] Walter Lippmann, *Public Opinion*, New York, Macmillan, 1922.
[14] Herta Herzog, "What Do We Really Know about Daytime Serial Listeners?" in Paul F. Lazarsfeld and Frank N. Stanton, editors, *Radio Research 1942–1943*, New York, Duell, Sloan & Pearce, 1944, pp. 3–33.
[15] From a study of the impact of party organization on political behavior in the Detroit area, by Daniel Katz and Samuel Eldersveld, in manuscript.
[16] Lippmann, *op.cit.*, p. 95.

TABLE 13.1. Determinants of Attitude Formation, Arousal, and Change in Relation to Type of Function

Function	Origin and Dynamics	Arousal Conditions	Change Conditions
Adjustment	Utility of attitudinal object in need satisfaction. Maximizing external rewards and minimizing punishments	1. Activation of needs 2. Salience of cues associated with need satisfaction	1. Need deprivation 2. Creation of new needs and new levels of aspiration 3. Shifting rewards and punishments 4. Emphasis on new and better paths for need satisfaction
Ego defense	Protecting against internal conflicts and external dangers	1. Posing of threats 2. Appeals to hatred and repressed impulses 3. Rise in frustrations 4. Use of authoritarian suggestion	1. Removal of threats 2. Catharsis 3. Development of self-insight
Value expression	Maintaining self identity; enhancing favorable self-image; self-expression and self-determination	1. Salience of cues associated with values 2. Appeals to individual to reassert self-image 3. Ambiguities which threaten self-concept	1. Some degree of dissatisfaction with self 2. Greater appropriateness of new attitude for the self 3. Control of all environmental supports to undermine old values
Knowledge	Need for understanding, for meaningful cognitive organization, for consistency and clarity	1. Reinstatement of cues associated with old problem or of old problem itself	1. Ambiguity created by new information or change in environment 2. More meaningful information about problems

Summary

The purpose of this paper was to provide a psychological framework for the systematic consideration of the dynamics of public and private attitudes. Four functions which attitudes perform for the personality were identified: the *adjustive function* of satisfying utilitarian needs, the *ego-defensive function* of handling internal conflicts, the *value-expressive function* of maintaining self-identity and of enhancing the self-image, and the *knowledge function* of giving understanding and meaning to the ambiguities of the world about us. The role of these functions in attitude formation was described. Their relevance for the conditions determining attitude arousal and attitude change was analyzed. [. . .]

Appeals to Image and Claims about Quality: Understanding the Psychology of Advertising

Mark Snyder and Kenneth G. DeBono

In three investigations we examined the evaluative and behavioral reactions of high and low self-monitoring individuals to two advertising strategies: appeals to a product's image and claims about a product's quality. High self-monitoring individuals reacted more favorably to image-oriented advertisements, were willing to pay more for products if they were advertised with an image orientation, and were more willing to try a product if it was marketed with an image appeal. By contrast, low self-monitoring individuals reacted more favorably to product-quality-oriented ads, were willing to pay more for products if they were advertised with a quality orientation, and were more willing to try a product if it was marketed with a quality claim. Theoretical and practical implications of these findings for advertising strategies, as well as theoretical implications of these findings for the nature of attitudes, are explored.

It has been called "the most potent influence in adapting and changing [our] habits and modes of life, affecting what we eat, what we wear, and the work and play of the whole nation" (Coolidge, cited by Fox, 1984, p. 97). It has been compared with "such long-standing institutions as the school and the church in the magnitude of its social influence" (Potter, 1954, p. 167). It "dominates the media, it has vast power in the shaping of popular standards, and it is really one of the very limited groups of institutions which exercise social control" (Potter, 1954, p. 167). "It" is advertising,

This research and the preparation of this manuscript were supported in part by National Science Foundation Grant BNS 82-07632 to Mark Snyder. We thank Russell Nettle for his assistance in conducting the investigations, and Allen M. Omoto, Jeffry A. Simpson, and Dave Smith for their helpful comments on the manuscript.

Requests for reprints should be sent to Mark Snyder, Department of Psychology, University of Minnesota, 75 East River Road, Minneapolis, Minnesota 55455.

whose messages reach out in words and in pictures, from newspapers and magazines, from radios and televisions.

For most people, advertising is all but impossible to avoid or to ignore. On television alone, viewers are exposed to tens of thousands of commercial messages every year (Hacker, 1984). These messages may be viewed as attempts at persuasion and social influence. Indeed, one of the giants of the advertising industry, William Bernbach of the Doyle Dayne Bernbach agency once said that "Advertising is persuasion, and persuasion is . . . an art. Advertising is the art of persuasion" (cited by Fox, 1984, p. 251). As persuasion artists, the creators of advertising seem to belong to two schools, each of which has flourished throughout the history of the advertising industry. Within the trade, these two schools are known, respectively, as the "soft-sell" approach and the "hard-sell" approach (cf. Fox, 1984).

Practitioners of the soft-sell approach typically create ads that appeal to the *images* associated with the use of the product, images that one may gain and project by using the product. Practitioners of this image-based approach to advertising believe that how a product is packaged by its advertising is as important as the product itself. Therefore, they tend to create advertisements that are very striking in their visual appeal; they pay particular attention to the finer details of form and color. Typically, the copy associated with these ads emphasizes the image of the product or, more specifically, the images associated with the use of the product. These image-oriented ads rarely, if ever, make any explicit mention of the quality of the product, and, indeed, little emphasis is placed on the product itself.

Consider the case of the ad campaign for Arrow shirt collars, which focused not on the product itself but on the image of the man who used it. In this case, the advertising agency "created a campaign stressing the accessories and background of the man who wore the product. Instead of picturing the collar by itself, [they] put it around the neck of a stylish young man, impossibly clear of eye, clean of jowl and square of jaw and surrounded with opulent possessions and women" (Fox, 1984, p. 44).

Or, consider the case of the DeSoto car ads, which pictured young people, happily at play, along with the simple message, "Expect to be stared at." Perhaps the best known example of image-oriented advertising is the Marlboro man, emphasizing the rugged, masculine image of the man who smokes Marlboro cigarettes. In not one of these cases does the ad contain any explicit information about the product itself, only allusions to the images to be gained by identifying oneself with the product.

By contrast, practitioners of the hard-sell approach to advertising have created rather different ads, ones that focus on claims about the intrinsic merit, inherent *quality*, and functional value of the product itself. Their ads tell the consumer how good the product is, how well it works, or, in the case of things to eat and drink, how good they taste. For these advertisers, it's the "matter, not the manner" that counts (Fox, 1984, p. 324). The earliest efforts of this school were on behalf of patent medicines and cure-alls, one of the very earliest of which was Lydia E. Pinkham's Vegetable Compound, advertised as "a sure cure for all female weaknesses, . . . efficacious and immediate in its effects" (cited by Fox, 1984, p. 141). Recent advertisements for Total cereal, emphasizing the nutritional benefits of the cereal, clearly fall into this category. So too do Pepsi Cola's now-famous series of Pepsi challenge taste tests, designed to communicate the supposedly superior taste quality of Pepsi and, in so doing, counter Coke's claim that "It's the real thing."

There is no doubt about it. The history of advertising testifies to the faith that these two strategies have engendered in their proponents (for a review, see Fox, 1984). Of course, some ads feature elements of both strategies, presenting information both about image and about quality. Nevertheless, the fundamental question to be asked is that of the basis of the effectiveness of either type of advertising appeal. What is it that makes image and quality appeals succeed in engaging, motivating, and persuading consumers? In other words, what are the psychological mechanisms involved that render each of these strategies successful?

One way to address a question such as this one is to identify categories of individuals who are especially responsive to either type of advertising: one category of individuals who are especially responsive to image-based advertising appeals and a contrasting category of individuals who are especially responsive to product-quality-based advertising appeals. Once identified, these categories of individuals can provide a more thorough understanding of the reasons why these two markedly different types of appeals are effective. Members of each category may serve as the ideal candidates in one's investigation of the dynamics of each strategy in operation. Moreover, susceptibility to one or other type of advertising strategy may be but one specific feature of a larger and more extensive syndrome of regular and consistent differences in how members of these categories think, feel, and act. Then the differing generalized interpersonal orientations characteristic of these contrasting categories of individuals may provide a framework within which to understand the effectiveness of advertising. (For a more elaborated discussion of this strategy of inquiry in personality and social psychology, see Snyder & Ickes, 1985.)

Are there, then, these two categories of individuals who are differentially influenced by these two types of advertising appeals? Specifically, are there individuals who typically are particularly responsive to advertisements that stress the image associated with the use of a product and, conversely, are there individuals who typically are especially influenced by advertisements that emphasize the quality of the product? There are reasons to believe that these two contrasting categories of individuals may be identified with the psychological construct of self-monitoring (Snyder, 1974, 1979).

High self-monitoring individuals typically strive to be the type of person called for by each situation in which they find themselves (Snyder & Monson, 1975). They are adept at tailoring their behavior to fit social and interpersonal considerations of situational appropriateness (Lippa, 1976) and, as a result, their behavior often displays marked situation-to-situation shifts in the images they convey to other people (Danheiser & Graziano, 1982; Shaffer, Smith, & Tomarelli, 1982). These high self-monitoring individuals are identified by their

relatively high scores on the Self-Monitoring Scale (Snyder, 1974).

Because of their concerns with being the right person in the right place at the right time, these high self-monitoring individuals ought to be very sensitive to the images of self that they project in social situations (indeed, there is some suggestion that they may be; Snyder, Berscheid, & Glick, 1985), and, as such, they may be especially attentive to and influenced by advertising messages that convey information about the images that they acquire and project by virtue of using particular consumer products. In other words, to the extent that an advertisement allows high self-monitoring individuals to perceive that a given product has the potential to be used to create or enhance an image, they should react favorably to it. They should respond to the cigarette ad that promises sophistication (even if the ad says nothing about the quality of the tobacco in the cigarette), to the car ad that features a sporty-looking car (even if the ad says nothing about the performance and handling characteristics of the car), and to the toothpaste ad that offers whiter teeth and brighter smiles (even if the ad says nothing about the cavity-fighting capability of the toothpaste).

By contrast, low self-monitoring individuals typically do not attempt to mold their behavior to fit situational and interpersonal considerations (Snyder & Monson, 1975). Instead, these individuals tend to guide their behavioral choices on the basis of information from relevant inner sources, such as attitudes, feelings, and dispositions (Snyder & Tanke, 1976). As a result, low self-monitoring individuals typically display substantial correspondence between their private attitudes and their actual behavior in social contexts (Snyder & Swann, 1976; Zanna, Olson, & Fazio, 1980). Low self-monitoring individuals are identified by their relatively low scores on the Self-Monitoring Scale (Snyder, 1974).

Unlike their high self-monitoring counterparts, low self-monitoring individuals are less concerned with the images they project to others in social situations; instead, they are more concerned that their behavior in social contexts be an accurate reflection of their underlying attitudes, values, and dispositions. As such, they may be particularly responsive to advertisements that feature appeals to a product's quality. Information about product quality may be readily interpreted by these individuals in terms of their underlying attitudes, values, and other evaluative reactions. Take, for example, a low self-monitoring individual who enjoys the taste of Scotch whisky and who also drinks Scotch whisky. To maximize the consistency between this individual's favorable attitude toward Scotch and the behavior of drinking a Scotch whose taste he or she actually enjoys, as well as to maximize the consistency between this individual's behavior of drinking Scotch and the accompanying evaluative reaction, "I am enjoying the taste of this Scotch," this individual ought to drink only those brands of Scotch that taste the way good Scotch should taste, brands whose taste this individual therefore would enjoy. Hence this individual should be particularly attentive and responsive to advertisements that inform him or her about the good taste of particular brands of Scotch. Such ads would provide information useful to this individual in making consumer decisions that provide opportunities to act in a manner consistent with underlying attitudes (in this case, to drink a Scotch the taste of which he or she enjoys), as well as opportunities to maximize the consistency between the behavior of drinking Scotch and the evaluative reaction of enjoying the taste of the Scotch he or she drinks.

Are high and low self-monitoring individuals differentially responsive to ads that promise images and to appeals that feature product quality? In our research, designed to answer this question, we have created advertisements that, in pictures and words, represent image-based and product-quality-based messages to consumers. Reactions to our ads, collected in a series of empirical investigations, suggest that high self-monitoring individuals are particularly responsive to image-oriented advertising appeals and that low self-monitoring individuals are particularly responsive to product-quality advertising appeals.

Study 1

In Study 1, we created three sets of magazine advertisements, each set containing two advertisements for a particular product. We advertised whisky, cigarettes, and coffee, three frequently advertised consumer products. The two advertisements for each product were identical in all respects except for one: the written message or slogan associated with the picture. One slogan was an appeal to the image associated with the use of the product; the other slogan was a claim about the product's quality.

Method

Participants

Fifty male and female undergraduates enrolled in introductory psychology at the University of Minnesota participated in this investigation for course credit. On the basis of a median split of their Self-Monitoring Scale scores (Snyder, 1974), obtained in an earlier questionnaire survey, we categorized half of the participants as high self-monitoring individuals and half as low self-monitoring individuals.

Stimulus materials

We created three sets of magazine type advertisements, each set containing two advertisements for a particular product. Specifically, we advertised Canadian Club whisky, Barclay cigarettes, and Irish Mocha Mint flavored coffee, with the following contents.

Canadian Club. The picture for this set of advertisements prominently displayed a bottle of Canadian Club resting on a set of house blueprints. The written copy for the image-oriented advertisement stated, "You're not just moving in, you're moving up," and the product-quality-oriented advertisement claimed that "When it comes to great taste, everyone draws the same conclusion."

Barclay cigarettes. Here, the pictorial content depicted a handsome gentleman, about to light up a cigarette, looking into a mirror at his female companion. The woman's hand is shown resting on the gentleman's shoulder. The image-oriented message read, "Barclay . . . you can see the difference," and the product-quality-oriented message read, "Barclay . . . you can taste the difference."

Irish Mocha Mint. For this set, the picture showed a man and a woman relaxing in a candle-lit room, smiling at each other while drinking Irish Mocha Mint coffee. The image-oriented ad promised to "Make a chilly night become a cozy evening with Irish Mocha Mint," and the product-quality ad informed the consumer about "Irish Mocha Mint: A delicious blend of three great flavors—coffee, chocolate, and mint." [1]

Procedure

When participants arrived for their individual appointments, the experimenter informed them that their task would be to help in evaluating the relative merits of advertisements currently being studied by researchers at the university. The experimenter then presented, sequentially, the three sets of advertisements (with their order of presentation counterbalanced across participants). After each set, participants filled out a 12-item questionnaire on which they were to make evaluative comparisons between the two advertisements in the set. For example, the questionnaire asked "Overall, which ad do you think is better?" "Which one appeals to you more?" "Which ad do you think would be more successful?"

Results and Discussion

We predicted that high self-monitoring individuals would react more favorably than low self-

monitoring individuals to the image-oriented advertisements, but that low self-monitoring individuals would respond more favorably than high self-monitoring individuals to the product-quality-oriented advertisements. To derive an index of favorability toward the advertisements, we assigned participants a score of 1 each time that, in making evaluative comparisons between two ads, they favored the image-oriented ad, and a 0 each time they favored the product-quality-oriented ad. For each product, the 12-item index created by this scoring procedure was internally consistent (for Canadian Club, KR-20 = .91; for Barclay, KR-20 = .95; for Irish Mocha Mint, KR-20 = .91). Therefore, to obtain for each product an index of favorability toward each type of ad, we summed the participants' scores over the 12 items for each product. This in essence creates, for each product, a 0–12 index of favorability toward the two types of ads; higher scores indicated greater favorability toward the image-oriented ad and lower scores indicated greater favorability toward the product quality ad. Means for this index of favorability toward each type of ad are presented, for each product, in Table 14.1

We then entered the participants' scores on the favorability index into an analysis of variance (ANOVA) with one between-subject factor (self-monitoring) and one within-subject factor (product). This analysis revealed a statistically significant main effect for self-monitoring propensity, $F(1, 18) = 4.21, p < .05$; that is, as predicted, high self-monitoring individuals reacted more favorably to the image-oriented ads than did low self-monitoring individuals, and low self-monitoring

---

[1] As a check on the effectiveness of the manipulation, we presented 10 judges with the three sets of advertisements and, after every set, asked them, "Which ad do you think is directed at concerns about product quality?" and "Which ad do you think is directed at concerns about product image?" All of the judges correctly classified all of the advertisements into the image-oriented and product-quality-oriented categories they had been designed to represent.

TABLE 14.1. Evaluations of Advertisements: Study 1

Self-monitoring category	Product		
	Canadian Club	Barclay	Irish Mocha Mint
High	6.84	5.00	7.40
Low	4.88	3.68	6.08

Note: Range = 0–12. Higher scores indicate greater favorability toward image-oriented advertisements, and lower scores indicate greater favorability toward product-quality-oriented advertisements.

individuals reacted more favorably than did high self-monitoring individuals to the product-quality-oriented ads. Moreover, the differential favorability of high and low self-monitoring individuals toward the image and quality advertisements was evident, to some extent, for each of the three products. Tests of simple main effects (cf. Keppel, 1982) indicated that the cell means on the favorability index were in the predicted direction for the Barclay ad, the Canadian Club ad, and the Irish Mocha Mint ad: $t(48) = 1.36, p < .10; t(48) = 1.84, p < .05$; and $t(48) = 1.34, p < .10$, respectively.

Clearly, individuals high and low in self-monitoring have different *evaluative reactions* to advertising that is based on appeals to image and claims about product quality. Although the effectiveness of an advertising campaign can, in part, be measured by the evaluative reactions to the advertisements, this is surely not the whole picture. The goal of any advertising strategy is not only to elicit a favorable reaction from the consumer, but also to induce the individual to purchase the particular product. Therefore, to determine how generalized these evaluative reactions to image-oriented and product-quality-oriented advertising are, and to examine the effects of these differential evaluations on actual consumer behavior, we next examined the impact of these two modes of advertising on one important feature of consumer behavior.

Study 2

[EDITORS' NOTE: Study 2 used the very same advertisements to examine how much participants would be willing to pay for the advertised products. High self-monitoring individuals were willing to pay more for products if they were advertised with image appeals, whereas low self-monitoring individuals were willing to pay more if the advertising focused on quality.]

Study 3

Are high self-monitoring individuals more willing to actually consume a product if it is advertised with an appeal to image than with a claim about product quality? And, conversely, are low self-monitoring individuals more willing to actually consume a product if it is advertised with a quality orientation than with an image orientation? To answer these questions, we conducted Study 3, in which consumers were offered the opportunity to try out a new shampoo.

Method

Participants

Forty introductory psychology undergraduates at the University of Minnesota participated in this study for course credit. On the basis of a median split of their scores on the Self-Monitoring Scale (Snyder, 1974), we categorized half of the participants as high self-monitoring individuals and half as low self-monitoring individuals.

Procedure

The experimenter, blind to the participant's self-monitoring score and posing as a market researcher, contacted participants by telephone and offered them the following opportunity to participate in a test marketing study:

> Hi, _____, my name is _____ and I work for a marketing research firm here in the Twin Cities. Presently, we are surveying college students to see if, in the future, they would be interested in trying out a new shampoo that our client plans to market. However, before you tell me if you would be interested in trying this shampoo, let me tell you a little about it.

At this point, the experimenter delivered one of the following messages, determined by random assignment.

> *Image message:* The results of recent laboratory tests have indicated that while compared to other shampoos, this brand usually rates about average in how it cleans your hair, it consistently rates above average in how good it makes your hair look.

> *Quality message:* The results of recent laboratory tests have indicated that while compared to other

shampoos, this brand usually rates about average in how good it makes your hair look, it consistently rates above average in how clean it gets your hair.

After delivering one of the two messages, the experimenter asked all of the participants the following two questions:

Now, _____ , what I would like you to do is to indicate for me which of the following verbal descriptions best describes your willingness to use this shampoo: definitely not, probably not, unsure, probably yes, or definitely yes. Also, with 0% indicating *not at all* and 100% indicating *definitely willing*, what percentage do you think best describes your willingness to try this shampoo?

The experimenter recorded the participants' responses, answered any questions they had, and then thanked them for their time.

Results and Discussion

To create an index of willingness to use the shampoo, we coded the participants' answers to the first dependent variable in the following manner: 1 point for answering *definitely not*, 2 points for *probably not*, 3 points for *unsure*, 4 points for *probably yes*, and 5 points for *definitely yes*. Because the participants' responses so scored were highly correlated with their percentage estimate scores on the second dependent variable ($r = .865$, $p < .01$), we decided to form a composite index of willingness to use the shampoo by summing the participants' responses over the two measures. To accomplish this, we first standardized scores on each measure and then used the sum of each participant's standardized scores as an indication of willingness to try the shampoo product. Means for this composite standardized "willingness to use" index are presented in Table 14.2.

We then entered the participants' scores on the composite index into a 2 × 2 (Self-Monitoring × Message) ANOVA. This analysis revealed a statistically reliable interaction, $F(1, 36) = 7.18$, $p < .05$. Evidently, high self-monitoring individuals were more willing than low self-monitoring individuals to try the shampoo if they believed that it would

TABLE 14.2. Willingness to Use the Product: Study 3

Self-monitoring category	Type of message received	
	Image	Quality
High	.7626	−.7008
Low	−.9106	.9201

Note: Higher scores indicate greater willingness to use the product.

leave their hair looking good, $t(36) = 2.06$, $p < .025$, and low self-monitoring individuals were more willing than high self-monitoring individuals to try the shampoo if they believed that it would leave their hair very clean, $t(36) = 1.99$, $p < .05$.

Clearly, then, when it came to actual choices to use or not to use this consumer product, high self-monitoring individuals invoked considerations of the images associated with a product (choosing, in this case, to use the shampoo that would make their hair look good, even if it meant that their great-looking hair would be less than perfectly clean) and low self-monitoring individuals responded to attributes of the product's quality in performing its defining function (choosing, in this case, to use the shampoo that would get their hair very clean, even if their very clean hair would have a less-than-beautiful look).

General Discussion

On the basis of the converging pattern of results of these three investigations, it seems that we have succeeded in identifying two types of advertising strategies (image and quality) and two types of individuals (those high and those low in self-monitoring) who react differentially to these two strategies. High self-monitoring individuals react favorably to image-oriented ads, they are willing to pay more money for products if they are advertised with an image orientation, and they will agree to try a product if it is marketed with an image appeal. By contrast, low self-monitoring individuals react favorably to product-quality-oriented ads, they are willing to pay more money for products if their advertisements stress product quality, and they will agree to try a product if an appeal is made to its quality.

How are we to understand the effectiveness of appeals to images and claims about product quality? One basis for such an understanding is provided by the generalized interpersonal orientations characteristic of high and low self-monitoring individuals. In other words, the propensity to respond favorably, at the level of evaluative reactions and at the level of behavioral choices, to image-oriented or quality-oriented advertising appeals may be one feature of the larger syndrome of differing cognitive, motivational, and behavioral processes that guide the behavior of high and low self-monitoring individuals in social contexts (for a review of the defining and characteristic features of these generalized interpersonal orientations, see Snyder, 1979). Responding favorably to image-based advertising may be yet another manifestation of a striving to be a pragmatic creature of one's situations, to project images appropriate to one's circumstances, a striving that is particularly pronounced in high self-monitoring individuals; thus these individuals are ideal candidates for the study of the role of appeals to images in the advertising process. Similarly, responding favorably to quality-oriented advertising may be yet another manifestation of a quest to be a principled being, one with congruence between one's actions and underlying attitudes, values, and dispositions, a quest that is especially evident in low self-monitoring individuals; thus these individuals are ideal candidates for the study of the role of claims about quality in the advertising process.

Before considering further the implications of our findings for understanding advertising as a process of persuasion and social influence, we examine more carefully the distinction between image-oriented and quality-oriented advertising strategies. As clearly defined as the distinction may be at the level of the operations used in these investigations, some further decision rules may be necessary in order to identify the general features that define and separate the two categories of advertisements. For example, is an advertisement whose message concerns "people of good taste" or one whose message concerns "quality-conscious

individuals" to be classified as an appeal to image or a claim about quality? From our perspective, if the message appeals to the image of having good taste or to the image of quality consciousness that one acquires by virtue of using the product, but at the same time the message does not claim that the product tastes good or that it has high quality, then the advertisement is an image-oriented one. As such, it ought to appeal preferentially to high self-monitoring individuals. By contrast, if the message actually makes claims about the good taste or the high quality of the product as expressions of one's intrinsic desires for things that taste good or one's inherent valuing of things high in quality, then the advertisement is a quality-oriented one. As such, its claims ought to be particularly effective with low self-monitoring individuals.

Furthermore, it is necessary to specify the conditions under which the differential reactions of individuals high and low in self-monitoring to image-oriented and quality-oriented advertising can be expected to be translated into actual consumer behaviors. Can high self-monitoring individuals be expected to buy every product that promises an image? And can low self-monitoring individuals be expected to buy every product that possesses high quality? Clearly not. How, then, can one specify which products advertised with appeals to images will actually be used by high self-monitoring individuals and which products advertised with claims about quality will actually be used by low self-monitoring individuals?

High self-monitoring individuals typically choose the images that they project on the basis of information about the appropriateness of particular images to specific social situations and interpersonal contexts. Such situational considerations also may be relevant in their responsiveness to information provided by advertising. Thus the high self-monitoring male smoker who seeks to project an image of rugged masculinity on his weekend trips with his hunting buddies to the hunting lodge may, in addition to choosing words, deeds, and expressive mannerisms appropriate to that image, also choose, at least while on hunting trips, to smoke the cigarettes (and perhaps prominently display the package) whose advertising promises just such an image of rugged masculinity. As well, this individual may choose not to smoke, at least in these same circumstances, the brand whose ads appeal to an image of cultural sophistication (even though, if asked, he might grant its ads highly favorable evaluative reactions). More generally, although high self-monitoring individuals may be expected to be favorable toward advertising that appeals to images, their actual choices among products so advertised may reflect the images that they actually choose to project in their social circumstances.

In the case of low self-monitoring individuals, just as their behavior in specific social contexts is thought typically to reflect their own general attitudes and dispositions, so too ought such considerations of their own personal attributes be relevant in their responsiveness to information provided by advertising. For example, the low self-monitoring individual who enjoys the taste of gin but who does not enjoy the taste of bourbon ought to be more likely to purchase the brand of gin whose advertising conveys information about its fine gin taste than the brand of bourbon whose advertising speaks of its fine bourbon taste, even though that individual ought to be expected to regard both advertisements as particularly appealing, engaging, and effective ones. More generally, low self-monitoring individuals may be expected to be generally favorable toward advertising that makes claims about product-quality attributes, but to choose among products advertised with this orientation on the basis of the fit between these products and their own attitudes, preferences, and dispositions. They would make these choices in ways that maximize the consistency between these personal attributes and their consumer behavior.

Not only does the self-monitoring conceptual framework provide a theoretical understanding of the effectiveness of advertising, but it provides some practical hints as well. One hint is that the most potent image-oriented advertisements are those that most effectively convey the message that the images associated with using the advertised products are particularly appropriate ones to project and are images that, if conveyed, will increase the likelihood that one will fit into important life situations. Another hint is that the most effective quality-oriented advertisements are the ones that most successfully include the message that one will, by using the advertised products, be gaining opportunities to be true to one's own personal attitudes and important values.

Our findings and our interpretation of them also provide a new perspective on the two longstanding traditions in the advertising industry: the image-oriented soft-sell approach and the claim-oriented hard-sell approach. Indeed, it very well may be that these approaches have succeeded, survived, and flourished because each one has managed to appeal to members of one category of consumers. Image-oriented advertising campaigns that have worked may have worked because they have succeeded in engaging and motivating the image concerns of high self-monitoring consumers. Claim-oriented advertising campaigns that have succeeded may have succeeded because they have been effective in engaging and motivating the quality concerns of low self-monitoring consumers.

Perhaps, too, advertisements that feature elements of both strategies (information about image and information about quality) may succeed because each type of information succeeds in drawing different sets of consumers; that is, the image elements of such *hybrid* ads may draw high self-monitoring consumers at the same time as their quality elements draw low self-monitoring consumers. However, a word of caution ought to be associated with this generalization from our findings: It is not yet known whether the relative preferences of high and low self-monitoring individuals for image-oriented and quality-oriented advertising are accompanied by an actual aversion to the other type of advertising. For example, are low self-monitoring individuals, who prefer quality-oriented messages, simply indifferent to image-oriented messages (so that a hybrid ad would appeal to them as much as a quality-only ad) or are they perhaps actively opposed to image-oriented messages (so that a hybrid ad might appeal to them less than a quality-only ad)? Answering this question would require comparisons of image and quality ads with "no-message" ads (ones that lack both appeals to images and claims about quality), although it is not clear, in the context of the design of our investigations, what operations would constitute such a "no-message" comparison condition.

Our concerns with appeals to image and claims about quality are not limited to the domain of advertising. Indeed, they ought to be considered in the context of several distinctions that have been made concerning the processes of persuasion. For one, Petty and Cacioppo (1981) introduced the distinction between the *central* route to persuasion, whereby persuasion is due to extensive thinking about and elaboration of the persuasive message, and the *peripheral* route to persuasion, whereby persuasion is mediated by nonmessage factors such as source attractiveness. In addition, Chaiken (1980) distinguished between the *systematic* processing of a persuasive message, whereby, as Petty and Cacioppo's central route, persuasion is dependent on extensive thinking about the content of the persuasive message, and the *heuristic* processive of a persuasive message, whereby agreement with the message is based on the use of simple decision rules (e.g., "Experts are usually correct").

Although the conceptual distinctions these investigators make may appear to be similar to the conceptual distinction we are advancing (e.g., one may be tempted to equate image-based appeals with the peripheral route to persuasion or to link them to heuristic processing), we believe that the research strategies used by these investigators and our research strategy are sufficiently dissimilar to render the conceptual similarity more apparent than real. In most persuasion research in which either central versus peripheral routes or systematic versus heuristic processing is examined, the content of the persuasive message is held constant and another variable (e.g., a source factor or subject's level of involvement) is manipulated (e.g., Petty, Cacioppo, & Goldman, 1981). By contrast, in our research, the only difference between the two advertisements for any given product was the message content; no peripheral cues were manipulated. Therefore, any differences that the image and product-quality advertisements engendered must have been due to reactions to the message content

itself. From this perspective, responsiveness to image-oriented and quality-oriented messages may both represent instances of central routes to persuasion.

Whether the processing of the message content itself was systematic or heuristic, we cannot say. One could engage in either systematic or heuristic processing of either type of persuasive message. Thus, for example, in processing the quality-oriented messages of our first two studies, one could invoke the heuristic, "If it promises taste, buy it," or one could systematically assess the fit between claims about the product's taste and one's abiding preferences. And, in processing the image-oriented messages of those studies, one could use the heuristic, "If it promises image, buy it," or one could systematically evaluate the strategic utility of using the product for particular image-fashioning purposes in specific situations. We suspect, in line with our previous discussion of when evaluative reactions to advertising are translated into consumer behavior, that ultimate behavioral responsiveness to advertising is the outcome of systematic processing, both for low self-monitoring individuals (who, we have suggested, assess the fit between products and their own attitudes, preferences, and dispositions) and for high self-monitoring individuals (who, we have suggested, evaluate the potential of products to aid them in creating the images they choose to project in social circumstances).

There is, in addition to the distinctions between central and peripheral routes to persuasion and between systematic and heuristic processing, another distinction that may be relevant to understanding responsiveness to messages that make appeals to image and those that make claims about quality. Kelman (1961) posited three processes of agreement with a communication: compliance, identification, and internalization. For our purposes, the most meaningful of this trio are the processes of identification and internalization. Identification is said to occur when an individual agrees with a message because that agreement allows him or her to project a desirable image and to fit into important situations and peer groups. This agreement is considered somewhat ephemeral in that it can easily change when the image projected is no longer desirable. As such, identification processes may be involved in the preferential responsiveness of high self-monitoring individuals to image-based appeals. By contrast, internalization is said to occur when an individual accepts a message because the message is congruent with the individual's personal value system. Accordingly, internalization processes may be implicated in the preferential impact of quality-based advertisements on low self-monitoring individuals.

Nevertheless, the applicability of Kelman's (1961) theory to our particular investigations may be limited by the fact that his theory is concerned primarily with reactions to attributes of the source of a persuasive message (i.e., expert sources tend to produce agreement by means of internalization, attractive sources tend to produce agreement by means of identification). Yet in our investigations we focused not on the source of the message but rather on the message itself. Nevertheless, it may be that messages that are linked to sources of high credibility are particularly effective with low self-monitoring individuals and that the very same messages, when linked to sources of high personal or social attractiveness, are particularly effective with high self-monitoring individuals.

In addition to having implications for understanding advertising strategies, our findings also may have implications for understanding the nature of attitudes themselves. Taken together, our studies provide evidence, albeit indirect, that attitudes may be serving different functions for high and low self-monitoring individuals. In our studies, high self-monitoring individuals seem to have formed more favorable attitudes toward objects that they potentially could use for the purpose of creating and displaying social images. In keeping with their pragmatic orientation toward their social worlds, high self-monitoring individuals reacted positively to objects that may have been useful to them as means for achieving the goals of presenting images appropriate to their social situations. By contrast, and in keeping with their principled orientation toward their social environs, low self-monitoring individuals in our studies reacted positively to objects and issues that allowed them the

opportunity to express their underlying attitudes and values.

This possibility—that the reactions of individuals high and low in self-monitoring to advertising may reflect differing functional bases of their attitudes toward consumer products—is an intriguing one. The notions that individuals may hold similar attitudes for different reasons, and that the same attitude may serve different functions for different individuals, are the fundamental tenets of the functional theories of attitudes (e.g., Katz, 1960; Smith, Bruner, & White, 1956). Although it may not be not possible, on the sole basis of the results of this series of investigations, to specify conclusively which of the particular functions proposed by these theories underlie either the specific domain of reactions to advertising or the general domain of social attitudes, theoretical analyses of self-monitoring (e.g., Snyder, 1979) do provide some basis for conjecture.

To the extent that the characteristic interpersonal orientation of high self-monitoring individuals is a pragmatic one of fitting themselves to their social circumstances, this characteristic interpersonal orientation may also include social attitudes that are formed on the basis of how well they serve the ends of behaving in ways appropriate to the various reference groups that form one's social circumstances. As such, the social attitudes of high self-monitoring individuals may be said, in the language of the functional theorists, to be serving a social adjustive function. By contrast, to the extent that the characteristic interpersonal orientation of low self-monitoring individuals is a principled one of choosing behaviors that accurately reflect and meaningfully communicate their own personal attributes, that interpersonal orientation may also include social attitudes formed on the basis of how well they reflect and communicate more fundamental underlying values. As such, the social attitudes of low self-monitoring individuals, once again in the language of the functional theorists, may be said to be serving a value-expressive function.

These conjectures about the links between the psychological construct of self-monitoring and the functional bases of social attitudes may hold the potential for dealing with a problem that has long plagued the functional theorists. The Achilles' heel of the functional theories has been the lack of a way to systematically test these notions (cf. Kiesler, Collins, & Miller, 1969). To assess the validity of a functional theory of attitudes, one must be able to identify a priori the functions being served by a given attitude for a given individual. In the past, this has proven very difficult to do and may, in part, explain why the functional theories have been in a state of hibernation for some two decades now.

However, the results of this series of studies suggest one way of overcoming this hurdle. Just as we were able to identify categories of individuals who were especially responsive to image-oriented and quality-oriented advertising messages, so too may it be possible to identify categories of individuals who are especially likely to hold attitudes serving particular types of functions. Thus, for example, if one were seeking candidates for the study of the social adjustive function of attitudes, one might seek out members of the category of high self-monitoring individuals. Similarly, if one wished to probe the dynamics of the value-expressive function of attitudes, one might focus one's efforts on members of the category of low self-monitoring individuals. In either case, the identification and investigation of these categories of individuals would serve not as ends unto themselves but as vehicles for understanding the functional underpinnings of attitudes. The application of this hybrid "personality–social psychology" strategy to the study of attitudes very well may have the potential to awaken the functional theories of attitudes, persuasion, and social influence from their long winter of hibernation.

REFERENCES

Chaiken, S. (1980). Heuristic versus systematic information processing and the use of source versus message cues in persuasion. *Journal of Personality and Social Psychology, 39,* 752–766.

Danheiser, P. R., & Graziano, W. G. (1982). Self-monitoring and cooperation as a self-presentational strategy. *Journal of Personality and Social Psychology, 42,* 497–505.

Fox, S. (1984). *The mirror makers.* New York: Morrow.

Hacker, A. (1984, June 24). Poets of packaging, sculptors of desire. *New York Times Book Review,* p. 1.

Katz, D. (1960). The functional approach to the study of attitudes. *Public Opinion Quarterly, 24,* 163–204.

Kelman, H. C. (1961). Processes of opinion change. *Public Opinion Quarterly, 25,* 57–78.

Keppel, G. (1982). *Design and analysis: A researcher's handbook* (2nd ed.). Englewood Cliffs, NJ: Prentice-Hall.

Kiesler, C. A., Collins, B. E., & Miller, N. (1969). *Attitude change: A critical analysis of theoretical approaches.* New York: Wiley.

Lippa, R. (1976). Expressive control and the leakage of dispositional introversion–extraversion during role-played teaching. *Journal of Personality, 44,* 541–559.

Petty, R. E., & Cacioppo, J. T. (1981). *Attitudes and persuasion: Classic and contemporary approaches.* Dubuque, IA: Wm. C. Brown.

Petty, R. E., Cacioppo, J. T., & Goldman, R. (1981). Personal involvement as a determinant of argument-based persuasion. *Journal of Personality and Social Psychology, 41,* 847–855.

Potter, D. M. (1954). *People of plenty: Economic abundance and the American character.* Chicago: University of Chicago Press.

Shaffer, D. R., Smith, J. R., & Tomarelli, M. (1982). Self-monitoring as a determinant of self-disclosure reciprocity during the acquaintance process. *Journal of Personality and Social Psychology, 43,* 163–175.

Smith, M. B., Bruner, J. S., & White, R. W. (1956). *Opinions and personality.* New York: Wiley.

Snyder, M. (1974). The self-monitoring of expressive behavior. *Journal of Personality and Social Psychology, 30,* 526–537.

Snyder, M. (1979). Self-monitoring processes. In L. Berkowitz (Ed.), *Advances in experimental social psychology* (Vol. 12, pp. 85–128). New York: Academic Press.

Snyder, M., Berscheid, E., & Glick, P. (1985). Focusing on the exterior and the interior: Two investigations of the initiation of personal relationships. *Journal of Personality and Social Psychology, 48,* 1427–1439.

Snyder, M., & Ickes, W. (1985). Personality and social behavior. In G. Lindzey & E. Aronson (Eds.), *Handbook of social psychology* (3rd ed., pp. 883–948). New York: Random House.

Snyder, M., & Monson, T. C. (1975). Persons, situations, and the control of social behavior. *Journal of Personality and Social Psychology, 32,* 617–644.

Snyder, M., & Swann, W. B., Jr. (1976). When actions reflect attitudes: The politics of impression management. *Journal of Personality and Social Psychology, 34,* 1034–1042.

Snyder, M., & Tanke, E. D. (1976). Behavior and attitude: Some people are more consistent than others. *Journal of Personality, 44,* 510–517.

Zanna, M. P., Olson, J. M., & Fazio, R. H. (1980). Attitude–behavior consistency: An individual difference approach. *Journal of Personality and Social Psychology, 38,* 432–440.

Received September 25, 1984
Revision received March 25, 1985 ■

Matching versus Mismatching Attitude Functions: Implications for Scrutiny of Persuasive Messages

Richard E. Petty and Duane T. Wegener

Two studies were conducted to examine the hypothesis that matching the content of a persuasive message to the functional basis of people's attitudes enhances message scrutiny. In Study 1, high and low self-monitors were exposed to a message that matched or mismatched the functional basis of their attitudes (i.e., image appeal for high self-monitors and quality appeal for low self-monitors) and that contained either strong or weak arguments. Attitudes were more strongly affected by message strength when the message arguments matched rather than mismatched the functional basis of the attitude. In Study 2, this outcome was especially characteristic of individuals who typically do not enjoy thinking (those low in need for cognition). These studies show that matching arguments to the functional basis of an attitude is not invariably beneficial for persuasion but can enhance or reduce attitude change (compared to mismatched arguments) depending on the cogency of the matched information.

Consider attitudes about a political candidate. There are many qualities of the candidate that might be relevant to citizens' views of the candidate such as his or her stand on domestic issues, a projected image of decisiveness and leadership, past congressional experience, and so forth. Which

Authors' note. This research was supported by National Science Foundation Grant SBR 9520854 to Richard E. Petty and an NIMH traineeship to Duane T. Wegener (T32 MH19728). We are grateful to the 1990–1994 Ohio State Groups for Attitudes and Persuasion for their comments on this research. Preliminary reports of these studies were presented at the 1995 meetings of the Midwestern Psychological Association in Chicago (Experiment 1), and the American Psychological Association in New York (Experiment 2). Address correspondence to Richard E. Petty, Department of Psychology, Ohio State University, 1885 Neil Avenue Mall, Columbus, OH 43210-1222, e-mail: petty.1@osu.edu, or to Duane T. Wegener, Department of Psychological Sciences, Purdue University, West Lafayette, IN 47907-1364, e-mail: wegener@psych.purdue.edu.

qualities should the candidate promote most? One answer to this question receiving renewed attention in recent years suggests that an effective procedure would be to provide people with information that matches the functional basis of their attitudes. Recent research on this functional approach has supported earlier notions (e.g., Smith, Bruner, & White, 1956) that attitudes toward objects, issues, or people can serve different functions for different individuals and that attempts to influence these attitudes are most effective when the content of the message matches the functional basis of the attitude (e.g., Clary, Snyder, Ridge, Miene, & Haugen, 1994).

A number of possible functions for attitudes have been proposed. For example, attitudes might serve an *ego-defensive* function whereby a person is protected from accepting undesirable or threatening truths about him or herself. Attitudes might also serve a *utilitarian* function whereby an attitude reflects rewards and punishments that the attitude object supplies to the holder of the attitude. People could also hold *value-expressive* attitudes that allow them to act in accordance with their underlying values or *social-adjustive* attitudes that allow them to identify with (or distance themselves from) particular social groups (e.g., Katz, 1960; Shavitt, 1990; Smith et al., 1956; see Kiesler, Collins, & Miller, 1969; Snyder & DeBono, 1989, for reviews).

A variety of methods for identifying which function an attitude serves have been developed. One method relies on individual differences and suggests that most attitudes serve different functions for different people. That is, for some people, most attitudes might serve a value-expressive function, but for others, most attitudes might serve a social-adjustive or ego-defensive function (see Clary et al., 1994, for direct self-report measures of functions, and Snyder & DeBono, 1985, 1989, for identification of functions through more global personality measures). An alternative to the individual difference approach suggests that attitudes toward particular issues or objects might serve a common function for most people. For example, attitudes toward air-conditioners might be based on utilitarian concerns for most people (e.g., Abelson

& Prentice, 1989; Prentice, 1987; Shavitt, 1990). Finally, it is possible that in some cases there is little consistency across attitude objects or people, and thus one must assess functions separately for each attitude object for each person (see Herek, 1987).

A key notion of the functional approach is that it is important to understand the functional basis of people's attitudes in order to understand how to change those attitudes. For example, one person might like a political candidate because the candidate's position regarding preservation of national parks allows the person to express an important value of caring for the environment (i.e., the value-expressive function). Another might like the same candidate because this person identifies with the well-known people supporting the candidate (i.e., the social-adjustive function). Functional theory offers the general proposition that persuasive appeals whose content addresses the function served by an attitude will be more persuasive than appeals that are irrelevant to the function served by that attitude. That is, one should offer value-relevant arguments to the person whose attitude serves a value-expressive function, but one should offer social-adjustment arguments to the person whose attitude serves a social-adjustment function (e.g., Clary et al., 1994; DeBono & Packer, 1991; DeBono & Rubin, 1995; Katz, 1960; Kiesler et al., 1969; Lavine & Snyder, 1996; Shavitt, 1990; Snyder & DeBono, 1989).

Various studies have provided support for the functional hypothesis that persuasive appeals are more effective when they present information addressing the function underlying an attitude. For example, Snyder and DeBono (1985) used the individual difference method of identifying people for whom attitudes likely served different functions. Specifically, because high self-monitors (Snyder, 1974) tailor their behavior to fit the socially appropriate considerations of different situations (i.e., they change their behavior in order to present themselves to others in a positive manner), Snyder (1979) Snyder and DeBono (1985) reasoned that their attitudes might typically serve the social-adjustive function. In contrast, because low self-monitors are guided by internal sources such as values and feelings, Snyder and DeBono (1985) reasoned that their attitudes would more likely serve the value-expressive function.

To test the idea that attitudes served these different functions for high versus low self-monitors and, thus, that attitudes could be changed more easily by presenting message arguments that matched these different functions, Snyder and DeBono presented research participants with advertisements for a variety of products. These advertisements either contained content that appealed to the social images that consumers could gain from use of the product (which should serve primarily a social-adjustive function) or presented content regarding the intrinsic quality or merit of the product (which should serve the value-expressive function to the extent that qualities of the product readily can be interpreted in terms of underlying values and other internal evaluations of the product; see Snyder & DeBono, 1989). For example, an ad for Canadian Club Whiskey containing image content showed a bottle of the whiskey resting on a set of blueprints for a house and stated, "You're not just moving in, you're moving up." The quality ad for the whiskey had the same picture, but used the statement, "When it comes to taste, everyone draws the same conclusion."

Across a number of studies, Snyder and DeBono (1985) found that high self-monitors rated ads with image content as better (more effective) than ads with quality content, were willing to pay more for products advertised with image rather than quality, and were more willing to use products advertised with image than with quality. In contrast, low self-monitors rated quality ads as better (more effective) than image ads, were willing to pay more for products advertised with quality rather than image, and were more willing to use products advertised with quality than with image. Individuals high versus low in self-monitoring have also been shown to rate product quality as better when the product has been advertised in a manner consistent with the functional base assumed to underlie the attitude (DeBono & Packer, 1991; see Clary et al., 1994, and Lavine & Snyder, 1996, for additional evidence consistent with matching functional message content to individuals' bases of attitudes

being more persuasive than mismatching content).

Using an object-oriented approach to classifying functions, Shavitt (1990) also found support for advertisements containing function-relevant arguments being more persuasive than function-irrelevant ads. That is, people preferred advertisements when the ad content matched the function served by the product, held more favorable attitudes toward brands advertised with the matching strategy, and preferred purchasing brands advertised with an ad when the content matched rather than mismatched the function of the object. Thus, the existing literature is consistent with the functional hypothesis that, all else being equal, messages containing arguments that match functional bases are more persuasive than messages containing contents that mismatch functional bases (see Shavitt, 1989; Snyder & DeBono, 1989, for reviews).

Why Does Matching Produce More Persuasion?

Although the effect of matching message content to the functional basis of a person's attitude has been clear and consistent in past research, the reason why such functional matching effects have been obtained has been less clear. As Lavine and Snyder (1996) noted recently, "the logic of the functional approach's matching hypothesis does not fully address the question of *how* such motivational appeals influence attitudes . . . in fact, the cognitive processes that mediate the functional matching effect are not yet well understood" (p. 581). Based on past work demonstrating that existing cognitive structures can bias the evaluation of message arguments (e.g., Cacioppo, Petty, & Sidera, 1982), Lavine and Snyder (1996) hypothesized that "functional match of a persuasive message should directly influence the recipient's perception of message validity . . . which in turn should influence postmessage attitudes" (p. 583). That is, functional matching of arguments should "bias recipients' evaluations of the persuasiveness of the arguments" and result in the message being "perceived as more persuasive than messages that contain functionally-irrelevant information" (p. 583). In two studies in which high and low self-monitors were presented with messages that either matched or mismatched the presumed functional basis of the attitude, matched messages elicited more favorable thoughts and were rated as more persuasive. That is, low self-monitors seemed motivated to generate favorable thoughts to a message that made an appeal to values, whereas high self-monitors seemed motivated to generate favorable thoughts to a message that made an appeal to image. Of greater interest, valenced thoughts and perceptions of message quality mediated the impact of functional argument matching on post-message attitudes. Thus, this study provided the first mediational evidence consistent with the view that arguments that match the functional basis of one's attitude produce greater attitude change because of biased processing of those arguments.

According to the Elaboration Likelihood Model of persuasion (ELM; Petty & Cacioppo, 1981, 1986), however, this biased processing effect should be most evident when the overall likelihood of message elaboration is high, such as when distractions are low (Petty, Wells, & Brock, 1976), and the message is high in personal relevance (Petty & Cacioppo, 1979; see also Chaiken & Maheswaran, 1994; Petty, Schumann, Richman, & Strathman, 1993). In fact, Lavine and Snyder (1996) noted that in their research, it was likely that "processing motivation was relatively high" (p. 600). On the other hand, according to the ELM, if the overall likelihood of thinking is quite low, functional matching might produce attitude change by a low-effort "peripheral route" even if there is little processing of the substantive merits of the information provided. For example, if the arguments simply seemed to suggest that values were relevant to the advocacy, a low self-monitor might be more inclined to agree than a high self-monitor by reasoning, "if it speaks to my values, it must be good." An analogous heuristic might be used by a high self-monitor to accept a message with arguments using image because the person might reason that "if the product is image related, I should buy it" (cf. Chaiken, 1987). These simple inferences could lead to message acceptance in the absence of thinking about the actual justifications for the value or image assertions contained in the message.

Both the "cue" and "biased processing" explanations for functional matching effects would predict main effects of functional matching. In fact, this is the only effect of functional argument matching that has been observed in the literature. The mechanisms behind the cue and biased processing explanations are different, of course, but the attitudinal outcome is similar. That is, messages that match the underlying basis of the attitude should be more effective than messages that mismatch—either because matching serves as a peripheral cue or because people engage in biased evaluation of functionally matched arguments. It is also possible, however, that past main effects of functional matching could be accounted for by differential processing of matched versus mismatched messages. According to the ELM, if people are unsure how much to process information and the background elaboration likelihood is not constrained to be either very high or low, a persuasion variable such as functional argument match might prompt people to effortfully scrutinize the message. In particular, people might give more careful thought to a message when the content of that message matches the functional basis of their attitudes than when the content mismatches. If past messages in the literature used relatively cogent information to support the attitude object, and content matching enhanced message processing, then people for whom the message matched the functional basis would be more persuaded than people for whom the message mismatched, because they would better recognize the cogency of the arguments presented. According to this analysis, however, if the supporting evidence was specious, then matching would be less effective than mismatching because people for whom the message matched would better recognize the weakness of the arguments. Thus, the enhanced scrutiny hypothesis suggests that functional matches of arguments could either be superior to or inferior to mismatches in producing persuasion, depending on the quality of the information presented in support of the advocated position.

To date, the possibility that functional matching of arguments enhances message scrutiny has not been tested. Nevertheless, some preliminary evidence consistent with this hypothesis has been found. In one study, DeBono and Packer (1991) found that people rated matching messages as more self-relevant than mismatching messages. Considerable prior research suggests that any feature of a message that invokes self-relevance increases information processing activity whether the self-relevance is based on linkage to one's possessions, social groups, or values (see Petty, Cacioppo, & Haugtvedt, 1992; Thomsen, Borgida, & Lavine, 1995, for reviews). In addition, DeBono and Packer (1991) found that low self-monitors made more memory errors regarding image ads (i.e., mismatching ads) than did high self-monitors (matching ads), although no difference was found for quality ads. Observed differences in memory are also consistent with the view that matched messages received greater elaboration than mismatched messages (Craik & Lockhart, 1972, p. 239).

Some indirect evidence for the possibility that arguments that match the function served by one's attitude can elicit greater scrutiny than arguments that mismatch comes from studies that examine functional matching without varying the actual content of the arguments that comprise the message. Although most studies addressing functional theory have varied the functional match of the arguments that comprise the message, some researchers have attempted to vary functional relevance by manipulating nonargument features of the communication such as whether the source of the message is one that appeals to individuals whose attitudes serve different functional bases. In fact, DeBono and colleagues (DeBono & Harnish, 1988; DeBono & Telesca, 1990) have provided strong support for the notion that functionally relevant sources can increase message scrutiny over functionally irrelevant sources even though the messages are not varied to differ in the actual functions they address. The notion is that expert sources provide a better functional match for individuals whose attitudes are based on values and the central merits of things (i.e., low self-monitors) but

that socially attractive sources provide a better functional match for individuals whose attitudes are based on social adjustment concerns (i.e., high self-monitors). This may be because of differential identification with these sources or because these sources might be expected to present different kinds of information (i.e., an expert might be more likely to present value-relevant arguments than an attractive source and an attractive source might be more likely to present image arguments than an expert source). Consistent with the notion that functional source matching increases message scrutiny, DeBono and Harnish (1988) found that attitudes were more dependent on argument quality and that issue-relevant thoughts were more predictive of attitudes when the source matched the presumed functional basis of the attitude than when it mismatched. The enhanced impact of argument quality on attitudes and the higher thought-attitude correlations are indicative of enhanced information processing activity (Petty & Cacioppo, 1986; Wegener, Downing, Krosnick, & Petty, 1995).

In another study varying noncontent features of the messages, DeBono (1987) presented recipients with a message containing both sides of an issue, but told recipients in advance that one position (i.e., the mentally ill should be institutionalized) was consistent with the functional basis of their attitudes. Following exposure to the message, people expressed more agreement with the side that was said to be a functional match. Because this study found that message-relevant thoughts were equally predictive of attitudes regardless of functional match, and these attitude results were replicated in a second study even when no messages were presented to process (i.e., recipients were simply told which side was associated with their function), DeBono concluded that "the pattern of results argues strongly for the notion that attitude change via a functional appeal may best be considered a peripheral process" (p. 284). We concur that this is probably the best interpretation of this research, and thus this research suggests that nonargument functional matching can serve as a peripheral cue when the elaboration likelihood is low either because no arguments are presented (DeBono, 1987, Study 2) or the message topic is a low relevance and/or low knowledge one that is unlikely to elicit much elaboration (e.g., "institutionalization of the mentally ill," DeBono, 1987, Study 1).

Of course, in the studies varying some feature of the communication other than the message arguments, the messages never directly matched or mismatched the functional bases of peoples' attitudes. Because of this, these studies provide no information as to whether message content that matches functional bases (which is the focus of most of the work on functional matches) receives greater thought or not. In addition, the research on source matching, which provides the best evidence for the notion that functional matching can increase information processing, might be subject to an alternative explanation. That is, if people form stronger expectations about what a message will say when the message is presented by someone matching the functional basis of the attitude than a mismatched source, they would be more surprised when the message violates these expectancies (i.e., because the messages at best provide a mix of functionally relevant and irrelevant arguments). Thus, surprise rather than functional matching per se might account for the enhanced information processing activity to functionally matched sources (e.g., Baker & Petty, 1994; Hastie, 1984; Maheswaren & Chaiken, 1991). This speculation should be tested in future research.

The Current Studies

In sum, the previous literature on functional argument matching indicates that matched arguments are more persuasive than nonmatched arguments, and the one mediational study suggests that the mechanism behind this matching effect is biased information processing (Lavine & Snyder, 1996). However, the ELM suggests that functional argument matching effects could result from other mechanisms such as the operation of peripheral cues or enhanced scrutiny of matched messages (Petty & Wegener, 1998).[1] In fact, studies that have examined functional relevance in ways that did not involve manipulating the functional match of the

message arguments themselves have provided support for both the cue (DeBono, 1987) and enhanced scrutiny hypotheses (DeBono & Harnish, 1988; DeBono & Telesca, 1990). Nevertheless, these studies do not address the possibility that matching the actual arguments in the message to the underlying function of one's attitude need not enhance persuasion as hypothesized and found by previous researchers. In particular, if the functionally matched arguments are weak, and receive greater scrutiny, less persuasion should result from functionally matched arguments. This effect has not been reported in the literature previously and, if obtained, would provide a strong counterpoint to the traditional view that functional matching of arguments invariably enhances persuasion.

Thus, in two experiments, we attempted to test the hypothesis that message arguments matching the functional basis of an attitude receive greater scrutiny than message arguments that mismatch the functional basis. We did this by manipulating the strength of the matching versus mismatching information in brief messages about new consumer products. If information that matches functional bases receives greater scrutiny than information that mismatches functional bases, then participants should form more favorable opinions of the products when the products are supported by strong, cogent information rather than weak, specious information to a greater extent when the information matches rather than mismatches functions. If either the cue or biased processing alternatives are operating in this context, however, one would find a main effect of functional match (with matching information leading to more favorable opinions than mismatching information) and no interaction between argument strength and functional match.

In sum, rather than suggesting that arguments that match the function served by one's attitude invariably will be more persuasive than arguments that mismatch, the processing view suggests that, under some circumstances at least, matching arguments are scrutinized more carefully. If information in matched messages is processed more thoroughly than information in mismatched messages, then matches should be more persuasive than mismatches if strong arguments are used (and baseline opinions are not already so favorable that little room is left for enhancement of opinions), but matches should also be less persuasive than mismatches if weak arguments are used.[2]

Argument Pretesting: Method

To create messages that systematically differed in argument strength and functional match for high versus low self-monitors, we pretested arguments adapted in part from prior functional studies (e.g., Snyder and DeBono, 1985) as well as some new ones.

Argument Strength

Strength was assessed using a procedure similar to that described by Petty and Cacioppo (1986). That is, we presented one group of 11 participants with four messages designed to represent each cell of a 2 (argument strength: strong, weak) $\times$ 2 (type of appeal: image, quality) within-participants design. Each of 11 participants received a strong-image, strong-quality, weak-image, and weak-quality message relevant to each of four categories of consumer products. Prior to receipt of the messages, participants were instructed to think carefully about the information about each product and to write down any thoughts that crossed their minds about whether the arguments stated in the messages constituted good reasons to buy and use the product and about whether the product possessed qualities that people wanted from that type of product. This instructed thought induction is used to examine differences in argument strength when task demands require effortful information processing. Thus, this induction should attenuate any natural tendencies for participants to process one type of claim more than others because all participants are instructed to process at a high level.

The different messages on each product shared the same introduction and conclusion, but the middle part of each message varied in the type and strength of the appeal. For example, the four messages for one of the products, shampoo, all began by stating that the shampoo would be available in a wide variety of sizes and concluded by stating that the price of the shampoo was competitive with other brands in that the shampoo sold for almost one-half cent less per ounce than other brands. The four variations of type and strength of appeal for the shampoo ads were as follows:

Strong Image: A brand new shampoo is being introduced whose primary qualities are related to how good it makes your hair look. That is, of people who have used the shampoo in tests of the product, over half of them thought the shampoo made their hair look better than the shampoo they used at home. Also, the shampoo seemed able to make people's hair manageable and attractive for a longer period of time than other shampoos.

Weak Image: A brand new shampoo is being introduced whose primary qualities are related to how good it makes your hair look. That is, of people who have used the shampoo in tests of the product, almost half of them thought the shampoo made their hair look better than the shampoo they used at home. Also, the shampoo seemed able to make people's hair manageable and attractive for some time as long as people did not go outdoors or otherwise mess up their hair following initial styling.

Strong Quality: A brand new shampoo is being introduced whose primary qualities are related to how well it cleans your hair. That is, of people who have used the shampoo in tests of the product, over half of them thought the shampoo cleaned their hair better than the shampoo they used at home. Also, the shampoo seemed able to keep hair clean for a longer period of time than other shampoos.

Weak Quality: A brand new shampoo is being introduced whose primary qualities are related to how well it cleans your hair. That is, of people who have used the shampoo in tests of the product, almost half of them thought the shampoo cleaned their hair better than the shampoo they used at home. Also, the shampoo seemed able to keep hair clean for some time as long as people did not go outdoors or otherwise soil their hair.

On the bottom of each page that contained the short message pertaining to one of the products, 10 double-spaced blank lines were provided on which participants were to record their thoughts. Following the blank lines, participants were asked to report what they thought about the product on three attitude scales anchored at 1 = *bad, negative,* and *harmful,* and 9 = *good, positive,* and *beneficial,* respectively. Messages for the products were presented in one of four orders, with the products always in the same order for each of the four blocks of messages (i.e., four blocks of messages were presented, each with one shampoo message, one coat message, one shoe message, and one toothpaste message) but varying the order of the four strength-by-appeal type combinations. Thus, for one set of participants, the strong image message was first in the first block, second in the second block, third in the third block, and fourth in the fourth block. For another set of participants, the strong image message was fourth in the first block, third in the second block, second in the third block, and first in the fourth block, and so on. The four orders represented a revised Latin square design.

Thoughts were categorized as favorable, unfavorable, or neutral toward the product by two judges unaware of the pretest hypotheses. Judges agreed on 84% of the thoughts listed. Disagreements were resolved by discussion. Finally, participants completed the 25-item self-monitoring scale (Snyder, 1974) and were identified as high or low on that measure by a median split (Median = 48.5).

Type of Argument

In a second pretesting study using the messages just described, 24 people participated in a 2 (argument quality) × 2 (type of appeal) × 4 (product) design with the first two factors constituting between-participants variables and the last factor being a within-participants variable. In this study, all participants were asked to rate messages for each of the four consumer products on a scale designed to assess the functional basis of the message presented. Specifically, participants were asked to "ignore your personal opinion about the merits of the message (i.e., how convincing or unconvincing it is) and indicate the extent to which

you think the message appeals to people concerned about the overall *quality* of the product (1) or the overall *image* of those who use the product (7)." The messages were presented in a different random order for each participant. Because product category had no impact in a preliminary analysis, ratings were averaged across the four products.

Argument Pretesting: Results

Argument Strength

An index of thought favorability was created for each message encountered by each pretest participant by subtracting the number of unfavorable thoughts from the number of favorable thoughts and dividing by the number of total thoughts reported. An attitude index was created by averaging the responses to the three attitude scales for each product and by averaging these responses across the four messages of the same type and strength (Cronbach alphas within combinations of type and strength were between .74 and .86). These indices were each submitted to a 2 (argument strength: strong, weak) × 2 (type of appeal: image, quality) × 2 (self-monitoring: low, high) mixed design analysis of variance (ANOVA). Because order of presentation did not influence the results reported, order was dropped from the analyses.

Results showed that our manipulation of argument strength was effective. That is, strong arguments led to mostly favorable thoughts ($M = .50$) and weak arguments led to mostly unfavorable thoughts ($M = -.33$), and these means were different from each other, $F(1, 9) = 105.3, p < .0001$. In addition, strong arguments led to more favorable attitudes toward the products ($M = 6.64$) than weak arguments ($M = 4.43$), $F(1, 9) = 86.4, p < .0001$. Argument strength × Type of appeal interactions on the attitude, $F(1, 9) = 19.12, p < .002$, and thought $F(1, 9) = 4.59, p < .06$, measures indicated that our manipulation of argument strength tended to be stronger for quality than for image ads. That is, although strong arguments led to more favorable thoughts ($M = .46$) and to more favorable attitudes ($M = 6.36$) than did weak arguments ($M = -.24$ for thoughts and 4.82 for attitudes) for image appeals, the effect was stronger for quality appeals ($Ms =$ .54 versus −.42 for thoughts, and 6.93 versus 4.04 for attitudes).[3]

Thus, although our manipulation of argument strength was successful for both image and quality messages, our manipulation of argument strength was somewhat stronger for quality than for image appeals. Because our primary hypothesis regards the extent to which a given message is differentially processed when that message matches versus mismatches the attitude function, it was not crucial that the argument quality manipulation be equated across type of appeal. In order to put the two manipulations on a common scale for presentation and analyses in the experiments to follow, however, we standardized attitude responses within type of appeal (across self-monitoring and argument strength). Using raw rather than standardized scores does not substantively change the results or conclusions.

Type of Message

Ratings of functional basis were submitted to a 2 (argument strength: strong, weak) × 2 (type of appeal: image, quality) ANOVA. As expected, the only significant result was a main effect for Type of appeal, $F(1, 20) = 38.8$, $p < .001$. Messages that were designed to represent quality were seen as making a quality appeal ($M = 3.4$), whereas messages that were designed to represent image were seen as making an image appeal ($M = 5.6$).

Experiment 1

In our initial experiment, we attempted to test the hypothesis that the quality of the information in a persuasive message would have greater impact if the information content matched, rather than mismatched, the functional base underlying attitudes toward the object. As with much past research (e.g., Snyder & DeBono, 1985), we used a measure of self-monitoring as our method for a priori identification of the likely functions of attitudes. That is, during a prescreening session, we administered

the 25-item self-monitoring measure (Snyder, 1974) using a 5-point response scale anchored at 0 = *not at all characteristic of me* and 4 = *extremely characteristic of me*. Items were scored such that high values corresponded to high levels of self-monitoring. Participants were recruited who had scored either high (score > 56) or low (score < 37) on the resultant measure (roughly from the top and bottom fourths of the distribution of scores in the prescreening session). This should increase the likelihood of obtaining categorization into the proper self-monitoring classification for this categorical individual difference (Gangestad & Snyder, 1985, 1991) and thus increase the likelihood of obtaining effects if they are present.

The basic procedure was as follows. Participants received descriptions of four products (i.e., a shampoo, a shoe, a coat, and a toothpaste). Each product was introduced and described with either strong or weak claims about product quality, or with strong or weak appeals to the image associated with use of the product. On the same page as the information about each product, participants provided their opinions of the product. Messages that matched the hypothesized functional bases of attitudes (i.e., image arguments to high self-monitors and quality arguments to low self-monitors) were classified as matches, and messages that mismatched the hypothesized functional bases of attitudes (i.e., quality arguments to high self-monitors and image arguments to low self-monitors) were classified as mismatches. This allowed us to represent tests of our hypothesis as the two-way interaction between argument strength and functional match.

Method

Participants

Thirty introductory psychology students were recruited to participate in the experiment in partial fulfillment of a class requirement. Participants were identified as either high ($n = 16$) or low ($n = 14$) in self-monitoring based on pretest responses to the version of the 25-item self-monitoring scale (Snyder, 1974) described previously.

Procedure

Participants received written instructions that the experiment concerned situations in which people form opinions based on limited sets of information. Participants were told that they would be given pieces of information about a number of products and that they would be asked to form overall opinions of the products based on the information they would receive. In addition, they were told to assume that characteristics of the products other than those noted in the passages were roughly equal to characteristics of similar items. Participants were given the example that if they were told only that a new car gets outstanding gas mileage, they should assume that other characteristics of the car (such as price and reliability) were basically the same for this car as for other cars in its class.

Next, participants received one message on each of the four products in the study (i.e., the shampoo, coat, shoe, and toothpaste) and reported their attitude toward each product on three scales at the bottom of the page below each message. Attitude reports were given on three 9-point scales anchored at 1 = *bad, useless,* and *harmful,* and 9 = *good, useful,* and *beneficial,* respectively. Products were always presented in the same order (i.e., the shampoo, coat, shoe, and toothpaste), and all four combinations of argument strength and type of appeal were represented across the four products. Participants received one of four orders of the message conditions that corresponded to a revised Latin square for the four combinations of argument strength and type of appeal. Because order of messages did not influence the pattern of results obtained, this factor was dropped from the following analyses.

Results and Discussion

A composite measure of attitude was constructed by summing responses to the three attitude scales and standardizing this composite within the type of appeal (image or quality) as noted previously (Cronbach alphas varied between .90 and .97). Corresponding to the experimental design described previously, the attitude measure was submitted to a $2 \times 2 \times 2$ mixed-design ANOVA. We

expected an interaction between functional match and argument strength, with matching information receiving greater scrutiny than mismatching information. The Match × Argument quality interaction was expected to hold equally for high and low self-monitors resulting in no three-way interaction.

Results showed that our manipulation of argument strength was effective. That is, as in the pretest, strong arguments led to more favorable opinions toward the products ($M = .59$) than weak arguments ($M = -.59$), $F(1, 28) = 63.87, p < .0001$. Consistent with the hypothesis that information matching the functional base of an attitude is naturally considered more extensively than information mismatching the functional base, the argument strength main effect was qualified by the two-way interaction between argument strength and functional match, $F(1, 28) = 4.77, p < .037$ (see Figure 15.1). That is, the effect of argument strength was greater when the message content matched the functional base of product attitudes (i.e., when image messages were presented to high self-monitors or quality messages were presented to low self-monitors) than when the message content mismatched the functional base of product attitudes (i.e., when quality messages were presented to high self-monitors or image messages were presented to low self-monitors). The Functional match × Argument strength interaction did not differ

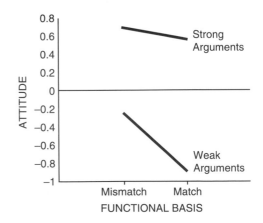

FIGURE 15.1 ■ Post-message attitudes as a function of argument strength and match of message content to functional basis of attitudes (Experiment 1).

across levels of self-monitoring ($p > .19$, for the three-way interaction).[4] Because the weak arguments were especially ineffective in persuading people when the message matched the function underlying the attitude, there was also a main effect of functional match such that matches ($M = -.19$) were *less* effective than mismatches ($M = .19$), $F(1, 28) = 7.93, p < .01$.

The results of Experiment 1 are consistent with the proposition that information matching the functional base underlying an attitude receives greater consideration than information mismatching the functional base. There was no support for the proposition that functional matches are simply more persuasive than functional mismatches regardless of the cogency of the supporting information presented. In fact, when the evidence is weak, content that matched the functional basis of attitudes was less persuasive than content that mismatched the functional basis. Thus, based on our first experiment, we can tentatively conclude that, all else being equal, matches per se are not necessarily more persuasive than mismatches.

If differential effectiveness of matching versus mismatching information is dependent upon the amount of processing given to matches versus mismatches (e.g., rather than differential weighting of information that was processed to the same extent), then this suggests some natural limiting conditions to this effect. For instance, if information matching the functional base of the attitude brings about greater processing than information mismatching the functional base (perhaps because it is viewed as more important or self-relevant as found by DeBono & Packer, 1991), then one should be especially likely to find differences in the impact of argument strength when the background likelihood of effortful scrutiny of information is moderate rather than very high or low. That is, matching should enhance information processing mostly when people are not already so highly motivated to engage in extensive scrutiny of the information that thinking cannot be enhanced further, nor so constrained from processing or so disinterested in the topic that motivation from functional matching alone is insufficient to enhance processing. For example, in our argument

pretesting, all participants were motivated to think by the task instructions and thus function matching would not be expected to (and did not) enhance information processing further. However, other factors that enhance the likelihood of thinking should also reduce the impact of functional matches on information processing. For example, if people are highly likely to scrutinize incoming information because of its high personal relevance (Petty & Cacioppo, 1979) or because they are high in their "need for cognition" (Cacioppo & Petty, 1982), then the functional match of the information would be less likely to enhance processing over a functional mismatch.

Therefore, to provide a replication of the results of our first experiment and to extend these findings by demonstrating one of the limiting conditions suggested by the hypothesized differences-in-processing view, we conducted a study in which functional matches and mismatches that varied in argument strength were presented to people who differed in both their self-monitoring and need for cognition tendencies.

Experiment 2

As noted above, if functional argument matches bring about greater processing of the arguments than functional mismatches, this should occur most strongly when some enhancement of processing is possible and least strongly when the likelihood of scrutiny is already high due to other factors. As just noted, one way of controlling the baseline level of processing is through classification of individuals as high versus low in need for cognition. The need for cognition scale provides an individual difference measure of the motivation to think about incoming information (Cacioppo & Petty, 1982), and the available research indicates that it provides a useful indicator of cognitive motivation in a wide variety of situations (see Cacioppo, Petty, Feinstein, & Jarvis, 1996, for a comprehensive review). Thus, according to the hypotheses noted above, functional matching of information should be least likely to enhance message processing for people who are high in their need for cognition because these individuals are already likely to be operating with a baseline level of message scrutiny that is quite high. In contrast, people low in need for cognition who are equally able to process messages as those high in need for cognition tend to avoid effortful processing of information and have been found to scrutinize the merits of persuasive appeals primarily when there is some special incentive to do so. For example, in one study (Priester & Petty, 1995), individuals low in need for cognition considered the merits of the arguments in a persuasive message when the source was described as untrustworthy, but not when the source was trustworthy. Individuals high in need for cognition processed the message extensively regardless of source trustworthiness. In another study (Smith & Petty, 1996), low need for cognition individuals processed the message arguments when the message was framed in a manner that was unexpected, but did not engage in careful scrutiny when the message framing was not surprising. High need for cognition individuals thought about the arguments to the same extent regardless of expectancies. In short, people high in need for cognition have tended to process message information regardless of the situational incentives to do so, whereas people low in need for cognition have required some special motivational incentive to undertake the cognitive work necessary to carefully evaluate the message arguments.[5]

If matching arguments to the basis of one's attitudes provides a motivational incentive to process, then low need for cognition individuals should be especially likely to scrutinize the message when the information matches the basis of their attitudes. High need for cognition individuals are expected to process the message regardless of its functional match. Therefore, functional match or mismatch of information should make less difference in information processing for individuals high in need for cognition.

To examine this implication of our enhanced processing account of functional matches, our second study followed the same design as Experiment 1 but added a need for cognition factor. Accordingly, we recruited people to participate in the study that fell into one of the four cells created by combining high versus low levels of need for cognition and high versus low levels of self-monitoring. We expected that the results of Experiment I would be replicated for people low in need for cognition (i.e., a Functional match × Argument quality interaction would be obtained), but we expected only a main effect of argument strength for people high in need for cognition. The attenuation of the matching effect for high need for cognition individuals should produce a three-way interaction overall (i.e., Need for cognition × Functional match × Argument quality). That is, functional matching should enhance consideration of argument quality for low but not high need for cognition individuals.

Method

Participants

Sixty-two undergraduate students were recruited to participate in the experiment for extra class credit. Participants were identified as either high (score > 45) or low (score < 42) in self-monitoring based on responses to the 13-item Lennox-Wolfe self-monitoring scale (Lennox & Wolfe, 1984), and as either high (score > 69) or low (score < 60) in need for cognition based on responses to the short (18-item) need for cognition scale (Cacioppo, Petty, & Kao, 1984). Both of these measures were available from a prescreening session.[6] Cell sizes for each of the combinations of self-monitoring and need for cognition were all between 12 and 18.

Procedure

The procedure and materials for the experiment were identical to those used in Experiment 1, with one exception. The materials for this experiment were embedded in a larger study that included an attitude survey on a variety of topics unrelated to the subject matter of the current experiment (e.g., participants provided their opinions on such issues as building nuclear power plants or changing lighting over to halogen bulbs).

Results and Discussion

As in Experiment 1, the attitude scales were summed to create a composite measure, and that measure was standardized within type of appeal (Cronbach alphas varied between .88 and .94). The resultant attitude measure was submitted to a 2 (functional match: match, mismatch) × 2 (argument strength: strong, weak) × 2 (self-monitoring: low, high) × 2 (need for cognition: low, high) mixed-design ANOVA with need for cognition and self-monitoring as between-participants factors and functional match and argument strength as within-participants factors.

Results showed that our manipulation of argument strength was again effective. Strong arguments led to more favorable opinions toward the products ($M = .59$) than weak arguments ($M = -.59$), $F(1, 58) = 62.29$, $p < .0001$. Of greater importance, this main effect of argument strength was qualified by the predicted three-way interaction between need for cognition, functional match, and argument strength, $F(1, 58) = 3.95$, $p < .05$. For participants low in need for cognition, the predicted interaction between functional match and argument quality was obtained, $F(1, 28) = 4.01$, $p < .05$ (see Figure 15.2). That is, consistent with the hypothesis that information matching the functional base of an attitude is processed more extensively than information mismatching the

functional base (at least when the baseline level of processing is not constrained to be low by inability to process or high because of other individual or situational factors), the effect of argument strength was greater when the message matched the functional base of product attitudes than when the message mismatched the functional base. The Functional match × Argument strength interaction did not differ across levels of self-monitoring ($p > .29$ for the three-way interaction) for people low in need for cognition.

In contrast, the only significant effect for individuals high in need for cognition was the main effect of argument strength, $F(1, 30) = 25.13$, $p < .0001$, such that strong arguments ($M = .31$) led to more favorable opinions of the products than weak arguments ($M = -.39$). There was no Match × Argument strength interaction, $p > .3$, for high need for cognition individuals.[7]

Thus, the results of Experiment 2 replicate the Functional match × Argument strength interaction found in Experiment 1 under conditions where ability to process was high but the baseline level of motivation to process was low enough to be enhanced by the functional match of the information. As predicted by the differential processing view, this enhancement of the argument strength effect did not occur when the baseline level of processing was already high. These results are consistent with the proposition that some past results favoring matching over mismatching of message content to attitude functions could have been obtained because strong arguments were used in the communications and the matching of message arguments to attitude functions led to enhanced message scrutiny over mismatching. It is important to note that when weak arguments were used, matching message content to the function served by the attitude is actually less effective than mismatching. Thus, Experiment 2 provides additional evidence that matching message arguments to attitude functions per se is not necessarily more effective than mismatching arguments, and our research provides some insight into one mechanism by which this occurs. That is, people scrutinize more carefully information in a message that matches the functional basis of their

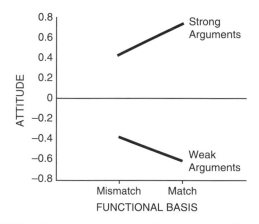

FIGURE 15.2 ■ Post-message attitudes as a function of argument strength and match of message content to functional basis of attitudes for individuals low in need for cognition (Experiment 2).

attitudes than informational content that does not match.

General Discussion

Whereas past studies have investigated whether the functional match of introductions to messages (e.g., DeBono, 1987) or sources that present messages (e.g., DeBono & Harnish, 1988; DeBono & Telesca, 1990) influence the processing of information in the messages, previous work has not examined whether matches of the substantive message content to the functional basis of one's attitude influence the extent of information processing (see Footnote 1). In fact, most functional theorists have assumed either explicitly or implicitly that matching of functional content to attitudinal basis should induce greater persuasion (e.g., see Clary et al., 1994; Snyder & DeBono, 1989; Shavitt, 1990) and that this effect is due to biased processing of the functionally matched message arguments (Lavine & Snyder, 1996). The current studies suggest that this is not invariably the case and, in fact, mismatching content to functional bases can be a superior strategy if the only available arguments are relatively weak and easy to counterargue. The current research also indicated why these matching versus mismatching effects might occur. Namely, these results are due to the fact that recipients can sometimes engage in greater scrutiny of content that matches the functional basis of their attitudes than content that does not match.

The view that matching persuasive messages to the functional bases of attitudes can increase the scrutiny the information receives might not only be useful for organizing past work on functional attitude change, but might also be used to organize work on changing attitudes with bases other than functional needs. For instance, research on the cognitive versus affective bases of attitudes has generally addressed the question of whether a message that is matched or mismatched to the base of the attitude is a more effective method of changing the attitude (e.g., Edwards, 1990; Millar & Millar, 1990). However, in contrast to the consistent prior findings that functional content matches produce

greater persuasion than mismatches (e.g., Shavitt, 1990; Snyder & DeBono, 1985), the work on affective versus cognitive bases of attitudes has not been so consistent. For example, Edwards (1990) found matching arguments to attitude bases was better than mismatching (e.g., an affective persuasion appeal was better than a cognitive persuasion appeal when the attitude under attack had an affective basis), but Millar and Millar (1990) found mismatches to be more effective. Although these researchers have arrived at seemingly opposite conclusions, their results can be made coherent by applying the framework from the current studies. In order to do so, one need only consider the implications of the differential processing perspective for the persuasiveness of the arguments used by Edwards (1990) and Millar and Millar (1990).

Edwards (1990) used attitude objects that were previously unfamiliar to research participants and arguments that appear difficult to counterargue (i.e., relatively strong information such as an aversive smell associated with a new beverage). In contrast, Millar and Millar (1990) used attitude objects familiar to participants and arguments that were relatively easy to counterargue (i.e., relatively weak information such as telling participants that a majority of other people liked a beverage that they disliked because the beverage made those people feel refreshed). Millar and Millar (1990) found that their counterattitudinal arguments were extensively counterargued, especially when the arguments attacked the basis of the attitude. Thus, if one assumes that the arguments in the Edwards (1990) studies were stronger than those in the Millar and Millar (1990) studies, then increased scrutiny of information that matched the attitudinal base could lead precisely to the results obtained by those researchers.

In general, our perspective suggests that a message that matches the basis of an attitude will receive greater scrutiny than one that mismatches (assuming that the elaboration likelihood is not constrained to be very high or very low; Petty, Gleicher & Baker, 1991; Petty & Wegener, 1998). Thus, the quality or cogency of the matched information—whether matched to a functional basis or an affective/cognitive basis—becomes critical in determining whether it would be more effective to match or mismatch the basis of the attitude. That is, if the matched arguments are strong and compelling, matching is more effective than mismatching because the strengths of the arguments will be especially appreciated. However, if the matched arguments are weak, mismatching is likely to be more effective than matching because the weaknesses of the matched arguments will be especially apparent. Future work should examine the limits of this effect by explicitly varying the overall elaboration likelihood to be very high or very low. Thus, although we observed the enhanced processing effects expected when the elaboration likelihood was not constrained to be very high or low, we did not observe any evidence for biased processing of functionally matched messages for high need for cognition individuals. Thus, it is unclear if our levels of processing were insufficiently high compared to the Lavine and Snyder (1996) research to observe biased processing (e.g., due to the reduced importance of our attitude issue—mundane consumer products—compared to theirs—an impending national election), whether our messages were not sufficiently ambiguous to observe biased processing (Chaiken & Maheswaran, 1994), or whether the Lavine and Snyder (1996) finding that matching was more effective than mismatching can be attributed to the fact that they only presented strong arguments and matching enhanced the extent of processing of these arguments (rather than biasing processing). Future work will have to determine the extent to which the functional matching of arguments works in only one way or in multiple ways under different elaboration likelihood conditions. Based on the current studies, at least, it is clear that functional matching of arguments can influence attitudes by influencing the extent of scrutiny given to the message and that, contrary to prior assumptions, functional matching of arguments need not increase persuasion.

Future work should also investigate the similarities between properties found for hypothesized functional bases of attitudes and other potential bases of attitudes (e.g., affective versus cognitive). To the extent that commonalities can be found, one might discover that phenomena related to attitudinal bases are more general than have been acknowledged in past work. That is, forming an attitude based on information that matches one's functional predispositions may imbue the attitude with properties very similar to those for attitudes based primarily on some other type of information (e.g., feelings associated with the object). If this is the case, then manipulations found to influence the properties of affective versus cognitive attitudes (e.g., focus manipulations meant to make one category of information more salient than the other and thus influence prediction of behavior by the attitude, see Millar & Tesser, 1986, Wilson, Dunn, Kraft, & Lisle, 1989) might also be found to influence attitudes based on specific attitude functions. For instance, one might find that focusing a respondent on a function other than that on which the attitude is based might undermine the prediction of later behavior from the reported attitude.

Alternatively, one might conceptualize bases of attitudes in terms of a hierarchy, with some categories of bases subdividing other superordinate categories. For instance, all of the arguments used in the current research might be considered cognitive. Thus, although past researchers have found differences in the effectiveness of persuasive information that matches versus mismatches the general category of affect or cognition (e.g., Edwards, 1990; Millar & Millar, 1990), we have also found differences in the scrutiny of (and thus effectiveness of) information that matched versus mismatched the functional basis of the attitude, even though all of the information provided fits the cognitive category. Future work will be needed in order to delineate which categories create meaningful differences in information processing and persuasion under which conditions. For instance, one might imagine that attitudes toward some classes of objects or for some people might naturally be organized along the affective/cognitive dimension, whereas other classes of objects or people might lead to attitudes organized along the functional dimensions.

Much work is left to be done regarding the role of functional bases of attitudes in the attitude change process. Thanks to recent advances in methods for a priori identification of attitudinal bases (Herek, 1987; Shavitt, 1990; Snyder & DeBono, 1985, 1989), the tools needed to make additional progress in this research domain are available. We believe that manipulations of the argument strength of matched versus mismatched persuasive information along with manipulations of baseline levels of elaboration likelihood could provide critical information regarding the processes underlying functional effects on attitude change processes.

NOTES

1. Lavine and Snyder (1996) examined the possibility that their functional matching result was produced because matching enhanced message scrutiny rather than biasing scrutiny, but concluded that it did not. This conclusion was based on the finding that functional matching of arguments enhanced persuasion even when the mere number of issue-relevant thoughts people generated was controlled. That is, when presumably controlling for the extent of processing of functionally matched messages, matching still led to greater persuasion. Their analysis assumes, of course, that the number of thoughts listed is a good indicator of the extent of processing. Petty and Cacioppo (1986), however, have noted that a number of studies suggest that extent of processing can be varied in the absence of any difference in the mere number of thoughts listed. In brief, this is because a nonthoughtful person might report six thoughts that reflect his or her a priori assessment of the issue (e.g., three negative thoughts and three favorable thoughts that reflect little message elaboration), whereas a thoughtful person would be more likely to report thoughts that reflect the quality of the arguments presented in the message (e.g., a strong message might elicit four favorable and two unfavorable thoughts, whereas a weak message might elicit four unfavorable and two favorable thoughts). Thus, the profile rather than the number of thoughts listed could reflect the extent of message scrutiny. If so, then the analysis by Lavine and Snyder does not rule out the possibility that they obtained greater persuasion for functionally matched messages because the matching elicited greater scrutiny of the strong arguments they presented.

2. As noted already, the ELM suggests that each of the explanations (i.e., cue effect, biased elaboration, enhanced elaboration) could account for functional matching effects under different baseline levels of thinking (see Petty & Cacioppo, 1986). We focus here on the enhanced elaboration hypothesis in that it is the one that can accommodate the heretofore unobtained result that matching arguments to functions can actually reduce persuasion. In addition, because prior work on functional matching of arguments has never manipulated the elaboration likelihood to render it especially high or low, the elaboration conditions

characterizing most past research might best be described as moderate. In any case, the current research examines the impact of functional matches when the elaboration likelihood is not constrained to be very high or low.

3. There was also an unexpected Self-monitoring × Argument strength interaction on both thoughts, $F(1, 9) = 5.79$, $p < .04$, and attitudes, $F(1, 9) = 4.85$, $p < .06$, such that low self-monitors were more affected by the argument quality difference than high self-monitors (although both groups were significantly affected by the argument quality manipulation). This effect does not occur in either of the reported studies, however, each of which is based on larger samples.

4. The Functional match × Argument strength interaction in our analysis is identical to a three-way interaction of type of appeal (quality/image), self-monitoring (low/high), and argument strength (weak/strong), $F(1, 28) = 4.77$, $p < .037$. That is, within each type of appeal, the self-monitoring group for which the message matched the function scrutinized that information more (was more persuaded by strong than weak arguments) than the group for which the information mismatched the function.

5. Our assumption is that the low need for cognition participants in our sample constitute a relatively moderate elaboration likelihood group. This is because elaboration likelihood depends on both motivational and ability factors and the ability of our low need for cognition participants to engage in message scrutiny in this setting is high (i.e., very simple message, no distractions, etc.). In any case, the low need for cognition students in this study were not constrained to remain low in thought (i.e., increases in motivation to scrutinize information could lead to increases in thought).

6. Because the prescreening battery included a large number of inventories (and was designed to accommodate the needs of various researchers), the 13-item Lennox and Wolfe (1984) version of the self-monitoring scale was selected instead of the 25-item Snyder (1974) scale (largely because it contained fewer items). Like the Snyder (1974) scale, however, respondents scoring high are expected to change their behaviors in order to present themselves in a positive manner to others, whereas respondents who score low are expected to act more in accordance with internal cues. Because researchers using this scale have found that high scorers attend more to situational cues, whereas low scorers attend more to internal cues to guide their behavior (e.g., Anderson & Tolson, 1989), high versus low self-monitors on this measure should roughly approximate the social-adjustive versus value-expressive functions that have been hypothesized for high and low scorers on the Snyder (1974) scale. In addition, in samples of respondents from the same participant pool as those in this experiment, scores on the Lennox-Wolfe (1984) and Snyder (1974) scales have been significantly correlated over a 5- to 7-week delay between administration of the scales ($r = .5$; $p < .0001$).

7. As in Experiment 1, classifying functional matches versus mismatches makes the test statistic for the three-way interaction presented identical to that of a four-way Need for cognition (low/high) × Type of appeal (image/quality) × Self-monitoring (low/high) × Argument strength (weak/strong) interaction, $F(1, 58) = 3.95, p < .05$. That is, within each type of appeal, the interaction from Experiment 1 was replicated for people low in need for cognition, but only a main effect of argument strength was found for people high in need for cognition such that strong arguments produced more favorable attitudes than weak ones.

REFERENCES

Abelson, R. P., & Prentice, D. A. (1989). Beliefs as possessions: A functional perspective. In A. R. Pratkanis, S. J. Breckler, & A. G. Greenwald (Eds.), *Attitude structure and function* (pp. 361–381). Hillsdale, NJ: Lawrence Erlbaum.

Anderson, L., & Tolson, J. (1989). Group members' self-monitoring as a possible neutralizer of leadership. *Small Group Behavior, 20,* 24–36.

Baker, S. M., & Petty, R. E. (1994). Majority and minority influence: Source-position imbalance as a determinant of message scrutiny. *Journal of Personality and Social Psychology, 67,* 5–19.

Cacioppo, J. T., & Petty, R. E. (1982). The need for cognition. *Journal of Personality and Social Psychology, 42,* 116–131.

Cacioppo, J. T., Petty, R. E., Feinstein, J., & Jarvis, W. B. G. (1996). Dispositional differences in cognitive motivation: The life and times of individuals varying in need for cognition. *Psychological Bulletin, 119,* 197–253.

Cacioppo, J. T., Petty, R. E., & Kao, C. (1984). The efficient assessment of need for cognition. *Journal of Personality Assessment, 48,* 306–307.

Cacioppo, J. T., Petty, R. E., & Sidera, J. (1982). The effects of salient self-schema on the evaluation of proattitudinal editorials: Top-down versus bottom-up message processing. *Journal of Experimental Social Psychology, 18,* 324–338.

Chaiken, S. (1987). The heuristic model of persuasion. In M. P. Zanna, J. M. Olson, & C. P. Herman (Eds.), *Social influence: The Ontario symposium* (Vol. 5, pp. 3–39). Hillsdale, NJ: Lawrence Erlbaum.

Chaiken, S., & Maheswaran, D. (1994). Heuristic processing can bias systematic processing: Effects of source credibility, argument ambiguity, and task importance on attitude judgment. *Journal of Personality and Social Psychology, 66,* 460–473.

Clary, E. G., Snyder, M., Ridge, R., Miene, P. K., & Haugen, J.A. (1994). Matching messages to motives in persuasion: A functional approach to promoting volunteerism. *Journal of Applied Social Psychology, 24,* 1129–1149.

Craik, F. I. M., & Lockhart, R. S. (1972). Levels of processing: A framework for memory research. *Journal of Verbal Learning and Verbal Behavior, 11,* 671–684.

DeBono, K. G. (1987). Investigating the social-adjustive and value-expressive functions of attitudes: Implications for persuasion processes. *Journal of Personality and Social Psychology, 52,* 279–287.

DeBono, K. G., & Harnish, R. J. (1988). Source expertise, source attractiveness, and the processing of persuasive information: A functional approach. *Journal of Personality and Social Psychology, 55,* 541–546.

DeBono, K. G., & Packer, M. (1991). The effects of advertising appeal on perceptions of product quality. *Personality and Social Psychology Bulletin, 17,* 194–200.

DeBono, K. G., & Rubin, K. (1995). Country of origin and perceptions of product quality: An individual difference perspective. *Basic and Applied Social Psychology, 17,* 239–247.

DeBono, K. G., & Telesca, C. (1990). The influence of source physical attractiveness on advertising effectiveness: A functional perspective. *Journal of Applied Social Psychology, 20,* 1383–1395.

Edwards, K. (1990). The interplay of affect and cognition in attitude formation and change. *Journal of Personality and Social Psychology, 59,* 202–216.

Gangestad, S. W., & Snyder, M. (1985). To carve nature at its joints: On the existence of discrete classes in personality. *Psychological Review, 92,* 317–349.

Gangestad, S. W., & Snyder, M. (1991). Taxonomic analysis redux: Some statistical considerations for testing a latent class model. *Journal of Personality and Social Psychology, 61,* 141–146.

Hastic, R. (1984). Causes and effects of causal attribution. *Journal of Personality and Social Psychology, 46,* 44–56.

Herek, G. M. (1987). Can functions be measured? A new perspective on the functional approach to attitudes. *Social Psychology Quarterly, 50,* 285–303.

Katz, D. (1960). The functional approach to the study of attitudes. *Public Opinion Quarterly, 24,* 163–204.

Katz, D., McClintock, C., & Sarnoff, D. (1957). The measurement of ego defense as related to attitude change. *Journal of Personality, 25,* 465–474.

Kiesler, C. A., Collins, B. E., & Miller, N. (1969). *Attitude change: A critical analysis of theoretical applications.* New York: John Wiley.

Lavine, H., & Snyder, M. (1996). Cognitive processing and the functional matching effect in persuasion: The mediating role of subjective perceptions of message quality. *Journal of Experimental Social Psychology, 32,* 580–604.

Lennox, R. D., & Wolfe, R. N. (1984). Revision of the self-monitoring scale. *Journal of Personality and Social Psychology, 46,* 1349–1364.

Maheswaren, D., & Chaiken, S. (1991). Promoting systematic processing in low-motivation settings: Effect of incongruent information on processing and judgment. *Journal of Personality and Social Psychology, 61,* 13–33.

Millar, M. G., & Millar, K. U. (1990). Attitude change as a function of attitude type and argument type. *Journal of Personality and Social Psychology, 59,* 217–228.

Millar, M. G., & Tesser, A. (1986). Effects of affective and cognitive focus on the attitude-behavior relation. *Journal of Personality and Social Psychology, 51,* 270–276.

Petty, R. E., & Cacioppo, J. T. (1979). Issue-involvement can increase or decrease persuasion by enhancing message-relevant cognitive responses. *Journal of Personality and Social Psychology, 37,* 1915–1926.

Petty, R. E., & Cacioppo, J. T. (1981). *Attitudes and persuasion: Classic and contemporary approaches.* Dubuque, IA: Wm. C. Brown.

Petty, R. E., & Cacioppo, J. T. (1986). The elaboration likelihood model of persuasion. In L. Berkowitz (Ed.), *Advances in Experimental Social Psychology* (Vol. 19, pp. 124–205). New York: Academic Press.

Petty, R. E., Cacioppo, J. T., & Haugtvedt, C. (1992). Involvement and persuasion: An appreciative look at the Sherifs' contribution to the study of self-relevance and attitude change. In D. Granberg & G. Sarup (Eds.), *Social judgment and intergroup relations: Essays in honor of Muzafer Sherif* (pp. 147–174). New York: Springer/Verlag.

Petty, R. E., Gleicher, F., & Baker, S. (1991). Multiple roles for affect in persuasion. In J. Forgas (Ed.), *Emotion and social judgments* (pp. 181–200). Oxford: Pergamon.

Petty, R. E., Schumann, D. W., Richman, S. A., & Strathman, A. J. (1993). Positive mood and persuasion: Different roles for affect under high and low elaboration conditions. *Journal of Personality and Social Psychology, 64,* 5–20.

Petty, R. E., & Wegener, D. T. (1998). Attitude change. In D. Gilbert, S. Fiske, & G. Lindzey (Eds.), *Handbook of social psychology* (4th ed., Vol. 1, pp. 323–390). New York: McGraw Hill.

Petty, R. E., Wells, G. L., & Brock, T. C. (1976). Distraction can enhance or reduce yielding to propaganda: Thought disruption versus effort justification. *Journal of Personality and Social Psychology, 34,* 874–884.

Prentice, D. A. (1987). Psychological correspondence of possessions, attitudes, and values. *Journal of Personality and Social Psychology, 53,* 993–1003.

Priester, J. M., & Petty, R. E. (1995). Source attributions and persuasion: Perceived honesty as a determinant of message scrutiny. *Personality and Social Psychology Bulletin, 21,* 637–654.

Shavitt, S. (1989). Operationalizing functional theories of attitude. In A. R. Pratkanis, S. J. Breckler, & A. G. Greenwald (Eds.), *Attitude structure and function* (pp. 311–338). Hillsdale, NJ: Lawrence Erlbaum.

Shavitt, S. (1990). The role of attitude objects in attitude functions. *Journal of Experimental Social Psychology, 26,* 124–148.

Smith, M. B., Bruner, J. S., & White, R. W. (1956). *Opinions and personality.* New York: John Wiley.

Smith, S. M., & Petty, R. E. (1996). Message framing and persuasion: A message processing analysis. *Personality and Social Psychology Bulletin, 22,* 257–268.

Synder, M. (1974). The self-monitoring of expressive behavior. *Journal of Personality and Social Psychology, 30,* 526–537.

Snyder, M., & DeBono, K. G. (1985). Appeals to image and claims about quality: Understanding the psychology of advertising. *Journal of Personality and Social Psychology, 49,* 586–597.

Snyder, M., & DeBono, K. G. (1989). Understanding the functions of attitudes: Lessons from personality and social behavior. In A. R. Pratkanis, S. J. Breckler, & A. G. Greenwald (Eds.), *Attitude structure and function* (pp. 361–381). Hillsdale, NJ: Lawrence Erlbaum.

Thomsen, C. J., Borgida, E., & Lavine, H. (1995). The causes and consequences of personal involvement. In R. E. Petty & J. A. Krosnick (Eds.), *Attitude strength: Antecedents and consequences* (pp. 191–214). Mahwah, NJ: Lawrence Erlbaum.

Wegener, D. T., Downing, J., Krosnick, J. A., & Petty, R. E. (1995). Strength-related properties of attitudes: Measures, manipulations, and future directions. In R. E. Petty & J. A. Krosnick (Eds.), *Attitude strength: Antecedents and consequences* (pp. 455–487). Mahwah, NJ: Lawrence Erlbaum.

Wilson, T. D., Dunn, D. S., Kraft, D., & Lisle, D. J. (1989). Introspection, attitude change, and attitude-behavior consistency: The disruptive effects of explaining why we feel the way we do. In L. Berkowitz (Ed.), *Advances in experimental social psychology* (Vol. 22, pp. 287–343). San Diego, CA: Academic Press.

Received August 30, 1995
Revision accepted February 7, 1997 ■

READING 16

Prejudice as Self-Image Maintenance: Affirming the Self through Derogating Others

Steven Fein and Steven J. Spencer

The authors argue that self-image maintenance processes play an important role in stereotyping and prejudice. Three studies demonstrated that when individuals evaluated a member of a stereotyped group, they were less likely to evaluate that person negatively if their self-images had been bolstered through a self-affirmation procedure, and they were more likely to evaluate that person stereotypically if their self-images had been threatened by negative feedback. Moreover, among those individuals whose self-image had been threatened, derogating a stereotyped target mediated an increase in their self-esteem. The authors suggest that stereotyping and prejudice may be a common means to maintain one's self-image, and they discuss the role of self-image-maintenance processes in the context of motivational, sociocultural, and cognitive approaches to stereotyping and prejudice.

A most striking testament to the social nature of the human psyche is the extent to which the self-concept—that which is the very essence of one's individuality—is integrally linked with interpersonal dynamics. Since the earliest days of the formal discipline of psychology, the significant influences of a number of social factors on the self-concept have been recognized. A central focus of sociocultural and social-cognitive approaches to psychology has concerned the ways in which individuals' self-concepts are defined and refined by the people around them. This is evident in early discussions of the social nature of individuals' self-concepts (Cooley, 1902; Mead, 1934) and of social

Steven Fein, Department of Psychology, Williams College; Steven J. Spencer, Department of Psychology, Hope College. Steven J. Spencer is now at Department of Psychology, University of Waterloo, Waterloo, Ontario, Canada.

Correspondence concerning this article should be addressed to Steven Fein, Department of Psychology, Bronfman Science Center, Williams College, Williamstown, Massachusetts 01267, or to Steven J. Spencer, Department of Psychology, University of Waterloo, Waterloo, Ontario N2L 3G1, Canada. Electronic mail may be sent via the Internet to steven.fein@williams.edu.

comparison theory (Festinger, 1954), and it continues to be evident in more recent work, such as that concerning self-fulfilling prophecies (e.g., Eccles, Jacobs, & Harold, 1990; Rosenthal & Jacobson, 1968; Snyder, 1984) and cultural influences (Abrams, 1994; Cameron & Lalonde, 1994; Cohen & Nisbett, 1994; H. R. Markus & Kitayama, 1991, 1994; Triandis, 1989; Turner, Oakes, Haslam, & McGarty, 1994).

The converse focus—the self-concept's influence on perceptions of and reactions toward others—has been recognized more fully within the last two decades, through, for example, research on self-schemas (H. Markus, 1977; H. Markus & Wurf, 1987), self-verification (Swann, Stein-Seroussi, & Giesler, 1992), self-discrepancies (Higgins, 1996; Higgins & Tykocinski, 1992), and a host of self-serving biases in individuals' perceptions, judgments, and memories involving the self (e.g., Ditto & Lopez, 1992; Greenwald, 1980; Klein & Kunda, 1992, 1993; Nisbett & Ross, 1980; Ross & Sicoly, 1979; Schlenker, Weigold, & Hallam, 1990).

Particularly within the past decade, research has converged on the role of self-image- and self-esteem-maintenance processes in people's perceptions and reactions regarding others. These approaches, whose roots can be seen in the earlier work of James, Festinger, Heider, Sherif, Tajfel, and others, include research on downward social comparison (Brown, Collins, & Schmidt, 1988; Brown & Gallagher, 1992; Gibbons & Gerrard, 1991; Gibbons & McCoy, 1991; Taylor & Lobel, 1989; Wills, 1981, 1991; Wood & Taylor, 1991), self-evaluation maintenance (Tesser, 1988; Tesser & Cornell, 1991), social identity (Abrams & Hogg, 1988; Brewer, 1993; Crocker, Thompson, McGraw, & Ingerman, 1987; Hogg & Abrams, 1988; Smith, 1993; Turner, 1982), terror management (Greenberg et al., 1992), and self-affirmation (Liu & Steele, 1986; Steele, 1988; Steele & Liu, 1983).

This article examines the role of self-image-maintenance processes in a particular set of reactions and perceptions: those concerning prejudice and negative evaluations of others. More specifically, we examine the thesis that many manifest-ations of prejudice stem, in part, from the motivation to maintain a feeling of self-worth and self-integrity. That is, self-image threat may lead people to engage in prejudiced evaluations of others. These negative evaluations can, and often do, make people feel better about themselves. Prejudice, therefore, can be self-affirming. By using available stereotypes to justify and act on prejudices, individuals may be able to reclaim for themselves a feeling of mastery and self-worth, often saving themselves from having to confront the real sources of self-image threat.

Several self-image-maintenance processes are described or implied in the existing literature, but the research reported in this article focuses on one in particular: self-affirmation. Steele and his colleagues (e.g., Steele, Spencer, & Lynch, 1993) have argued that people seek to maintain "an image of self-integrity, that is, overall moral and adaptive adequacy" (p. 885). If an individual experiences a threat to this image, he or she attempts to restore this image by reevaluating and reinterpreting experiences and events in ways that reaffirm the self's integrity and value. Supported by research on self-affirmation effects in cognitive dissonance, Steele et al. (1993) argued that when facing a potential threat, even an important one, people have "the option of leaving the threat unrationalized—that is, accepting the threat without countering it or its implications—and affirming some other important aspect of the self that reinforces one's overall self-adequacy" (p. 885).

We argue that prejudice often serves a self-affirming function for individuals, and providing people with other means of self-affirmation should reduce their desire to make prejudiced evaluations. The link between self-image threats and the use of prejudice should be weakened by providing people with the opportunity to self-affirm, that is, by providing them with information that restores their positive sense of self-integrity. This approach is distinct from many of the classic approaches to stereotyping and prejudice, such as frustration–aggression theory and scapegoating (Dollard, Doob, Miller, Mowrer, & Sears, 1939; Miller & Bugelski, 1948), social identity theory (Tajfel, 1982), and downward social comparison theory

(Wills, 1981). We argue that this process of self-affirmation should reduce the desire to make prejudiced evaluations even though it does not release pent-up anger or aggression, as frustration–aggression theory would require; enhance social identity, as social identity theory would require; make self–other comparisons, as downward social comparison theory would require; or confront the threat itself in any way. Only a self-affirmational perspective suggests that restoring a positive sense of self-integrity in this way would result in the decrease of prejudiced evaluations. Of course, this thesis shares many assumptions with these other theoretical positions. Our approach, however, can be seen as extending previous approaches by examining self-image maintenance as both cause and effect of prejudiced evaluations and by integrating these approaches with contemporary views of the self.

Taken together, the studies reported in this article examined both sides of this process: the roles of self-affirmation and self-image threat in influencing the likelihood that individuals will use stereotypes or prejudice and the role of prejudice in helping individuals restore a positive sense of self.

Study 1

In Study 1, we examined the hypothesis that self-affirmation should make participants less likely to evaluate another individual in ways that reflect their prejudice toward the individual's group. Participants in this study were asked to evaluate a target person who apparently was either a member of a group for which there was a readily available negative stereotype or a member of some other outgroup for which there was not a strong available stereotype. Before being exposed to this target person, participants were either self-affirmed or not affirmed. That is, half of the participants completed a task designed to affirm and make salient an important aspect of their self-concepts, and the other half completed a task designed not to affirm any important aspects of their self-concepts.

We believe that many stereotypes and prejudices are such readily available and cognitively justifi-

able means of self-enhancement that individuals often use their stereotypes and prejudices to self-enhance in the face of everyday vulnerabilities and frustrations (e.g., see Wood & Taylor, 1991). That is, unless other motives are activated, such as a goal of accurate perception (Darley, Fleming, Hilton, & Swann, 1988; Neuberg & Fiske, 1987), accountability (Tetlock, 1983), or social desirability or egalitarian motives (Dovidio & Gaertner, 1991; Monteith, 1993), people may find stereotyping and prejudice to be a reliable and effective way to protect their self-esteem in a frequently threatening world. To the extent, then, that the use of stereotypes and prejudice stems in part from self-image maintenance needs, self-affirmation should make individuals less likely to resort to this use. Study 1 was designed to test this hypothesis.

Method

Participants

Seventy-two introductory psychology students from the University of Michigan participated in this experiment as partial fulfillment of a course requirement.[1]

Procedure

The participants were told that they would participate in two experiments in this session. The first experiment was portrayed as a study of values. The second experiment was portrayed as an investigation of how employees evaluate candidates in the hiring process.

Manipulation of self-affirmation. Half of the participants completed a self-affirmation procedure, and half did not. This procedure was a modified version of that used by Steele and Liu (1983; see also Steele, 1988; Tesser & Cornell, 1991) to affirm and make salient an important part of individuals' self-concepts. Participants were given

---

[1] Although 72 people participated in the experiment, 18 were excluded because they were Jewish, for reasons that are described in the *Manipulation of target's ethnicity* section. Thus, the data from 54 participants were included in all analyses.

a list of several values (adapted from values characterized by the Allport–Vernon Study of Values), including *business/economics, art/music/theater, social life/relationships*, and *science/pursuit of knowledge*. Participants in the self-affirmation condition were asked to circle the value that was most important to them personally and then to write a few paragraphs explaining why this value was important to them.[2] In contrast, participants in the no-affirmation condition were asked to circle the value that was least important to them personally and then to write a paragraph explaining why this value might be important to someone else. Steele and his colleagues (e.g., Spencer & Steele, 1990; Steele, 1988) have found that causing participants to think about a value that is personally very important to them is an effective means of producing self-affirmation and that, in the absence of self-image threat, it does not affect participants' state self-esteem.

Evaluation task. For what we portrayed as the second experiment, participants were placed in individual cubicles and were told that their task was to evaluate an individual who had applied for a job as a personnel manager at a particular organization. The participants were given general information about the responsibilities of a personnel manager at this hypothetical organization and were encouraged to try to make an accurate assessment of the candidate's suitability for the job.

All participants next examined information about a fictitious job candidate who was about to graduate from their university. Participants were given the candidate's completed job application to examine. The application contained questions about the candidate's previous work experience, academic and extracurricular skills and interests, and other résumé-type information. The completed application was constructed to suggest that the applicant was fairly well qualified for the position but was not necessarily a stellar candidate.

Attached to the application was a photograph of the candidate. All of the participants saw virtually the same application and photograph; the variations are noted in the section below. After examining this material, participants watched an 8-min videotape presented as excerpts from the candidate's job interview. All participants saw the same videotape, which featured a fairly neutral performance by the candidate—that is, her responses tended to be adequate but not extremely positive or negative. After watching the excerpts, participants completed a questionnaire about the candidate and her qualifications.

Manipulation of target's ethnicity. Although all participants saw the same job interview excerpts, saw the same woman in the photograph attached to the job application, and read the same information about her work experiences, academic record, and other job-relevant information, we included two minor variations in the photograph and three in the application to suggest either that the candidate was Jewish or that she was not Jewish (and probably was Italian).

We used this distinction for several reasons. At the time and place in which this study was conducted, there was a very well known and relatively freely discussed stereotype concerning the "Jewish American princess" (JAP). There was a fairly sizable and salient minority of students at this campus who were Jewish women from New York City and Long Island, New York, and these women were the targets of a number of JAP jokes that spread across campus. In contrast to stereotypes about African Americans, gay men and lesbians, and many other groups, the JAP stereotype was one that many students were willing to discuss quite candidly, with many of them openly endorsing it.[3]

---

[2] None of our participants wrote paragraphs concerning prejudice or tolerance. Moreover, the effects of the manipulation were not related to which value—business/economics, art/music/theater, social life/relationships, or science/pursuit of knowledge—the participants chose.

[3] One of the reasons for this may be that the stereotype is diffused across two types of prejudice: anti-Semitism and sexism. That is, those who endorse the stereotype are protected against being considered anti-Semitic because they are not implicating Jewish men in their derogatory comments or beliefs, and they are protected against being considered sexist because they are not implicating most women. A second reason may be that the targeted group is perceived as being relatively privileged, and thus, disparaging them may not seem as harmful.

Another factor that played a role in our decision to examine this form of prejudice was that we were able to select a stimulus person who could be considered representative of the Jewish American princess and yet, with a few subtle manipulations, could just as easily be considered representative of a non-Jewish group—one that also was an outgroup to most participants but about which there was no strong negative stereotype or prejudice on this campus. This alternative categorization was of an Italian American woman. Although also a minority on campus, this group was not nearly as salient on campus, and as pilot testing confirmed, there was no strong, consensual stereotype or prejudice on campus concerning this group.

To manipulate the target's ethnic background, we varied the following elements of her application: her name (Julie Goldberg vs. Maria D'Agostino), an extracurricular activity (volunteering for a Jewish or Catholic organization), and her sorority (either of two sororities that shared similar reputations in terms of status, but one of which consisted predominantly of Jewish women and one of which consisted predominantly of non-Jewish women of European, but not Hispanic, descent). All the other information on the application, including all of the job-relevant information, was identical.

In both conditions, the photograph attached to the job application was of the same woman (who was also featured in the videotape). We had chosen a female undergraduate, unknown to the participants, who could be seen either as fitting the prototypic image of a Jewish American princess or as non-Jewish (and probably Italian). The photograph varied slightly, however, so that "Julie" was wearing a necklace featuring the Star of David and had her hair clipped up in back (in a clip that some pilot test students referred to as a JAP clip), whereas "Maria" was wearing a cross and had her hair down. Pilot testing suggested that our manipulation was successful.

This woman appeared in the video wearing a sweater that covered her necklace, and her hair was down but brushed in such a way that its length seemed somewhere in between the styles depicted in the two photographs. As indicated above, all participants saw the same 8-min video.

Dependent measures. Participants rated the candidate in terms of her overall personality and her qualifications for the job. Her personality was assessed by the extent to which participants agreed (on a 7-point scale) that each of the following traits described her: intelligent, insensitive, trustworthy, arrogant, sincere, inconsiderate, friendly, self-centered, down-to-earth, rude, creative, materialistic, motivated, cliquish, ambitious, conceited, happy, vain, warm, superficial. Negative traits were reverse scored. Her job qualifications were assessed by the extent to which participants agreed (on a 7-point scale) with the following statements: "I feel this person would make an excellent candidate for the position in question," "I would likely give this person serious consideration for the position in question," "I would guess that this person is in the top 20% of people interviewed," and "I felt favorably toward this person." Both scales showed good internal reliability (Cronbach's alphas of .93 and .91, respectively). Finally, participants were asked to indicate their own and the target's ethnicity and religion.

Results

Recall that our prediction was that when participants were not self-affirmed, they would evaluate the target more negatively when she was portrayed as Jewish than when she was portrayed as Italian, whereas when participants were self-affirmed, this difference would be reduced or eliminated.

The critical measure in this study was participants' ratings of the target's personality across a variety of dimensions. These ratings were subjected to a two-way analysis of variance (ANOVA). The ANOVA revealed that there was no significant main effect for the manipulation of affirmation, $F(1, 50) = 1.8, p > .15$, but that there was a significant main effect for the manipulation of the apparent ethnicity of the target, as the target was rated more positively when she appeared to be Italian than when she appeared to be Jewish, $F(1, 50) = 4.9, p < .05$. Most importantly, this main effect was qualified by a significant interaction, $F(1, 50) = 8.5, p < .01$. As can be seen in Figure 16.1, and consistent with our predictions, not affirmed

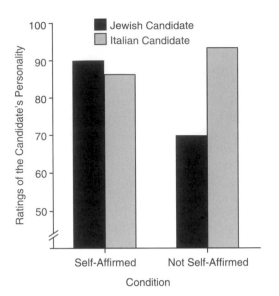

FIGURE 16.1 ■ Rating of candidate's personality as a function of self-affirmation condition and ethnicity of the candidate. Higher numbers indicate more favorable evaluations.

participants who evaluated the Jewish target were significantly more negative in their evaluations of the target's personality than were participants in all other conditions, $t(50) = 3.7$, $p < .001$. None of the other conditions differed significantly from each other.[4]

Ratings of how qualified the target was for the job in question also were consistent with our predictions. A two-way ANOVA revealed that participants who had not been affirmed tended to rate the target more negatively than did participants who had been affirmed, $F(1, 50) = 4.6$, $p < .05$. The ANOVA revealed further that participants rated the

candidate more positively when she was depicted as Italian than when she was depicted as Jewish, $F(1, 50) = 6.3$, $p < .05$. These main effects were qualified, however, by a marginally significant interaction between the two independent variables, $F(1, 50) = 3.0$, $p < .10$. Consistent with our predictions, not affirmed participants evaluated the qualifications of the candidate more negatively when she was portrayed as Jewish ($M = 14.9$) rather than Italian ($M = 20.6$), whereas affirmed participants did not make this discrimination ($Ms = 20.2$ and 21.2, respectively). The planned comparison indicated that not affirmed participants who evaluated the Jewish target were significantly more negative in their evaluations of the target's job qualifications than were participants in all other conditions, $t(50) = 3.7$, $p < .001$. None of the other conditions differed significantly from each other.

Discussion

The results of this study demonstrate that self-affirmation can reduce the likelihood that individuals will derogate members of stereotyped groups. In the absence of self-affirmation, participants' evaluations of the job candidate were biased as a function of her apparent ethnicity. That is, these participants evaluated the target more negatively if she was a member of a stereotyped group than if she was not. Among participants who had been self-affirmed, however, this difference was eliminated.

These results, therefore, highlight the significant role played by the self-concept in prejudice. More specifically, they support the idea that thinking about a self-relevant value, even one completely unrelated to prejudice, can reduce the expression of prejudice. Thinking about a self-relevant value has this effect even though it need not release pent-up anger or aggression, enhance social identity, or involve self–other comparisons, as frustration–aggression theory, social identity theory, and downward social-comparison theory would require.

In a replication of this study, we also examined the potential mediating role of participants' mood in this paradigm with an independent sample of 71

---

[4] We used this planned comparison for both dependent measures in this study, as well as a comparable planned comparison for each of the dependent measures in Studies 2 and 3, because it was the most direct test of our theoretically derived hypotheses (see, e.g., Hays, 1981; Keppel, 1973; Rosenthal & Rosnow, 1991; Winer, 1971). For each of these measures, we also conducted the more conservative Newman–Keuls post hoc comparisons. In each case, the Newman–Keuls comparisons indicated the difference tested in the planned comparison to be significant and revealed further that none of the other conditions differed significantly from each other.

participants. We measured participants' mood using the Mehrabian and Russell (1974) mood scale after the manipulation of self-affirmation but before the participants evaluated the target. The mood scale consists of three subscales, each consisting of six sets of bipolar adjectives. These subscales measure pleasure (e.g., happy–unhappy, pleased–annoyed), arousal (e.g., stimulated–relaxed, excited–calm), and dominance (e.g., controlled–controlling, influential–influenced). Consistent with the findings of Liu and Steele (1986), the manipulation of self-affirmation had no significant effects on any one or any combination of these subscales (all $Fs < 1$). Moreover, participants' mood was unrelated to their evaluation of the target's personality, $r(69) = -.120$, ns, or of her qualifications for the job, $r(69) = .04$, ns. Replicating the results of Study 1, not affirmed participants who evaluated the Jewish target rated the target's personality significantly more negatively than did participants in all other cells, $t(67) = 2.4$, $p < .01$. Similarly, not affirmed participants who evaluated the Jewish target tended to rate the target's job qualifications more negatively than did participants in all other cells, $t(67) = 1.8$, $p < .05$.

The results of these studies suggest that at least part of the negative evaluation of people who are stereotyped may result from people trying to affirm their self-image. To the extent that people's self-images have been buffered by other means of self-affirmation, they should be less drawn to such a strategy. In the absence of such self-affirmation, however, stereotyping and prejudice may provide a mechanism by which people protect or bolster their self-esteem. Stereotyping and prejudice may be reinforced, therefore, because they can make people feel better about themselves.

Study 2

The results of Study 1 suggest that self-affirmation can play an important role in reducing the effects of stereotyping or prejudice on individuals' evaluations of a member of a stereotyped group. In Study 2, we focused on the other side of this self-image maintenance coin by examining whether a

self-image threat would exacerbate the effects of stereotyping or prejudice on individuals' evaluations of a member of a stereotyped group.

Study 2 differed from Study 1 in two other important ways, thereby providing a better test of the generalizability of our hypotheses. First, rather than varying the target's apparent ethnicity, in Study 2 we manipulated the target's apparent sexual orientation. Thus, whereas the stereotyped group in Study 1 was contrasted with a nonstereotyped group that was also a distinct minority, the stereotyped group in Study 2 was contrasted with the nonstereotyped majority. Second, rather than measuring participants' general derogation of a target as a function of her membership in a stereotyped group, Study 2 measured participants' stereotyping of an individual as a function of his membership in a stereotyped group.

More specifically, some participants in this study received self-image-threatening information in the form of bogus negative feedback on an intelligence test; the other participants received no such threat. Later, all participants evaluated a target on a series of trait dimensions relevant to popular stereotypes of gay men. The biographical information about the target was manipulated so as to suggest to some of the participants that the target may have been gay and to suggest to the other participants that he was straight (heterosexual). The hypothesis tested in Study 2 was that participants should be more likely to exhibit stereotyping of the (apparently) gay target if they had previously received negative feedback on the intelligence test than if they had not.

Method
Participants

Sixty-one male undergraduates from Williams College participated in this experiment either for extra credit for their introductory psychology course or for the chance to win money in a random drawing.

Procedure

Participants reported to the laboratory individually and completed the tasks in individual rooms containing a desk and a Macintosh computer. Participants first read a sheet of paper containing the cover story, which stated that the study involved a series of different cognitive and social judgment tasks. The first part of the study involved the manipulation of self-relevant feedback (described below). After some filler tasks (e.g., a simple word-stem completion task) designed to preserve the integrity of the cover story, participants completed the social judgment task, in which the participants read information about a male target. The information was designed to suggest either that the target was gay or that he was straight. After rating the target on a series of dimensions, the participants were probed for any suspicions, debriefed thoroughly, and thanked for their participation.

Manipulation of feedback. Half of the participants were assigned randomly to the negative feedback condition, and the other half were assigned to the neutral condition. To the former half, the experimenter introduced the first set of tasks as "a new form of intelligence test that is given on the computer. It measures both verbal and reasoning abilities." To the latter half, the experimenter explained that they had been assigned to a control condition in which they were simply to read the materials contained in a bogus test of intelligence. The experimenter revealed to these participants that the participants in the treatment condition of the study would be told that the test was a real, valid measure of intelligence. In other words, the experimenter told the neutral condition participants the truth. These participants were instructed to refrain from trying hard to answer the questions on the bogus test because many of the questions had no correct answer and because the time limits were unrealistically quick. The experimenter also told them that the computer would present them with bogus scores at the conclusion of the test. To assure the participants that these scores were indeed bogus, the experimenter told them what these scores would be. The experimenter explained that the participants in the treatment condition would be led to believe that the scores were real. The purpose of having the participants in the neutral condition learn this cover story and go through the

test was so that they would be exposed to the same test and specific items as the participants in the negative feedback condition, but that the test would have no relevance to their self-image.[5]

All subsequent instructions for the test were presented on the computer. The instructions were presented in a professional-looking design that introduced the intelligence test as "The Reasoning and Verbal Acuity Battery." The instructions explained that the test had been validated in numerous studies throughout the United States and Canada. The test consisted of five parts, each tapping different sets of intellectual skills. The first four parts consisted of analogies, antonyms, sentence completions, and syllogisms. The fifth part was called a "verbal–nonverbal matching test" and involved matching difficult vocabulary words to various pictures; this was a modified version of the Ammons and Ammons (1962) Quick Test of Intelligence. The instructions to this battery of tests explained that research had shown that this combination of tasks was the ideal, most valid method to measure individuals' general intelligence.

To emphasize the relevance of these intellectual skills, each test within the battery was introduced with an explanation of what it measured. Many of the specific items in these tests were taken from advanced tests used for admission to graduate school or law school. To make the tests seem even more challenging (and thus to help to justify the bogus feedback for the participants in the negative feedback condition), we modified several of the items so that there was no correct answer among the options given. Moreover, the time limits for each item were very short (ranging from 10 to 20 s, depending on the test), and a clock showing the seconds ticking away appeared on the screen for each item.

---

[5] Consistent with the intent of the manipulation, pilot testing of 36 other participants from the same population revealed that the state self-esteem (as measured by Heatherton & Polivy's [1991] state self-esteem scale) of participants in the neutral condition was not significantly lower than that of participants who were not exposed to the test or cover story ($F < 1$). In addition, the state self-esteem of these participants (in either condition) was significantly higher than that of pilot test participants who were led to believe the test was real ($Fs > 6$).

At the conclusion of this battery of tests, the computer program indicated that it was calculating the scores. After 7 s a new screen appeared that indicated the participant's percentile rankings (relative to other college students tested in the United States and Canada) for each test. Each participant received an identical set of scores: 51st percentile for the analogies test, 54th for the antonyms, 56th for the sentence completions, 33rd for the syllogisms, and 38th for the verbal–nonverbal matching. Given the prestige of the college in which this study was conducted and the students' previous scores on tests such as the Scholastic Achievement Test, these scores are extremely disappointing to the students from this population. (See Footnote 5.)

Manipulation of target's apparent sexual orientation. After administering a series of brief cognitive tasks designed to enhance the integrity of the cover story, the experimenter introduced the "social judgment tasks" by informing the participants that they would read some information about an individual and make some judgments about him or her.

All participants read about a target named Greg, a 31-year-old struggling actor living in the East Village in New York City. The information summarized Greg's ambitions and career struggles and listed some of the many odd jobs that Greg had taken to pay the rent while he pursued his dream. The information continued by detailing a recent event in Greg's life concerning landing "a fairly large part in a serious and rather controversial play directed by a young director." Participants read that Greg was excited about the play and, in particular, about working with this young director. The director's name was not mentioned, but gender pronouns indicated that the director was a man. The participants read that after the first week of rehearsals, Greg approached the director and asked him whether he wanted to get "a drink or something" with him after that night's rehearsal so that they could talk about his role in some more depth. The story continued for a few paragraphs, summarizing the play's opening and reviews, and it concluded with the information that while continuing

to act in the play, Greg was writing his own play and had already gotten a commitment from the director to help him with it.

The information about Greg was identical across conditions with the following exceptions. In the first sentence, the participants in the straight-implied condition read that Greg "has been living with his girlfriend, Anne, in a small apartment" for several years. Anne's name was mentioned three more times in subsequent parts of the story about Greg, and there was one additional reference to his "girlfriend." For the gay-implied condition, in the first sentence we replaced the word "girlfriend" with "partner" and dropped reference to Anne. Neither the partner's name nor the partner's gender was specified, and there were no subsequent references to this partner.

Many of the details of the story about Greg (e.g., his living in the East Village, his caring "for a very close and very ill friend for the last 2 months of his friend's life," and his relationship with the director) were included to support the implication in the gay-implied condition that Greg was gay. Because each piece of information by itself very plausibly could describe a straight actor's life, however, we believed that the participants who were introduced immediately to references to Greg's girlfriend would not entertain the idea that Greg was gay.[6]

Dependent measures. Participants used an 11-point scale ranging from 0 (*not at all*) to 10 (*extremely*) to rate Greg's personality on each of 10 dimensions. Three of these (intelligent, funny, and boring) were included as stereotype-irrelevant fillers. The stereotype-relevant traits included sensitive, assertive/aggressive, considerate, feminine,

---

[6] An obvious question is why we did not simply state that Greg was gay. Pilot testing of students from this campus revealed quite strongly that many of the participants became suspicious of the purpose of the study if they read that the target was gay. More than half of the participants told the experimenter that they suspected that the study concerned their stereotypes about gay men. When we eliminated any explicit references to Greg's sexuality, our pilot test participants did not raise these suspicions, although most of them did spontaneously entertain the thought that Greg was gay.

strong, creative, and passive (see Fein, Cross, & Spencer, 1995; Kite & Deaux, 1987). Assertive/aggressive and strong were reverse-coded so that for each item, higher ratings indicated greater stereotyping. An index of this set of seven traits showed moderate internal reliability (Cronbach's $a = .77$). It may be worth noting that these traits, when taken out of a stereotyped context, are not necessarily negative and may indeed be rather positive. But to the extent that participants perceived these traits as more descriptive of a target if they thought that the target was gay than if they thought he was straight, this would indicate stereotyping, and the valence of these traits would be debatable.

In addition, participants used the same 11-point scale to indicate the degree to which they would like Greg as a friend and the degree to which their own personality was similar to Greg's. These measures, of course, were less ambiguous in terms of valence: Lower ratings on these two measures clearly indicated more negative feelings toward the target.

Results

Recall that we predicted that if participants read information about a target that implied that he was gay, they would be more likely to evaluate this target consistently with the gay stereotype if they had received threatening, negative feedback about their performance on the intelligence test than if they had not received any threatening feedback. If the information about the target indicated that he was straight, however, the manipulation of feedback should not have had a strong effect on participants' evaluation of the target. The results supported these predictions.

Stereotyping

A two-way ANOVA on the ratings of the target on the set of seven stereotype-relevant trait dimensions revealed a significant main effect for the manipulation of feedback, $F(1, 57) = 11.3$, $p < .001$, indicating that participants who had received negative feedback on the intelligence test rated the target more stereotypically (i.e., gave higher

ratings on the stereotype-consistent items) than did participants who had not received any feedback. In addition, the ANOVA revealed a significant effect for the manipulation of the target's apparent sexual orientation, $F(1, 57) = 5.3$, $p < .03$, indicating that participants who read information that implied that the target was gay rated him more stereotypically than if they read information suggesting that he was straight. Most importantly, the ANOVA revealed a significant interaction, $F(1, 57) = 4.4$, $p < .05$. As can be seen in Figure 16.2, and consistent with our predictions, participants who had received negative feedback and read information implying that the target was gay rated the target much more stereotypically than did participants in all other conditions, $t(57) = 4.1$, $p < .001$. None of the other conditions differed significantly from each other (see Footnote 4).

Although the stereotype-irrelevant traits were used as filler to make the participants less likely to be suspicious of the intent of our questions, we did conduct an ANOVA on the ratings concerning those traits. The independent variables did not have any significant effects on participants' ratings

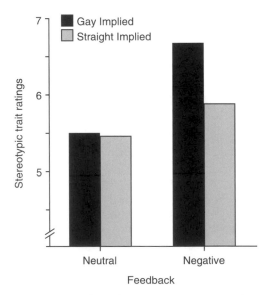

FIGURE 16.2 ■ Rating of target on stereotype-relevant traits as a function of feedback and implied sexual orientation of the target. Higher numbers indicate greater stereotyping.

of the target on any or all of these traits (all Fs < 1).

Liking and similarity

The measure of stereotyping yielded results consistent with our predictions. But would self-esteem threat also make participants less willing to indicate that they would like the target as a friend or that their own personality was similar to the target's? To address this question, we conducted an ANOVA on each of these measures.

The ANOVA on participants' ratings of the degree to which they would like the target as a friend revealed a significant main effect for the manipulation of feedback, $F(1, 57) = 5.7$, $p < .03$, indicating that participants who had received negative feedback on the intelligence test rated themselves as less inclined to like the target ($M = 5.81$) than did participants in the neutral condition ($M = 6.87$). The main effect for the manipulation of the information about the target's apparent sexual orientation did not approach significance ($F < 1$), but the interaction between the two variables was significant, $F(1, 57) = 4.1$, $p < .05$. Participants who had received negative feedback on the intelligence test were significantly less inclined to like the target than were those who had not received the feedback, whether or not the target information suggested he was gay, but the interaction reflects the tendency for this difference to be greater in the gay-implied condition ($Ms = 5.48$ vs. 6.98) than in the straight-implied condition ($Ms = 6.11$ vs. 6.75).

The ANOVA on participants' ratings of how similar their own personality was to the target's revealed a significant main effect for the manipulation of feedback, $F(1, 57) = 5.3$, $p < .03$, reflecting the tendency for participants to rate their personality as less similar to the target's if they had received negative feedback on the intelligence test ($M = 4.16$) than if they had received no feedback ($M = 5.33$). The manipulation of information about the target's sexual orientation did not have a significant effect ($F < 1$). More important, the independent variables produced a significant interaction, $F(1, 57) = 4.1$, $p < .05$. Consistent with our predictions, participants were particularly unlikely

to rate their personality as similar to the target's if they had received negative feedback and read information implying that the target was gay ($M = 3.94$), $t(57) = 2.3$, $p < .03$. None of the other conditions differed significantly from each other.

Discussion

Consistent with our predictions, participants showed more stereotyping in their evaluations of the target if they had previously received negative feedback about their own performance on an intelligence test. In addition to resulting in greater stereotyping, the negative feedback led participants to psychologically distance themselves from the target if they had reason to suspect that he was gay, by rating themselves as less likely to be friends with or be similar in personality to the target. If the information about the target suggested he was straight, however, the negative feedback had less effect on these measures.

These results support the hypothesis that self-esteem threat can increase individuals' likelihood of exhibiting stereotyping or prejudice toward members of stereotyped groups. Using a different stereotype, a different stereotype comparison condition (i.e., a majority rather than alternative minority group condition), and different dependent measures from those used in Study 1, Study 2 yielded results consistent with the hypothesis that self-image-maintenance processes can play an important moderating role in stereotyping or prejudice.

But does stereotyping or prejudice in response to self-image threat restore an individual's self-esteem? This question was addressed in Study 3.

Study 3

Our view suggests that one motivation for stereotype- or prejudice-based evaluations is that these sorts of evaluations can restore a threatened self-image. Study 3 provides the first complete test of this hypothesis by examining both sides of this process: the role of a threatened self-image in causing participants to derogate a member of a stereotyped group and the role of this derogation in restoring participants' threatened self-image. Thus, an important goal of Study 3 was to provide the first evidence that negative evaluation of a stereotyped target in response to self-image threat mediates increase in self-esteem.

Participants in Study 3 took what they thought was an intelligence test. Unlike in Study 2, all participants in Study 3 were led to believe that the test was real. They received bogus positive or negative feedback.[7] After the feedback, all participants completed a questionnaire that measured their state self-esteem. In an ostensibly unrelated experiment that followed, participants evaluated a woman portrayed as Jewish or Italian, as in Study 1. Following this evaluation, participants again completed the state self-esteem questionnaire so that we could monitor changes in their self-esteem.

We predicted that (a) participants who received negative feedback would have lower state self-esteem than participants who received positive feedback, (b) participants who received negative feedback and evaluated the Jewish target would rate the target more negatively than would the participants in the other conditions, (c) participants who received negative feedback and evaluated the Jewish target would exhibit a greater increase in state self-esteem than would participants in the other conditions, and (d) this increase in state self-esteem would be mediated by their evaluations of the target.

Method

Participants

One hundred twenty-six introductory psychology students from the University of Michigan participated in this experiment for partial fulfillment of a course requirement.[8]

Procedure

Overview. Participants reported to the laboratory in pairs and were told that they would be participating in two experiments: an intelligence test and a social interaction. Participants first were given an intelligence test and were given bogus feedback about their performance. They next completed a measure of their state self-esteem (Heatherton & Polivy, 1991) and were asked to indicate their score on the intelligence test, after which they were thanked for their participation, dismissed, and sent to the "social evaluation" experiment, where they were met by a different experimenter. The social evaluation experiment involved the same procedure as that used in Study 1. That is, participants received information about a job candidate who was depicted as either Jewish or Italian. After evaluating this candidate's personality and job qualifications by using the same measures as those used in Study 1, participants again completed the Heatherton and Polivy measure of state self-esteem, after which they were asked to indicate their own and the target's race and ethnicity. Finally, they were probed for any suspicions, debriefed thoroughly, and thanked for their participation.

Manipulation of feedback. When participants arrived for what was portrayed as the first experiment, they were told that the study was concerned with a new, improved form of intelligence test. The rationale and instructions were similar to but briefer than those given to the participants in Study 2. The intelligence test used in this study consisted of a longer but less difficult version of one of the tests from the battery of tests used in Study 2: the verbal–nonverbal matching test in which participants tried to match difficult vocabulary words to

---

[7] We believed that it would be difficult or impossible to provide performance feedback that would be neutral for most participants, unless, as in Study 2, we did not lead the participants to believe that the test was real. An average score was quite threatening to our participants, and determining how much above average would be neutral for all participants seemed impossible.

[8] Although 126 participants participated in the experiment, 17 were excluded because they were Jewish, 7 because they were foreign students and, consequently, would have been less likely to be familiar with the stereotype about Jewish American women, 4 because they misidentified the target's ethnicity, and 2 because they did not believe the false feedback about their performance on the intelligence test. Thus, the data from 96 participants were included in all analyses.

various pictures. This test was purported to be a very valid test of verbal and nonverbal skills. The experimenter began by giving each participant a pencil and a form commonly used for exams featuring multiple-choice questions that are graded via a computer. The test consisted of three sets of 10 words each.

The test was designed to be difficult and ambiguous enough for students to believe either positive or negative performance feedback. Some of the words were difficult or obscure for the average student (e.g., *capacious, celerity*), and some were easier (*forlorn, imminent*), but all had the feel of the kinds of vocabulary items that are included in college entrance exams, and many were such that participants felt as if they may have known what they meant but could not be sure. Moreover, the match between words and pictures often was not obvious, particularly given the fast pace of the test. Pretests and postexperiment interviews confirmed that participants tended to be unsure of how they were doing during the test and to believe the feedback that was given them.

At the completion of the test, the experiment took the participants' answers and went into an adjacent room. The door to this room was left open, and the participants could hear what sounded like a Scantron machine grading the tests. The experimenter returned each participant's answer form to him or her. The experimenter explained that a red mark appeared next to each incorrect answer, that the first number on the bottom of the form indicated the number of correct answers, and that the second number indicated the participant's percentile ranking relative to all the other students who had taken the test thus far.

The feedback was, of course, bogus. Half of the participants received positive false feedback about their test performance (i.e., a high score that ostensibly put them in the 93rd percentile for the university), whereas the other half received negative false feedback (i.e., a low score that ostensibly put them in the 47th percentile). Although the 47th percentile is close to the median, pretesting had indicated that participants uniformly found this to be very negative feedback (see also Stein, 1994).

Recall that we predicted that if participants had received threatening, negative feedback about their performance on the intelligence test, they would be more likely to derogate the target as a function of her apparent ethnicity than if they had received positive feedback about their performance. We also predicted that derogating the stereotyped target would help restore threatened participants' self-esteem. The results were consistent with these predictions.

Evaluations of the target

Participants' ratings of the target's personality were subjected to a two-way ANOVA, which revealed strong support for our predictions. Two significant main effects emerged: Participants who had received negative feedback about their performance on the intelligence test rated the target's personality more negatively than did participants who had received positive feedback, $F(1, 92) = 9.1$, $p < .05$, and participants who were led to believe that the woman was Jewish rated her qualifications more negatively than did participants who were led to believe that the woman was Italian, $F(1, 92) = 5.2$, $p < .01$. More importantly, these main effects were qualified by a significant interaction between the manipulations of feedback and ethnicity, $F(1, 92) = 7.1$, $p < .01$. As can be seen in Figure 16.3, participants who had received positive feedback did not evaluate the personality of the target as a function of her apparent ethnicity, whereas participants who had received negative feedback evaluated the qualifications of the target much more negatively if she was portrayed as Jewish than if she was portrayed as Italian. The planned comparison indicated that participants who had received negative feedback and evaluated the Jewish target were significantly more negative in their evaluations of the target's personality than were participants in all other conditions, $t(92) = 4.5$, $p < .001$. None of the other conditions differed significantly from each other (see Footnote 4).

The ANOVA of the ratings of the target's job qualifications yielded a similar pattern of results. The two main effects were again significant: Participants who had received negative feedback about their performance on the intelligence test rated the

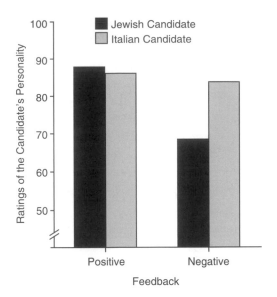

FIGURE 16.3 ■ Rating of candidate's personality as a function of feedback and ethnicity of the candidate. Higher numbers indicate more favorable evaluations.

target's qualifications more negatively than did participants who had received positive feedback, $F(1, 92) = 3.7$, $p = .05$, and participants who were led to believe that the woman was Jewish rated her qualifications more negatively than did participants who were led to believe that the woman was Italian, $F(1, 92) = 6.3$, $p < .05$. Although the interaction was not significant for this measure, $F(1, 92) = 2.3$, $p < .12$, the pattern of cell means was consistent with our predictions. Participants who had received positive feedback did not evaluate the target very differently as a function of her apparent ethnicity ($M_{Jewish} = 18.8$ vs. $M_{Italian} = 19.7$), but participants who had received negative feedback evaluated the qualifications of the target much more negatively if she was portrayed as Jewish ($M = 15.3$) than if she was portrayed as Italian ($M = 19.3$). The planned comparison indicated that participants who had received negative feedback and evaluated the Jewish target were significantly more negative in their evaluations of the target's qualifications than were participants in all other conditions, $t(92) = 3.4$, $p < .001$. None of the other conditions differed significantly from each other.

These results, therefore, provide a conceptual replication of those found in Study 2 and support

the generalizability of the findings by demonstrating them in the context of a different stereotype, a different kind of nonstereotyped group, and different dependent measures.

Self-esteem

In Study 3 we measured participants' state self-esteem at two points: after the feedback manipulation and after they rated the target. The theoretical range for this scale is 20 to 100, with higher numbers indicating higher state self-esteem. As expected, feedback had a significant effect on participants' state self-esteem. Participants who received the positive feedback felt better about themselves ($M = 77.5$) than did those who received the negative feedback ($M = 72.9$), $F(1, 94) = 4.4$, $p < .05$.

The change in state self-esteem from this first measure to the measure taken after participants evaluated the target was also consistent with predictions. The ANOVA revealed a marginally significant interaction between feedback and ethnicity, $F(1, 92) = 2.7$, $p = .10$. As can be seen in Figure 16.4, and consistent with our predictions, participants who received negative feedback and

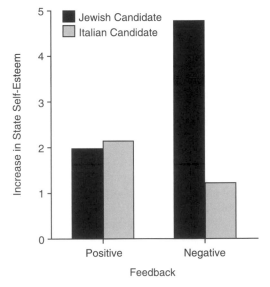

FIGURE 16.4 ■ Change in state self-esteem as a function of feedback and ethnicity of the job candidate. Higher numbers indicate greater increase in state self-esteem.

evaluated the Jewish target had a significantly greater increase in state self-esteem than did participants in the other conditions, $t(92) = 2.3$, $p < .05$. None of the other conditions differed significantly from each other on this measure.

These results suggest that the participants who received negative feedback and rated the Jewish woman restored their self-esteem by engaging in negative evaluation of the stereotyped target. We conducted a path analysis to test this reasoning (Baron & Kenny, 1986). Figure 16.5 depicts the results of this analysis. We allowed the planned interaction contrast to predict change in participants' self-esteem. This direct effect was significant, $\beta = .23$, $t(92) = 2.3$, $p < .05$. Next we allowed the planned interaction contrast to predict participants' ratings of the target's personality. This path was significant as well, $\beta = .42$, $t(92) = 4.6$, $p < .01$. Finally, we allowed the planned interaction contrast and participants' ratings of the target's personality to predict participants' change in state self-esteem. The path from participants' ratings of the target was significant, $\beta = .37$, $t(92) = 3.5$, $p < .01$, but the direct effect of the planned interaction contrast on participants' change in self-esteem was no longer significant, $\beta = .07$, $t(92) = 0.7$, $p > .40$. Thus, this path analysis suggests that the direct effect of the manipulations in this experiment on participants' change in state self-esteem was mediated by their evaluations of the stereotyped target's personality. These analyses suggest that the negative feedback led to increased derogation of the

Jewish target, which in turn led to increased state self-esteem, rather than suggesting that positive feedback led to a reduced derogation of the Jewish target.

Taken together, these results provide the first demonstration that self-image threats, such as negative feedback, can lead to negative evaluations of a stereotyped target and that these negative evaluations, in turn, can restore people's threatened self-images. Moreover, these findings support our hypothesis that derogating a stereotyped target in response to self-image threat mediates increase in self-esteem. These results, therefore, strongly corroborate the idea that negative evaluations of a stereotyped target may often result from an effort to affirm a threatened self-image.

General Discussion

This set of three studies examined evaluations of a member of a stereotyped group. Study 1 found that participants evaluated an individual target person more negatively if they thought she was a member of a stereotyped group than if they thought she was a member of a nonstereotyped group, but this effect did not occur if the participants' self-images had been bolstered through an affirmation procedure. Study 2 found that receiving self-image-threatening information led participants to evaluate an individual more stereotypically if he appeared to be a member of a stereotyped group. Study 3 demonstrated that receiving self-image-threatening information led participants to negatively evaluate an individual if she appeared to be a member of a stereotyped group, and these negative evaluations in turn were particularly effective in restoring participants' self-esteem. Moreover, the degree to which these participants made negative evaluations of the stereotyped target mediated the restoration of their self-esteem. Taken together, this research suggests that a threat to one's positive self-image or a self-affirmation that provides a buffer against self-image threats can moderate negative evaluations of a member of a stereotyped group and that these biased evaluations can in turn affect one's sense of self-worth.

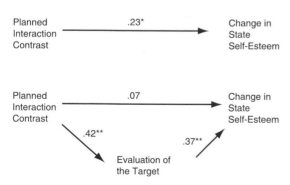

FIGURE 16.5 ■ Change in state self-esteem as mediated by negative evaluations of the job candidate's personality. *$p < .05$. **$p < .01$.

Self-Affirmation and Negative Evaluations of Others

This set of studies highlights the role of self processes in the perceptions of others. Information that threatens perceivers' sense of self-worth leads to the need to restore a positive self-image. Research by Steele and others (Steele, 1988; Steele & Liu, 1983; Steele et al., 1993) has shown that people can restore a threatened self-image in a number of ways, including by drawing on their own self-concept resources or by taking advantage of affirmational opportunities available in the situation. Steele et al. (1993) have suggested, however, that it may be difficult for people to spontaneously draw upon their self-concept resources to affirm their self-image. Therefore, people will often look to the situation to find opportunities to affirm their self-image. The studies presented here demonstrate that stereotyping or derogation of a member of a stereotyped group can provide such situational opportunities to restore a threatened self-image. Because it is likely that people often will encounter others in situations where it is personally and socially acceptable to evaluate them negatively, stereotyping and prejudice may be common reactions to self-image threat. However, when perceivers encounter someone who is a member of a group for which they do not have strong, accessible negative stereotypes, such as the woman in Studies 1 and 3 who is Italian or the man in Study 2 who apparently was straight, stereotyping or derogation is unlikely to be used as a self-affirmational strategy.

These studies also suggest that self-affirmation processes may affect a wide range of phenomena. Most of the research on self-affirmation theory has examined how self-affirmation affects cognitive dissonance processes (Steele, 1988; Steele & Liu, 1983; Steele et al., 1993), but some research has suggested that self-affirmation can also influence self-evaluation maintenance (Tesser & Cornell, 1991), learned helplessness reactions (Liu & Steele, 1986), and the academic performance of women and minorities (Steele & Aronson, 1995). The present research, in which self-affirmation affected stereotyping and prejudice, provides further evidence that self-affirmation and self-image

maintenance processes have broad applicability to a wide range of important phenomena.

Relations to Other Theories

Our approach emphasizes that stereotyping others is one of several possible self-image-maintenance strategies (Steele, 1988; Tesser & Cornell, 1991). We argue that negatively evaluating others has the potential to restore a positive self-image. Because these evaluations are part of a larger self-system that seeks to maintain an overall image of the self as morally and adaptively adequate, the state of the self-image—specifically, the extent to which it is threatened or affirmed—will influence when people will engage in stereotyping and when that stereotyping will restore a positive self-image. This approach clearly is related to other theories of stereotyping and prejudice, such as frustration–aggression, social identity, and downward social comparison. However, there are distinct theoretical differences between our approach and these approaches. In addition, the findings of the current studies support our approach and would not be predicted by these other theories.

In contrast to frustration–aggression theory, which argues that people may displace aggression by derogating others in response to blocked goals and frustrations in their life, our approach emphasizes that threats to the self-image in particular, rather than any source of frustration, lead to derogation of others. The results of Study 1 highlight this difference. Consistent with our predictions, we found that self-affirmation reduced participants' tendency to derogate a stereotyped target. It is unclear from frustration–aggression theory how a self-affirmation procedure such as that used in Study 1 would reduce frustration, unless frustration is defined more broadly than it has been in the past.

Social identity theory suggests that people favor their own groups over other groups in an effort to boost their group's status, which in turn boosts their own self-esteem. Although our approach would suggest that favoring one's own group over another group can restore one's self-image, we argue that negatively evaluating a stereotyped target can restore one's self-image even if group evaluations and in-group–out-group comparisons are not made. In the current studies there is no evidence that people are making in-group–out-group evaluations or comparisons. Both the threats and the affirmation were directed at the self, rather than at the group, and the evaluations were always of a single individual. Given that the self-affirmation manipulation in Study 1 was irrelevant to participants' group identity or status, it is unclear how social identity theory could account for the results of this study. Moreover, from a perspective that emphasizes in-group–out-group differences, one might predict that the negative feedback in Study 3 should have caused participants to derogate the Italian candidate because the Italian candidate could be considered an out-group member for most of the participants. In addition, such derogation should have been associated with a greater increase in self-esteem. The results do not support this account.

Downward social comparison theory argues that people make negative evaluations of others to bolster their self-esteem. A more precisely defined conception of downward social comparison, however, might require that social comparisons involve self–other distinctions. Our approach suggests that such self–other distinctions might indeed restore one's self-image, but negative evaluations of stereotyped others that do not involve self–other comparisons should also restore one's self-image. In the current studies there is no evidence that our participants made self–other comparisons when evaluating the targets. Moreover, even if participants made self–other distinctions, downward social comparison theory would predict that the self-image threats should have led to derogation of all other targets, whether or not they appeared to be members of a stereotyped group. The results of our studies do not support such a prediction.

At a theoretical level, therefore, our approach is consistent in many ways with other theories, such as frustration–aggression, social identity, and downward social comparison theory, although there are some important differences. In addition, only our account can explain the set of results found in the current studies.

At an empirical level, several studies have shown that self-image threat can lead to negative evaluations of others (Brown & Gallagher, 1992; Crocker et al., 1987; Gibbons & Gerrard, 1991), and other studies have demonstrated that negative evaluations of others can lead to increased self-esteem (Brickman & Bulman, 1977; Taylor & Lobel, 1989; Wills, 1991; Wood & Taylor, 1991). Our studies differ from these previous studies by demonstrating that when people experience self-image threats, their negative evaluations of stereotyped others can mediate an increase in self-esteem. Furthermore, the current studies are the first to show that thinking about a self-relevant value unrelated to prejudice can lead to a reduction in stereotyping. Thus, the findings of the current studies support our contention that stereotypic evaluations of others can serve a self-image-maintenance function.

In our view, any negative evaluation of others—through downward social comparisons, intergroup discrimination, or stereotyping and prejudice—has the potential to serve a self-image-maintenance function. Because of the prevalence, consensual nature, and potential subtlety of negative stereotypes in particular, stereotyping and prejudice may be an especially common and effective means of self-affirmation.

The Role of Motivation in Stereotyping and Prejudice

Major reviews of the stereotyping and prejudice literature (e.g., Ashmore & Del Boca, 1981; Brewer & Kramer, 1985; Hamilton & Trolier, 1986; Hilton & von Hippel, 1996; Snyder & Miene, 1994; Stroebe & Insko, 1989) acknowledge the role of motivational factors (which may be paired with or subsumed under a personality or psychodynamic approach) as one of the principal perspectives or approaches to the study of stereotyping and prejudice, along with the sociocultural and cognitive approaches. Typically, however, relatively little empirical evidence beyond research concerning psychodynamic-based constructs and theories from the 1940s and 1950s or intergroup relations and related phenomena (e.g., realistic group conflict and social identity theory) is cited in support of this perspective. The present research, along with recent examinations of the roles of affect and emotion (Esses, Haddock, & Zanna, 1994; Forgas, 1995; Islam & Hewstone, 1993; Mackie & Hamilton, 1993) and inhibition in stereotyping and prejudice (Bodenhausen & Macrae, in press; Devine, 1989; Devine, Monteith, Zuwerink, & Elliot, 1991; Monteith, 1993), examinations of the functions of stereotyping and prejudice (Snyder & Miene, 1994), examinations of the influence of desired beliefs on person perception (Klein & Kunda, 1992), and examinations of the roles of self-esteem and collective self-esteem in intergroup perceptions and discrimination (Branscombe & Wann, 1994; Crocker et al., 1987), reflects a burgeoning interest in processes that are relevant to this underdeveloped motivational perspective.

The results of the studies reported in this article suggest that prejudiced perceptions of members of stereotyped groups can, under the appropriate conditions, help perceivers restore a positive self-image. Engaging in stereotyping and prejudice, therefore, can be an attractive way for many individuals to feel better about themselves in the absence of more readily available means of alleviating self-image threats or of affirming oneself. Given the same sociocultural context, and given the same cues and information and information-processing conditions, perceivers who are motivated to restore a feeling of overall self-worth should be more likely than other perceivers to seek out or take advantage of stereotypes.

This is not to suggest, however, that sociocultural and cognitive factors are not also critically important in the processes examined in our studies. Rather, these studies reflect an interplay of each of these factors. This is reflected in the interaction between ethnicity or sexual orientation of the target and the manipulation of self-affirmation (Study 1) or self-esteem threat (Studies 2 and 3). If the need to restore a positive overall sense of self-worth influenced prejudice independently of social –cognitive factors, then the manipulations of self-affirmation and self-threat should have resulted simply in more positive (when self-affirmed) or

more negative (when the self was threatened and not affirmed) evaluations of the target individual. Rather, the manipulations of self-affirmation and self-threat significantly influenced participants' evaluations of the target only when they thought she or he was a member of a group for which there was a strong and negative stereotype, but not when they thought the target was not a member of such a group. Furthermore, evaluating the target negatively was associated with greater self-esteem boost in the former but not in the latter condition. Thus, the presence of the stereotype, stemming from sociocultural and cognitive factors, facilitated the process of derogating the target person and restoring self-esteem.

Only after recognizing the interplay among sociocultural, cognitive, and motivational factors can one adequately address the question of why derogating *any* target would not make participants feel better about themselves. In other words, if a threat to perceivers' self-esteem makes them want to restore their self-esteem, why not derogate an Italian woman if she is more available than a Jewish woman? Cognitive and sociocultural factors provide an answer to this question. Within the culture in which Studies 1 and 3 were conducted, there was a strong negative stereotype of Jewish American women but not of Italian American women. The JAP stereotype provided participants with the cognitive basis for perceiving the individual in a negative light. Similarly, the gay man stereotype provided participants in Study 2 with the cognitive basis for perceiving the individual in a stereotypical and negative light. Derogation would seem less justifiable in the absence of the stereotype because participants' judgments would not have been biased by the stereotype. Rather than feel better about themselves, most individuals likely would feel worse if they realized that they had disparaged another person in order to restore their own sense of self-worth (e.g., Devine et al., 1991). Stereotypes, through social–cognitive processes such as assimilation, illusory correlations, and schematic processing, can therefore facilitate self-image maintenance, particularly to the extent that perceivers are not aware of this influence.

The Nature of Stereotyping

Most of the stereotypes that we can think of are predominantly negative. Although they are very different from each other, stereotypes about African Americans, people with disabilities, Latinos, women, Native Americans, older people, gay men, lesbians, and those low in social economic status are similar in that they are primarily negative. The current analysis provides a possible explanation for the predominantly negative character of these stereotypes. Although there are undoubtedly other mechanisms that create and perpetuate negative stereotypes (e.g., illusory correlations, out-group homogeneity, in-group bias, and social roles), our analysis suggests that stereotypes may often take on a negative character because the negativity can help restore people's self-images. When people form stereotypes about a group, they may be more likely to characterize the group in negative terms because such characterizations allow evaluations of the group that can be used for later self-affirmation. Similarly, these stereotypes may be particularly resistant to change because they can make perceivers feel better about themselves.

This analysis emphasizes the important role that motivation can play in stereotyping and prejudice. People may be more likely to stereotype others or engage in prejudicial evaluations to the extent that they are motivated to restore or enhance their self-images. Thus, understanding people's motivations may be critical in determining whether they will stereotype others, how they will stereotype others, and what form these stereotypes will take. Stereotyping and prejudice are clearly an important problem in our society. Our analysis suggests that a complete understanding of these processes, and ways of mitigating them, requires an understanding of the role of the self in people's perceptions of others.

REFERENCES

Abrams, D. (1994). Social self-regulation, *Personality and Social Psychology Bulletin, 20,* 473–483.

Abrams, D., & Hogg, M. A. (1988). Comments on the motivational status of self-esteem in social identity and intergroup discrimination. *European Journal of Social Psychology, 18,* 317–334.

Ammons, R. B., & Ammons, C. H. (1962). The quick test: Provisional manual. *Psychological Reports, 11,* 111–161.

Ashmore, R. D., & Del Boca, F. K. (1981). Conceptual approaches to stereotypes and stereotyping. In D. L. Hamilton (Ed.), *Cognitive processes in stereotyping and intergroup behavior* (pp. 1–35). Hillsdale, NJ: Erlbaum.

Baron, R. M., & Kenny, D. A. (1986). The moderator–mediator variable distinction in social psychological research: Conceptual, strategic, and statistical considerations. *Journal of Personality and Social Psychology, 51,* 1173–1182.

Bodenhausen, G. V., & Macrae, C. N. (in press). The self-regulation of intergroup perception: Mechanisms and consequences of stereotype suppression. In C. N. Macrae, M. Hewstone, & C. Stangor (Eds.), *Foundations of stereotypes and stereotyping.* New York: Guilford Press.

Branscombe, N. R., & Wann, D. L. (1994). Collective self-esteem consequences of outgroup derogation when a valued social identity is on trial. *European Journal of Social Psychology, 24,* 641–657.

Brewer, M. B. (1993). Social identity, distinctiveness, and in-group homogeneity. *Social Cognition, 11,* 150–164.

Brewer, M. B., & Kramer, R. M. (1985). The psychology of intergroup attitudes and behavior. *Annual Review of Psychology, 36,* 219–243.

Brickman, P., & Bulman, R. J. (1977). Pleasure and pain in social comparison. In J. M. Suls & R. L. Miller (Eds.), *Social comparison processes: Theoretical and empirical perspectives* (pp. 149–186). Washington, DC: Hemisphere.

Brown, J. D., Collins, R. L., & Schmidt, G. W. (1988). Self-esteem and direct versus indirect forms of self-enhancement. *Journal of Personality and Social Psychology, 55,* 445–453.

Brown, J. D., & Gallagher, F. M. (1992). Coming to terms with failure: Private self-enhancement and public self-effacement. *Journal of Experimental Social Psychology, 28,* 3–22.

Cameron, J. E., & Lalonde, R. N. (1994). Self, ethnicity, and social group memberships in two generations of Italian Canadians. *Personality and Social Psychology Bulletin, 20,* 514–520.

Cohen, D., & Nisbett, R. E. (1994). Self-protection and the culture of honor: Explaining Southern violence. *Personality and Social Psychology Bulletin, 20,* 551–567.

Cooley, C. H. (1902). *Human nature and the social order.* New York: Schocken Books.

Crocker, J., Thompson, L. J., McGraw, K. M., & Ingerman, C. (1987). Downward comparison, prejudice, and evaluations of others: Effects of self-esteem and threat. *Journal of Personality and Social Psychology, 52,* 907–916.

Darley, J. M., Fleming, J. H., Hilton, J. L., & Swann, W. B. (1988). Dispelling negative expectancies: The impact of interaction goals and target characteristics on the expectancy confirmation process. *Journal of Experimental Social Psychology, 24,* 19–36.

Devine, P. G. (1989). Stereotypes and prejudice: Their controlled and automatic components. *Journal of Personality and Social Psychology, 56,* 5–18.

Devine, P. G., Monteith, M. J., Zuwerink, J. R., & Elliot, A. J. (1991). Prejudice with and without compunction. *Journal of Personality and Social Psychology, 60,* 817–830.

Ditto, P. H., & Lopez, D. F. (1992). Motivated skepticism: Use of differential decision criteria for preferred and nonpreferred conclusions. *Journal of Personality and Social Psychology, 63,* 568–584.

Dollard, J., Doob, L. W., Miller, N. E., Mowrer, O. H., & Sears, R. R. (1939). *Frustration and aggression.* New Haven, CT: Yale University Press.

Dovidio, J. F., & Gaertner, S. L. (1991). Changes in the expression and assessment of racial prejudice. In H. J. Knopke, R. J. Norrell, & R. W. Rogers (Eds.), *Opening doors: Perspectives on race relations in contemporary America* (pp. 119–148). Tuscaloosa: University of Alabama Press.

Eccles, J. S., Jacobs, J. E., & Harold, R. D. (1990). Gender role stereotypes, expectancy effects, and parents' socialization of gender differences. *Journal of Social Issues, 46,* 183–201.

Esses, V. M., Haddock, G., & Zanna, M. P. (1994). The role of mood in the expression of intergroup stereotypes. In M. P. Zanna & J. M. Olson (Eds.), *The psychology of prejudice: The Ontario Symposium* (Vol. 7, pp. 77–101). Hillsdale, NJ: Erlbaum.

Fein, S., Cross, J. A., & Spencer, S. J. (1995, August). *Self-esteem maintenance, stereotype consistency, and men's prejudice toward gays.* Paper presented at the 103rd Annual Convention of the American Psychological Association, New York.

Festinger, L. (1954). A theory of social comparison processes. *Human Relations, 7,* 117–140.

Forgas, J. P. (1995). Mood and judgment: The affect infusion model (AIM). *Psychological Bulletin, 117,* 39–66.

Gibbons, F. X., & Gerrard, M. (1991). Downward social comparison and coping with threat. In J. M. Suls & T. A. Wills (Eds.), *Social comparison: Theory and research* (pp. 317–345). Hillsdale, NJ: Erlbaum.

Gibbons, F. X., & McCoy, S. B. (1991). Self-esteem, similarity, and reaction to active versus passive downward comparison. *Journal of Personality and Social Psychology, 60,* 414–424.

Greenberg, J., Solomon, S., Pyszczynski, T., Rosenblatt, A., Burling, J., Lyon, D., Simon, L., & Pinel, E. (1992). Why do people need self-esteem? Converging evidence that self-esteem serves an anxiety-buffering function. *Journal of Personality and Social Psychology, 63,* 913–922.

Greenwald, A. G. (1980). The totalitarian ego: Fabrication and revision of personal history. *American Psychologist, 35,* 603–618.

Hamilton, D. L., & Trolier, T. K. (1986). Stereotypes and stereotyping: An overview of the cognitive approach. In J. F. Dovidio & S. L. Gaertner (Eds.), *Prejudice, discrimination, and racism: Theory and research* (pp. 127–163). Orlando, FL: Academic Press.

Hays, W. L. (1981). *Statistics* (3rd ed.). New York: Holt, Rinehart & Winston.

Heatherton, T. F., & Polivy, J. (1991). Development and validation of a scale for measuring state self-esteem. *Journal of Personality and Social Psychology, 60,* 895–910.

Higgins, E. T. (1996). Emotional experiences: The pains and pleasures of distinct regulatory systems. In R. D. Kavanaugh, B. Zimmerberg, & S. Fein (Eds.), *Emotion: Interdisciplinary perspectives* (pp. 203–241). Mahwah, NJ: Erlbaum.

Higgins, E. T., & Tykocinski, O. (1992). Self-discrepancies and biographical memory: Personality and cognition at the level of psychological situation. *Personality and Social Psychology Bulletin, 18,* 527–535.

Hilton, J. L., & von Hippel, W. H. (1996). Stereotypes. *Annual Review of Psychology, 47,* 237–271.

Hogg, M. A., & Abrams, D. (1988). *Social identifications: A social psychology of intergroup relations and group processes.* London: Routledge.

Islam, M. R., & Hewstone, M. (1993). Dimensions of contact as predictors of intergroup anxiety, perceived out-group variability, and outgroup attitude: An integrative model. *Personality and Social Psychology Bulletin, 19,* 700–710.

Keppel, G. (1973). *Design and analysis: A researcher's handbook.* Englewood Cliffs, NJ: Prentice Hall.

Kite, M., & Deaux, K. (1987). Gender belief systems: Homosexuality and the implicit inversion theory. *Psychology of Women Quarterly, 11,* 83–96.

Klein, W. M., & Kunda, Z. (1992). Motivated person perception: Constructing justifications for desired beliefs. *Journal of Experimental Social Psychology, 28,* 145–168.

Klein, W. M., & Kunda, Z. (1993). Maintaining self-serving social comparisons: Biased reconstruction of one's past behaviors. *Personality and Social Psychology Bulletin, 19,* 732–739.

Liu, T. J., & Steele, C. M. (1986). Attributional analysis as self-affirmation. *Journal of Personality and Social Psychology, 51,* 531–540.

Mackie, D. M., & Hamilton, D. L. (Eds.). (1993). *Affect, cognition, and stereotyping: Interactive processes in group perception.* San Diego, CA: Academic Press.

Markus, H. (1977). Self-schemata and processing information about the self. *Journal of Personality and Social Psychology, 35,* 63–78.

Markus, H., & Wurf, E. (1987). The dynamic self-concept. *Annual Review of Psychology, 38,* 299–337.

Markus, H. R., & Kitayama, S. (1991). Culture and the self: Implications for cognition, emotion, and motivation. *Psychological Review, 98,* 224–253.

Markus, H. R., & Kitayama, S. (1994). A collective fear of the collective: Implications for selves and theories of selves. *Personality and Social Psychology Bulletin, 20,* 568–579.

Mead, G. H. (1934). *Mind, self, and society.* Chicago: University of Chicago Press.

Mehrabian, A., & Russell, J. (1974). *An approach to environmental psychology.* Cambridge, MA: MIT Press.

Miller, N. E., & Bugelski, R. (1948). The influence of frustrations imposed by the in-group on attitude expressed toward out-group. *Journal of Psychology, 25,* 437–442.

Monteith, M. J. (1993). Self-regulation of prejudiced responses: Implications for progress in prejudice-reduction efforts. *Journal of Personality and Social Psychology, 65,* 469–485.

Neuberg, S. L., & Fiske, S. T. (1987). Motivational influences on impression formation: Outcome dependency, accuracy-driven attention, and individuating processes. *Journal of Personality and Social Psychology, 53,* 431–444.

Nisbett, R. E., & Ross, L. (1980). *Human inference: Strategies and shortcomings of social judgment.* Englewood Cliffs, NJ: Prentice Hall.

Rosenthal, R., & Jacobson, L. (1968). *Pygmalion in the classroom: Teacher expectation and pupils' intellectual development.* New York: Holt, Rinehart & Winston.

Rosenthal, R., & Rosnow, R. L. (1991). *Essentials of behavioral research: Methods and data analysis* (2nd ed.) New York: McGraw-Hill.

Ross, M., & Sicoly, F. (1979). Egocentric biases in availability and attribution. *Journal of Personality and Social Psychology, 37,* 322–336.

Schlenker, B. R., Weigold, M. F., & Hallam, J. R. (1990). Self-serving attributions in social context: Effects of self-esteem and social pressure. *Journal of Personality and Social Psychology, 58,* 855–863.

Smith, E. R. (1993). Social identity and social emotions: Toward new conceptualizations of prejudice. In D. M. Mackie & D. L. Hamilton (Eds.), *Affect, cognition, and stereotyping: Interactive processes in group perception* (pp. 297–315). San Diego, CA: Academic Press.

Snyder, M. (1984). When belief creates reality. In L. Berkowitz (Ed.), *Advances in experimental social psychology* (Vol. 18, pp. 248–306). New York: Academic Press.

Snyder, M., & Miene, P. (1994). On the functions of stereotypes and prejudice. In M. P. Zanna & J. M. Olson (Eds.), *The psychology of prejudice: The Ontario Symposium* (Vol. 7, pp. 33–54). Hillsdale, NJ: Erlbaum.

Spencer, S. J., & Steele, C. M. (1990, May). *The role of self-esteem functioning in IQ estimation.* Paper presented at the 62nd meeting of the Midwestern Psychological Association, Chicago.

Steele, C. M. (1988). The psychology of self-affirmation: Sustaining the integrity of the self. In L. Berkowitz (Ed.), *Advances in experimental social psychology* (Vol. 21, pp. 261–302). New York: Academic Press.

Steele, C. M., & Aronson, J. (1995). Stereotype threat and the intellectual test performance of African Americans. *Journal of Personality and Social Psychology, 69,* 797–811.

Steele, C. M., & Liu, T. J. (1983). Dissonance processes as self-affirmation. *Journal of Personality and Social Psychology, 45,* 5–19.

Steele, C. M., Spencer, S. J., & Lynch, M. (1993). Self-image

resilience and dissonance: The role of affirmational resources. *Journal of Personality and Social Psychology, 64,* 885–896.

Stein, K. F. (1994). Complexity of the self-schema and responses to disconfirming feedback. *Cognitive Therapy and Research, 18,* 161–178.

Stroebe, W., & Insko, C. A. (1989). Stereotype, prejudice, and discrimination: Changing conceptions in theory and research. In D. Bar-Tal, C. F. Graumann, A. W. Kruglanski, & W. Stroebe (Eds.), *Stereotyping and prejudice: Changing conceptions* (pp. 3–34). New York: Springer-Verlag.

Swann, W. B., Stein-Seroussi, A., & Giesler, R. B. (1992). Why people self-verify. *Journal of Personality and Social Psychology, 62,* 392–401.

Tajfel, H. (Ed.). (1982). *Social identity and intergroup relations.* Cambridge, England: Cambridge University Press.

Taylor, S. E., & Lobel, M. (1989). Social comparison activity under threat: Downward evaluation and upward contacts. *Psychological Review, 96,* 569–575.

Tesser, A. (1988). Toward a self-evaluation maintenance model of social behavior. In L. Berkowitz (Ed.), *Advances in experimental social psychology* (Vol. 21, pp. 181–227). New York: Academic Press.

Tesser, A., & Cornell, D. P. (1991). On the confluence of self processes. *Journal of Experimental Social Psychology, 27,* 501–526.

Tetlock, P. E. (1983). Accountability and the perseverance of first impressions. *Social Psychology Quarterly, 46,* 285–292.

Triandis, H. C. (1989). The self and social behavior in differing cultural contexts. *Psychological Review, 96,* 506–520.

Turner, J. C. (1982). Toward a cognitive redefinition of the social group. In H. Tajfel (Ed.), *Social identity and intergroup relations.* Cambridge, England: Cambridge University Press.

Turner, J. C., Oakes, P. J., Haslam, S. A., & McGarty, C. (1994). Self and collective: Cognition and social context. *Personality and Social Psychology Bulletin, 20,* 454–463.

Wills, T. A. (1981). Downward comparison principles in social psychology. *Psychological Bulletin, 90,* 245–271.

Wills, T. A. (1991). Similarity and self-esteem in downward comparison. In J. M. Suls & T. A. Wills (Eds.), *Social comparison: Theory and research* (pp. 51–78). Hillsdale, NJ: Erlbaum.

Winer, B. J. (1971). *Statistical principles in experimental design* (2nd ed.). New York: McGraw-Hill.

Wood, J. V., & Taylor, K. L. (1991). Serving self-relevant goals through social comparison. In J. M. Suls & T. A. Wills (Eds.), *Social comparison: Theory and research* (pp. 23–50). Hillsdale, NJ: Erlbaum.

Received December 21, 1995
Revision received November 1, 1996
Accepted November 8, 1996 ■

On the Functional Value of Attitudes: The Influence of Accessible Attitudes on the Ease and Quality of Decision Making

Russell H. Fazio,* Jim Blascovich,** and Denise M. Driscoll***

A series of experiments relevant to the functional value of accessible attitudes is reported. Experiment 1 established that diastolic blood pressure was sensitive to the task demands involved in subjects' expression of a preference between pairs of abstract paintings. In Experiments 2 and 3, subjects who had developed and rehearsed attitudes toward the individual paintings displayed a smaller elevation in diastolic blood pressure while performing this pairwise preference task than control subjects, suggesting that attitudes can ease decision making. Experiment 4 provided converging evidence for this hypothesis in that faster decision latencies were observed during the pairwise preference task when subjects had previously developed accessible attitudes toward the individual paintings. Evidence was also obtained suggesting that accessible attitudes enhanced the quality of the decisions made during the pairwise preference task.

The issue that this article addresses concerns the functionality of having an attitude. A quotation from Gordon Allport (1935) nicely illustrates what we have in mind.

Without guiding attitudes the individual is confused and baffled. Some kind of preparation is essential before he can make a satisfactory observation, pass suitable judgment, or make any but

* Indiana University.
** State University of New York at Buffalo.
*** Purdue University.
Authors' note. The present research was supported by Research Scientist Development Award MH00452 and Grant MH38832 from the National Institute of Mental Health to the first author and by National Science Foundation Grant BNS-9010231 to the second author. The authors thank Kathy Greene for her assistance with data collection and analysis and John Cacioppo, Tory Higgins, Richard Rose, Eliot Smith, and Timothy Smith for their helpful feedback during various stages of the research project. Address correspondence to Russell H. Fazio, Department of Psychology, Indiana University, Bloomington, IN 47405.

the most primitive reflex type of response. Attitudes determine for each individual what he will see and hear, what he will think and what he will do. To borrow a phrase from William James, they "engender meaning upon the world"; they draw lines about and segregate an otherwise chaotic environment; they are our methods for finding our way about in an ambiguous universe. (p. 806)

Like Allport, numerous theorists have considered attitudes to be functional constructs that accomplish a great deal for the individual. They structure one's social universe and, in so doing, ease decision making. They facilitate the individual's movement through the diverse array of objects and people encountered daily. In delineating various functions that attitudes might serve, both Katz (1960) and Smith, Bruner, and White (1956) commented on this knowledge or object appraisal function. For example, Smith et al. (1956) argue that an attitude toward an object saves the person from "the energy-consuming and sometimes painful process of figuring out *de novo* how he shall relate himself to it" (p. 41). Presumably, having categorized the elements in one's social world into good and bad enables the individual to progress easily through daily life. What to approach and what to avoid is clear. In this way, the individual is also in a position to maximize the likelihood of having positive day-to-day life experiences and to minimize the occurrence of aversive experiences.

This object appraisal function can be considered the primary value of possessing an attitude. In contrast to the many other functions that attitudes can also serve, this one is applicable to all attitudes. The other functions that theorists have discussed have more to do with the content or direction of attitudes than with the general utility of simply holding an attitude, regardless of its valence (e.g., DeBono, 1987; Herek, 1987; Shavitt, 1990). For example, the utilitarian function that has been posited centers on the development of positive attitudes toward those objects that have previously produced satisfaction or reward and the development of negative attitudes toward objects that have thwarted needs or desires or generally have produced some dissatisfaction. Similarly, in

discussing an ego-defensive function that attitudes might serve, functional theorists have noted that an attitude of a particular valence can help maintain or enhance an individual's self-esteem. For example, concerns about one's own self-esteem may be lessened by the development of a negative attitude toward some outgroup and the noting of one's superior relative standing.

In all these cases, the resulting attitudes, whether they stem from the utilitarian value of the attitude object, the ego-protective benefits of the attitude, or something else, serve an object appraisal function. When the attitude object is encountered, the attitude, in the words of Smith et al. (1956), "provides a ready aid in 'sizing up' objects and events in the environment" (p. 41). That is, regardless of why the individual's attitude took on a particular valence, the mere possession of any attitude serves the individual by orienting him or her to the object in question.

To our knowledge, however, no direct evidence exists documenting the functionality of possessing an attitude. The most closely related literature concerns research examining the extent to which people rely on their attitudes when they are experiencing varying levels of time pressure to reach a judgment. A number of studies have revealed that individuals are more likely to base a decision on their attitudes when they lack the time to consider the details of the stimulus information carefully (e.g., Jamieson & Zanna, 1989; Kruglanski & Freund, 1983; Sanbonmatsu & Fazio, 1990). These findings certainly imply that attitudes are useful constructs. However, the research is not informative with respect to the question whether individuals who lack a relevant attitude experience more difficulty in decision making than individuals who have the "ready aid" of a previously formed attitude.

The present research aims to demonstrate the validity of our argument regarding the functionality of possessing an attitude. More specifically, the series of experiments to be reported will suggest that possessing an attitude is functional in the sense that it increases the ease, speed, and quality of decision making. The particular approach that we took to investigating this functionality was heavily determined by past work concerning attitudes and, in particular, by a conceptualization of attitudes and their activation from memory that has guided research on the process by which attitudes influence behavior (e.g., Fazio, 1986, 1989). Within this model, an attitude is viewed as an association between a given object and a given evaluation. When an attitude is viewed as an association, it becomes obvious that the strength of an attitude, like any construct based on associative learning, can vary. That is, the strength of the association between the object and the evaluation can vary. This associative strength is postulated to be the major determinant of the likelihood that the attitude will be activated from memory when the individual encounters the attitude object.

This view allows us to consider what we call the attitude/nonattitude continuum. At the nonattitude end of the continuum is the case of an individual not having any a priori evaluation of the object stored in memory (Converse, 1970). It is not available. As we move along the continuum, an evaluation is available in memory and the strength of the association between the object and the evaluation increases. Toward the upper end of the continuum is the case of a well-learned strong association—sufficiently strong that the evaluation is capable of being activated automatically from memory upon observation of the attitude object (see Fazio, Sanbonmatsu, Powell, & Kardes, 1986).

This continuum provides an interesting means of conceptualizing the strength of an attitude. Position along the continuum determines the power of the attitude. The attitudes of two individuals with identical scores on some attitude measurement instrument may still differ markedly in their strength—that is, their likelihood of activation upon the individual's encountering the attitude object. The attitude of one individual may be activated in such a situation whereas the attitude of the other may not be. As a result, the attitude of the former individual is in a better position to influence judgments and behavior. Evidence supporting this assertion has been obtained in a number of investigations. Both correlational investigations in which the strength of object-evaluation associations in memory has been measured and laboratory experiments in which associative strength has been manipulated experimentally have found position along the attitude/nonattitude continuum to moderate the influence of attitudes on judgments and behavior (e.g., Fazio, Chen, McDonel, & Sherman, 1982; Fazio, Powell, & Williams, 1989; Fazio & Williams, 1986; Houston & Fazio, 1989).

The present research aims to extend this reasoning to the issue of the functional value of possessing an attitude. As mentioned earlier, even though the object appraisal function has been discussed in the literature for a long time, we know of no evidence that documents that attitudes are characterized by this functionality. The implications of our model for this notion of functionality are obvious. The degree to which an attitude adequately fulfills this object appraisal function would appear to depend on the extent to which the attitude is capable of being activated automatically from memory when the individual observes the attitude object. The likelihood of such automatic activation depends on the strength of the object-evaluation association. It is attitudes that involve a strong association that are truly functional. By virtue of their accessibility from memory, such attitudes do indeed provide the individual with the "ready aid" mentioned earlier. They free the individual from the processing required for reflective thought about his or her evaluation of the object. Simply put, the individual does not have to work so hard.

An experimental paradigm was developed to investigate these notions regarding functionality. The paradigm involved examining the degree to which individuals expended effort while performing a task for which attitudes were relevant. As attitude objects we chose abstract paintings, because we wanted novel objects toward which individuals were unlikely to have preexisting attitudes. The critical task, which will be referred to as the pairwise preference task, involved subjects' expressions of a preference between the members of pairs of such paintings.

We were interested in the degree to which individuals might exert effort while coping with the task demands involved in performing this pairwise preference task. Taking a lead from the literature on cardiovascular reactivity, we decided to use blood pressure as an indicant of any such effort expenditure. A number of investigations have found blood pressure to be sensitive to both cognitive and social task demands that individuals might be attempting to fulfill (e.g., Bittker, Buchsbaum, Williams, & Wynne, 1975; Obrist et al., 1978; Smith, Allred, Morrison, & Carlson, 1989; Williams, Bittker, Buchsbaum, & Wynne, 1975; Wright, Contrada, & Patane, 1986).

Three experiments employing the paradigm outlined above and blood pressure as a dependent measure were conducted. Experiment 1 was designed to test the assumption that measures of blood pressure would be sensitive to the task demands involved in the pairwise preference task. Experiments 2 and 3 examined whether the possession of accessible attitudes eased whatever demand for attentional resources might be produced by performing the pairwise preference task.

Experiment 1

Experiment 1 was designed to examine whether blood pressure was at all sensitive to the level of effort expenditure required by decision making during the pairwise preference task. We compared two conditions that differed in the extent to which the pairwise preference task placed demands on the subject. Task demand was manipulated by having subjects perform under self-paced or rushed conditions.

Method

Subjects

Thirty undergraduates participated in the experiment in partial fulfillment of an introductory psychology course requirement. Fifteen were assigned randomly to each of the two conditions.

Procedure

On arrival, the subject was told that the experiment concerned blood pressure during performance of a variety of tasks. The experimenter showed the sub-

ject the apparatus and attached the cuff. The subject's arm rested on a table at the side of the chair in which the subject was seated. On another table were a slide projector, an audiocassette recorder, and the blood pressure apparatus. The instrument was a Norelco Model HC3501, which had an automatically inflatable cuff and the capacity to store a number of readings in memory.[1] Immediately following this brief introduction, two consecutive baseline readings of blood pressure were taken. The average of the two served as the baseline.

All subjects then performed a task involving naming the colors in a series of slides of abstract paintings. This color-naming task will be described more fully in the presentation of the later experiments. In those experiments, this task was performed only by the subjects in the control conditions and constituted part of the manipulation. In the present experiment, all subjects performed the task, which was included only to bolster the cover story of our being interested in blood pressure fluctuation while individuals are performing a variety of tasks.

The second task that subjects performed was the critical pairwise preference task. The stimuli for this task were slides of 30 abstract paintings. The paintings were paired randomly, each painting being included in three unique pairings so as to form a total of 45 pairs. Subjects were told to indicate which member of the pair they preferred by saying "Left" or "Right" aloud. (These preference decisions were recorded by the audiocassette recorder.) In order to induce subjects to take this task seriously, the experimenter stressed the importance of responding accurately and led subjects to believe that some of the pairs would be repeated a second time so that their consistency could be checked.

Manipulation. The experimental manipulation centered on the nature of this pairwise preference task. In the rushed condition, the experimenter continued her description of the task by informing subjects that the task would be difficult because the slides would be advanced at a fairly rapid rate. They would have to decide on and indicate their preferences quickly. In fact, the slide projector automatically advanced every 2.5 s. In contrast, the subjects in the other condition were simply handed the remote control that operated the slide projector and instructed to advance the projector whenever they had reached a decision on any given trial. Thus, the control subjects operated in a self-paced fashion.

Dependent measures. Given the time that it took for the cuff to inflate automatically, it was possible to collect only one blood pressure reading during the pairwise preference task. The extent to which this reading deviates from the baseline reading constituted the major dependent variable. A subsequent reading was collected immediately after the task was concluded.[2] Subjects then completed a questionnaire regarding their subjective reactions to the pairwise preference task. The subjects indicated on 0-to-10 scales how difficult, hurried, and stressful they had found the task.

Finally, the experimenter handed the subject prints of the 30 paintings and gave the subject unlimited time to rank-order the entire set in terms of his or her liking for each painting. The intent here was to obtain data that would permit us to assess the quality of decision making during the pairwise preference task.

Results and Discussion

Manipulation check

The experimenter had used a stopwatch to time self-paced subjects' performance on the pairwise preference task. It was evident that these subjects operated at a more leisurely pace than the subjects in the rushed condition. The average time that subjects spent viewing each slide was 3.27 s in the self-paced condition, which differs significantly from the fixed viewing time of 2.5 s in the rushed condition, $t(14) = 4.80, p < .001$.

The self-report data also provide an indication that subjects in the rushed condition found the pairwise preference task more problematic than subjects in the self-paced condition. The two conditions differed significantly on an index that averaged the three ratings of how difficult, hurried, and stressful subjects found the pairwise preference task (rushed $M = 4.62$; self-paced $M = 3.38$), $t(28) = 2.19, p < .05$.

Thus, there is good reason to believe that the manipulation succeeded in making the pairwise preference task differentially demanding and, consequently, that the experiment can provide a test of the assumption that blood pressure will be sensitive to such task demands.

Dependent variables

Blood pressure. Neither systolic nor diastolic baseline readings differed between the two conditions (Ms of 132/78 and 127/72 mmHg for the self-paced and rushed conditions, respectively). The blood pressure data from the pairwise preference task were examined for changes from these baseline readings.[3] A significant difference was apparent on changes in diastolic blood pressure during the pairwise preference task as a function of whether the subjects were rushed or operated under self-paced conditions, $t(28) = 3.09, p < .005$. The rushed subjects ($M = 8.03$) displayed a greater increase in diastolic blood pressure than the self-paced subjects ($M = -6.80$). We doubt that the negative change score for the self-paced condition should be taken very seriously. The negative sign likely reflects an overestimate of baseline diastolic blood pressure stemming from the difficulty of inducing subjects, who may be initially apprehensive about the experimental procedures, to relax sufficiently at the beginning of the experiment. The important point is that a difference between the conditions did emerge on diastolic blood pressure.

The findings for systolic blood pressure were less dramatic. Although the data pattern was similar to that for diastolic blood pressure, the difference between the conditions did not reach a conventional level of statistical significance (rushed $M = -1.60$; self-paced $M = -8.03$), $t(28) = 1.65, p = .11$. As will become apparent, this has held true in all the experiments that were conducted. Diastolic blood pressure has proved to be the more sensitive measure.

The blood pressure readings that were collected

immediately following the pairwise preference task revealed no differences between the conditions for either diastolic (rushed $M = -3.50$; self-paced $M = -7.73$) or systolic blood pressure (rushed $M = -7.80$; self-paced $M = -4.90$), both ts < 1, suggesting that the greater elevations in blood pressure prompted by the rushed pairwise preference task dissipated quickly.

Concurrences. As mentioned earlier, subjects rank-ordered the 30 paintings at the end of the experiment. To assess the quality of subjects' decision making during the pairwise preference task, the extent to which the pairwise decisions corresponded with these rank-orderings was examined. We simply counted the times each subject's expressed pairwise preferences concurred with the rank-orderings. Thus, if a subject ranked Slide #4 as more likable than Slide #12, then the subject was given credit for a concurrence if the subject had chosen Slide #4 over Slide #12 when the two were presented together during the pairwise preference task. A perfect score would be a 45, as there were 45 trials in the pairwise preference task. By chance alone, the subject should receive a score of 22.5.

Scores in both conditions were well above chance (rushed $M = 33.8$, $t(14) = 8.37$, $p < .001$; self-paced $M = 33.53$, $t(14) = 6.51$, $p < .001$), providing assurance that the subjects did take the pairwise preference task seriously. The number of concurrences did not differ between the two conditions, $t < 1$, suggesting that the reliability of decision making during the pairwise preference task did not suffer as a consequence of subjects' being rushed.

To summarize, although subjects in the rushed condition were able to maintain an equivalent and better-than-chance reliability in their decision making during the pairwise preference task, they experienced a greater elevation in diastolic blood pressure while doing so than subjects in the self-paced condition. Apparently, rushed subjects had to bring additional resources to bear on their decision making during the pairwise preference task in order to achieve an equivalent level of performance. This suggests that diastolic blood pressure is

sufficiently sensitive to the demands of the pairwise preference task that it may be fruitful to employ diastolic blood pressure in a test of the functional value of possessing an accessible attitude. Hence, we went on to examine this question in the next experiment.

Experiment 2

All subjects in Experiment 2 performed the pairwise preference task under rushed conditions. That is, we took the condition that had proved the more demanding in Experiment 1 and sought to determine whether individuals who had developed attitudes in an earlier phase of the experiment would need to call on fewer additional resources in order to meet the demands of the rushed pairwise preference task. Subjects in the attitude rehearsal condition were exposed to each of the 30 paintings multiple times and, upon each exposure, announced an attitudinal judgment of the painting aloud. Thus, these subjects were induced to note and express their attitudes toward each painting multiple times. This attitude rehearsal, or repeated expression, manipulation has been used in past work as a convenient way to increase the strength of the association in memory between attitude object and one's evaluation of the object. The manipulation has been shown to be effective in enhancing the accessibility of the attitude from memory (e.g., Fazio et al., 1982, 1986; Houston & Fazio, 1989).

In contrast, we attempted to ensure that subjects in the control condition would not develop accessible attitudes toward the paintings. Indeed, we attempted to distract them from their evaluations of the paintings. These subjects were asked to judge the predominant color apparent in each painting and to estimate the percentage of the painting that consisted of that color. For example, in response to a given painting, the subject might say, "Red—40%." If the subject had sufficient time before the slide projector automatically advanced, the subject was then to name any other colors appearing in the painting. Thus, a subject might say, "Red—40%; yellow, orange, blue." As the paintings included an average of over six distinct colors, this task occupied the subject for virtually the entire time that any given slide was presented.

Thus, all subjects were exposed to each slide the same number of times. However, some subjects developed attitudes and expressed them repeatedly. Control subjects received no such inducement, and any attitudes they may have developed were formed spontaneously in spite of the color-naming task. Consequently, the manipulation permits us to compare subjects whose attitudes are at very different positions along the attitude/nonattitude continuum discussed earlier. On the basis of the findings from Experiment 1, we hypothesized that subjects in the attitude rehearsal condition would display a lesser elevation in diastolic blood pressure during the pairwise preference task than subjects in the control condition.

Method

Subjects

A total of 58 undergraduates participated in the experiment in return for monetary payment. Instrument malfunctions led to omitting the data from 2 subjects from the analysis. The data from another subject were excluded because she indicated, in response to the experimenter's questions during debriefing, that she had taken art history/appreciation courses and recognized many of the paintings. The analyses were based on 28 subjects in the attitude rehearsal condition and 27 in the control condition.

Procedure

Generally speaking, the procedure was identical to that for the rushed condition of Experiment 1, with the exception that the manipulation creating the attitude rehearsal and control conditions preceded the pairwise preference task. After the two initial blood pressure readings were taken, the experimenter introduced the subject's first task. During this task, all subjects were exposed to each abstract painting a total of four times. The 30 paintings were arranged in four blocks of slides; each painting appeared once in each block for a period of 5 s.

The paintings were ordered randomly within each block. Subjects in the attitude rehearsal condition were instructed to indicate their liking for each slide by saying aloud either "Like strongly," "Like," "Dislike," or "Dislike strongly." Subjects in the control condition were asked to judge the predominant color apparent in each painting, to estimate the percentage of the painting that consisted of that color, and then, if they had sufficient time during the 5-s presentation of that slide, to name any other colors appearing in the painting. Blood pressure was assessed twice during the 120 trials that constituted these manipulation tasks.

From this point on, the experimental procedure did not vary from that used in the rushed condition of Experiment 1. All subjects performed the pairwise preference task with 2.5 s for each trial, then completed the self-report measure in which they made subjective judgments of the pairwise preference task, and, finally, rank-ordered the 30 paintings from most to least liked.

Results

Blood pressure

Changes in diastolic pressure. Initial baseline diastolic blood pressure was equivalent in the two conditions (Ms of 73 and 74 for the color-naming and attitude rehearsal conditions, respectively). Mean changes in diastolic blood pressure from this baseline measure are displayed in Figure 17.1. Consider first diastolic blood pressure during the tasks that constitute the manipulation: the color-naming task and the attitude rehearsal task. The two readings taken during the manipulation tasks were averaged, and the difference between this average and the baseline measure was computed. The color-naming task produced a substantial elevation in diastolic blood pressure ($M = 14.35$). In contrast, the attitude rehearsal task was significantly less demanding ($M = -0.13$), $t(53) = 4.59$, $p < .001$. (This difference does pose some difficulties for interpreting the remaining findings—an issue that is discussed shortly and addressed directly by Experiment 3.)

The data of major interest concern diastolic blood pressure during the pairwise preference task. Just as predicted, the control condition displayed a significantly greater elevation in blood pressure ($M = 6.37$) than the attitude rehearsal condition ($M = -1.52$), $t(53) = 2.48$, $p < .02$. This difference suggests that accessible attitudes do indeed ease decision making. As in Experiment 1, the reading taken immediately after the pairwise preference task revealed no difference in diastolic blood pressure (control $M = -1.65$; attitude rehearsal $M = -6.10$), $t(53) = 1.08$, $p > .25$, suggesting that the elevation in diastolic blood pressure experienced during the pairwise preference task dissipated quickly.

Changes in systolic pressure. Baseline systolic blood pressure did not differ between the conditions (Ms of 126 and 125 for the color-naming

and attitude rehearsal conditions, respectively). Changes in systolic blood pressure from this baseline were, once again, less sensitive to the experimental manipulations. A difference between the conditions was apparent on changes in systolic blood pressure during the manipulation tasks (control $M = 1.98$; attitude rehearsal $M = -5.45$), $t(53) = 2.48$, $p < .02$, although the difference was not as dramatic as had been apparent for diastolic blood pressure. No effect of the manipulation was apparent on changes in systolic blood pressure either during the pairwise preference task (control $M = -0.24$; attitude rehearsal $M = -4.41$), $t(53) = 1.35$, $p > .15$, or after the task (control $M = -4.71$; attitude rehearsal $M = -8.31$), $t(53) = 1.16$, $p > .25$.

Additional findings

Concurrences. The correspondence between the decisions that subjects made during the pairwise preference task and their final rank-orderings of the paintings was again examined by counting the concurrences. As in Experiment 1, subjects in both conditions performed far better than the expected chance level of 22.5. The mean number of concurrences was 32.85 in the control condition, $t(26) = 11.35$, $p < .001$, and 36.93 in the attitude rehearsal condition, $t(27) = 18.23$, $p < .001$. Although both conditions surpassed the level expected by chance alone, concurrences were significantly more numerous in the attitude rehearsal condition, $t(53) = 3.38$, $p < .002$, suggesting that the reliability of decision making during the pairwise preference task was enhanced by the possession of accessible attitudes.

Self-reports. Despite the clear evidence from the blood pressure data that subjects found the pairwise preference task more demanding in the control condition than in the attitude rehearsal condition, subjects' self-reports revealed no awareness of any accompanying subjective state of distress. No effect was apparent on the index that averaged subjects' ratings of how difficult, hurried, and stressful they found the pairwise preference task (control $M = 5.69$; attitude rehearsal $M = 6.07$), $t < 1$.

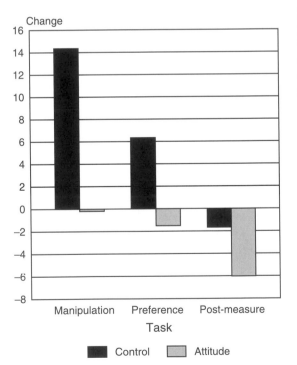

FIGURE 17.1 ■ Changes in diastolic blood pressure as a function of condition at three phases of Experiment 2: during the manipulation task (attitude rehearsal vs. color naming), during the pairwise preference task, and following the pairwise preference task.

Discussion

The results of Experiment 2 provide the first indication of the functional value of accessible attitudes. Such attitudes appear to ease decision making. Relative to control subjects, those subjects who developed and rehearsed attitudes toward each single painting displayed a smaller elevation in diastolic blood pressure while choosing between pairs of paintings. Apparently, fewer additional resources were necessary for attitude rehearsal subjects to perform the pairwise preference task than for control subjects.

The data on concurrences point to a second distinct benefit of possessing an attitude—one concerning the quality of the decision making. Concurrences between the decisions made during the pairwise preference task and the rank-orderings that subjects were given unlimited time to provide were significantly more numerous in the attitude rehearsal condition than in the control condition. Thus, control subjects did not attain as high a performance level as attitude rehearsal subjects, despite apparently having expended greater effort while performing the pairwise preference task.

Experiment 3

The third experiment was a replication of Experiment 2—a replication motivated by two concerns. First, and more important, we were quite astounded by the observation that accessible attitudes eased decision making to the point that subjects displayed a lesser elevation in diastolic blood pressure—despite the theoretical reasoning that underlay the experiment in the first place. Therefore, in the interests of obtaining evidence that the effect was robust, we decided to attempt a replication.

There was yet another motivation. One aspect of the blood pressure data concerned us. Recall that the color-naming task was itself more demanding than the attitude task.[4] Might the control subjects not have returned to baseline before the pairwise preference task and, for that reason, shown elevated blood pressure during the task? There is some reason to doubt an alternative explanation based on this notion. The blood pressure readings

taken immediately after the pairwise preference task revealed no differences between the conditions in either Experiment 1 or Experiment 2. This finding suggests that the elevations produced by the pairwise preference task dissipated rapidly. Such dissipation should also have occurred between the control subjects' performance of the color-naming task and the pairwise preference task. Nonetheless, Experiment 3 was designed to address the possibility directly by including a rest period between the tasks forming the manipulation (color naming vs. attitude rehearsal) and the pairwise preference task.

[EDITORS' NOTE: Experiment 3 included a 5-minute rest period prior to the pairwise preference task. A reading taken at the end of the rest period showed diastolic blood pressure to have returned to baseline. Nevertheless, all the earlier findings replicated.]

Discussion

Experiments 2 and 3 have yielded evidence suggesting two distinct benefits of possessing an attitude. Attitudes can both (a) ease decision making and (b) result in decisions that are of better quality in the sense that one is less likely to indicate later that one would have made a different decision. We wish to interpret these results as showing that the attitude rehearsal task led subjects to develop strong associations in memory between each painting and their evaluation of the painting. Activation of these evaluations during the pairwise preference task made that task less demanding for these subjects. In contrast, the control subjects had to construct their evaluations of each painting during the pairwise preference task, which is more effortful.

However, some alternative possibilities need to be addressed. Owing to the between-subjects nature of the attitude rehearsal manipulation, there exists a "family" of interrelated alternative explanations for the results presented thus far. Whereas subjects in the attitude rehearsal condition were concerned with their liking for each painting in both the manipulation phase of the experiment and the pairwise preference task, subjects in the control condition were not required to focus on their liking for each painting until they faced the pairwise preference task. In this sense, the pairwise preference task is more novel for the control subjects than for the attitude rehearsal subjects. Might differential task novelty, in itself, have yielded the difference observed in elevations in diastolic blood pressure? In a closely related fashion, it is also possible to consider the data in terms of procedural efficiency (e.g., Smith, 1989; Smith, Branscombe, & Bormann, 1988). Some subjects, those in the attitude rehearsal condition, had more trials devoted to evaluating paintings (and hence more practice at evaluating paintings) than other subjects did. Might the attitude rehearsal task simply have made the subjects more efficient at the procedure of evaluating paintings? Such increased efficiency might have made the pairwise preference task less demanding. Experiment 4 was conducted to examine these possibilities.

Experiment 4

Unlike the earlier experiments, Experiment 4 involved a within-subjects manipulation. The 30 paintings were divided randomly into three sets of 10. For one set, subjects engaged in attitude rehearsal; for another set, they performed the color-naming task; for the third, they received no exposure to the paintings. The pairwise preference task involved three types of randomly ordered trials: On one third of the trials, the subject indicated a preference between two paintings that had both been in the attitude rehearsal set; on another third, both paintings had been in the color-naming set; the remaining third involved pairs in which neither painting had been displayed during the first phase of the experiment.

Experiment 4 also involved a change in the dependent measure, necessitated by the logistics of the within-subjects design and the slow recording qualities of our blood pressure instrument. The apparatus did not permit collection of blood pressure data on a trial-by-trial basis. Hence, we turned to another indicant of the effort expended in making a decision on each trial of the pairwise preference task—the latency with which subjects could express their preferences.

What is important about this within-subjects experiment is that all subjects undergo the same task experiences. All subjects have the same number of trials devoted to color naming and to attitude rehearsal. All subjects receive equal levels of practice at judging paintings. So, if all that occurs as a consequence of attitude rehearsal is a diminution of the novelty of the pairwise preference task and/or an increase in procedural efficiency, we would expect no difference among the three kinds of trials that were included in the pairwise preference task. Task novelty and procedural practice have been held constant. If, however, object-evaluation associations are being developed in the memory as a consequence of attitude rehearsal, then the subjects should be faster at indicating a preference when they have rehearsed attitudes toward both alternatives than when they have not.

Method

Subjects

A total of 38 undergraduate students participated in the experiment in return for monetary payment. As many as four subjects participated in any given experimental session. Each subject was situated in an individual booth equipped with a monitor, a response box, and an audiocassette recorder.

Procedure

Subjects were informed that they would be performing a variety of tasks, all of which were to involve stimuli presented on their monitor. They were told that on some tasks they would respond aloud so that their answers could be recorded by the tape recorder in their booth. On other tasks they were to use the response box, and the controlling computer would record their answers.

The 30 paintings had been randomly divided into three sets of 10. One set was assigned to the attitude rehearsal condition, one to the color-naming condition, and one to the no-exposure condition. Which set served which purpose was counterbalanced across experimental sessions. All subjects performed both the attitude rehearsal and the color-naming tasks, exactly as in the earlier experiments. The order in which the two tasks was performed was counterbalanced.[5]

All subjects then performed a task intended to familiarize them with the nature of the pairwise preference task they were to perform next. This practice task involved the display of two adjacent words on the subjects' monitors (e.g., *coffee-tea, Coke-Pepsi*). Subjects were instructed to indicate whether they preferred the item on the left or the item on the right by pressing the appropriately labeled button on the response box. They were instructed to respond as quickly and as accurately as possible. This practice task consisted of 15 trials and merely served to acquaint the subjects with what was to be required of them in the task of major interest.

Subjects then were informed that the next task would also involve their indicating preferences as quickly and accurately as possible using the response box. This time they would be choosing between two abstract paintings on each trial. A total of 30 such pairwise preference trials occurred. Each of the original 30 paintings was paired with two different paintings, so as to form 30 unique pairs. Ten of the pairs involved two paintings from the attitude rehearsal condition, another 10 pairs involved two from the color-naming condition, and another 10 involved two from the no-exposure condition. The 30 trials were arranged in two blocks of 15; each of the 30 paintings appeared once in each block. Responses and response latencies were collected by a microcomputer, which also controlled the slide projector and video system that transmitted the stimulus slides to the subjects' monitors. These response latencies from the pairwise preference task constitute the dependent measure.

Results and Discussion

All latencies were subjected to a reciprocal transformation prior to analysis. Mean latencies, following retransformation back to the original metric of seconds, are displayed in Figure 17.2. A 3 (Condi-

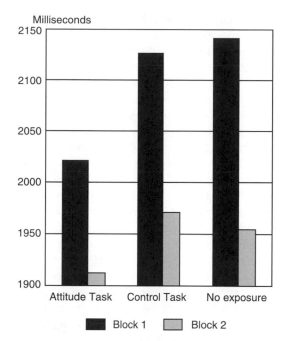

FIGURE 17.2 ■ Mean latency to express a preference in Experiment 4 on the various trials of the pairwise preference task as a function of block and the condition to which each painting had been assigned.

tion: attitude rehearsal, color naming, and no exposure) × 2 (Block) within-subjects analysis of variance was conducted on the transformed latency data. The analysis revealed a main effect of block, such that subjects were faster at indicating preferences in the second block, during which they were encountering each painting for the second time of the pairwise task, $F(1, 37) = 40.55, p < .001$. More important, the predicted main effect of condition was apparent, $F(2, 74) = 6.37, p < .005$, and was not qualified by any interaction with block, $F(2, 74) = 1.43, p > .20$. Further analyses showed this main effect of condition to be due to attitude rehearsal. Subjects were significantly faster on the pairwise trials on which they were choosing between paintings toward which they had rehearsed attitudes ($M = 1,963$ ms) than on trials involving paintings from either the color-naming set ($M = 2,045$), $t(74) = 3.08, p < .005$, or the no-exposure set ($M = 2,043$), $t(74) = 3.10, p < .005$.

The findings from this within-subjects experiment cast doubt on the plausibility of the "family" of alternative explanations discussed earlier. In contrast to Experiments 2 and 3, all subjects in Experiment 4 were equally familiar with the sort of evaluative judgments involved in the pairwise preference task. They all received equal amounts of practice at the general procedure of evaluating paintings before the pairwise preference task. That is, all subjects expressed an attitude toward the 10 paintings in the attitude rehearsal set four times. Nevertheless, subjects were able to make decisions during the pairwise preference task more easily when the paintings involved were ones toward which they had developed and rehearsed attitudes. Apparently, then, the attitude rehearsal task accomplishes much more than simply improving efficiency at the general procedure of evaluating paintings or familiarizing subjects with the nature of the pairwise preference task. Instead, it appears that the task leads to the development of associations in memory between a given painting and the evaluation of that painting.

The equivalence of the latencies stemming from decisions involving pairs of paintings from the color-naming set and pairs of paintings from the no-exposure set is also of interest. Two implications are suggested by this equivalence. First, the color-naming task apparently was quite successful in preventing subjects from spontaneously developing attitudes toward the paintings, just as had been hoped. If the subjects had spontaneously developed attitudes (albeit less accessible ones than those stemming from the attitude rehearsal task) in spite of having been kept busy by naming colors, latencies should have been faster for color-naming pairs than for no-exposure pairs.

The second implication of the equivalence between the color-naming and no-exposure conditions concerns a fairly complex, but nonetheless potential, alternative explanation for Experiments 2 and 3. Recall that the color-naming task was apparently quite demanding; it produced substantial elevations in diastolic blood pressure. Any accompanying subjective experience of stress may have been conditioned to the paintings. By associating such stress with the paintings in general, subjects may have felt some negative affect toward every painting. When attitudes were then

constructed during the pairwise preference task, the color-naming subjects may have been choosing between two paintings that were each judged more negative than was true for the attitude rehearsal subjects. Through such a mechanism, color-naming subjects might have found themselves "choosing between two negatives" more frequently during the pairwise preference task than attitude rehearsal subjects. The frequency of such decisions may, then, have been responsible for the greater elevations in diastolic blood pressure observed among color-naming subjects during the pairwise preference task. However, the plausibility of this argument is diminished by the latency findings. If paintings from the color-naming task were more likely to be judged negatively and more extensive deliberation were required in order to choose between two similarly negative paintings, then average latencies should have been slower on such trials than on trials involving pairs of paintings from the no-exposure set. Obviously, such was not the case.

The plausibility of this explanation is also diminished by a brief experiment that we conducted in order to examine whether the color-naming task led to the development of generally more negative attitudes toward the paintings than was true of the attitude rehearsal task. In brief, 30 subjects engaged in the color-naming task for 15 of the 30 paintings and the attitude rehearsal task for the other half of the paintings. Subjects later rated each painting on a −3 (*very much dislike*) to +3 (*very much like*) scale. No difference was apparent in the average ratings for the paintings that formed the color-naming set and those that formed the attitude rehearsal set (*M*s of 0.09 and 0.11, respectively), *t* < 1.

The strongest evidence against the conditioning explanation is provided by a recently conducted experiment that was modeled after Experiment 3 (Blascovich, Ernst, Tomaka, Kelsey, & Fazio, 1990). This experiment included not only the two between-subjects conditions of attitude rehearsal and color naming but also a third condition in which subjects received no exposure to the paintings prior to the pairwise preference task. Thus, there was no opportunity for these last subjects to associate any stress created by the color-naming task with the paintings. Yet, the physiological effects observed in this condition during the pairwise preference task were equivalent to those observed for the color-naming condition; subjects in both conditions displayed more autonomic activity than subjects in the attitude rehearsal condition.

General Discussion

The blood pressure data from Experiments 2 and 3 and the latency data from Experiment 4 provide converging evidence for the functional value of attitudes. The findings clearly point to one benefit of having an attitude. Just as is suggested by the so-called object appraisal function, an attitude provides the individual with a "ready aid" in sizing up objects. Having an attitude frees the individual from the processing required for reflective thought about his or her evaluation of the object. As a result, having an attitude can ease decision making.

The quality of these decisions also seems to be affected by having a preexisiting attitude. Recall the data on concurrences. Subjects who had developed and rehearsed their attitudes made more reliable decisions—ones that they were relatively unlikely to modify later—than control subjects. Our interpretation of this finding relates to the work we have done on attitude accessibility and the attitude-to-behavior process. An attitude that is highly accessible from memory is likely to be activated upon one's observation of the attitude object. As a result, an individual who possesses such a preexisting attitude is likely to arrive at immediate perceptions of the object that concur with his or her affect. When a person lacks an accessible attitude, the person is more likely to be influenced by momentarily salient, potentially idiosyncratic features of the object (see Fazio et al., 1989). As a result, the individual may make a decision that is not reflective of his or her attitude. It is as a consequence of such a mechanism that accessible attitudes may result in decisions that ultimately are more satisfying. By making decisions that are less attitudinally based, individuals who lack accessible attitudes risk deciding on courses of action that

they very well might alter when a later opportunity for reappraisal arises.

The present findings regarding blood pressure are not very informative about the physiological mechanisms that underlie performance during the pairwise preference task. In each of the three experiments, diastolic readings proved to be more sensitive to the experimental manipulations than systolic blood pressure. However, it may well be that more sophisticated physiological assessment involving continuous recording (as opposed to the relatively simple, discrete measurements that were available to us) would reveal reliable effects on both diastolic and systolic blood pressure. In any case, continuous recording of a wide array of physiological measures is needed to achieve an understanding of the precise physiological profile that is associated with decision making that does or does not involve accessible attitudes (see Blascovich & Kelsey, 1990; Cacioppo & Tassinary, 1990). All we can conclude on the basis of the present findings is that individuals who developed and rehearsed attitudes expended less effort while making attitudinally relevant decisions.

It is interesting that subjects' retrospective self-reports regarding the pairwise preference task did not reveal any effect of the manipulation in Experiments 2 and 3. Only in Experiment 1, for which the subject's own control of the pace of the pairwise task provided a very obvious external cue regarding the ease of the task (as well as a potential demand characteristic), were self-reports at all sensitive to the manipulations. Nor was a significant correlation between diastolic blood pressure and ratings of the task evident in either condition of any of the three experiments. Such a lack of concordance between self-reports and observed physiological reactions is not without precedent in this literature and has been discussed by a number of investigators (e.g., see Blascovich & Katkin, 1983; Krantz, Manuck, & Wing, 1986; Weinberger, Schwartz, & Davidson, 1979). A number of interpretations are possible in the present case. It may be that the three scales on which subjects judged the task are simply insensitive and that the null effects stem from measurement error. Alternatively, it is possible that, although control subjects exerted additional effort in order to perform the pairwise preference task, this extra expenditure was not itself distressing subjectively. According to this possibility, control subjects were accurate in judging the task as no more difficult, hurried, or stressful than attitude rehearsal subjects did. Finally, it is possible that the elevated blood pressure displayed by control subjects did indeed reflect a momentary state of distress but that subjects were unable to report such distress, at least retrospectively. Obviously, additional research with more refined physiological and self-report measures is necessary to disentangle these possibilities.

In closing, let us return to the notion of the attitude/nonattitude continuum. The present series of experiments have provided converging evidence regarding the relation between position along this continuum and the functional value of attitudes. The strength of the association in memory between an object and one's evaluation of the object appears critical in determining both the power and the functionality of the attitude. Attitudes that are highly accessible from memory, as a result of being characterized by strong object-evaluation associations, accomplish a great deal for the individual. They can guide behavior in a relatively spontaneous, nonreflective manner (see Fazio, 1990). One does not have to deliberate and reason; one does not have to construct an affective judgment. Instead, the evaluation is available in memory and is activated automatically when one encounters the attitude object. As a result, these kinds of attitudes ease decision making. Such attitudes also appear to produce decisions that are superior in quality, in the sense that individuals are less inclined to modify those decisions when later given an opportunity. Apparently because behavioral decisions involving accessible attitudes are more likely to be consistent with one's affect toward the objects in question, people are less likely to alter their judgments when reappraising the objects.

Thus, accessible attitudes—those that involve strong object-evaluation associations in memory—are very functional. There is very good reason to be skeptical of the power and functionality of some kinds of attitudes—those characterized by weak object-evaluation associations in memory. However, as we move along the attitude/nonattitude continuum, the functionality of the attitude increases. These more accessible attitudes are extremely useful in the day-to-day life of the individual.

The benefits of possessing an attitude that we have identified may not be unique to attitudes per se. The same may hold true for virtually any construct that people might form. Possessing a representation of a group or an impression of an individual may be similarly functional. Such social constructs help the individual make sense of, organize, and orient toward the diverse array of people that are encountered regularly. Decisions that have to be made can be made more easily. Likewise, having some preexisting appraisal of one's ability in a given domain probably eases decision making with respect to ability-relevant choices that might arise. Having that a priori self-knowledge also reduces the likelihood that the individual will make an error and expose himself or herself to a riskier situation than the ability level warrants. Thus, summary constructs regarding knowledge of one's self and of one's social world generally may be useful. Such constructs—at least relatively accessible ones—provide the same sort of "ready aid" that characterizes accessible attitudes.

Given the apparently general functionality of accessible attitudes, it is interesting to speculate about circumstances in which the possession of an accessible attitude might not prove helpful. Two potential exceptions to this general principle of functionality are worth noting. First, there is a sense in which accessible attitudes can leave the individual fairly closed-minded. By virtue of their automatic activation from memory and their influence on subsequent information processing, such attitudes can inhibit the individual from giving sufficient due to qualities of the object in question that are incongruent with the attitude. Thus, opportunities for experiencing a change of heart are likely to be diminished. In particular, when the attitude object has changed over time, an individual with a relatively accessible attitude may be less inclined to judge the object in terms of the new qualities that it exhibits than an individual with a less accessible attitude. In this sense, the former individual is less open to a new experience with the attitude object.

The second difficulty that may arise with accessible attitudes concerns situations or tasks in which one is motivated to be very deliberative, objective, and data driven in one's decision making (see Fazio, 1990). Desiring to overcome and adjust for the influence of one's highly accessible attitude, by whatever means, may make such judgmental processes all the more difficult. A more open-minded individual, one who lacks an accessible attitude, may find it easier to be data driven when motivated to be.

NOTES

1. The instrument also recorded heart rate. Because the heart rate data revealed no effects in any of the experiments we conducted, these data are not reported.

2. The experimenter pressed the control button that initiated cuff inflation immediately after presentation of the first slide of the pairwise preference task. About a minute was needed for the instrument to complete the reading. Thus, blood pressure was measured approximately midway through the task. The experimenter then pressed control buttons to have the instrument store this pairwise preference task reading in its memory and then to have the data printed on the instrument's thermal printer. Once printing was completed, the experimenter initiated cuff inflation for the postmeasure. As a result, this reading always occurred shortly after completion of the pairwise preference task.

We were well aware that this procedure would mean that the actual readings were not taken on the very same trial of the pairwise preference task for subjects in the rushed and the self-paced conditions. At a given point in time, the rushed subjects would have completed more trials than the self-paced subjects. This is the obvious dilemma that is faced when a time pressure manipulation is employed. Does one equate the measurements in the two conditions with respect to the amount of absolute time that has elapsed or the number of trials that the subjects have completed? We chose to do the former—in no small part, because of the inaccuracy and variability that would have arisen from attempting to adjust initiation of a measurement for a subject's self-dictated pace. This issue does not arise for Experiments 2 and 3, in which the two experimental conditions performed the pairwise preference task at the same externally imposed rate. Given the findings of these later experiments, it does not appear that the differential number of trials completed in the rushed and self-paced conditions

at the time of measurement is responsible for the observed effects. If the effects were due to the cumulative number of trials completed, instead of the differential task demand involved in making each decision, then there would have been no reason to expect differences to emerge in these subsequent experiments. This same argument applies to the unavoidable confounding of subjects' vocalization rates with the time pressure manipulation (see Lynch, Long, Thomas, Malinow, & Katcher, 1981, for an investigation of the effects of talking on blood pressure). Because the later experiments involved a set pace for all subjects, those experiments avoid comparing subjects who were forced to vocalize at differential rates.

3. The data in this and the later studies were also examined in analyses involving the use of the baseline readings as a covariate. These analyses of covariance yielded the same effects as the analyses of change scores, which are presented for ease of comprehension.

4. We can only speculate on the reasons for this difference. The color-naming task necessitated the constant attention of the subject, for the subject was occupied in naming colors for virtually the entire 5-s period that each slide was displayed, and the slides were presented every 5 s. In contrast, the attitude task did permit the subject a brief rest between slides if the subject was able to indicate an attitudinal judgment early in the 5-s period. Further, the color-naming task involved much more vocalization than the attitude rehearsal task, and this in and of itself may have elevated blood pressure (Lynch et al., 1981). Either or both of these factors may have contributed to the differential effects observed on blood pressure during the manipulation tasks.

5. These counterbalancing factors exerted no influence on the data and hence receive no further consideration.

REFERENCES

Allport, G. W. (1935). Attitudes. In C. Murchison (Ed.), *Handbook of social psychology*. Worcester, MA: Clark University Press.

Bittker, T. E., Buchsbaum, M. S., Williams, R. B., & Wynne, L. C. (1975). Cardiovascular and neurophysiologic correlates of sensory intake and rejection: II. Interview behavior. *Psychophysiology, 12,* 434–438.

Blascovich, J., Ernst, J. M., Tomaka, J., Kelsey, R. M., & Fazio, R. H. (1990). Attitude as a moderator of autonomic reactivity. *Psychophysiology, 27,* S17. (Abstract)

Blascovich, J., & Katkin, E. S. (1983). Visceral perception and social behavior. In J. T. Cacioppo & R. E. Petty (Eds.), *Social psychophysiology: A sourcebook* (pp. 493–509). New York: Guilford Press.

Blascovich, J., & Kelsey, R. M. (1990). Using cardiovascular and electrodermal measures of arousal in social psychological research. *Review of Personality and Social Psychology, 11,* 45–73.

Cacioppo, J. T., & Tassinary, L. G. (1990). Inferring

psychological significance from physiological signals. *American Psychologist, 45,* 16–28.

Converse, P. E. (1970). Attitudes and non-attitudes: Continuation of a dialogue. In E. R. Tufte (Ed.), *The quantitative analysis of social problems* (pp. 168–189). Reading, MA: Addison-Wesley.

DeBono, K. (1987). Investigating the social-adjustive and value-expressive functions of attitudes: Implications for persuasion processes. *Journal of Personality and Social Psychology, 52,,* 279–287.

Fazio, R. H. (1986). How do attitudes guide behavior? In R. M. Sorrentino & E. T. Higgins (Eds.), *The handbook of motivation and cognition: Foundations of social behavior* (pp. 204–243). New York: Guilford Press.

Fazio, R. H. (1989). On the power and functionality of attitudes: The role of attitude accessibility. In A. R. Pratkanis, S. J. Breckler, & A. G. Greenwald (Eds.), *Attitude structure and function* (pp. 153–179). Hillsdale, NJ: Lawrence Erlbaum.

Fazio, R. H. (1990). Multiple processes by which attitudes guide behavior: The MODE model as an integrative framework. In M. P. Zanna (Ed.), *Advances in experimental social psychology* (Vol. 23, pp. 75–109). Orlando, FL: Academic Press.

Fazio, R. H., Chen, J., McDonel, E. C., & Sherman, S. J. (1982). Attitude accessibility, attitude-behavior consistency, and the strength of the object-evaluation association. *Journal of Experimental Social Psychology, 18,* 339–357.

Fazio, R. H., Powell, M. C., & Williams, C. J. (1989). The role of attitude accessibility in the attitude-to-behavior process. *Journal of Consumer Research, 16,* 280–288.

Fazio, R. H., Sanbonmatsu, D. M., Powell, M. C., & Kardes, F. R. (1986). On the automatic activation of attitudes. *Journal of Personality and Social Psychology, 50,* 229–238.

Fazio, R. H., & Williams, C. J. (1986). Attitude accessibility as a moderator of the attitude-perception and attitude-behavior relations: An investigation of the 1984 presidential election. *Journal of Personality and Social Psychology, 51,* 505–514.

Herek, G. M. (1987). Can functions be measured? A new perspective on the functional approach to attitudes. *Social Psychology Quarterly, 50,* 285–303.

Houston, D. A., & Fazio, R. H. (1989). Biased processing as a function of attitude accessibility: Making objective judgments subjectively. *Social Cognition, 7,* 51–66.

Jamieson, D. W., & Zanna, M. P. (1989). Need for structure in attitude formation and expression. In A. R. Pratkanis, S. J. Breckler, & A. G. Greenwald (Eds.), *Attitudes structure and function* (pp. 383–406). Hillsdale, NJ: Lawrence Erlbaum.

Katz, D. (1960). The functional approach to the study of attitudes. *Public Opinion Quarterly, 24,* 163–204.

Krantz, D. S., Manuck, S. B., & Wing, R. R. (1986). Psychological stressors and task variables as elicitors of reactivity. In K. A. Matthews, S. M. Weiss, T. Detre, T. M. Dembroski, B. Falkner, S. B. Manuck, & R. B. Williams (Eds.), *Handbook of stress, reactivity, and cardiovascular disease* (pp. 85–107). New York: Wiley.

Kruglanski, A. W., & Freund, T. (1983). The freezing and unfreezing of lay-inferences: Effects on impressional primacy, ethnic stereotyping, and numerical anchoring. *Journal of Experimental Social Psychology, 19,* 448–468.

Lynch, J. J., Long, J. M., Thomas, S. A., Malinow, K. L., & Katcher, A. H. (1981). The effects of talking on blood pressure in hyptertensive and normaltensive individuals. *Psychosomatic Medicine, 43,* 25–33.

Obrist, P. A., Gaebelein, C. J., Teller, E. S., Langer, A. W., Grignolo, A., Light, K. C., & McCubbin, J. A. (1978). The relationship among heart rate, carotid dP/dt, and blood pressure in humans as a function of the type of stress. *Psychophysiology, 15,* 102–115.

Sanbonmatsu, D. M., & Fazio, R. H. (1990). The role of attitudes in memory-based decision making. *Journal of Personality and Social Psychology, 59,* 614–622.

Shavitt, S. (1990). The role of attitude objects in attitude functions. *Journal of Experimental Social Psychology, 26,* 124–148.

Smith, E. R. (1989). Procedural efficiency: General and specific components and effects on social judgment. *Journal of Experimental Social Psychology, 25,* 500–523.

Smith, E. R., Branscombe, N. R., & Bormann, C. (1988). Generality of the effects of practice on social judgment tasks. *Journal of Personality and Social Psychology, 54,* 385–395.

Smith, M. B., Bruner, J. S., & White, R. W. (1956). *Opinions and personality.* New York: Wiley.

Smith, T. W., Allred, K. D., Morrison, C. A., & Carlson, S. D. (1989). Cardiovascular reactivity and interpersonal influence: Active coping in a social context. *Journal of Personality and Social Psychology, 56,* 209–218.

Weinberger, D. A., Schwartz, G. E., & Davidson, R. J. (1979). Low-anxious, high-anxious, and repressive coping styles: Psychometric patterns and behavioral physiological responses to stress. *Journal of Abnormal Psychology, 88,* 369–380.

Williams, R. B., Bittker, T. E., Buchsbaum, M. S., & Wynne, L. C. (1975). Cardiovascular and neurophysiologic correlates of sensory intake and rejection: I. Effect of cognitive tasks. *Psychophysiology, 12,* 427–433.

Wright, R. A., Contrada, R. J., & Patane, M. J. (1986). Task difficulty, cardiovascular response, and the magnitude of goal valence. *Journal of Personality and Social Psychology, 52,* 837–843.

Received March 18, 1991
Revision received July 28, 1991
Accepted August 2, 1991 ■

Thinking Too Much: Introspection can Reduce the Quality of Preferences and Decisions

Timothy D. Wilson* and Jonathan W. Schooler**

In Study 1, college students' preferences for different brands of strawberry jams were compared with experts' ratings of the jams. Students who analyzed why they felt the way they did agreed less with the experts than students who did not. In Study 2, college students' preferences for college courses were compared with expert opinion. Some students were asked to analyze reasons; others were asked to evaluate all attributes of all courses. Both kinds of introspection caused people to make choices that, compared with control subjects', corresponded less with expert opinion. Analyzing reasons can focus people's attention on nonoptimal criteria, causing them to base their subsequent choices on these criteria. Evaluating multiple attributes can moderate people's judgments, causing them to discriminate less between the different alternatives.

When faced with a difficult decision, people sometimes spend a good deal of time thinking about the advantages and disadvantages of each alternative. At one point or another, most of us have even reached for a sheet of paper and made a list of pluses and minuses, hoping that the best course of action would become clear. Reflection of this kind is generally thought to be beneficial, organizing what might otherwise be a confusing jumble of thoughts and feelings. Benjamin Franklin, for example, relayed the following advice to the British scientist Joseph Priestley about how to make a difficult choice:

> My way is to divide half a sheet of paper by a line into two columns, writing over the one Pro, and over the other Con. Then, during three or four days consideration, I put down under the different heads short hints of the different motives, that at

This research was supported by National Institute of Mental Health Grant MH41841 to Timothy D. Wilson and a grant from the University of Pittsburgh Office of Research to Jonathan W. Schooler. We would like to thank Jack McArdle for his statistical advice.

Correspondence concerning this article should be addressed to Timothy D. Wilson, Department of Psychology, Gilmer Hall, University of Virginia, Charlottesville, Virginia 22903-2477.

*University of Virginia.
**University of Pittsburgh.

different times occur to me, for or against each measure . . . I find at length where the balance lies; and if, after a day or two of further consideration, nothing new that is of importance occurs on either side, I come to a determination accordingly . . . When each [reason] is thus considered, separately and comparatively, and the whole lies before me, I think I can judge better, and am less likely to make a rash step. (Quoted in Goodman, 1945, p. 746)

Franklin's advice has been captured, at least in spirit, by many years of research on decision analysis (e.g., Edwards, 1961; Keeney, 1977; Koriat, Lichtenstein, & Fischhoff, 1980; Raiffa, 1968; Slovic, 1982). Though the terms *decision theory* and *decision analysis* describe a myriad of theoretical formulations, an assumption made by most of these approaches is that decisions are best made deliberately, objectively, and with some reflection. For example, Raiffa (1968) states that

the spirit of decision analysis is divide and conquer: Decompose a complex problem into simpler problems, get your thinking straight in these simpler problems, paste these analyses together with a logical glue, and come out with a program for action for the complex problem (p. 271).

Janis and Mann (1977) go so far as to predict that a "balance sheet" procedure similar to Benjamin Franklin's will become as commonplace among professional and personal decision makers as recording deposits and withdrawals in a bankbook.

Curiously, however, there has been almost no research on the effects of reflection and deliberation on the quality of decision making. One reason for this lack of research is the difficulty of assessing how good any particular decision is. For example, Janis and Mann (1977) arrived at the "somewhat demoralizing" conclusion that there is "no dependable way of objectively assessing the success of a decision" (p. 11). Whereas we agree with Janis and Mann that any one measure of the quality of a decision has its drawbacks, we argue that it is not impossible to evaluate people's decisions, particularly if converging measures are used. The purpose of the present studies was to examine the effects of two different kinds of introspection on decision making. We hypothesized that

contrary to conventional wisdom, introspection is not always beneficial and might even be detrimental under some circumstances.

Our studies can be viewed as part of a growing literature on the drawbacks of introspection and rumination. Recent research from a variety of sources casts doubt on the view that introspection is always beneficial. Morrow and Nolan-Hoeksema (1990), for example, found that ruminating about a negative mood was less successful in improving this mood than was engaging in a distracting task. Schooler and Engstler-Schooler (1990) documented a deleterious effect of a different kind of reflection: Subjects who verbalized their memory for nonverbal stimuli (such as faces) were less likely than control subjects to recognize these faces on a subsequent recognition test. Most relevant to the present concerns, Wilson and his colleagues found that introspecting about the causes of one's attitudes can have disruptive effects, such as reducing attitude–behavior consistency and changing people's attitudes (Wilson, 1990; Wilson, Dunn, Kraft, & Lisle, 1989; see also Millar & Tesser, 1986a).

Effects of Analyzing Reasons

Forming preferences is akin to riding a bicycle; we can do it easily but cannot easily explain how. Just as automatic behaviors can be disrupted when people analyze and decompose them (Baumeister, 1984; Kimble & Perlmuter, 1970; Langer & Imber, 1979), so can preferences and decisions be disrupted when people reflect about the reasons for their feelings (Wilson, Dunn, Kraft, & Lisle, 1989). We suggest that this can occur as follows. First, people are often unaware of exactly why they feel the way they do about an attitude object. When they reflect about their reasons, they thus focus on explanations that are salient and plausible. The problem is that what seems like a plausible cause and what actually determines people's reactions are not always the same thing (Nisbett & Wilson, 1977). As a result, when asked why they feel the way they do, people focus on attributes that seem like plausible reasons for liking or disliking the stimulus, even if these attributes have no actual effect on their evaluations.

It might seem that people would focus only on attributes of the stimulus that are consistent with their initial attitude, to justify how they feel. That is, even if people do not know why they feel the way they do, and have to construct reasons, they might focus only on factors that could account for their present feelings. Undoubtedly such a justification process can occur. We suggest that under some circumstances, however, people will focus on reasons that imply a different attitude than they held before and will adopt the attitude implied by these reasons. These circumstances are hypothesized to be as follows. First, people often do not have a well-articulated, accessible attitude and thus do not start out with the bias to find only those reasons that are consistent with an initial reaction. They conduct a broader search for reasons, focusing on factors that are plausible and easy to verbalize even if they conflict with how they felt originally.

Even when people's initial attitude is inaccessible, analyzing reasons will not always change their attitude. A cause of people's attitude might be so powerful and obvious that it is difficult to miss when they analyze their reasons. For example, if we knew nothing about a stranger except that he was convicted of child abuse and then were asked why we felt the way we did about him, we would have little difficulty in pinpointing the actual cause of our feelings. Second, even if people miss an important cause of their feelings when they analyze reasons, they will not change their attitudes if the reasons that are salient and plausible are of the same valence as the actual cause. Thus, people might not realize that Attribute A was a major determinant of their reaction and instead might focus on Attribute B. If Attributes A and B imply the same feeling, however, no attitude change will occur.

In sum, we suggest that reflecting about reasons will change people's attitudes when their initial attitude is relatively inaccessible and the reasons that are salient and plausible happen to have a different valence than people's initial attitude. A considerable amount of evidence has been obtained

that is consistent with these hypotheses. It is well documented, for example, that when people are asked to think about why they feel the way they do, they sometimes bring to mind reasons that are discrepant from their initial attitude and that they adopt the attitude implied by these reasons (e.g., Millar & Tesser, 1986a; Wilson, Dunn, Bybee, Hyman, & Rotondo, 1984; Wilson, Kraft, & Dunn, 1989). In addition, Wilson, Hodges, and Pollack (1990) found that thinking about reasons was most likely to change people's attitudes when their initial attitude was relatively inaccessible.

It has not been clear, however, whether there is any harm done by the attitude change that occurs when people analyze reasons. We suggest that thinking about reasons can alter people's preferences in such a way that they make less optimal choices. In many domains, people have developed an adaptive, functional means of how to weight different information about a stimulus. For example, when evaluating food items with which they are familiar, people have little difficulty deciding which ones they prefer the most. Asking people to think about why they feel that way might focus their attention on attributes that seem like plausible reasons for liking or disliking the items but that in fact have not been heavily weighted before. Similarly, people might dismiss attributes that seem like implausible reasons but that in fact had been weighted heavily before. As a result, they change their mind about how they feel. To the extent that their initial reaction was adaptive and functional, this change might be in a less optimal direction.

Effects of Evaluating Multiple Attributes of Stimuli

A related kind of introspection might also influence people's decisions in disadvantageous ways, but in a different manner. Sometimes, when evaluating a stimulus, people decompose it into many different attributes. For example, potential car buyers sometimes consider a wide array of information about cars—such as their price, safety, repair record, gas mileage, and resale value. There is evidence that evaluating a stimulus on several different dimensions causes people to moderate their evaluations. Linville (1982), for example, asked people to evaluate five different brands of chocolate chip cookies. She asked some subjects to consider six different attributes of the cookies before rating them, such as how sweet they were and the number of chocolate chips they contained. She asked others to consider only two of these attributes. As predicted, those who evaluated six attributes made more moderate evaluations than those who evaluated two attributes: The range and standard deviation of their ratings of the five cookies were significantly smaller.

This moderation effect is most likely to occur when the different attributes people consider are uncorrelated, so that some are positive and some are negative (Judd & Lusk, 1984; Millar & Tesser, 1986b). The more such attributes people consider, the more all the alternatives will seem to have some good and some bad qualities and thus will appear more similar to each other. To our knowledge, no one has examined the effects of considering multiple attributes of a set of alternatives on the quality of people's decisions. If this type of introspection makes the alternatives more difficult to distinguish from one another, people may be more likely to make a poor choice. And, as noted earlier, to the extent that people's initial preferences (before introspecting) are adaptive, any form of thought that changes people's preferences might lead to less optimal choices.

The present studies examined the effects of analyzing reasons (in Studies 1 and 2) and considering multiple attributes of the alternatives (in Study 2) on people's preferences and choices. We hypothesized that both types of introspection would lead to less optimal decisions, by means of the different mechanisms we have just reviewed. Our measure of the quality of people's preferences and choices was expert opinion. In Study 1, we compared subjects' preferences for different brands of a food item, strawberry jam, with the ratings of these brands by trained sensory experts. We assumed that left to their own devices, people's preferences would correspond reasonably well to the ratings of the experts. We predicted that analyzing the reasons for one's reactions to the jams would

change people's preferences. Consistent with our hypothesis that analyzing reasons can produce attitudes that are nonoptimal, we predicted that the preferences of people in the reasons condition would not correspond very well with the experts' ratings of the jams. In Study 2, we examined college students' choices of which courses to take and compared these choices with various kinds of expert opinion about what the best choices were.

Study 1

Method

Subjects

Subjects were 49 undergraduate psychology students (39 men, 10 women) at the University of Washington. They volunteered for a study entitled "Jam Taste Test" in return for course credit and were instructed not to eat anything for 3 hours before the study.

Materials and ratings of the experts

We purchased five brands of strawberry jams or preserves that varied in their overall quality, as reported by *Consumer Reports* magazine ("Strawberry Jams," 1985). The *Consumer Reports* rankings were based on the ratings of seven consultants who were trained sensory panelists. These experts rated 16 sensory characteristics (e.g., sweetness, bitterness, aroma) of 45 jams; these ratings were averaged to compute the ranking of each jam (L. Mann, *Consumer Reports* magazine, personal communication, May 15, 1987). The jams we purchased were ranked 1st, 11th, 24th, 32nd, and 44th.

Procedure

Subjects, seen individually, were told that the purpose of the study was to evaluate different kinds of jams under different conditions, as part of a consumer psychology experiment. Experimenter 1 explained that some subjects would taste the jams on crackers, whereas others would taste the jams on plastic spoons. All subjects were told that they had been randomly assigned to the condition in which they would taste the jams on spoons and that after tasting the jams, they would be asked to rate their liking for each one. After receiving these initial instructions and signing a consent form, subjects were randomly assigned to a control or a reasons analysis condition. Reasons analysis subjects received written instructions asking them to "analyze *why* you feel the way you do about each" jam, "in order to prepare yourself for your evaluations." They were told that they would be asked to list their reasons for liking or disliking the jams after they tasted them, the purpose of which was to organize their thoughts. They were also told that they would not be asked to hand in their list of reasons. Control subjects did not receive any additional instructions.

All subjects were then asked to sit at a table with five plates, each containing a plastic spoon with approximately ½ teaspoon (3.3 ml) of strawberry jam. The jams were labeled with a letter from A to E and were presented in one random order. Experimenter 1 left the room, during which time the subjects tasted each of the five jams.

Version 1. The first five subjects in each condition followed a slightly different procedure than did those who followed. The initial subjects in the reasons analysis condition completed the reasons questionnaire while they tasted the five jams; that is, they tasted Jam 1, listed their reasons for liking or disliking Jam 1, tasted Jam 2, listed their reasons for liking or disliking Jam 2, and so on. The experimenter reiterated that the purpose of this questionnaire was to organize the subjects' thoughts and that they would not be asked to hand it in. When she returned, she picked up the reasons questionnaire, explained that it would not be needed anymore, and deposited it in a trash can. The initial subjects in the control condition tasted all five jams and then rated each one, without filling out any questionnaires.

Version 2. To equalize the amount of time subjects spent on the tasting part of the study, subsequent subjects followed a slightly different procedure. All subjects tasted the jams without

filling out any questionnaires and then were given a questionnaire to fill out when the experimenter returned. Subjects in the reasons condition received the reasons questionnaire. As in Version 1, they were told that they would not hand in this questionnaire, and the experimenter deposited it in the trash when she returned. Subjects in the control condition received a filler questionnaire instructing them to list reasons why they chose their major. The experimenter also left the room while control subjects completed this questionnaire. She collected the questionnaire when she returned.

The remainder of the experiment was identical for all subjects. Experimenter 1 introduced subjects to Experimenter 2, who was unaware of whether they had analyzed reasons. Experimenter 2 gave subjects a questionnaire on which to evaluate the jams, which consisted of a 9-point scale ranging from *disliked* (1) to *liked* (9) for each jam. Subjects were instructed to complete the questionnaire and to place it through a slot in a covered box, to maintain anonymity. Experimenter 2 left the room while subjects made their ratings. He fully debriefed subjects when he returned.

Results

We predicted that asking subjects to think about reasons would change their evaluations of the jams. Consistent with this prediction, a multivariate analysis on the mean ratings of the five jams found a significant effect of the reasons analysis manipulation, $F(5, 43) = 3.09$, $p = .02$. Individual t tests were significant on two of the jams, as seen in Table 18.1. We also predicted that analyzing reasons would produce preferences that were, in some sense, nonoptimal. To test this prediction, we computed the Spearman rank-order correlation between each subject's ratings of the five jams and the rank ordering of the jams by the *Consumer Reports* taste experts (for all analyses, these within-subject correlations were converted to z scores by means of Fisher's r-to-z transformation; the means reported here have been converted back to correlation coefficients). The mean correlation in the control condition was .55, reflecting a fair amount of agreement with the taste experts. As

TABLE 18.1. Study 1: Mean Liking Ratings for the Five Jams

Condition	Jam 1	Jam 2	Jam 3	Jam 4	Jam 5
Control					
M	6.52	7.64	6.12	2.72	4.68
SD	2.22	1.66	2.05	2.26	2.66
Reasons					
M	4.54	6.25	5.42	2.88	4.92
SD	2.00	2.38	2.70	2.13	2.89
t	3.27	2.38	1.03	−.25	−.30
p	.002	.02	.31	.81	.77

Note: The jams are listed in order of their rankings by the *Consumer Reports* experts; Jam 1 was the highest ranked jam, Jam 2 was the second highest, and so on. The liking ratings were made on 9-point scales that ranged from *disliked* (1) to *liked* (9).

predicted, the mean correlation in the reasons condition was significantly lower ($M = .11$), $t(47) = 2.53$, $p = .02$.[1] The mean correlation in the control condition was significantly higher than zero, $t(24) = 4.27$, $p = .0003$, whereas the mean correlation in the reasons condition was not, $t(23) = .80$, $p = .43$.

We noted earlier that some kinds of introspection cause people to moderate their evaluations. We have not found this to be the case with analyzing reasons in previous studies (e.g., Wilson, Lisle, & Schooler, 1990). Nor does analyzing reasons reduce people's confidence in their attitudes (Wilson, Dunn, Kraft, & Lisle, 1989). Nonetheless, it is important to see if in the present study, asking people to explain their preferences led to moderation. If so, this reduced variability in people's ratings might account for the lower correlation between their ratings and the opinions of the *Consumer Reports* experts. Though the mean ratings of the jams displayed in Table 18.1 seem to support this interpretation (i.e., the range in ratings of the five jams was lower in the reasons condition), it is more appropriate to test this possibility on a

within-subject basis.[2] We computed the range between each subject's highest and lowest rating of the jams, as well as the standard deviation of each subject's ratings. On average, these values were quite similar in both the reasons and control conditions, $ts(47) < .39, ps > .71$. Thus, there was no evidence that analyzing reasons caused people to evaluate the jams more similarly than did control subjects.

Instead, people seemed to have come up with reasons that conflicted with the experts' ratings and adopted the attitude implied by these reasons. Support for this interpretation comes from analyses of the reasons people wrote down in the reasons condition. Subjects' responses were first divided into individual reasons by a research assistant and then put into different categories of reasons for liking or disliking the jams. (Another research assistant coded a subset of the questionnaires and agreed with the first assistant's initial divisions into reasons 95% of the time and agreed with her placement of the reasons into individual categories 97% of the time.) Subjects gave an average of 2.93 reasons per jam. These reasons concerned some aspect of their taste (e.g., sweetness, tartness, fruitiness, 52%), texture (e.g., thickness,

---

[1] Initial analyses revealed that the effects of analyzing reasons did not differ according to which version of the procedure was used. Subjects in both conditions who followed the initial procedure—in which the jams were rated right after tasting them, without an intervening questionnaire—had higher correlations between their ratings of the jams and the *Consumer Reports* experts' ratings of the jams, as indicated by a significant main effect of version ($p = .02$). The difference in correlations between the reasons and control conditions, however, was in the same direction in both versions, and the Reasons × Version interaction was nonsignificant ($p = .60$). Initial analyses also

revealed that there were no significant effects of gender; thus subsequent analyses were collapsed across this variable.

[2] For example, consider two hypothetical subjects in the reasons condition, one of whom gave ratings of 9, 7, 5, 3, and 1 to the five jams, the other of whom gave ratings of 1, 3, 5, 7, and 9. The mean of these two subjects' ratings would be 5 for every jam, making it appear as though they were not discriminating between the jams, when in fact they were making very strong discriminations.

chunkiness, ease of spreading, 35%), appearance (e.g., color, how fresh they looked, 8%), smell (1%), naturalness or artificiality of the ingredients (1%), and miscellaneous (3%). Two research assistants also coded, on a 7-point scale, how much liking for each jam was expressed in subjects' reasons (reliability $r = .97$). Consistent with our hypothesis that the reasons people came up with would not match expert opinion, this index did not correlate significantly with the experts' ratings of the jams ($M = .25$), $t(23) = 1.74$, $p > .09$. Consistent with our hypothesis that people would base their attitude on the reasons they listed, this index correlated very highly with subjects' subsequent ratings of the jams (mean within-subject correlation = .92), $t(23) = 8.60$, $p < .0001$.

A closer look at how analyzing reasons changed people's attitudes is illuminating. In some of our previous studies, people who analyzed reasons changed their attitudes in the same direction, possibly because similar attributes of the stimuli became salient when people analyzed reasons, and people held similar causal theories about how these attributes affected their judgments (e.g., Wilson et al., 1984). In other studies, the attitude change was more idiosyncratic (e.g., Wilson, Kraft, & Dunn, 1989), which can occur for at least two reasons. First, for some stimuli, the attributes that become salient might differ from person to person. For example, when asked why they feel the way they do about a political candidate, people draw on different knowledge bases. The fact that is most salient to one person (e.g., that the candidate is antiabortion) may be completely unknown to another. Second, even if the same fact, such as the candidate's stance on abortion, is available to everyone, it may be evaluated quite differently by different people, leading to attitude change in different directions.

The fact that there were significant differences between conditions on ratings of two of the jams (see Table 18.1) indicates that at least some of the change in the present study was in a common direction: Subjects who analyzed reasons became more negative, on average, toward Jams 1 and 2. However, other changes may have occurred in idiosyncratic directions, so that some people who analyzed reasons became more positive, whereas others became more negative. To test this possibility, we correlated each subject's ratings of the five jams with the ratings of every other subject in his or her condition and then averaged these correlations, using Fisher's r-to-z-to-r transformation. The average correlation in the control condition was .55, indicating a fair amount of consensus about how likable the jams were. If subjects in the reasons condition changed their attitudes in a common direction, then their ratings should have correlated as highly, or possibly even higher, with other subjects in this condition. If these subjects changed their attitudes in idiosyncratic directions, then there should have been less consensus in the reasons condition. Supporting this latter possibility, the mean intercorrelation in the reasons condition was significantly lower than in the control condition ($M = .18$), $t(47) = 4.38$, $p < .0001$.[3]

Discussion

Left to their own devices, control subjects formed preferences for strawberry jams that corresponded well to the ratings of trained sensory experts. Subjects asked to think about why they liked or disliked the jams brought to mind reasons that did not correspond very well with the experts' ratings. They then seem to have based their preferences on these reasons (i.e., the correlation between the attitude implied by their reasons and their subsequent

[3]Two points should be made about these mean intercorrelations: one statistical and one conceptual. First, the lowered consensus in the reasons condition might show that people's evaluations became more random – that is, by becoming unsure of how they felt, subjects' ratings contained more "error," and thus were not as correlated with each other. Though we cannot completely rule out this interpretation, the fact that analyzing reasons did not reduce the range in sub-

jects' ratings and the fact that in previous studies, analyzing reasons has not made people less confident in their evaluations, reduces its plausibility (see Wilson, Dunn, Kraft, & Lisle, 1989). Second, note that to avoid the problem of lack of independence of the intercorrelations (e.g., there were 300 intercorrelations among the 25 subjects in the control condition), the t test was computed on the mean of each subject's intercorrelations with every other subject in his or her condition, so that there was one data point for each subject.

preferences was extremely high). As a result, their preferences did not correspond as well with expert opinion. No evidence was found for the possibility that analyzing reasons moderated subjects' judgments. Instead it changed people's minds about how they felt, presumably because certain aspects of the jams that were not central to their initial evaluations were weighted more heavily (e.g., their chunkiness or tartness).

It might be argued that there should have been a greater correspondence between the experts and subjects who analyzed reasons, because both sets of people made their ratings in an analytical frame of mind. The ratings made by the two groups, however, differed in important ways. First, the experts were provided in advance with a list of 16 criteria on which to evaluate the jams (L. Mann, *Consumer Reports* magazine, personal communication, May 15, 1987). In contrast, our reasons subjects had to decide for themselves which criteria to use, increasing the probability that they would focus on a few attributes that were salient and plausible as causes of their preferences. Second, the experts were trained sensory panelists with a good deal of experience in tasting food items. Wilson, Kraft, and Dunn (1989) found that people who are knowledgeable about the attitude object are unaffected by analyzing their reasons. Thus, even if the experts evaluated the jams analytically, we would expect their ratings to differ from the subjects in our reasons condition, who were not experts.

It might also be argued that the different attitudes reported by subjects in the reasons condition were due to demand characteristics. Though we went to some length to convince these subjects that no one would see their reasons, they still might have believed we would compare their attitude responses with their reasons, and thus they might have purposely exaggerated the similarity of their attitudes to their reasons because of concerns about consistency. Note, however, that even if this interpretation were true, it would not explain why the reasons generated by subjects implied an attitude that was different from those held by control subjects and the *Consumer Reports* experts.

One way to rule out a demand characteristics explanation more definitively would be to allow people to choose one of the attitude objects for their own personal use. For example, suppose we had told subjects in Study 1 that they could choose one of the jams to take home and had set up the study in such a way that no one would know which brand subjects chose. If subjects in the reasons condition acted on their reported attitudes—that is, if they chose jams that they had rated highly—it would seem that they had genuinely changed their attitudes, rather than simply reporting a new attitude to please the experimenter. Though we did not follow such a procedure in Study 1, we did in two studies by Wilson et al. (1990). For example, in one study, subjects examined five art posters and chose one to take home. The results were inconsistent with a demand characteristics explanation: Subjects who analyzed reasons chose different posters, even though they believed that the experimenter would not know which one they chose.

The Wilson et al. (1990) studies addressed another possible concern with Study 1: the use of expert opinion as our criterion of decision quality. It might be argued that even though subjects in the reasons condition formed preferences that were at variance with the experts, there was no cost in doing so. As long as people like a particular kind of jam, what difference does it make that experts disagree with them? We suggest it can make a difference, because the attitude change caused by analyzing reasons is often temporary. Over time, people probably revert to the weighting schemes they habitually use. If they made a choice on the basis of a different weighting scheme, they might come to regret this choice. To test this prediction, Wilson et al. (1990) contacted subjects a few weeks after they had been in the study, and asked them how satisfied they were with the poster they had chosen. As predicted, subjects who analyzed reasons expressed significantly less satisfaction with their choice of poster. Thus, analyzing reasons has been shown to reduce the quality of preferences in two different ways: It can lower the correspondence between these preferences and expert opinion, and it can cause people to make decisions they later regret.

Study 2 attempted to extend these findings in a number of respects. First, it was a field experiment that examined a real-life decision of some importance to college students: their choice of which courses to take the following semester. Students were presented with detailed information about all of the sophomore-level psychology courses being offered the next semester, and we examined their ratings of each course and whether they actually registered for the different courses. As in Study 1, we included a measure of expert opinion of the desirability of the alternatives. The "experts" were students who had previously taken the courses. We predicted that subjects in the control conditions would be most likely to choose courses recommended by these experts; that is, they should be most likely to register for the courses that had received the highest course evaluations. Subjects who analyzed reasons, however, might change the criteria they used to make their decision and thus be less likely to sign up for the highly rated ones.

Second, as discussed in the Introduction, we examined the effects of another form of introspection, in addition to analyzing reasons. Some subjects were asked to consider how every attribute of every course (e.g., the topic matter, the time it met) influenced their preferences. We hypothesized that this form of introspection would moderate subjects' ratings of the courses, by making them more cognizant of the fact that every course had pluses and minuses (Linville, 1982). We also hypothesized that this form of introspection might confuse subjects about which information was the most important, causing them to assign more equal weights to the different information. This change in subjects' weighting scheme was also expected to

change their decisions about which courses to take, possibly in a nonoptimal direction.

Third, we included a long-term measure of subjects' behavior: the courses they were enrolled in at the end of the following semester. Subjects had the opportunity to add and drop courses at the beginning of the semester; thus, even if our manipulations influenced their initial decision of which courses to take, they could revise these decisions later. Whether the manipulation would influence subjects' long-term behavior was an open question. On the one hand, we have argued that the attitude change caused by analyzing reasons is relatively temporary and will not influence long-term behavior. Consistent with this view, Wilson et al. (1984, Study 3) found that analyzing reasons did not influence dating couple's decision about whether to break up several months after the study was completed. On the other hand, if analyzing reasons changes subjects' decisions about the courses for which they register, they might experience a certain amount of inertia, so that they remain in these courses, even if they change their mind at a later point. Furthermore, Millar and Tesser (1986a, 1989) found that analyzing reasons highlights the cognitive component of attitudes and that these cognitively based attitudes will determine behaviors that are more cognitively based than affectively based. Given that the decision of whether to take a college course has a large cognitive component (e.g., whether it will advance one's career goals), the attitude change that results from analyzing reasons might cause long-term changes in behavior.[4]

---

[4] We should address some possible ethical objections to Study 2. It might be argued that it was unfair to ask subjects to reflect about their decision of which courses to take, given our hypothesis that it would change the courses for which they preregistered and possibly even change the courses they actually took the following semester. We struggled with this issue before conducting the study and discussed it with several colleagues. In the end, we decided that the potential knowledge gained—discovering some detrimental effects of introspection—outweighed the possible harmful effects on the participants. It would have been unacceptable to give subjects misinformation about the courses—for example, telling them that a course was highly rated by students when in fact it was not. However, we gave all subjects accurate information and

then asked some of them to reflect more than they might ordinarily do when forming their preferences. According to the predominant theories of decision making (e.g., Janis & Mann, 1977), asking people to be more reflective about their choices should have beneficial effects. Probably thousands of decision analysts, counselors, and academic advisers urge people to make decisions in ways similar to subjects in our reasons and rate all conditions. Given that the effects of our manipulations were predicted to be relatively benign (altering the psychology courses for which subjects preregistered and possibly altering the courses they took the following semester), we felt it was worth testing the wisdom of such advice. We did not, of course, make this decision alone. The study was approved by a Human Subjects Committee.

Fourth, to test more directly the hypothesis that people who analyze reasons change the criteria they use to make decisions, we included some additional dependent measures assessing the criteria subjects used, and we compared these criteria with another kind of expert opinion: ratings by faculty members in psychology of the criteria students ought to use when choosing courses. We predicted that the criteria used by control subjects would correspond at least somewhat to the criteria faculty members said students ought to use but that there would be less of a correspondence in the reasons condition. This would be consistent with our hypothesis that analyzing reasons can cause people to alter the criteria they use in nonoptimal ways.

Study 2

Method

Subjects

Two hundred and forty-three introductory psychology students at the University of Virginia volunteered for a study entitled "Choosing College Courses." The sign-up sheet indicated that participants would receive detailed information about all of the 200-level courses being offered by the psychology department the following semester (i.e., sophomore-level courses) and that only students who were considering taking one of these courses should volunteer for the study. Thirteen students were eliminated from the analyses for the following reasons: One participated in the study twice, 2 reported that they would not be enrolled in college the next semester, and 10 reported that they had already registered for classes, which was one of the major dependent variables. Other subjects failed to complete some of the individual questions and were eliminated from the analyses of these measures. Subjects received course credit for their participation.

Procedure

Subjects were run in large groups in the first 2 days of the preregistration period, when students register for the classes they want to take the following semester. Subjects received written instructions indicating that the purpose of the study was both to provide people with more information than they would ordinarily receive about 200-level psychology courses and to "look at some issues in decision making of interest to psychologists, such as how people make decisions between alternatives." They were given a packet of materials and told to go through it page by page without looking ahead, though they could look back at any point. After filling out some demographic information, they received descriptions of the nine 200-level psychology classes.

Course descriptions. Each course description included the name of the professor teaching the course, when and where it would meet, the required and recommended prerequisites for the course, the requirements for the psychology major satisfied by the course, whether a term paper was required, the format of the course (lecture or discussion), evaluations of the course by students who took the course the last time it was taught by the same professor, whether there was a required or optional discussion section, a description of the course contents, and a list of the books to be used. The course evaluations included a frequency distribution of the responses to two ratings, the overall teaching effectiveness of the instructor and the intellectual stimulation of the course, as well as the mean response to these two questions. Most, though not all, of this information was available for all nine courses. For example, one course was being taught by a new instructor—thus course evaluations were not available—and the format of one course was unknown. The course descriptions were presented in one of two counterbalanced orders.

Experimental conditions. Subjects were randomly assigned to one of three experimental conditions within each group session. In the rate all information condition (hereafter referred to as rate all), subjects were asked to stop and think about each piece of information about every course and then to rate the extent to which it made them more or less likely to take the course. Underneath each item, subjects were reminded to "stop and think about this piece of information," after which they rated it on a 9-point scale ranging from *makes me much less likely to take it* (1) to *makes me much more likely to take it* (9). Subjects in the reasons condition were instructed to think about why they might want or not want to take a course as they read the course descriptions. They were told that they would be asked to write down their reasons and were asked to prepare themselves by "analyzing why you feel the way you do about each course." After reading the course descriptions (without making any ratings of the information), these subjects did in fact write down their reasons for each of the nine courses. They were told that the purpose of this was to organize their thoughts and that their responses would be completely anonymous. They were also reminded that they could refer back to the course descriptions if they wanted. Subjects in the control condition were instructed to read the information about the nine courses carefully, after which they received a filler questionnaire that asked their opinion of some university issues (e.g., what they thought about the advising and honor systems) and their leisure-time activities.[5]

Dependent measures

All subjects rated the likelihood that they would take each course on a scale ranging from *definitely will not take this course* (1) to *definitely will take*

this course (9). If they had already taken a course, they were asked to indicate this and to not complete the rating scale. The courses were rated in the same order as they were presented in the course description packet. Subjects next rated each type of information they had received about the courses (e.g., the course evaluations, the course content), as well as two additional pieces of information (what they had heard about the courses from other students or professors and how interested they were in the topic), according to how much it influenced their decision about which courses to take. These ratings were made on scales ranging from *did not influence me at all* (1) to *influenced me a great deal* (9). The information about the courses was rated in one of two counterbalanced orders.

At this point, subjects handed in their packets and were given, unexpectedly, a recall questionnaire. They were asked to recall as much information about the courses as they could and to write it down in designated spaces for each course. Their responses were later coded by a research assistant who was unaware of the subjects' condition. She assigned subjects a 1 for each piece of information recalled correctly, a 0 for each piece not recalled, and a −1 for each piece recalled incorrectly. One of the authors also coded the recall questionnaires of 7 subjects; his codings agreed with the research assistant's 94% of the time.

After completing the recall measure, subjects were asked to sign a release form giving us permission to examine the registrar's records so that we

---

[5] The inclusion of the filler questionnaire in the control condition solved one problem but possibly created another. The problem it solved was controlling for the amount of time that elapsed between the examination of the course descriptions and the completion of the dependent variables in the reasons condition. It also, however, made the control and reasons conditions different in the amount of time spent thinking about unrelated matters between the examination of the courses and the dependent measures. That is, subjects in the reasons condition read the descriptions, spent several minutes thinking about why they felt the way they did about the courses, and then rated the courses. Control subjects spent several minutes thinking about unrelated matters after reading the course descriptions, which might have adversely affected their memory for the courses. To correct this problem, two versions of the control condition were run: one in which subjects

completed the filler questionnaire between reading the descriptions and completing the dependent measures, to equalize the delay between these activities, and one in which subjects completed the dependent measures immediately after reading the descriptions so that they would not be distracted by thinking about unrelated matters before completing the dependent measures. As it happened, the presence or absence of the delay in the control group produced very few significant differences on the dependent measures. The only difference was that subjects who had no delay between the course descriptions and the dependent measures reported that they were significantly less likely to take two of the nine courses. Because there were no other differences on any other dependent measure (including the actual registration and enrollment figures and the recall data), the data from the two versions of the control condition were combined in all analyses reported later.

could record the courses for which they actually registered. All subjects agreed to sign this form. They were then given a written explanation of the study that explained it in general terms; that is, that the study was concerned with the kinds of information people use when deciding what courses to take. Neither the hypotheses nor the different conditions of the study were discussed. At the end of the following semester, all subjects were sent a complete written description of the purpose of the study.

Expert opinion on the criteria for choosing courses

A questionnaire was distributed to the 34 faculty members in psychology in residence at the University of Virginia. They were given a description of the 10 pieces of information subjects had received about the psychology courses (e.g., "whether or not a term paper is required"), as well as the two other pieces of information that subjects had rated (what the student had heard about the courses from other students or professors and how interested the student was in the topic), in one of two counterbalanced orders. The faculty rated how much students should use each piece of information "to make sure they make the best decision they can" about which 200-level psychology course to take. These ratings were made on scales ranging from *should be given very little weight* (1) to *should be weighted very heavily* (9). A total of 18 (53%) of the faculty completed the questionnaire.

Results

Initial analyses revealed that neither the order in which the courses were presented, the order in which subjects rated how much the information about the courses influenced their likelihood of taking them, nor subjects' gender interacted significantly with the independent variables. There were a few significant main effects of gender and course order; for example, women recalled more information about the courses than did men, and the order in which the courses were presented had a significant effect on subjects' ratings of how likely they

were to take some of the courses. Because the distributions of men and women and of people who received the courses in each order were nearly identical in each condition, however, we collapsed across gender and order in all subsequent analyses.

Recall for and ratings of influence of the course Information

We predicted that the two introspection manipulations would alter the way subjects weighted the different information about the courses. To test this, we examined their recall for the information and their ratings of how much each type of information had influenced their decisions. We would certainly not argue that these measures were perfectly correlated with the weights subjects actually assigned to the different criteria. As one of us has noted elsewhere, subjects' causal reports are often inaccurate (Nisbett & Wilson, 1977). It is also well known that recall is often uncorrelated with people's weighting schemes (Hastie & Park, 1986). Few would argue, however, that such measures were orthogonal to the weights people used. Thus, relative differences in reported influence and recall between different conditions can be taken as rough indicators of what subjects in those conditions found important about the courses (Anderson & Pichert, 1978).

Recall. Interestingly, the total amount of information subjects recalled did not differ across the three conditions, $F(2, 226) < 1$. There were, however, differences in the kinds of information subjects recalled. Subjects' recall scores were averaged across the nine courses and analyzed in a 3 (introspection condition) × 10 (type of information, e.g., when the course met, whether a term paper was required) analysis of variance (ANOVA), with the last factor treated as a repeated measure. There was a very strong effect for type of information, $F(10, 217) = 59.53$, $p < .001$, reflecting the fact that subjects were more likely to recall some kinds of information about the courses than they were others. More interestingly, there was also a significant Condition × Type of Information interaction, $F(20, 434) = 2.53$, $p < .001$, indicating that the kinds of information subjects were most likely to remember differed by condition.

How well did subjects' recall correspond to the opinion of faculty as to how much people should weight each piece of information? We predicted that subjects in the control condition would do a reasonably good job of attending to the information that was important about the courses, whereas the introspection manipulations might disrupt this process. To test this prediction, we averaged subjects' recall for the three pieces of information faculty rated as most important (who was teaching the class, the course content, and the prerequisites for the class) and subjects' recall for the three pieces of information faculty rated as least important (when the class met, whether there was a required term paper, and whether the course had a discussion section). As seen in Table 18.2, control subjects recalled more of the "important" than "unimportant" information, $F(1, 226) = 10.09, p < .01$. As predicted, this was not the case in the two introspection conditions. Subjects in the reasons condition were no more likely to recall important than unimportant information, and subjects in the rate all condition actually recalled more of the unimportant information, $F(1, 226) = 3.46, p = .06$. These results were reflected by a significant Condition × Importance of Information interaction, $F(2,226) = 8.28, p < .001$. This interaction was also significant when the control condition was compared with the reasons condition alone, $F(1, 226) = 5.25, p < .05$, and with the rate all condition alone, $F(1, 226) = 12.69, p < .001$.

Ratings of influence of the course information. Subjects rated how much each of the 10 pieces of information about the courses influenced how likely they were to take them, as well as the influence of 2 additional items: what they had heard about the course from others and how interested they were in the topic of the course. A 3 (condition) × 12 (information type) between/within ANOVA revealed a significant main effect for condition, $F(2, 223) = 8.46, p < .001$, reflecting the fact that subjects in the rate all condition ($M = 5.78$) thought that all of the information had influenced them more than did subjects in the control and

TABLE 18.2. Recall for and Reported Influence of the Course Information as a Function of the Importance Attributed to These Items by Faculty

Variable	Condition		
	Control	Reasons	Rate all
Recall			
Recall for 3 highest items	0.23	0.19	0.16
Recall for 3 lowest items	0.14	0.19	0.21
Ratings of influence			
Ratings of 3 highest items	6.41	6.47	6.26
Ratings of 3 lowest items	4.73	5.11	6.32

Note: The higher the number, the more subjects recalled the information or thought the information influenced their decision of what courses to take.

reasons conditions ($Ms = 5.17$ and 5.26, respectively). The ANOVA also yielded a significant Condition × Information Type interaction, $F(22, 426) = 2.81, p < .001$, indicating that the manipulations influenced what kinds of information subjects thought influenced them.

As seen in Table 18.2, control subjects reported that the important information influenced them more than did the unimportant information, $F(1, 223) = 50.42, p < .001$. In contrast, subjects in the rate all condition reported that the two types of information had influenced them about equally, $F(1, 223) < 1$. Unexpectedly, subjects in the reasons condition responded similarly to control subjects. A 3 (condition) × 2 (importance of information) between/within ANOVA revealed a highly significant interaction, $F(2, 223) = 9.20, p < .001$. This interaction was also significant when considering the control and rate all conditions alone, $F(1, 223) = 30.91, p < .001$. It was not significant when the control condition was compared with the reasons condition, $F(1, 223) = 1.06$.[6]

---

[6] Subjects' ratings of the influence of and their recall for the course information were analyzed in several alternative ways. For example, we computed the within-subject correlations between subjects' recall and the faculty members' ratings of importance and then averaged these correlations across conditions. The results of these and other analyses were very similar to those reported in the text.

We predicted that the rate all manipulation might confuse people about which attributes of the courses were most important, causing them to assign more equal weights to the different information. One piece of evidence for this prediction was that as just seen, subjects in the rate all condition rated all of the information, on average, as more influential than subjects in the other two conditions. Another was that the mean, within-subject range in subjects' ratings of the influence of the information was significantly smaller in the rate all condition ($M = 6.78$) than in the control and reasons conditions (Ms = 7.35 and 7.47, respectively), ts(224) > 3.31, ps < .001. An identical pattern of results was found in an analysis of the within-subject standard deviations of the ratings of the course information.

Reported likelihood of taking each course

We expected that people instructed to reflect about their decision (i.e., those in the reasons and rate all conditions) would change their minds about which courses were the most desirable and that this change would be in a nonoptimal direction. To test this prediction, we computed the mean of subjects' reported likelihood of taking the five courses that had received the highest course evaluations by students who had taken the classes and the mean ratings of the three that had received the lowest ratings plus one for which no ratings were available (the results are nearly identical if this latter course is eliminated from the analyses). These means were analyzed with a 3 (condition) × 2 (course evaluation) between/within ANOVA.

The main effect for condition was not significant, $F(2, 199) = 1.88$, $p > .15$, indicating that subjects' condition did not influence their reported likelihood of taking psychology courses. The main effect for course evaluation was highly significant, $F(2, 199) = 195.61$, $p < .001$, reflecting the fact that subjects in all conditions preferred the highly rated courses to the poorly rated courses (see Table 18.3). Most relevant to our hypotheses, the Condition × Course Evaluation interaction was also significant, $F(2, 199) = 10.80$, $p < .001$. As predicted,

TABLE 18.3. Ratings of Likelihood of Taking the Courses

	Condition		
Evaluation of course	Control	Reasons	Rate all
Highly rated	4.77	4.55	4.45
Poorly rated	3.18	2.85	3.74

Note: The higher the number, the greater the reported likelihood that students would take the class.

subjects in the control condition showed more of a preference for highly rated courses than for poorly rated courses than subjects in the rate all condition (see Table 18.3). Considering these two conditions alone, the Condition × Course interaction was significant, $F(1, 199) = 14.25$, $p < .001$. Unexpectedly, there were no significant differences in the reports of subjects in the control versus reasons condition.

To see if subjects in the rate all condition moderated their ratings of the courses, we examined the range of each subject's ratings of the nine courses. As predicted, the average range was significantly smaller in the rate all condition ($M = 5.19$) than in the control condition ($M = 6.01$), $t(224) = 3.18$, $p < .001$. The mean in the reasons condition was actually larger than in the control condition ($M = 6.53$), $t(224) = 1.95$, $p = .05$. An identical pattern of results was found in an analysis of the within-subject standard deviations of the ratings of the courses. Finally, we examined the intercorrelations between subjects' ratings within each condition, as we did in Study 1. The mean intercorrelations in the control and reasons conditions were very similar (Ms = .24 and .23, respectively). Both of these means were significantly higher than the mean in the rate all condition ($M = .16$), ts(221) > 2.31, ps < .02. The lower agreement in the rate all condition may be a result of the fact that there was less variation in these subjects' ratings—that is, the restricted variance in their ratings placed limits on the magnitude of the intercorrelations.

Course preregistration and enrollment

In the few days after our study, all the participants registered for the courses they wanted to take the next semester. We obtained the preregistration records for the nine psychology courses and assigned subjects a 1 if they had preregistered for a course, a 0 if they had not, and a missing value if they had already taken the course. We also analyzed the actual course enrollment data at the conclusion of the following semester, to see if any differences found in the preregistration data persisted, even after students had had the option to add and drop courses. These data were coded in an identical fashion to the preregistration data.

Preregistration for courses. As predicted, the two introspection manipulations influenced the kind of courses for which subjects preregistered. As seen in Table 18.4, subjects in the introspection conditions (especially those who analyzed reasons) were less likely than control subjects to take the highly rated courses but about equally likely to take the poorly rated courses. The number of courses of each type that subjects registered for were analyzed in a 3 (condition) $\times$ 2 (course evaluation) between/within ANOVA, which yielded the predicted Condition $\times$ Course Evaluation interaction, $F(2, 206) = 6.40$, $p = .002$. This interaction was significant when the control and reasons conditions were considered alone, $F(1, 206) = 12.58$, $p < .001$, and when the control and rate all conditions were considered alone, $F(1, 206) = 4.12$, $p < .05$.

It can be seen by the low averages in Table 18.4 that the modal response in all conditions was not to take any of the nine psychology courses. Despite our request that people only participate in the study if they were considering taking a 200-level psychology course, many subjects opted not to take any. This created a bit of a statistical anomaly, in that the people who did not take any psychology classes lowered the variance and increased the sample size, thereby increasing the power of the significance tests. To avoid this problem, a 3 (condition) $\times$ 2 (course evaluation) chi-square analysis was performed after eliminating those students who did not register for any of the nine courses. This analysis was also significant, $\chi^2(2, N = 74) = 8.25$, $p = .02$, reinforcing the conclusion that the manipulations influenced the courses for which subjects registered.

Enrollment at the conclusion of the following semester. We did not make firm predictions about whether the effects of the introspection manipulations on people's choice of courses would persist over the long run. To see if they did, we analyzed the course enrollment data at the conclusion of the semester in the same manner as the preregistration data. The results were similar, though not as strong (see Table 18.4). The interaction effect in a 3 (condition) $\times$ 2 (course evaluation) ANOVA was significant, $F(2, 206) = 3.05$, $p = .05$. This interaction was significant when the control condition was compared only with the reasons condition, $F(1, 206) = 5.90$, $p < .05$, but not with the rate all condition, $F(1, 206) = 2.37$, $p = .13$. The chi-square on only those subjects enrolled in at least one course was not significant, $\chi^2(2, N = 74) = 2.84$, $p = .24$.

To test more definitively whether the effect of the manipulations had weakened over time, the preregistration and final enrollment data were entered into a 3 (condition) $\times$ 2 (course evaluation) $\times$ 2 (time of measurement: registration vs. final enrollment) ANOVA; the last two factors were treated as repeated measures. The Condition $\times$ Course Evaluation interaction was highly significant, $F(2, 206) = 5.31$, $p = .006$, reflecting the fact that at both times of measurement, subjects in the introspection conditions were less likely to take the highly rated courses but about equally likely to take the poorly rated courses. The Condition $\times$ Course Evaluation $\times$ Time of Measurement interaction was not significant, $F(2, 206) = 1.13$, $p =$

TABLE 18.4. Courses Preregistered for and Actually Taken

Variable	Condition		
	Control	Reasons	Rate all
Preregistration			
Highly rated courses	.41	.15	.21
Poorly rated courses	.04	.10	.01
Actual enrollment			
Highly rated courses	.37	.21	.24
Poorly rated courses	.03	.08	.03

Note: Subjects were assigned a 1 if they registered for or actually took a course and a 0 if they did not register or take a course.

.32, indicating that the attenuation of the Condition × Course interaction over time was not reliable.

Other analyses

Coding of reasons given in the reasons condition. The reasons protocols were coded as described in Study 1, with similar levels of reliability. Subjects gave an average of 2.06 reasons for liking or disliking each course. The most frequently mentioned reasons were interest in the material (33%), the course evaluations (23%), the course content (13%), whether a term paper was required (7%), and when the course met (6%). The reasons were also coded according to how much liking for each course they conveyed (reliability $r = .98$). The average within-subject correlation between these ratings and subjects' ratings of how likely they were to take each course was .70, $t(63) = 10.93$, $p < .0001$.

Other factors potentially influencing course selection. Some preference is given to upper-level students and majors when they enroll for psychology courses. This could not have accounted for the present results, however, because the number of such students was randomly distributed across conditions, $\chi^2(6, N = 229) = 4.49$, $p = .61$, for upper-level students; $\chi^2(2, N = 230) = 1.07$, $p = .58$, for majors.

Grades obtained in the psychology courses. The grades received by those subjects who took one or more of the nine psychology courses were obtained from the final grade sheets. There were no significant differences between conditions in these grades. The means for the control, reasons, and rate all conditions, on a 5-point scale ranging from A (4) to F (0), were 2.82, 2.78, and 3.20, respectively.

Discussion

We predicted that subjects who introspected about their decision about which courses to take would change the way they evaluated the courses, causing them to make less optimal choices. The results in the rate all condition, in which subjects rated each piece of information about every course according to how it influenced their decision, were entirely consistent with this prediction. These subjects' recall and reports of how they had weighted the information differed significantly from control subjects' and were significantly less likely to correspond to the ratings of faculty members of how this information ought to be used. In addition, these subjects were less likely to register for and somewhat less likely to remain in courses that students who had taken the courses previously said were the best courses. Thus, regardless of whether the opinions of faculty members or students' peers (those who had previously taken the courses) were used as the criteria of an optimal choice, subjects in the rate all condition appeared to have made less optimal choices than control subjects. We predicted that the rate all manipulation would change subjects' choices by moderating their evaluations, so that the courses appeared more similar to each other. We found two pieces of evidence in support of this prediction. Both the range in their ratings of how likely they were to take the courses and the range in their ratings of how much they were influenced by the different information about the courses were significantly smaller than the ranges in the other two conditions.

Asking subjects to analyze the reasons for their evaluations of the courses also caused them to weight the course information in a less optimal way and to make less optimal choices. The effects of this manipulation, however, were not as strong as the effects of the rate all manipulation. On some measures, subjects who analyzed reasons responded similarly to control subjects, such as on their reports of how the different kinds of course information influenced their decisions. On those measures that were most objective and consequential, however, our predictions were confirmed. For example, subjects in the reasons condition were significantly less likely than control subjects to preregister for and enroll in courses that had received high course evaluations (see Table 18.4). In addition, the correspondence between their recall of the course information and faculty members' ratings of this information was significantly lower than it was for control subjects (see Table 18.2).

As predicted, analyzing reasons did not make the courses seem more similar to subjects. In fact, the range in their ratings of the courses was significantly larger than it was in the control condition. Nor did analyzing reasons lower the range in their ratings of how much they were influenced by the different kinds of information about the courses. Thus, subjects in the reasons condition seemed to have had little difficulty in forming an opinion about which courses they liked and how the course information influenced them; it is just that their opinions differed from control subjects' (at least as assessed by their recall of the course information and the courses for which they registered and in which they were enrolled). These results are consistent with our hypothesis that when people analyze their reasons, they often change their criteria by focusing on attributes that seem like plausible reasons for liking or disliking the attitude object, but that in fact have not been heavily weighted before. Similarly, they dismiss attributes that seem like implausible reasons, but that in fact have been weighted heavily before. As a result, people change their mind about how they feel.

Despite this support for our predictions, we should not overlook the inconsistent effects of the reasons manipulation in Study 2 (e.g., the failure of this manipulation to influence subjects' reported likelihood of taking the courses). We offer the following, speculative explanation for these inconsistent findings. Both Wilson, Dunn, Kraft, and Lisle (1989) and Millar and Tesser (1986a) suggested that analyzing reasons is most likely to change attitudes that have a large affective component, because people are less likely to know the actual causes of these attitudes and because analyzing reasons is likely to emphasize cognitions and obscure the affect (the Millar & Tesser (1986a) explanation). People's attitudes toward college courses may have less of an affective component than their attitudes toward food items (e.g., strawberry jams), explaining why the effects were less consistent in Study 2. In addition, analyzing reasons may have a greater effect when the different dimensions of the stimuli are ill-defined,

because this increases the likelihood that people will overlook factors that initially influenced their judgments. Consistent with this view, the criteria used to evaluate the courses in Study 2 were much more explicit than were the criteria in Study 1. That is, in Study 2, we gave subjects a list of all the relevant attributes of the different courses, whereas in Study 1, subjects had to define the set of relevant attributes themselves (e.g., whether to consider the color or consistency of the jams). Clearly, further research is needed to verify these speculations.

Finally, we should mention a possible alternative explanation for the effects of the introspection manipulations. The manipulations may have caused people to attend less to the information about the courses, because they were concentrating on why they felt the way they did. According to this argument, any intervention that distracts people from the information about the alternatives would have similar deleterious effects to our introspection manipulations. The results of our recall measure, however, reduce the plausibility of this interpretation. If subjects in the introspection conditions were distracted, they should have recalled less information about the courses than did control subjects; in fact, there were no significant differences between conditions in the amount of information they recalled—only, as predicted, in the kinds of information they recalled (see Table 18.2).

General Discussion

Previous studies demonstrated that thinking about why we feel the way we do could change our attitudes (Wilson, 1990; Wilson, Dunn, Kraft, & Lisle, 1989). It has not been clear, however, whether the direction of this change is beneficial, detrimental, or neutral. The present studies demonstrated that analyzing reasons can lead to preferences and decisions that correspond less with expert opinion. This result, taken together with Wilson et al.'s (1990) finding that analyzing reasons reduces people's satisfaction with their choices, suggests that it may not always be a good idea to analyze the reasons for our preferences too carefully. In the present studies, analyzing reasons focused subjects' attention on characteristics of the stimuli that were, according to expert opinion, nonoptimal and caused them to use these characteristics to form preferences that were also nonoptimal. Nor may it be wise to analyze the effects of every attribute of every alternative. Evaluating multiple attributes led to nonoptimal preferences in Study 2 by moderating people's evaluations, so that the college courses seemed more equivalent than they did to subjects in the other conditions.

We do not mean to imply that the two kinds of introspection we examined will always lead to nonoptimal choices, and we certainly do not suggest that people studiously avoid all reflection before making decisions. Such a conclusion would be unwarranted for several reasons. First, we used stimuli in the present studies that were evaluated fairly optimally by control subjects, who were not instructed to reflect about the alternatives. That is, the evaluations and choices of control subjects in both studies corresponded fairly well with the experts' ratings. If people start out with feelings or preferences that are nonoptimal, the change that often results from introspection may be in a positive direction. Consistent with this possibility, Tesser, Leone, and Clary (1978) found that when people who experienced speech anxiety were asked to think about why they felt anxious, their anxiety was reduced.

Second, some people might be more likely to know why they feel the way they do about an attitude object and thus will be less likely to be misled by thinking about their reasons. Consistent with this hypothesis, Wilson, Kraft, and Dunn (1989) found that people who were knowledgeable about the attitude object and thus more likely to have attitudes that were based on objective, easily verbalizable attributes of it were relatively immune to the effects of thinking about reasons. Finally, in our studies, people were asked to reflect for a relatively brief amount of time. A more intensive, in-depth analysis, such as that advocated by Janis and Mann (1977), may have very different effects on the quality of people's decisions (see, for example, Mann, 1972).

We have just begun to explore the conditions under which people should and should not reflect about the reasons for their preferences, thus to make broad claims about the dangers of introspection would be inappropriate (or at least premature). Perhaps the best conclusion at this point is a variation of Socrates' oft-quoted statement that the "unexamined life is not worth living." We suggest that, at least at times, the unexamined choice *is* worth making.

REFERENCES

Anderson, R. C., & Pichert, J. W. (1978). Recall of previously unrecallable information following a shift in perspective. *Journal of Verbal Learning and Verbal Behavior, 17,* 1–12.

Baumeister, R. F. (1984). Choking under pressure: Self-consciousness and paradoxical effects of incentives on skillful performance. *Journal of Personality and Social Psychology, 46,* 610–620.

Edwards, W. (1961). Behavioral decision theory. *Annual Review of Psychology, 12,* 473–498.

Goodman, N. G. (Ed.). (1945). *A Benjamin Franklin reader.* New York: Crowell.

Hastie, R., & Park, B. (1986). The relationship between memory and judgment depends on whether the judgment task is memory-based or on-line. *Psychological Review, 93,* 258–268.

Janis, I. L., & Mann, L. (1977). *Decision making: A psychological analysis of conflict, choice, and commitment.* New York: Free Press.

Judd, C. M., & Lusk, C. M. (1984). Knowledge structures and evaluative judgments: Effects of structural variables on judgmental extremity. *Journal of Personality and Social Psychology, 46,* 1193–1207.

Keeney, R. L. (1977). The art of assessing multiattribute utility functions. *Organizational Behavior and Human Performance, 19,* 267–310.

Kimble, G. A., & Perlmuter, L. C. (1970). The problem of volition. *Psychological Review, 77,* 361–384.

Koriat, A., Lichtenstein, S., & Fischhoff, B. (1980). Reasons for confidence. *Journal of Experimental Psychology: Human Learning and Memory, 6,* 107–118.

Langer, E. J., & Imber, L. G. (1979). When practice makes imperfect: Debilitating effects of overlearning. *Journal of Personality and Social Psychology, 37,* 2014–2024.

Linville, P. W. (1982). The complexity–extremity effect and age-based stereotyping. *Journal of Personality and Social Psychology, 42,* 193–211.

Mann, L. (1972). Use of a "balance sheet" procedure to improve the quality of personal decision making: A field experiment with college applicants. *Journal of Vocational Behavior, 2,* 291–300.

Millar, M. G., & Tesser, A. (1986a). Effects of affective and cognitive focus on the attitude–behavior relationship. *Journal of Personality and Social Psychology, 51,* 270–276.

Millar, M. G., & Tesser, A. (1986b). Thought-induced attitude change: The effects of schema structure and commitment. *Journal of Personality and Social Psychology, 51,* 259–269.

Millar, M. G., & Tesser, A. (1989). The effects of affective–cognitive consistency and thought on the attitude–behavior relation. *Journal of Experimental Social Psychology, 25,* 189–202.

Morrow, J., & Nolan-Hoeksema, S. (1990). Effects of responses to depression on the remediation of depressive affect. *Journal of Personality and Social Psychology, 58,* 519–527.

Nisbett, R. E., & Wilson, T. D. (1977). Telling more than we can know: Verbal reports on mental processes. *Psychological Review, 84,* 231–259.

Raiffa, H. (1968). *Decision analysis.* Reading, MA: Addison-Wesley.

Schooler, J. W., & Engstler-Schooler, T. Y. (1990). Verbal overshadowing of visual memories: Some things are better left unsaid. *Cognitive Psychology, 22,* 36–71.

Slovic, P. (1982). Toward understanding and improving decisions. In W. C. Howell & E. A. Fleishman (Eds.), *Information processing and decision making* (pp. 157–183). Hillsdale, NJ: Erlbaum.

Strawberry jams and preserves. (1985, August). *Consumer Reports,* pp. 487–489.

Tesser, A., Leone, C., & Clary, G. (1978). Affect control: Process constraints versus catharsis. *Cognitive Therapy and Research, 2,* 265–274.

Wilson, T. D. (1990). Self-persuasion via self-reflection. In J. M. Olson & M. P. Zanna (Eds.), *Self-inference processes: The Ontario Symposium* (Vol. 6, pp. 43–67). Hillsdale, NJ: Erlbaum.

Wilson, T. D., Dunn, D. S., Bybee, J. A., Hyman, D. B., & Rotondo, J. A. (1984). Effects of analyzing reasons on attitude–behavior consistency. *Journal of Personality and Social Psychology, 47,* 5–16.

Wilson, T. D., Dunn, D. S., Kraft, D., & Lisle, D. J. (1989). Introspection, attitude change, and attitude–behavior consistency: The disruptive effects of explaining why we feel the way we do. In L. Berkowitz (Ed.), *Advances in experimental social psychology* (Vol. 19, pp. 123–205). San Diego, CA: Academic Press.

Wilson, T. D., Kraft, D., & Dunn, D. S. (1989). The disruptive effects of explaining attitudes: The moderating effect of knowledge about the attitude object. *Journal of Experimental Social Psychology, 25,* 379–400.

Wilson, T. D., Lisle, D. J., & Schooler, J. (1990). *Some undesirable effects of self-reflection.* Unpublished manuscript, University of Virginia, Department of Psychology, Charlottesville.

Wilson, T. D., Hodges, S. D., & Pollack, S. (1990). *Effects of explaining attitudes on survey responses: The moderating effects of attitude accessibility.* Unpublished manuscript, University of Virginia, Department of Psychology, Charlottesville.

Received January 5, 1990
Revision received July 9, 1990
Accepted July 12, 1990 ■

PART 5

Impact of Attitudes on Perception and Judgment

The final two sections of this collection of readings concern the consequences of attitudes. What impact do they have on an individual's processing of information, judgment, and behavior? In introducing the concept of attitude at the very beginning of this book, we discussed Allport's (1935) writing in which he proposed his definition of attitude. It is useful to re-visit Allport's discussion at this point, for he viewed attitudes as being characterized by sweeping power. "Time and again, the phenomena of perception, judgment, memory, learning, and thought have been reduced largely to the operation of attitudes . . . Without guiding attitudes the individual is confused and baffled . . . Attitudes determine for each individual what he will see and hear, what he will think and what he will do . . . they draw lines about and segregate an otherwise chaotic environment; they are our methods for finding our way about in an ambiguous universe" (Allport, 1935, p. 806).

With its emphasis on attitudes as tools for organizing and structuring the environment, this quotation underscores the knowledge function of attitudes. However, Allport also ascribes considerable power to attitudes in terms of their influencing perception, thought, and behavior. Allport's view certainly has been challenged over the years. Many scientists have been much more skeptical about the potential influence of attitudes. Most contemporary attitude theorists acknowledge that extreme theoretical stances, in either direction, are not appropriate and not justified by the available empirical research. The field now knows that just how impactful an attitude might be in any given situation depends on many factors including properties of the attitude itself (i.e., its "strength" as indexed by such factors as the accessibility of the attitude from memory and the confidence with which the attitude is held) and properties of the situation (e.g., its ambiguity).

If an event is crystal clear, then there is no room for multiple interpretation. Everyone will view it the same way. Witnesses will confidently assert that a driver has erred if the stoplight has been red for 10 seconds prior to the driver's speeding through the intersection. However, judgments will vary considerably more if the event involves the proverbial "pink" light. Was it yellow, or red? In such cases of ambiguity, what the perceiver brings to the situation may be just as (if not more) important as the actual physical reality. Perceptions and judgments reside in the "eye of the beholder," and attitudes are among the forces that can determine what the beholder sees. So, the driver in the pink light situation might be viewed very differently if he is one's best friend or one's worst enemy. Indeed, put yourself in the role of a police investigator querying witnesses to a traffic accident that occurred just as the stoplight was changing. How much trust would you place in the eyewitness reports of a friend of the driver, or someone who has just had an argument with the driver, versus a complete stranger?

The readings in this section concern perceptions and judgments of exactly this sort. Together, they illustrate the multiple ways in which attitudes can affect information processing. The impact can be observed on a full spectrum of cognitive processes, ranging from very global judgments of information related to the attitude object to more fundamental processes of visual attention and memory. The research findings attest to the importance of attitudes as determinants of the workings of the "eye of the beholder." Indeed, the artwork on the paperback cover of this book ("Eye of the Beholder" by Valerie Lorimer) was selected to highlight this very theme.

The first two readings focus on the impact of attitudes on judgments. Reading 19 is a classic article by Hastorf and Cantril (1954) reporting findings that any sports fan will have personally experienced. The opposing team, not the team for which the avid sports fan is rooting, commits more fouls, often of a more serious nature, and yet these infractions are more often overlooked by the referees. Two fans rooting for different teams seem to see very different games. Hastorf and Cantril document this very phenomenon with respect to a football game between Dartmouth and Princeton.

Attitudinally-biased judgments are evident in many realms beyond sports. A conceptually parallel effect is often observed in any contest that involves a subjective element, including those in the political domain. For example, in a study of the 1984 presidential election, Fazio and Williams (1986) found that judgments of the candidates' performance during the televised debates were strongly related to the candidate preferences that the viewers had expressed weeks earlier. Who was viewed as having won the debate was very much influenced by the attitudes that viewers brought to the situation. Moreover, this attitude–judgment relation was all the stronger among individuals whose attitudes toward the candidates were especially accessible from memory. (This article is reprinted in the final section of this collection, as Reading 27, because it concerns not only the relation between attitudes and judgments, but also the relation between attitudes and behavior, in this case voting behavior.)

But, one might argue, sports and politics are

inherently partisan. What about situations that, by their very essence, call for a more objective perspective? Surely, judging the methodological soundness and scientific merits of empirical research is such a domain. Yet, research by Lord, Ross, and Lepper (1979) indicates that attitudes can bias information processing even in situations in which judgments are supposed to be more objective in nature. Their article is reprinted as Reading 20. These researchers exposed participants with extremely-pro or extremely-con attitudes toward capital punishment to summaries of two purported scientific studies regarding the deterrent efficacy of the death penalty. The two studies reached different conclusions about the value of capital punishment as a deterrent. Participants' judgments of the quality of the research varied as a function of their own attitudes toward the death penalty. Proponents viewed the study that reached an unfavorable conclusion about capital punishment as more methodologically flawed than the study that reached a favorable conclusion, whereas the reverse was true among those opposed to the death penalty.

Even more fundamental cognitive processes than global judgments can be affected by attitudes. Memory is one such process. Recall for the past is not a matter of locating a document in some file cabinet and, hence, having available all the original details, as comprehensive and vivid as they were initially. To the contrary, memory processes are known to be constructive in nature. Considerable embellishment occurs. Yes, a few details surrounding the event might be recalled, but we tend to fill in the gaps based upon our general knowledge, thoughts about what was likely in that situation, and our intuitive theories relating the past and the present (see Ross, 1989, for an influential model of reconstructive memory). Our hopes, wishes, and desires—more generally speaking, our attitudes—can be among the factors that influence our reconstructions of the past. Reading 21 reprints an article by Ross, McFarland, and Fletcher (1981) concerning this phenomenon. Their research convincingly demonstrated that attitudes can have a causal influence on individuals' recall of their personal histories.

Attitudes also can influence visual attention. Of the multitude of objects that enter our visual field, which attract attention? Which do we actually come to notice? That is the question posed by Roskos-Ewoldsen and Fazio (1992) in the article reprinted as Reading 22. Following from the object-appraisal function of attitudes and from research that we discussed earlier concerning attitudes that are capable of automatic activation from memory, these researchers suggested that the activation of an attitude may play a very early role in visual attention. They suggested that even minimal processing of an attitude object that enters the visual field may be sufficient to activate a strongly associated evaluation. Once activated, this attitude—whether it is positive or negative—can direct further attention to that location in the visual field. Essentially, the object has been tagged as hedonically relevant and potentially consequential and, hence, as meriting further attention. A series of experiments provided support for this hypothesis. Attitude-evoking objects—ones toward which individuals held attitudes that were highly accessible from memory—automatically attracted attention. Thus, accessible attitudes are functionally beneficial in yet another sense. They orient visual attention to objects that can give us pleasure or cause pain, increasing the likelihood that we will notice (and, hence, can approach) the liked objects and also notice (and, hence, can avoid) the disliked.

It is important to recognize that the various potential consequences of attitudes for attention, memory, and judgment can have significant, cumulative effects. In any given experiment considered thus far, we have been concerned only with a momentary slice in time. Which objects did people notice when presented with a stimulus array? What is their current recollection of the past? What judgment do they offer of some single event or currently available set of information? Over time, however, these various processes can accumulate in such a manner that people who begin with different attitudes may, in effect, find themselves in very different social worlds.

Consider the multitude of news media that we encounter in any given day. We are likely to have our attention drawn to television, magazine, and newspaper stories that involve issues that are attitude-evoking for us. However, whether we choose to approach or avoid that story can be affected by whether the activated attitude is positive or negative. Certainly, sometimes we choose to read newspaper articles that advocate a position that is contrary to our own attitudes. However, over the long term, we are less likely to do that than to expose ourselves to information that is congenial with our attitudes and, hence, pleases us in one sense or another. As we gain such information, our knowledge and the support for our attitudinal position grow. The end result is that we accrue a very different knowledge base over time than people whose attitudes pushed them in a different direction.

This "selective exposure" hypothesis is the focus of Reading 23, an article by Sweeney and Gruber (1984). These researchers examined reactions to an important, real-world event as it unfolded over time—the Watergate affair that led to the resignation of President Richard Nixon. By interviewing a sample of voters at multiple points in time, Sweeney and Gruber were able to consider the relation between initial attitudes toward Nixon (comparing voters who had supported him to those who had voted for his opponent George McGovern), interest in the televised Senate Watergate hearings, and knowledge gained about Watergate-related matters. Nixon supporters were less interested in Watergate stories and, when queried the final time, also knew fewer relevant facts about the Watergate affair. The study provides an informative illustration of how attitudes can affect knowledge acquisition over time.

REFERENCES

Allport, G. W. (1935). Attitudes. In C. Murchison (Ed.), *Handbook of social psychology* (pp. 798–844). Worcester, MA: Clark University Press.

Fazio, R. H., & Williams, C. J. (1986). Attitude accessibility as a moderator of the attitude-perception and attitude-behavior relations: An investigation of the 1984 presidential election. *Journal of Personality and Social Psychology, 51,* 505–514.

Ross, M. (1989). Relation of implicit theories to the construction of personal histories. *Psychological Review, 96,* 341–357.

Suggested Readings

Ditto, P. H., & Lopez, D. F. (1992). Motivated skepticism: Use of differential decision criteria for preferred and nonpreferred conclusions. *Journal of Personality and Social Psychology, 63*, 568–584.

Eagly, A. H., Kulesa, P., Chen, S., & Chaiken, S. (2001). Do attitudes affect memory? Tests of the congeniality hypothesis. *Current Directions in Psychological Science, 10*, 5–9.

Houston, D. A., & Fazio, R. H. (1989). Biased processing as a function of attitude accessibility: Making objective judgments subjectively. *Social Cognition, 7*, 51–66.

McDonald, H. E., & Hirt, E. R. (1997). When expectancy meets desire: Motivational effects in reconstructive memory. *Journal of Personality and Social Psychology, 72*, 5–23.

Smith, E. R., Fazio, R. H., & Cejka, M. A. (1996). Accessible attitudes influence categorization of multiply categorizable objects. *Journal of Personality and Social Psychology, 71*, 888–898.

Vallone, R. P., Ross, L., & Lepper, M. R. (1985). The hostile media phenomenon: Biased perception and perceptions of media bias in coverage of the Beirut massacre. *Journal of Personality and Social Psychology, 49*, 577–585.

They Saw a Game: A Case Study

Albert H. Hastorf* and Hadley Cantril**

On a brisk Saturday afternoon, November 23, 1951, the Dartmouth football team played Princeton in Princeton's Palmer Stadium. It was the last game of the season for both teams and of rather special significance because the Princeton team had won all its games so far and one of its players, Kazmaier, was receiving All-American mention and had just appeared as the cover man on *Time* magazine, and was playing his last game.

A few minutes after the opening kick-off, it became apparent that the game was going to be a rough one. The referees were kept busy blowing their whistles and penalizing both sides. In the second quarter, Princeton's star left the game with a broken nose. In the third quarter, a Dartmouth player was taken off the field with a broken leg. Tempers flared both during and after the game. The official statistics of the game, which Princeton won, showed that Dartmouth was penalized 70 yards, Princeton 25, not counting more than a few plays in which both sides were penalized.

Needless to say, accusations soon began to fly. The game immediately became a matter of concern to players, students, coaches, and the administrative officials of the two institutions, as well as to alumni and the general public who had not seen the game but had become sensitive to the problem of big-time football through the recent exposures of subsidized players, commercialism, etc. Discussion of the game continued for several weeks.

One of the contributing factors to the extended discussion of the game was the extensive space given to it by both campus and metropolitan newspapers. An indication of the fervor with which the discussions were carried on is shown by a few excerpts from the campus dailies.

For example, on November 27 (four days after the game), the *Daily Princetonian* (Princeton's student newspaper) said:

> This observer has never seen quite such a disgusting exhibition of so-called "sport." Both teams were guilty but the blame must be laid primarily on Dartmouth's doorstep. Princeton, obviously the better team, had no reason to rough up Dartmouth. Looking at the situation rationally, we don't see why the Indians should make a deliberate attempt to cripple Dick Kazmaier or any other Princeton player. The Dartmouth psychology, however, is not rational itself.

The November 30th edition of the *Princeton Alumni Weekly* said:

> But certain memories of what occurred will not be easily erased. Into the record books will go in indelible fashion the fact that the last game of Dick Kazmaier's career was cut short by more than half when he was forced out with a broken

* Dartmouth College.
** Princeton University.

nose and a mild concussion, sustained from a tackle that came well after he had thrown a pass.

This second-period development was followed by a third quarter outbreak of roughness that was climaxed when a Dartmouth player deliberately kicked Brad Glass in the ribs while the latter was on his back. Throughout the often unpleasant afternoon, there was undeniable evidence that the losers' tactics were the result of an actual style of play, and reports on other games they have played this season substantiate this.

Dartmouth students were "seeing" an entirely different version of the game through the editorial eyes of the *Dartmouth* (Dartmouth's undergraduate newspaper). For example, on November 27 the *Dartmouth* said:

> However, the Dartmouth-Princeton game set the stage for the other type of dirty football. A type which may be termed as an unjustifiable accusation.
>
> Dick Kazmaier was injured early in the game. Kazmaier was the star, an All-American. Other stars have been injured before, but Kazmaier had been built to represent a Princeton idol. When an idol is hurt there is only one recourse—the tag of dirty football. So what did the Tiger Coach Charley Caldwell do? He announced to the world that the Big Green had been out to extinguish the Princeton star. His purpose was achieved.
>
> After this incident, Caldwell instilled the old see-what-they-did-go-get-them attitude into his players. His talk got results. Gene Howard and Jim Miller were both injured. Both had dropped back to pass, had passed, and were standing unprotected in the backfield. Result: one bad leg and one leg broken.
>
> The game was rough and did get a bit out of hand in the third quarter. Yet most of the roughing penalties were called against Princeton while Dartmouth received more of the illegal-use-of-the-hands variety.

On November 28 the *Dartmouth* said:

> Dick Kazmaier of Princeton admittedly is an unusually able football player. Many Dartmouth men traveled to Princeton, not expecting to win— only hoping to see an All-American in action. Dick Kazmaier was hurt in the second period, and played only a token part in the remainder of the game. For this, spectators were sorry.
>
> But there were no such feelings for Dick Kazmaier's health. Medical authorities have confirmed that as a relatively unprotected passing and running star in a contact sport, he is quite liable to injury. Also, his particular injuries—a broken nose and slight concussion—were no more serious than is experienced almost any day in any football practice, where there is no more serious stake than playing the following Saturday. Up to the Princeton game, Dartmouth players suffered about 10 known nose fractures and face injuries, not to mention several slight concussions.
>
> Did Princeton players feel so badly about losing their star? They shouldn't have. During the past undefeated campaign they stopped several individual stars by a concentrated effort, including such mainstays as Frank Hauff of Navy, Glenn Adams of Pennsylvania and Rocco Calvo of Cornell.
>
> In other words, the same brand of football condemned by the *Prince*—that of stopping the big man—is practiced quite successfully by the Tigers.

Basically, then, there was disagreement as to what had happened during the "game." Hence we took the opportunity presented by the occasion to make a "real life" study of a perceptual problem.[1]

Procedure

Two steps were involved in gathering data. The first consisted of answers to a questionnaire designed to get reactions to the game and to learn something of the climate of opinion in each institution. This questionnaire was administered a week after the game to both Dartmouth and Princeton undergraduates who were taking introductory and intermediate psychology courses.

---

[1] We are not concerned here with the problem of guilt or responsibility for infractions, and nothing here implies any judgment as to who was to blame.

The second step consisted of showing the same motion picture of the game to a sample of undergraduates in each school and having them check on another questionnaire, as they watched the film, any infraction of the rules they saw and whether these infractions were "mild" or "flagrant."[2] At Dartmouth, members of two fraternities were asked to view the film on December 7; at Princeton, members of two undergraduate clubs saw the film early in January.

The answers to both questionnaires were carefully coded and transferred to punch cards.[3]

Results

Table 19.1 shows the questions which received different replies from the two student populations on the first questionnaire.

Questions asking if the students had friends on the team, if they had ever played football themselves, if they felt they knew the rules of the game well, etc. showed no differences in either school and no relation to answers given to other questions. This is not surprising since the students in both schools come from essentially the same type of educational, economic, and ethnic background.

Summarizing the data of Tables 19.1 and 19.2, we find a marked contrast between the two student groups.

Nearly all *Princeton* students judged the game as "rough and dirty"—not one of them thought it "clean and fair." And almost nine-tenths of them thought the other side started the rough play. By and large they felt that the charges they understood were being made were true; most of them felt the

charges were made in order to avoid similar situations in the future.

When Princeton students looked at the movie of the game, they saw the Dartmouth team make over twice as many infractions as their own team made. And they saw the Dartmouth team make over twice as many infractions as were seen by Dartmouth students. When Princeton students judged these infractions as "flagrant" or "mild," the ratio was about two "flagrant" to one "mild" on the Dartmouth team, and about one "flagrant" to three "mild" on the Princeton team.

As for the *Dartmouth* students, while the plurality of answers fell in the "rough and dirty" category, over one-tenth thought the game was "clean and fair" and over a third introduced their own category of "rough and fair" to describe the action. Although a third of the Dartmouth students felt that Dartmouth was to blame for starting the rough play, the majority of Dartmouth students thought both sides were to blame. By and large, Dartmouth men felt that the charges they understood were being made were not true, and most of them thought the reason for the charges was Princeton's concern for its football star.

When Dartmouth students looked at the movie of the game they saw both teams make about the same number of infractions. And they saw their own team make only half the number of infractions the Princeton students saw them make. The ratio of "flagrant" to "mild" infractions was about one to one when Dartmouth students judged the Dartmouth team, and about one "flagrant" to two "mild" when Dartmouth students judged infractions made by the Princeton team.

It should be noted that Dartmouth and Princeton students were thinking of different charges in judging their validity and in assigning reasons as to why the charges were made. It should also be noted that whether or not students were spectators of the game in the stadium made little difference in their responses.

---

[2] The film shown was kindly loaned for the purpose of the experiment by the Dartmouth College Athletic Council. It should be pointed out that a movie of a football game follows the ball, is thus selective, and omits a good deal of the total action on the field. Also, of course, in viewing only a film of a game, the possibilities of participation as spectator are greatly limited.

[3] We gratefully acknowledge the assistance of Virginia Zerega, Office of Public Opinion Research, and J. L. McCandless, Princeton University, and E. S. Horton, Dartmouth College, in the gathering and collation of the data.

TABLE 19.1. Data from First Questionnaire

Question	Dartmouth students (N= 163) %	Princeton students (N= 161) %
1. Did you happen to see the actual game between Dartmouth and Princeton in Palmer Stadium this year?		
Yes	33	71
No	67	29
2. Have you seen a movie of the game or seen it on television?		
Yes, movie	33	2
Yes, television	0	1
No, neither	67	97
3. (Asked of those who answered "yes" to either or both of above questions.) From your observations of what went on at the game, do you believe the game was clean and fairly played, or that it was unnecessarily rough and dirty?		
Clean and fair	6	0
Rough and dirty	24	69
Rough and fair[a]	25	2
No answer	45	29
4. (Asked of those who answered "no" on both of the first questions.) From what you have heard and read about the game, do you feel it was clean and fairly played, or that it was unnecessarily rough and dirty?		
Clean and fair	7	0
Rough and dirty	18	24
Rough and fair[a]	14	1
Don't know	6	4
No answer	55	71
(Combined answers to questions 3 and 4 above)		
Clean and fair	13	0
Rough and dirty	42	93
Rough and fair[a]	39	3
Don't know	6	4
5. From what you saw in the game or the movies, or from what you have read, which team do you feel started the rough play?		
Dartmouth started it	36	86
Princeton started it	2	0
Both started it	53	11
Neither	6	1
No answer	3	2
6. What is your understanding of the charges being made?[b]		
Dartmouth tried to get Kazmaier	71	47
Dartmouth intentionally dirty	52	44
Dartmouth unnecessarily rough	8	35
7. Do you feel there is any truth to these charges?		
Yes	10	55
No	57	4
Partly	29	35
Don't know	4	6
8. Why do you think the charges were made?		
Injury to Princeton star	70	23
To prevent repetition	2	46
No answer	28	31

[a] This answer was not included on the checklist but was written in by the percentage of students indicated.
[b] Replies do not add to 100% since more than one charge could be given.

TABLE 19.2. Data from Second Questionnaire Checked while Seeing Film

Group	N	Total number of Infractions checked against			
		Dartmouth team		Princeton team	
		Mean	SD	Mean	SD
Dartmouth students	48	4.3*	2.7	4.4	2.8
Princeton students	49	9.8*	5.7	4.2	3.5

* Significant at the .01 level.

Interpretation: The Nature of a Social Event [4]

It seems clear that the "game" actually was many different games and that each version of the events that transpired was just as "real" to a particular person as other versions were to other people. A consideration of the experiential phenomena that constitute a "football game" for the spectator may help us both to account for the results obtained and illustrate something of the nature of any social event.

Like any other complex social occurrence, a "football game" consists of a whole host of happenings. Many different events are occurring simultaneously. Furthermore, each happening is a link in a chain of happenings, so that one follows another in sequence. The "football game," as well as other complex social situations, consists of a whole matrix of events. In the game situation, this matrix of events consists of the actions of all the players, together with the behavior of the referees and linesmen, the action on the sidelines, in the grandstands, over the loud-speaker, etc.

Of crucial importance is the fact that an "occurrence" on the football field or in any other social situation does not become an experiential "event" unless and until some significance is given to it: an "occurrence" becomes an "*event*" only when the

happening has significance. And a happening generally has significance only if it reactivates learned significances already registered in what we have called a person's assumptive form-world [1].

Hence the particular occurrences that different people experienced in the football game were a limited series of events from the total matrix of events *potentially* available to them. People experienced those occurrences that reactivated significances they brought to the occasion; they failed to experience those occurrences which did not reactivate past significances. We do not need to introduce "attention" as an "intervening third" (to paraphrase James on memory) to account for the selectivity of the experiential process.

In this particular study, one of the most interesting examples of this phenomenon was a telegram sent to an officer of Dartmouth College by a member of a Dartmouth alumni group in the Midwest. He had viewed the film which had been shipped to his alumni group from Princeton after its use with Princeton students, who saw, as we noted, an average of over nine infractions by Dartmouth players during the game. The alumnus, who couldn't see the infractions he had heard publicized, wired:

> Preview of Princeton movies indicates considerable cutting of important part please wire explanation and possibly air mail missing part before showing scheduled for January 25 we have splicing equipment.

The "same" sensory impingements emanating from the football field, transmitted through the visual mechanism to the brain, also obviously gave rise to different experiences in different people. The significances assumed by different happenings for different people depend in large part on the purposes people bring to the occasion and the assumptions they have of the purposes and probable behavior of other people involved. This was amusingly pointed out by the New York *Herald Tribune's* sports columnist, Red Smith, in describing a prize fight between Chico Vejar and Carmine Fiore in his column of December 21, 1951. Among other things, he wrote:

> You see, Steve Ellis is the proprietor of Chico Vejar, who is a highly desirable tract of Stamford,

---

[4] The interpretation of the nature of a social event sketched here is in part based on discussions with Adelbert Ames, Jr., and is being elaborated in more detail elsewhere.

Conn., welterweight. Steve is also a radio announcer. Ordinarily there is no conflict between Ellis the Brain and Ellis the Voice because Steve is an uncommonly substantial lump of meat who can support both halves of a split personality and give away weight on each end without missing it.

This time, though, the two Ellises met head-on, with a sickening, rending crash. Steve the Manager sat at ringside in the guise of Steve the Announcer broadcasting a dispassionate, unbiased, objective report of Chico's adventures in the ring. . . .

Clear as mountain water, his words came through, winning big for Chico. Winning? Hell, Steve was slaughtering poor Fiore.

Watching and listening, you could see what a valiant effort the reporter was making to remain cool and detached. At the same time you had an illustration of the old, established truth that when anybody with a preference watches a fight, he sees only what he prefers to see.

That is always so. That is why, after any fight that doesn't end in a clean knockout, there always are at least a few hoots when the decision is announced. A guy from, say, Billy Graham's neighborhood goes to see Billy fight and he watches Graham all the time. He sees all the punches Billy throws, and hardly any of the punches Billy catches. So it was with Steve.

"Fiore feints with a left," he would say, honestly believing that Fiore hadn't caught Chico full on the chops. "Fiore's knees buckle," he said, "and Chico backs away." Steve didn't see the hook that had driven Chico back . . .

In brief, the data here indicate that there is no such "thing" as a "game" existing "out there" in its own right which people merely "observe." The "game" "exists" for a person and is experienced by him only in so far as certain happenings have significances in terms of his purpose. Out of all the occurrences going on in the environment, a person selects those that have some significance for him from his own egocentric position in the total matrix.

Obviously in the case of a football game, the value of the experience of watching the game is enhanced if the purpose of "your" team is accomplished, that is, if the happening of the desired consequence is experienced—i.e., if your team wins. But the value attribute of the experience can, of course, be spoiled if the desire to win crowds out behavior we value and have come to call sportsmanlike.

The sharing of significances provides the links except for which a "social" event would not be experienced and would not exist for anyone.

A "football game" would be impossible except for the rules of the game which we bring to the situation and which enable us to share with others the significances of various happenings. These rules make possible a certain repeatability of events such as first downs, touchdowns, etc. If a person is unfamiliar with the rules of the game, the behavior he sees lacks repeatability and consistent significance and hence "doesn't make sense."

And only because there is the possibility of repetition is there the possibility that a happening has a significance. For example, the balls used in games are designed to give a high degree of repeatability. While a football is about the only ball used in games which is not a sphere, the shape of the modern football has apparently evolved in order to achieve a higher degree of accuracy and speed in forward passing than would be obtained with a spherical ball, thus increasing the repeatability of an important phase of the game.

The rules of a football game, like laws, rituals, customs, and mores, are registered and preserved forms of sequential significances enabling people to share the significances of occurrences. The sharing of sequential significances which have value for us provides the links that operationally make social events possible. They are analogous to the forces of attraction that hold parts of an atom together, keeping each part from following its individual, independent course.

From this point of view it is inaccurate and misleading to say that different people have different "attitudes" concerning the same "thing." For the "thing" simply is *not* the same for different people whether the "thing" is a football game, a presidential candidate, Communism, or spinach. We do not simply "react to" a happening or to some impingement from the environment in a determined way (except in behavior that has become reflexive or habitual). We behave according to what we bring to the occasion, and what each of us brings to the occasion is more or less unique. And except for these significances which we bring to the occasion, the happenings around us would be meaningless occurrences, would be "inconsequential."

From the transactional view, an attitude is not a predisposition to react in a certain way to an occurrence or stimulus "out there" that exists in its own right with certain fixed characteristics which we "color" according to our predisposition [2]. That is, a subject does not simply "react to" an "object." An attitude would rather seem to be a complex of registered significances reactivated by some stimulus which assumes its own particular significance for us in terms of our purposes. That is, the object as experienced would not exist for us except for the reactivated aspects of the form-world which provide particular significance to the hieroglyphics of sensory impingements.

REFERENCES

1. Cantril, H. *The "why" of man's experience.* New York: Macmillan, 1950.
2. Kilpatrick, F. P. (Ed.) *Human behavior from the transactional point of view.* Hanover, N. H.: Institute for Associated Research, 1952.

Received October 9, 1952 ■

Biased Assimilation and Attitude Polarization: The Effects of Prior Theories on Subsequently Considered Evidence

Charles G. Lord, Lee Ross, and Mark R. Lepper

People who hold strong opinions on complex social issues are likely to examine relevant empirical evidence in a biased manner. They are apt to accept "confirming" evidence at face value while subjecting "disconfirming" evidence to critical evaluation, and as a result to draw undue support for their initial positions from mixed or random empirical findings. Thus, the result of exposing contending factions in a social dispute to an identical body of relevant empirical evidence may be not a narrowing of disagreement but rather an increase in polarization. To test these assumptions and predictions, subjects supporting and opposing capital punishment were exposed to two purported studies, one seemingly confirming and one seemingly disconfirming their existing beliefs about the deterrent efficacy of the death penalty. As predicted, both proponents and opponents of capital punishment rated those results and procedures that confirmed their own beliefs to be the more convincing and probative ones, and they reported corresponding shifts in their beliefs as the various results and procedures were presented. The net effect of such evaluations and opinion shifts was the postulated increase in attitude polarization.

This research was supported in part by Research Grants MH-26736 from the National Institute of Mental Health and BNS-78-01211 from the National Science Foundation to Mark R. Lepper and Lee Ross. The authors would like to express their appreciation to Daryl Bem, Richard Nisbett, Robert Zajonc, and Mark Zanna for their thoughtful comments and suggestions on earlier drafts of this article, and to Lisa Burns for acting as the experimenter.

Requests for reprints should be sent to any of the authors, Department of Psychology, Stanford University, Stanford, California 94305.

The human understanding when it has once adopted an opinion draws all things else to support and agree with it. And though there be a greater number and weight of instances to be found on the other side, yet these it either neglects and despises, or else by some distinction sets aside and rejects, in order that by this great and pernicious predetermination the authority of its former conclusion may remain inviolate. (Bacon, 1620/1960)

Often, more often than we care to admit, our attitudes on important social issues reflect only our preconceptions, vague impressions, and untested assumptions. We respond to social policies concerning compensatory education, water fluoridation, or energy conservation in terms of the symbols or metaphors they evoke (Abelson, 1976; Kinder & Kiewiet, Note 1) or in conformity with views expressed by opinion leaders we like or respect (Katz, 1957). When "evidence" is brought to bear it is apt to be incomplete, biased, and of marginal probative value—typically, no more than a couple of vivid, concrete, but dubiously representative instances or cases (cf. Abelson, 1972; Nisbett & Ross, in press). It is unsurprising, therefore, that important social issues and policies generally prompt sharp disagreements, even among highly concerned and intelligent citizens, and that such disagreements often survive strenuous attempts at resolution through discussion and persuasion.

An interesting question, and one that prompts the present research, involves the consequences of introducing the opposing factions to relevant and objective data. This question seems particularly pertinent for contemporary social scientists, who have frequently called for "more empirically based" social decision making (e.g., Campbell, 1969). Very likely, data providing consistent and unequivocal support for one or another position on a given issue can influence decision makers and, with sufficiently energetic dissemination, public opinion at large. But what effects can be expected for more mixed or inconclusive evidence of the sort that is bound to arise for most complex social issues, especially where full-fledged experiments yielding decisive and easy-to-generalize results are a rarity? Logically, one might expect mixed evidence to produce some moderation in the views expressed by opposing factions. At worst, one might expect such inconclusive evidence to be ignored.

The present study examines a rather different thesis—one born in an analysis of the layperson's general shortcomings as an intuitive scientist (cf. Nisbett & Ross, in press; Ross, 1977) and his more specific shortcomings in adjusting unwarranted beliefs in the light of empirical challenges (cf. Ross, Lepper, & Hubbard, 1975). Our thesis is that belief polarization will *increase*, rather than decrease or remain unchanged, when mixed or inconclusive findings are assimilated by proponents of opposite viewpoints. This "polarization hypothesis" can be derived from the simple assumption that data relevant to a belief are not processed impartially. Instead, judgments about the validity, reliability, relevance, and sometimes even the meaning of proffered evidence are biased by the apparent consistency of that evidence with the perceiver's theories and expectations. Thus individuals will dismiss and discount empirical evidence that contradicts their initial views but will derive support from evidence, of no greater probativeness, that seems consistent with their views. Through such biased assimilation even a random set of outcomes or events can appear to lend support for an entrenched position, and both sides in a given debate can have their positions bolstered by the same set of data.

As the introductory quotation suggests, the notions of biased assimilation and resulting belief perseverance have a long history. Beyond philosophical speculations and a wealth of anecdotal evidence, considerable research attests to the capacity of preconceptions and initial theories to bias the consideration of subsequent evidence, including work on classic Einstellung effects (Luchins, 1942, 1957), social influence processes (Asch, 1946), impression formation (e.g., Jones & Goethals, 1971), recognition of degraded stimuli (Bruner & Potter, 1964), resistance to change of social attitudes and stereotypes (Abelson, 1959; Allport, 1954), self-fulfilling prophecies (Merton, 1948; Rosenhan, 1973; Snyder, Tanke, & Berscheid, 1977), and the persistence of "illusory correlations" (Chapman & Chapman, 1967, 1969). In a particularly relevant recent demonstration, Mahoney (1977) has shown that trained social scientists are not immune to theory-based evaluations. In this study, professional reviewers' judgments about experimental procedures and resultant publication recommendations varied dramatically with the degree to which the findings of a study under review agreed or disagreed with the reviewers' own theoretical predilections.

Thus, there is considerable evidence that people

tend to interpret subsequent evidence so as to maintain their initial beliefs. The biased assimilation processes underlying this effect may include a propensity to remember the strengths of confirming evidence but the weaknesses of disconfirming evidence, to judge confirming evidence as relevant and reliable but disconfirming evidence as irrelevant and unreliable, and to accept confirming evidence at face value while scrutinizing disconfirming evidence hypercritically. With confirming evidence, we suspect that both lay and professional scientists rapidly reduce the complexity of the information and remember only a few well-chosen supportive impressions. With disconfirming evidence, they continue to reflect upon any information that suggests less damaging "alternative interpretations." Indeed, they may even come to regard the ambiguities and conceptual flaws in the data *opposing* their hypotheses as somehow suggestive of the fundamental *correctness* of those hypotheses. Thus, completely inconsistent or even *random* data—when "processed" in a suitably biased fashion—can maintain or even reinforce one's preconceptions.

The present study was designed to examine both the biased assimilation processes that may occur when subjects with strong initial attitudes are confronted with empirical data concerning a controversial social issue and the consequent polarization of attitudes hypothesized to result when subjects with differing initial attitudes are exposed to a common set of "mixed" experimental results. The social controversy chosen for our investigation was the issue of capital punishment and its effectiveness as a deterrent to murder. This choice was made primarily because the issue is the subject of strongly held views that frequently do become the target of public education and media persuasion attempts, and has been the focus of considerable social science research in the last twenty years. Indeed, as our basic hypothesis suggests, contending factions in this debate often cite and derive encouragement from the same body of inconclusive correlational research (Furman v. Georgia, 1972; Sarat & Vidmar, 1976; Sellin, 1967).

In the present experiment, we presented both proponents and opponents of capital punishment first with the results and then with procedural details, critiques, and rebuttals for two studies dealing with the deterrent efficacy of the death penalty—one study confirming their initial beliefs and one study disconfirming their initial beliefs. We anticipated biased assimilation at every stage of this procedure. First, we expected subjects to rate the quality and probative value of studies confirming their beliefs on deterrent efficacy more highly than studies challenging their beliefs. Second, we anticipated corresponding effects on subjects' attitudes and beliefs such that studies confirming subjects' views would exert a greater impact than studies disconfirming those views. Finally, as a function of these assimilative biases, we hypothesized that the net result of exposure to the conflicting results of these two studies would be an increased polarization of subjects' beliefs on deterrent efficacy and attitudes towards capital punishment.

Method

Subjects

A total of 151 undergraduates completed an in-class questionnaire that included three items on capital punishment. Two to four weeks later, 48 of these students were recruited to participate in a related experiment as partial fulfillment of a course requirement. Twenty-four were "proponents" who favored capital punishment, believed it to have a deterrent effect, and thought most of the relevant research supported their own beliefs. Twenty-four were "opponents" who opposed capital punishment, doubted its deterrent effect, and thought that the relevant research supported *their* views.

Procedure

Upon entering the experiment, mixed groups of proponents and opponents were seated at a large table. The experimenter, blind to subjects' attitudes, told them that they would each be asked to read 2 of 20 randomly selected studies on the deterrent efficacy of the death penalty and asked them to use their own "evaluative powers" in thinking about what the author(s) of the study did, what the critics had to say, and whether the research provided support for one side or the other of this issue.

The experimenter next showed subjects a set of 10 index cards, each containing a brief statement of the results of a single study. Each subject was asked to choose one card and read it silently. In reality, all 10 cards in any one session were identical, providing either prodeterrent information, for example:

> Kroner and Phillips (1977) compared murder rates for the year before and the year after adoption of capital punishment in 14 states. In 11 of the 14 states, murder rates were *lower after* adoption of the death penalty. This research supports the deterrent effect of the death penalty.

or antideterrent information, for example:

> Palmer and Crandall (1977) compared murder rates in 10 pairs of neighboring states with different capital punishment laws. In 8 of the 10 pairs, murder rates were *higher* in the state *with* capital punishment. This research opposes the deterrent effect of the death penalty.

To control for order effects, half of the proponents and half of the opponents saw a "prodeterrence" result first, and half saw an "antideterrence" result first. The studies cited, although invented specifically for the present study, were characteristic of research found in the current literature cited in judicial decisions.

After reading one of these "result cards," subjects answered two sets of questions, on 16-point scales, about changes in their attitudes toward capital punishment (from −8 = more opposed, to 8 = more in favor) and their beliefs about the deterrent efficacy of the death penalty (from −8 = *less* belief that capital punishment has a deterrent effect, to 8 = *more* belief in the deterrent effect). One set of questions examined change occasioned by the single piece of information they had just finished reading; a second set of questions assessed the cumulative change produced by all of the materials read since the start of the experiment.[1]

Next the experimenter distributed detailed research descriptions bearing code letters corresponding to those on the result cards. The descriptions gave details of the researchers' procedure, reiterated the results, mentioned several prominent criticisms of the study "in the literature," listed the authors' rebuttals to some of the criticisms and depicted the data both in table form and graphically. After reading this more detailed description and critique of the first study, subjects were asked to judge how well or poorly the study had been conducted (from −8 = very poorly done, to 8 = very well done), and how convincing the study seemed as evidence on the deterrent efficacy of capital punishment (from −8 = completely unconvincing, to 8 = completely convincing).[2] Following this evaluation, subjects were asked to write why they thought the study they had just read did or did not support the argument that capital punishment is a

---

[1] Since most of our subjects had reported initial positions at, or very close to, the ends of the attitude and belief scales used for selection purposes, our initial plan to assess attitude polarization—in terms of difference scores assessing changes in subjects' attitudes and beliefs on these same scales from their initial measures to the completion of the experiment—proved impossible. As a substitute, we employed three sorts of measures to assess attitude change. First, we asked subjects, after each new piece of information, to indicate any changes in their attitudes and beliefs occasioned by that single piece of information. Second, we asked subjects, at these same points, to report on "cumulative" changes in their attitudes and beliefs since the start of the experiment. Third, subjects were asked to keep "running records" of their attitudes and beliefs on enlarged versions of the scales initially used for selection purposes. Although all of these measures individually raise some

problems, the congruence of data across these different measurement devices gives us some confidence concerning the results reported. Indeed, because the results obtained on the "running record" measure so completely parallel the findings obtained on the cumulative change question depicted in Figures 20.1 and 20.2, in terms of both the array of means and the obtained significance levels, the data from this measure will not be reported separately.

[2] Subjects were also asked, at this point, whether they thought the researchers had favored or opposed the death penalty and whether they thought an unbiased consideration should lead one to treat the study as evidence for or against capital punishment. Analyses on the first question showed only that subjects believed the researchers' attitudes to coincide with their stated results. Analyses on the second question proved wholly redundant with those presented for the "convincingness" and "well done" questions.

deterrent to murder, and then to answer a second set of attitude and belief change questions on the effects of the description alone and the effects of all experimental materials (i.e., the results and subsequent description and critique) up to that point in time.

Following completion of these questions, the entire procedure was repeated, with a second fictitious study reporting results opposite to those of the first. Again, subjects initially received only a brief description of the results of this second study but were then provided with a detailed presentation of the procedure, results, and critiques. As before, subjects were asked to evaluate both the impact of each single piece of evidence and the impact of all experimental materials up to that point in the experiment on their attitudes toward capital punishment and their beliefs concerning its deterrent efficacy.

To control for possible differences in the inherent plausibility of the two studies, two sets of materials were employed that interchanged the ostensible results of the two invented experiments. The overall design was thus completely counterbalanced with respect to subjects' initial attitudes, order of confirming vs. disconfirming evidence, and the association of the "before-after" vs. "adjacent states" designs with positive or negative results.[3] At the end of the procedure, subjects were carefully debriefed concerning the fictious nature of the studies and were asked not to reveal this deception to others. In addition to insuring that subjects understood the fictional nature of the experimental materials, this debriefing included discussion of the processes underlying the assimilation of evidence to previous theories and reassurance that a skeptical reaction to poorly designed research is often a praiseworthy cognitive response.

Results

Evaluations of the Two Studies

Our first hypothesis was that subjects holding different initial positions would differentially evaluate the quality and "convincingness" of the same empirical studies and findings. The relevant evaluations, presented in Table 20.1, revealed strong support for the hypothesized bias in favor of the study that confirmed subjects' initial attitudes.

A two-way analysis of variance (Initial Attitude × Order of Presentation) on the differences between ratings of convincingness of the prodeterrence and antideterrence studies yielded only a main effect of initial attitude, $F(1, 44) = 32.07, p < .001$. Proponents regarded the prodeterrence study as significantly more convincing than the antideterrence study, $t(23) = 5.18, p < .001$,[4] regardless of whether it was the "before-after" design that suggested the efficacy of capital punishment and the "adjacent states" design that refuted it, or vice versa. Opponents, by contrast, regarded the prodeterrence study as significantly less convincing than

TABLE 20.1. Evaluations of Prodeterrence and Antideterrence Studies by Proponents and Opponents of Capital Punishment

Study	Proponents	Opponents
Mean ratings of how well the two studies had been conducted		
Prodeterrence	1.5	−2.1
Antideterrence	−1.6	−.3
Difference	3.1	−1.8
Mean ratings of how convincing the two studies were as evidence on the deterrent efficacy of capital punishment		
Prodeterrence	1.4	−2.1
Antideterrence	−1.8	.1
Difference	3.2	−2.2

Note: Positive numbers indicate a positive evaluation of the study's convincingness or procedure. Negative numbers indicate a negative evaluation of the study's convincingness or procedure.

---

[3] Preliminary analyses were conducted to see if the particular association of positive versus negative results with either the before–after or adjacent-states designs would affect the results obtained. There were no significant effects or interactions involving this variation in stimulus materials; hence, the data were collapsed across this factor.

---

[4] All *p* values reported in this article are based on two-tailed tests of significance.

the antideterrence study, $t(23) = -3.02$, $p < .01$, again irrespective of which research design was purported to have produced which type of results. The same was true of the difference between ratings of how well done the two studies had been, $F(1, 44) = 33.52$, $p < .001$.[5] As above, proponents found the prodeterrence study to have been better conducted than the antideterrence study, $t(23) = 5.37, p < .001$, whereas opponents found the prodeterrence study to have been less well conducted, $t(23) = -2.80$, $p < .05$. As one might expect, the correlation between the "convincingness" and "well done" questions was substantial, $r = .67$, $p < .001$.

These differing opinions of the quality of the two studies were also reflected in subjects' written comments. At the risk of opening ourselves to a charge of "biased assimilation," we present a set of subjects' comments—selected for dramatic effect but not unrepresentative in content—in Table 20.2. As these comments make clear, the same study can elicit entirely opposite evaluations from people who hold different initial beliefs about a complex social issue. This evidence of bias in subjects' evaluations of the quality and convincingness of the two studies is consistent with the biased assimilation hypothesis and sets the stage for testing our further predictions concerning attitude and belief polarization.

Overall Attitude Polarization

Given such biased evaluations, our primary hypothesis was that exposure to the "mixed"[6] data set comprised by the two studies would result in a

further polarization of subjects' attitudes and beliefs rather than the convergence that an impartial consideration of these inconclusive data might warrant. To test this hypothesis requires a consideration of subjects' final attitudes, after exposure to both studies and related critiques and rebuttals, relative to the start of the experiment.

The relevant data provide strong support for the polarization hypothesis. Asked for their final attitudes relative to the experiment's start, proponents reported that they were *more* in favor of capital punishment, $t(23) = 5.07$, $p < .001$, whereas opponents reported that they were *less* in favor of capital punishment, $t(23) = -3.34$, $p < .01$. In a two-way analysis of variance (Initial Attitude × Order of Presentation), the effect of initial attitude was highly significant, $F(1, 44) = 30.06$, $p < .001$, and neither the order effect nor the interaction approached significance. Similar results characterized subjects' beliefs about deterrent efficacy. Proponents reported greater belief in the deterrent effect of capital punishment, $t(23) = 4.26$, $p < .001$, whereas opponents reported less belief in this deterrent effect, $t(23) = -3.79$, $p < .001$. Final attitudes toward capital punishment and beliefs concerning deterrent efficacy were highly correlated, $r = .88, p < .001$.

Such results provide strong support for the main experimental hypothesis that inconclusive or mixed data will lead to increased polarization rather than to uncertainty and moderation. Moreover, the degree of polarization shown by individual subjects was predicted by differences in

---

[5] In order to examine possible main effects of either study direction or initial attitude on subjects' ratings of how convincing and how well done the studies were—findings that would not be portrayed in the difference score analysis reported—a three-way analysis of variance (Initial Attitude × Order of Presentation × Direction of Study) was also performed. There were no main effects of study direction on either measure. A main effect of initial attitude—indicating that opponents evaluated the total set of evidence more negatively than did proponents—proved significant for the "well done" question, $F(1, 44) = 4.69$, $p < .05$, but not for the "convincing" question, $F(1, 44) = 1.53$, *ns*.

[6] The term *mixed*, we should emphasize, refers to the fact that one study yielded evidence confirming the deterrent efficacy of the death penalty, whereas the other study yielded evidence disconfirming such efficacy (with appropriate counterbalancing of purported procedures and purported results). Subjects, regardless of initial position, clearly recognized this discrepancy between results, as will be apparent in our analyses of their responses to the simple statements of the study's main findings. We do not mean to imply that the subjects "phenomenologically" judged the two studies to be of equal probative value; indeed, as indicated in the preceding discussion, identical procedures were clearly judged to differ in their probativeness depending on the congruity between the study's outcomes and the subject's initial beliefs.

TABLE 20.2. Selected Comments on Prodeterrence and Antideterrence Studies by Proponents and Opponents of Capital Punishment

Subject	Comments on	
	Prodeterrence study	**Antideterrence study**
	Set 1 materials	
S8 Proponent	"It does support capital punishment in that it presents facts showing that there is a deterrent effect and seems to have gathered data properly."	"The evidence given is relatively meaningless without data about how the overall crime rate went up in those years."
S24 Proponent	"The experiment was well thought out, the data collected was valid, and they were able to come up with responses to all criticisms."	"There were too many flaws in the picking of the states and too many variables involved in the experiment as a whole to change my opinion."
S35 Opponent	"The study was taken only 1 year before and 1 year after capital punishment was reinstated. To be a more effective study they should have taken data from at least 10 years before and as many years as possible after."	"The states were chosen at random, so the results show the average effect capital punishment has across the nation. The fact that 8 out of 10 states show a rise in murders stands as good evidence."
S36 Opponent	"I don't feel such a straightforward conclusion can be made from the data collected."	"There aren't as many uncontrolled variables in this experiment as in the other one, so I'm still willing to believe the conclusion made."
	Set 2 materials	
S14 Proponent	"It shows a good direct comparison between contrasting death penalty effectiveness. Using neighboring states helps to make the experiment more accurate by using similar locations."	"I don't think they have complete enough collection of data. Also, as suggested, the murder rates should be expressed as percentages, not as straight figures."
S15 Proponent	"It seems that the researchers studied a carefully selected group of states and that they were careful in interpreting their results."	"The research didn't cover a long enough period of time to prove that capital punishment is not a deterrent to murder."
S25 Opponent	"The data presented are a randomly drawn set of 10. This fact seems to be the study's biggest problem. Also many other factors are not accounted for which are very important to the nature of the results."	"The murder rates climbed in all but two of the states after new laws were passed and no strong evidence to contradict the researchers has been presented."
S38 Opponent	"There might be very different circumstances between the sets of two states, even though they were sharing a border."	"These tests were comparing the same state to itself, so I feel it could be a fairly good measure."

subjects' willingness to be less critical of procedures yielding supportive evidence than of procedures yielding nonsupportive evidence. Significant correlations were found between overall attitude change regarding capital punishment and differences in ratings of both how convincing, $r = .56$, $p < .001$, and how well done, $r = .56$, $p < .001$, the studies were. Overall changes in beliefs in deterrent efficacy produced comparable correlations of .53 and .57, both $ps < .001$.

Components of Attitude Polarization

In view of this strong evidence of overall attitude polarization, it is worth examining the course of attitude polarization as subjects' opinions were successively assessed after exposure to the first study, the details and critiques of the first study, the results of the second study, and the details and critiques of the second study. At each stage, it will be recalled, subjects were asked about the impact of the single piece of information they had just considered and the cumulative impact of all information presented to that point. Let us first examine the reported effects of single segments of evidence and then the effects of accumulated evidence over time.

Effect of Exposure to the Results of Each Study

Considering the result cards as single pieces of evidence, both proponents and opponents reported shifting their attitudes in the direction of the stated results for both the prodeterrence, $t(47) = 4.67$, $p < .001$, and antideterrence, $t(47) = -5.15$, $p < .001$, studies. As shown in the top half of Table 20.3, however, subjects' responses to the two studies also varied with initial attitude. Proponents tended to be influenced more by the prodeterrence study and opponents more by the antideterrence study.

TABLE 20.3. Mean Attitude and Belief Changes for a Single Piece of Information

Issue and study	Initial attitudes	
	Proponents	Opponents
Results only		
Capital punishment		
Prodeterrence	1.3	0.4
Antideterrence	−0.7	−0.9
Combined	0.6	−0.5
Deterrent efficacy		
Prodeterrence	1.9	0.7
Antideterrence	−0.9	−1.6
Combined	1.0	−0.9
Details, data, critiques, rebuttals		
Capital punishment		
Prodeterrence	0.8	−0.9
Antideterrence	0.7	−0.8
Combined	1.5	−1.7
Deterrent efficacy		
Prodeterrence	0.7	−1.0
Antideterrence	0.7	−0.8
Combined	1.4	−1.8

Note: Positive numbers indicate a more positive attitude or belief about capital punishment and its deterrent effect. Negative numbers indicate a more negative attitude or belief about capital punishment and its deterrent effect.

Thus a two-way analysis of variance (Initial Attitude × Order of Presentation) on combined change from the two result cards considered individually yielded only a main effect of initial attitude for both attitudes toward the death penalty, $F(1, 44) = 6.35$, $p < .02$,[7] and beliefs about its deterrent effect, $F(1, 44) = 10.37$, $p < .01$. Interestingly, the analysis of beliefs regarding deterrent efficacy also showed an unanticipated interaction effect, $F(1, 44) = 7.48$, $p < .01$, with proponents showing a differential response to results alone regardless of order of presentation but opponents showing a differential response to results alone only when the confirming study was presented first.

Effect of Exposure to Procedures and Data, Critiques and Rebuttals

When provided with a more detailed description of the procedures and data, together with relevant critiques and authors' rebuttals, subjects seemed to ignore the stated results of the study. As shown in the bottom half of Table 20.3, both proponents and opponents interpreted the additional information, relative to the results alone, as strongly supporting their own initial attitudes. Detailed descriptions of either the prodeterrence or the antideterrence study, with accompanying critiques, caused proponents to favor capital punishment more and believe in its deterrent efficacy more, but caused opponents to oppose capital punishment more and believe in its deterrent efficacy less. A two-way analysis of variance (Initial Attitude × Order of Presentation) on attitude change for the two descriptions combined yielded only a significant main effect of initial attitude for both the capital punishment issue, $F(1, 44) = 28.10$, $p < .001$, and the deterrent efficacy question, $F(1, 44) = 26.93$, $p < .001$.

---

[7] In order to rule out the possibility that direction of study interacted with initial attitude, a three-way analysis of variance (Initial Attitude × Order of Presentation × Direction of Study) was also performed on these data. The relevant interaction term did not approach significance, $F(1, 44) = 1.62$, *ns*.

Changes in Attitudes Across Time

Subjects' reported changes in attitudes and beliefs, relative to the start of the experiment, following exposure to each of the four separate pieces of information are depicted in Figure 20.1 for attitudes concerning capital punishment and in Figure 20.2 for beliefs concerning deterrent efficacy. These data, portrayed separately for subjects who received first either the prodeterrence study or the antideterrence study, provide a more detailed view of the attitude polarization process. They allow, as

well, an examination of the hypothesized "rebound effect," that the provision of any plausible reason for discounting data that contradict one's preconceptions will eliminate the effects that mere knowledge of those data may have produced.

The existence of such a "rebound effect" is obvious from examination of these figures. Whether they encountered the disconfirming result first or second, both proponents and opponents seemed to be swayed momentarily by this evidence, only to revert to their former attitudes and

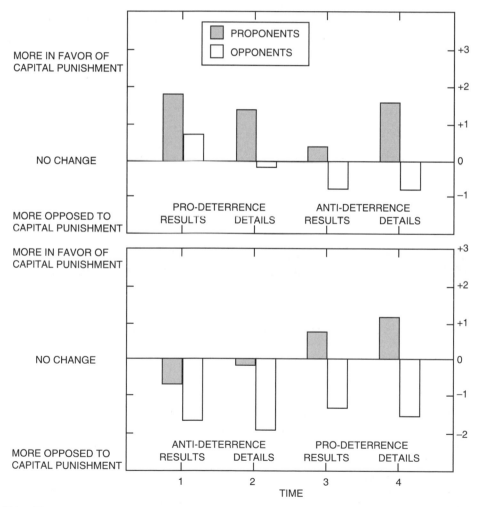

FIGURE 20.1 ■ Top panel: Attitude changes on capital punishment relative to start of experiment as reported across time by subjects who received prodeterrence study first. Bottom panel: Attitude changes on capital punishment relative to start of experiment as reported across time by subjects who received antideterrence study first.

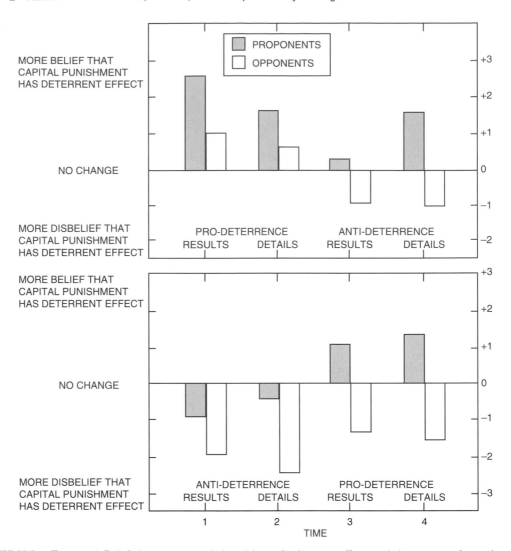

FIGURE 20.2 ■ Top panel: Belief changes on capital punishment's deterrent efficacy relative to start of experiment as reported across time by subjects who received prodeterrence study first. Bottom panel: Belief changes on capital punishment's deterrent efficacy relative to start of experiment as reported across time by subjects who received antideterrence study first.

beliefs (and in 23% of the individual cases, to even more extreme positions) after inspecting the procedural details and data, and the critiques and rebuttals found in the literature. Across all subjects, this rebound in opinions proved significant for both the capital punishment, $t(47) = 4.43$, $p < .001$, and deterrent efficacy, $t(47) = 4.58$, $p < .001$, issues. By contrast, no compensating rebound effects resulted from reading the descriptions and

critiques of studies supporting subjects' initial attitudes, for either capital punishment, $t(47) = .60$, ns, or deterrent efficacy, $t(47) = .23$, ns.

Discussion

The results of the present experiment provide strong and consistent support for the attitude polarization hypothesis and for the biased assimilation mechanisms postulated to underlie such polarization. The net effect of exposing proponents and opponents of capital punishment to identical evidence—studies ostensibly offering equivalent levels of support and disconfirmation—was to increase further the gap between their views. The mechanisms responsible for this polarization of subjects' attitudes and beliefs were clearly suggested by correlational analyses. Subjects' decisions about whether to accept a study's findings at face value or to search for flaws and entertain alternative interpretations seemed to depend far less on the particular procedure employed than on whether the study's results coincided with their existing beliefs.

The Normative Issue

It is worth commenting explicitly about the normative status of our subjects' apparent biases. First, there can be no real quarrel with a willingness to infer that studies supporting one's theory-based expectations are more probative than, or methodologically superior to, studies that contradict one's expectations. When an "objective truth" is known or strongly assumed, then studies whose outcomes reflect that truth may reasonably be given greater credence than studies whose outcomes fail to reflect that truth. Hence the physicist would be "biased," but appropriately so, if a new procedure for evaluating the speed of light were accepted if it gave the "right answer" but rejected if it gave the "wrong answer." The same bias leads most of us to be skeptical about reports of miraculous virgin births or herbal cures for cancer, and despite the risk that such theory-based and experience-based skepticism may render us unable to recognize a miraculous event when it occurs, overall we are surely well served by our bias. Our subjects' willingness to impugn or defend findings as a function of their conformity to expectations can, in part, be similarly defended. Only the strength of their initial convictions in the face of the existing inconclusive social data and arguments can be regarded as "suspect."

Our subjects' main inferential shortcoming, in other words, did not lie in their inclination to process evidence in a biased manner. Willingness to interpret new evidence in the light of past knowledge and experience is essential for any organism to make sense of, and respond adaptively to, its environment. Rather, their sin lay in their readiness to use evidence already processed in a biased manner to bolster the very theory or belief that initially "justified" the processing bias. In so doing, subjects exposed themselves to the familiar risk of making their hypotheses unfalsifiable—a serious risk in a domain where it is clear that at least one party in a dispute holds a false hypothesis—and allowing themselves to be encouraged by patterns of data that they ought to have found troubling. Through such processes laypeople and professional scientists alike find it all too easy to cling to impressions, beliefs, and theories that have ceased to be compatible with the latest and best evidence available (Mahoney, 1976, 1977).

Polarization: Real or Merely Reported?

Before further pursuing the broader implications of the present demonstration, it is necessary to consider an important question raised by our procedure: Did our subjects really show change (i.e., polarization) in their private beliefs about the desirability and deterrent efficacy of capital punishment? Certainly they told us, explicitly, that their attitudes and beliefs did change after each new piece of evidence was presented, and from the beginning to the end of the experiment. Moreover, they did show a willingness to report a shift in their attitudes in the direction of findings that were contrary to their beliefs, at least until those findings were exposed to methodological scrutiny and possible alternative interpretations. Nevertheless, it could be argued that subjects were not reporting real shifts in attitudes but instead were merely reporting what they believed to be a rational or appropriate response to each increment in the available evidence. Although we believe that it remains an impressive demonstration of assimilation biases to show that contending factions both believe the same data to justify their position "objectively," the potential limitations of the present measures should be kept in mind in evaluating the relationship of this study to prior polarization research. As noted earlier (see Footnote 1) our intended strategy of assessing direct changes from our initial selection measures of attitudes and beliefs, rather than asking subjects to report such changes within the experiment, was neither feasible nor appropriate, given the necessity of selecting subjects with strong and consistent initial views on this issue. Potentially such methodological problems could be overcome in subsequent research through the use of less extreme samples or, perhaps more convincingly, by seeing whether biased assimilation of mixed evidence will make subjects more willing to *act* on their already extreme beliefs.

Belief Perseverance and Attribution Processes

The present results importantly extend the growing body of research on the perseverance of impressions and beliefs. Two of the present authors and their colleagues have now amassed a number of studies showing that, once formed, impressions about the self (Ross et al., 1975; Jennings, Lepper, & Ross, Note 2; Lepper, Ross, & Lau, Note 3), beliefs about other people (Ross et al., 1975), or theories about functional relationships between variables (Anderson, Lepper, & Ross, Note 4) can survive the total discrediting of the evidence that first gave rise to such beliefs. In essence, these prior studies demonstrate that beliefs can survive the complete subtraction of the critical formative evidence on which they were initially based. In a complementary fashion, the present study shows that strongly entrenched beliefs can also survive the addition of nonsupportive evidence.

These findings pose some fundamental questions for traditional attribution models. To the extent that beliefs and impressions can be shown to persevere in the face of subsequent challenging data, we need a "top down" rather than—or perhaps in conjunction with—a "bottom up" approach (cf. Bobrow & Norman, 1975) to the question of how individuals extract meaning from their social environment. Instead of viewing people as impartial, data-driven processors, the present research suggests our models must take into account the ways in which intuitive scientists assess the relevance, reliability, representativeness, and implications of any given sample of data or behavior within the framework of the hypotheses or implicit theories they bring to the situation (Lepper, 1977). In everyday life, as well as in the course of scientific controversies (cf. Kuhn, 1970), the mere availability of contradictory evidence rarely seems sufficient to cause us to abandon our prior beliefs or theories.

Social Science Research and Social Policy

We conclude this article, as we began it, by considering the important links between social policy, public attitudes and beliefs about such policy, and the role of the social scientist. If our study demonstrates anything, it surely demonstrates that social scientists can not expect rationality, enlightenment, and consensus about policy to emerge from their attempts to furnish 'objective' data about burning social issues. If people of opposing views can each find support for those views in the same body of evidence, it is small wonder that social science research, dealing with complex and emotional social issues and forced to rely upon inconclusive designs, measures, and modes of analysis, will frequently fuel rather than calm the fires of debate.

REFERENCE NOTES

1. Kinder, D. R., & Kiewiet, D. R. *Economic grievances and political behavior: The role of personal discontents and symbolic judgments*. Paper presented at the meeting of the American Psychological Association, San Francisco, August 1977.
2. Jennings, D. L., Lepper, M. R., & Ross, L. *Persistence of impressions of personal persuasiveness: Perseverance of erroneous self assessments outside the debriefing paradigm*. Unpublished manuscript, Stanford University, 1978.
3. Lepper, M. R., Ross, L., & Lau, R. R. *Persistence of inaccurate and discredited personal impressions: A field demonstration of attributional perseverance*. Unpublished manuscript, Stanford University, 1979.
4. Anderson, C. A., Lepper, M. R., & Ross, L. *Theory perseverance: The persistent influence of discredited information*. Unpublished manuscript, Stanford University, 1979.

REFERENCES

Abelson, R. P. Modes of resolution of belief dilemmas. *Conflict Resolution*, 1959, *3*, 343–352.

Abelson, R. P. Are attitudes necessary? In B. T. King & E. McGuinnies (Eds.), *Attitudes, conflict, and social change.* New York: Academic Press, 1972.

Abelson, R. P. Script processing in attitude formation and decision making. In J. S. Carroll and J. W. Payne (Eds.), *Cognition and social behavior.* Hillsdale, N.J.: Erlbaum, 1976.

Allport, G. W. *The nature of prejudice.* Reading, Mass.: Addison-Wesley, 1954.

Asch, S. Forming impressions of personality. *Journal of Abnormal and Social Psychology*, 1946, *41*, 258–290.

Bacon, F. *The new organon and related writings.* New York: Liberal Arts Press, 1960. (Originally published, 1620.)

Bobrow, D. G., & Norman, D. A. Some principles of memory schemata. In D. G. Bobrow & A. Collins (Eds.), *Representation and understanding: Studies in cognitive science.* New York: Academic Press, 1975.

Bruner, J. S., & Potter, M. C. Interference in visual recognition. *Science*, 1964, *144*, 424–425.

Campbell, D. T. On reforms as experiments. *American Psychologist*, 1969, *24*, 409–429.

Chapman, L., & Chapman, J. The genesis of popular but erroneous psychodiagnostic observations. *Journal of Abnormal Psychology*, 1967, *72*, 193–204.

Chapman, L., & Chapman, J. Illusory correlation as an obstacle to the use of valid psychodiagnostic signs. *Journal of Abnormal Psychology*, 1969, *74*, 271–280.

Furman v. Georgia, 408 U.S. 238, 1972.

Jones, E. E., & Goethals, G. R. Order effects in impression formation. Attribution context and the nature of the entity. In E. E. Jones et al. (Eds.), *Attribution: Perceiving the causes of behavior.* Morristown, N.J.: General Learning Press, 1971.

Katz, E. The two-step flow of communication: An up-to-date report on an hypothesis. *Public Opinion Quarterly*, 1957, *21*, 61–68.

Kuhn, T. S. *The structure of scientific revolutions* (2nd ed.). Chicago: University of Chicago Press, 1970.

Lepper, M. R. Cognition and social behavior. *Science*, 1977, *196*, 765–766.

Luchins, A. S. Mechanization in problem solving: The effect of Einstellung. *Psychological Monographs*, 1942, *54*, 1–95.

Luchins, A. S. Experimental attempts to minimize the impact of first impressions. In C. I. Hovland (Ed.), *The order of presentation in persuasion.* New Haven, Conn.: Yale University Press, 1957.

Mahoney, M. J. *Scientist as subject: The psychological imperative.* Cambridge, Mass.: Ballinger, 1976.

Mahoney, M. J. Publication prejudices: An experimental study of confirmatory bias in the peer review system. *Cognitive Therapy and Research*, 1977, *1*, 161–175.

Merton, R. K. The self-fulfilling prophecy. *Antioch Review*, 1948, *8*, 193–210.

Nisbett, R., & Ross, L. *Human inference: Strategies and shortcomings of social judgment.* Englewood Cliffs, N.J.: Prentice-Hall, in press.

Rosenhan, D. L. On being sane in insane places. *Science*, 1973, *179*, 250–258.

Ross, L. The intuitive psychologist and his shortcomings: Distortions in the attribution process. In L. Berkowitz (Ed.), *Advances in experimental social psychology* (Vol. 10). New York: Academic Press, 1977.

Ross, L., Lepper, M. R., & Hubbard, M. Perseverance in self-perception and social perception: Biased attributional processes in the debriefing paradigm. *Journal of Personality and Social Psychology*, 1975, *32*, 880–892.

Sarat, A., & Vidmar, N. Public opinion, the death penalty, and the Eighth Amendment: Testing the Marshall hypothesis. *Wisconsin Law Review*, 1976, 171–197.

Sellin, T. (Ed.). *The death penalty.* New York: Harper & Row, 1967.

Snyder, M., Tanke, E. D., & Berscheid, E. Social perception and interpersonal behavior: On the self-fulfilling nature of social stereotypes. *Journal of Personality and Social Psychology*, 1977, *35*, 656–666.

Received February 16, 1979 ■

READING 21

The Effect of Attitude on the Recall of Personal Histories

Michael Ross, Cathy McFarland, and Garth J. O. Fletcher

Two studies were conducted to examine the relation between attitudes and the recall of past behaviors. The same paradigm was utilized in both experiments. First, subjects' attitudes on an issue were manipulated. Subjects were then asked to recall past behaviors relevant to the newly formed attitude. The results indicated that attitudes can exert a directive influence on recall of personal histories. The implications of the results for investigations of the relations between attitudes, behavior, and recall are discussed.

The concept of attitude has had a variable status in social psychology. In one famous quote, attitude was described as the "primary building stone in the edifice of social psychology" (Allport, 1968, p. 63). In recent years, however, some social psychologists have been more inclined to agree with Wicker's (1971) suggestion that "it may be desirable to abandon the attitude concept" (p. 29). This disenchantment stems from the evidence that attitudes fail to predict behavior in a variety of circumstances (Calder & Ross, 1973; Wicker, 1969). Although this view is overly pessimistic (Ajzen & Fishbein, 1977; Fazio & Zanna, in press), it seems clear that attitudes play a limited role in the etiology of many behaviors.

The importance of attitudes is not circumscribed by their role in predicting behavior, however. The function of attitudes examined in the present research was suggested by Bartlett (1932) in the context of his work on recall of pictures and prose passages. Bartlett proposed that attitudes influence memory: "Recall is ... a construction, made largely on the basis of an attitude, and its general effect is that of a justification of the attitude"

This research was supported in part by a Social Sciences and Humanities Research Council research grant to Michael Ross. The studies were conducted while Cathy McFarland was receiving an SSHRC doctoral fellowship. The authors thank Susan Fiske, Jim Olson, and Mark Zanna for their comments on an earlier version of the manuscript.

Requests for reprints should be sent to Michael Ross, Department of Psychology, University of Waterloo, Waterloo, Ontario, Canada N2L 3G1.

(p. 207). Bartlett deduced this from the content of subjects' recall and their self-reports of how they prodded their memories.

Following Bartlett, there has been a considerable amount of research relating cognitive schemata to recall that suggests, albeit indirectly, that attitudes might be expected to influence memory. This research demonstrates that recall can be biased by evaluations and impressions. For example, in a study testing Heider's (1958) balance theory, Zajonc and Burnstein (1965) found that errors in recall of hypothetical relationships tended to be in the direction of producing cognitively balanced rather than imbalanced structures. Also, memory of the characteristics of hypothetical individuals has been shown to be influenced by impressions of the target people formed after the characteristics have been described (Lingle, Geva, Ostrom, Leippe, & Baumgardner, 1979; Snyder & Uranow-itz, 1978).

Research on the selective learning hypothesis is more directly relevant to the present concerns. This research has provided less compelling evidence for a relation between attitudes and recall. Levine and Murphy (1943) described the selective learning hypothesis as follows: An individual "notes and remembers material which supports his social atti-tudes better than material which conflicts with these attitudes" (p. 515). The paradigm utilized by Levine and Murphy and subsequent researchers consists of exposing subjects to material that is consistent or inconsistent with their attitudes and asking them to reproduce the material at a later time. Although early studies provided support for the hypothesis (e.g., Jones & Kohler, 1958; Levine & Murphy, 1943), subsequent research has often yielded inconsistent or negative results (e.g., Greenwald & Sakumura, 1967). There is some recent evidence that the selective learning hypoth-esis may hold only for certain kinds of people (Olson, 1980).

It is reasonable to expect that attitudes will at times affect the recall of prose passages or opinion statements. Anyone who has examined the compli-cated and esoteric passages employed by Bartlett, for example, will not be surprised to learn that sub-jects forgot the details quickly and reconstructed

them using vague residual feelings or attitudes as guides.

For the social psychologist, however, a more interesting question concerns whether attitudes guide or shape the recall of events that occur in everyday life. Accordingly, in the present research we examined whether attitudes affect the recall of personal histories. We have been unable to locate any previous research that attempts to show that people's attitudes shape their memories of their own past behaviors. A possible cause of this neg-lect is that there are a number of reasons to believe that people may not base their recall on their atti-tudes. For example, many of our actions are well practiced, even routinized. As a result, we may be able to recall them without difficulty, not necessar-ily by remembering each instance but simply by remembering that the activities are performed habitually. Second, actions occur in social and environmental contexts that limit severely the range of potential behaviors. Thus, remembering the context may serve to evoke the behavior enacted. Third, many attitudes are related in a loose and multifaceted fashion to a network of behaviors rather than to one specific behavior (Fishbein & Ajzen, 1974). Moreover, a number of different attitudes may relate to the same behavior, and, alternatively, some behaviors may not be con-nected to any salient attitudes. In sum, attitudes often may appear to be indirect and unnecessary vehicles for recalling past actions.

With these concerns in mind, the following question was examined in the present research: Can attitudes be shown to exert a directive influ-ence on individuals' recall of their past behaviors when the conditions are optimal for demonstrating such an effect? To answer this question, we changed subjects' attitudes on an issue. We then measured recall of past behaviors relevant to the newly formed attitudes.

There were a number of considerations that guided our selection of attitude issues and experi-mental design. First, for the hypothesis to receive a fair test, it is necessary to produce quite sizable shifts in attitude. It would hardly be surprising if recall of past behaviors were unaffected by a minor change in attitudes. McGuire (1964) has shown that beliefs that are widely shared and rarely questioned ("cultural truisms") are vulnerable to attack. For this reason, we chose to manipulate attitudes on two issues of this nature. Second, we selected issues for which we could identify unambiguously relevant and specifiable behaviors. Third, we incorporated procedures that were intended to reduce the possible experimental demands inherent in asking subjects to recall actions that may be related to their attitudes. Thus, we manipulated but did not assess the attitudes of subjects who answered the behavior recall questions. This procedure was designed to decrease the likelihood that subjects would view the experiment as a study of the relation between attitudes and recall. Also, the behavior recall items were imbedded in a lengthy questionnaire that was administered in a "second experiment." This second study was allegedly unrelated to the first one, in which attitudes were manipulated. Finally, to verify that the attitude manipulation was indeed effective, we ran an additional group of subjects whose attitudes were measured in the absence of behavior recall.

In summary, the purpose of the present study was to examine the effects of attitudes on the recall of personal histories. Would recall be biased by subjects' attitudes?

Experiment 1

Method

Subjects. The subjects were 54 males and 47 females recruited from the voluntary subject pool at the University of Waterloo. Thirty-five of the subjects completed the questionnaire that assessed attitudes, and 66 of the subjects completed the questionnaire that assessed behavior recall. The data from four subjects were eliminated from the analysis. Three of these subjects were suspicious of the link between the two studies, and the other subject did not follow the instructions correctly in filling out the questionnaire. Of the three suspicious subjects, one was in the negative toothbrushing condition, attitude assessment; one was in the negative toothbrushing condition, recall

assessment; and one was in the positive bathing condition, recall assessment.

Procedure. A pretest was conducted to select the attitude issues for the study. Twenty-eight students were stopped on campus and asked for their opinions on a series of health-related issues; opinions were assessed on a 7-point scale (1 = strongly disagree; 7 = strongly agree). On the basis of this pretest, two items that showed reasonably high agreement were selected for the experiment: "It is important for health reasons to shower or bathe at least once a day" ($M = 5.41$, $SD = 1.07$), and "It is important for proper dental care to brush one's teeth after every meal" ($M = 5.83$, $SD = 1.34$). Toothbrushing was one of the cultural truisms employed by McGuire (1964).

In the experiment proper, some subjects were exposed to a communication that was either favorable or unfavorable toward toothbrushing; the remaining subjects were exposed to a communication that was either favorable or unfavorable toward bathing frequently. In the context of a second experiment, subjects were then asked to indicate either their attitudes on the relevant issues (toothbrushing and bathing) or to indicate how often they had brushed their teeth and bathed in the preceding 2 weeks.

Subjects were contacted for the experiment by telephone. The caller identified herself as a secretary for the psychology department. Subjects were informed that they would participate in two brief studies that were to be conducted one after the other due to scheduling ease. Subjects were told that the first study examined factors influencing the effectiveness of communications and that the second study concerned the relation of personality type to lifestyle.

Upon arrival at the first experiment, subjects were taken to a room in groups of two to five and told that they would be listening to tape recordings of a university radio program dealing with current health problems. They were informed that this show typically consisted of a brief interview with a medical or social scientist.

The subjects were told that they would listen to two of these interviews and write down the most important points. They were informed that the experimenter wanted to determine if there was agreement among nonexperts as to which were the key points. They would also be asked to generate an argument of their own that was consistent with the material being presented. They were told that their judgments and arguments would be used in the construction of health appeals that would eventually be presented to the Canadian public. They were asked to not put their names on their answer sheets; their responses were to be anonymous.

Subjects were taken to individual rooms to listen to the tape recordings through headphones. All subjects listened first to a filler tape arguing for higher seat belt usage in automobiles and then to either the positive or negative toothbrushing tape or the positive or negative bathing tape.

The interviews on the issues of toothbrushing and bathing were allegedly with officials of the Canadian Dental Association and the Canadian Medical Association, respectively. In the positive toothbrushing condition, the official described how frequent brushing strengthened tooth enamel and protected the teeth and gums against disease. In the negative toothbrushing condition, the same official argued the dangers of frequent brushing: Abrasive toothpastes cause erosion of the enamel, and frequent brushing may harm the gums, leading to infection and tooth loss. Further, it was emphasized that flossing was much superior to toothbrushing.

In the positive bathing condition, the official suggested that infrequent bathing can create skin complaints and that body odor can only be eliminated by frequent use of soap and water. In the negative bathing condition, he stated that frequent bathing removes a layer of skin that protects one against infection and that it also causes increased oil production in the skin, which can cause skin complaints.

The seat belt interview was allegedly with a representative of the Ontario Government Safety Division who argued for increased seat belt usage. We presented the seat belt tape to obscure the connection between the two studies. In the second study, there were no items on the questionnaire that pertained to the seat belt issue.

After listening to the tapes and making their

evaluations, subjects were thanked and dismissed. They returned to the waiting area and were contacted by the experimenter for the second study. This experimenter took subjects to a large "survey research" room. They were told that they would anonymously complete a questionnaire designed to assess the relation between personality type and life-style. They were informed that previous studies relating personality to life-style had focused on the abnormal personality and the everyday activities he or she engaged in. The present study would be concerned with this relationship in normal individuals.

The behavior recall groups responded to a version of the questionnaire that contained questions asking them to estimate the frequency with which they had engaged in various activities during the past 2 weeks. The target questions, which were imbedded among many other health-related items, were "How many times have you brushed your teeth in the past two weeks? (a) after breakfast, (b) after lunch, (c) after dinner." and "How many baths (or showers) have you taken in the past two weeks? (a) in the morning, (b) between 10 a.m. and 6 p.m., (c) in the evening."

The attitude assessment groups responded to a questionnaire that asked them to give their opinions of the same everyday activities that appeared in the recall version of the questionnaire. Three 9-point semantic differential scales were used to assess attitudes on the two target issues. The items were worded as follows: "Brushing your teeth after every meal is: important–unimportant, healthy–unhealthy, beneficial–harmful," and "Taking showers and baths often is: healthy–unhealthy, hygienic–unhygienic, beneficial–harmful."

After answering either the recall or opinion questions, all subjects filled out the personality section of the questionnaire. The personality test was Snyder's (1974) self-monitoring scale. Finally, subjects were probed for suspiciousness. They anonymously completed a questionnaire that required them to describe the purposes of the study and to discuss any confusing or odd aspects of the procedures. The experimenter also asked subjects directly if they had noticed a connection between the two studies. Subjects were informed of the

TABLE 21.1. Mean Attitude and Behavior Recall Scores for Experiment 1

	Toothbrushing			Bathing		
	Positive message	Control	Negative message	Positive message	Control	Negative message
Attitude						
M	3.62	4.17	12.75	3.70	5.87	11.63
n	8	18	8	10	16	8
Behavior recall						
M	35.85	32.8	28.62	11.06	11.35	10.89
n	13	36[a]	13	18	26	19

Note: The higher the attitude score, the more negative the attitude. The behavior recall scores indicate the number of times subjects reported brushing their teeth or bathing in the preceding 2 weeks.
[a] The n in this condition is 36 rather than 37, because one of the subjects failed to answer the relevant control question.

purposes of the experiment and fully debriefed following the suspiciousness probe.

Results

Attitude change. The three semantic differentials for each issue were summed, with higher scores reflecting more negative attitudes. All of the subjects responded to both the toothbrushing and bathing items on their attitude questionnaires. Accordingly, subjects who listened to the persuasive message on toothbrushing served as controls for subjects who heard the bathing message, and vice versa. The mean attitude in each condition is shown in Table 21.1. Subjects who listened to the positive messages were substantially more favorable toward toothbrushing and bathing than were subjects who heard the negative messages: For toothbrushing, $t(7.36) = 3.46, p < .002$; for bathing, $t(8.03) = 5.23$, $p < .001$.[1]

The attitudes of control subjects were similar to those of the pretest group, which were very positive. Not surprisingly, therefore, it was the negative message that exerted the stronger influence on attitudes. Subjects who heard the messages derogating toothbrushing and bathing held more negative attitudes toward these activities than did control subjects: For toothbrushing, $t(7.45) = 3.25, p < .01$; for bathing, $t(22) = 3.34, p < .003$. The tendency for

subjects who heard the positive message to hold more favorable attitudes than control subjects approached significance on the bathing message only, $t(19.48) = 2.07, p < .052$.

Behavior recall. Subjects who heard a message derogating toothbrushing reported brushing their teeth significantly fewer times in the preceding 2 weeks than did subjects who heard the positive message, $t(24) = 2.16, p < .05$ (means are shown in Table 21.1). However, the difference between the negative and positive bathing groups was slight and nonsignificant $(t < 1)$.[2]

Once again, subjects who listened to the persuasive message on one of the target issues could serve as controls for subjects who heard the persuasive message on the other issue. The control mean was intermediate to and nonsignificantly different from the mean behavior recall scores of subjects who heard the positive, $t(36.4) = 1.20, p < .24$, and negative, $t(47) = 1.20, p < .24$, toothbrushing messages. The control mean was virtually identical to the means obtained from subjects who heard the positive and negative bathing messages $(ts < 1)$.

Discussion

Relatively large shifts in attitudes toward toothbrushing and bathing were obtained. Behavior

---

[1] The degrees of freedom used were fractional, because the variances were heterogeneous and a separate variance *t* value was calculated. This procedure is described in Myers (1979).

[2] The results are not altered when the data from the suspicious subjects are included in the analysis.

recall appeared to be biased by attitudes only on the toothbrushing issue, however.

There are a number of differences between the two types of events that may account for the discrepant behavior recall results. Bathing takes longer than toothbrushing and constitutes a more complex series of behaviors. Bathing is also usually carried out no more than once per day. Perhaps for these reasons, bathing is a more vivid and memorable event than toothbrushing and therefore less prone to memory distortion over relatively short periods of time.

On this basis, it appears plausible to suggest that a longer time period than 2 weeks may be necessary for changes in attitudes toward bathing to significantly influence behavior recall. To test this hypothesis, the bathing recall condition in the first experiment was replicated in Experiment 2, with subjects being asked to recall the number of times they had bathed or showered in the previous month rather than in the preceding 2 weeks.

Experiment 2

Method

Subjects.   The subjects were 12 females and 30 males obtained from the voluntary subject pool at the University of Waterloo. Four subjects (three in the negative bathing condition and one in the positive bathing condition) were suspicious of the link between the two experiments; their data were therefore excluded from the analysis.

Procedure.   The positive and negative bathing tapes were identical to those used in the previous experiment. The bathing recall question was altered; subjects were asked how many baths or showers they had taken over the last month. The filler items in the questionnaire were also changed to assess recall over a 1-month period.

Results

Subjects who were exposed to the negative bathing message reported bathing fewer times in the preceding month ($M = 17.15$) than did subjects who were exposed to the positive message ($M = 25.33$), $t(36) = 2.51, p < .02$. Thus, the shift from a 2-week to a 1-month recall period produced the hypothesized effect (see Footnote 2). Because only one issue was used in this study, no control comparisons were derived.

Self-Monitoring and the Relation Between Attitudes and Recall

The self-monitoring scale was included largely to provide subjects with a rationale for distinguishing the second part of each study from the first part. Based on Snyder's (1979) characterization of low and high self-monitors, however, one might expect low self-monitors in particular to show the assimilation of behavior recall to current attitudes. As the behaviors of low self-monitors generally correspond to their attitudes, their attitudes may be a useful cue by which to recall their behaviors. The attitudes of high self-monitors should not serve this function to the same degree, because their behavior tends to be guided by the situation rather than by their attitudes (Snyder, 1979).

A median split on the self-monitoring dimension produced some support for this reasoning in both experiments. In the first experiment, low self-monitors who received the negative toothbrushing message ($M = 26.43$) reported brushing their teeth significantly fewer times than low self-monitors who received the positive toothbrushing message ($M = 38.00$), $t(22) = 2.29, p < .05$. This contrast was not significant among high self-monitors (for negative toothbrushing, $M = 31.1$; for positive toothbrushing, $M = 34.5$; $t < 1$). Similarly, in the second experiment, low self-monitors who received the negative bathing message ($M = 14.20$) reported bathing fewer times than low self-monitors who received the positive bathing message ($M = 27.40$), $t(27) = 2.28, p < .05$. High self-monitors who received the negative bathing message ($M = 19.20$) did not differ significantly in their recall from high self-monitors who received the positive bathing message ($M = 25.50$; $t = 1.16$, $p < .30$).[3]

These data should be considered with caution, however. The two-way interaction between self-monitoring and the direction of the persuasive message was not statistically significant in either experiment, $F(1, 22) = 1.44$, $p < .25$ (Experiment 1), and $F(1, 27) < 1$ (Experiment 2). Also, the cell ns were low, ranging from 5 to 10 subjects. The pattern is intriguing, though, and replication with higher ns seems warranted.

General Discussion

The results indicate that attitudes can exert a directive influence on recall of personal histories under carefully controlled and specifiable conditions. Presumably, the attitude serves as a retrieval cue. Individuals either reconstruct their actions in light of the attitude, or they focus on the subset of their behaviors that is consistent with the attitude. The present research does not reveal whether this effect on retrieval can be explained purely in information processing terms (different cues, i.e., attitudes, prompting different retrieval) or whether motivational concerns need be posited. (Attitude-consistent material arouses positive affect, and attitude-inconsistent material evokes negative affect, resulting in selective attention to attitude-consistent material.) The quote from Bartlett presented earlier allows for both possibilities, which seems to be the most reasonable hypothesis at the moment.

The data also reveal that attitudes do not always affect the recall of past behaviors, even within the limits of our experimental paradigm. The results for the recall of bathing behavior in Experiment 1 suggest that attitudes may not influence reconstructive memory when the behavior is vivid or readily recalled. Note that this lack of effect

argues against simple demand and self-presentation interpretations of the significant results. If subjects had formulated the experimental hypothesis and were responding to confirm it, or if subjects were responding on the behavior recall assessment to present themselves in a positive way, they were certainly free to do so on the 2-week bathing measure used in Experiment 1. Yet they did not.

There are two other reasons for disputing a self-presentation interpretation of the data. First, the anonymity of subjects' responses and the separation of the attitude and behavior recall portions of the study should have attenuated concerns for self-presentation. Second, Snyder's (1979) characterization of the self-monitoring dimension suggests that high self-monitors are more concerned about self-presentation than are low self-monitors. Thus, the impact of attitude on behavior should be greater with high self-monitors, assuming that the effect is mediated by a concern for self-presentation. If anything, though, the effect was stronger among low self-monitors, a result that is congruent with the hypothesis that attitudes rather than concerns for self-presentation guide recall.

The current research has shown that attitudes affect recall, whereas much of the research on selective learning has failed to demonstrate such selectivity (e.g. Greenwald & Sakumura, 1967). There are differences between the paradigms that could contribute to the discrepant results. In the typical selective learning study, subjects are provided with arguments on both sides of an issue. Although it might be expected that subjects will remember arguments consistent with their attitudes better than arguments inconsistent with their attitudes, the procedure introduces a number of factors that may influence memory and obscure the relation between attitudes and recall. For example, the relative familiarity or novelty of the arguments may be related to the subject's own position on the issue. For many subjects, the arguments that contradict their attitudes may be more novel and elicit greater attention than the arguments that support their attitudes (Greenwald & Sakumura, 1967). Because both attention and familiarity should enhance memory, there may not be a difference in

---

[3] Note that there was no relation between self-monitoring and amount of attitude change (for bathing, $F = 1.69$, ns; for toothbrushing, $F < 1$) and that results from the control conditions revealed that high and low self-monitors did not differ in the frequency with which they reported brushing their teeth or bathing in the absence of persuasive messages ($ts < 1$).

recall between the familiar supporting arguments and the novel opposing arguments.

The current paradigm sidesteps this difficulty. The source of recall is the subject's personal history rather than material containing novel arguments provided by the experimenter. Furthermore, an inconsistency between attitudes and own behaviors may arouse more negative affect and, hence, greater motivation to reduce the disparity than an inconsistency between attitudes and information provided by an experimenter.

A series of studies by Feather (1969-a, 1969-b, 1969-c) and a recent experiment by Weldon and Malpass (Note 1) offer some support for these contentions. Feather simply asked subjects to list the arguments pertinent to an issue. Subjects were able to report more arguments that supported their position than arguments that contradicted their position. Thus, selectivity is evidenced when recall is based on personal experience rather than on experimentally contrived materials. In addition, Weldon and Malpass (Note 1) demonstrated that attitudes are related to recall in a standard selective learning paradigm when factors such as familiarity with the arguments and intellectual skills are controlled for.

The current results complement those of past research on attitudes, behaviors, and recall of behaviors. Previous studies have shown that (a) attitudes can, at times, direct behavior (Ajzen & Fishbein, 1977; Fazio & Zanna, 1978), (b) behavior can affect attitudes (Bem, 1972), (c) current behaviors can affect the recall of past attitudes (Bem & McConnell, 1970), and (d) current attitudes are affected by the selective recall of past behaviors (Salancik, 1974). The present study adds another link. Attitudes can influence the recall of past behaviors.

It is intriguing to speculate about the possible associations among these causal sequences. For example, the results of the present experiment have methodological implications for the study of attitude–behavior relations. In some investigations of the effects of attitudes on behavior, subjects' recall of actions relevant to the attitude being investigated serves as the measure of behavior (e.g., Fishbein & Ajzen, 1974; Kahle & Berman,

1979; Ostrom, 1969). Our research suggests that behavioral recall may be biased by attitudes; as a result, the obtained degree of attitude–behavior consistency in such studies may be inflated spuriously (i.e., attitudes may exert a stronger influence over behavior recall than over behavior). The possibility of such a confound provides one more reason why actual behavior should be examined in studies of this kind, though we appreciate how difficult an investigative imperative this can be.

In addition, it is plausible to postulate a feedback loop between behavior recall and attitude. The present research indicates that attitudes may bias the recall of past behaviors. It follows that a review of previous behavior may lead individuals to conclude (perhaps inappropriately) that their past actions are consistent with their current attitudes and, hence, increase the confidence with which current attitudes are held.

The ramifications may not stop at this point, however. Fazio and Zanna (in press) have shown that the more confident individuals are of their attitudes, the better these attitudes predict future behavior. Thus, much like a self-fulfilling prophecy, the process of behavioral review may increase the control that attitude exerts over future behavior and produce a genuine increase in attitude–behavior consistency.

In a more general vein, the current data support Greenwald's (1980) characterization of the self or ego as analogous to a totalitarian political regime in which history is revised and fabricated to suit present concerns. Individuals appear to be revisionist historians with respect to their personal memories.

REFERENCE NOTE

1. Weldon, P. E., & Malpass, R. S. *The effects of attitudinal, cognitive, and situational variables on recall of biased communications.* Unpublished manuscript, University of Washington, 1980.

REFERENCES

Ajzen, I., & Fishbein, M. Attitude–behavior relations: A theoretical analysis and review of empirical research. *Psychological Bulletin*, 1977, *84*, 888–918.

Allport, G. W. The historical background of modern social

psychology. In G. Lindzey & E. Aronson (Eds.), *The handbook of social psychology* (Vol. 1). Reading, Mass.: Addison-Wesley, 1968.

Bartlett, F. C. *Remembering: A study in experimental social psychology*. Cambridge, England: Cambridge University Press, 1932.

Bem, D. J. Self-perception theory. In L. Berkowitz (Ed.), *Advances in experimental social psychology* (Vol. 6). New York: Academic Press, 1972.

Bem, D. J., & McConnell, H. K. Testing the self-perception explanation of dissonance phenomena: On the salience of premanipulation attitudes. *Journal of Personality and Social Psychology*, 1970, *14,* 23–31.

Calder, B. J., & Ross, M. *Attitudes and behavior*. Morristown, N.J.: General Learning Press, 1973.

Fazio, R. H., & Zanna, M. P. On the predictive validity of attitudes: The roles of direct experience and attitude. *Journal of Personality*, 1978, *46,* 228–243.

Fazio, R. H., & Zanna, M. P. Direct experience and attitude–behavior consistency. In L. Berkowitz (Ed.), *Advances in experimental social psychology* (Vol. 14). New York: Academic Press, in press.

Feather, N. T. Attitude and selective recall. *Journal of Personality and Social Psychology*, 1969, *12,* 310–319. (a)

Feather, N. T. Cognitive differentiation, attitude strength, and dogmatism. *Journal of Personality*, 1969, *37,* 111–126. (b)

Feather, N. T. Differentiation of arguments in relation to attitude, dogmatism, and tolerance of ambiguity. *Australian Journal of Psychology*, 1969, *21,* 21–29. (c)

Fishbein, M., & Ajzen, I. Attitudes toward objects as predictors of single and multiple behavioral criteria. *Psychological Review*, 1974, *81,* 59–74.

Greenwald, A. G. The totalitarian ego: Fabrication and revision of personal history. *American Psychologist*, 1980, *35,* 603–618.

Greenwald, A. G., & Sakumura, J. S. Attitude and selective learning: Where are the phenomena of yesteryear? *Journal of Personality and Social Psychology*, 1967, *7,* 387–397.

Heider, F. *The psychology of interpersonal relations*. New York: Wiley, 1958.

Jones, E. E., & Kohler, R. The effects of plausibility on the learning of controversial statements. *Journal of Abnormal and Social Psychology*, 1958, *57,* 315–320.

Kahle, L. R., & Berman, J. J. Attitudes cause behaviors: A

cross-lagged panel analysis. *Journal of Personality and Social Psychology*, 1979, *37,* 315–321.

Levine, J. M., & Murphy, G. The learning and retention of controversial statements. *Journal of Abnormal and Social Psychology*, 1943, *38,* 507–517.

Lingle, J. H., Geva, N., Ostrom, T. M., Leippe, M. R., & Baumgardner, M. H. Thematic effects of person judgments on impression organization. *Journal of Personality and Social Psychology*, 1979, *37,* 674–687.

McGuire, W. J. Inducing resistance to persuasion: Some contemporary approaches. In L. Berkowitz (Ed.), *Advances in experimental social psychology* (Vol. 1). New York: Academic Press, 1964.

Myers, J. L. *Fundamentals of experimental design*. Boston: Allyn & Bacon, 1979.

Olson, J. M. *Selective recall: Attitudes, schemata, and memory*. Unpublished doctoral dissertation, University of Waterloo, 1980.

Ostrom, T. M. The relationship between the affective, behavioral, and cognitive components of attitude. *Journal of Experimental Social Psychology*, 1969, *5,* 12–30.

Salancik, J. R. Inference of one's attitude from behavior recalled under linguistically manipulated cognitive sets. *Journal of Experimental Social Psychology*, 1974, *10,* 415–427.

Snyder, M. Self-monitoring of expressive behavior. *Journal of Personality and Social Psychology*, 1974, *30,* 526–537.

Snyder, M. Self-monitoring processes. In L. Berkowitz (Ed.), *Advances in experimental social psychology* (Vol. 12). New York: Academic Press, 1979.

Snyder, M., & Uranowitz, S. W. Reconstructing the past: Some cognitive consequences of person perception. *Journal of Personality and Social Psychology*, 1978, *36,* 941–950.

Wicker, A. W. Attitudes versus actions: The relationship of verbal and overt behavioral responses to attitude objects. *Journal of Social Issues*, 1969, *25,* 41–78.

Wicker, A. W. An examination of the "other variables" explanation of attitude–behavior inconsistency. *Journal of Personality and Social Psychology*, 1971, *19,* 18–30.

Zajonc, R. B., & Burnstein, E. The learning of balanced and unbalanced social structures. *Journal of Personality*, 1965, *33,* 570–583.

Received September 15, 1980 ▪

On the Orienting Value of Attitudes: Attitude Accessibility as a Determinant of an Object's Attraction of Visual Attention

David R. Roskos-Ewoldsen* and Russell H. Fazio**

Four experiments tested the hypothesis that objects toward which individuals hold attitudes that are highly accessible from memory (i.e., attitude-evoking objects) are more likely to attract attention when presented in a visual display than objects involving less accessible attitudes. In Experiments I and 2, Ss were more likely to notice and report such attitude-evoking objects. Experiment 3 yielded evidence of incidental attention; Ss noticed attitude-evoking objects even when the task made it beneficial to ignore the objects. Experiment 4 demonstrated that inclusion of attitude-evoking objects as distractor items interfered with Ss' performance of a visual search task. Apparently, attitude-evoking stimuli attract attention automatically. Thus, accessible attitudes provide the functional benefit of orienting an individual's visual attention toward objects with potential hedonic consequences.

Recently, there has been a resurgence of interest in the functional value of attitudes (e.g., Pratkanis, Breckler, & Greenwald, 1989). For example, the utility of attitudes as a means of expressing various aspects of one's social identity has received attention (e.g., DeBono, 1987; Herek,

* University of Alabama.
** Indiana University, Bloomington.
This research was supported by Research Scientist Development Award MH00452 and Grant MH38832 from the National Institute of Mental Health to Russell H. Fazio. We thank Asher Cohen, Jeffrey Franks, Igor Gavanski, Edward Hirt, Paula Niedenthal, Steven J. Sherman, and Richard Shiffrin for their helpful comments on a draft of this article.

Correspondence concerning this article should be addressed to Russell H. Fazio, Department of Psychology, Indiana University, Bloomington, Indiana 47401.

1987; Shavitt, 1989). Likewise, it has been demonstrated that attitudes are useful constructs that individuals rely on as the basis for a decision when situational constraints do not permit them the time and opportunity to consider the details of the available information carefully (e.g., Jamieson & Zanna, 1989; Sanbonmatsu & Fazio, 1990). In addition, support has been found for the object appraisal function of attitudes (Smith, Bruner, & White, 1956). Attitudes can constitute "ready aids" that eliminate the need to appraise an object anew and, hence, ease decision making (Fazio, Blascovich, & Driscoll, in press).

In this article, we propose that another function that attitudes can serve is what we term the *orienting value* of attitudes. Given the incredible number of objects that enter the visual field during any given day, individuals must, in some way, select what stimuli receive attention. Indeed, Kahneman and Treisman (1984) argue that one purpose of selective attention is to allow the cognitive system to adequately process specific information from a very complex and diverse world. It would be functional for a system to direct its attention to those stimuli that have the potential for some hedonic consequences, that is, those objects from which an individual can attain positive or negative outcomes. In other words, a functional system would, through some mechanism, attend to stimuli that it likes or dislikes. Thus, attitudes, or at least certain kinds of attitudes, could serve an orienting function in the sense that they direct our attention to objects that one might find beneficial to approach or to avoid. However, as Bargh (1989) has observed, little evidence exists that clearly documents that attitudes, or other social stimuli, do influence the attraction of attention.

Some data suggesting that positively or negatively valued objects *might* attract attention are available. For example, Erdelyi and Appelbaum (1973) briefly exposed Jewish subjects to a display of a central item (a swastika, Star of David, or the outline of a window) surrounded by eight objects. On both the Star of David and swastika trials, subjects recalled significantly fewer of the other eight objects. Presumably, the Star of David and the swastika, both evaluatively laden objects for Jewish subjects, attracted attention. However, given the design of the stimulus displays in the Erdelyi and Appelbaum (1973) study, it is difficult to argue, as some have done (e.g., Srull & Wyer, 1986), that these items actually *attracted* attention. Subjects were instructed to focus on the center of the display, which is where the critical items appeared. Because the subjects' attention was already focused on the critical items, it is difficult to maintain that the items attracted attention. Instead, it may be the case, as Erdelyi and Blumenthal (1973) and Paulhus and Levitt (1987) have suggested, that the emotional items in the center of the display held individuals' attention and, consequently, disrupted any further processing of the display.

Further suggestive evidence is found in a study by Renninger and Wozniak (1985). Using a measure of eye gaze, these experimenters found that children presented with a number of items simultaneously tended to look both initially, and a greater number of times, at toys in which they had greater interest, as measured earlier by playing time. To the extent that interest in a toy corresponds to a child's attitude toward the toy, these results would suggest that the child's attention was attracted to a positively valued object. Although it is possible that the subjects' attitudes toward the toys could explain these results, it is equally possible that greater familiarity with the toys guided the allocation of attention in these studies.

How might attitudes influence visual processing? Consistent with the hypothesis that affective responses may precede cognitive responses to a stimulus (Wilson, 1979; Zajonc, 1980), an attitude toward an object in the visual field may be activated from memory at an early stage in the processing of visual information. Once the attitude is evoked, it may orient further attention toward the object, so that ultimately the stimulus receives sufficient processing that the individual is able to report having noticed the presence of the object. This possibility raises an important question concerning whether *all* attitudes serve the orienting function. The reasoning implies that the attitude must be activated from memory on some coarse, preliminary, and possibly nonconscious identification of the object. Thus, the extent to which an attitude is capable of such automatic activation may be critical. It may be that some kinds of attitudes, namely more accessible ones, would be more likely than other kinds of attitudes to serve an orienting value. Recent research concerning the functional value of attitudes has observed that the ease of decision making varies directly with the accessibility of the attitudes toward the decision alternatives (Fazio et al., in press). The same may hold true for the orienting of visual attention.

Our approach to the issue of attitude accessibility is based on a view of attitudes as associations in memory between the attitude object and one's evaluation of the object (Fazio, 1989; Fazio, Chen, McDonel, & Sherman, 1982; Fazio, Powell, & Herr, 1983). The strength of these object–evaluation associations in memory can vary. This associative strength between the object and the evaluation of the object has been observed to act as a determinant of the likelihood that the evaluation will be automatically activated from memory on one's encountering the attitude object (Fazio, Sanbonmatsu, Powell, & Kardes, 1986).

This view of varying associative strength allows for the consideration of the attitude–nonattitude continuum (Fazio, 1989; Fazio et al., 1986). At the nonattitude end of the continuum is the case of the individual not possessing any *a priori* evaluation of the object stored in memory. As one moves along the continuum, an evaluation is available in memory and the strength of the association between the object and the evaluation increases. The stronger the association, the greater the likelihood of the attitude being activated on observation of the attitude object. At the upper end of the continuum is the case of the well-learned association. In this instance, the association between the attitude object and the evaluation of the object is sufficiently strong that the evaluation is capable of being activated automatically from memory on mere observation of the attitude object. We suggest that attitudes at this end of the continuum, those that are likely to be activated from memory on the mere observation of the attitude object, serve the

orienting function. Because the terminology is sometimes cumbersome, we often refer to objects toward which a given individual possesses such highly accessible attitudes as attitude-evoking or attitude-activating objects. The question of interest, then, is whether such attitude-evoking objects are more likely to attract attention when presented in an individual's visual field than are objects that are characterized by less accessible attitudes.

The first two experiments examine whether objects that are capable of activating a given individual's attitude are more likely to be noticed, and subsequently reported, when presented in a visual display. The first experiment involved the measurement of attitude accessibility, whereas attitude accessibility was manipulated in the second experiment. The third experiment was intended to demonstrate that subjects were not using any type of intentional search strategy to notice the attitude-activating objects. Specifically, subjects were involved in a number–letter discrimination task with various objects acting as distractor items. Of interest was whether subjects would incidentally notice, and at the end of the task recall, more of the attitude-evoking objects, despite having been told to ignore the distractor items. The fourth experiment was an attempt to show that attitude-evoking items attract attention independent of any processes involving memory for the attitude objects. Subjects were involved in a visual search task, and the accessibility of attitudes toward the to-be-ignored objects was manipulated. To-be-ignored objects that are characterized by highly accessible attitudes were hypothesized to interfere with subjects' ability to search the display effectively, thus indicating that these objects attracted attention (Shiffrin & Schneider, 1977).

Experiment 1

The first experiment involved the measurement of attitude accessibility. To return to the attitude–nonattitude continuum, an individual's attitude can be located along this continuum by measuring the latency with which the individual can respond to an inquiry about the attitude (Fazio et al., 1986; Powell & Fazio, 1984). The faster the individual can respond, the stronger the object–evaluation association and the more likely the attitude is capable of automatic activation on mere observation of the attitude object. It was predicted that subjects would be more likely to notice and report those objects that were capable of such attitude activation. Attitude accessibility was operationally measured using latency of response to an attitudinal inquiry. At an operational level, then, it was predicted that subjects would be more likely to notice, and report having seen, those objects toward which they could indicate their attitudes relatively quickly when asked to do so.

Method

Subjects. Twenty-eight subjects participated in this study. All subjects received partial credit toward fulfillment of a class requirement. Subjects were randomly assigned to the conditions.

Design. The basic design was 2 (order of tasks) × 3 (blocks of trials) mixed factorial. The experiment involved two major tasks. In the visual display task, subjects were briefly presented with displays of six objects and, immediately after each display, were asked to list as many of the objects as they noticed. In the other task, the accessibility of each subject's attitude toward each of the objects was measured. The order of these two tasks was counterbalanced across subjects.

Procedure. On arrival at the experimental session, subjects were placed in individual cubicles. There were two stages to the experiment. One stage involved the visual display task. Subjects were told that a picture with six objects arrayed in a circle would appear on the monitors in front of them. They were instructed that the display would appear very briefly and their task was to try to see as many of the objects as possible. Immediately after the display was terminated, they were to write down the names of as many of the objects as possible. The subjects were supplied with a booklet.

Each page was numbered to correspond to each display slide, and the numbers 1–6 appeared on the page. Each display was presented for approximately 1,500 ms. A pretest found that subjects recorded approximately half of the items on the display given this time period, which reduced any risk of ceiling or floor effects. After the display was terminated, subjects were given 25 s to write down as many of the items as possible. During the pretest, subjects indicated that 25 s provided ample time to write down the objects they had noticed in the display. Subjects were given 5 practice trials before the actual experiment began. There were 3 blocks of 18 displays for a total of 54 trials. Subjects were given a short break between each block. The slide projector and video system that transmitted the stimulus displays to the subjects' individual monitors was controlled by a microcomputer.

The other major experimental task involved determining the accessibility of subjects' attitudes toward each of the 108 items presented during the visual display task. Subjects were instructed that an object would appear on the screen and they were to indicate whether they liked or disliked the object by pressing the appropriate key. Subjects were given standard speed versus accuracy trade-off instructions. A series of practice trials preceded the actual experimental task. Responses and response latencies were collected by the microcomputer that also controlled the display of the stimulus objects.

One half of the subjects completed the visual display task first and then completed the attitude response latency task. The other half of the subjects did these two tasks in the reverse order. Between the two tasks, subjects completed an irrelevant filler task (two personality scales), which took approximately 10 min.

Stimulus materials. The stimuli consisted of slides containing pictures of common animals and objects (e.g., a bicycle, a jet, a squirrel, a flower, and a purse). Each of the displays had pictures of six objects arranged in a circle (see Figure 22.1). The items were taken from Snodgrass and Vanderwart's (1980) standardized set of 260

FIGURE 22.1 ■ An example stimulus display.

pictures. In selecting stimuli from this set, the pictures were restricted to those that were above the median on the normative data that Snodgrass and Vanderwart (1980) provided regarding name agreement. Thus, the selected objects were easily identifiable and nameable. Second, the pictures were limited to those objects toward which one intuitively could make an affective judgment (e.g., a picture of a human arm was excluded).

Snodgrass and Vanderwart (1980) also provided normative data concerning the familiarity of the pictures. They asked subjects "to judge the familiarity of each picture 'according to how usual or unusual the object is in your realm of experience.' Familiarity was defined as 'the degree to which you come in contact with or think about the concept' " (p. 183). These judgments were made along a 1 (*very unfamiliar*) to 5 (*very familiar*) scale. We used these normative data to ensure that the six objects in any given display were equivalently familiar. The six most familiar items were placed in the same display, the next six most familiar items in the next display, and so forth. Eighteen such displays were constructed. Averaged across displays, the range of familiarity scores within a display was a mere 0.15 units on Snodgrass and Vanderwart's 5-point scale. But, there was a range of familiarity across the displays; mean within-

display familiarity scores ranged from 1.56 to 4.75.

For each display, the six pictures were randomly assigned to each of the positions. For the second and third blocks of trials, the same six objects on any given display were rearranged so that the objects appeared in new positions.

Results

Number of objects reported. One way in which the data can be examined is by classifying the items within each display as those three objects toward which a given subject had more accessible attitudes versus the three objects with less accessible attitudes. Were those objects characterized by greater attitude accessibility more likely to be noticed? If objects toward which subjects have more accessible attitudes attract attention, then a greater number of these objects should be reported. To determine whether this was true, the items from each display were divided in half on the basis of each individual subject's latencies of response to the attitudinal inquiries. For any given subject and any given display, the three objects associated with the faster latencies were considered the high attitude accessibility items and the three associated with the slower latencies the low attitude accessibility items. The number of items characterized by high and low attitude accessibility that were noticed was then averaged across the displays.

These data were analyzed using a 2 (order of tasks) × 2 (high vs. low attitude accessibility) × 3 (blocks of trials) mixed analysis of variance (ANOVA). As expected, there was a main effect of attitude accessibility, $F(1, 26) = 16.15, p < .001$. A greater number of objects toward which subjects had more accessible attitudes were noticed ($M = 1.75$) than were objects toward which subjects had less accessible attitudes ($M = 1.61$). There was also a significant effect of block, $F(2, 52) = 10.17, p < .001$. A post hoc Scheffé test indicated that subjects noticed significantly fewer items in Block 1 ($M = 1.62$) than in Block 2 ($M = 1.69$) or Block 3 ($M = 1.73$). Finally, there was a significant effect of the order in which the two tasks were completed, $F(1,$

26) = 9.89, $p < .005$. Subjects noticed significantly more items if they completed the attitude judgment task first ($M = 1.81$) than if they completed the visual display task first ($M = 1.56$). No other main effects or interactions were significant.[1]

Judgment times. The data also can be examined in terms of the judgment latencies associated with objects that were or were not noticed during the visual display task. According to the hypothesis, the objects in a visual display that a subject notices are likely to be those toward which the subject has a relatively accessible attitude. Thus, subjects should be able to indicate evaluative judgments more quickly for those objects that are noticed and subsequently listed than for those objects that subjects did not list. In analyzing these data, whether the subject had reported the item or not was recorded for each visual display. The mean latency of response within these two categories was calculated for any given display.[2] These means were then averaged across the displays within a given block of trials.

The data were analyzed using a 2 (order of

tasks) × 2 (object was noticed or not noticed) × 3 (blocks of trials) mixed ANOVA. Order of task was a between-subjects variable. Whether the object was noticed and blocks were within-subject variables. As predicted, there was a significant main effect for whether the object was noticed or not, $F(1, 26) = 15.08$, $p < .001$. Those items that were noticed during the visual display task were indeed characterized by faster latencies of response during the attitude judgment task ($M = 2,029$ ms) than those items that were not noticed ($M = 2,060$ ms). These results indicate that objects toward which subjects could express their attitudes quickly were more likely to be noticed and subsequently reported.

There was also a main effect for the order of the tasks, $F(1, 26) = 9.30$, $p < .01$. Subjects who completed the visual display task first were able to express their attitudes quicker (1,954 ms) than subjects who completed the attitude judgment task first (2,140 ms). This is not surprising because the subjects who completed the notice task initially had seen the objects three times before participating in the attitude judgment task. However, the order variable did not interact with any other

---

[1] The items available in the Snodgrass and Vanderwart (1980) picture set made analysis of the effect of valence difficult because there are relatively few negative items among the stimulus items. On the average, subjects judged 29.2 of the 108 stimulus items negatively (range of 6–59). Nevertheless, to determine whether the observed effect depended on valence, we conducted an analysis in which positively and negatively valued objects within any given display were classified as involving high or low attitude accessibility on the basis of median splits on the latencies associated with the positive and negative responses, respectively. The analysis was restricted to subjects who had evaluated at least two objects negatively on a minimum of three visual displays. This criterion, which 4 subjects did not meet, ensured that at least three observations were available for each subject within each cell of a 2 (attitude accessibility) × 2 (valence) matrix. The proportion of items that were noticed within any of the four possible categories that were represented on any given display was calculated. Each of the four proportions was then averaged across displays (i.e., the sum of the within-cell proportions was divided by the number of displays on which the category had been represented). These data were analyzed with a 2 (order of tasks) × 2 (levels of attitude accessibility) × 2 (valence of the objects: positive or negative) × 3 (blocks of trials) mixed ANOVA. As before, a main effect of block (Ms of .54, .57, and

.58 for blocks 1, 2, and 3, respectively) emerged, $F(2, 44) = 4.27$, $p < .05$, as did a main effect of task order, $F(1, 22) = 11.29$, $p < .005$. Subjects reported a greater proportion of objects when they performed the visual display task second ($M = .62$) instead of first ($M = .51$). Also significant was a main effect of valence such that subjects reported more of the objects that they considered positive ($M = .59$) than those that they considered negative ($M = .54$), $F(1, 22) = 7.85$, $p < .02$. However, this latter effect was qualified by an interaction with task order, $F(1, 22) = 6.21$, $p < .025$. The higher reporting of positive than negative objects was evident when subjects performed the visual display task first (Ms of .55 vs. .46), but not when they performed it second (both Ms = .62). Most relevant to our concerns is the fact that the main effect of attitude accessibility was significant (Ms of .59 and .53 for high and low attitude accessibility, respectively), $F(1, 22) = 10.10$, $p < .005$, and was not qualified by any interaction with valence, $F(1, 22) = 1.05$, $p > .25$.

[2] Given the skewness that characterizes latency data, all analyses of latency scores reported throughout this article were conducted after a reciprocal transformation of the latency data (see Fazio, 1990). Means reported in the text and displayed in the figure have been retransformed back to the original metric.

variable. No other main effects or interactions were significant.[3]

Discussion

Overall, these results are consistent with our reasoning and our hypothesis. The experiment demonstrates an association between the accessibility of attitudes toward an object, as measured by latency of response to an attitudinal inquiry, and the likelihood that the object will receive attention. On the basis of this finding, one might suggest that objects toward which subjects have accessible attitudes are more likely to attract attention and, consequently, to be noticed.

Obviously, the results, although encouraging, are correlational in nature and open to multiple interpretations. It is possible that other variables that are associated with the accessibility of attitudes from memory also increase the likelihood that an object will receive attention when presented in a visual display. As an example, let us consider familiarity. Familiar objects may generally be characterized by greater attitude accessibility and also may be more likely to be noticed in a visual display. Indeed, in Experiment 1, the correlation between the rank order familiarity of each display (based on Snodgrass and Vanderwart's, 1980, norms) and the average number of items noticed in that display was substantial, $r(17) = .81, p < .001$. On the average, more items were noticed and reported from those displays that contained the more familiar items. It is also the case that the items in the more familiar displays tended to be characterized by faster latencies of response to the attitudinal inquiries. Across the 18 displays, the correlation between the rank order familiarity of each display and the average latency of response to those display items was .45, $p < .07$.

Fortunately, our arrangement of the stimulus items informs us that the observed covariation between an item's being noticed and the accessibility of attitudes toward that item holds true over and above any relations with familiarity. Recall that each display was constructed so as to include equally familiar items and that we found the objects characterized by greater attitude accessibility *within a given display* more likely to be reported. Although we controlled for familiarity in this way, other correlates of preexisting attitude accessibility unquestionably exist (see Fazio, 1989) and may have operated. Experiment 2 addressed this concern directly by examining performance on the visual display task after an experimental manipulation of attitude accessibility. Experiments 3 and 4 also involved manipulating, instead of measuring, attitude accessibility.

Another reason why the findings from Experiment 1 are open to multiple interpretations is that subjects' very task was to notice as many of the items in the display as possible. To address this issue, in Experiment 3 we used a paradigm that involved subjects' incidentally noticing, and at the end of the task recalling, items that they were instructed to ignore. These items were irrelevant to the task that subjects were performing, and subjects were attempting to perform as well as they had when these distractors had not been involved.

Finally, Experiment 1 (as well as Experiments 2

---

[3] Once again, a further analysis was conducted to examine whether the observed effect was qualified by an interaction with valence. We recorded whether the subject had or had not noticed a given item from a given display and whether the subject judged the object positively or negatively during the response latency task. The mean latency of response for any of these four categories that were present for a given display was calculated. Then, means were computed across the displays (i.e., the sum of the latency means within a given category was divided by the number of displays on which the category had been represented). The data were analyzed using a 2 (order of tasks) × 2 (object was noticed or not noticed) × 2 (positive or negative valence) × 3 (blocks of trials) mixed ANOVA. There was a significant main effect for whether the object was noticed or not, $F(1, 26) = 4.60, p < .05$ (noticed, $M = 2,071$ ms; not noticed, $M = 2,101$ ms). This main effect was not qualified by an interaction with valence, $F < 1$. It held true for both positively and negatively valued objects (positive and noticed, $M = 2,001$ ms; positive and not noticed, $M = 2,018$ ms; negative and noticed, $M = 2,144$ ms; negative and not noticed, $M = 2,188$ ms). A main effect for the order of the tasks did emerge, $F(1, 26) = 6.19, p < .05$ (visual display task first, $M = 2,007$ ms; attitude judgment task first, $M = 2,166$ ms). There was also a significant main effect of valence, $F(1, 26) = 18.09, p < .001$. Subjects expressed positively valenced attitudes faster (2,042 ms) than negatively valenced attitudes (2,227 ms). No other main effects or interactions were significant.

and 3) does not establish that any effect of attitude accessibility is due to attention per se. The locus of the observed effect could be anywhere from attention to learning to memory to report. This issue is most directly addressed by Experiment 4, which examined subjects' performance in a visual search task involving their detecting whether a visual display did or did not include a target item. In this way, attention could be examined independent of any processes involving memory for the attitude objects. This experiment will serve to illustrate that an attentional component was responsible, at least in part, for the findings from the earlier experiments.

Experiment 2

Earlier research has found that repeatedly expressing one's attitude enhances the strength of the object–evaluation association and, as a consequence, increases the likelihood that the evaluation will be capable of automatic activation on observation of the object (Fazio et al., 1986; Houston & Fazio, 1989; Powell & Fazio, 1984). In this experiment, attitude accessibility was manipulated by inducing subjects to make repeated like–dislike judgments of three items that were randomly selected from each display of six objects. To control for exposure to the pictures, subjects made repeated animate–inanimate judgments of the remaining pictures. In this way, the object–evaluation association was strengthened for one-half of the objects, yet, exposure to all the pictures was held constant. Thus, we are comparing two conditions in which attitudes differ with respect to their position along the attitude–nonattitude continuum. If our reasoning is correct, and attitude-evoking objects do attract attention, then subjects should notice and subsequently report a higher proportion of the objects from the attitude judgment task.

Method

Subjects. A total of 33 subjects participated in this experiment. An advertisement was run in the campus newspaper to recruit subjects in return for payment. Subjects were randomly assigned to conditions.

Design. The design was a 2 (set of pictures) × 2 (types of judgment: like–dislike vs. animate–inanimate) × 2 (order of judgment task). For each display, one half (three) of the pictures were randomly assigned to one set (Set A), and the remaining pictures were assigned to a second set (Set B). Half of the subjects completed the attitude rehearsal task with Set A pictures and the remaining subjects completed the attitude rehearsal task with Set B pictures. Each object within the set appeared at three different locations in the subject's booklet. Thus, subjects were induced to express their attitudes toward each object a total of three times. To control for any effects of exposure on later tasks, subjects judged whether the objects in the second set of pictures were animate or inanimate (the control judgment). Each object within this set also appeared three times.

Finally, the order of the two judgment tasks was counterbalanced. One half of the subjects completed the attitude rehearsal task first, whereas the remaining subjects completed the control (animate–inanimate) task first.

Procedure. On arrival to the experimental session, the subjects sat in individual cubicles. There were three stages to the main part of this experiment. One stage involved manipulating the accessibility of subjects' attitudes toward the various objects. Subjects were given booklets and told that the experiment concerned their judgments of a number of objects. One judgment involved whether the subjects liked or disliked the pictured object. Subjects indicated their judgment by circling the appropriate response below each picture. The response was a dichotomous like–dislike judgment. For another set of pictures, subjects judged whether the objects were animate or inanimate. Again, they circled the appropriate response. Both tasks were self-paced. The order of these two tasks was counterbalanced across subjects. Subjects were warned that they might see certain items more than once. They were told that this occurred because part of the experiment concerned whether the judgments became any easier with practice. Subjects were instructed to answer each time they saw a picture. After subjects completed each judgment task, they indicated on a 7-point scale how difficult they found the task and whether the task got any easier as they completed it, so as to bolster the cover story. After completing the picture judgment task, subjects engaged in an irrelevant filler task (completing two personality scales) for approximately 10 min.

At this point, subjects participated in the same visual display task that was used in Experiment 1. Each visual display was presented briefly (1,500 ms), and immediately after each display, the subjects listed as many of the items that had appeared as they could. The only difference from Experiment 1 was that subjects completed only one block of trials instead of the three blocks that were used in Experiment 1, so as to shorten the experiment. (Recall that no interaction involving block had been observed in Experiment 1.)

After completing this task, the subjects participated in a response latency task similar to that used in Experiment 1. Each object was presented on the screen, and subjects indicated whether they liked or disliked the object as quickly as possible. Standard speed versus accuracy trade-off instructions were used. These data were collected to provide a check of the attitude rehearsal manipulation. At this point, subjects were debriefed, paid, and dismissed.

Results

Manipulation check. The latency of response data were analyzed to ensure the attitude rehearsal task had indeed strengthened the association between the object and the evaluation of the object. As predicted, and as has been observed in a number of past experiments, the response latencies were faster for those items that had been assigned to the attitude rehearsal task ($M = 2,058$ ms) than for those items that had been assigned to the control task ($M = 2,115$ ms), $t(32) = 2.07, p < .05$.

Proportion reported. The major prediction of this study was that subjects would notice more objects toward which they had repeatedly expressed their attitudes than objects involved in the control task. In other words, subjects should be more likely to notice and subsequently report those objects that had been moved toward the more accessible region of the attitude–nonattitude continuum. To test this, we calculated two proportions for each visual display: the proportion of objects from the attitude rehearsal set that were noticed and the proportion from the control set that were noticed. These proportions were then averaged across the 18 trials of the experiment. These mean proportions were analyzed using a 2 (sets of pictures) × 2 (levels of attitude accessibility) × 2 (order of judgment task) mixed ANOVA. Subjects reported having seen a greater proportion of the attitude rehearsal objects ($M = .59$) than of the control objects ($M = .54$), $F(1, 29) = 7.83, p < .01$. Rehearsing one's attitude increased the probability that the subject would notice the object when it was later presented. Thus, when an object was experimentally made more capable of activating an associated evaluation, the object was more likely to receive attention. No other main effects or interactions were significant.[4]

---

[4] As in Experiment 1, the data also were analyzed to determine whether valence had any effect on the orienting of attention. The valence information stemmed from individual subjects' responses to each item during the manipulation check task. It proved necessary to limit this analysis to 20 of the 33 subjects. Recall that each of the 18 displays contained three objects from the attitude rehearsal set and three from the control set. Subjects were included in the analysis only if they judged at least one attitude rehearsal item negatively on at least three displays and judged at least one control item negatively on at least three displays. Thus, a subject's data were included in the analysis only if a minimum of three observations were available within each cell of a 2 (valence) × 2 (attitude rehearsal vs. control set) matrix. The proportion of items that were noticed within any of the four possible categories that were represented on any given display (positively valued objects from the attitude rehearsal set, negatively valued from the attitude rehearsal set, positively valued from the control set, and negatively valued from the control set) was calculated. Each of the four proportions was then averaged across displays (i.e., the sum of the within-category proportions was divided by the number of displays on which the category had been represented). These data were analyzed with a 2 (sets of pictures) × 2 (levels of attitude accessibility) × 2 (order of judgment task) × 2 (valence of the objects: positive or negative) mixed

Discussion

The findings from these two experiments demonstrate that objects toward which subjects had accessible attitudes were more likely to be reported as having been seen in the visual display. This held true regardless of whether attitude accessibility was measured, as in Experiment 1, or manipulated, as in Experiment 2. Apparently, then, attitude-evoking stimuli do receive attention when presented in a visual field. As argued earlier, it is functional for an organism to be able to detect and attend to those items in the environment that have the potential for hedonic consequences.

The central question of this research concerns whether objects toward which an individual holds a highly accessible attitude *attract* attention. Experiments 1 and 2 indicate that such attitude-evoking items *receive* attention when subjects are actively studying a visual display. Unfortunately, the results of Experiments 1 and 2 do not unambiguously demonstrate that such objects generally attract attention. First, although we do not believe it to be plausible, it is possible that subjects used a search and encoding strategy that relied on their attitudes toward the objects (e.g., somehow focusing on objects they felt strongly about, whether positively or negatively). If subjects relied on such an intentional strategy, it is unclear whether the attitude-evoking objects attracted attention or were noticed as a consequence of the particular strategy that subjects pursued. Second, and more important, the subjects in these two experiments were instructed to notice as many items as possible. Thus, even if we were to accept the premise that attitude-activating objects attracted attention, an important question arises concerning generalizability. Do attitude-evoking objects attract attention only when an individual is

actively searching and encoding the environment, or do they attract attention in more general circumstances as well?

If subjects were to perform a task in which it was functional to ignore the attitude-evoking items and yet these items still received attention, then we would be more justified in inferring that neither an intentional strategy nor actively searching a visual display is necessary to obtain this effect. Finding that subjects attended to attitude-activating objects when it is clearly counter to the task demands would constitute stronger support for the orienting value of accessible attitudes.

Experiment 3

In this experiment, we used an incidental learning paradigm to test whether attitude-evoking stimuli attract attention even when task demands do not require that the stimuli receive attention. Specifically, subjects performed a number–letter discrimination task. On certain trials, the item to be identified was surrounded by six distractor items. Subjects were instructed to ignore these distractor items and perform the number–letter judgment as quickly as possible. The accessibility of subjects' attitudes toward three of the six distractor items was manipulated as in Experiment 2. To the extent that attitude-evoking objects attract attention, subjects should be more likely to notice, and subsequently report, those items concerning which they had made repeated attitudinal judgments— despite the fact that the task demands made it profitable for the subjects to ignore these distractor items.

Method

Subjects. A total of 59 subjects participated in this study. All subjects received partial credit toward fulfillment of a class requirement. Subjects were randomly assigned to the conditions in the experiment.

Design. The design was 2 (set of pictures) × 2 (type of judgment: attitude or animate) × 2 (order

---

ANOVA. The only significant effect to emerge was the main effect of attitude accessibility, $F(1, 18) = 6.50$, $p < .05$. Subjects were more likely to report having seen a greater proportion of the attitude rehearsal objects ($M = .62$) than the control objects ($M = .52$). This effect was not qualified by valence, $F(1, 18) = 1.22$, $p > .25$. Thus, the effects of attitude rehearsal held true for both positively valued (Ms of .58 and .52 for attitude rehearsal and control items, respectively) and negatively valued objects (Ms of .65 and .52).

of judgment tasks) factorial. The accessibility of subjects' attitudes toward the various objects was manipulated in the same manner as Experiment 2. For each display, half (three) of the pictures were randomly assigned to one set (Set A), and the remaining pictures were assigned to a second set (Set B). Half of the subjects completed the attitude rehearsal task with Set A objects and the remaining subjects completed the attitude rehearsal task with Set B objects. The order of the two judgment tasks was counterbalanced: one half of the subjects completed the attitude rehearsal task first, and the remaining subjects completed the control (animate) task first.

Stimulus materials. For the first part of the number–letter discrimination task, two blocks of slides were prepared with solely a number or letter appearing in the center of the display (i.e, no distractor stimuli were present). Each block consisted of nine trials (four numbers and five letters). The same items appeared in each block, but the order of the items was randomized within each block.

Two blocks of 9 displays each were used in the actual experimental task involving distractors. Nine of the 18 displays used in Experiments 1 and 2 were randomly selected for this purpose. Either a number or a letter appeared in the center of the display, and the six objects surrounded it. The displays in the second block contained the same six distractor items, but the items appeared in different places on the display. The displays were randomly ordered within the two blocks.

The pictures used in the initial rating tasks were identical to the stimuli used in Experiment 2. Although there were only 54 distractor items (9 displays with 6 items per display) in the main part of the experiment, subjects rated all 108 items used in Experiments 1 and 2. The extra 54 items served as foils in a surprise recognition task. If the recognition foils had not been included in the initial rating tasks, subjects may have relied on a strategy of indicating that an item appeared as a distractor *because* they had made an earlier judgment of that item.

Procedure. On arrival at the experimental session,

subjects sat in individual cubicles. There were three stages to the main part of this experiment. The first stage involved manipulating the accessibility of subjects' attitudes toward the various objects. The tasks were identical to the judgment tasks in Experiment 2. Subjects made judgments of all 108 items used in Experiments 1 and 2.

After subjects completed the judgment tasks, they were told that the next phase of the experiment involved how well they could discriminate numbers and letters. Subjects were instructed that either a number or a letter would appear in the middle of their monitor and they should indicate as quickly as possible whether it was a number or a letter by pressing one key if it was a letter and a different key if the object was a number. Subjects were given standard speed versus accuracy trade-off instructions. Each item appeared for a total of 2 s. In fact, the key pads were not operative and no latencies were actually collected. Subjects completed two blocks of trials in this task, which lasted approximately 5 min.

Subjects then were told that, to make the task more difficult, distractors would be added to the displays. Specifically, a set of six pictures would surround each number or letter. Subjects were informed that

> [t]he experiment is concerned with how well you can ignore the distractors. Your task is to ignore the distractors and to respond whether the item was a number or letter as quickly as possible. It is important that you ignore the distractors because your task will be much simpler if you completely ignore the pictures surrounding the number/letter. The goal of the experiment is to determine whether you can, in fact, totally ignore the distractor items.

As in the first set of trials, there were two blocks of 9 trials each, and each display appeared for a total of 2 s.

At this point in the experiment, subjects were given a surprise recall test. They were instructed to list as many of the distractor items as they could and were told to be sure that the items they listed had in fact appeared as distractors and not solely in the early part of the experiment. Subjects were given as much time as they wanted to complete this task. Then subjects were given a surprise recognition test. They were presented with the 108 items that they had judged earlier and told to indicate which of those items had appeared as distractor items. Again, the subjects were instructed to indicate that an item had been a distractor only if they were certain they had seen the item during the number–letter discrimination task, and not just during an earlier phase of the experiment.

Finally, subjects were presented with the 54 items that appeared as distractor items and asked to indicate their attitudes toward each object. Specifically, they were given a 6-point scale ranging from −3 (*very bad*) to 3 (*very good*). The scale had no neutral (0) point, because subjects were not allowed to express a neutral attitude when they earlier indicated whether they liked or disliked each object. These data were collected so as to permit an examination of the possible role of attitude extremity. After subjects completed this task, they were debriefed, thanked, and dismissed.

Results

Two observations indicate that this experiment did involve the incidental learning of the distractor items. First, subjects expressed a great deal of surprise when they were asked to list as many of the objects as they could. A number of subjects indicated that they had been told to ignore the objects and, because they had done that, they did not think they could recall any objects. In fact, 2 subjects were upset enough by the surprise recall task that they refused to do it (they did, however, complete the recognition measure). Second, the overall number of distractors recalled was very low. Subjects were able to list, on average, just 3.97 of the total 54 distractors (7.3%). Yet, subjects had been exposed to each distractor twice during the discrimination task. Thus, it appears that we were successful in convincing subjects that their task was to ignore the distractors.

Correct recall and recognition. The first analysis concerned the number of distractor objects that were correctly recalled or recognized as having been present. The data from 2 subjects were omit-

ted from the recall analysis because they failed to complete the measure. The recall and recognition data each were analyzed using a 2 (sets of pictures) × 2 (order of judgments) × 2 (levels of attitude accessibility) mixed ANOVA. As predicted, there was a significant main effect of attitude accessibility for the recall data, $F(1, 53) = 4.91, p < .05$, such that a greater number of objects toward which subjects had highly accessible attitudes were incidentally noticed ($M = 2.30$) than objects toward which subjects had less accessible attitudes ($M = 1.67$). No other main effects or interactions were significant in the analysis of the recall data.

A similar effect was apparent on the recognition measure. Those objects made more capable of automatic attitude activation were more likely to be correctly recognized ($M = 11.14$) than were objects toward which subjects had less accessible attitudes ($M = 10.31$), $F(1, 55) = 5.80, p < .05$. Again, no other main effects or interactions were significant. Furthermore, the effect of attitude accessibility does not appear to be due to a simple bias toward identifying the more attitude-evoking objects as having been presented during the distractor task. The number of objects falsely believed to have been presented did not differ as a function of having made attitudinal ($M = 8.20$) versus animate–inanimate ($M = 8.60$) judgments regarding the object ($F < 1$). Thus, superior recognition was observed for the distractor objects toward which subjects had developed more accessible attitudes. Both the recall and the recognition findings, then, suggest that subjects were more likely to notice those distractors that were experimentally made more capable of attitude activation—even though it was not useful for subjects to attend to the pictures given the nature of the task they were performing.

Effects of repeated attitudinal expression on attitude extremity. Repeatedly expressing one's attitude toward an object has the potential to make the attitude more extreme, in addition to increasing the strength of the object–evaluation association in memory and the consequent accessibility of the attitude (see Judd & Brauer, in press). Although a number of studies have found no effect of repeated expression on attitude extremity (e.g., Fazio et al.,

1986; Powell & Fazio, 1984), the data from this experiment were analyzed to ensure that the manipulation of accessibility did not have any unanticipated polarizing effects.

To test whether repeated expression resulted in more extreme attitudes, we conducted two analyses. The first involved comparing the attitude extremity (absolute value of the attitude scores) of those subjects who had engaged in attitude rehearsal with respect to a given object with the attitude extremity of those subjects who had performed the control task with respect to that same object. A between-subjects t test was conducted for each and every attitude object. Of the 54 t tests, only four were significant and one marginally significant: giraffe, $t(57) = 2.07$, $p < .05$, attitude rehearsal $M = 2.24$, control $M = 1.80$; truck, $t(57) = 2.74$, $p < .01$, attitude rehearsal $M = 1.76$, control $M = 1.30$; leaf, $t(57) = 2.79$, $p < .01$, attitude rehearsal $M = 1.87$, control $M = 2.38$; necklace, $t(57) = 2.27$, $p < .05$, attitude rehearsal $M = 1.77$, control $M = 2.24$; heart, $t(57) = 1.86$, $p < .10$, attitude rehearsal $M = 2.76$, control $M = 2.47$. For two of these objects, attitude rehearsal actually *decreased* the extremity of the attitude (necklace and leaf).

To take advantage of the even greater statistical power that was available, we conducted a final analysis using a paired t test to compare the mean extremity associated with objects when they had been assigned to the attitude rehearsal set versus the control set. Averaged across the 54 objects, the means were virtually equivalent (Ms of 2.10 and 2.14 for the control and attitude expression conditions, respectively), $t(53) = 1.47$, $p > .10$. Despite the large number of observations involved in this test (59 subjects expressing attitudes toward 54 objects) and the resulting statistical power, no effect of repeated expression was apparent. As expected, then, it does not appear that the manipulation of attitude accessibility had any influence on attitude extremity.

Relation between attitude extremity and attention. Although the attitude rehearsal manipulation did not polarize attitudes, it is interesting to examine whether attitude extremity relates to the attraction of attention. Given that studies simultaneously measuring (not manipulating) preexisting attitude accessibility and attitude extremity have observed moderate correlations between the two variables (e.g., Fazio & Williams, 1986; Houston & Fazio, 1989; Powell & Fazio, 1984), we certainly would expect such a relation. More extreme attitudes are generally more accessible and, thus, are more likely to meet the hypothesized prerequisite that the attitude be activated from memory on some preliminary identification of the attitude object. Furthermore, once activated, more extreme attitudes may induce all the more attention to the attitude-evoking stimulus, precisely because the object is considered so hedonically relevant.

To examine the relation between attitude extremity and attention, we computed the proportion of distractor items correctly recalled within each cell of a 2 (attitude rehearsal or control objects) × 3 (high, −3 or 3; moderate, −2 or 2; or low, −1 or 1, extremity) matrix for each subject. The data were analyzed with a 2 (sets of pictures) × 2 (order of judgment tasks) × 2 (levels of attitude accessibility) × 3 (levels of extremity) mixed ANOVA. As one would expect on the basis of the findings reported earlier, the recall data displayed a main effect of attitude accessibility, $F(1, 53) = 4.84$, $p < .05$. Objects toward which subjects had highly accessible attitudes were recalled in greater proportion ($M = .084$) than objects toward which subjects had low accessible attitudes ($M = .057$). There also was a main effect of extremity, $F(2, 106) = 6.28$, $p < .005$. Subjects were more likely to report a greater proportion of objects toward which they held more extreme attitudes (Ms = .050, .068, and .094 for the low, moderate, and high extremity conditions, respectively). As mentioned earlier, the main effect of attitude extremity is not surprising given that studies in which attitude extremity and accessibility have been measured have found more polarized attitudes to be relatively more accessible from memory. Importantly, the interaction between attitude accessibility and attitude extremity was not significant, $F(2, 108) = 1.46$, $p > .23$. Thus, it does not appear that the consequences of attitude rehearsal on attention are limited to certain levels of attitude extremity.

The recognition data, which were analyzed in a similar manner, mirror the recall data. The main effect of attitude accessibility was significant, $F(1, 55) = 4.10$, $p < .05$ (Ms of .41 and .37 for the high and low attitude accessibility conditions, respectively). However, the main effect of extremity only approached significance, $F(2, 110) = 2.29$, $p < .11$ (Ms of .35, .39, and .42 for the low, moderate, and high extremity conditions, respectively). The interaction between the attitude accessibility and attitude extremity was not significant, $F(2, 110) = 2.07$, $p > .13$.

Discussion

The data from this experiment provide additional support for our theoretical perspective. Apparently, certain objects—those characterized by greater attitude accessibility—were more likely to attract subjects' attention. Furthermore, this study extended the earlier studies by demonstrating that this effect occurred in a situation in which subjects were not required to attend to the stimuli. Even though the six objects were distractors, the objects toward which subjects had more accessible attitudes were relatively more likely to attract attention. Although it is possible that subjects used some kind of intentional strategy to attend to the attitude-evoking objects in Experiments 1 and 2, it is difficult to conceive that subjects were using an intentional strategy to attend to objects that they were instructed to ignore.

The data from Experiment 3 also demonstrate that attitude extremity cannot explain the results of these experiments. The manipulation of attitude accessibility did not affect the extremity of subjects' attitudes towards the objects. This is not to say that attitude extremity is irrelevant to visual processing, for a main effect of extremity on the recall of the distractor items was observed. However, this effect was independent of the manipulation of attitude accessibility. Given that more extreme attitudes tend to be more accessible from memory (Fazio & Williams, 1986; Houston & Fazio, 1989; Powell & Fazio, 1984),

they are more likely to meet what we theorize to be the prerequisite condition for an attitude to influence visual attention—namely, that it be capable of automatic activation. Furthermore, once activated, extreme attitudes also are apt to more powerfully draw attention to the objects; such objects are, by virtue of their strongly associated extreme evaluations, more hedonically relevant than attitude objects associated with more mild evaluations.

Clearly, the results of the third experiment support the idea that objects toward which an individual possesses a strongly associated evaluation are relatively likely to attract attention. Nevertheless, a fourth experiment was conducted to provide converging evidence for the proposition. Instead of examining incidentally noticed items, we conducted a traditional visual search task (Shiffrin & Schneider, 1977) in Experiment 4. Specifically, the subjects' task was to search for a target among a number of items. However, subjects knew that the target could not appear in certain positions in the display. Of interest is whether the to-be-ignored stimuli that were characterized by relatively high attitude accessibility interfered with the subjects' ability to search the displays.

Experiment 4 also sought to test the possible role of memory in the first three experiments. Memory for the objects was involved in all three of the earlier experiments. In Experiments 1 and 2, even though subjects reported the objects they had noticed in each display immediately after its presentation, they had to briefly rely on their memory for the pictures. In Experiment 3 there was a clear memory component, because subjects were asked to recall and recognize objects from displays they had seen several minutes earlier. It is possible that subjects can simply remember attitude-evoking objects better or longer. The search task used in Experiment 4 removes any role of memory. The issue was not whether subjects could later report the presence of attitude-evoking distractors, but instead whether the presence of these items in to-be-ignored positions interfered with the subjects' ability to search for a target item.

Experiment 4

The experiment was modeled after Shiffrin and Schneider's (1977) "diagonal" study. In this study, displays of four letters were presented and the subjects' task was to search for a target that may have been present in the display. However, through instruction and training, the subjects understood that the target could only appear in the upper left or lower right corner of the display. Items in the to-be-ignored, off-diagonal positions that had been trained earlier to a level of automatic detection interfered with the subjects' visual search performance, indicating that these distractor items were automatically attracting the subjects' attention.

In this experiment, subjects searched for two targets in a display of six objects. The subjects' task was to determine as quickly as possible whether either of the two targets was present. However, the target could only appear in one of three positions in the display. The accessibility of subjects' attitudes toward the three distractor items was manipulated. If the trials that involved distractors characterized by greater attitude accessibility were to take longer to complete, then further support would be available for the hypothesis that attitude-activating stimuli inescapably attract attention.

Method

Subjects. A total of 31 subjects participated in this study. All subjects received partial credit toward fulfillment of a class requirement. Subjects were randomly assigned to conditions.

Design. The design of the experiment was a 2 (sets of pictures) × 2 (order of judgment task) × 2 (levels of attitude accessibility) × 2 (target present or absent). The set and order variables were identical to those in Experiments 2 and 3, as was the manipulation of the accessibility of attitudes toward the distractors. For half of the displays, the attitudes toward the three distractor objects were made more accessible by having subjects make repeated attitudinal judgments of the objects. For the remaining objects, the subjects made repeated

control (animate–inanimate) judgments to ensure that subjects had been exposed to all the distractors an equal number of times. Target presence simply dealt with whether one of the targets the subjects were searching for was or was not present in the display. On half the trials the target was present.

Procedure. On arrival to the experimental session, subjects were placed in individual cubicles. The initial stage of the experiment involved manipulating the accessibility of subjects' attitudes toward the various objects. After subjects completed the attitudinal and control judgment task, they were given instructions for the second part of the experiment. Subjects were told that the names of two objects would appear on their monitors for 2 s and then disappear. These were the target items. One s after the two target words had disappeared, a display of six pictures would appear and the subject's task was to indicate as quickly as possible whether either of the target items was present among the six objects. If a target was present, they were to press the *yes* button, and if a target was not present, the *no* button. Then subjects were told that to make the task easier, the target would only appear in one of three positions. Specifically, the target would only appear in Positions 2, 4, and 6 (see Figure 22.2). Subjects were

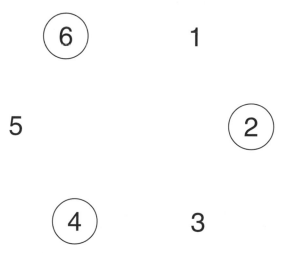

FIGURE 22.2 ■ Circled positions represent the potential location of target items; the other positions were occupied by the irrelevant distractor items.

told that to complete the task as quickly as possible, they should ignore the other three positions (Positions 1, 3, and 5) and that it was in their best interest not to scan the to-be-ignored positions. Subjects were given a sheet containing the six positions, with positions 2, 4, and 6 circled. This was to help them remember the positions where the target could possibly appear. Subjects were given standard speed versus accuracy trade-off instructions.

Subjects first underwent five blocks of practice trials. The practice trials were to familiarize the subjects with the task and to confirm to the subjects that the targets only appeared in positions 2, 4, and 6. Each block consisted of 6 trials, for a total of 30 practice trials. In each block, there were 3 target-present trials. Pretesting indicated that subjects were comfortable with the task after 30 trials. After each block, subjects were asked whether they had any questions and reminded how important it was to be accurate. The instructions and practice trials lasted approximately 15 min. After the 30 practice trials, subjects completed the experimental trials, which consisted of one block of 12 displays. Subjects were then debriefed, thanked, and dismissed.

Stimulus materials. The pictures used for the like–dislike and animate–inanimate judgements were identical to those used in Experiments 2 and 3. Because the experimental design involved both target presence (two levels) and the accessibility of subjects' attitudes toward the to-be-ignored items (also two levels), it was necessary that the number of stimulus displays be a multiple of four. Pretesting indicated that subjects made a disproportionately large number of errors on 3 of the original 18 displays. This limited the potential displays to 15, from which 12 were randomly selected for this experiment. This allowed for three observations in each of the four cells of a 2 (target presence) × 2 (attitude accessibility) matrix. In the initial judgment task, subjects rated only the three distractor items from each of the 12 displays. For half of these items, they performed attitude rehearsal and for the other half the control judgment task.

Results

Latencies for trials on which subjects made errors were excluded from the following analysis. Twelve subjects committed no errors. Each of the remaining subjects made only one error.

The latency data were analyzed using a 2 (sets of objects) × 2 (order of judgments) × 2 (levels of attitude accessibility) × 2 (presence of target) mixed ANOVA. As predicted, the main effect of attitude accessibility was significant, $F(1, 27) = 4.10, p < .05$. When subjects had highly accessible attitudes toward the distractors, they took significantly longer to determine whether the target was present ($M = 2,377$ ms) than when their attitudes toward the distractors were relatively less accessible from memory ($M = 2,300$ ms). As Figure 22.3 shows, this held true whether the target was present or not present in the display. Apparently, the presence of attitude-evoking distractors interfered with subjects' ability to efficiently search the display, indicating that these objects attracted subjects'

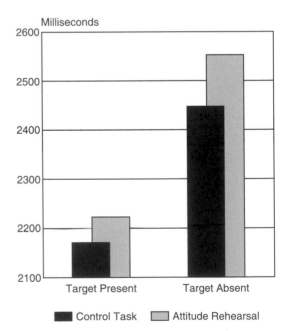

FIGURE 22.3 ■ Mean latencies to respond correctly in the visual search task as a function of whether a target item was present or absent and as a function of whether the distractor items were from the attitude rehearsal task or the control task.

attention—even though subjects were told to ignore those positions.

There also was a main effect of target presence, $F(1, 27) = 46.16$, $p < .001$. As one would expect, subjects were significantly faster to respond when a target was present ($M = 2,197$ ms) than when a target item was not present ($M = 2,442$ ms). This indicates that subjects probably did not search the entire display when a target was present. Rather, they stopped their search and replied that a target was present. No other main effects or interactions were significant.

Discussion

These data further substantiate the results from Experiments 1–3 by demonstrating that objects toward which subjects have highly accessible attitudes inescapably attract attention. Clearly, the situation in this experiment was such that subjects should not attend to the three to-be-ignored positions. Yet, when these off-positions contained distractors toward which subjects had made repeated attitudinal judgments, it took the subjects longer to search the display to determine whether the target was present. This effect occurred for both target-present and target-absent conditions. For the target-present condition, this interference was 54 ms, whereas for the target-absent condition, the attitude-evoking distractors slowed subjects' responses an average of 103 ms.

This experiment also ruled out the possibility that the evidence from the earlier experiments was somehow dependent on memory processes. Although Experiments 1–3 relied on subjects' memory for the objects, that was not the case in this experiment. Even if items characterized by highly accessible attitudes might be easier to remember, it is difficult to understand how the ease of remembering such attitude-evoking objects could explain the results of this experiment. Instead, this experiment lends further credence to the attentional explanation of Experiments 1, 2, and 3.

General Discussion

On the basis of these experiments, it would appear that certain attitudes do, in fact, serve an orienting function. These data indicate that objects that are likely to activate an associated evaluation from memory are themselves more likely to be noticed when presented in a visual display. This was true whether attitude accessibility was measured (Experiment 1) or manipulated (Experiment 2). Furthermore, it appears that this attraction of attention is not based on any intentional strategy that subjects might adopt, as demonstrated in Experiment 3. When the objects were presented as distractors to be ignored, the objects toward which subjects had more accessible attitudes were more likely to be noticed incidentally. Further support for the orienting value of accessible attitudes was found in Experiment 4. When the attitude-evoking items were presented as distractors in a search task, the speed of the search was disrupted. As a result, it can be concluded that objects capable of attitude activation do attract attention and that this attraction of attention appears to be inescapable (Shiffrin & Schneider, 1977).

The present findings provide additional corroboration for Zajonc's (1980) contention that affective responses may precede cognitive responses to a stimulus. The findings indicate that attitudes can exert an influence at a very early stage in an individual's processing of visual information. Apparently, preattentive identification of a visual stimulus can be sufficient to activate an associated evaluation of the object from memory. Such activation serves to direct further attention to the visual stimulus, increasing the likelihood that the stimulus receives sufficient processing for it to be consciously noticed and reported. The data from Experiment 3 further suggest that the more extreme the activated evaluation, the more attention is directed to the object. However, the major conclusion suggested by the four experiments is that the accessibility of the attitude, regardless of whether the evaluation is mild or extreme in its degree of polarization, plays an important role in such an attentional process. Some attitudes, those that involve relatively strong object–evaluation associations in memory, are more likely to be activated in response to the attitude object and, hence, are more likely to orient attention toward the object.

The manipulation of attitude accessibility that was used in Experiments 2–4 merits further discussion. To enhance the strength of object–evaluation associations in memory, we induced subjects to rehearse their attitudes toward some objects. Other objects were seen equally often, but subjects made judgments about whether the object depicted was animate or inanimate. Past research indicates that repeated attitudinal expression enhances the accessibility of the attitude from memory (e.g., Fazio et al., 1982; Powell & Fazio, 1984) and the likelihood that the attitude will be activated from memory on observation of the attitude object (Fazio et al., 1986). Importantly, the data from Experiment 3 established that such repeated attitude expression did not introduce any unanticipated confound concerning the extremity of the resulting attitudes. Repeated expression did not polarize attitudes. However, in the present context, one can raise the question of whether the two tasks that constituted the manipulation differed in their consequences not only for the accessibility of attitudes toward the objects, but also for the accessibility of the objects' memorial representations. In other words, might affective judgments be a deeper process that more effectively primes the object representation than do animate–inanimate judgments (Craik & Tulving, 1975)? Perhaps differential accessibility of the object's representation, as opposed to differential attitude accessibility, influenced the attraction of attention.

A number of observations cast doubt on this possibility. Both attitudinal and animate judgments involve accessing semantic knowledge about the object. Clearly the judgment of whether an object is animate requires consideration of the nature of the object, as does an expression of one's like or dislike of the object. If both judgments involve semantic knowledge, why should affect be considered a deeper judgment?

The difficulty of the initial encoding decision is often viewed as an indication of the depth of processing involved (Craik & Tulving, 1975; Jacoby,

Craik, & Begg, 1979). In terms of this criterion, it does not appear to be the case that the affective judgments were deeper than the animate–inanimate judgments. In a pretest for one of the experiments, we timed 37 subjects as they made the repeated like–dislike versus animate–inanimate judgments of 54 items. Completing the animate–inanimate judgment task took significantly longer ($M = 329.07$ s) than completing the attitude expression task ($M = 300.04$ s), $t(36) = 2.37, p < .05$.

Also, phenomenologically, the subjects found the evaluative judgments to be no more difficult than the animate–inanimate judgments. As part of the cover story for Experiment 2, subjects were asked to rate the difficulty of both the like–dislike and animate–inanimate judgment tasks on a 7-point scale (1 = *extremely easy*; 7 = *extremely difficult*). Not only did no significant difference emerge, but the direction of the means suggested that, if anything, the animate–inanimate judgment was perceived as more difficult ($M = 2.33$) than the like–dislike judgment ($M = 2.06$), $t(32) = 1.47$, $p = .15$.

Together, these decision time and perceived difficulty data suggest that, rather than contributing to the attentional effects that we observed, any difference between the depth of processing involved in the two manipulation tasks, if anything, worked against the hypothesis.

A second reason exists for doubting the alternative possibility regarding differential accessibility of the objects' memorial representations. Although it is evident that making repeated judgments of stimulus materials temporarily increases the accessibility of an object's memorial representation, this activation fades across time, beginning almost immediately after the object has been primed (e.g., Benton & Moscovitch, 1988; Higgins, Bargh, & Lombardi, 1985; Ratcliff, Hockley, & McKoon, 1985). However, in Experiments 2, 3, and 4, the order of the attitude and control judgment tasks was counterbalanced. Furthermore, in Experiments 2–4, there was a 5- to 15-min delay between the judgment tasks and the critical task in the experiment. If priming of object representations were all that was occurring in these experiments, stronger effects of the attitude judgment should have been observed when it was completed last (hence, closer to the experimental trials). But, there were no effects of order of the judgment task in Experiments 2, 3, or 4. Although this argument relies on a null effect, the absence of order effects in three experiments, using three different paradigms, does cast doubt on any alternative interpretation based on the acute accessibility of object representations.

A similar lack of support for an explanation based on differential accessibility of object representations is found in subjects' recognition performance in Experiment 3. If making repeated attitudinal judgments were to have enhanced the acute accessibility of an object's representation more so than making repeated animate-inanimate judgments did, then one might expect recognition for items that had been presented as distractors in the discrimination task to have been affected in a particular way. Subjects might have been expected to mistakenly believe that any greater sense of familiarity with the objects from the attitude rehearsal condition stemmed from their having been presented as distractors. Such reasoning implies that relatively more false alarms might have been observed in the case of objects that had appeared in the attitude task than in the case of those that appeared in the animate–inanimate task. Yet, the proportion of false alarms did not differ as a function of the manipulation. Only correct recognition was affected by the manipulation of attitude accessibility.

Finally, it should be kept in mind that the data from Experiment 1 were consistent with the hypothesis that attitude-evoking objects attract attention and that, in Experiment 1, preexisting attitude accessibility was measured rather than manipulated. Furthermore, familiarity, which, as mentioned earlier, Snodgrass and Vanderwart (1980) defined for their subjects in terms of the frequency of their coming in contact with or thinking about the object, should represent an approximate indication of the chronic accessibility of an object's memorial representation (Bargh, 1989; Higgins, 1989; Higgins, King, & Mavin, 1982). Familiarity was effectively controlled for in Experiment 1 by the arrangement of the stimuli. Within displays containing objects of equivalent

familiarity, those objects associated with greater attitude accessibility were more likely to be noticed and reported. Although it is possible that some other third variable influenced the accessibility of subjects' attitudes and the orienting of subjects' attention, familiarity with the objects is not responsible for the relation that was observed. Thus, the most parsimonious explanation of the results of all four experiments is that attitude accessibility influenced the extent to which the object attracted attention.

It is useful to consider the implications of our findings for theories of attention. Much of the research on attention has been focused on very basic processing of simple features, letters, or digits. By comparison, little research or theorizing has concerned the attentional processing of more complex displays such as those used in these experiments. However, the results of the four experiments seem to indicate that theories of attention need to accommodate such factors as subjects' attitudes toward objects in the visual environment. Attitudes can influence what objects individuals attend to in the environment.

These findings add to an emerging body of literature suggesting that affect is extracted preattentively and influences subsequent perception (see Dixon, 1981; Niedenthal, in press, for reviews). For example, a number of studies have found the presentation of undetectable affective stimuli to have consequences for subsequent perception and judgment (e.g., Greenwald, Klinger, & Liu, 1989; Niedenthal, 1990). Kitayama (1990) has observed that, under certain conditions, briefly displayed words that are affectively charged can be identified more accurately than neutral words. Hansen and Hansen (1988) have obtained evidence suggesting a preattentive processing of faces for features of facial threat (see also Hampton, Purcell, Bersine, Hansen, & Hansen, 1989), and Pratto and John (1991) have provided evidence indicating that attention is automatically directed toward undesirable trait terms. All of these findings point to an important role of affect in attention, perception, and judgment processes.

In some of the research mentioned above, as well as Taylor's (1991) recent review, the specific focus has involved a comparison of positive and negative affect in the interest of testing the proposition that attending to negative stimuli is more adaptive and more critical to the individual's well-being than attending to positive stimuli. The research by Hansen and Hansen (1988) found angry faces to attract attention more so than happy faces. Similarly, the work of Pratto and John (1991) revealed undesirable trait terms to attract attention more so than desirable ones. In this context, it is interesting to note that our findings revealed no such asymmetry favoring negative objects (see footnotes 1–3). However, we also must emphasize that our stimuli were not selected with this specific comparison in mind. A more systematic examination involving carefully equated positive and negative objects may reveal a tendency for individuals to be particularly attentive to negative objects. It also is possible, however, that the person domain constitutes a rather special case. Negative information about other people may be relatively unexpected (Kanouse & Hanson, 1972). Thus, being extra vigilant for, and directing attention to, negative stimulus persons, such as those with threatening facial gestures or those described by negative traits, may be especially adaptive. In the object domain, it may prove just as functional to have attention drawn to those objects from which one can attain desirable outcomes as it is to have attention drawn to those objects that pose the potential for some form of dissatisfaction.

In any case, our specific focus was not a comparison of positive and negative objects, but an examination of the role of attitude accessibility. Regardless of whether people generally display more vigilance for negative objects, our findings indicate that attitude accessibility is relevant to the attraction of attention to both positive and negative objects. We did not find the effect of attitude accessibility to depend on the valence of the individual's judgment of the object.

Conclusion

This research concerned the role that attitudes might play in directing attention among the multi-tude of objects that enter the visual field. Attitudes can be distinguished in terms of their accessibility from memory, that is, their likelihood of being activated automatically from memory on observation of the attitude object. The findings from this series of experiments indicate that, not only can some attitudes be activated automatically from memory on mere presentation of the attitude object, but that these attitude-evoking objects also can attract attention automatically. The extent to which objects within the visual field attract attention depends, at least in part, on the accessibility of one's attitudes toward the objects. If a strongly associated evaluation of an object exists in memory, then that object attracts greater attention.

Consider how functional this orienting value of accessible attitudes can be. As objects enter our visual field, we are likely to notice those that we have personally defined as likable—those that can help us, those that can provide some reward or satisfaction, or, in other words, those that we wish to approach. Likewise, we are likely to notice those objects toward which we have a strongly associated negative evaluation—those that can hurt us, or, in other words, those that we wish to avoid. What a benefit it is then to have strongly categorized one's world into good and bad, likes and dislikes. What we "see" appears to be influenced by these judgments. Accessible attitudes orient our attention to objects that have the potential for hedonic consequences and thus ready us to respond appropriately. In this way, such attitudes can promote an individual's maximizing positive outcomes and minimizing negative ones.

REFERENCES

Bargh, J. A. (1989). Conditional automaticity: Varieties of automatic influence in social perception and cognition. In J. S. Uleman & J. A. Bargh (Eds.), *Unintended thought* (pp. 3–51). New York: Guilford Press.

Benton, S., & Moscovitch, M. (1988). The time course of repetition effects for words and unfamiliar faces. *Journal of Experimental Psychology: General, 117,* 148–160.

Craik, F. I. M., & Tulving, E. (1975). Depth of processing and the retention of words in episodic memory. *Journal of Experimental Psychology: General, 104,* 268–294.

DeBono, K. (1987). Investigating the social-adjustive and value-expressive functions of attitudes: Implications for persuasion processes. *Journal of Personality and Social Psychology, 52,* 279–287.

Dixon, N. F. (1981). *Preconscious processing.* New York: Wiley.

Erdelyi, M. H., & Appelbaum, A. G. (1973). Cognitive masking: The disruptive effect of an emotional stimulus upon the perception of contiguous neutral items. *Bulletin of the Psychonomic Society, 1,* 59–61.

Erdelyi, M. H., & Blumenthal, D. G. (1973). Cognitive masking in rapid sequential processing: The effect of an emotional picture on preceding and succeeding pictures. *Memory and Cognition, 1,* 201–204.

Fazio, R. H. (1989). On the power and functionality of attitudes: The role of attitude accessibility. In A. R. Pratkanis, S. J. Breckler, & A. G. Greenwald (Eds.), *Attitude structure and function* (pp. 153–179). Hillsdale, NJ: Erlbaum.

Fazio, R. H. (1990). A practical guide to the use of response latency in social psychological research. In C. Hendrick & M. S. Clark (Eds.), *Review of personality and social psychology* (Vol. 11, pp. 74–97). Newbury Park, CA: Sage.

Fazio, R. H., Blascovich, J., & Driscoll, D. M. (in press). On the functional value of attitudes: The influence of accessible attitudes upon the ease and quality of decision making. *Personality and Social Psychology Bulletin.*

Fazio, R. H., Chen, J., McDonel, E. C., & Sherman, S. J. (1982). Attitude accessibility, attitude-behavior consistency, and the strength of the object-evaluation association. *Journal of Experimental Social Psychology, 18,* 339–357.

Fazio, R. H., Powell, M. C., & Herr, P. M. (1983). Toward a process model of the attitude-behavior relation: Accessing one's attitude upon mere observation of the attitude object. *Journal of Personality and Social Psychology, 44,* 723–735.

Fazio, R. H., Sanbonmatsu, D. M., Powell, M. C., & Kardes, F. R. (1986). On the automatic activation of attitudes. *Journal of Personality and Social Psychology, 50,* 229–238.

Fazio, R. H., & Williams, C. J. (1986). Attitude accessibility as a moderator of the attitude-perception and attitude-behavior relations: An investigation of the 1984 presidential election. *Journal of Personality and Social Psychology, 51,* 505–514.

Greenwald, A. G., Klinger, M. R., & Liu, T. J. (1989). Unconscious processing of dichoptically masked words. *Memory and Cognition, 17,* 35–47.

Hampton, C., Purcell, D. G., Bersine, L., Hansen, C. H., & Hansen, R. D. (1989). Probing "pop out": Another look at the face-in-the-crowd effect. *Bulletin of the Psychonomic Society, 27,* 563–566.

Hansen, C. F., & Hansen, R. D. (1988). Finding the face in the crowd: An anger superiority effect. *Journal of Personality and Social Psychology, 54,* 917–924.

Herek, G. M. (1987). Can functions be measured? A new perspective on the functional approach to attitudes. *Social Psychology Quarterly, 50,* 285–303.

Higgins, E. T. (1989). Knowledge accessibility and activation: Subjectivity and suffering from unconscious sources. In J.

S. Uleman & J. A. Bargh (Eds.), *Unintended thought* (pp. 75–123). New York: Guilford Press.

Higgins, E. T., Bargh, J. A., & Lombardi, W. (1985). Nature of priming effects on categorization. *Journal of Experimental Psychology: Learning, Memory, and Cognition, 11,* 59–69.

Higgins, E. T., King, G. A., & Mavin, G. H. (1982). Individual construct accessibility and subjective impressions and recall. *Journal of Personality and Social Psychology, 43,* 35–47.

Houston, D. A., & Fazio, R. H. (1989). Biased processing as a function of attitude accessibility: Making objective judgments subjectively. *Social Cognition, 7,* 51–66.

Jacoby, L. L., Craik, F. I. M., & Begg, I. (1979). Effects of decision difficulty on recognition and recall. *Journal of Verbal Learning and Verbal Behavior, 18,* 585–600.

Jamieson, D. W., & Zanna, M. P. (1989). Need for structure in attitude formation and expression. In A. R. Pratkanis, S. J. Breckler, & A. G. Greenwald (Eds.), *Attitude structure and function* (pp. 383–406). Hillsdale, NJ: Erlbaum.

Judd, C. M., & Brauer, M. (in press). Repetition and evaluative extremity. In R. E. Petty & J. A. Krosnick (Eds.), *Attitude strength: Antecedents and consequences.* Hillsdale, NJ: Erlbaum.

Kahneman, D., & Treisman, A. (1984). Changing views of attention and automaticity. In R. Parasuraman & D. R. Davis (Eds.), *Varieties of attention* (pp. 29–61). San Diego, CA: Academic Press.

Kanouse, D. E., & Hanson, L. R. (1972). Negativity in evaluations. In E. E. Jones, D. E. Kanouse, H. H. Kelley, R. E. Nisbett, S. Valins, & B. Weiner (Eds.), *Attribution: Perceiving the causes of behavior* (pp. 47–62). Morristown, NJ: General Learning.

Kitayama, S. (1990). Interaction between affect and cognition in word perception. *Journal of Personality and Social Psychology, 58,* 209–217.

Niedenthal, P. M. (1990). Implicit perception of affective information. *Journal of Experimental Social Psychology, 26,* 505–527.

Niedenthal, P. M. (in press). Affect and social perception: On the psychological validity of rose-colored glasses. In R. Bornstein & T. Pittman (Eds.), *Perception without awareness.* New York: Guilford Press.

Paulhus, D. L., & Levitt, K. (1987). Desirable responding triggered by affect: Automatic egotism? *Journal of Personality and Social Psychology, 52,* 245–259.

Powell, M. C., & Fazio, R. H. (1984). Attitude accessibility as a function of repeated attitude expression. *Personality and Social Psychology Bulletin, 10,* 139–148.

Pratkanis, A. R., Breckler, S. J., & Greenwald, A. G. (1989). *Attitude structure and function.* Hillsdale, NJ: Erlbaum.

Pratto, F., & John, O. P. (1991). Automatic vigilance: The attention-grabbing power of negative social information. *Journal of Personality and Social Psychology, 61,* 380–391.

Ratcliff, R., Hockley, W., & McKoon, G. (1985). Components of activation: Repetition and priming effects in lexical decision and recognition. *Journal of Experimental Psychology: General, 114,* 435–450.

Renninger, K. A., & Wozniak, R. H. (1985). Effect of interest on attentional shift, recognition, and recall in young children. *Developmental Psychology, 21,* 624–632.

Sanbonmatsu, D. M., & Fazio, R. H. (1990). The role of attitudes in memory-based decision making. *Journal of Personality and Social Psychology, 59,* 614–622.

Shavitt, S. (1989). The role of attitude objects in attitude functions. *Journal of Experimental Social Psychology, 26,* 124–148.

Shiffrin, R. M., & Schneider, W. (1977). Controlled and automatic human information processing: Il. Perceptual learning, automatic attending, and a general theory. *Psychological Review, 84,* 127–190.

Smith, M. B., Bruner, J. S., & White, R. W. (1956). *Opinions and personality.* New York: Wiley.

Snodgrass, J. G., & Vanderwart, M. (1980). A standardized set of 280 pictures: Norms for name agreement, image agreement, familiarity, and visual complexity. *Journal of Experimental Psychology: Human Learning and Memory, 6,* 174–215.

Srull, T. K., & Wyer, R. S. (1986). The role of chronic and temporary goals in social information processing. In R. M. Sorrentino & E. T. Higgins (Eds.), *Handbook of motivation and cognition: Foundations of social behavior* (pp. 503–549). New York: Guilford Press.

Taylor, S. E. (1991). Asymmetrical effects of positive and negative events: The mobilization–minimization hypothesis. *Psychological Bulletin, 110,* 67–85.

Wilson, W. R. (1979). Feeling more than we can know: Exposure effects without learning. *Journal of Personality and Social Psychology, 37,* 811–821.

Zajonc, R. B. (1980). Preferences need no inferences. *American Psychologist, 35,* 160–171.

Received September 5, 1991
Revision received December 20, 1991
Accepted January 6, 1992 ■

Selective Exposure: Voter Information Preferences and the Watergate Affair

Paul D. Sweeney* and Kathy L. Gruber*

A survey of political preferences and attitudes conducted during the Senate Watergate hearings of 1973 was used to examine hypotheses developed from selective exposure theory. Three groups of voters—Nixon supporters, McGovern supporters, and undecideds—participated in a three-wave panel survey conducted (a) just before the Watergate hearings started, (b) midway through the hearings, and (c) just before the end of the hearings. Responses that reflected interest in and attention to Watergate-related matters gave support to both the selective approach and avoidance components of the selective exposure hypothesis: The Nixon supporters reported less interest in and attention paid to Watergate-related matters than did members of the other groups. Responses to questions that probed for general knowledge about Watergate committee matters complemented the selective exposure analyses: Nixon supporters appeared to know less about the committee proceedings than the undecideds or McGovern supporters. Finally, analyses of behavioral intentions and evaluations of the attitude object illustrated the importance of studying selective exposure effects. This research is compared with previous studies of selective exposure, and a theoretical speculation about the sequence of modes of reducing inconsistency, which includes a stage analysis of selective exposure, is offered.

*University of Pittsburgh.
The data used in this article were made available by the Inter-University Consortium for Political and Social Research in Pittsburgh. The data were originally collected by John D. Holm. Neither the original collectors of the data nor the Consortium bear any responsibility for the analyses or interpretations presented here.

We would like to thank Victor Benassi, Dieter Frey, Richard Moreland, and Robert Ross for their help.

Requests for reprints should be sent to Paul D. Sweeney, who is now at the Program in Social Psychology, 744 Ballantine Hall, Indiana University, Bloomington, Indiana 47405.

People often apparently choose to pay attention to information that supports their point of view and avoid or give less credence to information that challenges their position. A short discussion of politics with a friend is usually enough to remind most of us of the truth inherent in this statement. The appeal of this "selective exposure" hypothesis has not been overlooked by social psychologists, as evidenced by the fact that it is a component of theories such as social comparison (Fazio, 1979) and cognitive dissonance (Festinger, 1957).

This intuitive appeal by itself is probably largely why one of the first reviews of this literature was both influential and rather devastating. The review concluded that there was little convincing evidence for the selective exposure hypothesis (Freedman & Sears, 1965). Thus the poor empirical showing coupled with our a priori belief in selective exposure was almost a death blow to this literature. Although research on selective exposure declined rather sharply after Freedman and Sears' review, some investigators persevered. A few research reports began to appear that tried to account for why early research was so surprisingly mixed. Several important variables were suggested as mediators of selective exposure effects, including (a) the utility of choosing to attend to potentially disconfirming information (Canon, 1964; Freedman, 1965), (b) the importance of the attitude under study (Clarke & James, 1967), (c) the degree of public commitment to an attitude (Clarke & James, 1967), (d) whether subjects have freely chosen to perform an attitude-relevant behavior (Frey & Wicklund, 1978), and (e) the setting (laboratory or field) in which selective exposure is studied (Katz, 1968).

These later two variables particularly seem to hold great promise for revealing consistent selective exposure effects. The degree of choice exercised by subjects and the setting in which exposure is examined have been relatively neglected. What little research there is, however, suggests that as choice is introduced into the research setting, and as the setting more closely approximates a real one, the more likely it is that selective exposure to information will occur (see Katz, 1968; Frey & Wicklund, 1978). In a recent experiment, for example, it was found that after subjects freely chose to engage in a behavior, they sought out information that would support the choice they made (Frey & Wicklund, 1978). Other results from this experiment also suggest that subjects actively avoided information inconsistent with their expressed behavior.

The results of Frey and Wicklund's (1978) study regarding selective *avoidance*, rather than selective *approach*, seem to be more difficult to find. Indeed, more recent reviews of this literature suggest that although some individual experiments may be open to question, their overall weight seems to establish selective approach to confirming evidence (Wicklund & Brehm, 1976). In contrast, although some data seem to support selective avoidance of disconfirming information (Canon, 1964; Frey, 1981; Frey & Wicklund, 1978; Lowin, 1969; Mills, 1965), the Wicklund and Brehm review suggests that selective avoidance of dissonant information has not been demonstrated conclusively.

There are at least two reasons for the lack of complementarity of approach and avoidance effects in the literature, both of which are related to the degree of choice and research setting variables mentioned earlier. First, investigators in this area have studied attitudes of little importance to subjects. This approach often requires subjects to commit themselves publicly to an attitude, a commitment that they may otherwise not have made (cf. Frey & Wicklund, 1978). Thus, in general, subjects may be less motivated to ardently defend their unimportant attitudes via selective exposure. Together with the data suggesting that subjects normally approach attitude consistent information regardless of its importance (*de facto* exposure; Sears & Whitney, 1973), this low level of motivation might account for the lack of consistency in approach and avoidance results. Thus arousal of dissonance and the more difficult selective avoidance effects may be less likely to occur in situations in which the attitude under study is relatively unimportant.

A second reason for the lack of complementarity between approach and avoidance effects concerns the way in which dissonance (and hence the need to engage in selective exposure) is aroused in subjects. That is, it is noteworthy that the *investigator* often, even in field studies of selective exposure (e.g., Rhine, 1967a), introduces the dissonance-creating event that potentially challenges subjects' attitudes. Although the manipulation of dissonance has clear advantages (such as control and precision), it also has corresponding disadvantages that are relevant to the present argument; for example, not all participants may agree that the investigator's definition of inconsistency is actually dissonance for them. Moreover, the strength of the dissonance-creating event is usually reduced when the investigator introduces such an event into a research setting. Under these circumstances it would be easy, for example, for subjects to attribute a lack of credibility to the source of dissonance arousal (the investigator), thereby reducing any need to engage in selective exposure. This effect, coupled with the data suggesting that subjects engage in de facto exposure, would lead to the observation of approach but not avoidance effects. Thus an explanation of the results found by Wicklund and Brehm (1976) may be tested by investigating selective exposure in a setting in which subjects have freely chosen to express an attitude (cf. Frey & Wicklund, 1978), and in which a powerful dissonance-inducing event is introduced by a relatively credible environmental event.

The present study examines these two factors as they affect selective approach and avoidance. Subjects who freely choose to express a strong attitude are tracked over time as a powerful attitude-relevant event unfolds. In particular, this study represents a three-wave panel survey of political and personal preferences conducted during the period of the Senate Watergate hearings in 1973. Three types of voters, Nixon supporters, McGovern supporters, and a group of undecideds, were identified and their responses to questions regarding approach and avoidance of Watergate-related information were examined. The undecideds were included as a control group. Researchers in selective exposure have generally not included a control group, even though the need for this condition has been recognized for some time (Rhine, 1967b). Rhine (1967b) points out that many of the

problems involved in determining whether a particular reaction represents selective approach or avoidance can be eliminated by including a control group of attitude-neutral subjects. Interviews with all three types of subjects were conducted just before the start of the Watergate hearings, during a break midway through the hearings, and again just before the end of the hearings.

The purpose of Senate Watergate hearings was to examine improprieties surrounding the conduct of the Nixon reelection committee. Eventually, however, the hearings centered on the President's White House staff and the President himself. We reasoned, therefore, that these hearings were likely to cause a substantial amount of dissonance on the part of our Nixon supporters, and hence we expected these participants to show selective *avoidance* of Watergate information, whereas McGovern supporters should show selective *approach* to such information (both relative to the control, or undecided, group). Questions regarding exposure to and knowledge of the Watergate hearings were used to examine these predictions. Finally, evaluations of Nixon's performance in office and subjects' behavioral intentions were also assessed to support the selective exposure analyses.

Method

Subjects

A total of 500 telephone numbers were randomly selected from the Cleveland Metropolitan directory. Of these, 360 subjects were contacted and interviewed 1 or 2 days before the Senate Watergate hearings began (May 15 and 16, 1973). A second interview was conducted during the committee's Memorial Day recess in which 193 subjects of the 360 who completed the first interview participated again. A third interview was conducted after John Dean's testimony (June 30 and July 1, 1973), in which he accused President Nixon of participating in the cover-up of the Watergate affair. In a third telephone interview, 135 subjects were contacted, all of whom had participated in at least one of the prior interviews. A total of 116 subjects participated in all three interviews, and it is from this group that our 82 subjects were chosen. All subjects were contacted by interviewers who received extensive training and who were supervised by the staff of the Institute of Social Research (ISR) at the University of Michigan (Holm, 1976).

Voter Identification Criteria

Three types of voters were identified: Nixon supporters, McGovern supporters, and undecideds. Two questions about voting choices that were asked in the first interview were used to classify subjects. The first question was, "In the last election which candidate did you vote for?" (Nixon, McGovern, and did not vote or do not remember). The second question was, "How do you feel about the outcome of the 1972 election?" (1 = not at all pleased, 2 = somewhat pleased, 3 = very pleased). Subjects who voted for Nixon and were very pleased with the outcome of the 1972 election were identified as Nixon supporters; subjects who voted for McGovern and were not at all pleased with the outcome of the election were identified as McGovern supporters; and those subjects who did not vote or who did not remember their vote were identified as undecideds. Using these criteria, 21 Nixon supporters, 42 McGovern supporters, and 13 undecideds who participated in all three interviews were identified.[1]

These strict identification criteria for Nixon and McGovern supporters were adopted so that a very committed subsample of subjects could be

identified. As research has shown (Wicklund & Brehm, 1976), the greater the commitment to a position, the more cognitive dissonance a person should feel about his or her decision. Thus, if selective exposure to information regarding the Watergate affair is likely to occur, it is this group of highly committed supporters that should show the predicted selective exposure effects.[2]

Results

Selective Exposure Variables

The responses to the selective exposure questions asked at all three survey administrations for the three types of voters are summarized in Table 23.1. A separate 3 × 3 repeated measures, least squares model analysis of variance (Winer, 1971, pp. 402–404) was performed for each selective exposure question.

The first selective exposure question probed the respondents' recent interest in politics: "Thinking back over the past four or five weeks, has your interest in politics been increasing or decreasing?" (1 = decreasing, 2 = neither/about the same, 3 = increasing). The overall sample mean for this question (2.38) was significantly greater than the midpoint of the scale ($Z = 4.75$, $p < .01$), indicating that the subjects' interest was generally increasing. The only significant result to emerge from the analysis of variance on this first question was a main effect

---

[1] It is clear that the ratio of Nixon voters to McGovern voters is much lower than one would expect given the landslide victory by Nixon in the 1972 election. We suspect this ratio is due to this particular sample of voters as well as our selection criteria. First, the sample was collected in a highly Democratic area, Cleveland, Ohio, which could account for a portion of the unexpected reversal in percentages of voters. Second, we suspect that because McGovern supporters were a clear minority, the degree of commitment to their candidate was higher than the commitment of our Nixon supporters to Nixon. Thus, our dual classification criteria was perhaps more likely to identify McGovern than Nixon supporters.

[2] Differential attrition rates among the three types of voters during the survey time period could potentially affect selective exposure responses. To examine this question, we used our selection criteria only for subjects who completed the first survey. We then looked to see if these subjects dropped out at different rates in our three groups across time. Although a fair percentage of subjects dropped out (15%), mostly due to our inability to contact them, this percentage did not differ across voter groups or survey times. Moreover, an identical question posed at all three survey administrations, "Do you mind if we contact you again about this survey?" revealed very high rates of intended compliance overall and no differences among our voter groups. In addition, subjects were not informed about the date and time of potential future interviews. Therefore, the notion that some subjects actively avoided participating (e.g., refusing to answer the phone) seems unlikely.

TABLE 23.1. Means and Standard Deviations for Selective Exposure Variables

| | Selective exposure question | | | | | |
| | Interest in politics | | Personal attention to Watergate | | Frequency of Watergate discussions | |
Type of Voter	M	SD	M	SD	M	SD
Nixon supporters (n = 21)						
Time 1	1.91	0.83	2.19	0.51	1.66	0.58
Time 2	2.38	0.67	2.10	0.70	1.82	0.68
Time 3	1.95	0.81	2.05	0.74	1.75	0.57
Undecideds (n = 13)						
Time 1	2.31	0.75	2.62	0.51	1.65	0.71
Time 2	2.15	0.80	2.31	0.63	1.83	0.75
Time 3	2.31	0.75	2.31	0.63	1.71	0.62
McGovern supporters (n = 48)						
Time 1	2.54	0.68	2.81	0.45	2.32	0.71
Time 2	2.65	0.60	2.68	0.47	2.34	0.70
Time 3	2.48	0.68	2.72	0.50	2.20	0.68

due to type of voter, $F(2, 79) = 6.20$, $p < .003$. Nixon supporters ($M = 2.04$) reported lower recent interest in politics than both the undecideds ($M = 2.26$) and the McGovern supporters ($M = 2.56$). Post hoc comparisons among these three means were conducted using Duncan's multiple-range test (Kirk, 1968, pp. 93–97). These tests revealed that all three means were significantly different from one another ($pS < .05$). No other significant effects emerged from the analysis of variance.

A second selective exposure question assessed attention that was focused more specifically on Watergate-related information: "In keeping up with the news these days, do you find you are paying a great deal of attention to what is going on in the Watergate affair; some attention; or no attention at all?" (1 = none, 2 = some, 3 = a great deal). The overall sample mean for this question (2.52) was also greater than the midpoint of the scale ($Z = 7.43$, $p < .01$), indicating that the general interest level in Watergate was fairly high throughout the hearings. Again, the only significant effect to emerge from the analysis of variance was a main effect due to type of voter, $F(2, 78) = 16.57$, $p <$

$.001$.[3] The Nixon supporters reported the lowest level of attention to Watergate news ($M = 2.11$), the undecideds an intermediate amount of attention ($M = 2.41$), and the McGovern supporters the highest level of attention ($M = 2.68$). Duncan mean comparisons once again revealed that all three groups differed significantly from one another ($ps < .05$). In the responses to the first selective exposure question (measuring personal interest in Watergate), we found similar results.

The previous question dealt with respondents' attention to information over which they had little participation in or contribution to (television news broadcasts). An equally important question is whether the subjects would engage in discussions of Watergate or seek information about Watergate from people that they know. To examine this question, three related questions were asked about how often subjects discussed Watergate with family, friends, and at work: "When you are [with family/

[3] Degrees of freedom change slightly from analysis to analysis due to missing data in one of the three voter categories. In no case, however, were the missing data differentially distributed among the three voter categories.

with friends/at work] these days, would you say
you discuss the Watergate case frequently,
occasionally, or never?" (1 = never, 2 = occasionally, 3 = a great deal). Subjects' responses to these
three questions were averaged to yield an index of
the frequency of Watergate discussion.[4] The overall sample mean for this question (2.01) did not
differ from the midpoint of the scale ($Z = .13$, ns),
indicating that the respondents generally reported
only occasional discussions of the Watergate
affair.

As in the earlier analyses, the only significant
effect that emerged from the analysis of variance
was a main effect due to type of voter, $F(2, 79) =$
10.04, $p < .001$. The Nixon supporters reported
slightly less frequent discussions of Watergate
($M = 1.70$) than did the undecideds ($M = 1.73$),
although both groups reported less discussion than
did the McGovern supporters ($M = 2.25$). Duncan
mean comparisons revealed that although the
means for the Nixon and undecided groups did not
differ, both were significantly lower than the mean
of the McGovern group ($ps < .01$). Thus on one
hand, the Nixon supporters reported relatively
infrequent discussions of the Watergate affair, an
event that almost daily presented information discrepant with their current views. On the other hand,
the McGovern supporters reported frequent discussion of these presumably attitude-consistent
events.

Knowledge About Watergate

If the above results are valid and selective exposure
is occurring, then differences in *knowledge* about
the Watergate affair should be noted among the
three types of voters. Most of the knowledge questions included in this study were asked during the
second and third interview periods, but none were
asked during all three periods. Nevertheless, an
examination of the responses to these knowledge
questions could bolster the previous selective
exposure analyses if consistent patterns of

responses over time are shown among the three
types of voters. The means and standard deviations
for the knowledge of Watergate questions are
shown in Table 23.2.

During the first interview, just before the hearings started, the respondents were asked to "Name
those who have been involved in the Watergate
affair; either by indictment or resignation from an
official position in government." The question was
scored as the number of correct names mentioned.
A one-way least squares analysis of variance performed on these data yielded a nonsignificant
effect due to type of voter, $F(2, 79) = 2.28$, $p <$
.13. Thus although the Nixon supporters ($M =$
2.27) were able to recall fewer names of those
involved in Watergate than were either the undecideds ($M = 2.47$) or the McGovern supporters
($M = 3.27$), the variances of the groups were too
large to yield a significant effect. When the same
question was asked at Time 3, however, a significant effect due to type of voter did emerge, $F(2, 79)$
$= 4.31$, $p < .02$. Again, the Nixon supporters ($M =$
3.17) were generally able to name fewer of those
involved in Watergate than the undecideds ($M =$
3.25) and the McGovern supporters ($M = 4.73$).
Mean comparisons showed that although the
Nixon and undecided groups did not differ, both
were significantly less than the McGovern group
($ps < .01$).

During the second interview, after the hearings
had started, subjects were again probed for their
degree of knowledge about the Watergate hearings:
"Can you tell me the names of the Senators who
are serving on the Watergate hearings committee?"
(responses ranged from 0 to 7 names correctly
mentioned). A one-way analysis of variance
yielded a significant effect, $F(2, 79) = 6.25$, $p <$
.003. The Nixon supporters were able to name very
few ($M = .19$), the undecideds an intermediate
number ($M = 1.09$), and the McGovern supporters
the largest number ($M = 1.69$) of Senators serving
on the committee. Duncan mean comparisons
showed that all three groups differed significantly
from one another ($ps < .01$). Analysis of responses
to an identical question from the third survey
yielded a similar significant effect for type of voter,
$F(2, 79) = 7.55$, $p < .001$. Again, the Nixon

---

[4] Analyses of responses to each of the three individual questions yielded results identical to the results of analysis performed on the following composite measure.

TABLE 23.2. Means and Standard Deviations for Knowledge About Watergate Questions

	Type of voter					
	Nixon supporters (N = 21)		Undecideds (N = 13)		McGovern supporters (N = 48)	
Dependent measure	M	SD	M	SD	M	SD
Name those indicted in the Watergate affair (0–7 correct)						
Time 1	2.28	1.71	2.46	2.51	3.27	1.85
Time 3	3.17	2.32	3.25	2.59	4.73	2.24
Name the senators on the Watergate Committee (0–7 correct)						
Time 2	0.19	0.40	1.08	1.80	1.69	1.88
Time 3	0.81	0.98	2.01	2.48	3.00	2.44
Name those who have testified before the Watergate Committee (0–7 correct)						
Time 2	1.05	0.87	1.39	1.76	2.41	1.73

supporters recalled the fewest number of Senators ($M = 0.81$) relative to the undecideds ($M = 2.01$) and the McGovern supporters ($M = 3.00$). Duncan comparisons once again showed all three groups to be significantly different from one another (*ps* < .01).

A final knowledge question was also asked during the second interview: "Can you tell me the names of persons who have testified before the committee?", with responses ranging from 0 to 7 correct names mentioned. The one-way analysis of variance for this measure also revealed a significant type of voter effect, $F(2, 79) = 6.50, p < .003$. In general the Nixon supporters ($M = 1.05$) could recall fewer of the people who testified before the Watergate committee than could either the undecideds ($M = 1.45$) or the McGovern supporters ($M = 2.41$). Duncan mean comparisons showed all three groups to be significantly different from one another (*ps* < .05). Thus a clear implication emerging on these knowledge-of-Watergate questions was that the Nixon supporters knew considerably less about Watergate-related events than did the McGovern supporters and in most cases knew less than did the undecideds as well.

General Political Interest/Knowledge[5]

The selective exposure and Watergate-related knowledge analyses just presented are predicated on the assumption that the Nixon supporters and McGovern supporters have equivalent levels of characteristic interest in politics and hence are equivalent in their general knowledge of political affairs. If this is not the case, the analyses of Watergate-specific interest and knowledge would be confounded with this general interest level— that is, if Nixon supporters are less interested and knowledgeable about politics in general, then they would not be interested in and would know little about any specific political event (Watergate).

To address this issue, several analyses were performed on measures of general political interest. First, subjects were asked about their characteristic interest in politics: 'Some people are quite interested, while others are not too interested in political affairs. What would you say your level of interest in politics has been the past year?" (1 = not

[5] We thank the editor and an anonymous reviewer for suggesting this section.

much interested, 2 = somewhat interested, 3 = very much interested). A one-way least squares analysis of variance performed on these data revealed a significant effect due to voter type, $F(2, 79) = 3.90$, $p < .02$. McGovern supporters and Nixon supporters ($Ms = 2.46$ and 2.38, respectively) reported a high level of general interest in politics relative to the undecided group ($M = 1.89$). Duncan mean comparisons show that although the means of the McGovern supporters and Nixon supporters did not differ, both were significantly greater than the mean rating of the undecideds ($ps < .05$).

This analysis seems to cast doubt on the notion that less general political interest among Nixon supporters than among McGovern supporters explains the differences in specific political interest presented earlier. A more powerful manipulation check, however, would be an assessment of knowledge of general political events by the two voter groups. Such an analysis would be less susceptible to self-report or motivational biases that may occur in the above general interest question. Unfortunately, the only political knowledge questions asked in this survey were specific to Watergate. We did, however, locate a study (Miller et al., 1979) conducted by the same organization responsible for the Watergate data set (ISR, University of Michigan). This study was conducted using similar data collection and summarization procedures, and it included several general political knowledge questions. An additional advantage of this survey is that the data were collected around the same point in time as this Watergate survey (from 3 to 6 months before this survey), thus making it highly comparable to the main analyses.[6]

Four measures of political knowledge as well as a similar self-report measure of general political interest from the new survey were analyzed. The knowledge questions included (a) How many times can a person be president? (b) How long is the term of a U.S. Senator? (c) How long is the term of a U.S. Congressman? and (d) Which party had the most members in Congress after the last (1972) election? The interest question was identical to the one discussed earlier. The knowledge questions were scored as either *correct* (1) or *incorrect* (0). A general knowledge index was then formed by summing each subject's scores on the four questions; thus the range of the index was from 0 to 4 answers correct. A one-way least squares analysis of variance computed on the general knowledge index showed no reliable differences among groups, $F(2, 801) = 0.86$, *ns*.[7] McGovern supporters ($M = 2.06$) had the lowest mean knowledge scores relative to both the Nixon supporters ($M = 2.16$) and the undecideds ($M = 2.30$), although no difference was reliable.

An analysis of the general interest question from the Miller et al. (1979) survey was also undertaken. An analysis of variance computed on this measure showed a nonsignificant effect due to type of voter, $F(2, 801) = 1.74$, *ns*. The general political interest of Nixon and McGovern supporters was similar ($Ms = 1.80$ and 1.83, respectively), and both means showed higher interest than the undecideds ($M = 1.92$), although the differences were not reliable. In addition, the correlation between general political interest scores and knowledge index scores was computed. The correlation was $-.42$ ($p < .001$),[8] indicating that self-reported interest is a fairly good estimator of true interest and knowledge. Thus, the congruence of the interest and knowledge questions in this new survey suggest that the self-report measure of interest in the Watergate survey is a valid one. In general, then, we are confident that the main selective exposure analyses reported are

---

[6] A hard-bitten skeptic might worry about the possibility that our voter groups in the Watergate survey are different somehow from the national sample just discussed. We should note that although this is a possibility, the comparability and clarity of results in the Watergate survey and the National Election Study (to be discussed) provide empirical evidence contradicting this possibility. Also, the "location-specific" model of political knowledge implied by this concern seems implausible a priori.

[7] No significant differences were found among groups for any of the knowledge items when the items were analyzed individually.

[8] This correlation is negative because of the differences in endpoints of the interest and knowledge questions. Thus, interpreted correctly, the correlation indicates that increasing interest in politics is associated with increasing political knowledge.

TABLE 23.3. Means and Standard Deviations for Behavioral Intention and Evaluation Questions

| Type of voter | Dependent measure | | | | | |
| | Likelihood of voting Republican in upcoming Congressional election | | Do you think Nixon has lost credibility? | | Should Nixon resign office? | |
	M	SD	M	SD	M	SD
Nixon supporters (N = 21)						
Time 1	1.91	0.44	1.21	0.42	1.00	0.00
Time 2	1.91	0.30	1.11	0.32	1.00	0.00
Time 3	1.95	0.38	1.32	0.48	1.00	0.00
Undecideds (N = 13)						
Time 1	2.18	0.60	1.55	0.52	1.45	0.52
Time 2	2.36	0.67	1.64	0.50	1.45	0.52
Time 3	2.55	0.52	1.73	0.47	1.37	0.50
McGovern supporters (N = 48)						
Time 1	2.61	0.49	1.76	0.43	1.67	0.48
Time 2	2.51	0.50	1.79	0.42	1.71	0.46
Time 3	2.40	0.49	1.81	0.40	1.57	0.50

not an artifact of some difference in general political interest or knowledge between Nixon supporters and McGovern supporters.[9]

Effects of Selective Exposure

Perhaps the most important and least investigated aspect of selective exposure is the implication of such biased exposure on attitude-relevant behavior and evaluations. To address this, we analyzed both a measure of intention to vote and several evaluations of Nixon's performance in office. Each of these questions were asked at all three survey administrations. The means and standard deviations for each of these questions are shown in Table 23.3.

First, subjects were asked, "Does the Watergate affair make you more or less likely than before to vote Republican in next year's congressional election?" (1 = more likely, 2 = makes no difference, 3 = less likely). A two-way repeated measures analysis of variance revealed a significant main effect due to type of voter, $F(2, 72) = 15.71$, $p < .001$. These data show that although Nixon supporters ($M = 1.92$) indicated that Watergate would have little effect on their future voting patterns, both the undecideds ($M = 2.36$) and the McGovern supporters ($M = 2.49$) indicated that Watergate clouded their evaluations of Republican politicians in general. Duncan mean comparisons revealed that although the mean of the Nixon group was significantly less than those of both the undecided and McGovern groups ($ps < .01$), the latter two groups did not differ from one another. Although no main effect was noted for the time of survey, an interaction between survey time and type of voter

[9] Yet another way to examine any potential differences in general political knowledge among voter groups was undertaken. Since at least some data show that demographic variables such as education level and income are positively related to political knowledge (Erskine, 1963; Sears, 1969), analysis of such data might reveal deficiencies in general knowledge among groups. If Nixon supporters are comparable or have higher education and income levels than McGovern supporters, we have yet another reason to believe that our Watergate-specific knowledge analyses are not artifactual. The only viable demo-graphic indicator included in the Watergate survey was an assessment of education level on a 1–5 scale (1 = 8th grade or less, 5 = college degree and above). The analysis of variance computed on these data shows no differences among groups, $F(2,81) = 0.41$. Analyses of income and education levels assessed in the larger CPS National Election Study showed that Nixon supporters have significantly higher income levels and equivalent levels of education. Thus, the demographic data give us no reason to believe that Nixon supporters were generally deficient in political knowledge.

emerged from the analysis, $F(4, 144) = 3.26$, $p < .02$. Mean comparisons showed that although the Nixon supporters and McGovern supporters did not change their voting intentions over time, the undecideds clearly became less likely ($p < .05$) to vote Republican as the survey progressed (*M*s for Time 1, Time 2, and Time 3 were 2.18, 2.36, and 2.55, respectively). Thus although the undecideds began to respond more like the McGovern supporters, the Nixon supporters and McGovern supporters remained steadfast in their opinions throughout the survey period.

The subjects were also asked several questions about Nixon's performance during the survey time period. First, subjects were asked, "Some people have said that President Nixon has lost so much credibility that it will be hard for him to be an effective president again. Do you agree or disagree?" (1 = *disagree*, 2 = *agree*). The two-way repeated measures analysis of variance computed on this question revealed only one significant effect, a main effect due to type of voter, $F(2, 69) = 25.42$, $p < .001$. Overall, the Nixon supporters ($M = 1.21$) were less likely to agree that Nixon had lost credibility than either the undecideds ($M = 1.64$) or the McGovern supporters ($M = 1.79$). Duncan mean comparisons revealed that all three groups differed significantly from one another ($ps < .05$). A related but more strongly stated question asked, "Do you think President Nixon should resign?" (1 = *no*, 2 = *yes*). Again, the only significant effect to emerge from the analysis was a main effect due to type of voter, $F(2, 71) = 25.57$, $p < .001$. Nixon supporters unanimously agreed that the President should not resign ($M = 1.00$), whereas the undecideds ($M = 1.42$) and the McGovern supporters ($M = 1.65$) were less in agreement about this question, but they tended more to favor resignation. Duncan mean comparisons revealed that all three groups differed significantly from one another ($ps < .05$).

Although the previous analyses suggest that differential exposure to Watergate-related information affected the respondents' behavioral intentions and evaluations, this analysis is at best indirect. A more direct assessment of the effects of selective exposure could be conducted at the individual level by correlating the exposure ratings with the behavioral intention and evaluation measures over time. Although there are a variety of ways to assess questions of possible causal precedence with correlational data, one technique that is particularly well-suited to our repeated measures design is cross-lag panel correlation (CLPC; Kenny, 1975, 1979; Rogosa, 1980). When properly applied, this test can determine whether the relation between any two variables (e.g., selective exposure and intentions/evaluations) results from the effects of some third, unspecified variable rather than from the effects of either (see Kahle & Berman, 1979, for an example of how CLPC is applied to similar data).

In order to apply CLPC to these data, two composite variables, a selective exposure variable and a behavioral intention/evaluation variable, were created for each of the three survey administrations. These composite variables represented both the average of the three selective exposure responses (see Table 23.1) and the average of the three behavioral intention/evaluation measures, respectively. Although both composite measures are based on relatively few items, a measure of internal consistency, Cronbach's alpha (Cronbach, 1951), revealed that these measures show respectable and about equal reliability (.62 and .58 for the exposure and the intention/evaluation measures, respectively).

As previously discussed, the design of this study allowed for assessments of subjects' responses at three different points in time. This situation is unusual in CLPC designs (cf. Kahle & Berman, 1979; Kenny, 1979) but is very beneficial because it allows one to replicate tests of a particular hypothesis. To test the hypothesis that intentions/evaluations are causally preceded by selective exposure, we first examined only the Time 1 to Time 2 portion of the complete cross-lag panel presented in Figure 23.1. The analysis of interest for this panel was the difference between the two cross-lag correlations [i.e., $r_{selexp_1 * beh_2} - r_{beh_1 * selexp_2}$]. If the difference between these two correlations were itself a significant value, then we would have evidence suggesting that exposure influences the subjects' behavioral intentions/evaluations. Because these two cross-lag correlations were not

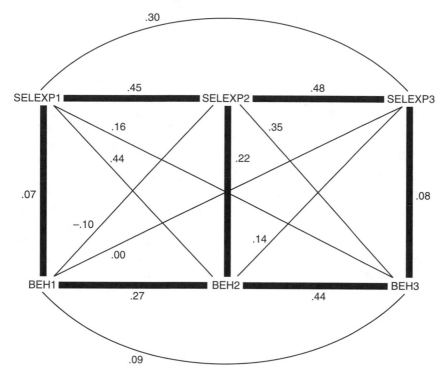

FIGURE 23.1 ■ Cross-lag correlation analysis. (Entries in the figure are Pearson correlations among selective exposure [SELEXP] and behavior [BEH] measures taken at three points in time.)

independent of one another, we applied a Pearson-Filon test so as to test for a significant difference between the two values (cf. Kenny, 1975). The difference between the two composite variables in the first panel was found to be significant ($Z = 4.09, p <$ .001). The difference between the cross-lag correlations when the two variables were assessed at Time 2 and Time 3 was marginally significant ($Z =$ 1.63, $p < $ .06). Finally, the third test of cross-lag correlations performed on the Time 1 to Time 3

panel proved to be nonsignificant ($Z = 1.05, p =$ .14).[10]

In all three cross-lag tests, the difference between the pairs of correlations ($r_{\text{selexp*beh}}$ − $r_{\text{beh*selexp}}$) was in the direction predicted by our rather simple model. That is, the effect of selective exposure on behavior was stronger than the reverse effect of behavior on selective exposure. In two cases we were able to show that this effect was significant. The third replication of this test of our

[10] Before computing significance tests on cross-lag correlation differences, it is necessary to satisfy several assumptions (cf. Kenny, 1975; Rogosa, 1980). The assumption of synchronicity of measurement was satisfied because both variables were assessed at the same time for each panel. The assumption of stationarity (cf. Kenny, 1975, p. 889) is tested by comparing the synchronous correlations. If a significant difference is found, it suggests that the relation between the two variables changes across the measured interval and thus renders any cross-lag comparison ambiguous. Fortunately, however, no significant differences between synchronous correlations were found for any of the three panels (from Time 1 to Time 2, $Z =$

−1.04; from Time 2 to Time 3, $Z = 1.02$; from Time 1 to Time 3, $Z = −0.07$). Finally, the assumption of equality of autocorrelations (cf. Rogosa, 1980) was also satisfied for all three panels (from Time 1 to Time 2, $Z = 1.43$; from Time 2 to Time 3, $Z = 0.38$; from Time 1 to Time 3, $Z = 1.43$). Two of these latter three tests, however, were close to traditional significance levels. We thus recommend that researchers conducting future empirical work specifically designed to test the causal precedence hypothesis via correlation designs should take note of this potential problem. One way to address this differential autocorrelation problem would be to develop highly reliable and valid scales of both measures.

hypothesis (cf. Kenny, 1979) was directional but not significant. Thus, even though this study was not designed to examine the effects of selective exposure, we have provided some preliminary evidence that suggests selective exposure may have an important influence on behavioral intentions and evaluations relevant to the attitude under study.

Discussion

The results of this study add to our understanding of selective exposure effects. We were able to replicate the selective approach results often found by selective exposure researchers (Wicklund & Brehm, 1976). On all of the questions used to assess only selective exposure effects, we found that the McGovern supporters showed the highest approach tendencies; moreover, this finding held in most other cases. Unfortunately, the study did not include questions that would allow us to examine whether the Nixon supporters actively sought out positive information to support their political preferences during the time of the Watergate hearings; that is, we had no information with which to assess their approach tendencies regarding *confirming* information.

The data also provide evidence for the avoidance component of the selective exposure hypothesis. Our Nixon supporters responded as though they were avoiding or paying relatively little attention to Watergate-related events. In all cases the Nixon supporters showed less interest than the McGovern supporters as well as the undecided subjects (although the latter difference was not always significant). Although the mean differences between Nixon and McGovern supporters could be accounted for by explanations other than selective avoidance (e.g., anchoring effects of prior attitudes), the consistently lower ratings given by the Nixon supporters relative to the undecideds are more difficult to account for with these other explanations. Apparently, the special challenge to the beliefs of the Nixon supporters was sufficient to produce the predicted avoidance effects. After all, a respected, bipartisan committee of U.S. Senators was investigating individuals closely associated

with a belief these voters have committed themselves to by overt action. Such a highly credible source was perhaps too difficult to challenge by other less serious and effortful means (e.g., attributions of low credibility to the source; suspected partisanship), leaving little recourse for the cognitive consistency of these committed voters. Selective ignorance of relevant Watergate-related information most likely resulted.

Analyses of the questions regarding knowledge of Watergate information support this conjecture. We reasoned that if selective avoidance of nonsupportive information was actually occurring (instead of response biases or simple partisanship, for example), then we should note differences in the amount of knowledge each group has about Watergate-related events. The results showed that the Nixon supporters evinced less knowledge about Watergate events than did the McGovern supporters and in most cases significantly less did than the undecideds. A priori we would not expect the undecideds to know more about Watergate than either the Nixon or McGovern supporters. After all, these undecided subjects were chosen to reflect a typical nonpartisan, perhaps politically apathetic group of individuals; such people generally pay little attention to political news of any kind. The Nixon supporters, in contrast, are committed voters and are presumably members of that surprisingly small percentage of Americans who do follow political happenings of most kinds relatively closely (Sears, 1969). Thus, the fact that Nixon supporters apparently know less than the undecided subjects in this arena of political affairs gives more credence to our selective avoidance results.

Analyses of the subjects' future voting intentions and evaluations of the attitude object also add validity to our explanation and in turn illustrate the importance of studying selective exposure. That is, although this study was not explicitly designed to examine whether selective exposure *causes* subsequent behavioral intentions and evaluations about Watergate-related objects, we did provide some preliminary evidence for this notion. The cross-lag analyses suggest that selective exposure does seem to have important influences that can be documented. Our data provide at least suggestive evidence that selectivity in information intake may affect subjects' evaluations of political figures and perhaps their intentions to vote for those politicians. The cross-lag analyses presented here are in no way meant to definitively answer the causal questions raised in this article. Indeed, studies that are explicitly designed to test such questions, either experimentally or with other correlational procedures (e.g., combinations of factor analysis and structural equations and other model-testing procedures), are clearly needed to document effects of motivated approach and avoidance of information.

Alternative Interpretations

In some ways the interpretation that these data indicate de facto selective exposure, rather than motivated exposure resulting from dissonance, could be seen as an inviting and more parsimonious explanation. The de facto reasoning makes salient the point that much of what appears to be motivated selectivity is actually an artifact of the disproportionate availability of supportive information in our environment. Republicans, for example, tend to affiliate with other Republicans, to vote Republican, and to be members of Republican-type clubs. Thus, we should not be surprised to find that a great deal of information they process in their daily lives is consistent with a Republican-type philosophy. This conclusion, however, does not imply that such people are actively seeking or avoiding such information; rather it suggests that their lives are constructed such that Republican-type information predominates. Although such a de facto explanation of exposure effects ignores exactly how people become immersed in such an attitude-confirming situation, it explains selective exposure without the need for the more complicated notion of motivated selectivity.

Several important points, however, argue *against* this more simple de facto exposure explanation. The first reason that these data seem to point to motivated selectivity by our subjects has to do with the sheer impact of the Watergate affair upon the American public in that period of 1973. The Watergate affair and hearings were quite simply the biggest news item with the American public in

years, and perhaps ever. There was, in fact, daily 5-hr long network coverage of the Watergate hearings, as well as a high volume of television and newspaper coverage. Thus differential availability of Watergate-related events (de facto exposure) seem intuitively implausible. Of all situations that would create sufficient availability or opportunity for attitude-inconsistent information, Watergate would certainly top the list. And, indeed, Gallup reported that by June of 1973 about 97% of the American public were at least familiar with the incident (Gallup, 1973); this is a figure that lies on the very high end of any political interest or knowledge assessment.

A second finding that also seems to argue against a de facto exposure explanation is the consistent differences reported between the Nixon supporters and the undecideds. Although mere opportunity or usefulness of Watergate information can perhaps explain the differences found between Nixon and McGovern supporters, such an explanation is lacking where the Nixon and undecided subjects are concerned. Undecided subjects would presumably be immersed in their relatively apolitical lives with little reason to increase their interest in political information. These undecideds, therefore, should be exposed to Watergate information relatively rarely if the de facto reasoning is extended. The results, however, suggest that even this group, although politically apathetic, received information about Watergate. These findings strongly suggest that such information was also *available* for processing by the Nixon supporters; we suggest that they selectively scanned their environment, purging that Watergate-related information that may have proven too uncomfortable.

Conclusions

Although previous research seemed to have difficulty documenting selective avoidance effects (Wicklund & Brehm, 1976), our data are clear on this point; moreover, we have suggested that the data go beyond simple demonstration of selective exposure to an illustration of some possible effects of such exposure. Several features of our research methods are worth highlighting in this regard. First, we included as subjects those with rather well-developed attitudes manifested before their participation in our study. Thus we avoided a problem that many previous studies have had to grapple with: that of having to "establish" an attitude before presenting a dissonance-producing event. Such newly created attitudes are necessarily weaker and probably succumb more easily to other dissonance-reducing mechanisms, as in a complete change in attitude. Second, as suggested above, we did not have to devise an event that would potentially challenge subjects' attitudes (and thereby create dissonance). Again, most studies of selective exposure have had to rely on the ingenuity of the particular investigator to devise a plausible scenario whereby subjects' beliefs would be legitimately challenged. Instead we serendipitously took advantage of a highly credible, real-world, dissonance-producing event: the Senate Watergate hearings.

We speculate that avoidance effects are less easily aroused and are thus more elusive than approach effects if weak attitudes are studied in situations in which dissonance is artificially created rather than naturally experienced. Clearly, under most conditions (dissonance inducing or otherwise), subjects "approach" consistent information (cf. Sears & Whitney, 1973; Snyder, 1981); thus it is not surprising that research supports this selective approach prediction (see Wicklund & Brehm, 1976). More of an effort is required of people, however, in cases in which selective avoidance effects are concerned. Considerable effort is often required to avoid attitude-disconfirming information, as in the Watergate case illustrated here. Thus we could conjecture that strength of an attitude situation (e.g., importance of previously held attitude and strength of dissonance-producing event) determines how inconsistency may be resolved via selective exposure effects. Our future research will examine whether the differential approach and avoidance effects can be resolved with this perspective. One could predict, for example, that the first step in attempting to resolve inconsistency would be an approach to consistent information—in a sense, a bolstering of a previously held attitude (Sherman & Gorkin, 1980). A second stage in resolving inconsistency, selective avoidance, may be necessary only when the approach effort is insufficient. As we have argued, the approach component is most likely to be inadequate when a strong and temporally consistent challenge (e.g., the Watergate hearings) is made to one's attitude. A final step in resolving inconsistency for those with strong previously held attitudes would be the reorganization of the attitude under attack. This would probably be a last resort because such a change would likely require modification of many other related attitudes (cf. Judd & Krosnick, 1982; Sherman & Gorkin, 1980).

REFERENCES

Canon, L. K. (1964). Self-confidence and selective exposure to information. In L. Festinger (Ed.), *Conflict, decision, and dissonance* (pp. 83–95). Stanford, CA: Stanford University Press.

Clarke, P., & James, J. (1967). The effects of situation, attitude intensity and personality on information-seeking. *Sociometry, 30,* 235–245.

Cronbach, L. J. (1951). Coefficient alpha and the internal structure of tests. *Psychometrika, 16,* 297–334.

Erskine, H. G. (1963). The polls: Textbook knowledge. *Public Opinion Quarterly, 27,* 133–141.

Fazio, R. (1979). Motives for social comparison: The construction–validation distinction. *Journal of Personality and Social Psychology, 37,* 1683–1698.

Festinger, L. (1957). *A theory of cognitive dissonance.* Stanford, CA: Stanford University Press.

Freedman, J. L. (1965). Confidence, utility, and selective exposure: A partial replication. *Journal of Personality and Social Psychology, 2,* 778–780.

Freedman, J. L., & Sears, D. O. (1965). Selective exposure. In L. Berkowitz (Ed.), *Advances in experimental social psychology* (Vol. 2, pp. 58–97). New York: Academic Press.

Frey, D. (1981). Postdecisional preference for decision-relevant information as a function of the consequence of its source and the degree of familiarity with this information. *Journal of Experimental Social Psychology, 17,* 51–67.

Frey, D., & Wicklund, R. A. (1978). A clarification of selective exposure. *Journal of Experimental Social Psychology, 14,* 132–139.

Gallup Opinion Index (June, 1973). Report No. 96.

Holm, J. D. (1976). *The Watergate hearings panel survey.* Ann Arbor: The University of Michigan Press.

Judd, C. M., & Krosnick, J. A. (1982). Attitude centrality,

organization, and measurement. *Journal of Personality and Social Psychology, 42,* 436–447.

Kahle, L. R., & Berman, J. J. (1979). Attitudes cause behaviors: A cross-lagged panel analysis. *Journal of Personality and Social Psychology, 37,* 315–324.

Katz, E. (1968). On reopening the question of selectivity in exposure to mass communications. In R. P. Abelson, E. Aronson, W. J. McGuire, T. M. Newcomb, M. J. Rosenberg, & P. H. Tannenbaum (Eds.), *Theories of cognitive consistency: A sourcebook* (pp. 788–796). Chicago: Rand McNally, 1968.

Kenny, D. A. (1975). Cross-lagged panel correlation: A test for spuriousness. *Psychological Bulletin, 82,* 887–903.

Kenny, D. A. (1979). *Correlation and causality.* New York: Wiley.

Kirk, R. E. (1968). *Experimental design: Procedures for the behavioral sciences.* Belmont, CA: Brooks-Cole.

Lowin, A. (1969). Further evidence for an approach–avoidance interpretation of selective exposure. *Journal of Experimental Social Psychology, 5,* 265–271.

Miller, W., Miller, A., Brody, R., Dennis, J., Kovenock, D., & Shanks, M. (1979). *The CPS American National Election Study, 1972.* Ann Arbor: The University of Michigan Press.

Mills, J. (1965). Avoidance of dissonant information. *Journal of Personality and Social Psychology, 2,* 589–593.

Rhine, R. J. (1967a). The 1964 presidential election and curves of information seeking and avoiding. *Journal of Personality and Social Psychology, 5,* 416–423.

Rhine, R. J. (1967b). Some problems in dissonance theory research on information selectivity. *Psychological Bulletin, 68,* 21–28.

Rogosa, D. (1980). A critique of cross-lag correlation. *Psychological Bulletin, 88,* 245–258.

Sears, D. O. (1969). Political behavior. In G. Lindsey & E. Aronson (Eds.), *The handbook of social psychology* (Vol. 5, pp. 315–458). Reading, MA: Addison-Wesley.

Sears, D. O., & Whitney, R. E. (1973). *Political persuasion.* Morristown, NJ: General Learning Press.

Sherman, S. J., & Gorkin, L. (1980). Attitude bolstering when behavior is inconsistent with central attitudes. *Journal of Experimental Social Psychology, 16,* 388–403.

Snyder, M. (1981). On the influence of individuals on situations. In N. Cantor & J. F. Kihlstrom (Eds.), *Personality, cognition, and social interaction* (pp. 309–329). Hillsdale, NJ: Erlbaum.

Wicklund, R. A., & Brehm, J. W. (1976). *Perspectives on cognitive dissonance.* Hillsdale, NJ: Erlbaum.

Winer, B. J. (1971). *Statistical principles in experimental design.* New York: McGraw-Hill.

Received September 17, 1982
Revision received September 19, 1983 ■

PART 6

Impact of Attitudes on Behavior

This final set of readings concerns the impact of attitudes on actual, overt behavior. They also provide an opportunity for drawing some connections to a number of the readings that have been assembled in this volume. Hence, while providing an overview of the readings that appear in this section, we will draw readers' attention to various ways in which the articles relate to issues that arose earlier. Essentially, we hope to provide some integrative links.

As we noted in introducing the very first section of this book, the assertion that attitudes guide behavior formed an integral part of many early definitions of attitudes. And, as we argued, the recognition that there need not be any one-to-one correspondence between attitudes and behavior was at least partly responsible for the more contemporary perspectives that do not make this assumption about the attitude–behavior relation as one of the defining features of the attitude concept. Instead, the extent to which attitudes might influence subsequent behavior is approached as a question open to theory and research.

By this point in time, an extensive literature has developed regarding the attitude–behavior relation. In fact, the literature is an excellent illustration of the cumulative nature of social psychology as a science. Theory and research have progressed in a very clear fashion, with later developments building upon earlier advances. In considering this progress, Zanna and Fazio (1982) noted that the field's understanding of attitude–behavior consistency can be viewed as having stemmed from three successive generations of research.

The "Is" question. The first such generation concerned the question: *"Is* there a relation between attitudes and behavior?" Despite the commonly held view, a few early skeptics did take issue with the assumption of attitude–behavior correspondence. The most noted of these was LaPiere, who wrote what became a classic and widely cited article concerning his research on attitude–behavior consistency back in 1934. The article, which is reprinted as Reading 24, concerned LaPiere's documentation of an apparent startling inconsistency between attitudes and behavior. At a time when discrimination against Orientals was not uncommon, LaPiere traveled extensively accompanied by a Chinese couple. During the course of their travels, they visited more than 200 hotels and restaurants and were refused service only once—an acceptance rate that surprised LaPiere. Some six months after having visited any given establishment, LaPiere wrote to each asking if they served Chinese guests. About 92% who responded said no! Thus, the verbal reports about the establishments' policies and the actual behavior exhibited toward LaPiere's companions seemed indicative of strikingly different attitudes toward Orientals. The result led LaPiere to question the very meaning of the verbal responses that are made to a questionnaire.

Just how relevant LaPiere's findings are to the issue of attitude–behavior consistency, and just how convincing they can be viewed, have been a matter of debate (e.g., Dillehay, 1973). For example, the persons who actually waited on the Chinese guests in LaPiere's study may not have been the same ones who responded to the questionnaire. Moreover, when answering the question about serving hypothetical Chinese guests, proprietors may have imagined slovenly unappealing persons instead of the clean, well-dressed and well-mannered individuals who actually entered the establishments. Despite these inadequacies, LaPiere's work was among the very first to question the prevailing assumption of attitude–behavior correspondence and, hence, is often cited in discussions of the topic.

Whether due to its methodological inadequacies or to the sheer plausibility of the argument that attitudes surely determine behavior, LaPiere's early skepticism did not prove very influential at the time. What had considerably more impact was Wicker's (1969) review of the literature. After considering the findings of 31 studies of the attitude–behavior relation, Wicker concluded: "Taken as whole, these studies suggest that it is considerably more likely that attitudes will be unrelated or only slightly related to overt behaviors than that attitudes will be closely related to actions . . . Correlation coefficients relating the two kinds of responses are rarely above .30 and often are near zero" (p. 65).

Wicker's conclusion certainly prompted skepticism about the value of the attitude concept, but it also prompted further research. At least some of these studies observed correlations substantially higher than the .30 ceiling of which Wicker spoke (e.g., Goodmonson & Glaudin, 1971; Seligman et al., 1979). The most striking example may be from the domain of voting behavior. In an analysis of data concerning four different presidential elections, Kelley and Mirer (1974) found that voting behavior could be predicted accurately from pre-election attitudes for some 85% of the respondents. Thus, as Zanna and Fazio (1982) noted, the answer to the "Is" question is a resounding "sometimes."

The "When" question. Given the range of observed outcomes, a second generation of research pursued a different approach to the matter of attitude–behavior consistency. Instead of asking whether attitudes predicted later behavior, researchers began to ask when they might do so. When will the attitude–behavior relation be strong or weak? In its most general form, the question of interest is: "Under what conditions do what kinds of attitudes of what kinds of individuals predict what kinds of behavior?" (Fazio & Zanna, 1981, p. 165).

Just as is implied by that particular wording of the "*When*" question, subsequent research has revealed the strength of the attitude–behavior relation to be moderated by qualities of the situation, the attitude, the individual, and the behavior. Summarizing these various moderating variables is well beyond the scope of the present overview. However, it may be valuable to mention a few variables that link to matters discussed earlier in the volume. Two of the personality variables that have been found to relate to attitude–behavior consistency are ones that received attention in the readings concerning the functions served by attitudes (Part 4). The construct of self-monitoring arose in Snyder and DeBono's consideration of image-based versus quality-based advertisements (Reading 14). Related research has shown low self-monitors, individuals who feel less need to accommodate themselves to the specific pressures of any given situation, to display greater attitude–behavior consistency than high self-monitors (e.g., Snyder & Kendzierski, 1982; Snyder & Swann, 1976). Similarly, the construct of need for cognition played a pivotal role in Petty and Wegener's consideration of the matching hypothesis (Reading 15). This personality variable also has been found to relate to attitude–behavior consistency. Generally speaking, individuals higher in need for cognition—those who enjoy thinking and, hence, tend to elaborate upon their beliefs and attitudes—tend to display greater consistency between

their attitudes and actual behavior (e.g., Cacioppo, Petty, Kao, & Rodriguez, 1986).

A number of additional moderators of the attitude–behavior relation are illustrated in the final three readings reprinted in this section. Reading 25 reprints an article by Lord, Lepper, and Mackie (1984) that relates to one of the criticisms we noted earlier regarding the LaPiere study. We wondered whether LaPiere's Chinese companions were representative of the persons the proprietors were imagining when they answered that their establishment would not accommodate Chinese guests. Lord *et al.* address the relevance of this very matter. Their research demonstrates that attitudes toward a social group are more likely to predict behavior toward a specific member of that group when that individual is prototypical, i.e., when the individual's characteristics match those of the typical group member. The findings lend all the more credence to the possibility that the Chinese couple in LaPiere's study simply did not match the proprietors' prototypes of Chinese and, hence, their attitudes toward Chinese proved irrelevant to their willingness to accommodate these specific, and presumably atypical, Chinese individuals.

Another moderating variable receives some consideration in the article by Ajzen and Fishbein (1973) that is reprinted as Reading 26. In this article, the authors summarize their model of the attitude–behavior relation, and review some relevant empirical research. One of the major tenets of the model relates to the specificity of the behavior in question and the attitude measure that is being used as a predictor. The model maintains that any given specific action is best predicted by an equally specific measure of attitude toward the act in question. Hence, if one is interested in whether a person will attend church services this Sunday, it is best to ask about the person's attitude toward that very specific act, not the person's attitude toward being religious. Subsequent research has shown that such general attitudes are most relevant when the goal is to predict an overall pattern of behavior (e.g., the number of religious behaviors of various sorts performed over the last few months). Thus, the extent to which the attitude and the behavior are measured at an equivalent level of specificity has been identified as a moderator of the attitude–behavior relation (Ajzen & Fishbein, 1977).

Yet another moderating variable—one that concerns a quality of the attitude itself, its accessibility from memory—forms the focus of the article by Fazio and Williams (1986) that is reprinted as Reading 27. Attitude accessibility received attention in earlier readings in this volume. It concerns the likelihood that the attitude will be activated automatically from memory when the individual encounters the attitude object (Reading 2) and impacts the extent to which the attitude proves functional as an aid for decision-making (Reading 17) and orients visual attention (Reading 22). Accessibility is one of the characteristics (along with affective–cognitive consistency, attitude confidence, and others) that give attitudes the "strength" to impact judgments and behavior. This quality of attitudes was examined as a determinant of the relation between attitudes and voting behavior in the present article by Fazio and Williams. Voting behavior was more strongly correlated with the attitudes that respondents expressed early in the presidential campaign within the subsample of participants whose attitudes were characterized by relatively greater accessibility from memory. As we noted in the preceding section when considering the impact of attitudes on judgments, the same moderating

effect of attitude accessibility was apparent for the relation between attitudes toward the presidential candidates and judgments of the candidates' performance during the televised debates.

Thus, research on the *"When"* question has identified a host of variables that determine the extent to which attitude–behavior consistency is observed. The findings make it all the more evident that the relation between attitudes and subsequent behavior can range from nil to nearly perfect.

The "How" question. Researchers have not been content to identify moderating variables. They also have sought to understand why some of these variables exert a moderating impact. Attempts to do so have spurred an even more general question, which Zanna and Fazio (1982) referred to as a third generation question. *How* do attitudes guide behavior? What are the processes by which attitudes influence behavior? The final two readings (26 and 27) actually are representative of broader programs of research that have sought to address this process issue. The Ajzen and Fishbein article details a model that the authors later came to refer to as the *theory of reasoned action* (Ajzen & Fishbein, 1980) and that evolved further into *theory of planned behavior* (Ajzen, 1991). As its name connotes, the model concerns a very deliberative reasoning process in which individuals carefully analyze the potential costs and benefits of engaging in a particular course of action. Decision-makers are presumed to consider their beliefs about the outcomes that will accrue and their evaluations of those outcomes in arriving at an attitude toward the behavioral option. (Note that this accords with the expectancy–value logic that we discussed earlier when considering attitudes as a function of beliefs; see Reading 8.) Attitudes toward the act, and beliefs about the normative expectations of others, influence individuals' intentions to perform or not perform the behavior. In turn, the behavioral intention or plan ultimately determines the behavior, unless some force beyond the individual's control intervenes. A considerable amount of evidence supports the idea that individuals do sometimes make behavioral decisions in this very way. For example, longitudinal research concerning family planning has found that decisions to have a child involve the consideration of beliefs, attitudes, and subjective norms in a manner that is very consistent with the model (Davidson & Jaccard, 1979).

This deliberative process can be contrasted to a much more spontaneous process by which attitudes can guide behavior. According to Fazio's (1986) process model, attitudes can guide behavior even without the individual's conscious deliberation, provided that the attitude is activated automatically from memory when the individual encounters the attitude object. In such a case, the attitude will color perceptions of the attitude object in the immediate situation. (Obviously, this postulate accords well with the research we considered in the previous section concerning the effects of attitudes on perception and the fact that accessible attitudes have this impact more than relatively inaccessible ones.) Biased as they are by the activated attitude, these immediate perceptions of the object will influence whether the person responds in a favorable or unfavorable manner, thus encouraging behavior that is consistent with the automatically activated attitude even though the individual may not have reflected carefully about the behavioral alternatives. By demonstrating the moderating role of attitude accessibility on the attitude–judgment relation, the Fazio and Williams study (Reading

27) provides some support for this process model. Additional support stems from research like that presented in Reading 6. Recall that in this research automatically activated racial attitudes were assessed implicitly. A priming procedure provided an estimate of the attitude automatically activated by the presentation of photos of African-Americans. These estimates proved predictive of how friendly the participant later acted in an interaction with an African-American. Presumably, the participants did not reason, deliberate, and decide to act warmly or coldly. Nevertheless, their relatively spontaneous behaviors—smiling, eye contact, tone of voice, body language, and the like—appear to have been influenced by their automatically activated racial attitudes.

The obvious question that next arises concerns the variables that will promote a spontaneous attitude-to-behavior process, a more deliberative one, or some combination of the two. This very concern is the focus of the *MODE model* (Fazio, 1990). MODE stands for Motivation and Opportunity as DEterminants of the attitude-to-behavior process. The model maintains that a deliberative process is necessarily effortful and, hence, requires that the individual be both motivated to engage in the effortful reasoning and have the opportunity to do so (i.e., have the time and the resources to deliberate). Given sufficient motivation and opportunity, individuals carefully consider the specific characteristics of the behavioral alternatives and construct attitudes regarding the specific options (Sanbonmatsu & Fazio, 1990). When either motivation or opportunity is lacking, however, individuals' decisions are more likely to be influenced not by a detailed consideration of the facts, but by any relevant and accessible attitudes they might possess. Spontaneous behaviors, like those involved in the tone of the interaction with the African-American target in the implicit measure study, are especially likely to be influenced by any automatically activated attitudes.

The MODE model also maintains that processes involving a mixture of spontaneous and deliberative elements can sometimes occur. With sufficient motivation, individuals may wish to correct for the influence of their automatically activated attitudes, and with sufficient opportunity they may succeed in doing so. This aspect of the MODE model also received some consideration in Reading 6. When completing a questionnaire that inquired very explicitly about their racial attitudes, individuals with a strong motivation to control prejudiced reactions showed evidence of correcting for their automatically activated negativity toward African-Americans. They presented themselves as much more favorable than did individuals with equally negative attitudes who lacked such motivation. Thus, verbal behaviors (responses to a questionnaire) were jointly determined by automatically activated racial attitudes and motivation to control prejudiced reactions.

Additional information about the MODE model and related research is available in some of the suggested readings.

REFERENCES

Ajzen, I. (1991). The theory of planned behavior. *Organizational Behavior and Human Decision Processes*, *50*, 179–211.

Ajzen, I., & Fishbein, M. (1977). Attitude–behavior relations: A theoretical analysis and review of empirical research. *Psychological Bulletin*, *84*, 888–918.

Ajzen, I., & Fishbein, M. (1980). *Understanding attitudes and predicting social behavior*. Englewood Cliffs, NJ: Prentice Hall.

Cacioppo, J. T., Petty, R. E., Kao, C. F., & Rodriguez, R. (1986). Central and peripheral routes to persuasion: An individual difference perspective. *Journal of Personality and Social Psychology*, *51*, 1032–1043.

Davidson, A. R., & Jaccard, J. J. (1979). Variables that moderate the attitude–behavior relation: Results of a longitudinal survey. *Journal of Personality and Social Psychology*, *37*, 1364–1376.

Dillehay, R. C. (1973). On the irrelevance of the classical negative evidence concerning the effect of attitudes on behavior. *American Psychologist*, *28*, 887–891.

Fazio, R. H. (1986). How do attitudes guide behavior? In R. M. Sorrentino & E. T. Higgins (Eds.), *The Handbook of motivation and cognition: Foundations of social behavior* (pp. 204–243). New York: Guilford Press.

Fazio, R. H. (1990). Multiple processes by which attitudes guide behavior: The MODE model as an integrative framework. In M. P. Zanna (Ed.), *Advances in experimental social psychology* (Vol. 23, pp. 75–109). New York: Academic Press.

Goodmonson, C., & Glaudin, V. (1971). The relationship of commitment-free behavior and commitment behavior: A study of attitude toward organ transplantation. *Journal of Social Issues*, *27*, 171–183.

Kelley, S., & Mirer, T. W. (1974). The simple act of voting. *American Political Science Review*, *68*, 572–591.

Sanbonmatsu, D. M., & Fazio, R. H. (1990). The role of attitudes in memory-based decision making. *Journal of Personality and Social Psychology*, *59*, 614–622.

Seligman, C., Kriss, M., Darley, J. M., Fazio, R. H., Becker, L. J., & Pryor, J. B. (1979). Predicting summer energy consumption from home-owners' attitudes. *Journal of Applied Social Psychology*, *9*, 70–90.

Snyder, M., & Kendzierski, D. (1982). Acting on one's attitude: Procedures for linking attitude and behavior. *Journal of Experimental Social Psychology*, *18*, 165–183.

Snyder, M., & Swann, W. B. (1976). When actions reflect attitudes: The politics of impression management. *Journal of Personality and Social Psychology*, *34*, 1034–1042.

Wicker, A. W. (1969). Attitudes versus actions: The relationship of verbal and overt behavioral responses to attitude objects. *Journal of Social Issues*, *25*, 41–78.

Zanna, M. P., & Fazio, R. H. (1982). The attitude-behavior relation: Moving toward a third generation of research. In M. P. Zanna, E. T. Higgins, & C. P. Herman (Eds.), *Consistency in social behavior: The Ontario symposium* (Vol. 2, pp. 283–301). Hillsdale, NJ: Erlbaum.

Suggested Readings

Dovidio, J. F., Kawakami, K., Johnson, C., Johnson, B., & Howard, A. (1997). On the nature of prejudice: Automatic and controlled processes. *Journal of Experimental Social Psychology*, *33*, 510–540.

Fazio, R. H., & Towles-Schwen, T. (1999). The MODE model of attitude–behavior processes. In S. Chaiken & Y. Trope (Eds.), *Dual process theories in social psychology* (pp. 97–116). New York: Guilford.

Fazio, R. H., & Roskos-Ewoldsen, D. R. (2005). Acting as we feel: When and how attitudes guide behavior. In T. C. Brock & M. C. Green (Eds.), *Persuasion: Psychological insights and perspectives* (2nd edition, pp. 41–62). Thousand Oaks, CA: Sage.

Maddux, W. W., Barden, J., Brewer, M. B., & Petty, R. E. (2005). Saying no to negativity: The effects of context and motivation to control prejudice on automatic evaluative responses. *Journal of Experimental Social Psychology*, *41*, 19–35.

Petty, R. E., & Krosnick, J. A. (Eds.) (1995). *Attitude strength: Antecedents and consequences*. Hillsdale, NJ: Erlbaum.

Sivacek, J., & Crano, W. D. (1982). Vested interest as a moderator of attitude–behavior consistency. *Journal of Personality and Social Psychology*, *43*, 210–221.

Attitudes vs. Actions

Richard T. LaPiere*

By definition, a social attitude is a behaviour pattern, anticipatory set or tendency, predisposition to specific adjustment to designated social situations, or, more simply, a conditioned response to social stimuli.[1] Terminological usage differs, but students who have concerned themselves with attitudes apparently agree that they are acquired out of social experience and provide the individual organism with some degree of preparation to adjust, in a well-defined way, to certain types of social situations if and when these situations arise. It would seem, therefore, that the totality of the social attitudes of a single individual would include all his socially acquired personality which is involved in the making of adjustments to other human beings.

But by derivation social attitudes are seldom more than a verbal response to a symbolic situation. For the conventional method of measuring social attitudes is to ask questions (usually in writing) which demand a verbal adjustment to an entirely symbolic situation. Because it is easy, cheap, and mechanical, the attitudinal questionnaire is rapidly becoming a major method of sociological and socio-psychological investigation. The technique is simple. Thus from a hundred or a thousand responses to the question "Would you get up to give an Armenian woman your seat in a street car?" the investigator derives the "attitude" of non-Armenian males towards Armenian females. Now the question may be constructed with elaborate skill and hidden with consummate cunning in a maze of supplementary or even irrelevant questions yet all that has been obtained is a symbolic response to a symbolic situation. The words "Armenian woman" do not constitute an Armenian woman of flesh and blood, who might be tall or squat, fat or thin, old or young, well or poorly dressed—who might, in fact, be a goddess or just another old and dirty hag. And the questionnaire response, whether it be "yes" or "no," is but a verbal reaction and this does not involve rising from the seat or stolidly avoiding the hurt eyes of the hypothetical woman and the derogatory states of other street-car occupants. Yet, ignoring these limitations, the diligent investigator will jump briskly from his factual evidence to the unwarranted conclusion that he has measured the "anticipatory behavior patterns" of non-Armenian males towards Armenian females encountered on street cars. Usually he does not stop here, but proceeds to deduce certain general conclusions regarding the social relationships between Armenians and non-Armenians. Most of us have applied the questionnaire technique with greater caution, but not I fear with any greater certainty of success.

Some years ago I endeavored to obtain comparative data on the degree of French and English

---

* Stanford University.
[1] See Daniel D. Droba, "Topical Summaries of Current Literature," *The American Journal of Sociology*, 1934, p. 513.

antipathy towards dark-skinned peoples.[2] The informal questionnaire technique was used, but, although the responses so obtained were exceedingly consistent, I supplemented them with what I then considered an index to overt behavior. The hypothesis as then stated *seemed* entirely logical. "Whatever our attitude on the validity of 'verbalization' may be, it must be recognized that any study of attitudes through direct questioning is open to serious objection, both because of the limitations of the sampling method and because in classifying attitudes the inaccuracy of human judgment is an inevitable variable. In this study, however, there is corroborating evidence on these attitudes in the policies adopted by hotel proprietors. Nothing could be used as a more accurate index of color prejudice than the admission or non-admission of colored people to hotels. For the proprietor must reflect the group attitude in his policy regardless of his own feelings in the matter. Since he determines what the group attitude is towards Negroes through the expression of that attitude in overt behavior and over a long period of actual experience, the results will be exceptionally free from those disturbing factors which inevitably affect the effort to study attitudes by direct questioning."

But at that time I overlooked the fact that what I was obtaining from the hotel proprietors was still a "verbalized" reaction to a symbolic situation. The response to a Negro's request for lodgings might have been an excellent index of the attitude of hotel patrons towards living in the same hotel as a Negro. Yet to ask the proprietor "Do you permit members of the Negro race to stay here?" does not, it appears, measure his potential response to an actual Negro.

All measurement of attitudes by the questionnaire technique proceeds on the assumption that there is a mechanical relationship between symbolic and nonsymbolic behavior. It is simple enough to prove that there is no *necessary* correlation between speech and action, between response to words and to the realities they symbolize. A parrot can be taught to swear, a child to sing "Frankie and Johnny" in the Mae West manner. The words will have no meaning to either child or parrot. But to prove that there is no *necessary* relationship does not prove that such a relationship may not exist. There need be no relationship between what the hotel proprietor says he will do and what he actually does when confonted with a colored patron. Yet there may be. Certainly we are justified in assuming that the verbal response of the hotel proprietor would be more likely to indicate what he would actually do than would the verbal response of people whose personal feelings are less subordinated to economic expediency. However, the following study indicates that the reliability of even such responses is very small indeed.

Beginning in 1930 and continuing for two years thereafter, I had the good fortune to travel rather extensively with a young Chinese student and his wife.[3] Both were personable, charming, and quick to win the admiration and respect of those they had the opportunity to become intimate with. But they were foreign-born Chinese, a fact that could not be disguised. Knowing the general "attitude" of Americans towards the Chinese as indicated by the "social distance" studies which have been made, it was with considerable trepidation that I first approached a hotel clerk in their company. Perhaps that clerk's eyebrows lifted slightly, but he accommodated us without a show of hesitation. And this in the "best" hotel in a small town noted for its narrow and bigoted "attitude" towards Orientals. Two months later I passed that way again, phoned the hotel and asked if they would accommodate "an important Chinese gentleman." The reply was an unequivocal "No." That aroused my curiosity and led to this study.

In something like ten thousand miles of motor travel, twice across the United States, up and down the Pacific Coast, we met definite rejection from those asked to serve us just once. We were received at 66 hotels, auto camps, and "Tourist Homes,"

---

[2] "Race Prejudice: France and England," *Social Forces*, September, 1928, pp. 102–111.

[3] The results of this study have been withheld until the present time out of consideration for their feelings.

refused at one. We were served in 184 restaurants and cafes scattered throughout the country and treated with what I judged to be more than ordinary consideration in 72 of them. Accurate and detailed records were kept of all these instances. An effort, necessarily subjective, was made to evaluate the overt response of hotel clerks, bell boys, elevator operators, and waitresses to the presence of my Chinese friends. The factors entering into the situations were varied as far and as often as possible. Control was not, of course, as exacting as that required by laboratory experimentation. But it was as rigid as is humanly possible in human situations. For example, I did not take the "test" subjects into my confidence fearing that their behavior might become self-conscious and thus abnormally affect the response of others towards them. Whenever possible I let my Chinese friend negotiate for accommodations (while I concerned myself with the car or luggage) or sent them into a restaurant ahead of me. In this way I attempted to "factor" myself out. We sometimes patronized high-class establishments after a hard and dusty day on the road and stopped at inferior auto camps when in our most presentable condition.

In the end I was forced to conclude that those factors which most influenced the behavior of others towards the Chinese had nothing at all to do with race. Quality and condition of clothing, appearance of baggage (by which, it seems, hotel clerks are prone to base their quick evaluations), cleanliness and neatness were far more significant for person to person reaction in the situations I was studying than skin pigmentation, straight black hair, slanting eyes, and flat noses. And yet an air of self-confidence might entirely offset the "unfavorable" impression made by dusty clothes and the usual disorder to appearance consequent upon some hundred miles of motor travel. A supercilious desk clerk in a hotel of noble aspirations could not refuse his master's hospitality to people who appeared to take their request as a perfectly normal and conventional thing, though they might look like tin-can tourists and two of them belong to the racial category "Oriental." On the other hand, I became rather adept at approaching hotel clerks with that peculiar crab-wise manner which is so

effective in provoking a somewhat scornful disregard. And then a bland smile would serve to reverse the entire situation. Indeed, it appeared that a genial smile was the most effective password to acceptance. My Chinese friends were skillful smilers, which may account, in part, for the fact that we received but one rebuff in all our experience. Finally, I was impressed with the fact that even where some tension developed due to the strangeness of the Chinese it would evaporate immediately when they spoke in unaccented English.

The one instance in which we were refused accommodations is worth recording here. The place was a small California town, a rather inferior auto-camp into which we drove in a very dilapidated car piled with camp equipment. It was early evening, the light so dim that the proprietor found it somewhat difficult to decide the genus *voyageur* to which we belonged. I left the car and spoke to him. He hesitated, wavered, said he was not sure that he had two cabins, meanwhile edging towards our car. The realization that the two occupants were Orientals turned the balance or, more likely, gave him the excuse he was looking for. "No," he said, "I don't take Japs!" In a more pretentious establishment we secured accommodations, and with an extra flourish of hospitality.

To offset this one flat refusal were the many instances in which the physical peculiarities of the Chinese served to heighten curiosity. With few exceptions this curiosity was considerably hidden behind an exceptional interest in serving us. Of course, outside of the Pacific Coast region, New York, and Chicago, the Chinese physiognomy attracts attention. It is different, hence noticeable. But the principal effect this curiosity has upon the behavior of those who cater to the traveler's needs is to make them more attentive, more responsive, more reliable. A Chinese companion is to be recommended to the white traveling in his native land. Strange features when combined with "human" speech and action seems, at times, to heighten sympathetic response, perhaps on the same principle that makes us uncommonly sympathetic towards the dog that has a "human" expression in his face.

What I am trying to say is that in only one out of 251 instances in which we purchased goods or services necessitating intimate human relationships did the fact that my companions were Chinese adversely affect us. Factors entirely unassociated with race were, in the main, the determinant of significant variations in our reception. It would appear reasonable to conclude that the "attitude" of the American people, as reflected in the behavior of those who are for pecuniary reasons presumably most sensitive to the antipathies of their white clientele, is anything but negative towards the Chinese. In terms of "social distance" we might conclude that native Caucasians are not averse to residing in the same hotels, auto-camps, and "Tourist Homes" as Chinese and will with complacency accept the presence of Chinese at an adjoining table in restaurant or cafe. It does not follow that there is revealed a distinctly "positive" attitude towards the Chinese, that whites prefer the Chinese to other whites. But the facts as gathered certainly preclude the conclusion that there is an intense prejudice towards the Chinese.

Yet the existence of this prejudice, very intense, is proven by a conventional "attitude" study. To provide a comparison of symbolic reaction to symbolic social situations with actual reaction to real social situations, I "questionnaired" the establishments which we patronized during the two year period. Six months were permitted to lapse between the time I obtained the overt reaction and the symbolic. It was hoped that the effects of the actual experience with Chinese guests, adverse or otherwise, would have faded during the intervening time. To the hotel or restaurant a questionnaire was mailed with an accompanying letter purporting to be a special and personal plea for response. The questionnaires all asked the same question, "Will you accept members of the Chinese race as guests in your establishment?" Two types of questionnaire were used. In one this question was inserted among similar queries concerning Germans, French, Japanese, Russians, Armenians, Jews, Negroes, Italians, and Indians. In the other the pertinent question was unencumbered. With persistence, completed replies were obtained from 128 of the establishments we had visited; 81

restaurants and cafes and 47 hotels, auto-camps, and "Tourist Homes." In response to the relevant question 92 per cent of the former and 91 per cent of the latter replied "No." The remainder replied "Uncertain; depend upon circumstances." From the woman proprietor of a small auto-camp I received the only "Yes," accompanied by a chatty letter describing the nice visit she had had with a Chinese gentleman and his sweet wife during the previous summer.

A rather unflattering interpretation might be put upon the fact that those establishments who had provided for our needs so graciously were, some months later, verbally antagonistic towards hypothetical Chinese. To factor this experience out responses were secured from 32 hotels and 96 restaurants located in approximately the same regions, but uninfluenced by this particular experience with Oriental clients. In this, as in the former case, both types of questionnaires were used. The results indicate that neither the type of questionnaire nor the fact of previous experience had important bearing upon the symbolic response to symbolic social situations.

It is impossible to make direct comparison between the reactions secured through questionnaires and from actual experience. On the basis of the above data it would appear foolhardy for a Chinese to attempt to travel in the United States. And yet, as I have shown, actual experience indicates that the American people, as represented by the personnel of hotels, restaurants, etc., are not at all averse to fraternizing with Chinese within the limitations which apply to social relationships between Americans themselves. The evaluations which follow are undoubtedly subject to the criticism which any human judgment must withstand. But the fact is that, although they began their travels in this country with considerable trepidation, my Chinese friends soon lost all fear that they might receive a rebuff. At first somewhat timid and considerably dependent upon me for guidance and support, they came in time to feel fully self-reliant and would approach new social situations without the slightest hesitation.

The conventional questionnaire undoubtedly has significant value for the measurement of "political

TABLE 24.1. Distribution of Results from Questionnaire Study of Establishment "Policy" Regarding Acceptance of Chinese as Guests (Replies are to the Question: "Will you Accept Members of the Chinese Race as Guests in your Establishment?")

	Hotels, etc., visited		Hotels, etc., not visited		Restaurants, etc., visited		Restaurants, etc., not visited	
Total	47		32		81		96	
	1[a]	2[a]	1	2	1	2	1	2
Number replying	22	25	20	12	43	38	51	45
No	20	23	19	11	40	35	37	41
Undecided: depend upon circumstances	1	2	1	1	3	3	4	3
Yes	1	0	0	0	0	0	0	1

[a] Column (1) indicates in each case those responses to questionnaires which concerned Chinese only. The figures in columns (2) are from the questionnaires in which the above was inserted among questions regarding Germans, French, Japanese, etc.

attitudes." The presidential polls conducted by the *Literary Digest* have proven that. But a "political attitude" is exactly what the questionnaire can be justly held to measure; a verbal response to a symbolic situation. Few citizens are ever faced with the necessity of adjusting themselves to the presence of the political leaders whom, periodically, they must vote for—or against. Especially is this true with regard to the president, and it is in relation to political attitudes towards presidential candidates that we have our best evidence. But while the questionnaire may indicate what the voter will do when he goes to vote, it does not and cannot reveal what he will do when he meets Candidate Jones on the street, in his office, at his club, on the golf course, or wherever two men may meet and adjust in some way one to the other.

The questionnaire is probably our only means of determining "religious attitudes." An honest answer to the question "Do you believe in God?" reveals all there is to be measured. "God" is a symbol; "belief" a verbal expression. So here, too, the questionnaire is efficacious. But if we would know the emotional responsiveness of a person to the spoken or written word "God" some other method of investigation must be used. And if we would know the extent to which that responsiveness restrains his behavior it is to his behavior that we must look, not to his questionnaire response. Ethical precepts are, I judge, something more than verbal professions. There would seem little to be

gained from asking a man if his religious faith prevents him from committing sin. Of course it does—on paper. But "moral attitudes" must have a significance in the adjustment to actual situations or they are not worth the studying. Sitting at my desk in California I can predict with a high degree of certainty what an "average" business man in an average Mid-Western city will reply to the question "Would you engage in sexual intercourse with a prostitute in a Paris brothel?" Yet no one, least of all the man himself, can predict what he would actually do should he by some misfortune find himself face to face with the situation in question. His moral "attitudes" are no doubt already stamped into his personality. But just what those habits are which will be invoked to provide him with some sort of adjustment to this situation is quite indeterminate.

It is highly probable that when the "Southern Gentleman" says he will not permit Negroes to reside in his neighborhood we have a verbal response to a symbolic situation which reflects the "attitudes" which would become operative in an actual situation. But there is no need to ask such a question of the true "Southern Gentleman." We knew it all the time. I am inclined to think that in most instances where the questionnaire does reveal non-symbolic attitudes the case is much the same. It is only when we cannot easily observe what people do in certain types of situations that the questionnaire is resorted to. But it is just here that the

TABLE 24.2. Distribution of Results Obtained from Actual Experience in the Situation Symbolized in the Questionnaire Study

	Hotels, etc.		Restaurants, etc.	
	Accompanied by investigator	Chinese not so accompanied at inception of situation[a]	Accompanied by investigator	Chinese not so accompanied at inception of situation
Total	55	12	165	19
Reception very much better than investigator would expect to have received had he been alone, but under otherwise similar circumstances	19	6	63	9
Reception different only to extent of heightened curiosity, such as investigator might have incurred were he alone but dressed in manner unconventional to region yet not incongruous	22	3	76	6
Reception "normal"	9	2	21	3
Reception perceptibly hesitant and not to be explained on other than "racial" grounds	3	1	4	1
Reception definitely, though temporarily, embarrassing	1	0	1	0
Not accepted	1	0	0	0

[a] When the investigator was not present at the inception of the situation the judgments were based upon what transpired after he joined the Chinese. Since intimately acquainted with them it is probable that errors in judgment were no more frequent under these conditions than when he was able to witness the inception as well as results of the situation.

danger in the questionnaire technique arises. If Mr. A adjusts himself to Mr. B in a specified way we can deduce from his behavior that he has a certain "attitude" towards Mr. B and, perhaps, all of Mr. B's class. But if no such overt adjustment is made it is impossible to discover what A's adjustment would be should the situation arise. A questionnaire will reveal what Mr. A writes or says when confronted with a certain combination of words. But not what he will do when he meets Mr. B. Mr. B is a great deal more than a series of words. He is a man and he acts. His action is not necessarily what Mr. A. "imagines" it will be when he reacts verbally to the symbol "Mr. B."

No doubt a considerable part of the data which the social scientist deals with can be obtained by the questionnaire method. The census reports are based upon verbal questionnaires and I do not doubt their basic integrity. If we wish to know how many children a man has, his income, the size of

his home, his age, and the condition of his parents, we can reasonably ask him. These things he has frequently and conventionally converted into verbal responses. He is competent to report upon them, and will do so accurately, unless indeed he wishes to do otherwise. A careful investigator could no doubt even find out by verbal means whether the man fights with his wife (frequently, infrequently, or not at all), though the neighbors would be a more reliable source. But we should not expect to obtain by the questionnaire method his "anticipatory set or tendency" to action should his wife pack up and go home to Mother, should Elder Son get into trouble with the neighbor's daughter, the President assume the status of a dictator, the Japanese take over the rest of China, or a Chinese gentleman come to pay a social call.

Only a verbal reaction to an entirely symbolic situation can be secured by the questionnaire. It may indicate what the responder would actually do when confronted with the situation symbolized in the question, but there is no assurance that it will. And so to call the response a reflection of a "social attitude" is to entirely disregard the definition commonly given for the phrase "attitude." If social attitudes are to be conceptualized as partially integrated habit sets which will become operative under specific circumstances and lead to a particular pattern of adjustment they must, in the main, be derived from a study of humans behaving in actual social situations. They must not be imputed on the basis of questionnaire data.

The questionnaire is cheap, easy, and mechanical. The study of human behavior is time consuming, intellectually fatiguing, and depends for its success upon the ability of the investigator. The former method gives quantitative results, the latter mainly qualitative. Quantitative measurements are quantitatively accurate; qualitative evaluations are always subject to the errors of human judgment. Yet it would seem far more worth while to make a shrewd guess regarding that which is essential than to accurately measure that which is likely to prove quite irrelevant.

Attitude Prototypes as Determinants of Attitude-Behavior Consistency

Charles G. Lord,* Mark R. Lepper,** and Diane Mackie*

This article addresses the questions of when we can predict from an individual's attitude toward a social group to the individual's behavior toward a specific member of that group. One possibility is that individuals determine their attitudes toward a social group by assessing their reactions to an imagined group representative who embodies the defining or central group characteristics—the prototypical group member. When they encounter a specific group member whose characteristics match well those of the "attitude prototype," individuals display attitude–behavior consistency; when the match is poor, they display attitude–behavior inconsistency. This proposition was tested in two experiments, and in each the attitude–behavior relationship was greater in relation to prototypical than to unprototypical group members. In addition, knowledge of an unprototypical group member had little or no effect on attitude prototypes. Rather, the unprototypical group member was dismissed as atypical, leaving the prototype intact to influence future social behavior. The implications for attitude change, and possible applications to more abstract attitudes, are discussed.

On a balmy evening in 1930, a smiling, well-dressed Chinese couple entered an elegant restaurant on the Pacific Coast. Because anti-Chinese attitudes were rampant at the time, they were unsure of their reception. To the couple's pleasant surprise, they were seated without incident, and the restaurant's staff and the other diners treated their presence as a matter of course. If anything, they were accorded more than ordinary consideration, even before they were joined by their friend, a

* Princeton University.
** Stanford University.
This research was supported in part by National Institute of Mental Health Grant MH36093 to Mark R. Lepper and Lee Ross. We thank John Darley, Walter Mischel, Lee Ross, and Abraham Tesser for helpful comments on previous versions of the manuscript.

Requests for reprints should be sent to Charles G. Lord, Department of Psychology, Princeton University, Princeton, New Jersey 08540.

Caucasian university professor. Six months later, the professor sent an attitude questionnaire to the restaurant's management, asking "Will you accept members of the Chinese race as guests in your establishment?" The answer was an unequivocal "No." Over the next 2 years, this scene was repeated at 81 restaurants and 47 hotels. Only once was the Chinese couple refused service, and yet over 90% of the 128 establishments answered the follow-up questionnaire by indicating an attitude opposed to serving Chinese (LaPiere, 1934). This was the first of a long line of empirical failures to demonstrate attitude–behavior consistency (see Schuman & Johnson, 1976, and Wicker, 1969, for comprehensive reviews).

One conclusion that could be drawn from these failures to demonstrate attitude–behavior consistency is that attitudes are not important determinants of behavior, that individuals react positively or negatively toward *specific* people, objects, and events as they occur rather than displaying any general tendencies to react positively or negatively toward entire classes of people, objects, or events. As for the common intuition that attitudes determine behavior, perhaps we so badly want to believe in attitude–behavior consistency that we misinterpret the evidence of our own senses. After all, it is perceived consistency between words and deeds that "enables men to participate in organized social life with good confidence that others will do what they say they will do, will be where they say they will be" (Dollard, 1949, p. 624). In addition, we may be unwilling to admit that our behavior is often inconsistent with our own values (Katz, 1960), so that we have good reason to exaggerate the attitude–behavior consistency of both other persons and ourselves. If attitudes cannot be shown to guide behavior, a half century of attitude research in social psychology has been nothing more than chasing after a phantom of our own imagination.

For those who continue to believe that general attitudes exist and influence behavior, the constructive approach involves an effort to discover the conditions under which the attitude–behavior relationship is weak or strong. Allport (1943), for example, noted that attitude–behavior consistency increases dramatically when individuals are heavily involved in and committed to the topic—conditions that may prompt monitoring of one's own actions along ideological lines (Snyder & Swann, 1976). A member of the National Association for the Advancement of Colored People might be more apt than a nonmember to display attitude–behavior consistency on civil rights legislation, but not necessarily on legislation about abortion. A related finding is that self-consciousness, which may increase phenomenological self-involvement, also increases attitude–behavior consistency (Carver, 1975). Attitude–behavior consistency is also more likely when the attitude in question has been thought about recently or seems especially relevant to the behavior (Synder, 1982). One's attitude toward Senator X seems relevant to the behavior of voting for him or her, but it is less clear what one's attitude on nuclear war has to do with voting for construction of a nuclear power plant. Another important variable is the attitude's origin. Some attitudes are developed from direct experience, whereas others are formed vicariously. Many people distrust gypsies even though they have never met one. Attitudes built upon a foundation of direct experience with the attitude object are more likely to generate attitude–behavior consistency (Fazio & Zanna, 1981).

LaPiere's (1934) explanation of empirical attitude–behavior inconsistency was that general tendencies to respond should not be inferred from questionnaire data. "The questionnaire is cheap, easy, and mechanical. The study of human behavior is time consuming, intellectually fatiguing, and depends for its success upon the ability of the investigator" (p. 237). Ajzen and Fishbein (1977) observed that in research on attitude–behavior consistency, the typical attitude question is general (e.g., "Do you like or dislike Chinese?") and the typical behavioral measure specific. They proposed that attitude–behavior consistency could be measured more accurately by using attitude questions whose degree of specificity corresponds with that of the behavior of interest. To determine whether a student will be on time for his or her 9:00 a.m. psychology class, ask him or her not "How much do you enjoy studying psychology?" but "How do you feel about being late for psychology courses?" or, even better, "How do you feel about being late for 9:00 a.m. psychology courses?" Each increase in question specificity returns higher attitude–behavior correlation coefficients (Ajzen & Fishbein, 1980), but to some extent this approach embraces behavioral specificity and obviates the need for a general attitude concept.

We propose a similar answer to the riddle of attitude–behavior consistency, but one that retains the concept of a general attitude. The proposal might be termed a mirror image of Ajzen and Fishbein's (1977) because it involves a more precise specification not of the attitude but of the attitude object. Ajzen and Fishbein's (1977) response to the potential mismatch between verbal and behavioral response measures is to increase the specificity of the verbal response. Ours is to expect consistency only when the stimulus in the behavioral response situation matches the *perceived* stimulus in the verbal response situation. This approach leaves the attitude question general, but accepts as relevant to attitude–behavior consistency only behavioral responses directed toward specific exemplars that match the image or prototype that individuals had in mind when asked about their general attitudes.

The restaurant and hotel proprietors in LaPiere's (1934) study responded to his questionnaire just as they anticipated encounters with any person or object that is not immediately present—by constructing and reacting to a cognitive prototype (Bartlett, 1932). A prototype is an exemplar or standard that incorporates the essential and most characteristic features of a class or group (Posner & Keele, 1968; Rosch, 1978). The problem with prototypes in person perception is that they may be inaccurate or unrealistic exemplars (cf. Cantor, Mischel, & Schwartz, 1982). If an attitude is an affective reaction toward and accompanying readiness to approach or avoid classes of objects, then imagined exemplars that are actually unrepresentative of their class will result in what appears to be attitude–behavior inconsistency (e.g., Baldwin, 1901–1905; Thurstone, 1946). Those of LaPiere's (1934) correspondents who imagined a "member of the Chinese race" as a barefoot coolie tracking mud across their lobbies were correct in stating that they

would refuse service to such an apparition. If LaPiere had entered these establishments with such a "prototypical Chinese" by his side, the proprietors' attitude–behavior consistency would have been nearly perfect. The reason that attitudes did not match behavior in LaPiere's study and, we suspect, in many similar studies since is that the target person toward whom the subject's behavior was measured did not match the prototype that the respondent had in mind when answering the general attitude question. Better prototype–target matches ought to result in greater attitude–behavior consistency.

Experiment 1

To test the contention that attitude–behavior consistency is greater when specific exemplars match an individual's prototype of a social group, we took advantage of the fact that Princeton undergraduates perceive each of their eating clubs (comparable to fraternities and sororities elsewhere) as attracting members who are similar to each other, and different from the members of other clubs, in personality. We first obtained general attitudes toward and personality profiles of the typical member of each of two eating clubs. Several months later, we presented the same students with an opportunity to interact with two persons who "happened" to belong to the two clubs in question. One target person matched the individual student's prototype profile perfectly on whichever six traits that student perceived as most characteristic of the typical member of one of the clubs; the other target person matched on three and mismatched on three of whichever six traits that student perceived as most characteristic of the typical member of the other club. The behavioral measure was willingness to work on a joint project with each of the target persons.

Method
Subjects

Forty-nine undergraduates completed a questionnaire that asked for their impressions of the Princeton eating club system, a topic of much current debate on campus. Among other filler questions, they were asked to rate on 6-point scales how likable they found the typical member of each of three well-known clubs, and how much they would like to work on a joint project with a member of each of the three clubs, given that "their membership in a particular eating club is all that you know about them." In addition, the students rated the typical member of each club on 20 trait adjectives representative of the 20 subscales of Jackson's (1974) Personality Research Form, a global personality measure. Examples are "ostentatious," "organized," "ambitious," and "humble." For each adjective, the students were instructed to check one of five columns labeled "very uncharacteristic," "somewhat uncharacteristic," "neither characteristic nor uncharacteristic," "somewhat characteristic," and "very characteristic." They were asked to place four checkmarks in each of the five columns. These ratings provided a profile of the trait attributes that each subject associated with the typical member, or prototype, of each eating club.

Materials

Two eating clubs, Dial and Cap & Gown, were selected as the most consistently described across prototype profiles. It should be noted, however, that the overlap of prototype profiles was accompanied by substantial individual differences. We therefore tailored our manipulation of prototypicality according to each individual's profiles. For each student, we constructed a "clinical interview description," supposedly written by a clinician, that provided 100% confirmation of that individual's prototype profile for one of the two clubs, and a second "clinical interview description" that provided 50% confirmation of that individual's prototype profile for the other club. No "clinical interview descriptions" were prepared for seven students who failed to complete the initial prototype profiles according to instructions.

In the 50% consistent description, the person described matched the individual student's prototype profile on three traits (randomly selected from the six most characteristic traits—the four traits that the individual had rated "very characteristic"

and a randomly drawn two of those rated "somewhat characteristic"), but did not match the student's prototype profile on the other three most characteristic traits. For example, for a student who rated the typical Cap & Gown member as very ambitious, aggressive, playful, approval-seeking, domineering, and persistent, the 50% consistent Cap & Gown member's description read as follows:

> Subject 11's first three responses to the WHO AM I test were "At Princeton," "Female," and "In Cap & Gown," which shows how important these aspects of her self-identity are to her. I noticed that her membership in Cap & Gown came up several times during our discussion. My brief interview revealed Subject 11 to be a rather ambitious young woman who already had clear plans for the future. She didn't seem at all aggressive, but on the contrary seemed quite docile. Even during our brief discussion I could see that she was a rather playful person, the type who can always lighten up a situation with a joke. I would imagine that she would not seek approval from others often or much care what anyone else thought about her. She gave me the impression of preferring not to be the one directing everything and everyone—clearly not the domineering type. My only other observation was that she was very persistent. I would guess that she would go on trying again and again to succeed at whatever she had started.

The 100% consistent description confirmed the student's own prototype on all six most characteristic adjectives. Thus stimulus materials were tailored for each individual student to provide a pair of "clinical interview descriptions" that drew attention to club membership and contained 100% prototypical information about a person said to be a member of one club and 50% prototypical information about a person said to be a member of the other club.

These pairs of clinical interview descriptions were pretested to ensure that they were of approximately equal likability. Twelve other undergraduates read the pairs of descriptions, but with *no* mention of club membership, and rated on 6-point scales how much they liked and how willing they would be to work with each person. For

almost all of the description pairs that we had prepared, these pretest raters viewed the two persons
as equally likable and as equally preferred work
partners ($p > .10$). In the few cases in which paired
descriptions differed significantly, changes were
made and new pretest ratings were obtained to
ensure that none of the paired descriptions differed
in likability or in work preference. Thus we determined in advance that raters who were unaware of
eating club membership thought that the two
descriptions that had been tailored for each student
were affectively equivalent.

Procedure

Approximately 3 months after the initial questionnaire sessions, we contacted the 42 students for
whom we had prepared "clinical interview descriptions" and asked them to participate in a psychology experiment. The earlier questionnaire was
not mentioned. Thirty-five students, none of whom
belonged to either Cap & Gown or Dial, agreed.
On arrival, each student was met by a female
experimenter who explained that we were asking
pairs of same-sex students to work together on an
unspecified joint project. Supposedly, three other
undergraduates were waiting in separate rooms, so
that the group would be split into two pairs. The
experimenter asked whether the student had participated in an earlier experiment on self-concepts,
"the one in which you were interviewed by a clinical psychologist on the faculty here?" All students
denied having participated in such an experiment.
The experimenter remarked, "So that's why I
couldn't find your card," and explained that participants in the present experiment were to read the
clinician's "thumbnail sketches" of the three other
participants in order to decide which of the others
they would prefer to work with on the joint project.
The experimenter then left the room and returned
with two index cards that contained the two per-
sonalized descriptions that we had prepared by reference to that student's own eating club prototype
profiles. She explained that one of the other three
students also had not participated in the earlier
clinical interviews, so that descriptions of only two
of the three potential partners were available.

Dependent measures

The experimenter asked the student to read both
descriptions carefully and then to complete a set of
scales that served as the dependent measures.
On scales labeled exactly as the initial questionnaire scales had been, the student rated how much
he or she would like to work on the project with
each of the two persons described, and how likable
each seemed. Once these primary measures had
been obtained, the experimenter asked the student
to describe each of the two target persons on the
same 20-trait form used to generate the initial
prototype profiles, asked which eating club each
target person belonged to, and asked how typical of
their club each target person seemed (also on 6-
point scales). These latter questions served as
checks on the effectiveness of the prototypicality
manipulation. Finally, to determine whether club
prototype profiles had been altered by exposure to
a non-prototypical member, the experimenter
asked the subject to complete again the initial liking, work preference, and 20-trait profile measures
for the typical member of each club.

In subsequent debriefing, the students expressed
surprise that they would not actually perform the
joint project, and that the target persons were
neither present nor real. We disqualified two subjects because they could not correctly recall the
target persons' eating clubs, and one subject
because we had inadvertently provided two 50%
consistent clinical interview descriptions. Thus the
final sample consisted of 32 undergraduates, each
of whom had expressed behavioral intentions
toward two target persons: one who matched their
prototype profile completely (100% prototypical
target person), and one who matched their prototype profile on some traits and mismatched on
others (50% prototypical target person). In addition, for 17 students the 100% prototypical target
person was said to be a Cap & Gown member, and
for the other 15 students the 100% prototypical
target person was said to be a Dial member.

Results and Discussion

None of the effects to be reported differed as a
function of gender or which club's prototype was

used to generate the 100% prototypical target person; consequently, these factors were ignored in the analyses reported.

Manipulation checks

The student subjects correctly perceived the 100% prototypical target person as more typical of his or her club ($M = 4.84$ on a scale of 1–6) than the 50% prototypical target person ($M = 4.00$), $t(31) = 3.00$, $p < .01$. Significantly, however, the students found the 100% prototypical target person no more likable[1] ($M = .94$) than the 50% prototypical target person ($M = 4.00$), $t(31) < 1$. Pretesting had successfully generated target persons who differed in how well they matched individual students' club prototypes, but did not differ in how likable they seemed to these same individual students. Thus differences in attitude–behavior consistency toward the two target persons could be attributed to prototype matching rather than to differences in likability.

Attitude–behavior consistency

The primary hypothesis was that behaviors are more likely to be consistent with attitudes when the target person (toward whom behavior is directed) matches the prototype that an individual had in mind when asked about his or her general attitude toward members of a social group. We tested this hypothesis in two ways. First, we examined differences between each individual's responses to the initial questionnaire attitude items and that same individual's responses to the later measures of preference for being paired with each target person. This might be termed a test of intra-individual consistency. A second analysis asked whether subjects had the same relationship to each other in their responses to the initial attitude question as in their responses to the later behavioral question. This might be termed a test of inter-individual consistency. For each test, we considered that

behavioral intentions as expressed on a measure of preference for working with a target person were functionally equivalent to behavior (Fishbein & Ajzen, 1975).

Intra-individual consistency. The absolute difference between each individual's answers to the initial attitude questions and the later behavioral intention questions served as a measure of attitude–behavior discrepancy. The larger the absolute difference, the less consistent that student's behavior was with his or her general attitude. One initial attitude question asked about the likability of members of a club; the other asked about working with members of a club. As Table 25.1 shows, for attitude on likability of club members, attitude–behavior consistency was greater for the 100% prototypical target person (mean absolute difference = 1.12 on a scale of 0–5) than for the 50% prototypical target person (mean absolute difference = 1.66), $t(31) = 2.42$, $p < .05$. For attitude on working with club members, attitude–behavior consistency was also greater for the 100% prototypical target person (mean absolute difference = 0.81) than for the 50% prototypical target person (mean absolute difference = 1.59), $t(31) = 4.13$, $p < .001$. Whether the attitude was expressed as liking for a social group or as preference for interacting with members of a social group, individuals' behavior was more consistent with their attitudes when confronted with a target person whose attributes matched those of their imagined prototypical group member than when confronted with a target person whose attributes did not match.

TABLE 25.1. Mean Absolute Differences Between Attitudes and Behavioral Intentions: Experiment 1

Attitude toward club members	Person–prototype match			
	100%		50%	
	M	SD	M	SD
Their likability	1.12	0.83	1.66	1.12
Working with them	0.81	0.82	1.59	1.24

Note: Absolute differences range from 0 to 5.

[1] Likability was significantly correlated with behavioral intentions toward both the 100% prototypical target person ($r = .61$) and the 50% prototypical target person ($r = .62$).

TABLE 25.2. Pearson Product-Moment Correlations Between Attitudes and Behavioral Intentions: Experiment 1

Attitude toward club members	Person–prototype match	
	100%	50%
Their likability	.49*	.27
Working with them	.69**	.32

* $p < .01$. ** $p < .001$.

Inter-individual consistency. Another way of looking at attitude–behavior consistency is through correlation coefficients. As shown in Table 25.2, attitude on likability of club members and preference for working with a particular club member were significantly correlated for the 100% prototypical target person ($r = .49$), but not for the 50% prototypical target person ($r = .27$). Similarly, attitude on working with club members and preference for working with a specific member were significantly correlated for the 100% prototypical target person ($r = .69$), but not for the 50% prototypical target person ($r = .32$). Students who more liked and wanted to work with members of a club were also more likely to prefer working on a joint project with a specific club member, but this inter-individual consistency proved significant only for the specific behavioral exemplar who matched their individual attitude prototypes. Although the difference between the first pair of correlations was not statistically significant ($z = 0.98$, $p > .10$), the difference between the second pair was ($z = 2.00$, $p < .05$).

Effect of a disconfirming target person on prototype profiles

One further question of interest is what happens to attitude prototypes when a specific target offers disconfirming evidence. Suppose that you despise cats and believe them to be haughty and aloof. One reaction to encountering a cat who fawns and obviously craves attention is to change your mind about the characteristics of (and presumably your attitude toward) cats in general. Another reaction is to decide that you have met an atypical cat, to con-

tinue to believe that the typical cat is haughty and aloof, and to continue to despise cats. We tested these two possible reactions to disconfirming evidence by examining the absolute differences between the premanipulation prototype profiles and the postmanipulation prototype profiles of both the specific target person and the prototypical club member. As shown in Table 25.3, when all 20 traits were considered, the 100% prototypical target person was described as a better match to the club prototype (mean difference = 16.03 on a scale of 0–64) than was the 50% prototypical target person (mean difference = 23.06), $t(31) = 5.49$, $p < .001$. This result is no more than a manipulation check. Of greater interest is the fact that subsequent prototype profiles were essentially unaffected by exposure to the target persons, with no greater change after encountering a 50% prototypical target person than after encountering a 100% prototypical target person ($p > .10$)

Much the same pattern was discovered in an analysis of the 6 traits explicitly confirmed or disconfirmed by the description of the 50% prototypical target person, who was described as a better match to the prototype on the 3 confirmed traits (mean difference = 2.16 on a scale of 0–15) than on the 3 disconfirmed traits (mean difference = 6.03), $t(31) = 6.38$, $p < .001$. On those same traits, the subsequent prototype profiles of the 50% prototypical target person's club differed only marginally in their match to disconfirming as opposed to

TABLE 25.3. Mean Absolute Differences Between Premanipulation and Postmanipulation Profiles: Experiment 1

Traits	Person profile		Prototype profile	
	M	SD	M	SD
All 20				
100% agreement	16.03	5.81	14.81	4.82
50% agreement	23.06	5.56	16.59	5.16
Explicitly confirmed or disconfirmed				
Confirmed	2.16	1.90	1.91	1.47
Disconfirmed	6.03	2.71	2.62	1.95

Note: Absolute differences range from 0 to 64 for all 20 traits, and from 0 to 15 for traits explicitly confirmed or disconfirmed.

confirming traits, $t(31) = 1.92$, $p < .10$. It seems that subjects in the present experiment were satisfied to label the 50% prototypical target person as atypical and retain their initial prototypes, a strategy that may usually serve them well. After all, one does not alter one's conception of the attributes of birds just because penguins do not fly. Robins do, and as long as "robin" remains the prototypical bird, birds will retain the attribute "fly." Similarly, subjects in the present experiment were justified in retaining their beliefs about the characteristics of typical club members even though they read about one member who did not fit the mold. It was probably easier for them to assume that the target person was regarded, even by other members of the club, as an "oddball" who was admitted by accident. The danger in such an inherently conservative cognitive strategy, of course, is that the prototype survives intact to influence later behavior toward those members of a social group who are subsequently encountered.

Experiment 2

Experiment 1 provided initial support for our proposal that attitude–behavior consistency depends importantly on attitude prototypes—that individuals display greater attitude–behavior consistency toward target persons who are similar rather than dissimilar to the prototype that they had in mind when they were asked about their general attitudes. We were concerned, however, with three aspects of our results. First, we had expected typicality ratings for the 50% prototypical target person to be nearer to the middle of the scale (neither typical nor atypical) than they were. Although the 50% prototypical target person was perceived as less typical than the 100% prototypical target person, the rating was still well above the scale's midpoint. In addition, we had expected attitude–behavior correlations for the 50% target person to be near 0; these correlations, however, were in the .30 range, indicating that our student subjects, who read 50% confirming and 50% disconfirming evidence, were still able to convince themselves that the 50% prototypical target remained more than a

random match to their club prototypes. One explanation was that some of the disconfirmed traits had been labeled only "somewhat characteristic," and that we had confirmed and disconfirmed only one extreme of the profile—the characteristic side. We never characterized a target person as displaying traits that an individual had rated as very uncharacteristic of the person's club.

A second aspect of our first experiment that concerned us was the ecological validity of the results. We had taken advantage of the presence at Princeton of naturally occurring social groups that students considered legitimate to like or dislike, and about whose members they had rather definite ideas. Princeton's eating clubs, however, may not be representative even of fraternities and sororities on other campuses, much less of more important social groups such as minority groups. A third potential problem lay in our interpretation of the effects of exposure to an atypical target person on the characteristics that subjects attributed to the typical club member. Because we had not asked the students how many members of each eating club they knew personally, we had no idea whether change should be expected on the basis of exposure to one atypical member. One might expect a student who knew only one member of Cap & Gown, for example, to change his or her prototype profile for the club significantly in response to the 50% prototypical target person, but not a student who knew 50 members of Cap & Gown.

To provide a more ecologically valid test of our major hypothesis, we designed a second experiment in which the group in question was a social group about whose members the average person might be expected to have a fairly consistent prototype—homosexuals. This group seemed an ideal choice both because college students might feel freer to express both positive and negative attitudes toward homosexuals than toward members of, for example, racial or ethnic minority groups (cf. Crosby, Bromley, & Saxe, 1980), and because pretesting had suggested that it would be unlikely that students would know a significant number of admitted homosexuals well enough to regard one target person as a small sample. Also in contrast to Experiment 1, we constructed 50% prototypical target persons by confirming and disconfirming half of the traits at each extreme of an individual's prototype profile, using only traits from the two most extreme categories.

Method

Subjects

Forty male Princeton undergraduates completed a questionnaire that asked for their impressions of male straight-A students, vegetarians, football lettermen, class presidents, social activists, right-to-life supporters, born-again Christians, and homosexuals. The students indicated on 10-point scales how likable they found the typical member of each group, and how willing they would be to interact socially with the typical member of each group. They also provided 30-trait profiles of the typical born-again Christian, vegetarian, and homosexual, using the profile forms described in Experiment 1, but with 30 instead of 20 traits. The 30 traits were those most frequently mentioned by six pretest judges who were asked to generate adjectives that discriminated homosexuals from heterosexuals. Again, however, prototype profiles were idiosyncratic. Some subjects, for example, rated "extraverted," "domineering," "playful," and "relaxed" as very characteristic of homosexuals, whereas other subjects rated the same traits as very uncharacteristic of homosexuals. Subjects all agreed, however, that homosexuals are "artistic," "creative," and not at all "athletic."

Materials

For each student who had completed the homosexual prototype profile according to instructions, we constructed a "counselor's report" that described John B., supposedly an Ivy League student who was thinking of transferring to Princeton. In addition to filler material (e.g., "grew up on Long Island, where his mother and elder sister still live"), the report conveyed information about 12 of John B.'s personality traits (e.g., "he was able to put his artistic inclinations to work in producing pictures and posters for the walls of his room"), and, at the

end of the second paragraph, mentioned that John B. had on his wall a photograph of himself waving a placard in "the Gay Rights rally in New York City in 1981." This "counselor's report" either confirmed all 12 most extremely placed traits on the individual student's profile of a typical male homosexual or confirmed 6 (3 very characteristic and 3 very uncharacteristic) and disconfirmed 6.

Procedure

Approximately 2 months after the initial questionnaire sessions, we contacted the 31 students for whom we had prepared "counselor's reports" and asked them to participate in a psychology experiment. The earlier questionnaire was not mentioned. Twenty-four students agreed. When a student appeared for the experiment, he was told that Princeton was participating with four other schools in a program designed to ease transition problems for students who were considering a transfer from one school to another within the Ivy League. Under this program, the experimenter continued, transfer students would make several weekend visits to the new university before the transfer date so that they could be introduced to social and academic life at their new institution by one or more volunteer student hosts.

Baseline measures. The experimenter maintained that the psychology department had been asked to investigate whether enough Princeton students would volunteer as hosts to make the plan workable. At this point, the student was asked to indicate his interest in the program by agreeing to one or more of the following activities: just be introduced; just meet them on arrival; spend time talking to them about life at Princeton; show them around campus; take them to dinner or a party; take them to a sporting event; introduce them to his friends; give them his phone number so they could call with any problems; host them for an entire weekend visit. Because we believed these activities to be arranged in a generally ascending order of social intimacy, we were interested in both the number of activities checked and their average level (counting "just be introduced" as 1 and "host a weekend visit" as 9). This measure served as a baseline from which we might detect later changes in willingness to interact with a particular target person after learning that the person in question was probably a homosexual.

Postmanipulation measures. Next, the experimenter explained that descriptions of the prospective transfer students had been compiled, with the student's consent, by counseling psychologists at each school, and were kept on file so that visitors and hosts could be well matched. Ostensibly to determine whether the student would be willing to participate in the visiting program for any potential visitor currently enrolled, he was asked to "read some of the descriptions and answer a series of questions about each one," with the understanding that the extent of involvement would be left up to the host. "Feel free to indicate clearly which person or persons you feel you could interact with best."

Twelve students read descriptions of John B. that matched their prototype profile of a homosexual on all 12 most extreme traits; the other 12 students read descriptions of John B. that matched their individual prototype profiles on 6 traits and mismatched on the other 6. After reading this counselor's report, the students indicated, on 13-point scales, labeled identically with the initial attitude question, how likable they thought the person was and how willing they would be to interact with the person socially. They then chose from the previously described list the activities that they would be willing to engage in should John B. visit Princeton, and completed 30-trait personality profiles of John B. and, finally, of the typical male homosexual. The experimenter then explained that we had no other reports for the student to read, and conducted a thorough debriefing. All students indicated that they had noticed John B.'s participation in a Gay Rights rally.

Results and Discussion

Attitude–behavior consistency

Conceptually, Experiment 2 provides a between-groups replication of Experiment 1. As in the first experiment, we analyzed both intra-individual and

TABLE 25.4. Mean Absolute Differences (in *z*-scores) Between Attitudes and Behavioral Intentions: Experiment 2

Attitudes toward homosexuals	Person–prototype match			
	100%		50%	
	M	SD	M	SD
Their likability	0.66	0.45	1.24	0.84
Interacting with them	0.87	0.65	1.12	0.78

Note: Means are absolute differences between z scores.

inter-individual consistency. Also as in the first experiment, the student subjects found the 100% prototypical target person no more likable[2] ($M = 9.08$ on a scale of 1–13) than the 50% prototypical target person ($M = 8.33$), $t(22) < 1$. The target persons differed in how well they matched individual students' prototypes but not in how likable they seemed to the same students.

Intra-individual consistency. Analyses of intra-individual consistency were complicated by the fact that the scales used for the postmanipulation measure of behavioral intention were longer than those used for the initial attitude questions; this produced an increase in the variance of responses for students who read about a 100% prototypical target person ($p < .001$), but not for students who read about a 50% prototypical target person ($p > .20$). Consequently, we first standardized responses to the likability and social interaction questions within condition, and then computed absolute differences in z-score units. The means are shown in Table 25.4. For attitude on likability of homosexuals, attitude–behavior consistency was greater for students who encountered a 100% prototypical target person (mean absolute difference = 0.66) than for students who encountered a 50% prototypical target person (mean absolute difference = 1.24), $t(22) = 2.10$, $p < .05$. A similar analysis of consistency between behavioral intentions and attitude on interacting with homosexuals produced a

---

[2] Likability was significantly correlated with behavioral intentions toward both the 100% prototypical target person ($r = .89$) and the 50% prototypical target person ($r = .79$).

similar but nonsignificant difference between conditions, $t(22) < 1$.

Inter-individual consistency. As shown in Table 25.5, attitude on likability of homosexuals was significantly correlated with preference for interacting socially with a 100% prototypical target person ($r = .66$), but not with preference for interacting socially with a 50% prototypical target person ($r = -.19$). Also, attitude on interacting with homosexuals was marginally correlated with preference for interacting with a 100% prototypical target person ($r = .37$), but not with preference for interacting with a 50% prototypical target person ($r = .02$). The difference between these pairs of correlations was statistically significant in the first case ($z = 2.09$, $p < .05$) but not the second case ($z = .78$, $p > .10$).

Another set of correlations relevant to inter-individual consistency involved changes in the social activities list, from subjects' premanipulation indications of willingness to meet and play host to a visiting transfer student to their later willingness to do so after discovering that the specific transfer student was probably a homosexual. In terms of changes in the number of activities checked, students who had relatively favorable attitudes toward homosexuals checked a greater number of activities, and students with relatively unfavorable attitudes fewer activities, after learning that the target person was a homosexual. This relationship was quite strong for students who read about a 100% prototypical target person ($r = .78$), but not for students who read about a 50% prototypical target person ($r = -.18$). The same pattern was found for correlations that involved change in the average level of social intimacy associated with

the activities checked ($r = .80$ for the 100% prototypical target person and .19 for the 50% prototypical target person). The difference between these pairs of correlations proved significant for the number of activities checked ($z = 2.60$, $p < .01$) and marginally significant for the level of intimacy endorsed ($z = 1.93$, $p < .06$).

Effect of a disconfirming target person on prototype profiles

As in Experiment 1, we were also interested in the effect of disconfirming evidence on prototype profiles. Would students change the traits that they attributed to the typical homosexual more after reading about a homosexual who did not match their beliefs than after reading about a homosexual who did match their beliefs? To answer this question we computed the absolute difference across the 30-trait profile between the premanipulation homosexual prototypes and both the postmanipulation target person profiles and the postmanipulation homosexual prototype profiles. The means are displayed in Table 25.6. The mean differences are higher than those of Experiment 1, but only because 30 traits were used rather than 20. In both instances the average subject's prototype profile changed by about 25% of the maximum possible change. Just as in Experiment 1, postmanipulation descriptions of the target person were more discrepant from premanipulation prototype descriptions in the 50% condition (mean difference = 37.67 on a scale of 0–96) than in the 100% condition (mean difference = 25.33), $t(22) = 3.91$, $p < .001$, but this difference was not reflected in

TABLE 25.5. Pearson Product-Moment Correlations Between Attitudes and Behavioral Intentions: Experiment 2

Attitudes toward homosexuals	Person–prototype match	
	100%	50%
Their likability	.66**	-.19
Interacting with them	.38*	.02

*$p < .10$. ** $p < .001$.

TABLE 25.6. Mean Absolute Differences between Pre-manipulation Prototype Profiles and Postmanipulation Profiles: Experiment 2

	Person–prototype match			
	100%		50%	
Profile	M	SD	M	SD
Person	25.33	9.87	37.67	8.40
Prototype	25.67	6.93	27.67	6.73

Note: Absolute differences range from 0 to 96.

corresponding prototype profile changes, $t(22) <$ 1). Target persons who matched an individual's prototype profile for the social group were responded to on the basis of the original prototype, whereas target persons who did not match the prototype profile were not, but the prototype itself emerged unscathed to influence behavior in new social situations.

General Discussion

These experiments provide an empirical referent for a frequently expressed idea—that attitudes toward a social group will match behavior toward a member of that group only to the degree that the target person matches the prototype that served as the basis for the attitude in the first place. In concluding an extensive review of the attitude–behavior consistency issue, Schuman and Johnson (1976) considered the LaPiere (1934) study and mused that "Leaving aside all the methodological points touched on in earlier pages, the result still puzzles us. Did the proprietors picture Chinese only as laborers in pigtails and coolie hats, and not ever recognize the couple before them as Chinese?" (pp. 201–202). In the same vein, LaPiere himself speculated that attitudes toward Armenian women were only symbolic responses to a symbolic situation (cf. Sears, Lau, Tyler, & Allen, 1979) and should not be confused with responses to a "woman of flesh and blood, who might be tall or squat, fat or thin, old or young, well or poorly dressed—who might, in fact, be a goddess or just another old and dirty hag" (LaPiere, 1934, p. 230).

The present approach to attitude–behavior consistency involves the assumption that "The key attitude concept is the 'disposition to place oneself into appreciated episodes of interaction with a class of objects' " (Abelson, 1972, p. 28). Whenever people have occasion to assess their attitude toward a particular group of people, they do so by first constructing an image of a concrete "best exemplar" or group prototype, and then placing themselves in imagined interaction with the prototype. Attitudes are the products of these imagined interactions. The interaction is not, however, with an abstract category, but rather with a specific concrete other—the group prototype—whether that prototypic person be a Chinese "coolie" or an Armenian "hag." It is probably far easier to assess one's attitude toward a prototype than toward the social group that the prototype represents. People gauge their reaction to an imagined interaction with a concrete rather than an abstract referent because they prefer to work with concrete representations (Nisbett, Borgida, Crandall, & Reed, 1976), and because concrete processing may often be much more compelling (Abelson, 1976; Nisbett & Ross, 1980).

The fundamental theoretical question that the present findings raise, of course, concerns the conceptual status of the prototype concept in this argument. At the simplest level, it is possible to view prototypes of attitude objects primarily as convenient devices for summarizing the attributes of those objects on which one's evaluative reactions are based. In this sense, the effects of our experimental manipulation can be viewed as a straightforward consequence of the differential information provided about the specific characteristics of different target objects. At a more complex level, however, it is also possible that such prototypes exert deeper organizing influences on people's attitudes and actions toward objects—that they frequently lead people to go "beyond the information given." In this view, for example, prototypicality along one set of dimensions (e.g., physical appearance) may lead to inferences, and more correspondent actions, based on assumed prototypicality along other dimensions (e.g., social attitudes or intellectual abilities).

The present approach suggests that one effective way to change attitudes might be to change individual prototypes. Here the difference between the present approach and previous work on stereotypes is most evident. A prototype is an exemplar of a category. A straightbacked wooden chair, for example, may be an individual's prototype for the category "chairs." What we have been calling a prototype profile is the set of attributes associated with the prototype. An individual who imagines a straightbacked wooden chair when he or she thinks of chairs may associate with the category attributes such as "hard" and "uncomfortable." An individual who instead imagines an overstuffed leather recliner may associate with the category opposite attributes such as "soft" and "comfortable." We believe that what has been termed a social sterotype in previous research (e.g., Katz & Braly, 1933) is actually the prototype profile, the set of attributes associated with a social category's prototype. Subjects in previous studies who were asked to describe "Turks," "Armenians," or "Jews" probably turned this difficult abstract problem into an easier concrete task by imagining a "best exemplar," sometimes a specific actual person and sometimes a caricature, and then generating that exemplar's attributes (cf. Lingle, Altom, & Medin, in press). As Brewer, Dull, and Lui (1981) note, "It is difficult to image an abstract 'fruit,' but when asked to represent the general category of fruit, most people will think first of a prototypic apple or orange" (p. 669). In the present experiments we made this cognitive translation explicit by asking subjects to describe the *typical* member of a social group.

The attitude prototype approach suggests optimism that group stereotypes can be changed, but through an indirect attack on the prototype rather than through a seemingly more direct attack on the prototype's attributes. If attitudes toward social groups are reactions to imagined group prototypes, then the most promising technique may be one of attempted "prototype substitution." One will never convince anyone that straightbacked wooden chairs are really soft and comfortable, but if one can get the individual to think instead of an overstuffed leather recliner whenever chairs are mentioned, changes in the attributes of the category "chairs" will follow automatically. We suggest that this is one way in which a Martin Luther King, for example, can have a positive effect on race relations. Sufficient exposure to King may have caused millions of white Americans to picture him, perhaps in the act of delivering his famous "I have a dream" speech, whenever they thought of blacks. A switch to King as the prototype of his race might well have substituted traits such as "intelligent," "noble," and "dignified" for less complimentary terms associated with previous "best exemplars."

We ought to be aware, at the same time, that it is all too easy to regard a Martin Luther King as atypical, as an "exception that proves the rule." Disconfirming evidence is often examined critically and explained away by differentiation of a social group into subtypes (Abelson, 1959; Weber & Crocker, 1983), whereas confirming evidence is welcomed enthusiastically (Lord, Ross, & Lepper, 1979), so that prototypes and attitudes remain essentially unchanged. Through the tactic of dismissing disconfirming group members as atypical, individuals may maintain both a negative attitude toward the group and the belief that "some of my best friends are" members of the group, and do so without necessarily being hypocritical (Locksley, Borgida, Brekke, & Hepburn, 1980). An interesting question for future research is whether some prototypes, perhaps those built upon a foundation of direct experience (Fazio & Zanna, 1978), may be more resistant to change through exposure to specific exemplars that do not match the prototype.

It is also interesting to speculate on the applicability of the attitude prototype approach to more abstract attitudes. The strict interpretation of the present results is that they apply only to attitudes about social groups. It is possible, however, that even attitudes on more abstract issues depend to some extent on attitude prototypes. An individual's attitude on capital punishment may depend on whether that individual's prototypical murderer is a cruel and calculating monster or an excitable and easily confused loner. In the same way, an individual's attitude on welfare reform may depend on whether that individual's prototypical welfare recipient is an alcoholic floozy or a struggling and concerned parent. Again, the present approach offers some hope that substituting a different prototype will elicit a different set of attributes and a changed attitude, even for these presumably more abstract attitudes.

REFERENCES

Abelson, R. P. (1959). Modes of resolution of belief dilemmas. *Conflict Resolution, 3,* 343–352.

Abelson, R. P. (1972). Are attitudes necessary? In B. T. King & E. McGinnies (Eds.), *Attitudes, conflict, and social change* (pp. 19–32). New York: Academic Press.

Abelson, R. P. (1976). Script processing in attitude formation and decision-making. In J. S. Carroll & J. W. Payne (Eds.), *Cognition and social behavior* (pp. 33–45). Hillsdale, NJ: Erlbaum.

Ajzen, I., & Fishbein, M. (1977). Attitude–behavior relations: A theoretical analysis and review of empirical research. *Psychological Bulletin, 84,* 888–918.

Ajzen, I., & Fishbein, M. (1980). *Understanding attitudes and predicting social behavior*. Englewood Cliffs, NJ: Prentice-Hall.

Allport, G. W. (1943). The ego in contemporary psychology. *Psychological Review, 50,* 451–478.

Baldwin, J. M. (1901–1905). *Dictionary of philosophy and psychology* (Vols. 1, 2, & 3). New York: Macmillan.

Bartlett, F. C. (1932). *Remembering: A study in experimental social psychology*. Cambridge, England: Cambridge University Press.

Brewer, M. B., Dull, V., & Lui, L. (1981). Perceptions of the elderly: Stereotypes as prototypes. *Journal of Personality and Social Psychology, 41,* 656–670.

Cantor, N., Mischel, W., & Schwartz, J. C. (1982). A prototype analysis of psychological situations. *Cognitive Psychology, 14,* 45–77.

Carver, C. S. (1975). Physical aggression as a function of objective self-awareness and attitudes toward punishment. *Journal of Experimental Social Psychology, 11,* 510–519.

Crosby, F., Bromley, S., & Saxe, L. (1980). Recent unobtrusive studies of black and white discrimination and prejudice: A literature review. *Psychological Bulletin, 87,* 546–563.

Dollard, J. (1949). Under what conditions do opinions predict behavior? *Public Opinion Quarterly, 12,* 623–632.

Fazio, R. H., & Zanna, M. P. (1978). Attitudinal qualities relating to the strength of the attitude–behavior relationship. *Journal of Experimental Social Psychology, 14,* 398–408.

Fazio, R. H., & Zanna, M. P. (1981). Direct experience and attitude-behavior consistency. In L. Berkowitz (Ed.), *Advances in experimental social psychology* (Vol. 14, pp. 161–202). New York: Academic Press.

Fishbein, M., & Ajzen, I. (1975). *Belief, attitude, intention and behavior: An introduction to theory and research*. Reading, MA: Addison-Wesley.

Jackson, D. (1974). *Personality Research Form Manual*. Port Huron, MI: Research Psychologists Press.

Katz, D. (1960). The functional approach to the study of attitudes. *Public Opinion Quarterly, 24,* 163–204.

Katz, D., & Braly, K. (1933). Racial stereotypes in one hundred college students. *Journal of Abnormal and Social Psychology, 28,* 280–290.

LaPiere, R. T. (1934). Attitudes vs. actions. *Social Forces, 13,* 230–237.

Lingle, J. H., Altom, M. W., & Medin, D. L. (in press). Of cabbages and kings: Assessing the extendability of natural object concept models to social things. In R. Wyer & T. Srull (Eds.), *Handbook of social cognition*. Hillsdale, NJ: Erlbaum.

Locksley, A., Borgida, E., Brekke, N., & Hepburn, C. (1980). Sex stereotypes and social judgment. *Journal of Personality and Social Psychology, 39,* 821–831.

Lord, C. G., Ross, L., & Lepper, M. R. (1979). Biased assimilation and attitude polarization: The effects of prior theories on subsequently considered evidence. *Journal of Personality and Social Psychology, 37,* 2098–2109.

Nisbett, R. E., Borgida, E., Crandall, R., & Reed, H. (1976). Popular induction: Information is not necessarily informative. In J. S. Carroll & J. W. Payne (Eds.), *Cognition and social behavior* (pp. 113–133). Hillsdale, NJ: Erlbaum.

Nisbett, R. E., & Ross, L. (1980). *Human inference: Strategies and shortcomings of social judgment*. Englewood Cliffs, NJ: Prentice-Hall.

Posner, M. I., & Keele, S. W. (1968). On the genesis of abstract ideas. *Journal of Experimental Psychology, 77,* 353–363.

Rosch, E. (1978). Principles of categorization. In E. Rosch & B. B. Lloyd (Eds.), *Cognition and categorization* (pp. 27–48). Hillsdale, NJ: Erlbaum.

Schuman, H., & Johnson, M. P. (1976). Attitudes and behavior. *Annual Review of Sociology, 2,* 161–207.

Sears, D. O., Lau, R. R., Tyler, T. R., & Allen, H. M. (1979). Self-interest vs. symbolic politics in policy attitudes and presidential voting. *American Political Science Review, 73,* 369–384.

Snyder, M. (1982). When believing means doing: Creating links between attitudes and behavior. In M. P. Zanna, E. T. Higgins, & C. P. Herman (Eds.), *Consistency in social behavior: The Ontario symposium* (Vol. 2, pp. 105–130). Hillsdale, NJ: Erlbaum.

Snyder, M., & Swann, W. B., Jr. (1976). When actions reflect attitudes: The politics of impression management. *Journal of Personality and Social Psychology, 34,* 1034–1042.

Thurstone, L. L. (1946). Comment. *American Journal of Sociology, 52,* 39–40.

Weber, R., & Crocker, J. (1983). Cognitive processes in the revision of stereotypic beliefs. *Journal of Personality and Social Psychology, 45,* 961–977.

Wicker, A. W. (1969). Attitudes versus actions: The relationship of verbal and overt behavioral responses to attitude objects. *Journal of Social Issues, 25,* 41–78.

Received July 22, 1983
Revision received December 7, 1983 ■

READING 26

Attitudinal and Normative Variables as Predictors of Specific Behaviors[1]

Icek Ajzen[2]* and Martin Fishbein**

Fishbein's modified version of Dulany's theory of propositional control was considered as an explanation for the reported lack of relationship between traditional measures of attitude and overt behavior and as an alternative for the prediction of specific actions. Evidence in support of the theory was reviewed. Specific behaviors were shown to be predictable from specific behavioral intentions, and these intentions were shown in turn to be a function of two components: (a) the attitude toward the act in question and (b) the perceived normative expectations of reference groups, multiplied by the person's motivation to comply with the expectations. Variables other than these two components were shown to affect behavioral intentions and overt behaviors indirectly by influencing one or both of the components. Traditional attitudes were treated like any other variable external to the theory, and their relations to behavior, if any, were also shown to be mediated by the theory's two components.

Allport (1935, 1968) pointed out that the concept of attitude "is probably the most distinctive and indispensable concept in contemporary American social psychology [1968, p. 59]." Although definitions vary considerably, there is general agreement that a person's attitude toward some

* University of Massachusetts.
** University of Illinois, Champaign.
[1] Preparation of this article was supported in part by National Institute of Mental Health Grant MH 20182-01 to the first author. A more comprehensive version of the theoretical analysis can be found in Technical Report 1-72 under this grant. Parts of this article were presented at a Workshop on Attitude Research and Consumer Behavior at the University of Illinois, Urbana, December 1970. The authors are indebted to Harry C. Triandis and Allan W. Wicker for their comments on an earlier draft of this article.
[2] Requests for reprints should be sent to Icek Ajzen, Department of Psychology, University of Massachusetts, Amherst, Massachusetts 01002.

object constitutes a predisposition on his part to respond to the object in a consistently favorable or unfavorable manner (cf. Allport, 1935). Indeed, social psychologists have used attitude as an explanatory device to account for observed consistency in overt behavior toward a stimulus object (cf. Campbell, 1963). It is hardly surprising, therefore, that attitude and overt behavior have been assumed to be closely related, despite an accumulation of contrary evidence (e.g., Berg, 1966; Bray, 1950; Kutner, Wilkins, & Yarrow, 1952; LaPiere, 1934).

In recent years, however, the assumption of a strong relationship between attitude and behavior has been questioned by an increasing number of investigators (e.g., DeFleur & Westie, 1958; Festinger, 1964; Linn, 1965; McGuire, 1969; Warner & DeFleur, 1969; Wicker, 1969). In fact, as indicated before, examination of empirical research available to date shows few consistent and mostly nonsignificant relations (cf. Fishbein, 1973; Wicker, 1969). Most of these studies (e.g., Bray, 1950; DeFleur & Westie, 1958; Linn, 1965; Rokeach & Mezei, 1966; Smith & Dixon, 1968) obtained a general measure of attitude toward a stimulus object (e.g., Negroes) and then observed the relation between a person's score on the attitude scale and some specific behavior toward the object. The present article attempts to explain the inconsistent findings, and it presents an alternative approach to the prediction of specific behavior from attitudinal variables.

There is no shortage of explanations to account for the low attitude–behavior relationship. It has been suggested (e.g., Rosenberg & Hovland, 1960) that attitudes are multidimensional, including cognitive, affective, and conative components. It follows that single attitude scores cannot adequately represent all of these attitudinal components and thus cannot predict behavior accurately. Others (e.g., Ehrlich, 1969; Triandis, 1967; Wicker, 1969) have argued that attitude is but one variable that influences behavior. Additional factors such as social norms, habits, personality characteristics, etc., also influence behavior and must therefore be taken into consideration. Discussions of these and other suggestions can be found

in Ehrlich (1969), Wicker (1969), and Fishbein (1973).

Most of the proposed explanations imply that traditional measures of attitude, while relevant to the prediction of behavior, are insufficient. However, most treatments of attitude have not systematically dealt with additional variables as determinants of behavior. Instead, they have usually viewed these other variables as sources of error variance. This article describes a theory that attempts to integrate these other determinants into a single conceptual framework. The theory deals with the prediction of specific behavior under a given set of conditions.[3] It specifies a small number of variables as antecedents of behavioral intentions and explicates the conditions under which additional factors are expected to contribute to behavioral prediction. At the same time, the theory also provides an explanation for the lack of any systematic relationship between traditional measures of attitude and overt behavior. Empirical research generated by the theory is presented and discussed in terms of its implications for the theoretical model and for the problem of attitudinal prediction of behavior.

The Theory

The present model for attitudinal prediction of behavior is a modified version of Dulany's (1968) theory of propositional control.[4] As in the original formulation, the modified version of the theory deals with prediction of a specific behavioral intention in a well-defined situation. The theory assumes that most behavior of interest to social psychology is under volitional control and that in a given situation, a person holds or forms a specific intention that influences his subsequent overt

---

[3] A discussion of attitudinal prediction of behavior in more general terms can be found in Fishbein (1973).

[4] A detailed account of the relationships between the original and the modified versions of the theory of propositional control can be found in Fishbein (1967).

behavior.[5] The intention in the present theory refers to performance of a given action in a given situation; it is the intention to perform the particular overt response that is to be predicted.[6]

According to Fishbein's (1967) modification of Dulany's (1968) theory, there are two major factors that determine specific behavioral intentions: a personal or "attitudinal" factor and a social or "normative" factor. These two components in the theory are given empirical weights. Symbolically, the central equation of the theory can be presented as follows:

$$B \sim BI = [Aact]w_0 + [NB(Mc)]w_1. \qquad (1)$$

In Equation 1, B = overt behavior; BI = behavioral intention; Aact = attitude toward the act; NB = normative belief; Mc = motivation to comply with the normative belief; and w_0 and w_1 are empirically determined weights.

It can be seen that behavioral intentions are a function of the weighted sum of two variables. The first, Aact, is the actor's attitude toward performing the behavior in question under the given circumstances. Unlike traditional attitudinal approaches, Aact is the person's attitude toward performing a particular act in a given situation with respect to a given object and *not* his attitude toward the object or class of objects per se.[7] Thus, as was the case with behavioral intentions, the attitude toward an act deals with the specific behavior that is to be predicted.

A person's evaluation of, or attitude toward, a specific act is proposed to be a function of the act's perceived consequences and of their values to the person. Consistent with Fishbein's earlier theorizing (Fishbein, 1963), and similar to formulations proposed by other theorists (e.g., Peak, 1955; Rosenberg, 1956; Rotter, 1954), Aact is conceptualized in terms of an expectancy-value model:

$$Aact = \sum_{i=1}^{n} B_i a_i, \qquad (2)$$

where B_i refers to the individual's belief about the likelihood that the behavior in question will result in Outcome i; a_i is the person's evaluation of (or attitude toward) Outcome i; and n is the number of beliefs.[8]

The normative component of the theory, NB(Mc), deals with the influence of the social environment on behavior. NB is the actor's belief about the likelihood that members of a given reference group expect him to perform the behavior in question. This normative belief is multiplied by Mc, the individual's motivation to comply with the reference group's perceived expectations. Of course, the potential reference groups or individuals whose expectations are perceived to be relevant vary with the behavioral situation. While in some instances the expectations of a person's family or friends may be most relevant, in others it may be the expectations of his supervisors or society at large that are most influential. Frequently, the expectations of more than one reference group have to be considered. It is then, of course, also necessary to measure the individual's motivation to comply with each of the relevant reference groups. In this case, the theory assumes the form presented in Equation 3:

$$B \sim BI = [Aact]w_0 + [\sum_{i=1}^{n} NB_i (Mc_i)]w_1. \qquad (3)$$

When only one referent is taken into account, or

---

[5] Clearly, reflexes and habitualized responses may not be under volitional control. For general discussions of the problem of volitional control see Kimble and Perlmuter (1970) and Ryan (1970).

[6] Social psychologists trying to measure the conative component of attitudes (e.g., Bogardus, 1925; Triandis, 1964) have also been concerned with behavioral intentions. However, these intentions were of a much more general type, such as intentions to show social distance, to show friendship, etc.

[7] It is worth noting that the attitude toward the act is similar to Rokeach's (1968) operationalization of "attitude toward the situation."

[8] Equation 2 is clearly very similar to the subjective expected utility model of behavioral decision theory (cf. Becker & McClintock, 1967; Edwards, 1961). While there are certain differences between these formulations which need not concern us here, both models specify that for any individual, the attractiveness of a given act is a function of the summed products of the subjective probabilities and utilities he assigns to the act's outcomes.

when a measure of the expectation of a "generalized other" is obtained, the theory takes the form of Equation 1.[9]

Motivation to comply can be viewed in two different ways. First, it can be seen as the person's motivation to comply with a given reference group, regardless of the referent's particular demands (i.e., as the person's general tendency to accept the directives of a given referent). Second, it is possible to view motivation to comply as specific to the given expectation of a reference group. While a person may be generally motivated to comply with, say his friends, he may not want to behave in accord with one of their specific expectations. Early studies related to the theory have failed to distinguish between these two possible conceptions of motivation to comply and have usually assessed specific motivation. Both on theoretical and empirical grounds it now appears that the general conception is more appropriate.

Our present understanding of the determinants of social normative beliefs and motivation to comply is rather limited. It can be argued that the person's (P) normative beliefs are related to his perception of the referent's (O) attitude toward P's performing a given behavior ($Aact_0$). That is, if P perceives that O has a favorable attitude toward P's engaging in the behavior, P will believe that O thinks he should perform the behavior. Further, and consistent with our earlier discussion, $Aact_0$ should be a function of P's perception of O's beliefs about the consequences of P's performing the act and P's perception of O's evaluation of those consequences:

$$Aact_0 = \sum_{i=1}^{n} B_{oi}a_{oi},\qquad(4)$$

where B_{oi} = P's perception of O's beliefs that performing the act will lead to outcome i; a_{oi} = P's perception of O's evaluation of outcome i; and n = the number of beliefs that P perceives O to hold. Thus, just as P's own attitude toward the act (Aact) can be described in terms of an expectancy-value model, his normative beliefs (NB) may be viewed in terms of an expectancy-value model attributed to a given referent. Some support for this notion is presented below.

The two major determinants, then, of specific behavioral intentions are the attitude toward the act and normative beliefs multiplied by motivation to comply. As indicated in Equation 1, the attitudinal and the normative components are given empirical weights in the prediction equation proportional to their relative importance in the prediction of behavioral intentions. These empirical weights (w_0 and w_1) are expected to vary with the kind of behavior that is being predicted, with the conditions under which the behavior is to be performed, and with the person who is to perform the behavior. Thus, for some behaviors, normative considerations (expectations of friends, family, etc.) may be more important in determining behavioral intentions than are attitudinal considerations (the expected outcomes of the act). For other behaviors, the reverse may be true. In a similar fashion, we may expect that the relative importance of the two components will be influenced by situational variables, such as the behavior's observability, and by personal characteristics and preferences.

The present version of the theory, therefore, can be viewed as a multiple regression equation where the two predictors are Aact and NB(Mc), and the criterion is BI, the specific behavioral intention. Standardized regression coefficients can serve as estimates of the empirical weights of the two predictors. Given a high correlation between BI and

---

[9] Fishbein's (1967) formulation of the theory also included a component dealing with personal normative beliefs, that is, with the person's own belief about what he should or ought to do and his motivation to comply with his own expectations. However, empirical findings have repeatedly indicated that a subject's report of his personal normative belief serves mainly as an alternative measure of his behavioral intention. Inclusion of personal normative beliefs in the theory, therefore, tended to confound, rather than clarify, the problem of understanding the determinants of behavioral intention. While there is a clear conceptual distinction between personal normative beliefs and behavioral intentions, the high relation between obtained measures of these variables suggests that it may be difficult to develop a satisfactory operationalization of personal normative beliefs. For this reason, personal normative beliefs have been deleted from the present version of the theory.

overt behavior, (B), the two components of the theory should also predict actual behavior. However, a high correlation between BI and B will not always obtain. It may be suggested that the more abstract or generalized the measure of intention, the lower will be its correlation with a specific behavior. Perhaps of greatest importance is the possibility that behavioral intentions may change after they have been measured but before the overt behavior has been observed. Clearly, the longer the time interval between the measurement of intention and the observation of behavior, the less likely it is that the intention measured will predict overt behavior accurately. New information about behavioral consequences and/or normative expectations may produce changes in Aact and NB(Mc) and may thus influence BI, reducing the correlation between the behavior and the previously measured intention. Finally, the relation of behavioral intention to overt behavior may be reduced if the behavior is not entirely under the person's volitional control. Thus, an individual may not be able to perform a given behavior, despite his intention to do so, if he lacks the required ability or if he is prevented from doing so by circumstances or by other people. When these problems can be avoided, a measure of intention is expected to be highly related to overt behavior.[10]

The theory suggests that variables other than Aact and NB(Mc) may influence behavioral intentions, and hence overt behavior, *indirectly* by influencing either of these two components or their relative weights. Thus, situational variables or personality characteristics are expected to be related to intention and overt behavior only if they affect Aact, NB (Mc), or the weights of these predictors (w_0 and w_1). The same principle applies with respect to the actor's attitude toward the object of the behavior. Thus, an individual's attitude toward some person or group of people (e.g., his attitude toward Negroes) must influence either Aact, NB (Mc), or their weights before it can be related to

intentions and overt behavior toward the person or group. Furthermore, even though a traditional measure of attitude may be correlated with one of the two components, it still should be unrelated to behavior if that component carries little or no weight in the determination of behavioral intentions and overt behavior.

The theory thus can provide an explanation for the lack of consistent relations between traditional measures of attitude and overt behavior. The above considerations indicate that traditional attitude measures (e.g., toward people, groups, institutions) will be related to behavior under some conditions but not under others. In addition, the theory suggests an alternative means of predicting socially relevant intentions and behaviors. The remainder of this article deals with some of the research that has been conducted in an attempt to find empirical support for the theory.

Empirical Support

Some evidence for the theory's validity has been accumulated by Dulany (1961, 1964, 1968) and his associates (Dulany & O'Connell, 1963; Schwartz, 1966) in studies of verbal conditioning and concept formation. Of greater relevance to the modified version of the theory, however, are a number of investigations performed by Fishbein and his associates (Ajzen, 1971; Ajzen & Fishbein, 1969, 1970, 1972; Carlson, 1968; Darroch, 1971; DeVries & Ajzen, 1971; Fishbein, 1966; Fishbein, Ajzen, Landy, & Anderson, 1970; Hornik, 1970). These studies have attempted to predict behaviors ranging from strategy choices in Prisoner's Dilemma games to premarital sexual intercourse among undergraduates. Table 26.1 summarizes the basic results concerning relationships between the theory's constructs. These correlations as well as additional findings are discussed on the following pages.[11]

---

[10] For a more complete discussion of factors influenceing the size of the behavioral intention-overt behavior relation, see Fishbein (1973).

[11] Most of the results to be reported have been presented in the original research reports; however, in a few cases, some additional analyses were performed on the data when this was necessary for purposes of the present review.

TABLE 26.1. Correlations, Regression Coefficients, and Multiple Correlations of Aact and NB(Mc) on BI; Correlations between BI and B in 10 Investigations

Study	N	Correlation coefficients		Regression coefficients		Multiple correlations on BI	Correlation BI–B
		Aact–BI	NB(Mc)–BI	Aact–BI	NB(Mc)–BI		
Fishbein et al. (1970)							
Communication	144	.599**	.666**	.295**	.478**	.704**	.690**
Compliance	144	.573**	.493**	.432**	.248**	.608**	.211**
Ajzen & Fishbein (1970)[a]							
Cooperation	32	.370*	.752**	.229	.707**	.785**	.571**
Individualism	32	.710**	.780**	.353*	.552**	.852**	.758**
Competition	32	.883**	.733**	.691**	.327**	.922**	.765**
Total	96	.754**	.838**	.378**	.601**	.888**	.897**
Ajzen (1971)							
Cooperation[b]	36	.562**	.834**	.112	.768**	.839**	.578**
Competition[b]	36	.550**	.247	.541**	.225	.594**	.528**
Total	216	.747**	.688**	.529**	.399**	.818**	.822**
Hornik (1970)[c]							
Grit	30	.854**	.695**	.757**	.131	.859**	.970**
RPM	30	.800**	.650**	.714**	.116	.804**	.858**
Hawk	30	.380*	.114	.371*	.061	.385	.521**
Total	90	.799**	.597**	.712**	.134	.806**	.867**
Darroch (1971)[d]	107	.675**	.537**	.629**	.049	.681**	.462**
Fishbein (1966)[e]							
Males	21	.518*	.843**	−.148	.947**	.860**	.394
Females	14	.918**	.759**	.757**	.232*	.935**	.676**
Total	35	.767**	.810**	.374**	.535**	.849**	.447**
DeVries & Ajzen (1971)[f]	146	.515**	.558**	.354**	.422**	.647**	.664**
Ajzen & Fishbein (1969)[g]	100	.623**	.551**	.470**	.345**	.766**	–
Ajzen & Fishbein (1972)[h]	56	.778**	.414**	.748**	.139	.793**	–
Carlson (1968)[i]	49	.811**	.726**	.629**	.273*	.913**	–

Note: Aact = attitude toward the act; BI = behavioral intentions; NB = normative beliefs; Mc = motivation to comply; B = behavior.
[a] Coefficients are given for one of the two Prisoner's Dilemma games. Results for the other game are very similar.
[b] Coefficients are based on data from control groups (no message).
[c] Results presented refer to Trial 25.
[d] Average coefficients over releases with respect to four different pictures.
[e] Correlations in column 6 are based on self-reports of behavior.
[f] Average coefficients over three related cheating situations. The behavioral measure is a self-report.
[g] Average coefficients over eight common behaviors.
[h] Average coefficients over four hypothetical situations of risk.
[i] Average coefficients over 30 behaviors toward an African Negro.
* $p < .05$.
** $p < .01$.

The Relation between Behavioral Intention and Overt Behavior

The theory assumes that behavioral intentions, appropriately measured, are highly predictive of actual behavior. The relationship between these variables has been examined in seven studies, two of which have only obtained self-reports of behavior (see Table 26.1). Measures of behavioral intentions have typically been very direct, asking

the subject to indicate what he intends to do or would do in the situation.

Two studies using different two-person Prisoner's Dilemma games (cf. Rapoport & Chammah, 1965) have attempted to relate these measures of behavioral intentions to the proportion of cooperative choices in the games. Ajzen and Fishbein (1970) had their subjects play two Prisoner's Dilemma games differing in the extent to which the payoff matrices encouraged cooperation. The games were played either under cooperative, individualistic, or competitive motivational orientations (cf. Deutsch, 1960). Behavioral intentions were measured after 8 "warm-up" trials, and the behavior predicted was the proportion of cooperative choices on the following 10 trials. Over the total sample of subjects, the correlations between behavioral intentions and game behavior were .897 and .841 ($p < .001$) for the two games. These high BI–B correlations are probably attributable to the fact that the measures of behavioral intentions were (a) behavior specific, (b) taken immediately prior to the behavior, and (c) were taken after 8 warm-up trials which allowed the subject to form fairly accurate beliefs about the consequences of cooperating and about his partner's expectations. The intentions, therefore, seemed to have changed very little in the course of the game and could provide accurate predictions of overt behavior.

Ajzen (1971) used a different Prisoner's Dilemma game in the context of a study designed to produce changes in intentions and behavior by means of persuasive communications. The game was played under cooperative and competitive motivational orientations. The correlation for the total sample between behavioral intentions and cooperative game behavior over 20 trials was .822 ($p < .001$).

These findings demonstrate that appropriate measures of behavioral intentions can predict specific overt behavior with a high degree of accuracy. Further support for this claim comes from a recent study by Hornik (1970) in which subjects played an extended Prisoner's Dilemma game against a simulated partner. In the game, the players could convert "missiles" into "factories" or reconvert factories into missiles (see Pilisuk & Skolnick, 1968). The simulated partner used either a Hawk strategy (deceptive play, retaining all or most of his missiles on each trial), a Grit strategy (taking small unilateral initiatives toward disarmament), or an RPM strategy (reward, punish, or match response to maximize the subject's disarmament). The measure of intention asked subjects to state how many missiles they intended to maintain until the end of

the next trial. Overt behavior was the number of missiles actually maintained. Measures of intention were obtained at the beginning and after each block of 5 trials. High correlations were found between behavioral intentions and actual behavior. For example, behavior on Trial 26 was predicted from the measure of intention taken after Trial 25. The average correlation (after transformation to Fisher's z) over the three strategy conditions was .867 ($p < .001$). The correlation, however, was lower in the Hawk condition (.521) than either in the Grit (.970) or in the RPM (.858) conditions.

There seem to be several factors that contributed to this difference. First, in both the Grit and RPM strategies, the simulated confederate behaved in a consistent, systematic manner. In the Grit conditions, the confederate always maintained one missile less than the subject had maintained on the preceding trial. In contrast, the Hawk strategy involved six deceptive and hostile response patterns that were employed in a random, predetermined sequence. Thus, while the Grit and RPM strategies permitted the subject to form fairly accurate expectations about his opponent's behavior and hence fairly accurate beliefs about the consequences of behaving in given ways, this was not the case in the Hawk condition. Second, the random behavior of the Hawk was to some extent matched by the subject. The subject's behavior in the Hawk condition was more erratic (i.e., less stable from trial to trial or over blocks of trials) than in either of the other two conditions. Third, the Hawk strategy seemed to create a uniformly negative orientation in the subjects. The variance of behavioral intentions in the Hawk condition was much lower than in the Grit and RPM conditions. The first factor may explain the lower reliability of intentions in the Hawk than in the other two conditions. This unreliability, as well as the low variance (i.e., restriction of range) in predictor and criterion, served to attenuate the size of the BI–B correlation in the Hawk condition.

Observing a completely different type of behavior, Darroch (1971) also obtained significant but moderate correlations with behavioral intentions. Darroch employed a modified version of the DeFleur and Westie (1958) picture-release technique. Pictures were taken of the subject with a black or a white confederate. The subject was then asked to release these pictures for a variety of purposes by signing appropriate release forms. Approximately 1 month prior to the picture-taking session, measures of specific behavioral intentions (as well as of other variables) had been obtained. Correlations between the number of releases signed and behavioral inintentions varied from .262 to .584 for the different pictures taken, with an average of .462 (The subject was photographed with confederates varying in race and sex.)

A number of reasons may be suggested for these relatively low correlations. Variance in the predictor (intentions) and the criterion (behavior) was found to be low; many subjects intended to sign and actually signed most release forms. In addition, approximately 4 weeks intervened between measurement of intentions and behavior. Moreover, at the beginning of the second session, a persuasive communication was introduced in an attempt to influence the subjects' normative beliefs. Unfortunately, no assessment was made of the effects of this manipulation on intentions. However, after this manipulation, measures were obtained of (a) the subject's felt comfort in each picture, (b) how pleased he would be if his parents saw each picture, (c) his perception of his friends' willingness to appear in a similar picture, and (d) his judgment of the quality of each picture. Assuming that these measures reflect to some degree the normative manipulation, as well as any other changes that may have occurred, it should be possible to improve the prediction of behavior by considering these variables in addition to intentions. This expectation was confirmed by multiple correlations that ranged from .590 to .767, with an average multiple correlation of .735.

The results presented so far indicate that high correlations can be obtained between specific behavioral intentions and corresponding overt behavior. However, the Hornik (1970) and Darroch (1971) studies also demonstrated how problematic such predictions can sometimes be. A study by Fishbein et al. (1970) looked more closely at some of the difficulties that can be encountered in trying to relate intentions and behavior. A series of three studies was conducted in which the task of three-person groups was to balance a board in the shape of an equilateral triangle by raising or lowering their respective corners of the board.[12] On each trial the group members were permitted to send a written communication to one of their co-workers instructing him to raise or lower his corner. Two behavioral measures were taken: the number of instructions the subject sent to each co-worker (communicative behavior) and the proportion of instructions from each co-worker with which the subject complied (compliance behavior). Differences between the two co-workers on these two measures were used as the dependent variables. Similarly, differences were computed between the intentions to communicate with the two co-workers and between the intentions to comply with them, measured immediately prior to the first trial.

While the correlation between intentions and communicative behavior was reasonably high ($r = .690, p < .01$), the correlation with compliance was much lower although still significant ($r = .211, p < .01$). There is reason to suspect that the subjects changed their behavioral intentions as a result of their interactions on the task. First, with regard to communication, a person may initially intend to send instructions to one of his co-workers. But if he learns in the course of the interaction that this group member tends not to comply with his instructions, he is likely to change his evaluation regarding communication to this member, and he will thus modify his behavioral intentions accordingly. In support of this argument, a significant correlation of .528 was obtained between compliance by a given partner and the subject's communicative behavior toward that partner.

Second, concerning compliance, it appears reasonable that a person's intention to comply with a given co-worker will be influenced by the nature of the instruction he receives from that co-worker. This argument is supported by the significant negative correlation ($r = -.456$) of compliance behavior with the absolute discrepancy between

---

[12] A detailed description of the apparatus can be found in Raven and Eachus (1963), Raven and Shaw (1970), and Fishbein et al. (1970).

the instructions received by a subject and his own perception of the best course of action. That is, compliance decreased as the perceived unreasonableness of the instruction increased.

If these claims are valid, we would expect that adding these mediating factors to the initial measures of behavioral intentions should improve the prediction of overt behavior. This expectation was confirmed when the subject's intention to communicate and the co-worker's compliance were regressed on communicative behavior. The regression weight of compliance by the co-worker was significant ($\beta = .328$, $p < .01$), and the multiple correlation was .756. Similarly, a multiple correlation was computed with intention to comply and the previously mentioned index of discrepancy as predictors and compliance behavior as the criterion. The regression weight of the index of discrepancy was $-.431$ ($p < .01$), and the multiple correlation with behavior was .484. It can thus be seen that the mediating variables made significant contributions to the prediction of overt behavior, independent of the specific intention measured at the beginning of the interaction.

More importantly, however, it is to be expected that the subject's intentions toward the end of the experiment will have been affected by these processes. In the study under consideration, posttest measures of behavioral intentions were obtained. When these posttest measures were used in multiple postdictions of behavior, the regression weights of the mediating variables dropped to nonsignificance. The regression weight of compliance by co-workers in postdicting communication was .076 while the weight of the index of discrepancy was .122 in the postdiction of compliance. The multiple postdictions of behavior were thus almost entirely due to the posttest behavioral intentions. The posttest multiple correlations with behavior were .885 for instructions and .513 for compliance.

These findings provide some support for the notion that processes intervening between the measurement of intention and the observation of behavior tend to reduce the relationship between these two variables. Further evidence in support of this notion was provided in Hornik's (1970) study in which behavioral intentions were measured at different stages in the interaction process. In the Grit and RPM conditions where the simulated confederate followed systematic cooperative strategies, the subjects' intentions became consistently and significantly more cooperative over trials. In the Hawk condition, where the simulated confederate played six competitive response patterns in a random fashion, there was no systematic change in the mean number of missiles the subjects intended to maintain from trial to trial, although as was previously mentioned, these intentions were not consistent (i.e., stable) over time. In addition, it can be predicted that the correlation between behavioral intentions and game behavior should be highest when the intention is measured in close proximity to the behavior that serves as the criterion and that this correlation should decline with increasing amounts of interaction between the measurement of intention and the observation of behavior. Hornik's data strongly support these predictions. For example, behavior on Trials 11 through 35 was highly related to intentions on Trial 25; the mean correlation across conditions was .866 ($p < .001$). The average correlation between intentions on Trial 10 and the same behavioral criterion was only .387 ($p < .05$), while intentions at the beginning of the experiment (before Trial 1) showed a nonsignificant correlation of .277 with the criterion.

It thus appears that the best measure of intentions for the prediction of a given behavior is one that is taken in close temporal proximity to the behavior that is to be predicted. Problems of a different type emerged in a study concerned with premarital sexual intercourse among undergraduates (Fishbein, 1966). Subjects rated their general intentions to engage in premarital sexual intercourse on a 7-point bipolar scale. On a second such scale they rated their intentions to engage in premarital sexual intercourse "this semester." The behavioral criterion was a self-report of behavior taken at the end of the semester. The general intention to engage in premarital sexual intercourse and self-reported behavior correlated .564 ($p < .05$) for female subjects and .174 (ns) for males. The more specific intention to engage in this behavior in the course of the semester showed somewhat stronger relationships with behavior: The correlations were .676 ($p < .01$) for females and .394 (*ns*) for males.

Thus, as expected, a specific measure of behavioral intentions yielded better predictions of behavior than did a more general measure. Also of interest is the significant sex difference in the accuracy with which subjects could predict their own sexual behavior. This finding is consistent with the argument that lack of ability or opportunity may lower the correspondence between behavioral intentions and behavior. Clearly, females in our society may meet fewer obstacles than males when they attempt to execute their intentions to engage in premarital sexual intercourse. The reason that the correlation between intentions and behavior was only .676 even for females can most likely be found in the fact that a whole semester intervened between the measurement of these two variables. Many uncontrolled factors may have produced changes in the behavioral intentions.

In sum, the results of studies concerned with a variety of behaviors indicate that accurate behavioral prediction is possible when appropriate measures of behavioral intentions are obtained. When appropriate measures are not available (e.g., when the measure is obtained far in advance of the behavior, or when feedback from the behavior per se may change the intentions), other variables may have to be taken into account if accurate behavioral prediction is to be obtained. Next to be considered are the factors that determine specific behavioral intentions.

Predicting Behavioral Intentions

All studies mentioned before, as well as some additional studies, have investigated the degree to which specific behavioral intentions are predictable from the attitudinal and normative components of the theory. Generally speaking, multiple correlations of Aact, the attitude toward the act, and of NB(Mc), the normative component, on behavioral intentions (BI) are very high. Aact is usually measured by rating the specific behavior in question on a few evaluative semantic differential scales. The normative beliefs (NB) are measured

by a direct question concerning perceived expectations of other people. Where appropriate, beliefs about more than one referent are assessed. For each referent, the subject's motivation to comply is measured on a single 7-point bipolar scale. Multiple correlations of the two components with behavioral intentions have been computed in at least 10 different studies (Ajzen, 1971; Ajzen & Fishbein, 1969, 1970, 1972; Carlson, 1968; Darroch, 1971; DeVries & Azjen, 1971; Fishbein, 1966; Fishbein et al., 1970; Hornik, 1970). The average multiple correlation in these studies was .808.

It is obvious, therefore, that the theory provides highly accurate predictions of behavioral intentions. For example, in the studies using two-person Prisoner's Dilemmas mentioned earlier (Azjen, 1971; Ajzen & Fishbein, 1970), the multiple correlations of Aact and NB(Mc) with BI ranged from 818. to .888. Carlson (1968) measured 30 behavioral intentions with respect to a Negro stimulus person. The multiple predictions of these intentions from the attitudinal and normative components ranged from .770 to .970, with a mean of .913. Ajzen and Fishbein (1969) measured intentions to engage in eight different behaviors on a Friday night. Multiple correlations ranging from .684 to .819 were obtained; the average over these correlations was .766.

It is worth noting that highly accurate predictions of behavioral intentions can be observed even when there is a low relationship of these intentions to overt behavior. For example, in the triangle-board study (Fishbein et al., 1970) previously discussed, multiple correlations of .704 and .608 were found for the prediction of pretest intentions to communicate and to comply, respectively. The corresponding correlations on the posttest were .807 and .765. Similarly, in the study concerned with premarital sexual intercourse (Fishbein, 1966), multiple correlations on behavioral intentions were .935 for females and .860 for males.

The evidence strongly supports the present theory by showing that the two predictors, Aact and NB(Mc), offer high multiple correlations with behavioral intentions. But perhaps of greater importance are the relative weights of the two components in the prediction of behavioral intentions. According to the theory, these weights should vary with the situation and with individual differences between actors. Over all studies conducted and across conditions within these studies, there is a slight tendency for the attitudinal component to take on a somewhat greater weight than does the normative component. However, such a comparison is theoretically meaningless. Different behaviors, different situations, and different individuals have to be compared.

The study on premarital sexual behavior (Fishbein, 1966) found evidence for individual differences in regression weights. For female subjects, the standardized regression coefficients in the prediction of specific intentions were .757 ($p < .01$) for the attitudinal component and .232 ($p < .05$) for the normative component. The strength of the regression weights was reversed for the male sample: The attitudinal component had a regression weight of −.148 (*ns*) while the regression coefficient of the normative component was .947 ($p < .01$). Thus it appears that attitudinal considerations of the consequences of premarital sexual behavior were more important than normative considerations for female students. Normative beliefs and motivation to comply, however, were the primary determinants of behavioral intentions for males.

Carlson (1968) observed differences in regression weights due to particular behaviors. His female subjects supplied measures of intentions, attitude toward the act, and normative beliefs[13] with respect to 30 different behaviors vis-à-vis a "21-year-old, male, African Negro student." A factor analysis of the behavioral intentions yielded five major factors that were labeled "formal social acceptance, informal social acceptance, marital acceptance, cooperation, and subordination-superordination." The loadings of the 30 intentions on these factors were found to correlate significantly with the regression coefficients of the attitudinal and normative components for each of the behaviors. For example, the regression coefficients

of the normative component correlated .60 with the loadings of the behavioral intentions on the marital acceptance factor; that is, the more a given behavior involved marital acceptance, the greater was the importance of the normative considerations. Similarly, there was a positive correlation ($r = .54$) between the regression weights of the attitudinal component and the formal social acceptance factor. The more a behavior involved formal social acceptance, the greater became the importance of attitudinal considerations.

Situational characteristics can also be shown to influence the relative weights of the attudinal and normative components. For example, these weights may take on different values in cooperative and competitive situations. It stands to reason that perceived expectations of others with whom a person is trying to cooperate are more important than expectations of others with whom he competes. Conversely, considerations of an act's consequences (i.e., attitudinal considerations) should carry a greater weight under competition than under cooperation.

These expectations were borne out in the studies by Ajzen and Fishbein (1970) and Ajzen (1971) using the Prisoner's Dilemma game. In the first study (Ajzen & Fishbein, 1970), the subjects played two games with different payoff matrices under one of three motivational orientations: cooperation, individualism, or competition. In the cooperative condition, the subjects were instructed to consider themselves to be partners; in the competitive condition they were told to do better than the other person; players in the individualistic condition were told to have no interest whatsoever in the fate of their partner. The regression coefficients of the attitudinal and normative components on behavioral intentions showed the expected patterns. Under cooperation, the regression coefficients of the normative component were .707 ($p < .01$) and .573 ($p < .01$) in the two games played. The corresponding weights of the attitudinal component were .229 and .239 (both nonsignificant). In the competitive conditions, the regression coefficients were .327 ($p < .01$) and .298 ($p < .01$) for the normative component and .691 ($p < .01$) and .669 ($p < .01$) for the attitudinal component.

---

[13] Personal normative beliefs were used in the multiple regression analyses of this study.

Clearly, norms were more important under cooperation while attitude toward the act was more important under competition. There were no great differences between the weights of the components in the individualistic conditions.

These findings were corroborated in an experiment where a different Prisoner's Dilemma game was played either under cooperative or competitive instructions (Ajzen, 1971). The regression coefficient of the normative component was .768 ($p <$ .01) under cooperation but only .225 (ns) under competition. The attitudinal component carried a significant ($p < .01$) regression weight under competition ($\beta = .541$) but not under cooperation ($\beta = .112$).

In conclusion, there is considerable evidence that behavioral intentions are predictable from the theory's attitudinal and normative components. Furthermore, the relative importance of these two components in the prediction of intentions varies with the type of behavior under consideration, with the situation in which the behavior is to be performed, and with individual differences between actors.

Determinants of the Attitudinal and Normative Components

Early research on Fishbein's summation theory of attitudes (e.g., Anderson & Fishbein, 1965; Fishbein, 1963; Kaplan & Fishbein, 1969) has provided considerable evidence that an individual's attitude toward an object (or person) is a function of his beliefs about the object and the evaluative aspects of those beliefs. A similar formulation was suggested in Equation 2 for the attitude toward an act; here, beliefs about an object were replaced by beliefs about an act's consequences.

Some studies have tested the attitudinal formulation with respect to Aact, the attitude toward an act. For example, Ajzen and Fishbein (1970) obtained measures of the likelihood that cooperative choices in the Prisoner's Dilemma would lead to the two possible payoffs for the players. These estimates were multiplied by the subject's evaluation of the payoffs, and the products were summed. This estimate of Aact was correlated with a direct measure of attitude toward cooperation obtained on four evaluative semantic differential scales. In the two Prisoner's Dilemma games that were played, the correlations were .632 and .672 ($p <$ .01).

Using four hypothetical decision situations involving a certain amount of risk, Ajzen and Fishbein (1972) obtained estimates of the probability that the risky option would lead to success or failure. Subjective evaluations of success and failure were then multiplied by these subjective probabilities, and the products were summed. The correlations between a direct measure of Aact and this estimate were significant in all four hypothetical situations, ranging from .299 to .814 with a mean of .611.

These findings, then, provide support for the expectancy-value model of the attitudinal component. The study involving hypothetical decisions under risk (Ajzen & Fishbein, 1972) has also tested the expectancy-value formulation for the normative component (see Equation 4). This study tried to manipulate the perceived expectations of reference persons by telling the subjects that a given referent believed there was either a high or a low probability that the risky alternative would lead to success. That is, the referents (close family and friends) were said to have low or high confidence in the risky alternative's chances of success. The subject's perception of the referent's beliefs about the act's possible consequences (success or failure) and the subject's perception of the referent's evaluations of success and failure were then measured. These two measures were multiplied and summed to yield an estimate of the referent's attitude toward the act as perceived by the subject ($Aact_0$). A direct measure of $Aact_0$ was also obtained using four evaluative semantic differential scales. Finally, a regular measure of normative beliefs (NB) was taken; that is, the perceived expectations of the referents were measured.

The three indices obtained (the estimate of $Aact_0$, the direct measure of $Aact_0$, and the measure of NB) correlated significantly with each other. The estimate of $Aact_0$ showed a mean correlation of .508 with the direct measure of $Aact_0$. More importantly, the measure of NB correlated, on the average, .635 with the direct measure of the referent's perceived attitude and .501 with the estimate of $Aact_0$. Thus, there is some empirical evidence that normative beliefs are related to the subject's perception of the referent's attitude toward the act in question. Also in support of this general idea, it was found that an experimental manipulation of the referent's estimate that the risky alternative would lead to success had a significant influence on the three related measures (i.e., the direct and indirect measures of $Aact_0$ and NB). Of greatest interest was the finding that the direct measure of normative beliefs showed the expected effects of this manipulation: The subject believed that the referent person expected him to engage in the risky behavior when he was told that the referent's estimate of success was high. The measure of normative beliefs was significantly lower (i.e., the perceived expectation of the referents was not to take the risky alternative) when the referents were said to have low estimates of success.

Clearly, then, the perceived attitude of a relevant reference group exerts a significant influence on the behavioral expectations attributed to them. It has been argued that the motivation to comply with the referent's expectations may be related, among other things, to the referent's power over the actor. Limited support comes from Ajzen's (1971) study using the Prisoner's Dilemma game. In this study, a measure was obtained of the subject's desire to please his partner. It is possible to argue that this measure is an indication of the other person's referent power (cf. French & Raven, 1959). Consistent with expectations, the correlation of this measure with motivation to comply was found to be .661 ($p < .01$).

The last few paragraphs have discussed some empirical support for notions concerning the nature and determinants of the normative component in the present theory. It appears that there is some relation between normative beliefs and the referent's perceived attitude toward the act. There also seems to be a relationship between motivation to comply and the referent's power. However, it is obvious that much more research is needed before any firm conclusions can be drawn.

Effects of "External" Variables

According to the theory, any variable other than Aact or NB(Mc) may influence behavioral intentions, and hence behavior, indirectly. Thus, any "external" factor such as demographic or personality characteristics of the actor, variables related to the particular behavior under investigation, or situational variables can affect intentions and overt behavior only if they influence the attitudinal or normative components or their relative weights.

Many of the studies previously discussed have provided support for this prediction. The conclusion emerging from these studies is that any variable found to be related to overt behavior is also related to at least one of the predictors in the theory, while external variables unrelated to overt behavior are also unrelated to either the attitudinal or normative components. Moreover, also consistent with expectations, whenever an external variable is related to intentions and overt behavior, this relation is considerably attenuated when Aact and NB(Mc) are statistically held constant. For example, Ajzen and Fishbein (1970) studied the effects of the players' F scores and sex on cooperation in the Prisoner's Dilemma. Further, it will be recalled that two games were played differing in their payoff matrices and that these games were played under one of three motivational orientations: cooperation, competition, and individualism. The results indicated that intentions and actual game behavior were affected significantly by the payoff matrix and by motivational orientation. There were no significant relations between game behavior and either sex or F score. Examination of findings with respect to normative beliefs and attitude toward the act showed the same pattern: significant effects of payoff matrix and motivational orientation; no significant effects of sex and F score on either of the theory's two predictors.

Analyses of covariance on intentions and behaviors were then performed in which attitude toward the act and normative beliefs were treated as simultaneous covariates. This procedure reduced the effect of the payoff matrix to nonsignificance. The effect of motivational orientation, although significant at the .05 level, was greatly attenuated.

These results demonstrate the intervening role played by the theory's two components. The effects of external variables on behavioral intentions and game behavior seem to have been mediated by attitudinal and normative considerations. Similar findings emerged in the experiment by Fishbein et al. (1970) in which three-person groups were to level a triangle board. This task was facilitated by spirit levels mounted on top of the triangle board in front of each group member. Two experimental conditions were created by varying the alignment of the spirit levels and thus affecting the information available to the group members. These variations had strong effects on behavioral intentions and on actual behavior. In one condition, approximately equal numbers of instructions were sent to the other two group members, and each subject complied to approximately the same degree with his instructions. In the second condition, however, considerably more instructions were sent to one group member, and more compliance was observed with respect to the other.

Exactly the same pattern of results were observed with respect to the attitudinal and normative components. Attitude toward the act and perceived expectations were affected by the experimental manipulation in the same way as were intentions and task behaviors, indicating again that the theory's two components tend to mediate the effects on behavior of external variables, in this case a situational variable.

Considering the effects of external variables on intentions and behavior brings us back to the starting point of this article; that is, to the relation between measures of general attitudes toward persons or objects and overt behavior with respect to them. The present theory denies the existence of a consistent and strong relation between the attitude toward an object (Ao) and any given behavior with respect to the object. Like any other variable external to the theory, Ao is expected to predict behavior only to the extent that it is related to one of the theory's components; and even then only if that component carries a significant weight in the regression equation.

Of the studies discussed in this article, five employed measures of general attitudes. In the three studies using two-person games (Ajzen, 1971; Ajzen & Fishbein, 1970; Hornik, 1970), the attitude toward the other player was measured on evaluative semantic differential scales. Fishbein et al. (1970) obtained similar attitude measures with respect to the other two group members working with the subject on the triangle-board task. Finally, Darroch (1971) used a Likert-type measure of attitude toward Negroes. Intentions concerning the task and actual task behavior were the dependent variables of the first four studies. DeFleur and Westie's (1958) photographic release signing procedure provided the dependent variable in the Darroch study.

Table 26.2 summarizes findings with respect to Ao, the attitude toward an object and its relations to behavioral intentions and behavior. The table also presents evidence on the mediating role of the attitudinal and normative components. In the first column of Table 26.2, it can be seen that the correlations of the traditional attitude measures with overt behavior were rather low, even though they did reach significance in some instances. Thus, in one of the two Prisoner's Dilemma games employed by Ajzen and Fishbein (1970), the correlation was .256 ($p < .01$), but in the other game, it did not reach significance ($r = .091$). Similarly, Ajzen (1971) found a low but significant Ao-B correlation ($r = .265$, $p < .01$). Fishbein et al. (1970) found that while the correlation of attitude and behavior was not significant for communicative behavior ($r = -.024$), for compliance it was significant ($r = .262$) at the .05 level. Darroch (1971) obtained equally low and inconsistent attitude-behavior correlations ranging from .088 to .248, using the picture-release technique.

Hornik's (1970) results are interesting in their inconsistency. While in the Grit and RPM conditions attitude toward the simulated partners was highly predictive of game behavior, the correlation broke down completely in the Hawk condition.

Thus, as one would expect on the basis of the present theory, sometimes moderate or even high correlations between attitude and behavior are obtained while at other times the correlations are low and nonsignificant. Similar findings can be observed with respect to the relation between

TABLE 26.2. Correlations between Attitude toward an Object and Various Criteria

Study	Product–moment correlations				Partial correlations	
	Ao–B	Ao–BI	Ao–Aact	Ao–NB(Mc)	Ao–BI[a]	Ao–B[b]
Ajzen & Fishbein (1970)	.256* .091	.237* .091	.354* .239*	.262* .015	−.126 −.197	.107 .161
Ajzen (1971)	.265**	.242*	.257**	.241*	.092	.119
Fishbein et al. (1970)	−.024 .262**	−.003 .279**	.059 .418**	.037 .163	−.072 .160	−.031 .164
Darroch (1970)	.212* .248*	.390** .415**	.300** .306**	.233* .334**	.259** .298**	.031 .083
	.110 .088	.118 .142	.082 .148	.109 .143	.084 .061	.070 .055
Hornik (1970)	.780** .730**	.771** .763**	.779** .718**	.684** .741**	.294 .444*	.208 .227
	−.117	−.085	−.015	.012	−.087	−.085

Note: Ao = attitude toward an object; B = behavior; BI = behavioral intentions; Aact = attitude toward the act; NB = normative beliefs; Mc = motivation to comply.
[a] Aact and NB(Mc) are held constant.
[b] BI is held constant.
* p < .05.
** p < .01.

attitude and behavioral intentions (see column 2 in Table 26.2). More important, however, are the correlations between the general attitude measure and the theory's two predictors. These correlations are presented in columns 3 and 4 of Table 26.2. Whenever Ao shows a significant correlation with intentions and behavior, it is also found to correlate significantly with Aact, with NB(Mc), or with both. The conclusion that the attitudinal and normative components mediate the effect of Ao on intentions and that intentions mediate its effect on behavior also finds support in the partial correlations that are presented in the last two columns of Table 26.2. In column 5 the partial correlations between Ao and intentions are presented, partialling out Aact and NB(Mc). It can be seen that the partial correlations are very low and mostly nonsignificant. One notable exception are two partial attitude–intention correlations reported by Darroch (1971) that remained significant. No explanation for this finding seems readily available. One of the partial correlations between Ao and BI reported by Hornik (1970) is also significant. It should be noted, however, that holding Aact and NB(Mc) constant greatly attenuated the original correlation from .730 (see column 1 of Table 26.2) to .444. Of greater importance for the attitude–behavior relation are the residual correlations of Ao and behavior, holding BI constant, which appear in column 6. It can be seen that in all cases, the correlations between attitude and behavior were reduced to nonsignificance. There appears to be little doubt that the inconsistent attitude–behavior relationships in these and other studies can be attributed to variations in the degree to which the general attitude measure is related to the specific determinants of overt behavior.

Changing Intentions and Behaviors

The low and inconsistent relations usually obtained between traditional measures of attitude and overt behavior suggest that there is little reason to assume that attitude change will result in behavioral change. Indeed, what little evidence there is on this point indicates that attitude change has relatively little effect on behavior (Festinger, 1964). In light of the present theory, this should not come as a surprise; behavioral change can best be effected by manipulation of the determinants of behavioral intentions and behavior, that is, the theory's two components. Thus, it is suggested that changes in attitudinal-type variables *may* result in behavioral change. However, rather than attempting to change traditional attitudes toward an object, one needs to deal with Aact and NB(Mc) which are more behavior-specific.

Although not always recognized, it is usually quite easy to influence behavior in specified directions. All that has to be done is to change the situation such that different behaviors will be called for. In terms of the present theory, situational changes have to affect either the consequences of the behavioral alternatives (i.e., Aact) or the normative expectations (i.e., NB[Mc]). It has been shown previously that such variations do indeed exert a strong influence on behaviors. Thus, a slight change in the alignment of the spirit levels on the triangle board completely altered the patterns of interaction among the members of the group (Fishbein et al., 1970). Similarly, variations in the pay-off matrix of a Prisoner's Dilemma game can strongly influence behavior (Ajzen & Fishbein, 1970). It was also shown that these effects were mediated by their influence on the theory's components.

More direct evidence in support of these notions is available in two experimental investigations. In the first (Ajzen & Fishbein, 1972), an attempt was made to change behavioral intentions in a hypothetical situation involving some risk. Specifically, the decision involved an investment of $1,000 in a building project. In a pretest, the subject's estimate of the project's chances of success were set at 70%. Furthermore, his close family and friends with whom the subject was said to have discussed the issue also had a 70% subjective probability of success. The subject's intention to invest the money was measured, as were his attitude toward the act and his normative beliefs (i.e., the perceived expectations of his close family and friends). Computing the multiple correlation of attitude toward the act and normative beliefs on behavioral intentions showed the attitudinal component to carry most of the weight in the prediction. The regression coefficient of the normative component was nonsignificant. It was therefore predicted that change in the attitudinal component would be reflected in corresponding change of intentions, while intentions would be relatively unaffected by change in the normative component.

In a posttest administered after an unrelated intervening activity, either the subject's own subjective probability of success or that of his close family and friends was lowered to 30%. As expected, these manipulations lowered attitude toward the act of investing money and normative beliefs about it, respectively. Intentions, however, were affected very little by the shift in normative

beliefs while the reduction in the attitude toward the act was accompanied by a strong decrease in behavioral intentions.

This study demonstrates that changes in normative beliefs are unrelated to behavioral intentions when the normative component has little predictive power. The study by Ajzen (1971) supported the same principle with respect to changes both in attitude toward the act or in normative beliefs. Moreover, the effects of such changes on actual behavior were also assessed. The experiment involved a Prisoner's Dilemma game played under a cooperative or a competitive motivational orientation. As mentioned previously, in predicting intentions and behavior, the normative component was of greater importance than was the attitudinal component in the cooperative condition while the reverse was true for the competitive condition. Shifts in intentions and game behavior should thus result from changes in normative beliefs in the cooperative condition but less so in the competitive condition. Similarly, changes in attitude toward the act should influence intentions and behavior more under competition than under cooperation.

To effect changes in the theory's components, one half of the groups in each motivational condition were given an "attitudinal message" while the other half were given a "normative message." The attitudinal message was designed to make the attitude toward cooperation either more favorable or less favorable. The normative message was designed to have similar effects on the perceived expectations of the other player.

The results for both intention and behavior strongly supported the prediction. A highly significant Motivational Orientation × Message-Type interaction was found: The attitudinal message changed intentions and game behavior under competition while the normative message was most effective under cooperation.

Clearly, then, the effectiveness of a persuasive communication designed to change behavior depends on the target variable that is attacked. Messages directed at the attitudinal component are effective only if that component carries a significant weight in the prediction of behavior. The same holds true for a message directed at the normative component. If one of the components is of little importance in the prediction of behavior, then any attempt to change it, even if successful, cannot be expected to have a strong effect on behavior.

Conclusion

This article has reviewed research related to a theory for the prediction of specific behavioral acts. It has been argued that traditional measures of general attitudes toward objects cannot be expected to adequately predict such specific behaviors. While measures of attitude toward an object, such as obtained by the Thurstone, Likert, or semantic differential techniques, may perhaps be related to a person's general behavioral tendency with respect to the object (cf. Fishbein, 1973), it appears that for the prediction of a given act, attitudinal variables more specific to the act in question will have to be considered.

The present theory represents one possible approach to the problem. It suggests that the most immediately relevant predictor of a specific action is the person's behavioral intention. Although problems can arise with regard to the intention–behavior relationship, empirical research has shown that high correlations between these variables can be obtained. It was also shown that behavioral intentions are predictable from the theory's two components: attitude toward the specific act and normative beliefs multiplied by the person's motivation to comply with the norms. Support was also provided for the prediction that the effects on behavior of variables other than those included in the model are mediated by their influence on one or the other of the two components.

In this context it was shown that the traditional attitude toward an object, a variable external to the theory, is also related to overt behavior only to the extent that it affects either the attitudinal or the normative component. Since such traditional measures of attitude need not correlate with either component, although they may in some situations, they cannot be expected to predict behavior consistently. Failure of previous investigations to find

consistent attitude–behavior relations supports this general line of reasoning.

REFERENCES

Ajzen, I. Attitudinal vs. normative messages: An investigation of the differential effects of persuasive communications on behavior. *Sociometry*, 1971, **34**, 263–280.

Ajzen, I., & Fishbein, M. The prediction of behavioral intentions in a choice situation. *Journal of Experimental Social Psychology*, 1969, **5**, 400–416.

Ajzen, I., & Fishbein, M. The prediction of behavior from attitudinal and normative variables. *Journal of Experimental Social Psychology*, 1970, **6**, 466–487.

Ajzen, I., & Fishbein, M. Attitudes and normative beliefs as factors influencing behavioral intentions. *Journal of Personality and Social Psychology*, 1972, **21**, 1–9.

Allport, G. W. Attitudes. In C. Murchison (Ed.), *A handbook of social psychology*. Worcester, Mass.: Clark University Press, 1935.

Allport, G. W. The historical background of modern social psychology. In G. Lindzey & E. Aronson (Eds.), *Handbook of social psychology*, Vol. 1. Reading, Mass.: Addison-Wesley, 1968.

Anderson, L. R., & Fishbein, M. Prediction of attitude from the number, strength, and evaluative aspect of beliefs about the attitude object: A comparison of summation and congruity theories. *Journal of Personality and Social Psychology*, 1965, **2**, 437–443.

Becker, G. M., & McClintock, C. G. Value: Behavioral decision theory. *Annual Review of Psychology*, 1967, **18**, 239–286.

Berg, K. E. Ethnic attitudes and agreement with a Negro person. *Journal of Personality and Social Psychology*, 1966, **4**, 215–220.

Bogardus, E. S. Measuring social distance. *Journal of Applied Sociology*, 1925, **9**, 299–308.

Bray, D. W. The prediction of behavior from two attitude scales. *Journal of Abnormal and Social Psychology*, 1950, **45**, 64–84.

Campbell, D. T. Social attitudes and other acquired behavioral dispositions. In S. Koch (Ed.), *Psychology: A study of a science*. Vol. 6. *Investigations of man as socius: Their place in psychology and the social sciences*. New York: McGraw-Hill, 1963.

Carlson, A. R. The relationships between a behavioral intention, attitude toward the behavior and normative beliefs about the behavior. Unpublished doctoral dissertation, University of Illinois, 1968.

Darroch, R. K. Attitudinal variables and perceived group norms as predictors of behavioral intentions and behavior in the signing of photographic releases. Unpublished doctoral dissertation, University of Illinois, 1971.

DeFleur, M. L., & Westie, F. R. Verbal attitudes and overt acts: An experiment on the salience of attitudes. *American Sociolgoical Review*, 1958, **23**, 667–673.

Deutsch, M. The effects of motivational orientation upon threat and suspicion. *Human Relations*, 1960, **13**, 123–139.

DeVries, D. L., & Ajzen, I. The relationship of attitudes and normative beliefs to cheating in college. *Journal of Social Psychology*, 1971, **83**, 199–207.

Dulany, D. E. Hypotheses and habits in verbal "operant conditioning." *Journal of Abnormal and Social Psychology*, 1961, **63**, 251–263.

Dulany, D. E. The separable effects of the information conveyed by a reinforcer. Paper presented at the meeting of the Psychonomic Society, St. Louis, October 1964.

Dulany, D. E. Awareness, rules, and propositional control: A confrontation with S-R behavior theory. In D. Horton & T. Dixon (Eds.), *Verbal behavior and S-R behavior theory*. New York: Prentice-Hall, 1968.

Dulany, D. E., & O'Connell, D. C. Does partial reinforcement dissociate verbal rules and the behavior they might be presumed to control? *Journal of Verbal Learning and Verbal Behavior*, 1963, **2**, 361–372.

Edwards, W. Behavioral decision theory. *Annual Review of Psychology*, 1961, **12**, 473–498.

Ehrlich, H. J. Attitudes, behavior, and the intervening variables. *American Sociologist*, 1969, **4**, 29–34.

Festinger, L. Behavioral support for opinion change. *Public Opinion Quarterly*, 1964, **28**, 404–417.

Fishbein, M. An investigation of the relationships between beliefs about an object and the attitude toward that object. *Human Relations*, 1963, **16**, 233–240.

Fishbein, M. Sexual behavior and propositional control. Paper presented at the meeting of the Psychonomic Society, St. Louis, October 1966.

Fishbein, M. Attitude and the prediction of behavior. In M. Fishbein (Ed.), *Readings in attitude theory and measurement*. New York: Wiley, 1967.

Fishbein, M. The prediction of behaviors from attitudinal variables. In C. D. Mortensen & K. K. Sereno (Eds.), *Advances in communication research*. New York: Harper & Row, 1973.

Fishbein, M., Ajzen, I., Landy, E., & Anderson, L. R. Attitudinal variables and behavior: Three empirical studies and a theoretical reanalysis. (Tech. Rept. No. 70–9, ARPA Order 454, Contract 177–473 N00014–67–A0103–0013) Seattle: University of Washington, 1970.

French, J. P. R., Jr., & Raven, B. H. The bases of social power. In D. Cartwright (Ed.), *Studies in social power*. Ann Arbor: University of Michigan Press, 1959.

Hornik, J. A. Two approaches to individual differences in cooperative behavior in an expanded Prisoner's Dilemma game. Unpublished master's level paper, University of Illinois, 1970.

Kaplan, K. J., & Fishbein, M. The source of beliefs, their saliency, and prediction of attitude. *The Journal of Social Psychology*, 1969, **78**, 63–74.

Kimble, G. A., & Perlmuter, L. C. The problem of volition. *Psychological Review*, 1970, **77**, 361–384.

Kutner, B., Wilkins, C., & Yarrow, P. R. Verbal attitudes and overt behavior involving racial prejudice. *Journal of Abnormal and Social Psychology*, 1952, **47**, 649–652.

LaPiere, R. T. Attitudes vs. actions. *Social Forces*, 1934, **13**, 230–237.

Linn, L. S. Verbal attitudes and overt behavior: A study of racial discrimination. *Social Forces*, 1965, **44**, 353–364.

McGuire, W. J. The nature of attitudes and attitude change. In G. Lindzey & E. Aronson (Eds.), *The handbook of social psychology*. (2nd ed.) Vol. 3. *The individual in a social context*. Reading, Mass.: Addison-Wesley, 1969.

Peak, H. Attitude and motivation. *Nebraska Symposium on Motivation*, 1955, **3**, 149–189.

Pilisuk, M., & Skolnick, P. Inducing trust: A test of the Osgood proposal. *Journal of Personality and Social Psychology*, 1968, **8**, 121–133.

Rapoport, A., & Chammah, A. M. *Prisoner's Dilemma: A study on conflict and cooperation*. Ann Arbor: University of Michigan Press, 1965.

Raven, B. H., & Eachus, H. T. Cooperation and competition in means-independent triads. *Journal of Abnormal and Social Psychology*, 1963, **67**, 307–316.

Raven, B. H., & Shaw, J. I. Interdependence and group problem-solving in the triad. *Journal of Personality and Social Psychology*, 1970, **14**, 157–165.

Rokeach, M. *Beliefs, attitudes, and values*. San Francisco: Jossey-Bass, 1968.

Rokeach, M., & Mezei, L. Race and shared belief as factors in social choice. *Science*, 1966, **151**, 167–172.

Rosenberg, M. J. Cognitive structure and attitudinal affect. *Journal of Abnormal and Social Psychology*, 1956, **53**, 367–372.

Rosenberg, M. J., & Hovland, C. I. Cognitive affective, and behavioral components of attitudes. In M. J. Rosenberg, C. I. Hovland, W. J. McGuire, R. P. Abelson, & J. W. Brehm (Eds.), *Attitude organization and change*. New Haven, Conn.: Yale University Press, 1960.

Rotter, J. B. *Social learning and clinical psychology*. Englewood Cliffs, N. J.: Prentice-Hall, 1954.

Ryan, T. A. *Intentional behavior: An approach to human motivation*. New York: Ronald Press, 1970.

Schwartz, S. Trial-by-trial analysis of processes in simple and disjunctive concept attainment tasks. *Journal of Experimental Psychology*, 1966, **72**, 456–465.

Smith, E. W. L., & Dixon, T. R. Verbal conditioning as a function of race of the experimenter and prejudice of the subject. *Journal of Experimental Social Psychology*, 1968, **4**, 285–301.

Triandis, H. C. Exploratory factor analyses of the behavioral component of social attitudes. *Journal of Abnormal and Social Psychology*, 1964, **68**, 420–430.

Triandis, H. C. Toward an analysis of the components of interpersonal attitudes. In C. W. Sherif & M. Sherif (Eds.), *Attitude, ego-involvement, and change*. New York: Wiley, 1967.

Warner, L. G., & DeFleur, M. L. Attitude as an interactional concept: Social constraint and social distance as intervening variables between attitudes and action. *American Sociological Review*, 1969, **34**, 153–169.

Wicker, A. W. Attitudes vs. actions: The relationship of verbal and overt behavioral responses to attitude objects. *Journal of Social Issues*, 1969, **25**, 41–78.

Received December 10, 1971 ■

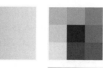

READING 27

Attitude Accessibility as a Moderator of the Attitude-Perception and Attitude-Behavior Relations: An Investigation of the 1984 Presidential Election

Russell H. Fazio and Carol J. Williams

It was hypothesized that the extent to which individuals' attitudes guide their subsequent perceptions of and behavior toward the attitude object is a function of the accessibility of those attitudes from memory. A field investigation concerning the 1984 presidential election was conducted as a test of these hypotheses. Attitudes toward each of the two candidates, Reagan and Mondale, and the accessibility of those attitudes, as indicated by the latency of response to the attitudinal inquiry, were measured for a large sample of townspeople months before the election. Judgments of the performance of the candidates during the televised debates served as the measure of subsequent perceptions, and voting served as the measure of subsequent behavior. As predicted, both the attitude-perception and the attitude-behavior relations were moderated by attitude accessibility. The implications of these findings for theoretical models of the processes by which attitudes guide behavior, along with their practical implications for survey research, are discussed.

The present research was supported by Grant MH 38832 from the National Institute of Mental Health.

The authors thank David Brown, the manager of the shopping mall where the attitude data were collected, for his cooperation; Sheri Rieth for her skillful assistance with all the phases of data collection; and Michael Bailey for designing and building the apparatus that was used to measure and record attitudes and response latencies. In addition, the authors are grateful to Paget Gross, David Sanbonmatsu, and Steven Sherman for their comments on an earlier draft of the article.

Correspondence concerning this article should be addressed to Russell H. Fazio, Department of Psychology, Indiana University, Bloomington, Indiana 47405.

Research on the consistency between individuals' attitudes and behavior toward an object has focused on the identification of variables that moderate the extent of the observed relation. This approach, which has been referred to as the *When?* generation of research due to its focus on the issue of when attitude scores are predictive of later behavior (Zanna & Fazio, 1982), has produced considerable progress. A variety of situational variables, personality factors, and qualities of the attitude itself have been identified as moderators of the attitude-behavior relation (see Fazio, 1986, for a recent review).

Yet another approach to the attitude-behavior issue has been initiated recently. This approach centers on the process(es) by which attitudes guide behavior, what Zanna and Fazio (1982) referred to as the *How?* question. Within this context, it has been suggested that the accessibility of an individual's attitude from memory assumes crucial importance. In fact, Fazio and his colleagues have proposed a model of the attitude-to-behavior process that focuses specifically on the chronic accessibility of the attitude from memory (Fazio, 1986; Fazio, Powell, & Herr, 1983). In brief, the model views behavior in any given situation as stemming from individuals' perceptions of the attitude object and the situation in which the attitude object is encountered. Consistent with the object appraisal function that attitudes presumably serve (Katz, 1960; Smith, Bruner, & White, 1956) and with the constructive nature of perception, individuals' attitudes may guide such perceptions. That is, selective processing of the qualities of the attitude object in the immediate situation can occur. However, selective processing in a manner that is congruent with the valence of the attitude is conceivable only given that the attitude has been activated from memory upon observation of the attitude object. Hence, the accessibility of the attitude is postulated to be a critical determinant of whether the attitude-to-behavior process is initiated. In this way, attitude accessibility is thought to affect both the attitude-perception and the attitude-behavior relations.

The present research involves both the *when* and the *how* approach in that it centers on attitude accessibility as a moderator of the attitude-behavior relation. Attitude accessibility was measured for each of the respondents in an attitude survey. The consistency between attitudes and later behavior toward the attitude object (as well as the consistency between attitudes and perceptions of the attitude object in a later situation) was examined as a function of attitude accessibility scores. In this way the present investigation serves as both a test of the proposed process model (the how question) and as an attempt to identify a variable that moderates the attitude-behavior relation (the when question).

According to the process model, the chronic accessibility of an attitude is a function of the associative strength of the attitude object and the evaluation that the individual holds of the object. That is, attitudes are characterized as object-evaluation associations and the strength of the association acts as a determinant of the accessibility of the attitude. The stronger the association, the greater the likelihood that the evaluation will be activated spontaneously upon the individual's encountering the attitude object. Support for this view stems from a number of experiments involving attempts to enhance the strength of the object-evaluation association by inducing individuals to note and express their attitudes repeatedly. Such repeated expression has been found to enhance both the speed with which individuals can respond to inquiries concerning their attitudes (Fazio, Chen, McDonel, & Sherman, 1982; Powell & Fazio, 1984) and the likelihood that the attitude will be activated automatically from memory upon the individual's mere observation of the attitude object (Fazio et al., 1983; Fazio, Sanbonmatsu, Powell, & Kardes, 1986).

The obvious implication of this view is that the attitudes of two individuals with identical scores from some attitude measurement instrument may still differ markedly. The strength of the object-evaluation association and, hence, the chronic accessibility of the attitude may differ. Consequently, when they encounter the attitude object in a given situation, the attitude of one individual may be activated automatically, whereas the attitude of the other may not be. Thus, the two individuals may construe any information that becomes available concerning the attitude object quite differently. Perceptions of the attitude object and, ultimately, behavior toward the object are more likely to be "guided" by the attitude in the case of the individual whose attitude has been activated.

To date, little research has been conducted linking attitude accessibility to attitude-behavior consistency. However, a number of findings suggest that such a moderating effect may occur. For example, the manner of attitude formation has been found to affect both attitude-behavior consistency (see Fazio & Zanna, 1981, for a review) and attitude accessibility (Fazio et al., 1982, Experiments 1 and 2; Fazio et al., 1983). In separate experiments, it has been observed that individuals who were introduced to a set of intellectual puzzles, via direct behavioral experience with example puzzles, formed attitudes that were both more accessible from memory and more predictive of their later behavior with those puzzles than did individuals who were provided only with indirect nonbehavioral experience. Enhancement of the strength of the object-evaluation association through repeated attitudinal expression has been found to produce similar effects. Again, in separate experiments, this manipulation has been observed to enhance both attitude accessibility, as mentioned earlier (Fazio et al., 1982; Experiment 3), and attitude-behavior consistency. The latter evidence is provided by an experiment in which repeated attitudinal expression increased the correspondence between attitudes toward a set of intellectual puzzles and subsequent behavior involving those puzzles (Fazio et al., 1982, Experiment 4).

Thus, although past findings are consistent with the hypothesis that attitude accessibility acts as a moderator of attitude-behavior consistency, no single investigation has examined this postulated relation directly. The present study does so by simultaneously assessing attitudes and the accessibility of those attitudes and then assessing relevant perceptions and relevant behavior at later points in time. Attitudes that are highly accessible from memory are hypothesized to be more predictive of subsequent perceptions of the attitude object and

subsequent behavior toward the attitude object than are attitudes characterized by relatively poor accessibility.

In the present investigation, attitude accessibility was measured via the latency of response to an attitudinal inquiry. Hence, it is important to review what is known about this measure. First, as indicated by the research involving repeated attitudinal expression, latency of response to an attitudinal inquiry does appear to index the strength of an object-evaluation association satisfactorily. Second, the latency measure appears to be a fairly good approximation of the likelihood of automatic activation of the evaluation upon mere observation of the attitude object. Experiments have shown that attitude objects preselected on the basis of an individual's having responded quickly to an attitudinal inquiry are more likely to be activated automatically upon subsequent presentation of the attitude object than are attitudes characterized by relatively slow latencies of response to an attitudinal inquiry (Fazio et al., 1986). Thus, how long it takes to respond to an attitudinal inquiry is reflective of the likelihood that the attitude will be activated spontaneously upon one's encountering the attitude object.

The specific latency measure used in the present research differs only slightly from the operationalization involved in the research upon which the preceding inferences are drawn. In the previous work, the response whose latency was measured involved a dichotomous judgment. For example, upon presentation of an attitude object, subjects would press either a control button labeled *good* or one labeled *bad* as quickly as possible. In the present investigation, we were interested in simultaneously obtaining a scalar measure of the attitude and the response latency. Subjects heard a tape-recorded attitude statement and, as quickly as possible, responded by pressing one of five buttons labeled *strongly disagree* to *strongly agree*.

Pilot Experiment

Given this desired modification, we were somewhat concerned about the extent to which response latency would still reflect the strength of the object-evaluation association. Hence, we conducted a preliminary experiment, modeled after that by Powell and Fazio (1984), involving the repeated expression manipulation. Fifty-five subjects expressed attitudes toward each of three target issues a total of three times and did not evaluate another three target issues. The target issues that were used concerned gun control, school prayer, and the United Nations as one set, and Reaganomics, the space program, and mandatory retirement age as the other set. Which set of issues comprised the repeated expression versus control items was counterbalanced across subjects. Each time that an issue appeared on the questionnaire it was evaluated with respect to a different semantic differential scale. For example, subjects might have evaluated gun control on a support/oppose scale, then on a beneficial/harmful scale, and so on. After completing the questionnaires, subjects participated in the response time task. Response latencies were affected by the repeated expression manipulation. Subjects were significantly faster at indicating the extent of their agreement or disagreement with attitudinal statements that concerned issues toward which they had repeatedly expressed their attitudes ($M = 2.65$ s) than statements that concerned issues toward which they had not ($M = 3.28$), $t(54) = 3.55$, $p < .001$. This finding suggests that increasing the number of response options from two to five did not affect the sensitivity of the latency measure as an indicant of the strength of the object-evaluation association.

Overview

The present investigation concerned attitudes, perceptions, and behavior relevant to the 1984 presidential election. Specifically, both attitudes toward each of the candidates, Reagan and Mondale, and the accessibility of those attitudes were assessed for a large sample of townspeople in the summer of 1984. The perception and behavior measures were collected months later. The perception measure concerned respondents' judgments of the performance of the candidates during the nationally tele-

vised debates. The behavior measure was collected by telephoning respondents within a few days after the election and asking them to indicate whether they had voted in the election and, if so, for whom.

It was predicted that individuals whose attitudes toward a candidate were relatively accessible, that is, individuals who were able to respond relatively quickly to the attitudinal inquiry, would display perceptions of debate performance that were more congruent with their attitudes than would individuals whose attitudes were marked by relatively low accessibility, that is, those who responded relatively slowly to the attitudinal inquiry. Such differential selective processing of the debates and, although not measured, of other information about the candidates that became available during the course of the campaign, was expected to affect the stability of respondents' attitudes. As a result, the likelihood that voting behavior would be congruent with the attitude scores obtained months earlier also was expected to be moderated by the accessibility of the attitude.

Method

Subjects

A total of 245 voting age residents of the Bloomington, Indiana area participated in the initial part of the study. Twenty-five of these individuals responded to an advertisement in the local newspaper. Another 16 people were recruited and interviewed at the public library. The majority of the sample, the remaining 204 individuals, were shoppers at a local mall who agreed to participate in a political survey. The subjects were paid $3.00 for participating in the survey. All interviews were conducted during June and July of 1984. Participants were interviewed either singly or, more commonly, in pairs.

Of these 245 respondents, 136 provided perception data in the manner described later and 153 provided usable data regarding their voting behavior. Because occasional missing values exist within the subsample of respondents for whom perception or voting data were available, the number of observations involved in the various analyses that were conducted is not always consistent. Sample sizes or degrees of freedom are reported for each analysis that was conducted.

Procedure

The initial part of the study was described to participants simply as a political survey. No mention was made of the experimenters' affiliation with the psychology department. The survey consisted of 25 attitudinal statements recorded on a cassette tape. Subjects were instructed to listen to each statement and indicate the extent of their agreement with the statement by pressing one of five buttons labeled *strongly agree, agree, don't care, disagree,* and *strongly disagree.* Subjects were instructed to respond as quickly as possible while being sure that their response accurately reflected their opinion on each issue. Each recorded statement was preceded by a warning signal, the word *ready*, to ensure the respondents' full attention. A 15-s interval separated each statement on the tape.

The apparatus that was used for this survey was specially designed for the investigation. It was a battery-powered, portable unit consisting of a Timex-Sinclair microcomputer, a two-channel cassette recorder, and two subject stations. The attitudinal statements and the *ready* signals were recorded on one channel of the tape. At the end of each statement, an electronic marker was recorded on the second channel. This marker served as a signal to the microcomputer to begin timing. Participants responded via a five-button control box. Two such response stations were attached to the apparatus. Subjects' responses stopped the timing. Both the responses and the response latencies (to the nearest millisecond) were recorded by the microcomputer.

The first five statements were intended to serve as practice items to acquaint subjects with the procedure. The experimenter monitored the subjects' performance during these trials to ensure that subjects did understand the procedure. Of the remaining 20 statements, 5 were factual items[1] (e.g., "The capital of Indiana is Terre Haute") and 15 were opinion items concerning attitudes toward such issues as school prayer, gun control, and nuclear power plants in addition to the two major-party candidates for the presidency. These two critical statements were "A good president for the next 4 years would be Ronald Reagan" and "A good president for the next 4 years would be Walter Mondale".[2]

When participants had finished, they were asked to complete a payment receipt, which involved their indicating their names, addresses, and telephone numbers. It was in this way that the information necessary to contact the respondents for the next two phases of the investigation was obtained.

The next phase concerned judgments of the candidates' performances during the nationally televised debates. The first debate involved the presidential candidates and was held on October 7; the second involved the vice-presidential candidates and was held on October 11. It was judgments of these two debates that served as our perception measures. A third debate in the series occurred on October 21, but was not included in our questionnaire because we were concerned that individuals might not complete and return the questionnaire prior to their actual casting of a vote on election day.

The day after the second debate, subjects were mailed a letter from the Political Behavior Research Laboratory on psychology department letterhead. (If two or more members of a household

[1] These factual fillers were included with the hope that they might provide a baseline measure of how quickly individuals generally respond to a query and thus serve to reduce some of the measurement error involved in latency indications of attitude accessibility. However, response latency to the factual items did not correlate substantially with latency to either of the target items. The average correlations of the factual latencies with the Reagan latency and the Mondale latency were a mere .186 and .174, respectively. Furthermore, the average interitem correlations among the latencies to the 15 opinion issues was an insubstantial .189. Thus, latencies of response within this data set appear to have been very content specific.

[2] The somewhat awkward wording of these statements was necessitated by a desire to have the name of the candidate appear at the end of the statement, which served as the location of the marker on the second channel of the tape that started the timing.

had participated in the initial survey, only one was sent this letter.) The letter asked for help in a study being conducted concerning public perceptions of the performance of the participants in the two debates that had been held thus far. It further explained that if individuals would complete and return the enclosed stamped postcard by October 25, they would receive a check for $2.00. In addition, subjects were urged to complete the postcard questionnaire regardless of whether they had only read or heard about the debates or whether they had actually watched the debates. The postcard contained an item concerning the presidential debate. Subjects were asked to endorse one of five statements: "Reagan was much more impressive," "Reagan was slightly more impressive," "The two candidates performed equally well," "Mondale was slightly more impressive," or "Mondale was much more impressive." A similarly worded item concerned the vice-presidential debate. In addition, subjects were asked to indicate whether they had watched each debate. Of the 216 letters that were mailed, 136 responses were received.

The final phase of the investigation concerned voting behavior. Beginning the day after the election, an attempt was made to contact by telephone all the individuals who had participated in the initial survey. One hundred sixty-three individuals were reached and were asked whether they had voted and, if so, for whom. Eight of these people chose not to reveal their votes. Two other respondents had voted for candidates other than Reagan or Mondale and their data were not included in subsequent analyses.

Results

Presentation of the results will be divided into two major sections. We will consider first the relations between attitudes and perceptions and between attitudes and voting behavior among the respondents as a whole. We then will turn our attention to tests of the hypotheses and to how the overall relations vary as a function of attitude accessibility.

Relations Within the Overall Sample

As is to be expected, attitudes toward Reagan and Mondale were negatively correlated, $r(239) = -.657$, $p < .001$.[3] Response latencies for the two questions inquiring about Reagan and Mondale correlated only moderately, $r(239) = .273$, $p < .001$. The average latency for the Reagan item ($M = 1.983$ s) did not differ significantly from the average latency for the Mondale question ($M = 1.954$), $t < 1$, suggesting that the strength of object-evaluation associations for the two candidates was roughly equivalent within the sample.[4]

The attitude-perception relation. It is commonly believed that pre-existing attitudes toward the candidates color viewers' judgments of the candidates' performances during the debates. The data provide clear support for this belief. Attitude toward Reagan and attitude toward Mondale were each predictive of respondents' judgments of performance during the presidential debate. The upper portion of Table 27.1 presents the relevant correlation coefficients. On the assumption that attitudes toward the presidential candidates also would be relevant to the other member of the respective ticket, correlations were also computed concerning the performance of the vice-presidential candidates during their debate. Selective processing of candidate performance is again evident (see Table 27.1). The more positive the attitude toward Reagan, the more positively the performance of the Republican vice-presidential candidate, George Bush, was judged relative to the performance of the Democratic candidate, Geraldine Ferraro. Likewise, individuals with positive attitudes toward Mondale were more likely to judge Ferraro's performance to have been better than Bush's than were individuals

---

[3] All significance levels reported in this article are two-tailed.
[4] In order to compare response latencies to the two questions, it was necessary to measure precisely the locations of the timing markers for the two questions. Using a storage oscilloscope, it was possible to determine the interval between the marker and the end of the acoustic signal for each statement to the nearest millisecond. These constants then were added to the recorded latencies. Thus, the response latencies reported refer to the interval between the precise conclusion of the acoustic signal and the subjects' responses.

TABLE 27.1. Correlations Between Attitudes and Perceptions and Attitudes and Voting Behavior

Sample and measure	Attitude toward		
	Reagan	Mondale	t
Perceptions			
All respondents			
Presidential debate	.474	.432	<1
	(134)	(134)	
Vice-presidential	.536	.398	2.21**
debate	(134)	(134)	
Both debates	.605	.496	1.88*
	(134)	(134)	
Watchers only			
Presidential debate	.458	.436	
	(101)	(101)	<1
Vice-presidential	.538	.358	
debate	(84)	(84)	2.28**
Both debates	.566	.486	
	(74)	(74)	<1
Voting behavior			
All respondents	.710	.565	2.96***
	(150)	(150)	
Voters only	.782	.632	3.28***
	(121)	(121)	

Note: The number of respondents upon which any given correlation is based is listed in parentheses. The *t* value refers to the significance test of the difference between two dependent correlation coefficients.
* *p* < .07. ** *p* < .05. *** *p* < .005.

with negative attitudes toward Mondale. Finally, an overall perception measure involving the sum of respondents' judgments regarding the two debates was also examined and revealed similar congruency between respondents' attitudes and judgments of the debate performances of the candidates. The pattern of relations that was observed on these three perception measures was essentially the same when we restricted the analyses to only those respondents who had indicated watching each debate (see Table 27.1).

Also presented in the upper portion of Table 27.1 is the *t* value of a statistical test of the difference between two correlation coefficients within the same sample (Cohen & Cohen, 1975). With respect to each of the three perception measures, when considering either all the respondents or only those who reported watching the debates, attitude

toward Reagan was more predictive of judgments of debate performance than was attitude toward Mondale. In three of the six cases, this difference approached or reached statistical significance.

The attitude-voting behavior relation. Of the 153 individuals who provided usable data regarding their voting behavior, 29 indicated that they had not voted. In one set of analyses that was conducted, those 29 individuals who indicated they had not voted were assigned a score of 0, and those who voted for Reagan or Mondale were assigned scores of +1 or −1, respectively. Thus, these analyses involved all the respondents. The correlation between each attitude measure and voting behavior is presented in the lower portion of Table 27.1. Despite having been assessed over 3 months prior to the election, attitudes toward Reagan and Mondale were each highly predictive of voting behavior. However, attitude toward Reagan was significantly more predictive of voting behavior than was attitude toward Mondale, suggesting that attitude toward Reagan might have been a more important determinant of voting behavior than attitude toward Mondale.

An additional set of analyses was performed only on the subsample of respondents who reported having voted. These analyses revealed similar but somewhat stronger relations between attitudes and voting behavior. Once again, the correlations between attitude toward Reagan and voting and between attitude toward Mondale and voting differed significantly, implying that feelings toward Mondale were less critical in determining how the respondents voted than were evaluations of Reagan.

Relations as a Function of Attitude Accessibility

Division into high and low accessibility groups. Findings from previous research (Powell & Fazio, 1984) have indicated the existence of a small, but nonetheless statistically reliable, relation between attitude extremity and latencies of response to an attitudinal inquiry. In the present case, attitude extremity, scored as deviation from the neutral point, was associated with faster response latencies with respect to Reagan, $r(240) = .531$, $p < .001$, and to Mondale, $r(242) = .532$, $p < .001$.

As a consequence of this relation between attitude extremity and latency, dividing subjects at the overall median response time with respect to each candidate would have resulted in more extreme attitudes in the high accessibility group than in the low accessibility group. In order to ensure that any inferences drawn about attitude accessibility were not confounded by attitude extremity, a much more conservative procedure was followed in classifying subjects into high and low accessibility groups. Median splits were performed at each and every response level for each of the two attitudes in question. For example, in considering the accessibility of attitudes toward Reagan, the latencies of all subjects who had responded *strongly agree* to the item were examined. Those whose latency was faster than the median for this subsample were assigned to the high accessibility group and those with latencies slower than the median were assigned to the low accessibility group. The same procedure was followed for each of the other response levels. As a result, attitude distributions in our high and low accessibility groups were perfectly equivalent, and we could examine whether knowledge of attitude accessibility enhances predictive power over and above any effect of attitude extremity.[5] Such division into high and low accessibility groups was conducted anew on the specific set of respondents who provided data for each perception and voting measure that was examined.

---

[5] Our procedure for controlling for attitude extremity involves observed attitude scores that obviously are not a perfect indication of true attitudes. Given that attitudes are measured with some error, it should be noted that underlying extremity differences may persist even when we equate individuals on the extremity of their measured responses. Ideally, we would have liked to control for error-free extremity by measuring extremity in multiple ways and controlling for an extremity latent variable. However, assessing the relevant attitudes in multiple ways was not feasible within the context of the present field situation. Thus, we focused on controlling for measured attitude extremity, which is clearly preferable to not attempting any control whatsoever for attitude extremity.

The attitude-perception relation. The hypothesis that attitude accessibility moderates the extent to which perceptions of the candidates' debate performance are congruent with attitudes toward the candidates was examined by comparing attitude-perception correlations within high and low accessibility groups. Those individuals who had responded to the questionnaire regarding the debates were assigned to high and low accessibility groups in the manner just described. This was done for attitudes toward each of the candidates. The correlations that were computed once again involved judgments of the performance of the candidates in the presidential debate, judgments of the vice-presidential debate, and the overall measure mentioned earlier. The upper portion of Table 27.2 displays the correlation coefficients within each group, along with the z value of the statistical test of the difference between the correlations in the high and low accessibility groups, for both the sample of all respondents and the subsample that reported viewing the debate(s) on television. In each and every case, the attitude-perception correlation is stronger in the high accessibility group than in the low accessibility group. Differences as a function of attitude accessibility were particularly evident with respect to attitude toward Reagan, especially when considering the vice-presidential debate. It was in such cases that the differences approached or achieved a conventional level of statistical significance.

The stronger effects of attitude accessibility for perceptions of the vice-presidential debate than for judgments of the presidential debate might have been a consequence of differential ambiguity. Whereas the media seemed to have viewed Mondale as the clear victor in the presidential debate, the vice-presidential debate was viewed much more evenly. Our own subjects appear to have concurred. The average rating of the outcome of the presidential debate on the 5-point scale was 2.27, which was reliably different from the neutral point value of 3, $t(135) = 7.14$, $p < .001$, in the direction of Mondale having performed more impressively than Reagan. In contrast, the vice-presidential debate was viewed as more of a toss-up. Although the average rating of 3.21 did reveal a preference

TABLE 27.2. Correlations Between Attitudes and Perceptions and Between Attitudes and Voting Behavior Within High Accessibility (HA) and Low Accessibility (LA) Groups

Sample and measure	Attitude toward					
	Reagan			Mondale		
	LA	HA	z	LA	HA	z
Perceptions						
All respondents						
Presidential debate	.471	.483	<1	.416	.468	<1
	(67)	(68)		(69)	(67)	
Vice-presidential	.409	.660	2.02**	.380	.448	<1
debate	(67)	(67)		(69)	(66)	
Both debates	.537	.673	1.23	.473	.546	<1
	(67)	(67)		(69)	(66)	
Watchers only						
Presidential debate	.394	.529	<1	.437	.438	<1
	(50)	(51)		(51)	(50)	
Vice-presidential	.410	.679	1.73*	.312	.403	<1
debate	(42)	(42)		(42)	(42)	
Both debates	.404	.738	2.13**	.381	.587	1.13
	(37)	(37)		(37)	(37)	
Voting behavior						
All respondents	.601	.816	2.73***	−.482	−.616	1.17
	(76)	(75)		(76)	(76)	
Voters only	.663	.891	3.39****	−.563	−.658	<1
	(61)	(61)		(62)	(61)	

Note: The number of respondents upon which any given correlation is based is listed in parentheses. The z value refers to the significance test of the difference between two independent correlation coefficients.
* $p < .10$. ** $p < .05$. *** $p < .01$. **** $p < .001$.

for Bush, $t(134) = 1.98$, $p = .05$, the extremity of this average judgment of the debate outcome was significantly less than had been the case for the presidential debate, $t(134) = 4.41$, $p < .001$. If, as these data suggest, the outcome of the presidential debate was less ambiguous than the vice-presidential debate, then it is not surprising that attitude accessibility appeared to exert a larger role with respect to the vice-presidential debate than the presidential debate.

With respect to attitude toward Mondale, a difference between high and low accessibility groups was evident consistently across the various samples and measures but in no case was the difference large enough to achieve statistical significance. As we shall see, this pattern of strong effects of accessibility for attitude toward Reagan and weaker effects for attitude toward Mondale was evident

consistently in the data set. More shall be said about this pattern following the presentation of additional results.

An additional set of analyses was performed to examine the extent to which attitudes toward Reagan and Mondale jointly predicted perceptions. The multiple correlation using the two attitude measures as joint predictors of perceptions was computed within high and low accessibility groups. To create two accessibility groups with equivalent attitude distributions, the sample of individuals who had provided data on a given perception measure was first divided into a series of subsamples. Any given subsample consisted of individuals with identical responses to the question concerning Reagan and identical responses to the question concerning Mondale. For example, all individuals who had responded *strongly agree* to the Reagan item and *strongly disagree* to the Mondale item comprised one subsample; all who had responded *agree* to the Reagan item and *strongly disagree* to the Mondale item comprised another subsample, and so on. The average latency of response to the two attitudinal inquiries was computed for each respondent. Within each subsample, the median average latency served as the division point. Those whose average latency was faster than the median within the subsample were assigned to the high accessibility group, and those whose average latency was slower than the subsample median were assigned to the low accessibility group. Although cumbersome, this procedure ensured that any differences that were observed as a function of accessibility were not confounded by differential attitude distributions in the two groups.

The results of these analyses are depicted in the upper portion of Table 27.3. The multiple correlations predicting perceptions from attitudes toward Reagan and Mondale were stronger in the high accessibility group than in the low. In two of the cases, these differences approached statistical significance (see Table 27.3).

The attitude-voting behavior relation. The hypothesis concerning the moderating role of attitude accessibility was examined by comparing the correlation between each attitude and voting behavior for groups displaying high versus low accessibility with respect to each attitude. Those individuals who had provided usable voting behavior data were divided into high and low accessibility groups in the manner described earlier. The correlation coefficients are presented in the lower portion of Table 27.2. In all cases, the relation between attitude and behavior is stronger, just as predicted, among subjects characterized by high attitude accessibility than among those characterized by low attitude accessibility. This was particularly true with respect to attitude toward Reagan. For both the entire sample and the subsample including only the voters, respondents whose attitudes toward Reagan were highly accessible displayed significantly greater attitude–behavior consistency than those whose attitudes were relatively less accessible. Indeed, among the voters in the

TABLE 27.3. Multiple Correlations Using Attitudes Toward Reagan and Mondale as Joint Predictors of Perceptions and of Voting Behavior Within High and Low Accessibility Groups

Sample and measure	Accessibility group		
	Low	High	z
Perceptions			
All respondents			
Presidential debate	.440	.580	1.08
	(67)	(68)	
Vice-presidential debate	.432	.658	1.86*
	(67)	(67)	
Both debates	.530	.721	1.81*
	(67)	(67)	
Watchers only			
Presidential debate	.446	.558	
	(51)	(50)	<1
Vice-presidential debate	.488	.623	
	(42)	(42)	<1
Both debates	.513	.669	
	(37)	(37)	1.00
Voting behavior			
All respondents	.637	.823	2.48**
	(75)	(75)	
Voters only	.723	.879	2.46**
	(61)	(60)	

Note: The number of respondents is listed in parentheses. The *z* value refers to the significance test of the difference between two independent correlation coefficients.
* $p < .075$. ** $p < .025$.

high accessibility group, nearly 80% of the variance in voting behavior, as compared with 44% among low accessibility voters, was predicted by attitude toward Reagan. The high correlation evident among respondents with a highly accessible attitude toward Reagan is all the more astounding when one keeps in mind that the attitude was measured via a single item some 3½ months prior to the election.

As with the findings concerning the attitude-perception relation, the moderating role of attitude accessibility was less apparent when considering attitude toward Mondale. Although the correlations between attitude toward Mondale and voting were stronger in the high than in the low accessibility groups, the differences were not as large as had been found for attitude toward Reagan and were not statistically significant.

Attitudes toward Reagan and Mondale as joint predictors of voting behavior were examined in the same way as had been done with respect to the perception measures. As before, subsamples of individuals who had responded identically to the Reagan question and identically to the Mondale question were divided into high and low accessibility groups on the basis of the subsample's median average response latency to the two questions. The multiple correlations predicting voting behavior from the two attitude measures was significantly higher in the high accessibility group than in the low for both the sample that included all respondents and the sample that included only voters. The lower portion of Table 27.3 presents the within-groups multiple correlations and the significance tests.

Discussion

The results of this investigation essentially confirmed the initial predictions. The accessibility of the attitude from memory was found to moderate both the attitude-perception and the attitude-behavior relations. Individuals with relatively accessible attitudes, as indicated by relatively fast latencies of response to the attitudinal inquiry, displayed greater selective perception as a function of those attitudes and greater attitude-behavior consistency than did individuals with less accessible attitudes.

One unexpected finding concerned the relative weakness of the results when considering attitude toward Mondale singly. Although this attitude measure was consistently more predictive of subsequent perceptions and behavior among the high accessibility respondents than among the low, the differences were small and not statistically reliable. What may account for the lesser robustness of the results with respect to attitude toward Mondale than with attitude toward Reagan?

When considering attitude-perception and attitude-behavior relations within the overall sample, it was observed that attitude toward Mondale tended to be less predictive than attitude toward Reagan. This suggests that Mondale and attitudes

toward him were relatively less important in determining perceptions of the debates and voting than were Reagan and attitudes toward him. How individuals felt toward Reagan appears to have influenced how they voted more so than how they felt about the alternative. Such differential influence may be typical of elections that involve an incumbent. Indeed, political scientists have shown that voting in such cases can be interpreted as a retrospective rewarding or punishing of the incumbent based on satisfaction or dissatisfaction with his first term (Fiorina, 1981; Key, 1966). If Mondale and attitudes toward him were less relevant to judgments of the outcomes of the debates and to the decision for whom to vote, then it is not surprising that consideration of the accessibility of this less relevant attitude did not produce robust benefits in the ability to predict the subsequent judgments and behavior.

The weakness of the results with respect to attitude toward Mondale should not detract from the strength and clarity of the other findings. The analyses involving attitude toward Reagan and the analyses using attitudes toward Reagan and Mondale as multiple predictors each revealed a substantial moderating role of attitude accessibility. As such, they provide excellent support for the hypotheses derived from the proposed model of the attitude-behavior process (Fazio, 1986). Just as suggested by the model, attitude accessibility acts as a determinant of both the attitude-perception and the attitude-behavior relations.

It should be noted, however, that within the context of the model perceptions that have been biased by an activated attitude are regarded as an immediate precursor of behavior. This is because the model is intended to address behavior that flows from one's definition of an event involving the attitude object. How one defines the event is viewed as the determinant of behavior. The critical issue is whether that definition is influenced by attitude, which in turn depends on whether the attitude is activated from memory on observation of the attitude object.

The present results provide support for the model's assertion that selective perception depends on the accessibility of the attitude from memory.

Recent research documents that latency of response to a direct attitudinal inquiry is at least roughly indicative of the likelihood that the attitude will be activated automatically upon mere presentation of the attitude object (Fazio et al., 1986). In the present case, individuals with accessible attitudes (as indicated by relatively fast latencies) were more likely to judge the performance of the candidates during the debates in a manner that was congruent with their attitudes. Such individuals held attitudes that presumably involved relatively strong object-evaluations associations. Consequently, their attitudes were probably more likely to be activated while they were viewing the debates and, hence, were more likely to color their perceptions of the outcomes of the debates. However, unlike the context addressed by the postulated attitude-behavior process model, these perceptions were not an immediate precursor of the voting behavior of ultimate interest in the present case.

Instead, the influence of attitude accessibility upon the consistency between attitudes, as assessed months earlier, and voting behavior seems to have been a function of the stability of those attitudes. The act of voting in a presidential election is clearly a reasoned, intentional action in which individuals would actively retrieve the relevant attitudes from memory if they had not been activated automatically. Thus, there is no need for attitudes to be highly accessible from memory for the attitudes to exert an influence upon the act of voting. Indeed, most voters enter the voting booth with a definite intention to vote for a particular candidate. However, whether the attitudes that form the basis for the behavioral intention are equivalent to those assessed months earlier does depend on the accessibility of those initial attitudes.

Initial attitudes characterized by high accessibility were likely to have biased people's interpretations of any information about the candidates that came to their attention during the course of the campaign, including the outcome of the debates. The present data indicate that such selective processing was less likely for individuals whose attitudes were relatively less accessible. The amount of selective processing, as in the judgments of the

debates, is apt to have determined the persistence of the attitude over time. Thus, greater selective processing on the part of those individuals with relatively accessible attitudes is likely to mean that their final voting decisions were affected by attitudinal positions more equivalent to the ones that they held months earlier than was the case for individuals with less accessible attitudes.

This reasoning implies that an association should exist between attitude-perception congruency and attitude-behavior correspondence. That is, individuals who held initial attitudes that were unlikely to bias their interpretations of subsequent information should display less attitude-behavior correspondence because those attitudes were potentially more subject to modification during the course of the campaign. Additional analyses of the present data revealed such an association. For the subset of respondents who had provided both perception and voting information (82 individuals when considering only voters, and 95 when also including those who reported not having voted), we computed two indices. The absolute value of the difference between standardized attitude scores and standardized perception scores served as an index of discrepancy between attitudes and perceptions. Similarly, the absolute value of the difference between standardized attitude scores and standardized voting scores served as an index of the discrepancy between attitudes and behavior.[6] These two indices were consistently and reliably associated. Regardless of whether the attitude examined concerned Reagan or Mondale, regardless of which of the three perception measures was used, and regardless of which of the two voting measures was examined, a significant correlation between attitude-perception and attitude-behavior discrepancies was apparent. The 12 correlation coefficients ranged from .264 to .523, with the

---

[6] Just as one would expect, comparison of mean index scores in high versus low accessibility groups confirmed the findings reported earlier concerning the differences in correlation coefficients in the high versus low groups. Index scores were generally lower, indicating less discrepancy between attitudes and perceptions and between attitudes and behavior, within the high than within the low accessibility groups.

average being .381 (all $ps < .02$).[7] Thus, the less the individual's attitude promoted selective processing of the debates, the less likely the individual was to vote in a manner that was consistent with that initial attitude.

These findings serve to illustrate the relevance of attitude accessibility and the likelihood of automatic attitudinal activation to behavioral decisions that are not themselves the immediate outcome of automatic processes but instead stem from conscious and deliberative reasoning. Fazio (1986) has discussed automatic versus controlled processing (see Schneider & Shiffrin, 1977; Shiffrin & Schneider, 1977) models of the attitude-behavior relation and has offered some thoughts about attempts to integrate the two into a more comprehensive model. The present investigation illustrates one such linkage. Voting behavior is most likely the result of a controlled process in which individuals reflect and arrive at a behavioral intention, conceivably in a manner consistent with Ajzen and Fishbein's (1980) theory of reasoned action. Yet, the sort of automatic processes that the model proposed by Fazio and his associates (Fazio, 1986; Fazio et al., 1983) focuses on are relevant to such decisions. Just as postulated by the automatic process model, a relatively accessible attitude is likely to bias interpretations of subsequently received information because it is likely to be activated automatically upon observation or mention of the attitude object. As a result, a relatively accessible attitude is apt to remain more persistent over time than one that is less accessible. Such greater persistence implies that the attitudinal position that is considered at the time that the controlled decision is made will be more equivalent to the initial position in the case of accessible than in the case of relatively inaccessible attitudes.

Our interpretation of the present findings rests on the validity of latency of response to an attitudinal inquiry as a measure of the chronic accessibility of the attitude. As indicated earlier, this measure has been found to relate to the likelihood of automatic activation of the attitude upon exposure to the attitude object (Fazio et al., 1986). Attitude objects concerning which an individual can indicate an attitude relatively quickly when faced with a direct inquiry are also likely to activate the attitude from memory automatically upon their presentation. In contrast, attitude objects for which response latencies to an inquiry are relatively slow are also unlikely to produce automatic attitudinal activation upon their presentation. Thus, we can be confident that the latency measure that was used in the present investigation does reflect the chronic accessibility of the attitude.

Nevertheless, the correlational nature of the present investigation should not be overlooked. Attitude accessibility may be related to other qualities of the attitude that are reflective of attitudinal "strength," such as attitude centrality, certainty, and affective-cognitive consistency (see Raden, 1985, for a recent review of such strength-related attitude dimensions). Indeed, precisely such covariation among the various indices of attitudinal strength has been hypothesized (e.g., Fazio et al., 1982; Fazio, 1986). It has been suggested that the attitudinal qualities that have been identified as moderators of the attitude-behavior relation all may do so because they reflect the strength of the object-evaluation association and, hence, in terms of the attitude-behavior process, the likelihood that the attitude will be activated from memory when the attitude object is encountered. Furthermore, it has been found that attitude accessibility is affected by the manner of attitude formation (Fazio et al., 1982; Fazio et al., 1983); attitudes based on direct behavioral experience are more accessible from memory than are those based on indirect experience. Also, attitude accessibility has been found to relate to the personality construct of self-monitoring (Snyder, 1974); low self-monitoring individuals possess attitudes that are generally more accessible from memory than do high self-monitors (Kardes, Sanbonmatsu, Voss, & Fazio, in press). Both the manner of attitude formation and self-monitoring have been shown to moderate the attitude-behavior relation.

Thus, although we can be confident that our

---

[7] This relation between attitude-perception discrepancy and attitude-behavior discrepancy also was evident within the high (average $r = .314$, $p < .05$) and within the low (average $r = .398$, $p < .01$) accessibility groups.

latency measure reflects attitude accessibility, a number of additional variables may be related to our classification of individuals in the present investigation as possessing attitudes of either high or low accessibility. Which single dimension or combination of dimensions is causally "responsible" for the moderating effects that were observed cannot be discerned given the correlational nature of the investigation. What we see as the advantage of focusing upon the construct of attitude accessibility is its clear relevance to the issue of the *process* by which attitudes influence perceptions and behavior. Unlike other indicants of the "strength" of an attitude, attitude accessibility operates at an information processing level of analysis. Nonetheless, the present findings are most appropriately viewed as simply *consistent* with the implications of the theoretical model of the attitude-behavior process that has been proposed. As such, they provide a real-world corroboration of past experimental findings that have indicated that the strength of the object-evaluation association (and, hence, attitude accessibility) has a causal impact on attitude-behavior consistency (Fazio et al., 1982, Experiment 4). Additional experimental work is necessary to isolate the causal influence of attitude accessibility. Such work appears warranted on the basis of the present correlational findings stemming from an important, real-world context.

Regardless of any ambiguity concerning the causal mechanism that might be operating in the present case, two additional, more practical, implications of the findings are worth noting. The data clearly indicate that behavioral prediction can be improved by consideration of the accessibility of respondents' attitudes. Differences as large as 35 percent in the amount of behavioral variance explained by attitude were observed as a function of attitude accessibility. The very simplicity of the latency measure that was used to index attitude accessibility makes it attractive for use in surveys in which one is concerned with the prediction of individuals' behavior from their attitudes. Our findings indicate that such an approach is not only feasible but also beneficial. The accessibility of respondents' attitudes provides an indication of the

degree to which attitudes are likely to guide subsequent behavior. Thus, one's ability to predict how a given individual will behave may be enhanced by the simultaneous measurement of attitude and attitude accessibility.

Although far more speculative, the technique also may be useful to a pollster interested not in the prediction of individual behavior but in the drawing of an inference about the future behavior of a population. A pollster who desires to obtain an estimate of the future behavior of some population by assessing the attitudes of a representative sample might achieve a more accurate estimate by also considering the accessibility of the respondents' attitudes. If those attitudes appear to be highly accessible, more faith could be placed in the validity of the sample's attitudes as an estimate of the population's future behavior. If those attitudes appear to involve rather weak object-evaluation associations and, hence, are less accessible, then the sample's attitudes are less likely to constitute a valid estimate of the population's behavior. One can easily imagine conducting research involving a large series of such polls and the collection of population behavioral data, in order to arrive at some weighting system by which a pollster might use the average accessibility of attitudes within a sample as an indication of the degree to which the sample attitudes provide a reasonable estimate of future behavior within the population.

The present data also suggest that the degree to which individuals' interpretations of information follow from their attitudes is a function of the accessibility of those attitudes. This, too, has a practical implication. Because relatively inaccessible attitudes seem to promote less selective processing, individuals who possess attitudes of this sort would seem to be more easily swayed by information about the attitude object. It is for such people, as opposed to those with highly accessible attitudes, that persuasive communications have the best chance to be effective agents of attitude change. Consistent with this reasoning, Wood (1982) has found that attitude change in response to a persuasive communication is moderated by the degree to which individuals can rapidly retrieve beliefs about the attitude object from memory.

Thus, whether the context be a political campaign, a marketing campaign, or whatever, the maximal use of resources might be made by targeting efforts at individuals whose attitudes are relatively low in accessibility. Especially in a situation in which various demographic variables are associated with attitude accessibility, such targeting would be possible. The measure of attitude accessibility used in the present study—latency of response to an attitudinal inquiry—would appear to provide a feasible means of identifying a target population for whom the campaigner's persuasive efforts might pay off.

REFERENCES

Ajzen, I., & Fishbein, M. (1980). *Understanding attitudes and predicting social behavior*. Englewood Cliffs, NJ: Prentice Hall.

Cohen, J., & Cohen, P. (1975). *Applied multiple regression/ correlation analysis for the behavioral sciences*. Hillsdale, NJ: Erlbaum.

Fazio, R. H. (1986). How do attitudes guide behavior? In R. M. Sorrentino & E. T. Higgins (Eds.), *The handbook of motivation and cognition: Foundation of social behavior* (pp. 204–243). New York: Guilford Press.

Fazio, R. H., Chen, J., McDonel, E. C., & Sherman, S. J. (1982). Attitude accessibility, attitude-behavior consistency, and the strength of the object-evalaution association. *Journal of Experimental Social Psychology, 18,* 339–357.

Fazio, R. H., Powell, M. C., & Herr, P. M. (1983). Toward a process model of the attitude-behavior relation: Accessing one's attitude upon mere observation of the attitude object. *Journal of Personality and Social Psychology, 44,* 723–735.

Fazio, R. H., Sanbonmatsu, D. M., Powell, M. C., & Kardes, F. R. (1986). On the automatic activation of attitudes. *Journal of Personality and Social Psychology, 50,* 229–238.

Fazio, R. H., & Zanna, M. P. (1981). Direct experience and attitude-behavior consistency. In L. Berkowitz (Ed.), *Advances in experimental social psychology* (Vol. 14, pp. 162–202). New York: Academic Press.

Fiorina, M. P. (1981). *Retrospective voting in American national elections*. New Haven, CT: Yale University Press.

Kardes, F. R., Sanbonmatsu, D. M., Voss, R., & Fazio, R. H. (in press). Self-monitoring and attitude accessibility. *Personality and Social Psychology Bulletin*.

Katz, D. (1960). The functional approach to the study of attitudes. *Public Opinion Quarterly, 24,* 163–204.

Key, V. O. (1966). *The responsible electorate*. New York: Vintage.

Powell, M. C., & Fazio, R. H. (1984). Attitude accessibility as a function of repeated attitudinal expression. *Personality and Social Psychology Bulletin, 10,* 139–148.

Raden, D. (1985). Strength-related attitude dimensions. *Social Psychology Quarterly, 48,* 312–330.

Schneider, W., & Shiffrin, R. M. (1977). Controlled and automatic human information processing: I. Detection, search, and attention. *Psychological Review, 84,* 1–66.

Shiffrin, R. M., & Schneider, W. (1977). Controlled and automatic human information processing: II. Perceptual learning, automatic attending, and a general theory. *Psychological Review, 84,* 127–190.

Smith, M. B., Bruner, J. S., & White, R. W. (1956). *Opinions and personality*. New York: John Wiley & Sons.

Snyder, M. (1974). The self-monitoring of expressive behavior. *Journal of Personality and Social Psychology, 30,* 526–537.

Wood, W. (1982). Retrieval of attitude-relevant information from memory: Effects on susceptibility to persuasion and on intrinsic motivation. *Journal of Personality and Social Psychology, 42,* 798–810.

Zanna, M. P., & Fazio, R. H. (1982). The attitude-behavior relation: Moving toward a third generation of research. In M. P. Zanna, E. T. Higgins, & C. P. Herman (Eds.), *Consistency in social behavior: The Ontario Symposium* (Vol. 2, pp. 283–301). Hillsdale, NJ: Erlbaum.

Received November 16, 1985
Revision received February 19, 1986 ■

How to Read a Journal Article in Social Psychology

Christian H. Jordan and Mark P. Zanna

When approaching a journal article for the first time, and often on subsequent occasions, most people try to digest it as they would any piece of prose. They start at the beginning and read word for word, until eventually they arrive at the end, perhaps a little bewildered, but with a vague sense of relief. This is not an altogether terrible strategy; journal articles do have a logical structure that lends itself to this sort of reading. There are, however, more efficient approaches — approaches that enable you, a student of social psychology, to cut through peripheral details, avoid sophisticated statistics with which you may not be familiar, and focus on the central ideas in an article. Arming yourself with a little foreknowledge of what is contained in journal articles, as well as some practical advice on how to read them, should help you read journal articles more effectively. If this sounds tempting, read on.

Journal articles offer a window into the inner workings of social psychology. They document how social psychologists formulate hypotheses, design empirical studies, analyze the observations they collect, and interpret their results. Journal articles also serve an invaluable archival function: They contain the full store of common and cumulative knowledge of social psychology. Having documentation of past research allows researchers to build on past findings and advance our under-standing of social behavior, without pursuing avenues of investigation that have already been explored. Perhaps most importantly, a research study is never complete until its results have been shared with others, colleagues and students alike. Journal articles are a primary means of communicating research findings. As such, they can be genuinely exciting and interesting to read.

That last claim may have caught you off guard. For beginning readers, journal articles may seem anything but interesting and exciting. They may, on the contrary, appear daunting and esoteric, laden with jargon and obscured by menacing statistics. Recognizing this fact, we hope to arm you, through this paper, with the basic information you will need to read journal articles with a greater sense of comfort and perspective.

Social psychologists study many fascinating topics, ranging from prejudice and discrimination, to culture, persuasion, liking and love, conformity and obedience, aggression, and the self. In our daily lives, these are issues we often struggle to understand. Social psychologists present systematic observations of, as well as a wealth of ideas about, such issues in journal articles. It would be a shame if the fascination and intrigue of these topics were lost in their translation into journal publications. We don't think they are, and by the end of this paper, hopefully you won't either.

Journal articles come in a variety of forms, including research reports, review articles, and theoretical articles. Put briefly, a *research report* is a formal presentation of an original research study, or series of studies. A *review article* is an evaluative survey of previously published work, usually organized by a guiding theory or point of view. The author of a review article summarizes previous investigations of a circumscribed problem, comments on what progress has been made toward its resolution, and suggests areas of the problem that require further study. A *theoretical article* also evaluates past research, but focuses on the development of theories used to explain empirical findings. Here, the author may present a new theory to explain a set of findings, or may compare and contrast a set of competing theories, suggesting why one theory might be the superior one.

This paper focuses primarily on how to read research reports, for several reasons. First, the bulk of published literature in social psychology consists of research reports. Second, the summaries presented in review articles, and the ideas set forth in theoretical articles, are built on findings presented in research reports. To get a deep understanding of how research is done in social psychology, fluency in reading original research reports is essential. Moreover, theoretical articles frequently report new studies that pit one theory against another, or test a novel prediction derived from a new theory. In order to appraise the validity of such theoretical contentions, a grounded understanding of basic findings is invaluable. Finally, most research reports are written in a standard format that is likely unfamiliar to new readers. The format of review and theoretical articles is less standardized, and more like that of textbooks and other scholarly writings, with which most readers are familiar. This is not to suggest that such articles are easier to read and comprehend than research reports; they can indeed be quite challenging. It is simply the case that, because more rules apply to the writing of research reports, more guidelines can be offered on how to read them.

The Anatomy of Research Reports

Most research reports in social psychology, and in psychology in general, are written in a standard format prescribed by the American Psychological Association (1994). This is a great boon to both readers and writers. It allows writers to present their ideas and findings in a clear, systematic manner. Consequently, as a reader, once you understand this format, you will not be on completely foreign ground when you approach a new research report—regardless of its specific content. You will know where in the paper particular information is found, making it easier to locate. No matter what your reasons for reading a research report, a firm understanding of the format in which they are written will ease your task. We discuss the format of research reports next, with some practical suggestions on how to read them. Later, we discuss how this format reflects the process of scientific investigation, illustrating how research reports have a coherent narrative structure.

Title and Abstract

Though you can't judge a book by its cover, you can learn a lot about a research report simply by reading its title. The title presents a concise statement of the theoretical issues investigated, and/or the variables that were studied. For example, the following title was taken almost at random from a prestigious journal in social psychology: "Sad and guilty? Affective influences on the explanation of conflict in close relationships" (Forgas, 1994, p. 56). Just by reading the title, it can be inferred that the study investigated how emotional states change the way people explain conflict in close relationships. It also suggests that when feeling sad, people accept more personal blame for such conflicts (i.e. , feel more guilty).

The abstract is also an invaluable source of information. It is a brief synopsis of the study, and packs a lot of information into 150 words or less. The abstract contains information about the problem that was investigated, how it was investigated, and the major findings of the study, and hints at the theoretical and practical implications of the findings. Thus, the abstract is a useful summary of the research that provides the gist of the investigation. Reading this outline first can be very helpful, because it tells you where the report is going, and gives you a useful framework for organizing information contained in the article.

The title and abstract of a research report are like a movie preview. A movie preview highlights the important aspects of a movie's plot, and provides just enough information for one to decide whether to watch the whole movie. Just so with titles and abstracts; they highlight the key features of a research report to allow you to decide if you want to read the whole paper. And just as with movie previews, they do not give the whole story. Reading just the title and abstract is never enough to fully understand a research report.

Introduction

A research report has four main sections: introduction, method, results, and discussion. Though it is not explicitly labeled, the introduction begins the main body of a research report. Here, the researchers set the stage for the study. They present the problem under investigation, and state why it was important to study. By providing a brief review of past research and theory relevant to the central issue of investigation, the researchers place the study in an historical context and suggest how the study advances knowledge of the problem. Beginning with broad theoretical and practical considerations, the researchers delineate the rationale that led them to the specific set of hypotheses tested in the study. They also describe how they decided on their research strategy (e.g., why they chose an experiment or a correlational study).

The introduction generally begins with a broad consideration of the problem investigated. Here, the researchers want to illustrate that the problem they studied is a real problem about which people should care. If the researchers are studying prejudice, they may cite statistics that suggest discrimination is prevalent, or describe specific cases of discrimination. Such information helps illustrate why the research is both practically and theoretic-ally meaningful, and why you should bother reading about it. Such discussions are often quite interesting and useful. They can help you decide for yourself if the research has merit. But they may not be essential for understanding the study at hand. Read the introduction carefully, but choose judiciously what to focus on and remember. To understand a study, what you really need to understand is what the researchers hypotheses were, and how they were derived from theory, informal observation, or intuition. Other background information may be intriguing, but may not be critical to understand what the researchers did and why they did it.

While reading the introduction, try answering these questions: What problem was studied, and why? How does this study relate to, and go beyond, past investigations of the problem? How did the researchers derive their hypotheses? What questions do the researchers hope to answer with this study?

Method

In the method section, the researchers translate their hypotheses into a set of specific, testable questions. Here, the researchers introduce the main characters of the study—the subjects or participants—describing their characteristics (gender, age, etc.) and how many of them were involved. Then, they describe the materials (or apparatus), such as any questionnaires or special equipment, used in the study. Finally, they describe chronologically the procedures of the study; that is, how the study was conducted. Often, an overview of the research design will begin the method section. This overview provides a broad outline of the design, alerting you to what you should attend to.

The method is presented in great detail so that other researchers can recreate the study to confirm (or question) its results. This degree of detail is normally not necessary to understand a study, so don't get bogged down trying to memorize the particulars of the procedures. Focus on how the independent variables were manipulated (or measured) and how the dependent variables were measured.

Measuring variables adequately is not always an easy matter. Many of the variables psychologists are interested in cannot be directly observed, so they must be inferred from participants behavior. Happiness, for example, cannot be directly observed. Thus, researchers interested in how being happy influences people's judgments must infer happiness (or its absence) from their behavior—perhaps by asking people how happy they are, and judging their degree of happiness from their responses; perhaps by studying people's facial expressions for signs of happiness, such as smiling. Think about the measures researchers use while reading the method section. Do they adequately reflect or capture the concepts they are meant to measure? If a measure seems odd, consider carefully how the researchers justify its use.

Oftentimes in social psychology, getting there is half the fun. In other words, how a result is obtained can be just as interesting as the result itself. Social psychologists often strive to have participants behave in a natural, spontaneous manner, while controlling enough of their environment to pinpoint the causes of their behavior. Sometimes, the major contribution of a research report is its presentation of a novel method of investigation. When this is the case, the method will be discussed in some detail in the introduction.

Participants in social psychology studies are intelligent and inquisitive people who are responsive to what happens around them. Because of this, they are not always initially told the true purpose of a study. If they were told, they might not act naturally. Thus, researchers frequently need to be creative, presenting a credible rationale for complying with procedures, without revealing the study's purpose. This rationale is known as a *cover story*, and is often an elaborate scenario. While reading the method section, try putting yourself in the shoes of a participant in the study, and ask yourself if the instructions given to participants seem sensible, realistic, and engaging. Imagining what it was like to be in the study will also help you remember the study's procedure, and aid you in interpreting the study's results.

While reading the method section, try answering these questions: How were the hypotheses translated into testable questions? How were the variables of interest manipulated and/or measured?

Did the measures used adequately reflect the variables of interest? For example, is self-reported income an adequate measure of social class? Why or why not?

Results

The results section describes how the observations collected were analyzed to determine whether the original hypotheses were supported. Here, the data (observations of behavior) are described, and statistical tests are presented. Because of this, the results section is often intimidating to readers who have little or no training in statistics. Wading through complex and unfamiliar statistical analyses is understandably confusing and frustrating. As a result, many students are tempted to skip over reading this section. We advise you not to do so. Empirical findings are the foundation of any science and results sections are where such findings are presented.

Take heart. Even the most prestigious researchers were once in your shoes and sympathize with you. Though space in psychology journals is limited, researchers try to strike a balance between the need to be clear and the need to be brief in describing their results. In an influential paper on how to write good research reports, Bem (1987) offered this advice to researchers:

> No matter how technical or abstruse your article is in its particulars, intelligent non-psychologists with no expertise in statistics or experimental design should be able to comprehend the broad outlines of what you did and why. They should understand in general terms what was learned. (p. 74)

Generally speaking, social psychologists try to practice this advice.

Most statistical analyses presented in research reports test specific hypotheses. Often, each analysis presented is preceded by a reminder of the hypothesis it is meant to test. After an analysis is presented, researchers usually provide a narrative description of the result in plain English. When the hypothesis tested by a statistical analysis is not explicitly stated, you can usually determine the hypothesis that was tested by reading this narrative description of the result, and referring back to the introduction to locate an hypothesis that corresponds to that result. After even the most complex statistical analysis, there will be a written description of what the result means conceptually. Turn your attention to these descriptions. Focus on the conceptual meaning of research findings, not on the mechanics of how they were obtained (unless you re comfortable with statistics).

Aside from statistical tests and narrative descriptions of results, results sections also frequently contain tables and graphs. These are efficient summaries of data. Even if you are not familiar with statistics, look closely at tables and graphs, and pay attention to the means or correlations presented in them. Researchers always include written descriptions of the pertinent aspects of tables and graphs. While reading these descriptions, check the tables and graphs to make sure what the researchers say accurately reflects their data. If they say there was a difference between two groups on a particular dependent measure, look at the means in the table that correspond to those two groups, and see if the means do differ as described. Occasionally, results seem to become stronger in their narrative description than an examination of the data would warrant.

Statistics *can* be misused. When they are, results are difficult to interpret. Having said this, a lack of statistical knowledge should not make you overly cautious while reading results sections. Though not a perfect antidote, journal articles undergo extensive review by professional researchers before publication. Thus, most misapplications of statistics are caught and corrected before an article is published. So, if you are unfamiliar with statistics, you can be reasonably confident that findings are accurately reported.

While reading the results section, try answering these questions: Did the researchers provide evidence that any independent variable manipulations were effective? For example, if testing for behavioral differences between happy and sad participants, did the researchers demonstrate that one group was in fact happier than the other? What were the major findings of the study? Were the researchers original hypotheses supported by their observations? If not, look in the discussion section for how the researchers explain the findings that were obtained.

Discussion

The discussion section frequently opens with a summary of what the study found, and an evaluation of whether the findings supported the original hypotheses. Here, the researchers evaluate the theoretical and practical implications of their results. This can be particularly interesting when the results did not work out exactly as the researchers anticipated. When such is the case, consider the researchers explanations carefully, and see if they seem plausible to you. Often, researchers will also report any aspects of their study that limit their interpretation of its results, and suggest further research that could overcome these limitations to provide a better understanding of the problem under investigation.

Some readers find it useful to read the first few paragraphs of the discussion section before reading any other part of a research report. Like the abstract, these few paragraphs usually contain all of the main ideas of a research report: What the hypotheses were, the major findings and whether they supported the original hypotheses, and how the findings relate to past research and theory. Having this information before reading a research report can guide your reading, allowing you to focus on the specific details you need to complete your understanding of a study. The description of the results, for example, will alert you to the major variables that were studied. If they are unfamiliar to you, you can pay special attention to how they are defined in the introduction, and how they are operationalized in the method section.

After you have finished reading an article, it can also be helpful to reread the first few paragraphs of the discussion and the abstract. As noted, these two passages present highly distilled summaries of the major ideas in a research report. Just as they can help guide your reading of a report, they can also help you consolidate your understanding of a report once you have finished reading it. They provide a check on whether you have understood the main points of a report, and offer a succinct digest of the research in the authors own words.

While reading the discussion section, try answering these questions: What conclusions can be drawn from the study? What new information does the study provide about the problem under investigation? Does the study help resolve the problem? What are the practical and theoretical implications of the study's findings? Did the results contradict past research findings? If so, how do the researchers explain this discrepancy?

Some Notes on Reports of Multiple Studies

Up to this point, we have implicitly assumed that a research report describes just one study. It is also quite common, however, for a research report to describe a series of studies of the same problem in a single article. When such is the case, each study reported will have the same basic structure (introduction, method, results, and discussion sections) that we have outlined, with the notable exception that sometimes the results and discussion section for each study are combined. Combined results and discussion sections contain the same information that separate results and discussion sections normally contain. Sometimes, the authors present all their results first, and only then discuss the implications of these results, just as they would in separate results and discussion sections. Other times, however, the authors alternate between describing results and discussing their implications, as each result is presented. In either case, you should be on the lookout for the same information, as outlined above in our consideration of separate results and discussion sections.

Reports including multiple studies also differ from single study reports in that they include more general introduction and discussion sections. The general introduction, which begins the main body of a research report, is similar in essence to the introduction of a single study report. In both cases, the researchers describe the problem investigated and its practical and theoretical significance. They also demonstrate how they derived their hypotheses, and explain how their research relates to past investigations of the problem. In contrast, the separate introductions to each individual study in reports of multiple studies are usually quite brief, and focus more specifically on the logic and rationale of each particular study presented. Such introductions generally describe the methods used in the particular study, outlining how they answer questions that have not been adequately addressed by past research, including studies reported earlier in the same article.

General discussion sections parallel discussions of single studies, except on a somewhat grander scale. They present all of the information contained in discussions of the single studies, but consider the implications of all the studies presented together. A general discussion section brings the main ideas of a research program into bold relief. It typically begins with a concise summary of a research program's main findings, their relation to the original hypotheses, and their practical and theoretical implications. Thus, the summaries that begin general discussion sections are counterparts of the summaries that begin discussion sections of single study reports. Each presents a digest of the research presented in an article that can serve as both an organizing framework (when read first), and as a check on how well you have understood the main points of an article (when read last).

Research Reporting as Story Telling

A research report tells the story of how a researcher or group of researchers investigated a specific problem. Thus, a research report has a linear, narrative structure with a beginning, middle, and end. In his paper on writing research reports, Bem noted that a research report:

... is shaped like an hourglass. It begins with broad general statements, progressively narrows down to the specifics of [the] study, and then broadens out again to more general considerations. (1987, p. 175)

This format roughly mirrors the process of scientific investigation, wherein researchers do the following: (1) start with a broad idea from which they formulate a narrower set of hypotheses, informed by past empirical findings (introduction); (2) design a specific set of concrete operations to test these hypotheses (method); (3) analyze the observations collected in this way, and decide if they support the original hypotheses (results); and (4) explore the broader theoretical and practical implications of the findings, and consider how they contribute to an understanding of the problem under investigation (discussion). Though these stages are somewhat arbitrary distinctions—research actually proceeds in a number of different ways—they help elucidate the inner logic of research reports.

While reading a research report, keep this linear structure in mind. Though it is difficult to remember a series of seemingly disjointed facts, when these facts are joined together in a logical, narrative structure, they become easier to comprehend and recall. Thus, always remember that a research report tells a story. It will help you to organize the information you read, and remember it later.

Describing research reports as stories is not just a convenient metaphor. Research reports *are* stories. Stories can be said to consist of two components: A telling of what happened, and an explanation of why it happened. It is tempting to view science as an endeavor that simply catalogues facts, but nothing is further from the truth. The goal of science, social psychology included, is to *explain* facts, to explain *why* what happened happened. Social psychology is built on the dynamic interplay of discovery and justification, the dialogue between systematic observation of relations and their theoretical explanation. Though research reports do present novel facts based on systematic observation, these facts are presented in the service of ideas.

Facts in isolation are trivia. Facts tied together by an explanatory theory are science. Therein lies the story. To really understand what researchers have to say, you need consider how their explanations relate to their findings.

The Rest of the Story

There is really no such thing as research. There is only search, more search, keep on searching. (Bowering, 1988, p. 95)

Once you have read through a research report, and understand the researchers findings and their explanations of them, the story does not end there. There is more than one interpretation for any set of findings. Different researchers often explain the same set of facts in different ways.

Let's take a moment to dispel a nasty rumor. The rumor is this: Researchers present their studies in a dispassionate manner, intending only to inform readers of their findings and their interpretation of those findings. In truth, researchers aim not only to inform readers, but also to *persuade* them (Sternberg, 1995). Researchers want to convince you their ideas are right. There is never only one explanation for a set of findings. Certainly, some explanations are better than others; some fit the available data better, are more parsimonious, or require fewer questionable assumptions. The point here is that researchers are very passionate about their ideas, and want you to believe them. It's up to you to decide if you want to buy their ideas or not.

Let's compare social psychologists to salesclerks. Both social psychologists and salesclerks want to sell you something; either their ideas, or their wares. You need to decide if you want to buy what they are selling or not—and there are potentially negative consequences for either decision. If you let a salesclerk dazzle you with a sales pitch, without thinking about it carefully, you might end up buying a substandard product that you don't really need. After having done this a few times, people tend to become cynical, steeling themselves against any and all sales pitches. This too is dangerous. If you are overly critical of sales pitches, you could end up foregoing genuinely useful products. Thus, by analogy, when you are too critical in your reading of research reports, you might dismiss, out of hand, some genuinely useful ideas—ideas that can help shed light on why people behave the way they do.

This discussion raises the important question of how critical one should be while reading a research report. In part, this will depend on why one is reading the report. If you are reading it simply to learn what the researchers have to say about a particular issue, for example, then there is usually no need to be overly critical. If you want to use the research as a basis for planning a new study, then you should be more critical. As you develop an understanding of psychological theory and research methods, you will also develop an ability to criticize research on many different levels. And *any* piece of research can be criticized at some level. As Jacob Cohen put it, "A successful piece of research doesn't conclusively settle an issue, it just makes some theoretical proposition to some degree more likely" (1990, p. 1311). Thus, as a consumer of research reports, you have to strike a delicate balance between being overly critical and overly accepting.

While reading a research report, at least initially, try to suspend your disbelief. Try to understand the researchers story; that is, try to understand the facts—the findings and how they were obtained—and the suggested explanation of those facts—the researchers' interpretation of the findings and what they mean. Take the research to task only after you feel you understand what the authors are trying to say.

Research reports serve not only an important archival function, documenting research and its findings, but also an invaluable stimulus function. They can excite other researchers to join the investigation of a particular issue, or to apply new methods or theory to a different, perhaps novel, issue. It is this stimulus function that Elliot Aronson, an eminent social psychologist, referred to when he admitted that, in publishing a study, he hopes his colleagues will "look at it, be stimulated by it, be provoked by it, annoyed by it, and then go ahead and do it better. . . . That's the exciting thing

about science; it progresses by people taking off on one another's work" (1995, p. 5). Science is indeed a cumulative enterprise, and each new study builds on what has (or, sometimes, has not) gone before it. In this way, research articles keep social psychology vibrant.

A study can inspire new research in a number of different ways, such as: (1) it can lead one to conduct a better test of the hypotheses, trying to rule out alternative explanations of the findings; (2) it can lead one to explore the limits of the findings, to see how widely applicable they are, perhaps exploring situations to which they do not apply; (3) it can lead one to test the implications of the findings, furthering scientific investigation of the phenomenon; (4) it can inspire one to apply the findings, or a novel methodology, to a different area of investigation; and (5) it can provoke one to test the findings in the context of a specific real-world problem, to see if they can shed light on it. All of these are excellent extensions of the original research, and there are, undoubtedly, other ways that research findings can spur new investigations.

The problem with being too critical, too soon, while reading research reports is that the only further research one may be willing to attempt is research of the first type: Redoing a study better. Sometimes this is desirable, particularly in the early stages of investigating a particular issue, when the findings are novel and perhaps unexpected. But redoing a reasonably compelling study, without extending it in any way, does little to advance our understanding of human behavior. Although the new study might be "better," it will not be "perfect," so it would *have* to be run again, and again, likely never reaching a stage where it is beyond criticism. At some point, researchers have to decide that the evidence is compelling enough to warrant investigation of the last four types. It is these types of studies that most advance our knowledge of social behavior. As you read more research reports, you will become more comfortable deciding when a study is "good enough" to move beyond it. This is a somewhat subjective judgment, and should be made carefully.

When social psychologists write up a research

report for publication, it is because they believe they have something new and exciting to communicate about social behavior. Most research reports that are submitted for publication are rejected. Thus, the reports that are eventually published are deemed pertinent not only by the researchers who wrote them, but also by the reviewers and editors of the journals in which they are published. These people, at least, believe the research reports they write and publish have something important and interesting to say. Sometimes, you'll disagree; not all journal articles are created equal, after all. But we recommend that you, at least initially, give these well-meaning social psychologists the benefit of the doubt. Look for what they are excited about. Try to understand the authors' story, and see where it leads you.

Acknowledgments

Preparation of this paper was facilitated by a Natural Sciences and Engineering Research Council of Canada doctoral fellowship to Christian H. Jordan. Thanks to Roy Baumeister, Arie Kruglanski, Ziva Kunda, John Levine, Geoff MacDonald, Richard Moreland, Ian Newby-Clark, Steve Spencer, and Adam Zanna for their insightful comments on, and appraisals of, various drafts of this paper. Thanks also to Arie Kruglanski and four anonymous editors of volumes in the series, Key Readings in Social Psychology, for their helpful critiques of an initial outline of this paper.

Correspondence concerning this article should be addressed to Christian H. Jordan, Department of Psychology, University of Waterloo, Waterloo, Ontario, Canada N2L 3G1. Electronic mail can be sent to chjordan@watarts.uwaterloo.ca

REFERENCES

American Psychological Association (1994). *Publication manual* (4th ed.). Washington, DC: APA.

Aronson, E. (1995). Research in social psychology as a leap of faith. In E. Aronson (Ed.), *Readings about the social animal* (7th ed., pp. 3–9). New York: W. H. Freeman & Company.

Bem, D. J. (1987). Writing the empirical journal article. In M. P. Zanna & J. M. Darley (Eds.), *The complete academic: A practical guide for the beginning social scientist* (pp. 171–201). New York: Random House.

Bowering, G. (1988). *Errata.* Red Deer, Alberta, Canada: Red Deer College Press.

Cohen, J. (1990). Things I have learned (so far). *American Psychologist, 45,* 1304–1312.

Forgas, J. P. (1994). Sad and guilty? Affective influences on the explanation of conflict in close relationships. *Journal of Personality and Social Psychology, 66,* 56–68.

Sternberg, R. J. (1995). *The psychologist's companion: A guide to scientific writing for students and researchers* (3rd ed.). Cambridge, UK: Cambridge University Press.

Author Index

Page numbers in **bold** denote whole chapter contributions.

Subject Index

Page entries for headings with subheadings refer to general aspects of that topic.
Page entries for figures/tables appear in **bold**.